CONTEMPORARY AMERICAN EDUCATION

An Anthology of Issues, Problems, Challenges

SECOND EDITION

Queens College, The City University of New York

COLLIER-MACMILLAN LIMITED, LONDON

CONTEMPORARY AMERICAN EDUCATION

Stan Dropkin | ***Harold Full*** | ***Ernest Schwarcz***

THE MACMILLAN COMPANY

PRINTED IN THE UNITED STATES OF AMERICA

The Macmillan Company
866 Third Avenue, New York, New York 10022

Collier-Macmillan Canada, Ltd., Toronto, Ontario

Library of Congress catalog card number: 78-93181

Fourth Printing, 1972

Preface

Students entering any profession can be expected to have a familiarity with and an understanding of the fundamental issues, problems, and challenges of their chosen field. In most professional careers the issues, problems, and challenges often deal with new information with which students have had little previous experience. Within the field of education, however, these conditions do not hold.

Every student who enters teaching brings to his career many years of experience with teachers and schools that have influenced and molded his thinking about education. Although the student cannot, or should not, ignore these experiences, it must be recognized that they tend to limit and, at times, distort his view of the function of education and the nature of teaching and learning. No matter how open or how biased are the student's views, these very personal relationships need to be expanded. He needs to develop a growing sense of the complex dimensions of the task of the school in a democratic society within a rapidly changing technological culture.

The selection of readings in this anthology offers a body of information on the philosophical, social, and historical backgrounds that influence education and are in turn influenced by education. The articles have been carefully chosen to give the student ready access to a representative sampling of ideas, theories, and proposals of some of the most respected educational thinkers of the twentieth century.

In revising this anthology, the editors have been conscious of the great turbulence that has taken place in the past five years both in the school and in society. The rapidity of change in these years has been so drastic as to border upon the cataclysmic. Almost no one could have predicted this upheaval. As a consequence, the editors have made the following major revisions in this edition: (1) "American Society in Transition" is now the opening section of the book, dramatizing the pervasive role society plays upon institutions, political structures, and individuals. Eighty per cent of the selections here reflect a considered judgment of the new trends that will characterize societal dynamics of the Seventies; (2) Section V,

"Persistent Problems and Current Concerns," has been drastically altered to give emphasis to the multitude of influences upon the school as a social institution. This section is divided into three new areas: "Youth in Transition" probes the underlying causes of the ferment among the current school population; "Teachers in Transition" explores the images teachers are projecting in a growing militancy concerning their rewards and changing responsibilities; "Schools in Transition" examines current challenges and controversies of the larger society as they are particularized in the schools. The special emphasis given here to education of children of minority groups is an acknowledgment of the continued effort toward the education of all American youth.

Other changes in this edition are centered on the updating of the problems and issues developed since the book was originally published and the incorporation of new points of view supported by current research. All introductions are expanded and newly selected references are included at the end of each section.

In selecting the readings in this book the editors have relied upon their many years of experience in teaching education at Queens College. In addition, they were guided by the following criteria: Do the articles raise significant questions that will lead the student to further exploration of these ideas on his own? Do the articles open new vistas for the student—is he able to see new problems or to see old problems in new perspectives? Do the articles help the student to see the larger dimensions of the functions of education? Are the articles pertinent to education in the last third of the twentieth century? Do the articles represent ideas that have been of continuing concern in the development of American education? Does each article offer an adequate representation of the author's point of view? Do the articles in each section present a representative sampling of the issues, problems, and challenges?

No particular philosophy, ideology, or educational theory is urged upon the reader; rather, the editors have endeavored to present the student with a variety of points of view that will enable him to study data in depth and to appreciate the authentic flavor of American education as it exists today.

Prospective teachers constitute the audience for which this book is primarily intended, but since the functions and processes of education are becoming increasingly a concern for all segments of our society, the contents of this book should have much wider applicability. The editors feel that this volume may be used profitably in several ways: (a) as a basic text for introductory courses in the study of education; (b) as supplementary reading in a basic foundations course with or without the use of a standard text; (c) as a source book for advanced students who are concerned with examining important views, trends, and issues in education; and (d) as a reference for interested laymen who may wish to gain an intelligent insight into the role of contemporary education in America.

The editors wish to thank Miss Maureen Nasse, Mrs. Lillian Leibowitz, Mrs. Martha Shapiro, Mrs. Ruth Myers, Mrs. Sylvia Noroff, and Robert H. Dropkin for their valuable secretarial help in compiling this book of readings.

S. D.
H. F.
E. S.

Contents

SECTION V | *Persistent Problems and Current Concerns*

SECTION I | *American Society in Transition*

PERHAPS THE GREATEST TASK facing our world society is the attempt to cope with the increasing tempo of change. So swift is the acceleration that trying to make sense of change will, in time, become one of society's major endeavors. Trying to predict, much less prepare for, near cataclysmic changes in every facet of societal life will require more and more of our intellectual efforts.

The articles that follow are designed to enable the student to gain an intimate knowledge and understanding of the individual's actions and reactions within his particular society. This reciprocal relationship constitutes the broad frame of reference around which the readings are organized. Urbanization, the rate of social change, automation, conservation, megalopolis, the formation of the inner cities are current social forces influencing today's school and shaping proposals for the future. Charles Frankel of Columbia University sees as the greatest challenge to man his ability to keep pace with the rapidity of change in his physical, social, intellectual, and emotional environment. He feels that education is the crucial factor in helping man transform both himself and his environment.

Another problem facing man today has become known as the "population explosion." Although Malthus wrote about population in 1790, the present dimension of the problem is of a greater order than that ever faced by mankind. Not only is the world's population soaring annually by over 60 million, an increase greater than the population of France and Czechoslovakia, but the rate of increase is accelerating. Believing that these population changes are intimately related to all aspects of human welfare, C. P. Snow, the great novelist and social critic, presents challenging ideas on how to prepare individuals and nations to agree to collaborate for human ends.

These human needs and ends should be served also by a conscious policy of conservation. A civilization reveals the nature of its goals and values in the environmental conditions it creates. Ecologists, such as Robert and Leona Rienow and former Secretary of the Interior Stewart L. Udall, warn us that unless rapid action is taken, irreparable imbalance will result from uncontrolled technological disturbance of natural systems. The spoiling of nature's beauty is aesthetically intolerable. A tiny fraction of the population of the earth uses—when it does not abuse—a disproportionate percentage of the world's resources to keep its wasteful, voracious economy in operation. This inequity is morally repugnant.

Man not only spoils the beauty of nature and wastes its resources, he also destroys his social environment. In the Spring of 1968, the National Advisory Commission on Civil Disorders shook the nation briefly with its findings on turmoils in the Negro slums of the American cities. The Commission's report bluntly assigns the blame for the riots to white racism. Its accounting of deprivation, despair, and frustration is unsparing. Its recommendations, a summary of which is printed in this anthology, take note of the fateful paradox of so much want and suffering in an affluent society. The Commission's findings emerge as a warning against "two societies, separate and unequal."

While it seems to be true that when we speak in the North of minority groups, of people in the ghettos, we mean the Black or Puerto Rican minorities, there are many other poverty groups that should not escape our attention. These include, the Mexican-American, the Appalachian, the migrant worker, and the American Indian. Lack of space does not permit us to focus on all these subgroups. We have chosen the groups that represent "subcultures of poverty," the poor of Appalachia and the American Indian. Anthropologists distinguish between sheer poverty as an economic phenomenon and what could be termed a "subculture of poverty." Within the subculture of poverty, some of the major factors are the sense of not belonging, the sense of marginality, and the deep sense that the institutions of the larger society do not serve these people and are not geared to them—hence the designation "Portraits of the Forgotten." Their problem is not just of economics; it is a whole set of interrelated attitudes.

Donald G. Cooley discusses the great advances at the frontiers of medicine and looks at the not too distant future when teachers may well be talking about enzyme-assisted instruction, protein memory consolidators, antibiotic memory repellers, and the chemistry of the brain. He examines the impact of biological science on our life in general and on the process of memory and learning in particular. We expect that education will play a crucial role in helping to solve the great social problems mentioned above. But the whole process of formal schooling is now wrapped inside an environment of speeded up technological change which is constantly influencing children and the way they learn. The jet-speed of this technological revolution, especially in the area of mass communication, has provided us with something new to reflect upon. The following two articles take up this challenge of the mass media. Erik Barnouw discusses the meaning of McLuhanism. The unnoticed fact of our present is the electronic environment created by new communication media. It is as pervasive as the air we breathe, yet its full import eludes the judgments of common sense. The environments set up by different media are not just containers for people, they are processes which shape people. Content always exists in some form and is, therefore, governed by the dynamics of that form. If you do not know the form, the medium, says McLuhan, you do not know the message. And according to Carroll Quigley each society develops its unique way of dealing with experiences by having its own cognitive system. Different people have different cognitive systems and it is the task of education to bring about the needed revolution in thinking by conveying the attitude that our own way of thinking is not the way things necessarily are.

The final selection is a shattering examination of the basic modes of thought that have represented the Greek influence on Western thought for over 2,000 years. Utilizing the contributions of the behavioral sciences, Lynn White, Jr. confronts four time honored canons with their future oriented challengers: Occident versus globe; rational versus unconscious; language and logic versus symbol; hierarchy of values versus spectrum of values. He stresses the fact of elemental changes in our society's standards of values and judgments. After removing the comforting reference points of 2,000 years, Dr. White asks those in education to share in the titanic task he proposes, "to smelt all human values down and to recast them as a unit." Who in education—in all our society—is ready?

CHARLES FRANKEL | ***The Third Great Revolution of Mankind***

Probably no event in recent years has had a greater impact on the American mood than the Soviet Union's success in launching artificial satellites. The sputniks stirred justified anxieties about America's position in the cold war and upset some of our tenderest assumptions about our situation. But more than this, the sputniks—and now our own Explorer—have turned loose some bewildering predictions about the future.

Trips to the moon and twenty-minute jaunts to Moscow, we are told, are on the agenda of human "progress"—though no one has yet said how to make the moon or Moscow more attractive places in which to land. It is even whispered that mankind may lose one of its oldest topics of conversation because it will be possible to control the weather.

But while predictions about man's future career in outer space have an undeniable interest, the satellites, it may be suspected, also have a significance that is a bit closer to earth and closer to home. For they are not merely events in an armaments race or science-fiction stories come true. They are peculiarly dramatic symbols of what has been going on backstage, East and West, during the last fifteen years—a sudden extension of scientific intelligence and technical resourcefulness which represents an extraordinary spurt of human intellect and power. And this spurt of the human mind has social and moral, as well as technological, consequences. The sputniks are signs in the skies that the normal human scene is changing in some of its fundamental characteristics and that we are living in the midst of a fundamental revolution in human affairs.

Some 25,000 years ago an "Agricultural Revolution" took place which changed man from a nomadic hunter and berry picker into a deliberate cultivator of his food supply. In the latter half of the eighteenth century an "Industrial Revolution" began, with results which we have not yet fully absorbed. Both these revolutions began as changes in the ideas and tools men had used to adjust themselves to nature. They ended by changing men's relations to each other, their moral and political outlooks, and the very substance of the things they thought worth seeking in life. It is easy to overestimate the significance of events that happen in one's own

From *The New York Times Magazine* (February 9, 1958).

day. But the revolution that has taken shape in the last fifteen years must be put in company like this to be seen in its proper perspective.

Indeed, in the natural energies it has released, and in the speed with which it has done so, the present shift in the relation of man to his environment dwarfs either of its predecessors. It is impossible to believe that its other consequences will not eventually be as great. Now that we have had a chance to absorb the first impact of the sputniks, it may be worth while to sit back and reflect on some of the long-range social issues of which the sputniks are a portent.

We can already see some of the more obvious issues. War, for example, has changed its character and has lost one of its traditional functions in international affairs. Leaving all issues of morality aside, large-scale war can no longer be used, as it has sometimes been used in the past, as an intelligent instrument even of national selfishness. While the danger of all-out nuclear war has not substantially receded, such war can only be an instrument of utter desperation.

Similarly, the problem posed by the expansion of population in the world promises to become even more acute as a result of the advances in medicine and technology that are almost surely in prospect. Through most of its history the human race has had to struggle to keep its numbers from declining. But our very success in improving the basic conditions of human existence now threatens to turn back upon us and to lead to incalculable human suffering unless organized measures are taken to control the birth rate.

But war and the growth of the world's population are relatively familiar problems, even though the penalty for failing to solve them has suddenly become astronomically high. The present revolution in human affairs is likely to bring other changes, however, to which somewhat less attention has been paid. And not the least important is a possible change in the way in which human work will be organized with the advent of new industrial processes such as automation.

One possible consequence of automation, for example, is a sharp increase in the ratio of skilled workers to unskilled workers. This means a host of new issues for industrial unions, and new problems for both labor leaders and industrial managers. Of equal significance is the possible impact of the automatic factory on the way in which the working day may be arranged. As the British engineer Landon Goodman has pointed out, the cost of introducing automation may be so high in many cases that it will be uneconomical to operate a plant only eight hours a day. If many industrial plants are going to find it necessary to operate around the clock, obvious consequences will follow for everything from the nature of home life to the way in which cities are organized. Even the old phrase, "as different as night and day," is likely to lose some of its force.

The new way in which work may be organized also affects the attitudes that men may take toward other parts of life. Most of the work that men have had to do in history has been disagreeable; most of the leisure that men have had has been the prerogative of the few. This fact has colored much of our thinking about the way in which life ought to be lived. The democratically-minded have been suspicious of what is "useless"; the aristocratically-minded have regarded the useful as just a bit vulgar. But if leisure becomes everybody's prerogative (and problem), and if automation can be used to make human work less routine and to give more workers the opportunity to exercise their individual skills and discretion, the sharp division between work and leisure will make even less sense than it makes today. The effects will be felt, to take only one example, in our ideals of "liberal" education, which are still primarily leisure-oriented, and in our conception of "vocational" education, which is already anachronistic in its view of what ordinary people need to be "prepared for life."

But the new processes of industrial production are parts of a larger trend which has even deeper implications of its own. During most of the past, developments in technology were largely independent of developments in pure scientific research. To some extent this remained true even in the nineteenth century. But technology has now become almost entirely the child of fundamental theoretical inquiry. This means that we can count in the future on a steady process of technological innovation, and at a steadily more rapid pace.

We come at this point to perhaps the profoundest consequence of the present revolution in human affairs. It is the simple change in the tempo of change. For nothing cuts more quickly or deeply into a society's way of doing things than changes in its technology.

This quickened tempo represents an unprecedented challenge to the human ability to adjust to social change. It took man roughly 475,000 years to arrive at the Agricultural Revolution. It required another 25,000 years to come to the Industrial Revolution. We have arrived at the "Space Age" in a hundred and fifty years—and while we do not know where we go from here, we can be sure that we shall go there fast. Our expectations of change, and the ability of our nervous systems or our social systems to withstand the shock of change, have been formed in the long experience of the race. And this experience, even in the nineteenth century, has not prepared us for the pace of events that lie ahead.

Such an extraordinary change in the basic tempo of human history means that new and deliberate efforts will be needed to control the processes of social change. As the last hundred years of Western history demonstrate, men can learn to change at a much quicker pace than before. But as these same years also suggest, there are limits, and it is difficult to imagine a day when it will not take time for men to adjust to new conditions, to learn new skills and habits, and to get over the nostalgia and resentments that come when old and familiar things are destroyed. There is a conservative in every man and, in the world into which we are moving, he is going to get a harder workout than ever before.

Accordingly, if the things we cherish from the past are not going to be carelessly destroyed, and if the best possibilities of the future are going to be realized, it seems probable that we shall have to have institutions that have been deliberately set up to exercise long-range social forethought. A steady process of technological innovation, for example, can mean recurrent crises of technological unemployment. If this is not to happen, institutions will have to exist to envisage the new skills that will be needed, to undertake the continuing task of retraining workers, and to control the pace at which new techniques are introduced so that we can make a sensible adjustment to them. Given the pace and magnitude of the technical changes that are in prospect, we cannot count on the market place and the price system to do this job alone. Technological innovation means social change; and there is no more reason to introduce such innovations, letting the chips fall where they may, than there is to introduce a new and powerful drug on the market without first making it meet the test of medical examination and control.

The need to exercise more deliberate control over the processes of social change raises, of course, a fundamental issue. It is the issue of freedom and regimentation, the question of the tension between personal liberty and initiative on the one hand, and the obvious and growing necessity, on the other, for an ever larger degree of social organization. This has been the central issue in industrial society for more than a century. In the world which the present revolution is forming it will be equally decisive. But the terms we have habitually employed in trying to solve it will almost certainly need to be revised.

The dangers that a larger degree of social organization can bring are obvious. It can mean, at the very least, a multiplication of the nuisances that exhaust individual energy in administrative forms to fill out, incessant committees, petty bureaucratic tyrannies. It can mean that power will steadily pile up at the center until it is impossible to place an effective check upon it. Perhaps worst of all, our ideals and attitudes can change.

Under the pressure of the need for organization, we can come slowly but painlessly to like the standard and the impersonal, and to prefer the man who fits the system to the man who is difficult to harness. If this happens, we can lose liberties we now cherish and never notice or regret the loss.

But the individual can be crushed just as easily in a subway rush as on an assembly line. When there is more traffic on the streets, more controls are necessary. And when these controls are inadequate or break down, the individual has less freedom to go where he wants to go, not more freedom. The question, in brief, is not whether we shall have a larger amount of conscious social organization or not, but what kind of social organization we shall have. It can be centralized or decentralized; it can be broken up into small units or cover only very large ones; it can concentrate authority up at the top or spread considerable authority down to lower levels. Most important of all, it can have as its conscious object the cherishing of individual differences and the promotion of individual talents. The dangers of a larger degree of social organization are unmistakable. But disorganization will be no healthier a climate for freedom.

The problems of social organization and of controlling the results of technological innovation bring us, however, to a final problem. It is the problem of the use and abuse of science, a problem that is likely to become steadily more acute as our world becomes more steadily and obviously a creature of science. In the future, as in the past, two extreme possibilities confront us. The first is to make an idol out of science. The second is to denigrate its importance on grounds of fixed moral or religious principle.

Illustrations of the tendency to make an idol out of science have suddenly blossomed all around us since the sputniks began their dance in space. With a hopefulness that is somewhat frightening, both scientists and laymen have predicted, for example, that science will soon be able to change human emotions and desires by biochemical means. Others have talked about the coming mastery of the principles of "group dynamics" and the ability that science will give us to choose the right leaders and to get people to work together harmoniously.

Such predictions represent revivals of Plato's ancient dream that, if philosophers became kings, man's political and moral troubles would come to an end. And they rest on precisely the same combination of political innocence and moral arrogance. There is, unhappily, no guarantee that those who dispense the pills that are going to change our desires and emotions will themselves have the right desires and emotions.

But it is a grave mistake to dismiss science as useless in solving moral and political problems. Objective knowledge of the conditions and consequences of our personal desires or our social institutions does help us to realize the actual nature of the ends we choose to pursue; and in this way we can frequently come to choose our ends and ideals more intelligently.

Even more than in the past, the world which the present revolution is creating will be one in which a process of steady re-examination of existing institutions will be a condition, not simply of a decent life, but in all probability of survival as well. Those who take fixed positions in such a world, and who deny the usefulness of scientific knowledge in resolving moral and political dilemmas, will be pleading merely for the rule of dogma or of their own private intuitions. It is unreasonable and unattractive to think that the society of the future should be ruled by a scientific élite masquerading as moral experts. It is equally unattractive to think that it should be ruled by those who make a principle of ignorance, and whose claim to be moral experts rests on their sense of superiority to the processes of sober scientific inquiry.

The attitudes that are aroused by science suggest, indeed, the fundamental educational problem which the present revolution puts before us. This revolution is at bottom the product of ideas and modes of thought which have remained closed secrets to most of the best educated men and women today. As a result, in what is alleged to be the most "scientific" of ages, science has the quality of magic for the popular mind. But while the problem is critical, it is not insurmountable.

The difficulties of acquainting college-trained men and women with the fundamental methods and ideals of contemporary science have been greatly exaggerated. It requires, of course, the imparting of factual information; but it requires, even more, the training of the imagination of the ordinary, educated layman so that he can grasp the general character of scientific problems even if he does not understand all their details, and can appreciate the kind of triumph which the solution of such problems represents.

Such an imaginative grasp of science, which would allow more members of modern culture to share vicariously in the most majestic achievements of their civilization, is possible for a great many more than now have it. And even more than the problem of training more scientists and engineers, this is the fundamental problem of education in the sciences.

As one looks ahead to the unfamiliar world that is emerging, it is possible, of course, to feel overwhelmed by this educational problem or by the other problems which this world puts before us. One can try to retreat from the unfamiliar, either by laughing off artificial satellites as mere basketballs in outer space or by concentrating almost hysterically on just one short-range issue—the military struggle for outer space—to the neglect of all the other issues that artificial satellites dramatize. And one can also take an apocalyptic attitude, and assume that the unfamiliar world that is emerging is also going to be absolutely unrecognizable, whether for the better or for the worse. But human traits like envy, malice and egoism are likely to remain with us no matter what moral medicines the druggist of the future has on his shelves. And once the initial thrill wears off, most honeymooners are probably going to prefer the moon overhead rather than underfoot.

But if utopia is not around the corner, neither is it inevitable that our powers are unequal to the problems that are appearing. In an age whose problems are almost all signs of mounting human powers, this would be a strange moral to draw. Man is now making his own stars and setting his own impress on the solar system. If these stars are as yet minuscule and only a very little way out in space, they still represent something of an achievement for a creature who is built rather close to the ground. The world that is taking shape can preserve old joys and it can also contain many new ones. The scientific imagination of the twentieth century has shown remarkable flexibility and daring. There is no reason in the nature of things why our social imagination cannot show some of the same qualities, or why it cannot escape, as modern science has, from the backyard of its old commonplaces and dogmas. If it did, its achievements could be even greater than the shooting of satellites into the sky.

C. P. SNOW | *World Population: Hope or Despair?*

Uneasiness seems to be becoming part of the climate of our time. Uneasiness with an edge of fear? Perhaps. It is a bad state. It can be a paralyzing and self-destructive state.

What is going wrong with us? Of course, we are not the first people in history to have this kind of experience or ask this kind of question. But we can deal only with our own time and speak only with our own words. It does seem—and though the feeling is subjective, it is strong and one can hear it expressed by the very young—that our world is closing in.

. . .

We know incomparably more than any human beings before us about what is going on in other cities, in other countries. Particularly the immediate prospect of human suffering. We know it is happening. We see people starving before they have died; we know that they are going to die. We know so much, and we can do so little. We turn away.

Yes, we turn away. We don't project ourselves outwards; we turn inwards. We draw what in England we call the curtains, and we try to make an enclave of our own.

. . .

Let us be honest. Most of us are huddling together in our own little groups for comfort's sake. We are turning inward more than is really natural. As I said before, we draw the curtains and take care not to listen to anything which is going on in the streets outside. We are behaving as though we were in a state of siege.

. . .

In many places and for many purposes, including some of the fundamental human purposes, there are already too many people in the world. Within a generation, there will be far too many. Within two or three generations—unless we show more sense, goodwill and foresight than men have ever shown—there will be tragically too many. So many that the ordinary human hopes will have disappeared.

. . .

We can't avoid any longer the fundamental trouble we are moving into: the trouble which, in truth, we are already in. This has certainly contributed to our state of siege. Never mind our mental states, though. The trouble is elemental.

The Rich and the Poor

It is the contrast between the rich countries of the world and the poor. The fact that half our fellow human beings are living at or below subsistence level. The fact in the unlucky countries the population is growing faster than the food to keep it alive. The fact that we may be moving —perhaps in 10 years—into large-scale famine.

Unfortunately, there are nearly twice as many people in the poor countries as in the rich. Further, there will—nothing can stop it—be an extra billion people added to the world population in the next 10 years. Of those, rather more than three-quarters will be added to the poor.

The most dreadful of all . . . is that many millions of people in the poor countries are going to starve to death before our eyes—or, to complete the domestic picture, we shall see them doing so upon our television sets.

How soon? How many deaths? Can they be prevented? Can they be minimized?

Those are the most important questions in our world today. Much more important than all the things which fret us in Western societies—student power, racial conflicts, the disaffection of the young. Though I believe there is an invisible connection between our local problems and the catastrophic world one.

To answer those questions we have to rely to an extent upon judgment —which is really informed guessing. Most of the expert demographers and the agronomists take the most pessimistic view.

It is common ground that, in large parts of the poor world, in sections of Asia, Africa, Latin America, the collision between rising population and available food is very near. . . .

. . .

. . . At best, this will mean local famines to begin with. At worst, the local famines will spread into a sea of hunger. The usual date predicted for the beginning of the local famines is 1975–80.

. . .

The major catastrophe will happen before the end of the century. We shall, in the rich countries, be surrounded by a sea of famine, involving hundreds of millions of human beings, unless three tremendous social tasks are by then in operation. Not just one alone, but all three. They are

1. A concerted effort by the rich countries to produce food money and technical assistance for the poor.
2. An effort by the poor countries themselves, on the lines of India and Pakistan, to revolutionize their food production.
3. An effort by the poor countries—with all the assistance that can be provided under 1.—to reduce or stop their population increase, with a corresponding reduction in the population increase in the rich countries also.

A Peak of Despair

Despair is a sin. Or, if you talk in secular terms as I do, it prevents one's taking such action as one might, however small it is. I have to say that I have been nearer to despair this year, 1968, than ever in my life.

I don't mean anything at all subtle. It goes without saying that to avoid major war, there has to be some sort of understanding between the U.S. and the U.S.S.R. It also goes without saying, I suggest, that to avoid the catastrophe I have just been discussing—the catastrophe a little further ahead—there has to be something more than uneasy understanding, something more positive than coexistence, between the two great power-centers of the world.

. . .

Now I want you to consider the alternatives, that is, what will probably happen. I am going to suggest three models for the next thirty years. They are all projections, in slightly different directions, from the first part of this discussion.

The Alternatives

Model A is the gloomiest. It is, I am afraid, the most likely. The relations between the superpowers will not alter much. They will still coexist, in the sense of avoiding major war. They will spend increasing sums on armaments, antiballistic missiles and so on: there will be no greater security for either, and probably not much less. Internally, they will change less than many who live in other countries would expect.

Both the American and Soviet societies will get richer. The rest of the advanced world will polarize, as now, towards one or the other of the superpowers.

Famine will take charge in many countries. It may become, by the end of the period, endemic famine. There will be suffering and desperation on a scale as yet unknown. This suffering will be witnessed—since our communications will be even better—by the advanced countries, whose populations will be living better than they are today.

It is hard to imagine the psychological and political conditions which will be created by such a gap.

Model B is a shade more cheerful version of Model A. Some sanguine observers believe that, with immense good fortune, this might conceivably be enough, not enough to avert serious suffering, but enough to tide it over, and give mankind a generation's breathing space to think and plan. I find it hard to believe that they are being realistic.

Model C is by far the most unlikely of the three, and yet we have to act as though it is more likely than it is. The only decent way to respond to a state of siege is to break out of it. Or at least to try to. Most of us are private citizens, who can only do little things. But the whole world is made up of private citizens, and if they can see the situation, then the situation may be changed.

Most of the time, human beings are rapacious and selfish. Some are capable of great nobility, but we can't build on that. Many in rich countries are so selfish that they would, and maybe will, be willing to get richer and use the technological superiority which their riches gives them to fight off the hungry millions outside.

I for one shouldn't like to live in such a world; and in purely material terms it couldn't be long maintained. But we have to take selfishness for granted. We can also, however, take human intelligence for granted. For all our faults, that has been the strength of the species. It is our best hope now.

We have to tell the facts. We have to make sure that people understand those ominous curves—the curve of population, the curve of food supply. We have to tell what the collision means.

It is going to need great sacrifices. Including one of the most difficult sacrifices of all, the sacrifice of our rigidities. For, in some ways, a state of siege is comfortable. If we break out, we are going into the harshness of the streets outside.

American citizens and Soviet citizens are called upon to face an unfamiliar harshness: the harsh but active assumption that the opposite society is not going to collapse, within foreseeable time. It is no use waiting until the U.S.S.R. becomes capitalist or the U.S. Communist. If we wait that long, the world population will have doubled, redoubled, redoubled, 7 billions, 14 billions, 28 billions.

The Ultimate 'Cause'

One hears young people asking for a cause. The cause is here. It is the biggest single cause in history, simply because history has never before presented us with such a danger. It is a very difficult cause to fight, because it will be long and drawn out, it is going to need using political means for distant ends.

We have to stop being trivial. Many of our protests are absurd, judged by the seriousness of the moment in which we stand. We have to be humble and learn the nature of politics. Politics is bound to be in essence short-term. That is no one's fault. Politicians have to cope with the day's tasks.

American governments have to try to keep their country safe, in the short term as well as the long. Soviet governments have to do exactly the same. But it is in the nature of politics that the short-term duties come first.

It is the duty of all the rest of us, and perhaps, most of all, of the generations which are going to live in what is now the future, to keep before the world its long-term fate. Peace. Food. No more people than the earth can take. That is the cause.

I should be less than honest if I told you that I thought it was likely to succeed. Yet we should be less than human if we didn't try to make it. We live in our time. This is the responsibility of our time, and it is our own. Sometimes I console myself with a piece of rabbinical wisdom:

If I am not for myself, who am I?
If I am for myself alone, what am I?
If not now, when?

ROBERT AND LEONA RIENOW | ***Conservation for Survival***

Conservation is no longer a "cause"; it is a crisis. Its features are drawn in taut lines by forces unprecedented in human history, like a human face contorted by foreboding and strain. Conservation today

From *The Nation* (August 26, 1968). Reprinted by permission of the publisher and authors.

bears scant resemblance to the historic pattern of the familiar wallflower at the ongoing dance of material progress.

Under the impact of a rocketing population, an insatiable spiral of economic expansion, as well as a gargantuan and pitiless technology, the very character of the concern of conservation has shifted. Once preoccupied with the quantity of resources, its attention is now focused on the quality of environment. Once a question of supply, conservation is now an issue of survival—of species, of habitat, of mankind.

Daily, the country is, or should be, shocked by the brinkmanship of the exploitation we live by. Dr. Barry Commoner has reported that some tested baby food has been found to contain enough nitrogen fertilizer to endanger life. Dr. Lamont C. Cole warns the American Association for the Advancement of Science that had a ship the size of the Torrey Canyon, loaded with concentrated herbicides rather than with crude oil, sunk off our coast, it would have erased the photoplankton of the sea which produce 70 per cent of the world's oxygen, and man and beast throughout the Northern Hemisphere would quickly have found themselves gasping for breath. As for air poisoning, despite mandatory crankcase and exhaust control devices on Los Angeles automobiles, the amount of hydrocarbons spit into the air daily has leaped from 1,870 tons in 1960 (before controls) to 10,860 tons a day, and the mustard blanket wraps that city—and most cities—more tightly than ever in its choking embrace.

Secretary Udall comes up with the mournful list of seventy-eight American species of wildlife which we have pushed to the brink of the never-never land—among them the American bald eagle, the national emblem. In December, 1967, thousands of oil-blackened waterfowl washed ashore on Maine's sub-zero coast, there to starve and freeze to death, victims of an illegal oil spill.

In the next thirty years, says Russel E. Larson, dean of the College of Agriculture at Pennsylvania State, the world must duplicate all the progress made through agriculture since the beginning of time, if we would avoid world-wide starvation. And in 1967, eighty nations of the world were for the first time moved to meet in Washington, D.C., in "a massive cooperative international effort to find solutions for man's water problems," in the President's words.

All these calamities and crises which now tread on one another's heels are symptoms, environmental warnings. We are burdening the land with more people, production, and machines than it can possibly sustain.

"The problem," observed biologist Hugh H. Iltis of the University of Wisconsin, "is one of a single species of animal who is making the earth unfit for habitation by conquering it." It is a problem unique to our age. Not until 1915 did the United States reach its first 100 million population. On November 20, 1967, an unthinking, if not an ignorant, crowd stood in the foyer of the Commerce Department and applauded wildly as the census clock registered the 200 millionth inhabitant. In thirty-five years, perhaps even in twenty-five, if bullish tendencies prevail, another 100 million Americans will appear on the scene. These are the increased hordes who will inundate the parks, blight the landscape, crowd the beaches, destroy the air and make life unbearable for one another.

They are also compounded of an individual and collective appetite that is driving society to dyspepsia. Every "7½ seconds a new American is born," begins our *Moment in the Sun.* "He is a disarming little thing, but he begins to scream loudly in a voice that can be heard for seventy years. He is screaming for 26,000,000 gallons of water, 21,000 gallons of gasoline, 10,150 pounds of meat, 28,000 pounds of milk and cream, 9,000 pounds of wheat, and great storehouses of all other foods, drinks, and tobaccos. . . .

"He is requisitioning a private endowment of $5,000 to $8,000 for school building materials, $6,300 worth of clothing, $7,000 worth of furniture—and 210 pounds of peanuts to pass through his hot, grasping little hand. He is yelping for a Paul Bunyan chunk, in his own right, of the nation's pulpwood, paper, steel, zinc, magnesium, aluminum, and tin. . . ."

This infant will grow into the world's most prodigious consumer, citizen of a nation that accounts for one-fifteenth of earth's people but consumes one-half of its total product (and aspires, by the year 2000, to consume 83 per cent of it). We wallow in statistics projecting a gross national product by the turn of the century that will be more than double our present GNP—and appear charmed by the vision of 244 million cars on the road in the same year. We plan on a building pace of five times present experience. It is this double threat of more people demanding more per capita production that makes the modern conservationist run scared.

Nor can he muster much hope to save the beauty and balance of man's surroundings when he considers the relentless, savage power of the forces of predation. The exploiters are armed with an artillery of modern machinery as to make the universe quake.

A "mechanical monkey," for instance, has been announced with cheers. It embraces a living tree in a death hug and climbs to the top, chewing off all branches as it goes. It promises to consume every last unprotected tree of our once vast forests. "We shake up the earth and make it tremble!" exulted one TV documentary on man's subjection of nature. In Florida, a land speculator has developed the giant "tree-crusher" which shaves a 27-foot swath through the region's great cypress swamps for more housing developments.

The replacement of the bulldozer with the immense earth-churning cats, plus powerful new chain saws, have enabled the lumbermen of the Pacific Coast to promise the extermination of *all* of the prehistoric coastal redwoods within this one generation. "The redwoods are commercially valuable," declared a lumber company spokesman, "and therefore *they must be cut.*"

True to their promised goal, as soon as the Senate, in November, 1967, cautiously approved a modest 66,000-acre park on Redwood Creek (with options for Secretary Udall to add to it the treasured "Emerald Mile," just upstream from its boundary) the barons acted. Overnight, the owners moved their mammoth machinery into the Emerald Mile, quickly felled a dozen of the 300-foot-tall giants, and rigged up the skidroads to strip down this breathtakingly beautiful spot. The old imperiousness of the 19th-century lumber baron was resurrected from ghosts Americans thought long banished.

Surface mining alone has defaced 3.2 million acres of land, and with the aid of a monstrous machine equipped with 200-ton jaws, the rate of disfigurement is now 150,000 acres a year which, it is estimated, we shall soon come near to doubling. Thus it is that today the defender of the environment tries to stand up against these demographic and economic forces with the breath of catastrophe and despair blowing down his neck. And as the forces of destruction expand, the land shrinks. No longer is the conservationist operating in a framework of almost wicked plenty—our virginal resource abundance which both dizzied and corrupted. Now each assailed spot becomes a final battle for its kind.

When the Eastern New York Chapter of Nature Conservancy wrenched Great Bear Swamp near Westerlo from the path of the Army Corps of Engineers' bulldozers, they were saving the last northern outcropping of the giant rhododendron in all New York State. When nature lovers rushed to stave off development of the Wild Buffalo River in Arkansas, it was the last such river left in that section of the country. When the Audubon Society and others joined forces to set aside habitat for the Kirtland's Warbler in Michigan and the Atwater prairie chicken in Texas, it was in each case the last such habitat available on planet earth.

Nor is the issue always confined so narrowly. The ecologist today worries about ecosystems. He sees us tampering with climates, willfully exterminating entire species, altering many thousand-year-old habitats. Says biologist Dan McKinley of the State University of New York at Albany in his colorful prose: "A broad ecological disaster will now be final, in a world where untapped frontiers no longer beckon us and temper our mistakes. . . . The man who burns his incense to an expanding economy must learn to investigate what is going up in smoke."

Today's conservationist must view the landscape not in spots and dabs as he once did but in its entirety. He must be concerned with a biotic community, with complete ecosystems. His vision has perforce come to encompass the whole web of life, including man. Thus he no longer sees just a poison bait carelessly planted here and there or an aerial spray drifting down on a field of cabbage, but bewails rather the systematic nation-wide saturation of the American environment with an annual 700 million pounds of biocides, herbicides and pesticides. He sees the predacious disruption of a whole watershed.

As a consequence he mourns not only a specific wildlife loss from an occasional chemical "spill"—but the blotting out of an entire species such as the Atlantic salmon, or the Great Lakes sturgeon. The California condor, the timber wolf, the grizzly bear, the roseate spoonbill, the southern sea otter and many more—even the Eastern bluebird—are struggling gamely against man's ingenuity in order to stay alive. Never before in history has there been concern over the ability of nature to defend herself, but Professor Iltis expresses the new attitude. "It is abundantly clear," he says, "that one of the most important jobs of the conservation movement today is to expose the fallacies of the indestructibility of nature."

Certainly no one who honestly confronts the assorted revolutions in population, in production and in expectations can ignore the limitations on resources. On this finite, raked-over little globe gluttony must soon have an end. Even the most optimistic find hope only in the "resources" of manipulation, foreign importation and scientific innovations—shaky piling indeed.

Lucky "breakthroughs" and scientific serendipity aside, however, the startling emphasis today is not primarily a statistical one. A *qualitative* deterioration is impoverishing and debauching our environment. Scientists no longer worry as much about the coal and oil supply as about the life-endangering contaminants their combustion throws into the atmosphere. Public officials have transferred their concern from the inventory of chemicals available, to septic rivers, the 100,000 defiled lakes, and the poisoned estuaries that have resulted from these products. The question as to whether we shall always have enough plastic and paper is blotted out of sight by the mountains of "discards" and trash we must wade over and through. Whether we have enough steel to make automobiles becomes secondary in urgency to the blight of junkyards and the aggressiveness of the motor vehicle.

Maybe the more visionary scientists are right when they assert that some day they will need "only mass and energy" in order to create *anything*; we can then stoke the stomachs of the most crowded population with tasty viands concocted of granite, industrial dust and kelp.

But the modern ecologist must weigh against the satisfactions of fecundity and stomach stoking the losses in quiet, in health, in open space, in dignity, in sanity itself, and in the preservation of natural beauty.

This qualitative malaise is nature's backlash that, at long last, is beginning to raise some welts. "Committing that sin of overweening bumptiousness, which the Greeks called hubris," wrote Aldous Huxley, "we behave as though we were not members of the earth's ecological community, as though we were privileged and in some sort, supernatural beings and could throw our weight around like gods."

The crisis has come upon us suddenly; by the same token, the sting of the ecological backlash can be countered only with emergency measures while we buy time. Harsh and limiting expedients are justified if they will allow us to come to grips with the basic economic and social distortions. This generation is experiencing the convulsions of a dying nature. Only mouth-to-mouth resuscitation will revive her now.

For example: the seas of the world are suffering progressive deterioration and mindless abuse. Whole species are being fished to death by unregulated mechanical rakes that comb the ocean floor, by percussion, explosion, and the greedy rivalry of prowling fleets of scores of nations existing in feudal maritime disorganization. Until international law can regulate in some measure the exploitation of the world's maritime waters, holding actions must be adopted. If, unilaterally, this country can prevent the fatal destruction of the estuaries, breeding grounds for two-thirds of the ocean's sea life within its jurisdiction, legislation to that end should be risked.

Again, 462 million tons of particulates are spewed into the air each year with catastrophes of deadly proportions impending when weather inversions press these masses of pollution too long and smotheringly over the metropolises. Any measures—restrictions on the automobile or tinkering with the smokestacks—are a boon.

If we would save the Emerald Mile, or the Northern Cascades, or the Grand Canyon from precipitant destruction, quick Congressional action is imperative. If we can stave off the rising tide of infectious hepatitis (50,000 new cases a year) and mononucleosis (resembling leukemia) by reducing the septic threat of the river sewers, we shall have to act boldly in this staying action. If New York Councilman Robert Low's bill to prohibit transistor radios in buses, subways and public places will aid in preserving the hearing, health of the heart and normalcy of the blood pressure (as Dr. Samuel Rosen declares), such a bill can hardly be tossed aside as "futile" or "immaterial."

However, to be realistic, it must be repeated that these holding actions are not solutions but expedients, and their most drastic implementation now promises, dismally, to offer little more than temporary relief. The real solution to this whole complex of civilized afflictions is a package of such cultural intricacy—it calls for revolutionary shifts in values and social goals—that time and intense effort alone can bring it about. In the long run, the conservationist cannot really save any natural wonder, any threatened species, any significant open space, breathable air, potable water, or the amenities of civilization unless he grapples with the self-destroying expansionism doctrine.

How can what Aldo Leopold termed "the ecological conscience" replace the ingrained American creed of unceasing growth? . . . How can we, in the words of Secretary Udall, "disentangle our minds and hearts from our purse strings?"—even to save ourselves?

By this time even the most crass and obdurate expansionist must face up to the pitiful incompetence of both industry and government to protect the natural heritage or safeguard the future. Industry is profit oriented; government is power oriented. The nation needs a stewardship of our remaining treasure that is posterity oriented.

Of late, many suggestions are springing forth as to how to effect this new sense of values and at the same time protect what is left. Federal Power Commissioner Charles R. Ross himself brought to attention the idea (publicized by Scenic Hudson Preservation Conference) of the British National Trust—guardians of the public weal—whose duty it is to examine all proposed projects in the light of historical as well as environmental damage. Composed of the most prestigious and impartial citizens personally selected by the Chancellors of Oxford, Cambridge and the University of London, the Trustees of the British Museum and National Art Gallery, the presidents of the Royal Academy of Arts, the Youth Hostels Association, the Entomological Society and Royal Horticultural Society, as well as heads of the National Trust for Scotland, Ramblers Association, Government of Northern Ireland, Commons Preservation Society, Society for the Promotion of Nature, and one or two others, it has served well "to save the pleasures of England from the social and economic revolution which is threatening our landscape."

"With the wealth of organizations in addition to the Sierra Club, such as the National Geographic Society, the Conservation Foundation, and the Wildlife Federation, this Nation could easily establish such an illustrious and influential body whose opinion would normally carry the day." "At the very least," adds the Commissioner, "the advantages of any development would have to be clearly in the Nation's interest before this Commission or the Secretary would overrule the objections of such a body." In the same vein, Rep. John V. Tunney of California is pressing hard for a "Council of Ecological Advisers"—eminent citizens divorced from commerce—to speak out for the public interest. It is certain that bureaucratic heads and pressure-tormented officials would, as Commissioner Ross has revealed, welcome such a trust for it would take the heat off their own necks. Best of all, for the first time in American history, the suicidal effects of the growth fixation would lie nakedly and honestly exposed.

Prof. Nathaniel Wollman, writing in *Daedalus* (Fall, 1967), is convinced that our only hope lies in the power of such a board of environmental experts to reduce our reliance "upon a technical elite for making the correct decision. . . ." And writer Robert Boyle restates the same idea in more earthy fashion when he says in *Sports Illustrated*: "Putting an engineer in charge of a resource such as a river is like hiring a plumber to design a fountain."

Always heretofore, when public agitation has risen to a head for some reform measure to save the land, the head has been neatly decapitated by the high-powered economists of the threatened interests. . . . Public rights and desires are left headless and speechless, and usually bleed quietly to death.

For another instance of this one-sided propaganda: right now when public anxiety is at its height concerning our foul rivers, we are slapped in the face with the statement that the $20 billion a year which it might cost to bring them back to a state of "pristine purity" is about as much as the nation spends for its public school education. Most people, we are assured, would find such an undertaking "ridiculous." The crusade falls on its face.

But if we had a public-oriented group of economists of the stature of Professor Wollman of the University of New Mexico, they might quickly tear such smug arguments to bits. Twenty billion dollars a year is "roughly one-third to one-half the amount by which one year's GNP exceeds the previous year's GNP. Should we decide, therefore, to restore our streams to purity," he concludes tellingly, "the cost is a delay by four to six months of the expected *increase* in all other goods and services that we would otherwise enjoy." Here at last we have both sides of the coin. Would that we now had at hand a National Ecological Trust where the rebuttal powers of Mr. Wollman and others like him might be broadcast to the entire populace rather than be hid, as they now are, in the esoteric covers of that weighty little Journal of the American Academy of Arts and Sciences, *Daedalus*.

For the findings of such a trust *would* be broadcast. By its very prestige, if not by the shock of its disclosures, it would command all communication media instantly. There arises here, however, the ancient enigma of the irresistible force and the immovable object. Once again the inborn growth obsession lifts its formidable head. We have built a whole set of sturdy institutions, economic and social, on the annually accelerated gouging of the environment. But in the words of architect

Robert W. Patterson, "You cannot multiply forever both people and the things that people want unless you plan to take over more territory than the sterile moon represents."

STEWART L. UDALL | ***The Urban Affliction***

Since 1965 the American political and social systems have been confronted by a test more demanding and ominous than any in the country's domestic history except the Civil War. This crisis represents the confluence of two tragic tributaries of failure: the century-long failure to build livable cities and the closely related failure to make a multiracial society work.

The trials of the nation in facing these failures have been painfully visible in fire, in violence, in the anguish of organized protest, in the anger and chaos of civil disorder, and in the extreme alienation of youth. U.S. citizens have openly advocated the wrecking of our cities, college campuses have seethed with protest, and a sense of community has disappeared in some urban sectors. For the first time since General Sherman's scorched-earth march to the sea in 1865, our cities have been put to the torch by Americans. These tragic occurrences and attitudes threaten the vitals of our system. They cast doubt on our ability to make the dream of brotherhood a reality. They call into question the competence of industry and government to eliminate poverty. They throw a garish spotlight on the failure of American urbanization. And they question both the quality of our leadership and the adaptability of our institutions.

No sudden lapse led to this emergency. In large measure it is the outgrowth of old errors and of shortcomings of previous generations. The seeds were planted by public and private policies of keeping a whole race in an inferior state; by approaches to economics that accepted poverty and slums as inevitable incidents of American life; by a division of power that strangled local government and demeaned local leadership; by a national default of conscience which produced the degradation of the environment; by the belief that producing goods for man was more important than the cultivation of the good in man. The truth is that our cities were on fire decades before the first flames at Watts. But the conflagration was, to use a phrase of Robert Frost's, "the slow, smokeless burning of decay." Yet, when physicians were finally put on the case (and the Cassandra-like forecasts of Lewis Mumford read plain), the diagnoses were consistent and clear-cut.

After the summer riots of 1967, at a time when the nation could boast of the most prolonged peacetime prosperity in history, a Detroit businessman peered into the pus-pocket slums of his city and exclaimed: "Absolutely terrifying. No wonder people riot." And Arnold Toynbee, always quick with prophecy, observed, "America seems to be heading for . . . a kind of permanent civil war within the principal cities of the United States." This was considered an alarmist judgment by most Americans. Conventional wisdom had held for two decades that a physical reconditioning of the slums would somehow arrest the destructive effects of race discrimination, and enough jobs would turn up to make life gradually better for the more than six million migrants who poured, unprepared, into the decaying cities of the North. The velocity of this mass migration can be indicated by two statistics: between 1960 and 1967 New Haven's nonwhite population rose from 15 to 24 per cent; Newark's rose from 34 to 52 per cent.

Slums, however, were only the worst sores on a sick urban body. Architect Edward Durell Stone looked at the U.S. cityscape and scathingly described it as "a main street with its neon wilderness, architecture without beauty or distinction, streets snarled up in automobiles, no harmony, no beauty, few trees, limited park areas . . . nothing but an asphalt jungle where the big idea is to sell merchandise, put gas in the automobile, and move on." Stone was right, but, given the blighted urban scene, right in a way that ironically subverts the best values of his own fine work. The cruelest part of the irony lies in society's limited use of men like Stone. To confine architecture, as Americans almost always do, to single structures rather than over-all designs is to guarantee that what few good buildings are built will be imbedded in personal or corporate privacy and make virtually no contribution to the essential fabric of the city.

Other self-appointed physicians of sick cities have echoed Stone's judgment: an eminent architect wondered aloud whether American cities were "too ugly to save"; a sensitive editor termed our largest city, New York, "something of an insult"; a *Fortune* writer, back from a nationwide tour, asserted that "the United States has let its public environment run to overpowering disorder," and concluded that "the whole place needs to be done over," and an elderly architect chided his countrymen for turning one of the "most beautiful continents into one of the ugliest" in the short space of half a century.

This spate of criticism raises basic questions. Why do we linger outside the door of distinction, so rich and so slovenly, so friendly and so filled with hate? Why should a people prideful of its science settle for a soiled and second-rate environment? Why has the most science-centered society in history *not* developed a science of human settlements? Why is our industrial complex able to build Saturn rockets but unable to fashion tools to renovate and renew the environment where most of us live? Why, if it is sound to spend billions of dollars on supersonic aircraft to whisk us to London in two hours, is it not equally important to devise systems of public transportation to get most of us to and from work in less than half that time? Above all, why have we been so slow to come to grips with the domestic shortcomings that vitiate the best intentions of our foreign policies?

The answers to some of these questions lie, of course, in our history. Until now we have possessed this continent and prepared our living spaces on it more with rapacity than with regard for man, more with force of machine power than with vision. In attempting to reconstruct the flaws that led to failure, one encounters a vicious circle of attitudes and events that have shaped our large and small municipalities. Agrarian roots and the rural suspicion of two centuries taught us to distrust city conglomerations; distrust led to the rigging of arrangements (rotten boroughs and rural malapportionment were only the most notorious disfranchising devices), which seriously weakened city action; weak city government led to a system of low priorities, then to even lower citizen expectations of the capability of local government. Low expectations, in turn, led to weak leadership; weak leadership led to lack of control over growth, and onward to the waste of the resources and opportunities of cities. Finally, waste and improvidence led to supposedly "insoluble" problems, and insoluble problems meant that cities were indeed "ungovernable." Thus the ring closed back to the anticity bias where it all began.

Another circle of failure and frustration revolved around the racial issue. A legalized policy of apartness, sanctioned by broadly based private opinion, for nearly a century shaped a two-color caste system in American society. This caste system was accepted by city builders, catering to the market, who began to create vast homogeneous areas within and around the cities. People preferred to live together with their look-alike, be-alike brethren and would willingly commute many miles in order to place a safe distance between their private lives and the everyday world of business. This American way resulted in a large-scale pattern of urban sprawl and suburban segregation. It was quite possible in the suburban sameness for a child to play, go to school, and grow up without really knowing human beings of other races or classes. This was socially suffocating and further entrenched the mistrust of the egalitarian brotherhood propounded by Jefferson and reaffirmed by Lincoln. Thus another ring was closed, and became a formidable fortress against the influx of rural Negroes as they moved toward their new "homes" in the central cities. The truth of the matter was that, without quite knowing it, we were trying a unique and potentially ennobling experiment for the first time in the history of civilization—the establishment of a multiracial society—but our private commitment fell far short of our professed principles.

The historical development of our cities was determined by piecemeal decisions that bespoke the urgencies of commerce, geography, and prejudice, not the needs of a mature civilization. Initially, they grew beside the natural harbors of the seacoast and along rivers, where waterborne shipments of goods and people were convenient. Many of them sprang up overnight; others straggled into existence in shapes created by the short-view vectors of free enterprise. It has been pointed out by Charles Abrams that in the empire-building era that followed the Civil War the horse did more to shape most cities than the early architects. As Abrams puts it: "The distance he could draw a tram to work places, and the distance and speed a team of horses could pull a fire engine, determined the boundaries of a neighborhood. It was an era of equine city planning, equine streets, equine architecture, and equine industrialization. The age was equine even in its effect on personality, for it slowed human pace to that of the horse whose limitations conditioned man's ideals."

The life of the urban dweller and his values were consistently submerged and sacrificed. Railroads were rammed into the heart of most cities; the asphalt and steel bands of highways and railroads took the water fronts and riversides from the people; and, as the twentieth century progressed, land speculation and the automobile largely determined the face and character of the cities.

At the same time, there was a certain beauty to life in the small towns, enhanced by the physical proximity of all sorts and conditions of men. Though the rich man lived on the corner and the Negro, even here discriminated against, lived in "the back" or over the stable or garage, they were in contact; their lives were at least tangentially related. But this, too, was lost as the cities grew in size beyond all rational bounds.

European-style city-making was alien to our experience. The architect side of Jefferson's nature "envied Europe their art," but even he never expected much of our cities. It was not that we disdained design, but, rather, that we had designed a political system that denied cities the power or wherewithal to create greatness, and made improvised development become the American way. The planning and building of great cities, as Solon and Phidias found in ancient Athens, is always a task for teamwork. Detail is important, control even more so, and the undertaking must enlist the talents and cooperation of the entire community. But our genius has run to parts, not wholes. We have been builders of efficient, soaring buildings, not master builders of city complexes. Our one notable contribution to architecture is the skyscraper—a singular structural stunt that somehow symbolized both the excess of individualism that has brought us to the edge of urban bankruptcy and the readiness to employ steel without style and put technology before taste.

Great cities put people first. They use land lovingly to create the kind of large and small boulevards, plazas, malls, vistas, squares, and waterscapes which form the *ambiance* of London, Paris, Rotterdam, Florence, and Athens. In our country, only in the nation's capital does space and distance dominate and define a significant part of the setting. The squares and circles and spaces of Washington show what control and planning can do to make a city unique. Only Washington limits the height of all buildings by law. Its vistas allow its monuments to soar; its low buildings soften the handiwork of man and give trees a chance to spread the good tidings of a green sheath. Only in Washington, of all our major cities, do the spires of cathedrals still dominate the horizon and deny the message of the skyscraper sky line that we are pre-eminently and everlastingly a commercial civilization. But even the nation's capital is only a partial triumph, for beyond its spires and spaces lie the ugly enclaves of ghettos.

Our Phidiases—Frederick Law Olmsted and Daniel Burnham—had only a brief hour at the edge of things; and Frank Lloyd Wright, the most renowned American designer of this century, never completed a structure built with public funds in his seventy years as an architect. The most esteemed Americans of the last century were not apostles of urban design. They were, instead, inventors, single-minded captains of industry, and imaginative engineers. It did not occur to the Carnegies, Edisons, Rockefellers, Roeblings, and Fords of an earlier era to turn their talents away from machines and industrial efficiency to the creation of superior cities. Machine production and great feats of engineering, not the manufacture of elegant, highly livable cities, were the objective.

The last three generations of Americans have exploited the cities as surely as our nineteenth-century ancestors stripped and raided the forestlands of this continent. For every corporation or individual who gave an asset to the people, a hundred selfishly subtracted from the common wealth. Every unwise rezoning for ill-planned buildings robbed us of sky, a sense of space, a glimpse of greenery. Poor transportation systems robbed men of time, and a rising crescendo of noise robbed them of peace and privacy. Worst of all, laws that discouraged the uprooting of slums gave birth to superghettos and robbed everyone of the precious fellowship of neighborhood feeling.

But one must quickly acknowledge that this robbery was as legal as the leveling of the forests, for more often than not local officials paved the way for the developers who gradually dehumanized the cities. "Take," not "give"; "hasten," not "consider"—these were the cardinal rules. And when, in New York, farsighted men built Rockefeller Center—a plaza with a fountain and open space enclosed by office skyscrapers—the shock was so great that it took nearly a generation for imitators to step forward and repeat this spacious gesture.

It is a sad fact that governments often conspired to encourage the forces of disorder and decay. The federal government abetted fragmentation and encouraged nonplanning. The Federal Housing Administration actively encouraged the worst forms of suburban sprawl. Federal public-housing programs more often than not replaced the old slums with superslums of tomorrow, and all too often urban renewal was perverted into Negro removal. Until the late 1960's federal aid for air and water-pollution control was negligible. The one vast public-works program of the 1950's—the highway act of 1956—sliced up cities and compounded the congestion of car-inundated streets.

The squandering of the land, water, air, light, sky, and open space of our cities has been the conservation scandal of this century. The misuse of our water estate is a case in point. No nation has ever had more superb, water-based sites for cities; the settings of San Francisco, New York, Seattle, San Diego, Chicago, Boston, and St. Louis, to name but a few, were unsurpassed. With wise land-use planning, their rivers and lakes and harbors might have been the threads on which could be strung beads of beauty and order. Yet most of our cities have fouled and marred and depleted these assets. New York has more water front than any city in the world—five hundred and forty miles of it, with thirty-five miles of beaches—but untreated sewage, misplaced highways, and rotting clutter have cut off New Yorkers from their own shorelands. San Francisco's incomparable bay, insulted in every way known to mechanized man, is now misshapen and reduced in beauty and humane value. Many of the water-oriented cities of the Great Lakes area and the Mississippi basin paradoxically are forced to look landward for outdoor recreation and lakeward for new airport sites. By contrast, Italy's Venice, the only city to make optimum use of a water endowment, is, many agree, one of the most serene and enjoyable urban areas in all the world, albeit a static relic of a frozen past.

The dissipation of irreplaceable land has been equally appalling. Today, most cities waste most of their streets, as well as most of their open space, their water fronts, their vistas, their riverscapes, their parks. Fifty acres for cars and streets and parking lots and one, if any, for playgrounds is the apparent policy of most cities.

If, as President John F. Kennedy once noted, the wise use of resources is "the highest form of national thrift," we have indeed been profligate. Nowhere is this more so than in California, an area with the finest overall climate of North America. There, glistening air, majestic mountainscapes, unspoiled beaches, and a lovely landscape of orchards and farms and small cities have been swallowed up in an orgy of land speculation, untrammeled commercialism, and bulldozed progress. Nor is there tangible hope for salvation by technology in many parts of Southern California. The large-lot sprawl of five decades has so thinly and evenly spread the population across the valleys that mass transit is now unfeasible and a proliferation of highspeed freeways is the only form of "relief" so far found possible. In this automobile-centered environment, U.C.L.A. now charges its students more for parking space than for tuition.

In this area of California can be found all the accumulated ills of unplanned growth: exclusive reliance on the most inefficient means of transportation (the individual auto); an enormous waste of time in travel; the triumph of the shopping center and the decline of the neighborhood; the garish crescendo of the commercial striphighway and the Chinese-wall invasions of the omnipresent freeway; the expenditure of billions of dollars for highways (so people can "escape" to the beaches) but only pennies for parklands so desperately needed in every neighborhood; an apparent consensus that the highest and best use of urban land—and even the air itself—is for automotive, not human, activity. This is, in fact, the final triumph of machines over men. The small-grained scale that once invited a safe stroll, a hike, or a bicycle outing and the multipurpose, but always human, use of streets have been lost. Is it any wonder that Watts, a rotting cul-de-sac in the heart of the nation's least controlled explosion of suburban sprawl, was the first urban ghetto to blow up and burn?

As long as local governments lacked budgets, plans, and power, and were dedicated to the proposition that any growth was acceptable, no new or exciting approaches to metropolitan progress were possible. We were a pragmatic, individualistic people, and if new industrial activity promised payrolls, no other questions were asked. Industry was welcome, and if the entrepreneurs gouged a community and mortgaged its future by building a hideous plant that usurped open space and emitted effluents that ruined a river or befouled the air, this was acceptable, whether it was a pulp mill in an unspoiled valley in Idaho or North Carolina, a packing house in Omaha, or a steel mill on the Great Lakes. Urban environments have become the end products of misguided concepts of property rights and short-term profits. This is a conclusion we never grasped.

The warping of the few good land-use plans that we did have also played a part in the rape of metropolitan values. To this day, breaking zoning regulations is a game played with zest, and considerable success, in most cities. A single vignette of suburban development dramatizes the sorry story and reveals a fatal weakness of local government as well. The rezoning of Merrywood, on the palisades of the Potomac near Washington, occurred in 1963. Among the participants were a county sheriff who acted as "broker," a group of developers, a suave zoning lawyer, and a Board of Supervisors (some of whose members were later convicted of conspiracy for actions in other rezoning cases). Rezoning was granted to allow high-rise apartments on the Potomac Palisades. This violated the metropolitan master plan, and in the end it was thwarted only by the purchase of a scenic easement by the National Park Service at a cost of nearly a million dollars.

Local government has not worked well in this country because we have not given it a fighting chance to function; its entities have been too weak to plan, too poor to act. But this, after all, was intended when we made the cities the starved stepchildren of government. Glib talk about "ungovernable" cities is a rationalization that masks an unwillingness to revitalize local governments and permit large-scale urban renovation to begin. Weak city and county government is the foreseeable result of past practices. Rural-run legislatures and Congresses have rationed local power and retained the superior sources of revenue. The "lower" governments have been saddled with welfare and public-education costs that in most modern countries are paid for by central governments. At the same time, the "higher" bureaucracies have sat by complacently while the overpowering problems of poverty, pollution, and racial discord were piled on the doorsteps of underfinanced, undermanned, and already floundering urban governments.

With such handicaps and disabilities, the lag of leadership at city hall is easy to understand. Politics, like physics, has its own immutable laws. One is: weak politics repels excellence and attracts mediocrity. The nineteenth century put the outrageous Boss Tweed in the history books, but beyond Tom L. Johnson, of Cleveland, who took office in 1901, who are the mayors the nation remembers in the twentieth century? Who have been the inspirers and innovators? How many truly great mayors have reinvigorated urban institutions and presided over the refurbishing of their cities? The names are pitifully few; that much is certain. Of course, flamboyant mayors like "Big Bill" Thompson, of Chicago, Michael Curley, of Boston, and New York's Jimmy Walker found a place in memory as shrewd showmen who entertained the populace while they presided over the slow decay of their cities. Tied to the patronage politics which captured the votes of the minority groups in the melting pot, unaware of the basic elements of urban grace, they readily sacrificed future livability to the selfish ambitions of developers and the agents of industrial growth. For all his panache, what, one is tempted to inquire, is the municipal legacy Fiorello La Guardia left New York? How well did he prepare his city for the postwar onslaught of change? For all his temporary triumphs in moving traffic, will not Robert Moses be remembered more for the wetlands and beaches he saved than for all his asphalt and bridges? And is it not sadly significant that New York City's most vivid postwar figure until John Lindsay took office in 1966 was the official "greeter," Grover Whalen, rather than any leader who attempted to modernize and humanize our most "vibrant" city?

Across the nation, leadership failed to involve the talents of industry and the design sector in the effort for municipal betterment. Until the riots of the 1960's, few businessmen bothered to involve themselves and their organizations in the future of the city. They paid their taxes, complained, commuted to the far edge of megalopolis—and left the rest to city hall. As for leadership from the design professions, the paucity of gifted city planners in this century is noteworthy. Apart from Daniel Burnham, of Chicago, and the younger Olmsted (and even they dealt too much in superficialities), one must race ahead to the last decade, to the work of Edward Logue in Boston and Edmund Bacon in Philadelphia, to find bold concepts and broad vision. Architects, it seemed, could be counted on to design individual buildings, but were not enlisted for the larger task of saving the city. After making a thankful bow to the best mayors of recent times—Richard Lee, of New Haven, David Lawrence, of Pittsburgh, Joseph Clark, of Philadelphia, Raymond Tucker, of St. Louis, and maybe William Hartsfield, John Collins, Jerome Cavanagh, and John Lindsay—one realizes how few of these excellent men have been able to marshal the energy, insight, and power needed to carry out large-scale projects to reshape entire cities.

It is, therefore, understandable that the best examples of city planning in this country grew out of tightly controlled and carefully implemented master plans. For example, both Washington, D.C., and Salt Lake City were offshoots not of ordinary politics but of authoritarian circumstance. L'Enfant could plan because he was the agent of a Founding Father who was authorized to plan a capital; Brigham Young could lay out Salt Lake City because he was the unquestioned leader of a theocratic state. But these efforts were atypical and ran against the American grain. Catch-as-catch-can speculative building, small-time profiteers, and racial bigotry were to fix the frame and face of most municipalities.

Unfortunately, even those social surgeons who correctly diagnosed the big-city sickness found their remedies impeded by the vested interests and obsolete institutions. Sound cities were impossible if outmoded charters forbade regional solutions to the over-all problems. How could there be a common plan or good design or programs of environmental rehabilitation when no one could do anything about upriver pollution, upwind air contamination, or the care and keeping of the land itself?

The whole sad story is epitomized by the political plight of metropolitan New York, with its seventeen county governments and five hundred autonomous zoning boards. How can the hopes and needs of such disparate groups be welded into a whole and wholesome entity? Westchester county, a classic piece of the metropolitan mosaic, itself has twenty-eight independent "master plans," thirty-seven different subdivision regulations, thirty-eight "official" maps, forty-four zoning regulations, two hundred and fifteen members of assorted planning groups, two hundred and eighty members of legislative boards, two hundred and forty-five school trustees, and twenty-eight members of county commissions.

With no agreement on common principles of planning, such diverse and numerous voices can only shout in the discord of competing ideas and conflicting standards that will inevitably doom entire regions to no-plan plans, to citizen apathy, and to localized aims and commonplace aspirations. If growth is to be decided *ad hoc,* by the day-to-day whims and maneuverings of "just grow" land speculation, random development will decide the shape and scale of the American city and guarantee a man-made mess of continental proportions. This, of course, has been a reflection of the inner drive of the suburbanite to establish easygoing environments insulated, temporarily at least, from the problems of interracial fellowship and high property taxes.

Into this complacent system, between 1950 and 1968, six million Southern Negroes spilled northward, bearing with them all the accumulated disabilities of a demoralizing social system that had left them wholly unprepared to succeed in the cities. The only reception these "immigrants" got was joblessness and the cold hospitality of a demeaning system of social welfare. This new American melting pot quickly became a cold cauldron of frustrated hopes. Unsolved human problems multiplied in urban areas functionally incapable of dealing with them. So we came, with slow understanding, to what we now call the "urban crisis of the 1960's."

Now that history has unmistakably certified our failures, I am convinced that it is a stroke of fortune that the many overriding issues of cities and human relations interlock and overlap. We cannot solve one problem without resolving the total problem; we must, as part of a single, unprecedented project, build beautiful cities and attempt to become a beautiful people ourselves. To reheat our melting pot, and stir it wisely and well, will require that the issues of racial fellowship, slums, ghettos, and urban imbalance be dealt with together, as part of an inspiring national plan. The miscalled "Negro problem" is now subsumed under the larger issue of how to redefine good cities and the good life in this country.

No great city will ever just grow. It must express a vision, a plan. There can be no common glory in a free society without a common plan, and such a plan can only exist as an expression of public purpose. The many mansions of the radiant city involve far more than the furnishing of attractive rooms for individual living. This is the lesson we have yet to learn.

There are some hopeful signs. Some leaders of business, labor, politics, and design are beginning to understand that the cities cannot be saved without their aid. But it is time to acknowledge that our troubles are too acute for repair work, little plans, or the patchwork programs of "urban renewal." Indeed, one can hope the turning point was reached sometime in the 1960's. In the last month of his life, in a noble address at Amherst, President John F. Kennedy elevated his gaze to "Look forward to the day when we will build handsome and balanced cities . . . ," and a few months later his successor, Lyndon B. Johnson, made city renewal a central theme of his Great Society program.

But the hard realities of the 1960's—the squalor, the ugliness, the inhumanity, and the police squads at the ready—tell us that the failure of American urbanization is now a judgment of history. The urban malady is severe and pervasive. Experience has taught us the hard lesson that far more is required than palliatives and pilot programs. The urban affliction will respond only to the sound surgery and humane therapy of a dedicated generation. If our social problems are great, so are our resources, our talents, our aspirations. Man's highest hopes, his most remembered experiments in living, have been acted out in cities throughout the course of history. The future of this nation can be no greater than the future of the American city.

REPORT OF THE NATIONAL ADVISORY COMMISSION ON CIVIL DISORDERS | ***Two Societies—Separate and Unequal***

The summer of 1967 again brought racial disorders to American cities, and with them shock, fear, and bewilderment to the nation.

The worst came during a two-week period in July, first in Newark and then in Detroit. Each set off a chain reaction in neighboring communities.

On July 28, 1967, the President of the United States established this Commission and directed us to answer three basic questions:

What happened?

Why did it happen?

What can be done to prevent it from happening again?

To respond to these questions, we have undertaken a broad range of studies and investigations. We have visited the riot cities; we have heard many witnesses; we have sought the counsel of experts across the country.

This is our basic conclusion: Our nation is moving toward two societies, one black, one white—separate and unequal.

Reaction to last summer's disorders has quickened the movement and deepened the division. Discrimination and segregation have long per-

From *The Report of the National Advisory Commission on Civil Disorders,* Otto Kerner, Chairman (New York: Bantam Books, 1968).

meated much of American life; they now threaten the future of every American.

This deepening racial division is not inevitable. The movement apart can be reversed. Choice is still possible. Our principal task is to define that choice and to press for a national resolution.

To pursue our present course will involve the continuing polarization of the American community and, ultimately, the destruction of basic democratic values.

The alternative is not blind repression or capitulation to lawlessness. It is the realization of common opportunities for all within a single society.

This alternative will require a commitment to national action—compassionate, massive, and sustained, backed by the resources of the most powerful and the richest nation on this earth. From every American it will require new attitudes, new understanding, and above all, new will.

The vital needs of the nation must be met; hard choices must be made, and, if necessary, new taxes enacted.

Violence cannot build a better society. Disruption and disorder nourish repression, not justice. They strike at the freedom of every citizen. The community cannot—it will not—tolerate coercion and mob rule.

Violence and destruction must be ended—in the streets of the ghetto and in the lives of people.

Segregation and poverty have created in the racial ghetto a destructive environment totally unknown to most white Americans.

What white Americans have never fully understood—but what the Negro can never forget—is that white society is deeply implicated in the ghetto. White institutions created it, white institutions maintain it, and white society condones it.

It is time now to turn with all the purpose at our command to the major unfinished business of this nation. It is time to adopt strategies for action that will produce quick and visible progress. It is time to make good the promises of American democracy to all citizens—urban and rural, white and black, Spanish surname, American Indian, and every minority group.

Our recommendations embrace three basic principles:

To mount programs on a scale equal to the dimensions of the problems.

To aim these programs for high impact in the immediate future in order to close the gap between promise and performance.

To undertake new initiative and experiments that can change the system of failure and frustration that now dominates the ghetto and weakens our society.

The programs will require unprecedented levels of funding and performance, but they neither probe deeper nor demand more than the problems which called them forth. There can be no higher priority for national action and no higher claim on the nation's conscience.

No American—white or black—can escape the consequences of the continuing social and economic decay of our major cities.

Only a commitment to national action on an unprecedented scale can shape a future compatible with the historic ideals of American society.

The great productivity of our economy, and a federal revenue system which is highly responsive to economic growth, can provide the resources.

The major need is to generate new will—the will to tax ourselves to the extent necessary to meet the vital needs of the nation.

We have set forth goals and proposed strategies to reach those goals. We discuss and recommend programs not to commit each of us to specific parts of such programs but to illustrate the type and dimension of action needed.

The major goal is the creation of a true union—a single society and a single American identity. Toward that goal, we propose the following objectives for national action:

Opening up opportunities to those who are restricted by racial segregation and discrimination, and eliminating all barriers to their choice of jobs, education and housing.

Removing the frustration of powerlessness among the disadvantaged by providing the means for them to deal with the problems that affect their own lives and by increasing the capacity of our public and private institutions to respond to these problems.

Increasing communication across racial lines to destroy stereotypes, to halt polarization, end distrust and hostility, and create common ground for efforts toward public order and social justice.

We propose these aims to fulfill our pledge of equality and to meet the fundamental needs of a democratic and civilized society—domestic peace and social justice.

Pervasive unemployment and underemployment are the most persistent and serious grievances in minority areas. They are inextricably linked to the problem of civil disorder.

Despite growing federal expenditures for manpower development and training programs, and sustained general economic prosperity and increasing demands for skilled workers, about two million—white and nonwhite—are permanently unemployed. About ten million are underemployed, of whom 6.5 million work full time for wages below the poverty line.

The 500,000 "hard-core" unemployed in the central cities who lack a basic education and are unable to hold a steady job are made up in large part of Negro males between the age of 18 and 25. In the riot cities which we surveyed, Negroes were three times as likely as whites to hold unskilled jobs, which are often part time, seasonal, low-paying and "dead end."

Negro males between the ages of 15 and 25 predominated among the rioters. More than 20 percent of the rioters were unemployed, and many who were employed held intermittent low status, unskilled jobs which they regarded as below their education and ability.

Education

Education in a democratic society must equip children to develop their potential and to participate fully in American life. For the community at large, the schools have discharged this responsibility well. But for many minorities, and particularly for the children of the ghetto, the schools have failed to provide the educational experience which could overcome the effects of discrimination and deprivation.

This failure is one of the persistent sources of grievance and resentment within the Negro community. The hostility of Negro parents and students toward the school system is generating increasing conflict and causing disruption within many city school districts. But the most dramatic evidence of the relationship between educational practices and civil disorders lies in the high incidence of riot participation by ghetto youth who have not completed high school.

The bleak record of public education for ghetto children is growing worse. In the critical skills—verbal and reading ability—Negro students are falling further behind whites with each year of school completed. The high unemployment and underemployment rate for Negro youth is evidence, in part, of the growing educational crisis.

We support integration as the priority education strategy; it is essential to the future of American society. In this last summer's disorders we have seen the consequences of racial isolation at all levels, and of attitudes toward race, on both sides, produced by three centuries of myth, ignorance, and bias. It is indispensable that opportunities for interaction between the races be expanded.

We recognize that the growing dominance of pupils from disadvantaged minorities in city school populations will not soon be reversed. No matter how great the effort toward desegregation, many children of the ghetto will not, within their school careers, attend integrated schools.

If existing disadvantages are not to be perpetuated, we must drastically improve the quality of ghetto education. Equality of results with all-white schools must be the goal.

The Welfare System

Our present system of public welfare is designed to save money instead of people, and tragically ends up doing neither. This system has two critical deficiencies.

First, it excludes large numbers of persons who are in great need, and who, if provided a decent level of support, might be able to become more productive and self-sufficient. No federal funds are available for millions of men and women who are needy but neither aged, handicapped, nor the parents of minor children.

Second, for those included, the system provides assistance well below the minimum necessary for a decent level of existence, and imposes restrictions that encourage continued dependency on welfare and undermine self-respect.

A welter of statutory requirements and administrative practices and regulations operate to remind recipients that they are considered untrustworthy, promiscuous, and lazy. Residence requirements prevent assistance to people in need who are newly arrived in the state. Regular searches of recipients' homes violate privacy. Inadequate social services compound the problems.

Housing

After more than three decades of fragmented and grossly underfunded federal housing programs, nearly six million substandard housing units remain occupied in the United States.

The housing problem is particularly acute in the minority ghettos. Nearly two-thirds of all non-white families living in the central cities today live in neighborhoods marked with substandard housing and general urban blight. Two major factors are responsible.

First, many ghetto residents simply cannot pay the rent necessary to support decent housing. In Detroit, for example, over 40 percent of the non-white occupied units in 1960 required rent of over 35 percent of the tenants' income.

Second, discrimination prevents access to many non-slum areas, particularly the suburbs, where good housing exists. In addition, by creating a "back pressure" in the racial ghettos, it makes it possible for landlords to break up apartments for denser occupancy, and keeps prices and rents of deteriorated ghetto housing higher than they would be in a truly free market.

To date, federal programs have been able to do comparatively little to provide housing for the disadvantaged. In the 31-year history of subsidized federal housing, only about 800,000 units have been constructed, with recent production averaging about 50,000 units a year. By comparison, over a period only three years longer, FHA insurance guarantees have made possible the construction of over ten million middle and upper-income units.

Two points are fundamental to the Commission's recommendations.

First, federal housing programs must be given a new thrust aimed at overcoming the prevailing patterns of racial segregation. If this is not done, those programs will continue to concentrate the most impoverished and dependent segments of the population into the central-city ghettos where there is already a critical gap between the needs of the population and the public resources to deal with them.

Second, the private sector must be brought into the production and financing of low and moderate rental housing to supply the capabilities and capital necessary to meet the housing needs of the nation.

Conclusion

One of the first witnesses to be invited to appear before this Commission was Dr. Kenneth B. Clark, a distinguished and perceptive scholar. Referring to the reports of earlier riot commissions, he said:

> I read that report . . . of the 1919 riot in Chicago, and it is as if I were reading the report of the investigating committee on the Harlem riot of '35, the report of the investigating committee on the Harlem riot of '43, the report of the McCone Commission on the Watts riot.
>
> I must again in candor say to you members of this Commission—it is a kind of Alice in Wonderland—with the same moving picture reshown over and over again, the same analysis, the same recommendations, and the same inaction.

These words come to our mind as we conclude this report.

We have provided an honest beginning. We have learned much. But we have uncovered no startling truths, no unique insights, no simple solutions. The destruction and the bitterness of racial disorder, the harsh polemics of black revolt and white repression have been seen and heard before in this country.

It is time now to end the destruction and the violence, not only in the streets of the ghetto but in the lives of people.

PETER FARB | ***Portraits of the Forgotten: The American Indian***

The quadrennial elections never fail to evoke compassion for "the Vanishing Americans," and this year the tragicomedy is again being played with style. "The poor Indian" is once more the theme of position papers and convention planks. As it did four years ago, the Administration has sent a message to Congress that repeats the aspirations of the Great White Father for his red children: better education, better housing, better health care, better job training. (Since "better" is a relative word, the Great White Father has pinpointed exactly how much "better" he has in mind: a mere 12 percent increase from last year's incredibly low, fantastically mismanaged budget.) Politicians of both parties are making their usual salutes to the "progress" of the red man in adapting to a white world. Vice President Humphrey states that tuberculosis among Indians declined 55 percent since 1955—but he neglects to add the fact that the Indian death rate from tuberculosis is still seven times that of the American population as a whole. Perhaps the least politically motivated obeisance to the red man was Senator Robert F. Kennedy's inquiry, just before his assassination, into the shame of Indian education.

The facts about Indian life today assuredly are bleak enough without election-year dramatization. Some 400,000 of the total 550,000 Indians in the United States live on approximately 200 reservations in twenty-six states. The reservations exist as poverty-stricken islands surrounded by an ocean of American bounty. The Indians are generally despised by whites; they are in ill health both physically and mentally, almost without political power, inarticulate in their attempts to win respect for their heritage. The amazing thing is not that they have managed to survive at all, but that they still possess patience about the white man's latest aspirations for them this election year. They hang on to a little piece of the future, but every year their grip slips a bit more. For this is their life today:

Housing. About 90 percent of Indians live in tin-roofed shacks, leaky adobe huts, brush shelters, and even abandoned automobiles. Approximately 60 per cent of Indians still haul their drinking water, frequently from more than a mile away and often from contaminated sources.

Income and Jobs. Indian unemployment ranges between 40 and 75 per cent in comparison with about 4 per cent for the nation as a whole. On one reservation in Utah I visited this summer, less than 25 per cent of the eligible work force had jobs—and most of these were employed by their own tribal organization. The average red family lives on $30 a week, while average white and black families earn at least $130 a week.

Health. The average age of death for an Indian today is forty-three years, for a white sixty-eight years. Death from dysentery is forty times greater among Indians than whites; influenza and pneumonia death rates are twice as high; middle-ear infections are so widespread that on some reservations a quarter of the children have suffered permanent hearing loss. Trachoma, an infectious eye disease that often causes blindness, is virtually nonexistent in the United States—except on the reservations. A survey made a few years ago on the San Carlos Apache Reservation in

Arizona showed that 61 per cent of the children between the ages of five and eighteen were afflicted.

Education. Indian education is the worst of any minority group. The Indian completes about five years of schooling—whereas all other Americans average 11.2 years. It is not only the quantity of education the Indian is deprived of but the quality, for the saddest fact of all is that the longer he stays in school, the farther behind his achievement falls in comparison with white children.

In Idaho's Blackfoot school district, for example, three-fourths of the students in the elementary school are Indian, yet every teacher is white. Speaking any Indian language is prohibited and nothing is taught of Indian culture. In the last few years there have been nearly fifteen suicides by the school children. One out of every five junior-high students was found to be sniffing glue. When Senator Robert Kennedy visited the district, he asked the principal whether Indian culture and traditions were taught. He was informed, "There isn't any history to this tribe"—although the grandfathers of these children had played an important role in the history of the West. When the Senator asked if there were any books in the library where the children could read about Indian culture, he was shown *Captive of the Delawares,* which had a picture on the cover of a white child being scalped by an Indian.

The Indian can probably survive the bad housing, lack of jobs, dismal health conditions, and poor education—but not the implication that he is irrelevant to American culture. For once the Indians are deprived of the last bit of the culture that has sustained them, they will disappear into the faceless American poor. Yet, the U.S. Bureau of Indian Affairs was founded a century ago with the stated aim to alienate Indian children "from their native culture and language so they could take their place in modern society"—and that has remained an implied aim to this day. A white policy has stripped the Indian of his identity and made him embarrassed about his rich oral literature, his customs and traditions, his native foods and dress. A white education system has turned out imitation whites who succumb to the bleakness of reservation life and the prejudice around them.

"The American Indian today is about to go over the brink—not only of poverty and prejudice, but of moral collapse," says William Byler, executive director of the Association on American Indian Affairs. The Indian has learned that no one wants to listen or to understand when he speaks his thoughts about his own future. He is bewildered by the capricious policies handed down in Washington—first telling him to leave the reservation and get jobs in the cities, next telling him to stay on the reservation and bring industry to it. Some politicians tell him that he is a child who must be protected by the kindly White Father—and other politicians tell him that he is man enough to be cast adrift to sink or swim in the capitalist tide. The result of such confusion is widespread apathy among Indians. They find it difficult to act in concert with other Indians because whites deliberately ripped apart the intricate web of their social and political relationships.

. . .

Many people concerned about the American Indian are coming to believe that we should simply stop offering the Indian pat solutions. Everything has been tried. The Indians have been herded from reservation to reservation, switched from hunting to agriculture or from agriculture to hunting, moved to cities to work in factories or told instead to make room for factories on their reservations. Indians exist today as the most manipulated people on earth—and yet our Indian policy has produced only failure after failure.

We have never recognized the Indian as someone who has his own historical rights to live and to act as an Indian within the framework of what remains of his culture. It is time that Washington allowed Indians on their own reservations to make their own decisions about their futures. Instead of dismantling the reservations, as some land-hungry Congressmen propose, let us begin by dismantling the U.S. Bureau of Indian Affairs. Indians directly concerned, and many impartial observers of the Indian scene as well, regard BIA as incredibly inefficient and unresponsive to the needs of modern Indians. Most BIA personnel still operate with the nineteenth-century attitudes of the Indian fighters and still regard the Indians as childlike wards of the federal government. BIA is distrusted, and even hated, by most Indians.

A model for a new Indian-Government relationship already exists and has been tested successfully for thirty-five years—the U.S. Soil Conservation Service. SCS is a service agency that provides farmers, ranchers, and timber growers with technical assistance that aids them in deriving the most benefits from various federal and state programs. But the actual policymaking and coordination of the work of many experts are firmly in the hands of some 3,000 soil conservation districts across the nation. Each district is a legal entity whose locally elected boards have the authority to work out constructive plans for their individual problems.

With such a new Indian-Government relationship, the sprawling federal programs in education, housing, employment, and so forth would be coordinated by local people who would adapt the programs to local need. With such a plan, it would be possible to take away the education responsibilities from BIA and place them in the Office of Education; the employment problems of Indians could be better handled by the Department of Labor; a start in decentralization has already been made in taking many health services away from BIA and having them carried on by the Public Health Service. Taking the human resource problems out of BIA leaves it free to concentrate on the land resource, a responsibility for which the U.S. Department of the Interior, of which it is a part, has a long history of competence.

But will the Indian be willing to participate in administering his own future? Promising indications that he will exist on many reservations. The Sioux of South Dakota, as just one example, impressed me this summer by their aggressive concern for taking what is best from American society while holding on to what remains of their own traditions. They are working hard to get the most benefits from the existing federal programs in health, education, welfare, employment, and housing while at the same time seeking to make their voices heard. Among other things, they have organized voter registration drives and elected Indians to school boards for the first time in history.

Clearly, it is time we stopped regarding Indians as living museum pieces with no relevance to America today. Their past and their future, for better or for worse, are intertwined with ours.

PETER SCHRAG | *Appalachia*

Once again Appalachia is becoming America's forgotten land. Seven years and more than seven billion federal dollars after John F. Kennedy brought the region to national attention, grand solutions have soured into new problems, the exploitation of land and people continues, and even the best and most hopeful efforts are jeopardized by a war 10,000 miles away and by ugly political machines all too close to home.

. . .

Appalachia, the original American frontier, extends from southern Pennsylvania to northern Alabama, covering 182,000 square miles of land rich in coal, timber, sandstone, natural gas, water, and some of the most magnificent scenery on the continent. In 1966, nearly 100 million tons of coal worth close to $400 million were mined in Kentucky alone. Where the strip mines have spared the hillsides, the folded mountains, covered by white oak, pine, walnut, beech, and other trees, extend in all directions to the blue-gray horizon. But in the half-abandoned coal camps that adjoin the sulphur-polluted creeks, on the streets of the little towns, and in the welfare offices, the poverty of the people stands in brutal contrast to the wealth of the land. Along the winding roads, the rotting carcasses of abandoned automobiles lie alongside smoldering coal dumps and the decaying tipples of exhausted mines, and in the brown and yellow streams, once rich with fish, the sad trash of poverty accumulates in rusty piles.

Appalachia, now growing its third welfare generation, has counties where more than a third of the population is unemployed, where the government check—social security, welfare, aid to dependent children—is the prime source of income, and where some men are so far from their last job that it cannot properly be said that they have a trade at all. Here the average adult has a sixth-grade education, three-fourths of the children who start school drop out before they complete the twelfth grade, and the statistics of human pathology—tuberculosis, silicosis, infant mortality—are so high that they do not belong in the Western world at all.

Everything has eroded: The best of the resources flow forever down stream and toward the industrial cities of the North. Heavy rains wash the topsoil from the hills and turn the rivers into muddy torrents, the coal fires the mills of the North and the generators of the TVA (which is the prime buyer of Appalachian fuel), while the most skilled and ambitious of the young leave the hills and hollows to find work in Cleveland, Chicago, or Detroit. "We've been the great pool of manpower for the Northeast," said a poverty worker in eastern Tennessee. "And the pool has been turned on and off at will. The rest of the country gets automobiles and the gadgets of affluence. All this region gets is silicosis."

. . .

In this sad economy of food stamps and subsistence, the coal company is no longer the great employer—and hence the paternalistic provider—it used to be. Gone are the days when the company owned the buildings, ran the store, and furnished the services, and even the most naïve have now abandoned the hope that some day "the mines will open up again." What remains is the condition of dependency: Through a half-century of rural industrialization, the once-independent mountaineer was reduced to reliance on a single enterprise, and, when it no longer required his labor, to nothing except the dole. The public payroll, and most notably the public schools, now furnish the prime source of employment. In Appalachia, schools mean jobs for bus drivers, clerks, lunchroom employees, coaches, and teachers, and hence they represent the most important source of political power at hand. In the isolated mountain counties, where kinship and tribal loyalties overshadow the abstractions of political ethics, the school superintendent is often a political boss who controls and contracts for insurance, construction, and fuel, appointment to other offices, and employment in the system.

. . .

The American romance with the happy hillbilly came to an end in the early Sixties. Prompted by Mr. Kennedy's concern with Appalachian poverty—which he saw first hand in the 1960 West Virginia primary—Americans began to discover the misery behind the moonshine. Television crews and magazine writers swarmed to the hills in such numbers that one Kentucky motel owner began to conduct photographic safaris to hollows that he promised "ain't been worked yet." While bands of hungry, desperate miners roamed the coal regions dynamiting trains and bridges, Congress passed the Manpower Development and Training Act, the Appalachia Redevelopment Act, and a variety of other measures designed to bring the heretofore invisible poor some share of the affluence that most Americans took for granted.

. . .

. . . the existing programs serve only to hide the misery: The new highways are beginning to make it possible to cross large portions of Appalachia without seeing a tarpaper shack or a coal dump; the food stamps run out before the end of the month, and the schools, though far better than they used to be, still remain a blind alley, graduating children who are approximately two years behind the national average on standardized tests. "The bare gut essentials are now being met," said Tom Gish, the editor of the Whitesburg, Kentucky, *Mountain Eagle,* who is undoubtedly the most outspoken and dedicated journalist in the region. "By and large people are getting fed and getting coal for the winter. If you go back to the early Sixties when there was mass hunger and violence, then you can say there's been improvement. Peace has been restored."

But the peace is shaky, and the economy remains dependent on the federal government. . . . Poverty remains endemic: Median family income in eastern Kentucky is $3,505, and Gish predicts that if poverty funds are reduced there will be more violence. In the county seats, the prosperous get roads and water lines and sewers, but only a few miles away the privies stand alongside the dirty creeks from which people draw their water, rain turns the unpaved roads into muddy ruts, and the youngsters can't go to school because they have no shoes.

The prime beneficiaries of government funds appear to be the swelling banks, which are afraid to invest their deposits in anything but government bonds; the small businesses; and the politicians. For all their ignorance and isolation, the economic and political interests of Appalachia have a highly developed knack for using outside help to perpetuate the existing structure and the conditions of dependency. In Perry County, Kentucky, a political enemy of a former county school superintendent used his influence as director of a poverty project to help elect a new school board and oust the superintendent; the new administration then rewarded him with the directorship of another federally financed program administered by the schools. In other areas, the directors of happy pappy programs discourage their charges from participating in community action groups that threaten local political machines, and in almost every community the traditions of nepotism are so powerful that many people still regard the poverty program as a source of employment rather than as a means of upgrading the skills of human beings and the social health of the community. "Jobs are coveted so much, and loyalties to kin are so strong," said a poverty worker in Kentucky, "that it's pretty hard to persuade anyone that you have to pick people on merit."

Although some training programs have brought new skills and confidence, and although many children who had once gone hungry through the school day are now receiving hot lunches (sometimes even in the most remote one-room schools), many school officials have refused to appoint outsiders, preferring to promote politically faithful employees to the uncertainties of new blood and new ideas. . . .

Given these conditions, the most promising idea for Appalachia has been community action—training individuals to organize local groups for social improvement, community welfare, and self-help. As originally conceived, the Community Action Program (CAP) of the Office of Economic Opportunity was to include "maximum feasible participation" of the poor: Community action agencies were, if possible, to be free from domination by local politicians. In some areas of Appalachia, the program worked effectively, despite the suspicions of county officials: Community centers have been built, small marketing cooperatives (selling quilts and other local products) have been organized, and new leadership has developed. In the eastern Kentucky counties of Leslie, Knott, Letcher, and Perry, a four-county Community Action Program (LKLP), which includes poor people as well as sympathetic county judges, has established a network of depots to inform people of their welfare rights, of new training programs, and of the availability of medical facilities. Among other things, LKLP operated a transportation system to bring the sick from the hollows to the area clinics, it is training local people in welfare work and social service, and it has prompted a number of projects to clear the region of decaying bridges and abandoned coal tipples.

Despite such successes, however—and there are others—many CAP agencies have been captured by established interests or abandoned after local battles destroyed embryonic organizations before they had a chance to function. Many of those that survive must straddle an uncertain line between ineffectiveness and the dangerous course of challenging the established order. . . .

. . .

Perhaps the chief consequence of the recent programs in Appalachia is the realization that poverty and exploitation, isolation and ignorance, are not susceptible to left-handed solutions, that they are linked to the general affluence, and that they raise moral questions which strike at the very heart of America's willingness to bring a decent life to all its citizens. . . .

It is difficult to cheer the results of Appalachian development or the war on poverty: The harmonious interplay of poverty, politics, and the welfare mind combine to frustrate even the most valiant effort. But it is even more difficult to criticize the intent of these programs or the officials who are charged with running them. They have been forced to live with a limited and reluctant mandate that prohibits them from anything more than making poverty bearable and, if possible, invisible. The vested Appalachian interests in the status quo—coal companies, railroads, banks, local bar associations, insurance agencies, politicians—are so vast that they represent a fair cross section of American society itself. Their stockholders and beneficiaries live all over the nation; they help sustain our affluence. If Appalachia hasn't changed, it may be in part because too many are dependent on it as it now is.

JOHN KENNETH GALBRAITH | Education and Economic Development

In these last years, as many new countries of Asia and Africa have escaped colonial bondage and turned as first-class citizens to the tasks of their national development, they have had to decide what priority to accord to investment in education. Should it have the very highest priority? Is education a prerequisite to all other progress? Or should a certain economic base be provided first? Only as increased production income is available does a good education become possible. Only from this will there be wherewithal to support schools and colleges and universities. Economic growth is necessary if a nation is to pay for schools and the teachers.

This has been the debate. It has been decided in various ways. Sometimes, too, it has been decided without anyone's seeing that there is an argument. Education has been given priority. Or other forms of expenditure—roads, airports, dams—have been put first because they seemed the first essential.

The problem of priority here is comparatively new. Uncertainty has entered with economics. Economic development in our day has come to be regarded overwhelmingly as a problem in economic analysis. In economic analysis, in turn, the role of education is ambiguous. This ambiguity has led to doubt and uncertainty as to what comes first.

More specifically, we think of economic development as the investment of present resources for increased future production—the investment of savings for growth. We regularly measure the development effort of a country by the volume of its investment—what it saves from its own consumption, and what it is borrowing from consumers abroad, to invest in future increases in output. And here is the problem, for education is both a form of consumption and a kind of investment. Like bread, it is something we use or consume. But, like a dam or canal, it is something in which we invest to produce more in the future. This difference leads on to very different attitudes toward education in development. When we think of education as a consumer service, it becomes something on which we should save. Savings are necessary for investment, and savings are obtained by economizing on consumption. But when we think of education as an investment, it becomes something we should emphasize. We seek to expand investment. The resulting conflict in policy could scarcely be greater.

The contrasting attitudes which underlie this conflict are evident in almost every discussion of education. Convocation speakers the world around remind their highly indifferent audiences that man does not live by bread alone. The enrichment of the mind is as important as the nourishment of the body. Intellectual activity is properly pursued for its own sake; the poet, artist, or writer rightfully scorns economic gain as a test of performance. It was their tendency to apply economic calculation to refreshment of the spirit and mind which caused Carlyle to characterize eonomists as the learned professors of the dismal science. And who would say that people should be rescued from the serfdom of ignorance only in order to make them more productive? In these attitudes education is defended for its own sake—by my more vulgar definition, it is a consumer good. Though it is a rather superior consumer good, it has nothing directly to do with production. And those who take a less poetic view of matters righteously insist on the priority of ditches, dams, and fertilizer plants. For it is these that feed poets.

But there is another view. Studies by Theodore Schultz among others in the United States have recently shown that outlays for education may bring large increases in production. By the kind of calculation that Carlyle would have most abhorred, a dollar or a rupee invested in the intellectual improvement of human beings will often bring a greater increase in national income than a dollar or a rupee devoted to railways, dams, machine tools, or other tangible capital goods. To rescue farmers and workers from illiteracy may certainly be a goal in itself. But it is also a first indispensable step to any form of agricultural progress. Nowhere in the world is there an illiterate peasantry that is progressive. Nowhere is there a literate peasantry that is not. Education, so viewed, becomes a highly productive form of investment.

And this is true of many kinds of education. Most of us would agree on the importance of scientists and engineers for economic development. Machines are no more important than the men who make them, maintain them, or improve them. But the productivity of doctors and public health specialists is also very high. The suppression of malaria brings great increases in energy and output, as the experience of the last fifteen years has shown. (It also brings an astonishing output of babies, and, while we have talked of birth control in these last years, science has so far accomplished much more in promoting births than in preventing them.) The suppression of yaws and hookworm has a similar effect on productivity.

But not only scientists, engineers, and doctors are a good educational investment. There are surprising returns to esoteric and even exotic forms of knowledge. The linguist obviously maintains the avenues to the technology of other cultures. Literacy leads on to a demand for writers who can supply its market. And the accomplished writer adds to gross national production in precisely the same way as a successful farmer. Not even the artist, as an object of investment, may be ignored. One of the most successful industries of modern India is motion picture production. This industry flourishes only in the presence of a secure artistic tradition in the theater, music, ballet, and the visual arts. It requires reasonably good artists to produce bad pictures; it takes very good ones to produce good pictures. No one ever invested in an artist with a view toward helping the balance of payments. Yet India's artistic tradition is serving admirably to earn foreign exchange.

The fact is that education is of high importance both as an object of immediate consumption and as a form of investment for future production. It is neither consumption nor investment, but both. To look at education as a form of consumption, given the importance that the developing country attaches to investment, is to risk assigning it an unduly low priority. Some new countries have almost certainly done so. They have regarded their steel mills, dams, and fertilizer factories as the tangible manifestation of such development. Aswan, Volta, or Bhakra-Nangal *are* development. They get the discussion, the money, the visitors, the glow of pride. Well-trained teachers may provide a greater promise of increased production. But they are not such tangible monuments to progress.

However, I have a feeling that this mistake is by way of being corrected—and I hasten to say that it has never been nearly so serious an error in India as in the less developed lands. India has held, on the whole, to the lesson of the nineteenth century, which is that education, or education abetted by honest and orderly government, comes first. I doubt, however, that any country has yet accepted all of the implications of education as a form of development investment. Neither university students nor faculties have yet seen the full significance of their claim as a form of investment on scarce development resources. Let me turn to this.

If education, and henceforth I speak more specifically of university education, is regarded as a consumer service, we will naturally bring to it the attitudes that seemed appropriate to other forms of consumption. These include a high degree of permissiveness. The phrase "consumer sovereignty" is one of the oldest in economics; it implies the right of the consumer to choose between various forms of consumption. It implies, above all, to consume or not to consume, as he wishes.

This notion of consumer sovereignty, when brought to education, suggests that the student has the right to study or not to study as the consumer has the right to consume or not to consume. It implies that the choice lies with the individual and the individual alone. It implies that his field of study is purely a matter of his own preference. No one may interfere with or guide his sovereign choice in these matters. But if, in fact, the student is the privileged object of the investment of scarce resources, the matter is not so clear. Society has given him some of its savings. Surely he has a clear obligation to return to society the increased production that society expects and for which it has spent its scarce substance. The more scarce the resources, the greater this obligation.

As I have noted, if education is viewed as a consumer good, it is the privilege of every individual to pursue the curriculum of his choice. Everyone has a right to an arts degree if that is the preferred and fashionable course of study. But if education is a form of investment, then planning of educational output becomes desirable and even imperative. Attention must be accorded to the distribution of talent between engineering, science, medicine, agriculture, and other needed specialties. I am not going so far as to suggest that students should be forced into a profession which they do not prefer. And the planning of university specialization is an exceedingly difficult matter. But I am certainly suggesting that when education is viewed as an investment, serious thought must be given to the accommodation of students to need and the incentives and other arrangements by which this is brought about.

To view education as an investment will, I venture, have some bearing on university direction and administration. The university must be responsive to development requirements and it must be so organized as to make this possible. This means strong and responsive leadership by the faculty and its duly constituted representatives. The needs of the larger community must be effectively translated into curricula, courses, and good academic discipline. It is hard ever to take a stand against democracy. But the schoolmaster, at his best and in the most democratic countries, has always been a rather authoritarian figure. I doubt that a university can be wholly successful unless it reposes strong and responsible power in those who teach and unless those who teach delegate as needed to their representatives. In recent times Latin American universities have been experimenting with highly democratic direction in which students, graduates, and faculty all participate more or less equally. Democratic or not, it is a formula for deterioration, incoherence, and chaos. I believe the university is by nature an oligarchy of its faculty. This is especially so if education is regarded purposefully as an investment from which the most of what is needed must be obtained.

But I have no intention of allowing the faculty to escape without comment. It, too, has special responsibilities when education is viewed as a development outlay. By no means all of the traditional university practices and habits fit the requirements of the developing country. Thus, in most older university communities—mine is one—many faculty members have come to take a rather lofty view of teaching. We say that our primary task is research, or writing, or intellectual leadership. Students, we agree, are sufficiently privileged if they can see us passing in the street or listen thrice weekly to some uninspired and badly delivered lectures. These attitudes cannot be afforded if education is being tested by its productivity. Then the task of the teacher must be to mold and shape and guide and inspire his students to ensure that they are indeed a more productive property. If he fails to do so, he is squandering scarce public resources.

Nor can subject matter or degrees be copied as a matter of course by the university in the developing countries. As an economist, I look with considerable discontent on much of the economics that is taught in the new countries. It is not clinically concerned with the problems of these countries and pragmatically with their solutions. Rather it is often a fashionable elucidation of the sophisticated models and systems which are currently in fashion at Cambridge, the London School, or even at Harvard. As a layman I have sometimes wondered if medical education has been really adapted to the situation of the poor country. In the United States and Europe and, indeed, also in New Delhi, we yearn for doctors who are trained and totally trustworthy. The provision of such total training is the *sine qua non* of modern medical education. But in the developing country, with scarce resources, if we insist on these high standards for the few, may we not deny medical assistance to the many? Do we not get good doctors in the capitals at the price of having no one to set a broken leg or prescribe some morphine in the villages?

The problem of investment is always to obtain the kind of capital most appropriate to requirement at the lowest cost. There is indication in fields as diverse as medicine and economics that a less costly form of capital, better adjusted to the requirements of the developing country, could in fact be obtained. Investment, to speak technically, could be rationalized. No one would urge the wrong tractors for the underdeveloped country merely because they exist in America or the Soviet Union. So with education.

But let me summarize and make a more general point. A developing country may rightfully regard its outlays for education as an investment. The fact that these have also the characteristics of consumption, and are rewarding to the individual in their own right, must not be allowed to confuse the issue. That something is both a consumer service and a source of productive capital for the society does not detract at all from its importance as an investment. Rather it enhances that importance.

But when we consider education as investment, we must consider it as purposefully as any other form of capital outlay. This the older and more developed countries do not necessarily do or need to do. Their traditions are different; wealth has made it possible for them to be much more easygoing. The new country cannot be so permissive toward those in whom it invests. They are a privileged group who must work to deserve their privileges. The teachers are custodians of scarce national resources which must not be wasted. The country must be sure that its educational investment is adapted to its needs.

In short, the developing country must consider its educational system in the light of the peculiar requirements of development. It cannot simply adapt from the older models. Having come late to development, it is the good fortune of the new countries that they can learn from others. But it is their misfortune that so much of what exists in other countries cannot be copied without serious cost. Adaptation, as I have earlier suggested, is as demanding in its own way as innovation.

DONALD G. COOLEY | ***Frontiers of Medicine***

Memory is the basis of learning. What wouldn't the educator give for a memory-triggering pill that could stir his dullest students to feats of flawless recitation! Or that he might himself take to dispel the image of the absentminded professor.

Such a pill is not an impossible dream, for chemical agents to improve mental functioning are dimly foreshadowed in work already going on in scores of research centers. Yet if a "memory pill" is ever achieved, it will owe its creation in no small measure to a variety of research that is not primarily concerned with memory.

New medical research trails fan out into thousands of paths that crisscross and interweave bewilderingly. Their common denominator is the vast microscopic world of the human cell, within which myriads of fleeting chemical reactions are at long last beginning to become scrutable. Great advances in chemistry and physics have brought mysterious life processes under study at the molecular level and even at that of the exchanges of electrons.

Rapid progress in molecular biology laid the footings for a new platform of knowledge from which medical researchers are poised to take off in ways that are much more sophisticated and rational than the empirical methods of the past. Well-taught high school biology students are knowledgeable about the DNA molecules in cell nuclei, which carry all the hereditary directives of an organism and express them through the synthesis of catalytic protein molecules—enzymes—with the assistance of a sister nucleic acid, RNA.

Soon, perhaps unexpectedly soon, we should have detailed structural maps of human genes, which are thought to be groupings of fairly simple chemical units strung along the DNA molecule. How odd to think that a particular constellation of atoms gives us brown eyes, say, or toes instead of hoofs! Besides genetic mapping, there is the gigantic task of visualizing all of our life processes in molecular terms and reducing them—as has been done in many instances—to chemical equations and physical interactions.

What we have achieved in recent years represents a quantum jump in knowledge—and ignorance. How, for instance, do we learn and remember? Scanty present knowledge brings old theories into question without furnishing a completely satisfying new one. The long-credited theory that experience leaves an imprint on electrical circuits in the nervous system and that reverberations of the circuit evoke recall of the experience no longer predominates.

Startling and controversial experiments with goldfish, flatworms, mice, and monkeys suggest that memory and learning can be transferred physically from one organism to another. Uneducated worms and fishes have seemingly acquired fears and memories and habit patterns by receiving injections of brain substance of educated colleagues. Such studies, inconclusive and warmly debated though they are, hint that the learning process has a persistent chemical component.

If so, how can mere molecules help us to remember? A current hypothesis is that experience induces a permanent biochemical change in the brain. To oversimplify, an event that has significance for us causes us to synthesize unique proteins in nervous tissue. These molecules persist and when they are somehow reawakened, we remember the original event. Changes in electrical, geometrical, and physical relationships are involved, but there is fair agreement that altered protein synthesis is an essential element of long-term memory.

Since protein synthesis is a chemical phenomenon, an inference is that we may be able to correct unsatisfactory mental functioning—psychosis, forms of mental retardation, irrational behavior, encroachments of senility—by providing the right chemical environment. Many mental disorders appear to arise from poor "molecular environment" of the brain.

Do patients with severe mental illness actually suffer from a disturbance of body chemistry? Controversy has for years surrounded reports of the isolation of abnormal substances from the blood and urine of schizophrenic patients. Cause-and-effect relationships between such excreted substances and mental disturbance are neither clearly defined nor clearly ruled out. But there are enough untraced chemical clues to give researchers hope that electro-shock treatments and the couch may eventually be dethroned by a capsule.

What medical advances may result from making thousands of molecular maps of life processes? For one thing, the unknown causes of many diseases are doubtless hidden in the molecular transactions of cells. Suppose, for example, that the unknown cause of multiple sclerosis or diabetes could be traced to a biochemical defect in some regulatory or feedback system of the body. We would then have a basis for designing a drug to attack the disease directly, rather than merely its symptoms. The disease would become a thing of the past.

A few biochemical defects have in fact been identified, particularly in disorders characterized as "inborn errors of metabolism." Many of these chemical errors produce forms of mental retardation as well as physical symptoms. The defect is inherited. The victim lacks an enzyme necessary for some body process because he failed to inherit a gene that directs its synthesis. Phenylketonuria is a familiar example. The affected infant does not produce an enzyme necessary for metabolism of phenylalanine, an amino-acid constituent of protein foods. Toxic by-products accumulate and impair mental development. At present we treat the disorder largely by restricting phenylalanine in the diet, but how much better if the defective gene could be repaired to turn on a normal enzyme factory!

Heredity is also a factor in gout, diabetes, and many other disorders—both rare and common. Predisposition to high blood pressure, cardiovascular disease, rheumatic fever, and other conditions often "runs in families." As the science of medical genetics progresses, more and more diseases will probably be found to have, at least in part, some genetic basis. Gene-mapping gives hope that we may be able to identify a malfunctioning gene long before disease is manifested. But how can we repair the molecules of a gene? It is secure within body cells; snug, defiant, inviolable. Even so, it may not remain forever thus.

Geneticists begin to speak with some assurance of "molecular surgery" —a far-off frontier indeed. Perhaps 20 years off. One possibility is that of training viruses to perform surgery inside cells. In fact, they do so already, but with results that are usually harmful to the host.

Viruses contain a core of nucleic acids, bundles of genes, within a protein coat. A disease-causing virus attaches itself to a cell and, like an infinitesimal hypodermic needle, squirts its genes through the cell wall. This disrupts the cell's own genes.

Some viruses are harmless, however. Why don't we load them with *good* information—instructions, say to repair or replace a defective gene —and send them into cells to wield atomic scalpels constructively? We can't do this today because we don't know enough. But someday we will, in the view of Arthur Kornberg, Nobel Prizewinning biochemist of Stanford University School of Medicine. Hardly a wide-eyed dreamer, Dr. Kornberg is highly knowledgeable about viruses. He and his colleagues have created a totally artificial "test tube" copy of the genetic material of a virus and demonstrated it to be as infectious as the original.

In discussing how "genetic engineering" can be applied to cure disease, Dr. Kornberg gives as an example a hereditary form of anemia due to defective hemoglobin molecules. Thus far, there is no cure; present treatment consists of blood transfusions. Someday, however, Dr. Kornberg expects that the gene for normal human hemoglobin will be identified and reproduced in quantity in test tubes. Then it should be possible to incorporate these genes in harmless viruses that would carry instructions for synthesizing normal hemoglobin into cells.

Complex overlapping of studies in genetics shows up in the convergence of virus and immunology research on the cancer problem. Cancer is a variety of diseases characterized by uncontrollable multiplication of cells. How does cancer get started? Today we believe the causes of most spontaneous cancers are multiple—primary factors acting in concert with secondary factors. Not the least of the latter factors are the person's genetic constitution and the immunological mechanisms of his body.

Viruses are known to cause many animal cancers but have not yet been proved guilty in human cancer. We rarely see virus particles in human cancers. Possibly viruses lie latent in cells in forms not recognizable as viruses. Many researchers expect that a virus or viruses will someday be implicated in human cancer. If so, we can reasonably hope to develop a vaccine that will immunize people against cancer.

We quite probably have natural immunities that protect us against cancer by rejecting occasional malignant cells or interposing a barrier to factors that might ignite them. If this protective machinery exists, we know very little about it or why it sometimes fails. Newly recognized ignorance has immensely complicated the entire discipline of immunology, which is too easily thought of as a simple matter of antigenic substances stimulating the production of antibody molecules that thereafter recognize and neutralize the antigen.

The body's incredible selectivity in rejecting millions of potential antigens—at the molecular level, where specific knowledge of chemical mechanisms lies hidden—is one of the great puzzles of biology that researchers confidently expect to solve. If we could rationally design drugs to intensify, obliterate, or modify specific immune mechanisms, we could offer entirely new kinds of medical treatments.

In laboratory animals, cancers have recently been shown to possess distinctive antigens, not present in the animal's normal cells. Different forms of cancer have antigens peculiar to them. These distinctive differences between malignant and normal cells are potentially exploitable. Were we able to identify comparable antigens in human cancer, we might well devise immunology treatments that could—by enhancing the body's response to the cancer's particular antigen—prevent the cancer or keep an existing cancer from metastasizing.

One may anticipate, too, future drugs to cure those strange human diseases that are classified as "auto-immune" because they reflect immunity gone wrong—inability of the body to "recognize" some of its own tissues, so that harmful sensitivities are set up. Diseases caused by or associated with autoimmune reactions include rheumatoid arthritis, acquired hemolytic anemia, glomerulonephritis, lupus erythematosus, thrombocytopenic purpura, ulcerative colitis, scleroderma, and possibly multiple sclerosis. Allergies also reflect perverse behavior of immune mechanisms. Researchers hope to pinpoint the structure-activity relationships of molecules and immune mechanisms, and from a new base of knowledge devise chemical means of curing a broad spectrum of disabling and sometimes deadly diseases.

Heart transplant operations have made the biggest medical headlines of the year. Kidney transplants have been done for years with less fanfare. We have experimentally transplanted the liver, lung, spleen, and other organs. But the body's tendency to reject donated organs is a great limiting factor. We use drugs, radiation, and antilymphocyte serum to suppress the patient's immune mechanisms while he adapts to the organ. Unfortunately, such measures dangerously reduce resistance to infection and interfere with synthesis of important proteins. What we need—and what may be forthcoming from immunologists—are chemical agents to turn immune reactions off selectively and harmlessly.

In the longer view, however, many researchers expect that transplants of completely artificial organs will supersede those of human organs. This is certainly the view of the American Society for Artificial Internal Organs. The supply of donated organs is not equal to the demand and probably never will be, even if techniques of organ preservation are perfected.

The first completely artificial organ will undoubtedly be the heart, a relatively simple pump, as organs go. Already in use are partially artificial hearts, with artificial valves or booster devices such as an artificial ventricle. The next step is a totally artificial heart that will replace the patient's doomed organ and run for the rest of his life. Several experimental models, somewhat resembling plastic bags with a tangle of tubing, are in a fairly advanced state of development. One model has kept animals alive and healthy for two or three days. We do not know how long it will take to perfect an artificial heart and to cure patients with coronary thrombosis by implanting a device taken off a shelf, but 10 years is a reasonable guess.

More far-out in the era of artificial man are artificial devices embodying miniature electronic components and highly sophisticated technology. An artificial ear that electronically simulates the auditory functions of nerves and structures is under development. Implantable pacemakers that deliver timed electrical impulses to regulate the heartbeat are forerunners of devices that can be preprogramed like computers to control malfunctioning body parts.

All of us who live long enough have intimations of aging. But we know very little about aging, other than its measurable manifestations. What is the biochemical process of growing old? Genetics, immunology, and chemistry furnish leads that remain to be spelled out in molecular language.

Perhaps body molecules become cross-linked in a chemical process resulting in an excess of connective tissue that gradually squeezes the working parts of vital organs. This, or processes unknown, may be programed into cells by our genes on a fateful time schedule. An excess of enzymes of our own making may spark an immunological reaction expressed in subtle deterioration. Even if we are not able to totally reverse these basically chemical phenomena, we should at least be able to slow them down so that people over 30 could be trusted by the young.

The frontiers of medicine are clouded by the vast areas of ignorance that new knowledge has disclosed. Medical progress presupposes the augmentation and support of education to gain ever sharper insights into the marvelous chemical processes we live by. Unexpected turns characterize research; to predict is hazardous. But prediction may serve a modest purpose if to some extent it mitigates dissatisfaction with the mortality of man.

ERIK BARNOUW | ***McLuhanism Reconsidered***

The globe, says Marshall McLuhan in *Understanding Media,* is becoming a tribal village. Lately the village has been buzzing with his ideas.

Marshall McLuhan is a medium who is bringing us a message from a world beyond our ken. The message concerns our psychic environment; all environments, he tells us, are "imperceptible." His tidings are therefore not subject to verification and we must accept them largely on the authority of his crystal ball. But he relays his message to us in such vivid images that he is likely to compel an awed acceptance. To some extent, we go along willingly.

The core of his message is a persuasive idea. It is that each new medium alters our psychic environment, imposing on us a particular pattern of perceiving and thinking that controls us to an extent we scarcely suspect. Our conscious attention is always on the "content" of a medium, but McLuhan sees content as comparable to "the juicy piece of meat carried by the burglar to distract the watchdog of his mind." While thus distracted, we slip into "subliminal and docile acceptance of media impact." Media become "prisons without walls for their human users," we are like wanderers under a hypnotic spell.

A spell that has held mankind for centuries is that of written language, mass-produced via print. Its hypnotic ramifications have been discussed by McLuhan both in *The Gutenberg Galaxy* (1962) and in *Understanding Media* (1964). He tells us that as print became the main cultural transmission belt for one generation after another, knowledge and ideas were necessarily processed into a linear, one-step-at-a-time form required by the medium. Man was thus pushed into sequential habits of thinking, quite unlike the complexity and richness and all-at-onceness of face-to-face communication, and without the resonance of the human voice.

All this encouraged a "civilized" detachment in the recipient of communication. However, the electronic media have restored the resonance (radio) and reintroduced the complexity and all-at-onceness (film, tele-

From *Saturday Review* (July 23, 1966).

vision), and done it on a scale that gives the world potentially a tribal unity. McLuhan sees modern man in a state of shock, unable to adjust to the rapidly changing state of communication, clinging to linear habits in an all-at-once world.

McLuhan sometimes seems exhilarated by his portrait of our plight. But he offers lines of hope, usually revolving around the arts. These provide "anti-environments" that help us perceive the environment itself. They provide a warning radar system. The artist helps us "sidestep the bully blow of new technology." He foresees the transforming impact and builds Noah's ark. One senses that it is as artist, rather than as scholar, that McLuhan is asking to be recognized. McLuhan habitually states his case in sweeping terms; that is, he overstates it, as in his succinct, "the medium is the message," which tends to make content and programing irrelevant concerns. But it is this boldness in his formulations that has centered unprecedented interest on the media and the environments they create, and for this we should be grateful to him.

In this work McLuhan carries forward explorations of various earlier observers. Among these predecessors was the late Harold Innis, whose *Empire and Communications* (1950) and *The Bias of Communication* (1951) analyzed in detail the relationship of media to power structures, beginning with those of ancient times. He saw each new medium upsetting an old monopoly and creating a new controlling alignment—to be threatened in time by other media, usually developing on the fringes of society.

The transition from stone to papyrus, Innis told us, helped monarchs rule over larger areas but made them dependent on armies of scribes, who became a privileged class, a bureaucracy. At the same time the shortage of papyrus made it necessary for government to control its production and distribution, which in effect centralized the control of communication. In the Middle Ages the shortage of parchment was a factor in maintaining a church monopoly of knowledge, eventually broken by the advent of paper, which could be produced in quantity and soon became an instrument in the rise of heresies. The Arabs, who had brought paper from the East, avoided parchment for religious reasons: It was not always possible to tell what animal hide had been used. Innis thus found innumerable factors—economic, social, religious—affecting the control and flow of information, and found these meshing with the rise and fall of power groups. Such observations have invited study of similar factors at work, particularly in regard to the electronic media.

Such study has hardly begun. We are vaguely aware that at the dawn of this era the control of patents—over tubes, circuits, etc.—conferred power over new media, and that military contracts—in two world wars —bolstered this power and placed the electronic industry in a central position in our society. The rise of commercial broadcasting conferred on large advertisers a sharing role in this power, helping create the "military-industrial complex" that worried Eisenhower toward the end of his Presidency, and which has been further strengthened by the computer. There is wide awareness of such a "complex," but few are in a position to know to what extent it may permeate our lives and govern our assumptions, conscious and unconscious; few of us have known any other environment and would therefore have no basis for comparisons and judgment.

The processing of the environment is largely taken for granted. To be sure, voices of education and religion and other interests are also heard, but—to use Innis's term—are pushed to the "fringes" of the social order. The voice of the individual, as opposed to that of the corporation, meanwhile, weakens as writers and artists assume employee status.

Our founding fathers tried to strengthen the individual by providing in the Constitution that only authors should be the beneficiaries of copyright law, but the 1909 copyright law (with dubious constitutionality) reversed this by changing the meaning of the word "author." The employer, the corporation, could also be an "author." Ours is thus the age of the corporate author. Individual author and artist are, in any case, separated from their audiences by an obstacle course of agents, editors, producers, financiers, distributors, jobbers, and retailers, all of whom are potential barriers to communication—censors with veto power.

Amid all this, what is the "message" of the electronic media?

Strangely enough, it is far more complex than the circumstances might lead us to expect, and more complex than we would infer from the McLuhan dictum, "The medium is the message." Such media as film and television have a richness and ambiguity not fully appreciated. A sponsor, scanning words in a script, might feel sure he knows what a film will "mean," but it may mean different things to different people, and different things at different times and in different places. The words fail to control meaning. The complexity of images may involve unsuspected ambivalences. The current administration has had an unprecedented range of means at its disposal for "selling" a war to the public; the electronic media and their sponsors have, on the whole, cooperated. Yet wide dissent remains and apparently grows.

Is it possible that the television image of war has communicated something different from the narrative words that came with it? Is it possible that "noncontroversial" sponsored extravaganzas such as *The Man From UNCLE,* with glossy heroes and villains and their marvelously "sophisticated" weapons, have merely conveyed the idea that international power struggles have been drained of meaning? Has *Get Smart,* with tongue in cheek, conveyed a similar message?

Scores of such questions assail us. Our film and television worlds have generally merchandised good living. Uneasy in poverty settings—which seem to raise unwelcome social issues—media officials have consistently pushed drama into *House Beautiful* atmospheres (facilitated by webs of promotional tie-ins). All this has seemed to the entrepreneurs uplifting and noncontroversial. It was, therefore, an unexpected shock to Hollywood when Sukarno, addressing a group of its executives in 1956, praised them for their role in fomenting the postwar revolutions of Asia. All those movie characters with refrigerators and cars, said Sukarno [*Variety,* June 6, 1956], had shown Asians that they had been deprived of their birthright. Was it possible the executives had been merchandising revolution along with wall-to-wall carpeting?

The Negro revolt raises similar questions. Before television the radio industry was close to lily-white but not, of course, in visible terms. Its replacement by a blatantly white television coincided with the gathering momentum of the Negro revolt. Was there a connection? Did mid-century television, virtually denying the existence of the Negro, serve as goad? Some observers think so. In any case, when demonstrations by the Negro began to win regular attention in television newscasts—helped by the journalistic tradition that gave special news value to violence or the threat of it—his very presence seemed revolutionary.

This foothold and the pressure it created seem to have facilitated a following step, which in our curious electronic society is perhaps more crucial and revolutionary: the entrance of the Negro into network commercials. Is it possible that the advancing Negro image on television is giving Americans an awareness of his existence in their midst, which might otherwise continue to yield to non-seeing? Is it possible that many problems—"poverty," for example—tend in our time to remain abstractions to us until they become physical realities on a screen, which is now our guide to seeing?

The kinds of inquiry stimulated by Innis, and carried forward by McLuhan, are surely worth pursuing. These two investigators, while similar in many ways, have had different emphases. While Innis was especially interested in economics and the growth of monopolies, McLuhan is more mystical. Around his principal theory—the pervasive effects of media—McLuhan constructs various subsidiary theories which are less satisfactory and are, in any case, not essential to his main theory. His classification of media into "hot" and "cool" is one of the embellishments that seems to lead, via labyrinths of confusion, to a dead end.

McLuhan, following up the idea of the "linear" impact of print, ascribes the influence of each medium largely to its technical characteristics. Thus he sees the mosaic pattern of the television image as all-important, and considers its impact "totally" different from that of film. His insistence on this seems odd. He feels that television stimulates intense audience participation because the viewer has to fill in the spaces between the dots in the mosaic; the film viewer, he says, doesn't have to do this, and therefore doesn't participate much.

One might well argue that because the film viewer is looking at a blank screen half the time, and has to fill in twenty-four gaps every second, he participates mightily. But the participation of a viewer can hardly be defined in such simple terms; it goes far beyond the "color me green" function. In all media, communication can bring into play inner conflicts usually held in suspension, and lead them into critical collision. In film and television alike, this participation is reinforced in countless ways. The constantly changing inclusions and exclusions of the frame, the attention-riveting magnifications, the shifting viewpoints and juxtapositions, the interplay and sometimes counterpoint of words and sounds and music, can involve the viewers in a fever of inferences and participating feelings. It is surely this complexity—not a mosaic or other pattern—that makes these media so rich and—from an establishment point of view—potentially treacherous. Add to this the omnipresence of television, and one hardly needs to search for mystical explanations of its impact.

McLuhan has another subsidiary theory that seems attractively neat at first, but contributes no enlightenment. This is that the "content" of a medium (McLuhan prefers to put "content" in quotes) is always an old medium. "The 'content' of TV," he says, "is the movie." On the contrary, as Innis made clear, every new medium has made itself felt by new content, and has in this way had its upsetting effect on existing power structures. The printing press presented material and ideas ignored by monastic copyists. And Negroes on television marching from Selma toward Montgomery in company with white men and women, and seen by Dixiecrats in a Selma country club via a network telecast —as so vividly described in *The New York Times*—were in no sense an old movie. They were "content," and not just a mosaic.

But perhaps media are not as easily pigeonholed as McLuhan believes. Each medium has technical limitations which, on further consideration, appear to yield special advantages, and the ultimate limitations are those of the mind. McLuhan writes in the medium of print. This is said to induce a sequential, assembly-line habit of thought. In spite of this, McLuhan's writings have had a resonant, all-at-once effect, precipitating coast-to-coast debates. He has used the medium to speak more than the Gutenberg message. Was it perhaps "content" that did it? How he has accomplished the miracle he will have to tell us, but it seems to require at least some modification of his message.

CARROLL QUIGLEY | *Needed: A Revolution in Thinking*

Every event, every human experience, is unique. It occurs at a certain place, at a certain moment, to persons at a specific age and condition, and in an arrangement of all these which will never be repeated. Never again will that event happen at that place, at that time, to those people, under those conditions.

Men can deal with such unique events by action. The baseball player at the plate faces that unique and never-to-be-repeated pitch and by making a never-to-be-repeated swing at it may be able to hit the ball over the fence for a home run. This is an example of how men, by action, can deal successfully with the unique events that make up the living experience of all men.

But men also try to deal with the continuous stream of unique events which make up their lives by other methods besides action. They try to think about them and to communicate with other men about them. To do this, they classify unique events into general classes or categories and they attach names or labels to such categories.

This process of classification and labeling ignores the qualities which make events unique and considers only those qualities which events are believed to share or to have in common. In this process, each society (and each person in that society) classifies its experiences and events into categories, and then gives labels to these categories and puts a relative value on them—regarding some of them as good or desirable and others as less good and less desirable.

Each society has such a system of categories and of valuations on categories, and it is known as the society's "cognitive system." It is the most important thing we can know about any society and the most difficult to learn. When someone speaks of the "inscrutable Chinese" or the "mysterious East," he is really saying these remote peoples have cognitive systems that are different from his own and are therefore more or less incomprehensible to him.

Getting to know the cognitive system of any people (or even of other persons in our own society, since no two persons have *exactly* the same cognitive system) is difficult because it is not easy even to take the first step—to recognize that we ourselves have a cognitive system, a

From *NEA Journal* (May 1968).

distinctive way of looking at the world *that is not the way the world actually is* but is simply the way that our group conventionally looks at our world.

The best way to recognize that one's own group has a distinctive way of looking at things and that our own way is *not* the way things necessarily are is to deal with other groups who have cognitive systems different from ours and who are just as certain that their way of seeing things is the way things actually are.

Such an experience, called "cultural shock," may lead to cognitive sophistication, the recognition that *all* cognitive systems are subjective, that each is misleading to those who have it, and that although each enables those who have it to function *within* their own group, it handicaps them in dealing with persons from other groups. Moreover, even within a single society or group, cognitive sophistication is necessary whenever the experiences of that society are changing so rapidly that the old ways of looking at actuality handicap rather than help in dealing with the society's problems.

When people or groups with different cognitive systems interact, frictions and clashes occur, in many cases, without anyone's being able to see why. This happens even where there may have been a maximum of good will on both sides. The difficulty occurs because each is unaware that he has a cognitive system of his own and, while seeing fully what the other person does that irritates him, he cannot see why anything he is doing should irritate anyone else.

Cognitive sophistication makes it possible to know both one's own cognitive system and that of the different group with which one works so that one may be able to translate both talk and actions from one such system into the other, while recognizing the conventional and arbitrary nature of both.

Cognitive sophistication is so rare and so difficult to acquire that interaction across cultural barriers is a frequent cause of conflict. This applies to *all* relationships across cultural barriers—not only to those with other nations and major cultures but also to those within a culture, such as relationships between suburbanites and slum dwellers or between races or social classes.

The cause of such cognitive conflicts may arise in large part from the different ways in which peoples look at time. Time is *undivided* duration, but in order to think or talk about it, each culture must divide it.

Our culture divides it into two parts, the past and the future, which meet at the present moment—an instant without duration. This is reflected in European languages, which have tenses in the past, present, and future. But some peoples, such as the Bantu of Africa, do not have time classes of this sort in their language or social outlook. Many Bantu tongues divide verbs into those concerned with completed and incompleted actions. They have no future tense because they categorize the future and the present together into a single form concerned with unfinished actions. (Similarly, in English we sometimes say, "I am going to school tomorrow," using the present tense for a future action.)

In the usual Bantu cognitive system, time is quite different from what it is to middle-class Americans, since it consists of a present of long duration and great importance, a past of less importance and moderate duration, such as can be held in personal memory, and almost no future distinguishable from the present.

Among some of these peoples, the future is not conceivable beyond the next few days and certainly has no meaning in terms of years or even of nine months. These people live in and value the present with all its problems, pleasures, and human relationships. Such people, even if they are given birth-control devices, are unlikely to use them simply because they have no training in subjecting present relations to a hypothetical event nine months in the future.

Such cognitive differences are of great significance, especially when their value systems are different. The African values the present, whereas many middle-class Americans put all emphasis on the importance of the future and are ready to make almost any sacrifice in the present for the sake of some hypothetical future benefit. In contrast to both, the aristocrat of today, like the ancient Greek, usually puts his highest valuation on the past.

In our society, the latter viewpoint is now generally ignored, but the conflict between the "future preference" of the American middle-class suburbanite and the "present preference" of the lower-class slum dweller leads the former to regard the latter as shiftless, irresponsible, and lacking in self-discipline, while the slum dweller may regard the suburbanite's constant present sacrifice for future benefit as making him dehumanized and inhibited.

In my opinion, the collapse, over the past two decades, of middle-class efforts to export our "self-enterprise" economic system to "undeveloped countries" or to abolish ignorance and poverty in our own cities has been caused primarily by the existence of cognitive barriers—especially the one associated with time.

But there is much more to the problem than this. Men can deal with their experiences consciously only if they have a cognitive system. This is why no one can remember the events of the first year or two of his own life, before he had acquired a cognitive system by learning to talk and rationalize. The events of that period of "infantile amnesia" are incorporated in the person's neurological and metabolic systems, as can be shown by getting him to relive an experience under hypnosis, but he cannot consciously recall and verbalize the experience until he has categorized it, something he could not do when it occurred.

The cognitive system of any people is of major importance because it includes all those unconscious classifications, judgments, and values which trigger most of an adult's initial responses to events. Every culture, including our own, has a cognitive system at its very foundation, and this is what really keeps it functioning, because it enables large numbers of people to live in the same society without constant clashes and conflicts. A few examples will serve to show this.

We divide the whole range of colors, as found in the rainbow, into six colors: red, orange, yellow, green, blue, violet. With our European background, we think a view is beautiful if it consists of alternating horizontal bands of green and blue, as in a landscape consisting of a foreground strip of green shore, with a blue lake beyond, a farther shore of green trees and hills, with a blue sky beyond that.

But to a Bantu of dry Africa, such a view is a rather boring panorama of a single color, for many natives of that language-group place green and blue in a single category with one name, although they divide the lower red-orange-yellow portion of the spectrum into a larger number of basic colors, with names. That is why what impresses us as a beautiful view of shore, lake, and sky strikes them as a rather monotonous field of one color, whereas, conversely, an African view, which to us seems to be a dull expanse of semiparched soil with dry grasses, may seem to them to be an exciting scene of many different colors.

(As Americans of European background have become familiar with the African-like views of Arizona and New Mexico, many have come to feel that these semidesert views are preferable to the more "conventional beauties" of New England, Wisconsin, or upper Michigan. And the Navaho or other natives of our Southwest show their preference for the red-orange-yellow portion of the spectrum by their extensive use of these colors of longer wave length and their scanty use of green, blue, or violet in their arts.)

A somewhat similar example exists in respect to distinguishing and naming the various states of H_2O. In our culture we divide that range into no more than five or six categories, such as ice, snow, slush, water, and steam. But some Eskimo groups, who are vitally concerned with how a dog sled moves on snow, divide snow alone into 50 or more different categories, each with a distinct name. Today, in our own culture, as the sport of skiing grows more popular, we are developing special and numerous names for snow conditions on ski slopes to describe different skiing conditions.

Another significant example of any culture's cognitive view of experience may be seen in the way it divides the life span, especially the preference it places on these divisions.

Many native societies of Africa, for example, are formally divided into six or seven rigid stages, and the transitions from one to another are marked by formal, often painful, "crisis ceremonies."

Frequently, there is little contact between different age classes. Thus youths of seven to 11 years may live together in bands, with almost no contact with parents, while the age group 18 to 28 may be almost totally devoted to war or hunting and forbidden to marry until they move, as a group, into the next age range, say from 28 to 45.

By contrast, in the medieval period, Christian Europe divided a person's life into only two stages, childhood and adulthood, separated about age seven by First Communion. There was a slight tendency, arising from the Jewish Bar Mitzvah, to make another division about age 13, marked by the sacrament of Confirmation, but generally, anyone over seven was spoken to and treated as an adult.

Over the last five centuries or more, however, our Western culture has changed its cognitive view of this matter to become more like the African, until today we have at least six or more age classifications: infants, children, teens or adolescents, the college crowd, the young marrieds, middle-aged, and retired persons. There is increasing segregation of these—in education, in living quarters, in reading and entertainment, and in commercial markets (as in a department store).

The generation gap has become a familiar problem, and communication across age-group barriers has become a major issue. Moreover, female preference for the adolescent period has given us hordes of 40-year-old women trying to look like adolescents, or even like Twiggy pre-adolescents. The influence of such cognitive changes on all aspects of life is evident.

The power and affluence of Western civilization do not result from our technology, our political structure, or even our economic organization, but from our cognitive system, on which they are based. That system began to develop before 500 B.C. with the introduction of the idea, in Palestine and Persia, of one God—omnipotent, omniscient, and perfect—and with the growth of two-valued logic in Persia and Greece.

Although our cognitive system has made our civilization the richest and mightiest in the world, its continued use *without cognitive sophistication* is leading us to disaster. Lynn White, Jr., points this out in his article, "The Historical Roots of Our Ecologic Crisis" in *Science* for March 10, 1967.

Professor White's thesis is that when the Judeo-Christian faith established the view that there is no spirit in nature other than man, the world was reduced to a created object to be exploited by man, and the way was thus opened to the destruction of nature and to the total pollution of the world—a consequence that may have become inevitable with the rejection, in the later thirteenth century, of the message of St. Francis to treat all nature as sacred.

The cognitive techniques derived from our underlying outlook have included (a) using analysis rather than synthesis in seeking answers to problems; (b) isolating problems and studying them in a vacuum instead of using an ecological approach; (c) using techniques based on quantification rather than on qualification study done in a contextual situation; (d) proceeding on the assumption of single-factor causation rather than pluralistic, ecological causation; and (e) basing decisions and actions on needs of the individual rather than the needs of the group.

In our society, if we want to know how something functions, we take it apart, cut it up, isolate it from its context; we analyze its factors and assume that only one is an independent variable; we then quantify the changes this independent variable makes in all the other variables that are assumed to be dependent on it. Then we make the independent variable one link in a chain of such independent variables, each surrounded by its system of dependent variables, the whole forming a chain going back to some original cause in the past, or extending forward, in a similar chain, to some ultimate goal in the future.

From such reasoning, given to us from the Greeks through Aristotle, we got the "final" causes [or goals] and the "Unmoved Mover" [that which is the first cause of all movement and does not itself move] of Aristotelean metaphysics, and, today, we still use this way of thinking, even though we no longer believe in Aristotle's metaphysics.

The now-obsolescent mode of thought and cognition just described might be contrasted with a newer method which is, incidentally, closer to the thinking processes of southern and eastern Asia, which were never much influenced by transcendental Hebrew monotheism or by Greek two-valued logic.

This newer (or older) way of looking at experience tries to find how anything functions by seeing its relationships to a larger system, and ultimately to the whole cosmos. To do so, it uses an ecological and qualitative approach, seeking to grasp the whole contextual situation of innumerable factors, all of which are changing at once, not only by quantitative changes within a fixed identity (such as Western logic *can* handle) but with constant shifts of identity and quality.

This more intuitive and less logical point of view is now sweeping the West as is evidenced by the fact that our traditional Western categories and cognitive assumptions are being rejected not only by youthful "hippies," but also by those hardheaded, analytical people on whom the survival of the West depends.

The stumbling block, of course, is that our whole institutional setup is based on the old method of thought. For example, our educational system is based on the methods of categorization, specialization, and quantification, which must be replaced. This old method of thought is seen on the lower levels, where objective tests assume such things as two-valued logic (True, False), the principle of contradiction. (Yes, No), and the principle of retained identity, just as, on the highest levels, the great increase in the use of computers assumes the possibility of objective analysis and quantification of life experiences.

It is difficult to change our old methods of thinking, no matter how bankrupt they may be. Standing in the way of change are the pressures exerted by institutionalized establishments, the profits of powerful groups producing equipment based on old ways of thinking, and the need which the large bureaucratized organizations of our society have for persons with narrow technical training in the older cognitive patterns.

On the other hand, if we do not make such a change, we may well be destroyed by problems that cannot be handled by the established methods of specialization, isolation, and quantification. These problems are already swallowing us up in the crises of environmental destruction, urban blight, social and racial tensions, poor mental health, and international conflict that threatens to lead to nuclear annihilation.

LYNN WHITE, JR. | ***The Changing Canons of Our Culture***

There is a pervasive conviction that our image of the person is changing. One symptom of this change is the assumption that one can no longer profitably discuss Man: one talks about people, about the ways in which they act and interact, think and feel in terms of the pattern of a given culture, and about how deviation from the norms of that culture molds individuals and eventually may remold the pattern of culture. Indeed, the most permeative idea in this book is the anthropologists' concept of culture: it has irrigated the whole field of humanistic study. Our new image of the person may therefore best be described and understood in terms of basic changes in our own culture.

There is consensus today that although inevitably we are the offspring of the past, we are mutants as well. We are living in a time of general shift more fundamental than any since agriculture and herding displaced food-gathering and hunting as the habit of human existence. Not only the outer forms of living are being remodeled: our standards of values, thought and conduct, our criteria of judgment, all of our yardsticks are altering as well. The very canons of our culture are changing.

What are these changes of canon?

For one thing, ever since the days of the Greeks our thinking has been framed within *the canon of the Occident.* This is the unexamined assumption that civilization par excellence is that of the Western tradition; that history is essentially the stream of events which began with the siege of Troy and which gradually expanded from its first drama in the Levant to find ever wider stages in the Mediterranean of the Pax Romana, the Europe of medieval Latin Christendom, and the North Atlantic civilization of so-called Modern Times. All else—the epic spectacles of Peru and Mexico, of Islam, India and further India, of China, Korea, and Japan, even of that extraordinary Eastern Christendom of Byzantium and Russia—was either irrelevant or at best a cabinet of curiosities. To us, Man has really meant European-American Man: the rest were "natives." We may snicker at the California country pastor who habitually prayed "for the conversion of the heathen in the heart of Africa where the foot of man has never trod," but his naïvete illustrates what we are outgrowing. Our image of the person is ceasing to assume tacitly that the white man is made peculiarly in the likeness of God.

The canon of the Occident has been displaced by *the canon of the globe.* Today everything from communism to Coca-Cola is becoming worldwide in its range. This has the ring of platitude only because we have accepted it so completely in the realm of international politics. Few of us realize the extent to which our most ordinary actions and thoughts are today being formed according to non-Occidental models. Admitting that we are change-prone, just why do we change as we do? There are superficial reasons indeed, but no really adequate explanations for such casual facts as that the use of vodka, for example, is growing so rapidly in America today, or that in any large liquor store one can buy saki, a beverage theoretically available but practically unknown among us a decade ago. Of making cookbooks there is no end; but why, suddenly, is there a market for innumerable ordinary kitchen-shelf cookbooks which, without cultural pretensions or hands-across-the-sea flourishes, simply assimilate the skewers of Armenia, the woks of China, and much else to everyday American cookery?

To be sure, no great culture of the Old World has ever been entirely isolated: borrowings have been constant. The eighteenth century loved *chinoiserie* and took to drinking tea out of porcelain cups—equipped, we may note, with unoriental saucers into which one might pour the tea if it were too hot. But this was consciously a fad; we today are different in the extent of our readiness to assimilate alien influences and our relative unconsciousness about the process. For several decades China and Korea have been the chief factors in furniture design from Los Angeles to Stockholm. A bride, recoiling from her mother's taste, today chooses the new without thinking of its Asian inspiration, which in any case is largely masked by the cliché of "functionalism." And Japan is the obvious source of most that is best in contemporary American and European domestic architecture. Not long ago a group of American ladies arranged to entertain some visiting Japanese students with a house-tour of the finest recently-built homes in their community. The students remained in a state of courteous boredom—after all, all this looked pretty much like grandmother's house on Kyushu—until they burst into arm-waving enthusiasm over the sparkling gingerbread of an immaculately preserved Victorian villa which their hostesses had added to the tour to show how we had progressed. Clearly, while the Western tourist wails that the Orient is being "ruined" by Occidental influences, the Oriental may rightly feel that from his standpoint the West too is losing its distinctive and "picturesque" qualities by overmuch orientalization.

"But," objects the diminished ghost of Plato, "tacos and pilaff, crockery and bedposts, are not the essence of a civilization: it is *ideas* that are really important. Quite naturally our Asian friends have been taking over the superb philosophical concepts which are in the public domain of the West, but can it be shown that we are absorbing anything equivalent from them?"

For the moment, but only for the moment, let us refrain from looking at the structure of values which underlies the question: it can perhaps be answered in its own terms.

For more than a century, since the days of Schopenhauer and Emerson at least, the professional thinkers of the North Atlantic civilization have been consciously subject to Asian influences, but these have been regarded as an exotic rather than an integral element in our thought. In the last two or three decades, however, the psychoanalytic movement, the study of semantics, and the intricate skein of philosophies and theologies labeled Existentialism have combined to challenge the ancient Platonic-Cartesian dualism which polarized experience between mind and body, spirit and substance, time and eternity, man and nature, natural and supernatural. Because of all this we are at the moment peculiarly vulnerable to influences drawn from the stream of Buddhist thought which rose first in India and flowed in a broadening current through China to Japan, where it came to be known as Zen. With an almost unbelievable sophistication, but naturally in terms of their own tradition, the Zen thinkers faced and pondered many of the issues which are uppermost in the minds of Western linguists, psychologists, and philosophers today; and these latter, whether directly or by reflection, are finding light from the East. Prophecy is rash, but it may well be that the publication of D. T. Suzuki's first *Essays in Zen Buddhism* in 1927 will seem in future generations as great an intellectual event as William of Moerbeke's Latin translations of Aristotle in the thirteenth century or Marsiglio Ficino's of Plato in the fifteenth. But in Suzuki's case the shell of the Occident has been broken through. More than we dream, we are now governed by the new canon of the globe.

One reason for the subtly pervasive influence of Zen among us, even upon those who have never heard of it, is its challenge to a second major canon which we inherited from the Greeks: *the canon of logic and language*. For more than two thousand years in the West it has been axiomatic that logic and language are perfected instruments of intellectual analysis and expression. The training of our minds has consisted essentially of getting skills in logic, whether in its philosophical or its mathematical form, and in language, by which we have meant the European and, until recently, the classical tongues. Much of our present discussion of education is still based on the premise that the mind which has mastered logic and language is able to achieve clear and efficient results in any field.

But there is a new and more complex canon today, one which does not deny the validity of the canon of logic and language but which puts it into a wider context, just as the canon of the globe does not negate the canon of the Occident but changes its nature by amplifying it.

This second new canon is *the canon of symbols*. It insists that logic and language are neither perfected nor infallible, but rather that they are simply two most marvellous—and still evolving—human devices closely related to a cluster of similar inventions of symbolic intellectual instruments: the visual arts, literature, music, dance, theatre, liturgy, mythology, formulations of scientific law, philosophical patterns, and theological systems. A symbol may be a novel, a creed, a formula, a gesture, or a cadence, as well as an image, a word, or a crescent, cross, or swastika. We are beginning to see that the distinctive thing about the human species is that we are a symbol-making animal, *Homo signifex*, and that without this function we could never have become *sapiens*.

For we have not only a capacity for making symbols: we are under necessity to create them in order to cope humanly with our experience. An orangutang or a tiny child may manage in terms of things immediately sensed or remembered as sensed. But thought or communication involving relationships or generalizations, much less any complex imagination of what might be as compared with what is, seems to demand symbols. For practical purposes we do not and cannot deal with things in themselves: we must deal with signs pointing toward things.

The fact that these signs are arbitrary to the point of whimsicality is not a defect but a virtue: each arbitrary creation may open new vistas to the mind's eye. If this book were in Hopi it would still convey much the same ideas, but some probably a bit more lucidly and some a bit more obscurely; for each convention of symbols has its peculiar capacities and weaknesses. Our race needs both Hopi and English.

The mathematicians above all other have discovered the utility of developing different symbolic grammars which may be mutually contradictory but which are functional so long as they are internally coherent. In 1733, as intellectual sport the Jesuit Girolamo Saccheri challenged Euclid's axiom of parallels and, substituting the "nonsensical" axiom that through a given point two lines may be drawn parallel to a given line, he constructed a self-consistent non-Euclidean geometry. Unfortunately he laughed it off as a *jeu d'esprit*. Not until four generations later did mathematicians realize that he had made a great discovery. Then a whole constellation of contrasting geometries burst forth, and it was with the light of Riemannian geometry that Einstein found the mathematical key for the release of atomic energy. The most astonishing part of the new canon of symbols is the discovery that we human beings can deal with facts only in terms of fantasies. We have only begun to understand the instrumental validity of arbitrary symbols.

Indeed, even the way our senses report experience to us may be structured by the conventions of language, art, or the like. Recently an American psychologist studied changes in perception and methods of solving problems which took place among members of the Baganda tribe in Uganda as they learned English and came under European influence. He gave them pieces of cardboard of different shapes, sizes, and colors and asked them to separate them into piles. Those who had been in English-language schools almost always divided them according to color, as Westerners do. Those who had had few European contacts built piles on the basis of size or shape, but almost never according to color: the language of the Bagandas is almost entirely lacking in words for colors, and evidently the tribesmen are simply not equipped to detect such variations. If Homeric Greek makes no distinction between blue and green, can we be sure that those less blind than Homer were able to see the difference? And when, toward the middle of the thirteenth century, Villard de Honnecourt appends to his sketch of a lion the proud scribble, "Note well that this lion was drawn from life," should we be astonished that his lion is exactly one of those tame little poodle-lions, with a mane of symmetrical ringlets, universally found in late Romanesque and early Gothic sculpture? In every society there is a convention of vision, and perhaps of each of the senses.

A most important aspect of the canon of symbols, therefore, is our realization that while symbols are created by us, these creatures in a peculiar way come alive, turn upon us, and coerce us and our experience to conform to their anatomy.

For example, any man who makes it his business to observe American women closely will quickly discover that in our land women are emotionally dependent on men in a way quite different from that in which men are dependent on women. Despite all the proud talk of sex equality, women themselves refer to "hen parties" with contempt and to "stag parties" with a twinge of envy. The reasons for this widespread and unwarranted feminine sense of being secondary are many, but at least one of them is linguistic. The grammar of English dictates that when a referent is either of indeterminate sex or of both sexes, it shall be considered masculine. The penetration of this habit of language into the minds of little girls as they grow up to be women is more profound than most people, including most women, have recognized; for it implies that personality is really a male attribute, and that women are a human subspecies. It is dramatized in the story of the suffragette fight in Britain, when a young recruit to the feminist forces burst into tears after a little clash with police over picketing. "My daughter, don't despair," said a seasoned campaigner. "Pray to God and She will give you strength!" It would be a miracle if a girl-baby, learning to use the symbols of our tongue, could escape some unverbalized wound to her self-respect; whereas a boy-baby's ego is bolstered by the pattern of our language.

Intuitions of this sort, related to the new canon of symbols, lead us on to the recognition of a third major change in the canons of our culture. From the Greeks, again, we inherit *the canon of rationality* which assumes that reason is the supreme human attribute and that anything other than rationality is "less" than rationality and to be deplored as subhuman. It assumes that disagreements are not fundamental, and that, with adequate reasonable discussion and examination of the evidence, a single truth will emerge acceptable to all men.

But now we dwell in a world dominated by *the canon of the unconscious.* Closer scrutiny of our mental processes has shown that a vast lot is happening in the shadowy iridescence, the black opal of the abyss which lies within each of us. Our scientists, in particular, have become fascinated by the problem of the genesis of original ideas, and have resuscitated the word "serendipity" to label one of the most curious aspects of intellectual creation: the seemingly instantaneous discovery of something entirely unexpected in the course of hard work toward a different goal. The word was invented in 1754 by Horace Walpole from the legend of the Princess of Serendip: she had three suitors to each of whom she assigned an impossible task; all three failed, but in the course of his heroic struggles each accomplished something even more marvelous. Every scholar and artist has in some measure experienced serendipity: the sudden welling up into consciousness of insights, intellectual structures, visions which clearly would never have come had the conscious mind not been in travail, but of whose gestation we had no forewarning. Reason is not all of the mind.

For many centuries such thinkers as St. Thomas Aquinas, so rationalist that they perceived some limitations of reason, groped towards a picture of the human mind as a shiny sheet of metal, part of which is bent back upon itself so that it is mirrored in itself. Reason is the part of the mind which is capable of reflection, that is, of contemplating its own processes. The rest of the mind perhaps does not differ from reason in its essential qualities, particularly in creativity. But unfortunately we cannot yet easily watch it in action.

Aldous Huxley in his essay on mescalin has pointed out that, as the chemistry and physiology of our nervous system become clearer, experimental means of peering into these mysteries may be developed. To date, the psychoanalytic assault on the problem of the unconscious has been the most sustained and probably the most rewarding. Yet its very success has opened up new complexities: the unconscious seems to be as deeply conditioned by cultural forms as is the conscious mind. Surely the relative scarcity in America of the Oedipus complex, at least in its "classic" Freudian form, is related to the contrast between the paternal monarchy of the nineteenth-century Viennese family and the chaotic town-meeting government of the typical American family of recent decades.

The social psychologists, anthropologists, and historians are proving helpful in this exploration of the unconscious. For example, it is becoming clear that episodes such as the slaughter of the Jews by the Nazis, the four centuries of the witch-mania during the European Renaissance, or the recent resurgence of witchcraft and witch hunting among the Navahos, are intelligible not in terms of the functioning of the rational faculty but as group responses to spiritual crises, as means of coping with and "explaining" deep psychic disturbances produced by catastrophic shifts in the cultural foundations. The linguists analyzing non-European tongues have reached similar insights: language structures, social relationships, and cosmologies often have a related pattern among a given people, and the emotions and unconscious attitudes as well as the verbalized ideas of participants in a culture seem to be shaped by these as definitely as a Flathead Indian's brain is shaped by the headboard of his papoose cradle.

The human mind is not completely conditioned. It can achieve an extraordinary degree of freedom and "objectivity." But we have come to see that logical reasoning and rational confrontation of relevant evidences is only part of the task if true freedom is to be won. The idea that there are unconscious areas of the mind is not new, but in no previous era, of Western thought at least, has it loomed so large or challenged us so insistently. The realization of the scope, the dangers, and the potentialities of the unconscious is essential to our new image of the person.

It is significant that, more and more, we are using the word *unconscious* rather than *subconscious*. The latter is involved in metaphorical association of up-and-down spatial relationships with value judgments, and it thus might trick us into assuming that the unconscious is in some way *sub* and therefore inferior or unworthy. This aspect of the new canon of the unconscious illustrates the fourth, and final, major change of canon which is observable in our culture.

Although some of the earlier Ionian philosophers seem to have had a different bent of mind, ever since the great days of Athens we have generally thought, felt and acted in terms of *the canon of the hierarchy of values*. We have assumed and consciously taught that some types of human activity are more worthy of study and reverence than others because the contemplation of them seemed to bring greater spiritual rewards. This hierarchy of values, expressed most clearly in the ancient concept of the liberal arts, was codified in the Middle Ages, expanded in the Renaissance and post-Renaissance, and has continued to be manifest in emphasis on the importance of mathematics, logic, philosophy, literature, and the unapplied sciences. Within its self-imposed limitations, this tradition of personal cultivation and of education had an unsurpassed richness and intellectual magnificence.

But large parts of human experience and creativity were omitted from the upper rungs of this ladder of values which provided the pattern and rationale of our inherited culture. Anything, above all, which required the use of the hands was excluded, not only rigorously but with some indignation, from the area of prestige which was reflected in the older liberal arts curricula. It was shut out because the top brackets of culture and education were the perquisite of an aristocracy which used not its hands but its brains.

The Greeks and Romans, living in a slave economy, considered use of the hands banausic and contemptible. Primitive Christianity, largely a proletarian movement, had contrary instincts which were perpetuated by the medieval monks and by their Protestant ascetic offshoot, the Puritans. But the notion that "to labor is to pray," that work with the hands is integral to the good life, was slow to make an impression on our cultural tradition, presumably because society remained largely aristocratic or hierarchical in organization. Today we have forgotten, or can scarcely believe, the degree to which manual operations were once avoided by those who were, or aspired to be, of the upper crust. For example, old pictures of the dissection of cadavers in medical schools show not only that the professor of anatomy almost invariably stood lecturing from a medical text while a barber-surgeon assistant actually wielded the scalpel but that, at a slightly later period when this assistant had come to achieve a certain social status, he too, although present to supervise, delegated the actual dissection to a second assistant.

The secret of the almost explosive originality of our times is the wiping out (save in certain cultural backwaters) of the ancient barrier between the aristocrat and the worker. Americans, whose ancestors first created a large-scale equalitarian community, should take particular pride in this reunion of the human hand and brain into their proper organic whole: the ideal image of the person is no longer the armless Venus of Milo. Yet even in America our language and our presuppositions are still so permeated by the inherited aristocratic tradition that it is hard to put into words just what is involved in the fact that the combined democratic and technological revolutions have made both workers of us all and aristocrats of us all; that the two sets of values, historically so sharply divided, are now confused and must be schematized according to a new plan.

This plan is emerging: the old canon of the hierarchy or ladder of values has turned at right angles to become a new *canon of the spectrum of values.* Whereas the old canon insisted that some human activities are by their nature more intellectually and spiritually profitable than others, the new canon holds that every human activity, whether changing diapers or reading Spinoza, whether plowing for barley or measuring galaxies, enshrines the possibility—perhaps not the actuality but the potentiality—of greatness: its proper contemplation and practice promise the reward of insight. "What is the Buddha?" asked the Zen novice. "Three pounds of rice," replied the abbot.

"All the road to heaven is heaven," said St. Teresa of Avila. The notion of a spectrum of values, as distinct from a hierarchy of values, challenges all the dualisms which, among us Occidentals, for over two thousand years have divided the seamless coat of actual human experience. The path and the goal, means and ends, becoming and being, process and purpose—all these fuse into nowness. We are no longer under compulsion to violate immediacy: each perception, whatever its nature, may be the beatific vision, each moment orchestrated for Gabriel's trumpet. Just as the economic and political revolutions of our time have produced an egalitarian society, so our intellectual revolution has insisted on—what would have seemed a logical and semantic absurdity to former ages—an equality of values. Indeed, we suddenly realize the weakness of our verbal symbols: clearly "value" is a monetary metaphor, inherently scaled up-and-down rather than sideways. Yet we have no other serviceable word, so we must use the term "value," understanding in what sense it is obsolete.

Just as aristocratic forebodings that a democratic social work would necessarily mean the end of personal cultivation and individualism have not been realized, so democratic insistence on the equal potential worth of what have been called "values" does not inevitably lead to mental or emotional drabness. On the contrary, it can open our eyes to the spiritual possibilities inherent in types of experience and creativity which, because of a divided society and class-centered education, could not be envisaged as a whole by any previous generation.

It compels us, for example, to redefine our notion of "genius" to embrace kinds of originality hitherto overlooked. Sometime about 1420 an unknown carpenter or shipwright, presumably a Fleming, invented the bit-and-brace, thus making possible continuous rotary motion in boring. By that act he invented the compound crank and precipitated the greatest single revolution in the design of machinery: by 1430 we find machines involving double compound cranks and two connecting rods. No unconscious "evolution" led to the brace: it was created by a leap of the mind which imagined and implemented a new kinetic pattern which has been fundamental to the development of modern society. Until we have learned to look at the carpenter's brace with a certain awe, we have not begun to absorb the cultural implications of the democratic revolution.

All four of the old canons which have suffered a sea change in the storms of our time were formulated by the first consciously Occidental society, that of Athens. In the realm of thought and emotion, twenty-four centuries of Hellenic dominance now are ended. The marvel is not that our vision is confused but rather that we are learning so quickly how to view mankind from vantage-points other than the Acropolis.

Whenever there is major change there is likewise risk of great loss. If we have made a correct analysis of the four mutations of canon which are going on around us, what are the cultural treasures which may be endangered by this flux?

Does the change from the canon of the Occident to the canon of the globe in any way diminish the wonder, the amazing variety and spontaneity of the Western tradition in which we Americans stand? No; but it imposes upon us the difficult problem of how to become citizens of the world without uprooting ourselves from our native soil. A superficial cosmopolitanism is no adequate substitute for a cultural parochialism which makes up in spiritual depth what it lacks in breadth. How are we to become cultivated in global terms when most of us don't manage it in Occidental terms?

The canon of logic and language has become the canon of symbols. Are logic and languages less important than formerly? No; now we can envisage and use them as parts of a vastly expanded set of tools of analysis and communication. But whereas once a person could confidently regard himself as educated if he were competent with these two instruments (including, of course, mathematics), how is each of us today to learn to handle the rest with facility, or even to know what is happening when other people are employing them? In a brief life which can accommodate only a short period of formal education, how can we learn the vocabulary, grammar, and semantics of drama, dance, music, and the like? How can we explore the mutually contradictory but often coherent thought structures of the major philosophers, and learn to use them, as a mathematician uses the different incompatible geometries, each to achieve a variant quality of vision? How can we find time or imagination enough to encompass the language of myth, which tells not what once happened but what is always happening? How can we come to understand, from the inside, why Newton considered himself almost more a theologian than a mathematician? The peril is that, like small children suddenly taken to a new land with a strange speech, we may become tongue-tied. Indeed, the state of much current literature, music, and art makes one fear that this is in fact happening.

Now that the canon of rationality has become the canon of the unconscious, does this mean that we should simply assume that we and all other people are essentially irrational and need no longer bother with the disciplines of reason? No; it means that we have come to realize more clearly than ever before the psychological, biological, and cultural context of the rational function. We have recognized the chances that self-interest or self-deception will mask itself quite honestly as rationality. That we name such cover-up thinking with the popular word "rationalizing" shows how deeply this conception has penetrated the general mind. We have put our idea of the conscious mind into the frame which in fact it has always had, and by this sharper delimitation of its bounds we can become more aware of the nature, the uses, and the glory of rationality. Yet, when all this is said, to many temperaments the canon of the unconscious is an invitation to let the reason become lazy.

Finally, since revolution has swept aristocracy into the cracks and corners, does the shift from the canon of the hierarchy of values to the canon of the spectrum of values mean that the values cultivated by the aristocracies of the past are obsolete? No; on the contrary, if we neglect them we are betraying the democratic revolution which was an effort to upgrade the masses and not to downgrade them. Yet in the long perspective of human history our revolution is so new that we do not really know what a high democratic culture would look like, much less what its formal education—that is, its organized plan for cultural transmission—would be. The task of understanding ourselves and the world we live in is vastly complicated by the democratic necessity of supplementing the well formulated aristocratic values with others, more nebulous at present because never adequately verbalized, which for millennia have been held by the common people to be equally necessary and worthy of respect. In general these latter values have centered not, like those of the aristocrats, in government, religion, and art but in the home, the daily relations of people in community, and the skills of production and craftsmanship. The task is not simply to add these to the traditionally cherished values of the upper class, but rather to smelt all human values down and to recast them as a unit. Until this is done we shall continue in a state of cultural confusion; but the blast furnace is only now beginning to glow hot.

Each of these four basic changes of canon is a green apple in the bad case of intellectual, social, artistic, and moral dyspepsia from which we are all suffering at present: there is more to be digested than our bellies can handle. There are some, of course, who think that they can vomit the substance of the modern world and nourish themselves on savors wafted from the past. But most of us will say with Adelard of Bath, eight centuries ago, "I'm not the sort of fellow who can be fed with the picture of a beefsteak!"

Only one aid to digestion appears. Practically every book we read, every speech we hear, every TV show or moving picture we see, every conversation around us is formulated and phrased, at least on the surface, in terms of the four old canons of the Occident, of logic and language, of rationality and of the hierarchy of values. This outer form, however, is a violation of the inner substance. In theological terms, our culture has experienced transubstantiation and it is our spiritual task to recognize the actualities and not be deceived by the accidents. It would be useful as an intellectual discipline to apply to our analysis of what goes on about us the four new canons of the globe, of symbols, of the unconscious, and of the spectrum of values. Since each of them is no more than a cultural reflection of a changed concept of what a human being is, these canons may help us to understand not only our age but ourselves.

Starting at one end of the Christian system of theological symbols, the Westminster Catechism of 1647 poses as its first question, "What is the chief end of man?" and answers, with the rolling thunder of Calvinism, "To glorify God and enjoy Him forever." In diametrical contrast, the Anglican Catechism of 1549 had begun with a most deceptive appearance of simplicity: "What is your name?" The latter question is really no easier than the other, but, given the temper of our times, most minds of the mid-twentieth century must start their pilgrimage from this earthier point of wondering who we are.

Selected References

BANTOCK, G. H. *Education in an Industrial Society.* London: Faber & Faber, 1963.

BENEDICT, RUTH. *Race: Science and Politics.* New York: Viking Press, 1962.

BRICKMAN, WILLIAM W. (ed.). *Educational Imperatives in a Changing Culture.* Philadelphia: University of Pennsylvania Press, 1967.

BRONOWSKI, JACOB. *The Identity of Man.* Garden City, N.Y.: The Natural History Press, 1966.

CLARK, KENNETH B. *Dark Ghetto: Dilemmas of Social Power.* New York: Harper and Row, 1965.

DE BONO, EDWARD. *New Think: The Use of Lateral Thinking in the Generation of New Ideas.* New York: Basic Books, 1968.

DRUCKER, PETER F. *The Age of Discontinuity: Guidelines to Our Changing Society.* New York: Harper and Row, 1969.

DUBOS, RENE. *So Human an Animal.* New York: Charles Scribner's Sons, 1968.

GALBRAITH, JOHN KENNETH. *The New Industrial State.* Boston: Houghton Mifflin Company, 1967.

GLAZER, NATHAN, and DANIEL P. MOYNIHAN. *Beyond the Melting Pot.* Cambridge, Mass.: M.I.T. Press, 1963.

GREEN, THOMAS F. *Work, Leisure, and the American Schools.* New York: Random House, 1968.

HARRINGTON, MICHAEL. *The Accidental Century.* New York: The Macmillan Company, 1966.

HENRY, JULES. *Culture Against Man.* New York: The Vintage Press, 1965.

HUUS, HELEN (ed.). *Values for a Changing America.* Philadelphia: University of Pennsylvania Press, 1966.

KAHN, HERMAN, and ANTHONY J. WIENER. *The Year 2000: A Framework for Speculation on the Next Thirty-Three Years.* New York: The Macmillan Company, 1967.

KING, EDMUND J. *Education and a Social Change.* New York: Pergamon Press, 1966.

KVARACEUS, WILLIAM C., *et al.* (ed.). *Poverty, Education, and Race Relations.* Boston: Allyn & Bacon, 1967.

LINTON, THOMAS E., and JACK L. NELSON (eds.). *Patterns of Power.* New York: Pitman Publishing Corp., 1968.

LUNDBERG, FERDINAND. *The Rich and the Super-Rich.* New York: Lyle Stuart, 1968.

MARCUSE, HERBERT. *One Dimensional Man: Studies in the Ideology of Advanced Industrial Society*. Boston: Beacon Press, 1966.

MCLUHAN, MARSHALL. *Understanding Media: The Extensions of Man*. New York: McGraw-Hill Company, 1964.

MICHAEL, DONALD N. *The Unprepared Society: Planning for a Precarious Future*. New York: Basic Books, 1968.

"Political Socialization" *Harvard Educational Review* (Summer 1968), entire issue.

"Science and Culture," *Daedalus* (Winter 1965), entire issue.

SENIOR, CLARENCE. *The Puerto Ricans: Strangers—Then Neighbors*. Chicago: Quadrangle Books, 1965.

SMITHSONIAN ANNUAL II. *The Fitness of Man's Environment*. Washington, D.C.: Smithsonian Press, 1968.

SNOW, C. P. *The Two Cultures and the Scientific Revolution*. New York: Cambridge University Press, 1960.

UDALL, STEWART L. *1976: Agenda for Tomorrow*. New York: Harcourt, Brace & World, 1968.

WALKER, DANIEL. *Rights in Conflict*. The Official Report of the National Commission on the Causes and Prevention of Violence. New York: The New American Library, 1968.

WARD, BARBARA. *The Rich Nations and the Poor Nations*. New York: W. W. Norton & Company, 1962.

WIENER, NORBERT. *The Human Use of Human Beings*. New York: Anchor Books, 1954.

SECTION II | *Historical Background of American Education*

HISTORY IS MORE than a record of events and dates; it is an understanding of why these events come about and how they develop. A critical examination into these questions forces the historian to explore the manner in which particular, specific events are closely associated with a broad range of relationships of the total culture. From a careful reflective study of historical data, valid interpretations and intelligent judgments can be made; misinterpretation and parochial judgments can be avoided. This type of scholarly study of the historical backgrounds of American education, one of the nation's most important matters of public policy, is needed to show its vital relationship to the culture.

In making selections for this section of the reader, the editors assume that future proposals must rely to some degree on informed judgments about what has gone before. Although the past cannot solve present problems nor chart clearly a future course, it can provide a vantage point from which to view old problems in new perspective or to discern newly emerging issues. Historical interpretation used in this fashion need not limit our thinking to conventional or traditional solutions. In fact, it is not to find answers but to ask more intelligent questions that the study of history can best serve present and future members of the profession. Bernard Berenson, recognized authority of Italian renaissance art, was once asked what he learned from viewing works of art in museums or galleries never previously visited. He replied that his greatest learning came from thinking about the questions he should ask when he visited the gallery again.

Insight into the past rests upon the ability to raise intelligent questions; it reveals the folly of attempting to provide simple answers to complex problems. Schools do not exist in a vacuum; they are influenced by the society of which they are a part, and in turn they influence that society. In this context educational history records the search for more meaningful aims and purposes, more vital curricula and more effective methods, by taking into account the complex nature of American education and by rejecting simple, easy solutions.

In recent times there has been a resurgence of scholarship devoted to a re-examination of the place of education in American history. The "new" history has attempted to place the developments in education within the broad stream of social, political, and intellectual ideas that have characterized the growth of American culture.

Viewing educational history from this broader perspective breaks sharply with traditional interpretation, which, almost exclusively, focused its concern on the development of the school as a formal institution divorced from society and analyzed in neat, chronological segments. As Oscar Handlin, Professor of History at Harvard, explains it:

> The breakthrough in the history of education, as in other fields, has come recently through a process which has risen above the limitations of institutional perspective. At the point at which historians began to look at the educational process rather than at the school, they were compelled to consider a broad range of relationships to the totality of the culture. The most promising developments have come through viewing the history of education as an aspect either of social or intellectual history. In the first context, the acculturation of a child is examined against the background of the environment within which he grows to maturity, and education is regarded as the process of transmitting to him the techniques and attitudes of the society in which he lives. In the second context, the emphasis is upon the subject matter which is taught and the broad intellectual forces that help form it.[1]

The selections of historical readings reflect largely this new emphasis in writing educational history. The articles cannot represent an exhaustive treatment of the development of American education; they are intended, however, to present a thoughtful choice from recent historical scholarship of some of the important phases in that development.

Those who read the articles should be aware of some fundamental questions if their study is to proceed in an intelligent manner, questions that aid the reader in asking further questions as his perspective is broadened. How does the culture affect education? In what manner does education act upon the culture? What misconceptions of the place of education in American life can be identified? What significant shifts in the meaning of and commitment to education can be perceived? What

[1] Oscar Handlin, "Introductory Note," *Harvard Educational Review, 31:* 121–123 (Spring 1961), pp. 121–122.

distinctive purposes has education served in American democracy? What trends, characteristics, or qualities of education can be discerned that have been of continuing concern in the development of American education?

R. Freeman Butts, in the opening article, gives a brief yet comprehensive survey of the historical development of American education. He traces the idea "the search for freedom" as a constant factor within changing demands of society from the beginnings of education in the colonies to the complex culture of today.

Robert Middlekauff, in his article, "Education in Colonial America" supports his belief that educational development in the colonies followed an uneven course: "Variety in support, in state participation, and in the forms institutions assumed characterized colonial education."

The development of the common schools to meet the need for popular education is discussed by Rush Welter as an expression of democratic thought in nineteenth-century America. The movement for popular education is treated from three perspectives: first, the workingmen's demand for an effective system of public schools to counteract the "monopolistic" and "aristocratic" sentiments; next, Horace Mann's views of the common school as an agency of liberal democracy; finally, the religious intransigence of the 1830's and 1840's which posed the greatest obstacle for the development and expansion of the public schools.

Lawrence A. Cremin of Columbia's Teachers College presents two interpretations of the changing role of the American secondary school in the twenty-five year period around the turn of the century. In his treatment of this brief period, Cremin demonstrates the mutual interaction between the school and society by pointing to the rapidity of change in the political, economic, and social sectors of society from 1893 to 1918 which was of such magnitude that its radical effect upon the schools constituted a "revolution in American education."

One of the important problems of the period Cremin identifies was the influx of new immigrants from Southern and Eastern Europe. The schools were, for the most part, unaware of the nature or complexity of the educational problem posed by the immigrant. The Americanization of children of the foreign born, viewed favorably by many educational historians including Dr. Butts in his lead article in this section, was achieved by denigrating the rich cultural background that immigrants brought from their homeland in Europe. Jane Addams, in a moving speech before the convention of the National Education Association in Chicago in 1897, portrays vividly the plight of the foreign born peasant in the public schools of that era. Even though exact parallels cannot be drawn between the inequalities in educational opportunities endured by the Italian immigrant at the turn of the century and those of the Negro and Puerto Rican in today's schools, Jane Addams' testimony reveals a depth of understanding of minority groups that has relevance to the current struggles of children of the ghettos in today's schools. In fact, it seems as though we have learned little in the intervening seventy years about how best to educate culturally different students.

Historical readings dealing with significant phases of American education must take into account the influence of John Dewey's ideas on one of the most important reform movements in the schools—"progressive" education. Lawrence A. Cremin sees Dewey's concerns related not only to the "qualities central to life in a free society," but as "an effort to realize for the first time in history the democratic commitments to equal educational opportunity." Critical of the excesses and perversions to which progressive education had been converted, Dewey restates the need for an education system where the process of moral-intellectual development is put into practice as a necessary element for the creation of a democratic society.

The article by Richard Hofstadter, "Democracy and Anti-Intellectualism in America," although directed specifically to higher education, has much wider application. Hofstadter treats a theme that has plagued the historical development of education in the United States. He feels that educators have lost confidence in "the importance and value of the life of the mind"; they have capitulated "to the non-intellectual and anti-intellectual criteria that many forces in our society wish to impose on education." In the perspective of history the tension between our popular democracy and intellectualism has come about because the complementary relationship between democracy and education has never been faced realistically: ". . . while populistic democracy has been on the side of many educational improvements and reforms, it has often been aligned as sharply with forces tending to constrain freedom . . . and to lower devotion to intellectual goals." This article should provoke thought about the present-day education establishment in its historical development. Hofstadter's thesis is, in one sense, an evaluation of the quantitative and qualitative aspects of education in the United States, a system that has had as its goal the education of all the children of all the people.

In retrospect the greatest force upon American public schools in the late 1950's, and with growing intensity throughout the 1960's, began with the landmark decision of the United States Supreme Court outlawing the "separate but equal" doctrine that for some sixty years had guided the organization and administration of the schools. What began as a patchwork of uneven, uncoordinated responses to this new Federal policy, eventually forced Americans into a painful reexamination of discriminatory practices against minority groups that led to a searching reappraisal of the values and purposes of public schools in a democracy.

Three new articles in this second edition help put in perspective the main currents of thought and action during the past fifteen years regarding the desegregation of schools. Two essays by an able, new historian of American education, David B. Tyack of Stanford, examine the struggle of Black America to obtain equal educational opportunities against a background of a broad range of socio-cultural relationships. In "Growing Up Black," Tyack recognizes the unavoidable consequences of placing upon schools much of the burden for bringing the Negro more completely into the mainstream of American life. Schools were charged with the responsibility for providing an emotional and intellectual climate for disadvantaged minorities to compensate, in some measure, for the distrust created by years of segregation and shame. Yet, Tyack concludes, "only as it makes progress in this arduous task can the *common* school fulfill its promise." Tyack's second article, "Catholic Power, Black Power," reflects upon similarities between the rebellion of American Catholics in the 19th century against the Protestantization of the public school and the current struggle of the largest minority in the United States for Black Power. There was, however, one important difference in these confrontations—Catholics were *forced* to assimilate, whereas Negroes were traditionally *refused* entrance into the life of American society.

This section on historical backgrounds of American education closes with a look at some present-day realities for education. President John H. Fischer of Teachers College, Columbia University, sees the current mood of uneasiness about schools as one brought about by the failure of the public school system to meet squarely the continuing challenge of educational opportunity equal for all. Throughout their history, American schools have been less than enthusiastic about change. Their response, says Fischer, has been at best reluctant, and not infrequently recalcitrant. Too often, school problems of the 1960's were met with 19th century solutions. They were not met with fresh, courageous, bold projections for a school system that would be the great equalizer of the conditions of man as envisioned by Horace Mann a century ago. Clearly, American schools are at a turning point in their two-hundred year history. If today's schools are to be a vital force for democracy, Fischer concludes, "it will take the vigor that we reserve for our most important tasks."

R. FREEMAN BUTTS | *Search for Freedom: The Story of American Education*

The story of American education needs constant retelling. It is a story that few of us know well enough. Yet, education directly involves more than one-half of all Americans and indirectly affects the lives, welfare, security, and freedom of everyone. Students, teachers, and other citizens cannot afford to ignore it.

Fortunately, most Americans have faith in education and believe that educated young people are better equipped to "get ahead" in the world than uneducated ones are. However, the really important reason for believing in the value of education is that it can be the foundation of freedom. In the first place, a truly democratic society must rest upon the knowledge, intelligence, and wisdom of all the people. Without the proper kind of education available to everyone, a free society cannot long endure. Therefore, all people must have the kind of education that will fit them for freedom as responsible citizens.

In the second place, without the proper kind of education, the individual will not be able to develop his own powers as a person. He will not be able to give direction to his own action and thought as he may wish. He will not be able to decide wisely for himself what he should do or think.

Freedom from arbitrary restraint, from compulsion, or from tyranny is essential for the free man, but that alone is not enough. If each person is to achieve the genuine freedom of self-direction and self-fulfillment, he must have an education befitting a free man.

Now, what kind of education will best develop the free citizen and the free person? This is the persistent question that runs through the story of American education. It has been answered in different ways at different times in our history. It is still being debated vigorously, and sometimes angrily, today.

This question is so important that every American—and above all, every student and teacher—should make it his business to learn all he can about it. The first requirement is a knowledge of the history of American education. Here are some of the fundamental questions that mark the high lights of the story:

From *NEA Journal* (March 1960), pp. 33–48. Reprinted by permission.

1. What kind of schools and colleges will promote maximum freedom in society? To what extent should a free society encourage public schools in contrast to private schools? Is freedom better served by religious schools or by secular schools? Is a free society better served by local controls or by central control of schools? Should a free society maintain common schools and colleges open equally to all, or should it divide students into separate schools and colleges according to their race, religion, social class, prospective vocation, or intellectual ability?

2. What kind of education program will promote maximum freedom for all individuals? Should schools and colleges stress practical training or purely intellectual studies? Should schools and colleges offer students preparation for many vocations or for just a few? Should educational methods stress learning by direct experience or by reading books? Should a liberal education be designed for the few or for the many?

If we can understand some of the major answers given to these questions during our history, we shall be on the way to understanding the central idea of American education.

I. Education Under Colonial Rule (1600 to 1770's)

For nearly 175 years, the source of governmental authority for the American colonies was the crown and parliament of England. The colonists were, however, ruled locally by legislative assemblies or by individual proprietors or by royal governors who received their authority from the English government in London.

This authority included jurisdiction over education. From the very beginning of American history, education was a function of government. It continued to be so after the states were independent.

The various colonies, however, handled educational matters differently. In the New England colonies, the governing bodies not only exerted general authority over education but also established, supported, and directly administered their own schools.

For example, the colonial legislature of Massachusetts passed a law founding Harvard College in 1636; in the following years it took hundreds of actions concerning the college. In the 1630's, the governments of several towns in New England established schools under their direct jurisdiction and supervision.

In 1642 the colonial legislature of Massachusetts passed a general educational law applying to all parts of the colony. It required all parents to see that their children were taught to read, learn the major laws, know the catechism, and learn a trade. It authorized and required the town officials to see that parents obeyed the law and to levy fines upon those parents who disobeyed.

In 1647 the Massachusetts legislature passed a second law, this time requiring all towns of fifty or more families to appoint a teacher and permitting the towns to pay him out of public taxes if the people so voted. Such a teacher was to teach reading and writing. (We would call him an elementary-school teacher.) Furthermore, the law of 1647 required towns of one hundred or more families to appoint a teacher of Latin grammar. (We would call him a secondary-school teacher.)

The New England version of state authority in education came to this: The colonial government could require parents to have their children educated; the central government of the colony could require local towns to appoint teachers (establish schools); public funds could be raised by taxation to pay the teachers; and public teachers were subject to direct supervision and control by governmental authorities (either the town meeting as a whole or the selectmen or the education committee).

In the Southern colonies the colonial governments had the same legal authority to legislate on educational matters, but they did not pass laws requiring *all* children to be educated. They rather assumed, as in England, that any parent who could afford to educate his own children should do so by making individual arrangements with a private tutor or by sending them to a private school.

The Southern legislatures, however, did pass laws requiring that poor children and orphaned children be apprenticed to a trade and taught the rudiments of reading and religion by their masters.

The governmental attention in the South was directed mainly at lower-class underprivileged children who had no parents or whose parents could not care for them. Even so, the parish or county governments sometimes legislated on educational matters through their boards of vestrymen or magistrates.

Some efforts were even made in the colonial legislatures of Maryland, South Carolina, and Virginia to establish colony-wide systems of public schools. These were unsuccessful, not because there was no governmental authority for education, but because the people at that time did not believe they were necessary.

In the Middle Colonies the same governmental authority was used by the Dutch to establish public schools in New Netherland and by the Quakers in Pennsylvania. But a more tolerant policy toward religion had attracted several different religious denominations to these colonies.

Each group wanted its own religious principles taught in its own school. It was consequently more difficult to teach a single religious outlook in a public school open to children of different faiths than it had been in New England where most people were Congregationalists or in the South where most people were Anglicans.

In the eighteenth century the colonial governments began to permit the different religious groups to establish their own schools in which they could teach their own religious doctrines and their own languages (whether German, Dutch, French, or Swedish). In this way the state gave to religious and charitable bodies the right to conduct schools.

In like manner the colonial governments began to grant charters to small groups of businessmen or landowners. An educational charter gave these groups the right to incorporate as a board of trustees. They could then buy land, build buildings, appoint teachers, and generally manage a school.

Some of these corporate schools came to be known as "academies." One of the most famous was the Philadelphia Academy founded in 1751 by Benjamin Franklin. Others were the Newark Academy in Delaware, the Washington Academy in New Jersey, and the Dummer Academy and Phillips Academy in Massachusetts.

These incorporated academies made education attractive and available to children of middle-class merchants who could afford the tuition. At first it was unclear whether these denominational schools and incorporated academies were public or private schools, but eventually they came to be known as "private" schools in American terminology.

Other private schools were run by individual teachers as profit-making, business enterprises. In the seacoast cities of the eighteenth century these private teachers began to give young people direct preparation for jobs in commerce and trade. In general, the private-school teacher accepted or rejected students as he pleased. He charged what fees he could get, and he managed his affairs as he saw fit—so long as he had enough students to stay in business.

By contrast, the "public" school in the eighteenth century was a non-profit school under the supervision of a governmental agency or a corporate board of control. The parents had the right to send their children to it; the governing body set the fees and employed the teacher. Hence a "public" school was not run for the teacher's private profit.

The standards of curriculum were established and the achievement of pupils evaluated by the board of control, whether governmental or corporate. Later on, the corporate school came to be known as a "private" school, because it was not operated directly by a governmental board.

In the seventeenth century the "public" or town schools of Massachusetts, Connecticut, and New Hampshire taught the doctrines of a specific religion, that is, Congregational Calvinism. This was so because the Congregational church was established by the law of the legislature in those colonies.

This practice, known as "an establishment of religion," was common throughout Europe in the sixteenth and seventeenth centuries. The laws of the state required all people to accept the doctrines and rituals of the established church and authorized punishment for those who objected. The law levied taxes on everyone to support the ministers of the established church or churches. The Church of England, for example, was the established church in several of the Southern colonies; therefore, orthodox Anglicanism was taught in their schools.

But in the course of the eighteenth century, the idea of religious freedom gained great headway in the American colonies. This meant that such minority religious groups as Quakers, Presbyterians, Baptists, Dutch Reformed, Lutherans, Methodists, Mennonites, and others gained freedom to worship as they pleased. As a result, such groups did not wish to send their children to town schools where their children would be obliged to accept a religion in which they did not believe. The established churches would not at first consent to the removal of their religion from the public schools.

The solution in the eighteenth century was to permit the minority religious groups to establish their own schools. This meant that private religious schools could operate alongside the public schools. Although the public schools were weakened, this arrangement contributed to freedom at a time when the majority religious groups insisted that the public schools teach *their* religion and *only* their religion.

A few voices began to argue that if public schools did *not* teach a sectarian religion then all children could attend them freely. This was argued by William Smith in Pennsylvania, by William Livingston in New York, and by Thomas Jefferson in Virginia.

But the time was not yet ripe for such a solution. Although it was a gain for freedom to permit people to pursue their own way in religion and education, most people were not yet convinced that *others* should have the same freedom *they* had. Nor were they convinced that an education separated from specific religious doctrines was desirable. The search for freedom continued.

Meanwhile, as people moved out of the New England towns and cities into the unsettled lands of the country, they could no longer send their children long distances back to the town schools. They therefore began to set up their own local schools. This was the origin of the "district" school.

Representing the ultimate in local control, the district system reflected a decline in central state control of schools as the eighteenth century came to a close. This system had the advantage that it kept the schools close to the people, but it had the disadvantage that some districts ran low-quality schools or none at all. Local control was no guarantee that the quality of schools would be uniformly high.

At the end of colonial rule, common schools in which children of different religions or races learned together were still the exception. It was generally felt that schools should perpetuate the religious or cultural beliefs of the sponsoring agency. Some groups did go so far as to try to set up schools for Indians. Few but Quakers tried to do so for Negroes.

Seldom was it argued in colonial times that the aim of education was to empower every individual to make the most of himself as a person. The first system of education set up in America served to maintain the class distinctions imported from Europe.

Children of poor, lower-class parents had no education at all or were bound out as apprentices to learn a trade. Children of upper-class parents (public officials, clergymen, wealthy landowners) were expected to have an education appropriate to their station in life. The New England colonies broke this pattern somewhat when they required the towns to provide a minimum amount of education for *all* children.

Not all children actually received an education, but the principle was established that a commonwealth must rest upon an educated citizenry even if the education amounted only to bare literacy. Added to this was the Protestant belief that all adherents to the true faith should be able to read the Bible for themselves so that they could know the grounds and reasons for their faith. In any case, the New England town schools went a long way in seeing that a large number of their children received some education. This was the first step toward an education for freedom.

Learning to read, write, recite the catechism, and possibly do some arithmetic was the essence of a beginning or elementary education. In the earliest days, school books were rare and materials were scarce. A common device for teaching reading was a hornbook, a piece of wood with the alphabet and Lord's Prayer on it. The child could carry this around with him until he had learned everything on it.

Somewhat later in the seventeenth century, books began to be used; the most famous was *The New England Primer.* This consisted of the alphabet, simple syllables, words, sentences, and stories, all of a religious and moral character. A child may have spent two or three years obtaining this kind of elementary education. Taking the thirteen colonies as a whole, probably only one child in ten went to school at all.

What we would call secondary education was offered in Latin grammar schools. The immediate reason for stress on Latin was that Harvard College required it for admission because the main bodies of knowledge throughout Europe since the days of the Roman Republic and the Roman Empire had been written in Latin.

Even though the common languages of the people (vernaculars) were being used more widely by the sixteenth and seventeenth centuries, it was still the custom for an educated person to know Latin—and some Greek, if possible.

So the Latin grammar school was designed to prepare sons of the privileged classes for college in order that they might eventually enter one of the "higher" professions, such as the ministry, law, medicine, teaching, or simply that of "gentleman." Relatively few in the total population were expected to attain these callings in life. Most were expected to be tradesmen, farmers, workers, mechanics, or servants. For these an elementary education was considered sufficient—or even more than necessary.

In the course of the eighteenth century, however, cities and towns grew rapidly in size, trade and commerce increased, immigration rose, and goods and services were much more in demand than in the seventeenth century.

The cry was heard that the old classical Latin education was no longer appropriate for preparing young people to engage in these new important occupations of making goods, distributing them, and selling them. Education, some said, should become more practical, not solely intellectual or literary.

Two types of intermediate or secondary schools tried to meet this need. Some were "English" schools, so called because they were taught in English rather than in Latin. The instructors tried to offer whatever studies the young people desired, for example, English language; French, German, Spanish, Italian (languages useful for trade); mathematics (useful for navigation and surveying); commercial arithmetic and bookkeeping (useful in business); geography, history, and drawing (useful for leisure).

In the early decades of the eighteenth century these private-venture schools responded to the needs of the growing middle classes (merchants and tradesmen). They gave an education directly aimed at occupations other than the learned professions, and they catered to girls as well as to boys.

A second type of practical school was the academy, which was usually residential and often under the auspices of a religious denomination or a nonsectarian board of control. The curriculum of these schools, at least as proposed by Benjamin Franklin, was likely to be much broader than that of the Latin grammar school. It might include geography, history, science, modern languages, and the arts and music, as well as the classical languages and mathematics.

Both of these types of schools contributed to freedom by increasing the range of occupations for which they gave preparation. In this way an increasing number of young people from all social classes could gain a larger measure of self-direction and improve their position in society. Both types of schools were frowned upon by the classicists, but the academy survived the opposition because it met the needs of the middle classes. It eventually drove the Latin grammar school out of existence.

Meanwhile, the opportunities for college education were expanding. Eight colleges besides Harvard were founded prior to the Revolutionary War. Most of them reflected specific denominational outlooks, and their courses of study were largely linguistic, mathematical and bookish.

Some outstanding leaders tried to change the character of college studies by stressing the new sciences and social sciences. Among these were William Smith at the College of Philadelphia, William Livingston and Samuel Johnson at the founding of Kings College (Columbia), and Thomas Jefferson at the College of William and Mary.

But the tradition of classical studies supported by religious discipline was too strong for these reformers. Harvard (1636), Yale (1701), and Dartmouth (1769) remained Congregational in outlook; William and Mary (1693) and Columbia (1754), Anglican; Princeton (1746), Presbyterian; Brown (1764), Baptist; and Rutgers (1766), Dutch Reformed. The College at Philadelphia, the only college to be nondenominational at the outset (1755), was a forecast of the future, but it soon came under Anglican domination.

In general, then, the colonial period saw gains for freedom in the growth of representative government, the spread of religious freedom, and the rise of energetic middle classes of free men in town and country alike. Education tried to respond to these social movements as well as to a growing liberalism in thought and belief.

At the beginning of the colonial period, orthodoxies in theology, philosophy, and politics dominated the schools. Children were looked upon as sinful creatures who could be ruled only by harsh discipline, fear, and unrelenting obedience. By the end of the period, a growing liberalism meant that, here and there, children and adults alike were treated more humanely and less brutally. Human dignity and respect for persons were safer than they had been.

During most of the colonial period, education for developing a free person moved slowly and haltingly. For the most part, education at all levels was concerned as much with moral training as with intellectual training. If anything, the moral was considered more important and closely bound up with orthodox religion. Teachers were expected to conform in their beliefs to the dictates of whatever group controlled the schools. It was seldom argued that the teacher had a claim to freedom of teaching as an essential characteristic of a free society, a claim to deal freely with ideas even though they might be distasteful to the immediate managers of the school.

The founding of nine colleges of liberal arts in the thirteen colonies was a remarkable achievement by men who would be free, but the dominant view was definitely that a liberal education (and thus the educational basis for freedom) was for the few, not for the many. There was reluctance to expand the range of liberal studies beyond the traditional classics, mathematics, and philosophy, even though the explosion of knowledge was already beginning to crackle and pop in the seventeenth and eighteenth centuries.

The notion that education had a clear responsibility for enabling each individual to develop himself to the utmost was beginning to be stated but was not yet widely accepted. Building schools for a colonial society prior to the Revolutionary War was a dress rehearsal for freedom, not the main performance.

II. A Century of Republican Education (1770's to 1870's)

From the 1770's to the 1870's, Americans planned, built, changed, argued, and fought over the kinds of free institutions that should replace colonial rule. One of these institutions was education. As they set up and operated a republican form of government dedicated to equality, democracy, and freedom, they found that they needed an educational system appropriate to such a government.

In many different ways they said that if a republican government—or society—were to prosper and endure, then the people who elected the government, held office, made laws, enforced laws, and consented to be ruled must be educated as responsible citizens.

James Madison, father of the Constitution and author of the Bill of Rights, put it this way:

A popular Government, without popular information, or the means of acquiring it, is but a Prologue to a Farce or Tragedy; or, perhaps both. Knowledge will forever govern ignorance; and a people who mean to be their own Governors must arm themselves with the power which knowledge gives.

But this was not easy to do. The people who had won the Revolutionary War—these so-called Americans—were not really Americans, at least *not yet.* They were English, Scottish, French, German, Dutch, Swedish, and a good many more. And they were soon to be Irish, Italian, Hungarian, Polish, and Russian as well. They spoke different languages and they had different customs. Some had no tradition of self-government and others were fiercely proud or jealous of rule by others.

When it was finally decided that they should all learn the same language and the same principles of republican government, how was this to be done?

The answer was that it could best be done by a common school, taught in English, to which all the children of all the people could go together and learn how to live together and govern themselves.

But some people were poorer and some richer; some had good manners and others were coarse and rude. Should *all* these people really be educated?

Yes, they must be—if free government is to endure.

Well, but who is to pay for the poor ones?

Everyone must pay for all. If there are weak spots anywhere, the whole community of freedom is weakened. So the common schools must be supported by taxes paid by all.

All right, but who is to control these schools?

The only institution of a free society which serves everyone equally and is controlled by everyone is the government. So the government should control the common schools. And to keep the schools close to the people, the state and local governments, rather than the national government, should control the schools.

But won't the schools be subject to political and partisan prejudice?

Well, they might be, so we must create something genuinely new, something that will give all the people their say but keep the schools free of narrow, partisan politics. This can be done by a series of local boards of education subject to but separate from the executive, legislative, and judicial branches of government.

These school boards, often elected directly by the people, could constitute a kind of "fourth branch of government." They would exert direct control over local education under the general authority set up by the state governments and subject to the guarantees of equality and freedom laid down in the United States Constitution and applying to all Americans.

So far so good, but what about religious education? Don't all these Americans with different religions have freedom to run their own schools under the First Amendment of the Constitution and under their state constitutions?

Yes, indeed, they do. But each American will have to decide for himself whether the education that supports a free society should be conducted in separate schools in which religion provides the fundamental framework for all studies or in common schools devoted primarily to the whole range of free institutions in America. If they decide the first way, the children will be divided into separate schools for their entire education and this division will be along religious lines. If the second way, the children will attend the same public school together for their common education and only be separated for their religious education, which can be conducted as may be desired by the home or by the church or by the synagogue.

In the century of republican education, most Americans chose the common school, controlled and supported in common, and embracing a nonsectarian religious outlook.

Their primary concern was to design a universal, free, public school that would promote free institutions and free citizenship. For the first one hundred years of the Republic, the need for creating the common bonds and loyalties of a free community was paramount.

Less attention was given to the claims of diversity and difference as the essence of freedom for individuals. This came later when the Union had been established, made secure against internal opposition, defended against outside invaders, and preserved despite a war between the states themselves.

The republican ideal of the first century of nationhood gave the following answers regarding the control of education:

A free society required the public elementary schools to provide the basic information, literacy, and moral teachings required by every free man. For most Americans the term "free man" was limited to white men, until the Civil War legally introduced Negroes to citizenship. Private elementary schools continued to exist but they were declining in numbers and in importance by the 1870's.

Under the effective and determined leadership of an extraordinary galaxy of "public-school men," the idea of universal common schooling was widely accepted in the new United States during the first half of the nineteenth century. Outstanding among these were Horace Mann and James G. Carter in Massachusetts, Henry Barnard in Connecticut, Calvin Stowe in Ohio, Caleb Mills in Indiana, John D. Pierce in Michigan, Ninian Edwards in Illinois, Calvin Wiley in North Carolina, and Charles F. Mercer in Virginia. These men and others made speeches before thousands of people; wrote hundreds of pamphlets, articles, and reports; organized scores of groups and societies to agitate for common schools; and held dozens of positions in state governments or school systems.

They argued that the payment of tuition for schooling was unfair to children of poor parents, who could not pay for an education. They argued that the older forms of public support, like land grants from the federal Land Ordinances of 1785 and 1787, would not support schools on the vast scale now necessary.

They argued that the term *free school* should no longer mean a school in which only the poor children were given free education and all others paid tuition.

They argued that class distinctions could be lessened only when a *free school* meant that *all* children were given a free education together and when the entire school system was supported by taxes levied upon everyone.

Aiding their efforts were the newly formed labor unions, which demanded that the public schools provide universal education.

The states gradually accepted this idea of a free public school. The state legislatures passed laws *permitting* local school districts to tax themselves for such schools; they sometimes gave state funds to *encourage* local districts to tax themselves; and they finally *required* all local districts to tax themselves and establish public schools.

By these means, the local freedom of districts to ignore schooling for their children gave way to the larger freedom to be gained by a total population enlightened by education of all. Local control by districts was gradually limited by requirements set by state constitutions, state legislatures, state boards of education, and state superintendents of schools. It was decided that a free society would be better served if education were planned by the central authority of the states rather than left wholly to the completely decentralized control of local school boards. This was not done without bitter conflict, for many believed that state, as opposed to local, control would be undemocratic and destroy freedom.

But in the 1820's, the 1830's, and 1840's it was decided that a state government, responsive to public control, could serve freedom as well as, if not better than, the hundreds of local school districts could do. If a local district were left free to provide a poor education or no education at all for its children, those children would be deprived of their birthright to an education that would prepare them for free citizenship. Thereby, the state's own freedom would be endangered.

A smaller freedom must be limited in the interests of a greater freedom. And to guarantee the larger freedom, the state must exert its authority to see to it not only that schools were available to all but that all children actually attended school. Massachusetts led the way by passing its compulsory attendance law in 1852.

The solution was a genuinely creative one. Authority for providing education was defined in state constitutions and in state laws. State authority for education was carried out by state superintendents of schools responsible to a state board of education, elected by the people or appointed by the governor. New York State created the office of state superintendent of schools in 1812. Massachusetts established a state board of education in 1837 with Horace Mann as secretary, and Connecticut did likewise in 1839 with Henry Barnard as secretary. Other states followed.

These state agencies could then set minimum standards for all the schools of the state. Meanwhile, the direct management of schools would be left in the hands of locally elected school boards, local superintendents, and locally appointed teachers. Local management served the cause of flexibility, diversity, and freedom.

This arrangement was designed to assure that schools would serve the whole *public* and would be controlled by the *public* through special boards of education, not through the regular agencies of the state or local governments. This is why in America we use the term *public schools,* not simply *state schools* or *government schools,* as they are often called in those countries that have centralized systems of education.

Since the United States Constitution had not mentioned education as a function of the federal government, the free states after the Revolution reclaimed the authority over education that had been the prerogative of the colonial legislatures.

But the United States Constitution and the state constitutions *did* proclaim freedom of religion and separation of church and state as one of the essentials of republican government. That is, neither the federal government nor state governments could interfere in the affairs of churches or use public funds to support them. Therefore, the states could not give public money to schools under the control of churches.

But what about religious instruction in the common public schools? It was soon evident that if common schools taught the doctrines of a particular church they would violate the freedom of conscience of all those who did not agree.

Could the common schools find a common religious outlook and teach that? Many Protestants thought so. They tried to find the common religious doctrines of Christianity and they found them in the Bible. If the schools would teach only the nonsectarian principles of Christianity as contained in the Bible, they argued, all sects would be satisfied. This might have been the case if America had remained exclusively Protestant.

But immigration had brought increased numbers of Roman Catholics and Jews. Besides, many Americans had never officially belonged to any church. Catholics charged that the so-called "nonsectarian" schools were really Protestant in character and that they were therefore sectarian. So Catholics established their own schools and many demanded a share in the public tax funds to support them. Most Protestants and Jews opposed the giving of public money to parochial schools.

Most states finally decided to prohibit any sectarian control over common schools and to prohibit use of public money for private schools under sectarian control. Especially bitter struggles between Protestants and Catholics were decided for the time being by legislation in New York in 1842 and by constitutional amendment in Massachusetts in 1855. Nearly every state had a similar struggle and enacted similar laws.

By the end of the first century of republican education, the general decision was that a free society was better served if the majority of children went to common, nonsectarian schools than if they went to separate, sectarian religious schools. This made it possible for the United States to build a universal system of free elementary schools sooner than any other country in the world.

The line of argument went like this: Nonsectarianism would provide a greater measure of national unity than could be achieved when each sectarian group shepherded its own children into its own schools. The range of communication among children would be restricted if each group continued to run its own schools differently in religion and language from others. Separate schools would create and perpetuate divisions among the people—thus narrowing their outlooks and reducing free interchange of ideas. Free common schools would more certainly serve the cause of free institutions.

At the end of the first century of the Republic, secondary schools, however, were still largely in private and religious hands. This fact did not seem undesirable to most Americans of that particular period.

The private academies provided considerable opportunity to those who could afford some education beyond the essentials. Likewise, most of the 200 colleges were under private and religious control. This, too, seemed reasonable to the majority of Americans at that time: Elementary education for all at public expense would be sufficient to guarantee the basic security of a republican government; advanced education for *leadership* in the state and in the professions could then be obtained privately by those who could afford it.

A few spokesmen, however, began to argue that a free society needed "free" secondary and higher institutions as well as free elementary schools. The public high school, for example, appeared as early as 1821 in Boston. The idea spread rapidly, but the public high schools did not dominate the secondary-school field till the late nineteenth century.

Advocates of free higher education tried to transform some of the private colleges into state institutions. This happened at the College of William and Mary in Virginia, at Columbia in New York, and at the College of Philadelphia.

The most notable attempt, however, occurred when the New Hampshire legislature tried to transform Dartmouth College into a state university. But the United States Supreme Court in 1819 (*Trustees of Dartmouth College v. Woodward*) decided that the college was a private corporation and that its charter was a contract which the state could not change unless "the funds of the college be public property."

Following the Dartmouth College decision, private colleges increased in numbers, most of them sponsored by religious denominations. Especially active were Presbyterians, Congregationalists, Episcopalians, Methodists, and Roman Catholics. But the advocates of public higher education also redoubled their efforts. State universities were established in twenty states before the Civil War. The earliest universities to be set up under state control (but not free of tuition) were in Georgia, North Carolina, and Vermont.

The ideal of freedom as a basis for a state university was most eloquently proclaimed by Thomas Jefferson at the University of Virginia, which opened in 1825. In Virginia, as elsewhere, religious groups were bitterly opposed to the state university and tried to prevent its establishment or to divert public funds to their own institutions.

Federal land grants authorized by the Morrill Act in 1862 gave a significant boost to the state-university movement. Funds from these grants were used by the states to establish agricultural and engineering colleges or to strengthen their state universities.

Despite the advocates of free and equal education for all, the era of republican education tried to get along with common schools at the elementary level, but with secondary and higher institutions divided along denominational lines. In general, while the elementary schools served everyone, the academies and colleges and universities catered to the wealthier and upper social classes rather than to the ordinary people.

The major failure to achieve the reformers' goal of a common universal school was the system of segregated schools for Negroes, which appeared occasionally in the North as well as generally in the South. In fact, it was the Roberts case in the Massachusetts Supreme Court in 1849 which set forth the principle that separate schools for Negroes were permissible so long as their facilities were equal to those of the white schools. Charles Sumner's argument that separate schools violated the equal rights of Negroes was rejected by the court, but, even so, Massachusetts and other Northern states moved soon thereafter to abolish their segregated schools by law.

Turning now to the kind and quality of education achieved in the first century of the Republic, we find the main elements of the common-school curriculum continued to be reading, writing, and arithmetic. These three R's were supposed to give the elements of literacy and the intellectual tools necessary for acquiring the knowledge and "popular information" of which Madison spoke.

But, said the school reformers, the citizen of the new Republic needed more than this—much more. He needed a knowledge of history and geography to instill feelings of patriotism, loyalty, and national pride. He needed moral teachings to instill habits of "republican" character. And he needed some practical studies, like bookkeeping or manual training, so that he could get and keep a job.

The common school was designed to do more than give intellectual training. It was to provide citizenship training, character education, and a means by which every child might advance up the economic and social scale as far as his talents would carry him.

By providing such equal opportunity, the common school would protect free institutions. It would promote progress and prosperity; it would reduce poverty and prevent crime. This was a big order to hand to the schools, but the optimism, energy, and faith of the times all prodded the schools to try to do their share—sometimes more than their share—in making the American dream come true.

The "new" school had to have new methods as well as new subjects. Such school reformers as Joseph Neef and Horace Mann argued that the customary strict discipline, corporal punishment, and slavish memorizing of textbooks were not good enough to carry the burden the school must carry. They therefore argued for the enthusiasm, excitement, interest, and eager learning that could come with a more humane and sympathetic attitude toward children.

Of course, the conservatives charged that the reformers would spoil the children if they spared the rod, but the reformers persisted despite the opposition.

The main trouble was that the teachers were not trained to deal with small children constructively. Would the liberal-arts colleges provide this training? Some proposals were made—at Amherst, at Brown, at Michigan, and elsewhere—that they should do so, but the colleges were not interested. So, entirely new institutions called normal schools were created to give their whole attention to the training of elementary-school teachers.

The first of these were founded as private normal schools in the 1820's by Samuel R. Hall at Concord, Vermont, and by James G. Carter at Lexington, Massachusetts. The first state normal school was opened in 1839 at Lexington, and the idea eventually spread throughout the country.

The normal schools taught young people of high-school age how to teach the elementary-school subjects. Compared with the better colleges of the day, their quality was low, but they made possible the rapid building of the common school systems in the several states. They raised school teaching above the level of incidental apprenticeship and began the process of making it a profession, narrow though the training was in the beginning. If the colleges of liberal arts had been as much interested in school teaching as they were in law, medicine, or other professions, the quality and status of the elementary-school teacher might have been higher much sooner than they were.

The curriculum of the secondary schools also began to respond to the political and economic progress of the times. The academies, replacing the Latin grammar schools, taught a wider range of subjects. Thus, students began to have some freedom of choice of studies. And some academies opened their doors to girls, a notable victory for freedom. By the 1870's some 6000 academies dotted the educational landscape.

But the common-school reformers felt that the private academies could never do the job that needed to be done. They therefore argued that free public high schools should be created to provide a practical education for those boys and girls who would not or could not go on to college.

Offering a practical nonclassical curriculum to youth who could live at home while attending secondary school, the public high school was destined to become ever more popular after the Civil War. It added to the range of vocations for which the schools prepared and in this way opened up possibilities of self-improvement through careers that had never before been within reach of the majority of youth.

Reformers such as George Ticknor at Harvard and Henry Tappan at Michigan also tried to broaden the curriculum of the colleges to make them serve the commercial business, and political needs of the rapidly growing nation. They wanted to make real universities out of the small colleges.

Classicists put up great resistance against such reforms. Especially powerful was the report of the Yale faculty in 1828, which condemned practical courses and argued that the colleges should continue to stress the mental discipline to be acquired by strict study of Greek, Latin, mathematics, and philosophy.

Colleges should give a *liberal* education, said the Yale faculty, not a vocational education. Colleges should lay the *foundation* for later professional study; they should not give the professional study itself.

By the 1870's the dominant view of higher education came down to this: Liberal education was the only proper education for a free man, but relatively few young men (and no young women) could profit from such a training. Universal education may be all right for the common man, but college education should be reserved for the uncommon man.

The republican ideal of free universal education had not yet been applied to secondary schools or to colleges. The second century of the Republic, the century of democracy in education, did just this.

III. Nearly a Century of Democratic Education (1870's to 1960's)

Whereas the republican ideal had been to provide *some* education for all and *much* education for a few, the democratic goal was to provide *as much education as possible for all.* The keynote of the century of democratic education was "more education for more people." It had its drawbacks, its setbacks, and its ups and downs, but nothing seemed able to stop for long the surge to education as the essence of the search for freedom.

The march to the schools came faster, the lines stretched longer, and the students grew older as the second century of the Republic moved from the 1870's to the 1960's. By 1900 the great majority of children aged six to thirteen were in elementary schools; by 1960 over 99 per cent were in attendance. Universal elementary schooling for all children had been won.

More remarkable, however, was the march to the secondary schools. By 1900 about 10 per cent of children aged fourteen to seventeen were actually in school; in 1930 more than 50 per cent attended; and by 1960 nearly 90 per cent were attending. This comes close to universal secondary education, something not dreamed of by the republican leaders of the first century of nationhood.

In 1760 the average colonist may have had two to three years of schooling; by 1960 the average American had ten to eleven years of schooling. And the end has not been reached. The average years of schooling will probably go to twelve or even to fourteen within a decade or two.

Still more remarkable was the stepped-up-tempo of the march to college. In 1910 about 5 per cent of all youth aged eighteen to twenty-one were attending college; by 1960 nearly 40 per cent of all such youth were attending institutions beyond high school. Millions more were attending adult-education classes and courses of instruction being offered by business, industry, labor, the armed services, churches, and voluntary agencies. And education by television and other automatic devices had scarcely begun. The potentials were staggering.

How did all this happen and why? The story is complicated, but a few elements are clear. Republican education may have been sufficient for a society marked by a relatively small population scattered over large areas of rich land and relying mainly upon farming and trading for subsistence. But in a society that relied on science and technology, the situation was radically different.

Not only did the leaders, scholars, experts, and professional men need more and better education, but also the kind of education that *everyone* needed grew steadily greater in quantity and higher in quality. For *this* kind of industrial society, a democratic education would be necessary if freedom were to be maintained.

A society based on steam power, electric power, or nuclear power can be managed and controlled by relatively few people. Technical power leads to political and economic power. To prevent autocratic, dictatorial use of political and economic power by a few, everyone must have an education devoted to freedom. There is no other satisfactory way to limit political or economic power.

So it became increasingly clear that the opportunity to acquire an expanded and extended education must be made available to *all*, to the poor as well as to the rich, to the slow student as well as to the bright, to the South and West as well as to the North and East, to girls as well as to boys, to Negroes as well as to whites, to immigrants as well as to native-born, to Catholic and Jew as well as to Protestant and nonchurchgoer.

The century of democratic education took the doctrines of the common school and applied them almost completely to the secondary school and in part to the college. Equality of opportunity stood alongside freedom as the prime goals of education.

Let us see what happened to the organization and control of education in the age of democratic education:

The nineteenth-century solution to the problem of public and private schools came to this: A system of public institutions ranging from primary school to university, open for everyone as long as his abilities justify, is the best guarantor of a free society based upon equality of opportunity. Private institutions are free to operate alongside the public institutions, but these should be supported voluntarily and should not be given public funds.

In the 1870's a series of court cases (especially the Kalamazoo case in Michigan) agreed that the people of the states could establish and support public high schools with tax funds if they so desired. Thereupon the public high-school movement spread rapidly, and the private academy shrank in importance. Furthermore, all states passed compulsory attendance laws requiring attendance to at least age sixteen. Provision of public secondary schools thereupon became an *obligation* of the states, not just a voluntary matter for the local districts to decide.

Children were permitted to attend properly approved nonpublic schools as a way of meeting state attendance laws. This principle was affirmed by the United States Supreme Court in the Oregon case of 1925 (*Pierce v. Society of Sisters*).

States had the right to supervise, inspect, and set minimum standards for *all* schools and to require children to attend *some* school, but the state could not compel students to attend public schools if their parents preferred private schools. Freedom to have a say in the education of their children was a constitutional right of parents under the Fourteenth Amendment. Besides, private schools were valuable property which could not be destroyed by action of the state without due process of law.

By 1930 the preference of most Americans for public schools was clear; only about 9 per cent of children attended nonpublic schools. The public policy hammered out in the nineteenth century was also clear: Public funds should not be used to support private schools. Beginning in the 1930's, however, the clamor began to rise again that the private schools should be given some public aid. Campaigns to get parents to send their children to private schools began to show results.

Today more than 16 per cent of children are in nonpublic schools, a gain so spectacular that the American people have to face up to certain questions more directly than at any time since the 1830's: Shall we encourage private schools as well as public schools with public money? Is the present balance among public and private schools about right? If not, should we favor private or public schools?

Through the years, much of the controversy over public and private schools has been basically sectarian. Today more than ninety per cent of children attending nonpublic schools are enrolled in parochial schools conducted by the Roman Catholic Church. A whole series of laws and court cases in the nineteenth century decided that religious freedom and separation of church and state meant that the states could not give tax money to support private education. But from 1930 onward, exceptions began to be made.

The Cochran case in 1930 permitted Louisiana to spend tax funds to give free textbooks to children in private as well as public schools; the Everson case in 1947 permitted New Jersey to provide bus transportation for parochial-school pupils; in 1948 the School Lunch Act gave federal money to parochial schools even though state funds could not be so used. Advocates of parochial schools were now arguing that public funds should be used to pay for auxiliary services that benefited the child but were not direct aid to the school as such.

In recent decades, the arguments for diverting public funds to private schools have changed. It is now argued that the states should aid all parents to send their children to the kind of school they wish. This would not aid *schools;* it would aid parents to exercise their freedom of educational choice. So if parents want their children to go to religious schools, they should receive their fair share of tax funds. If they want their children to go to all-white schools, they should receive tax funds to help them to do this. Obviously, the whole idea of a common school is now under severe attack.

What the American people will decide in the years to come is in doubt. In fact, the whole idea inherited from republican days that a free society rests upon a common school system maintained and controlled by the free government is in peril.

"Freedom" may come to mean that parents can divide up among themselves the public funds which had originally been designed to support a free educational system which in turn was designed to perpetuate the free society itself. Does freedom of choice for parents mean that the state is obligated to support and pay for that choice?

Such questions as these came to focus sharply in the problem of central and local control. If some towns or regions in a state could not or would not provide good schools for their children, should the children suffer, or should the state try to equalize the burden by giving financial aid to those towns? The answer turned out to be clear: Equalize the burden in fairness to the children.

Most states use tax money, raised all over the state, to support schools in all parts of the state wherever and whenever local property taxes did not provide enough money to operate good schools. Central control in state hands seemed desirable for the purpose.

But what about the federal government? Will the same answer be given? If some *states* cannot or will not provide good schools for their children, should the federal government try to equalize the burden by giving financial aid to the states? If all states try hard, and still some states cannot provide acceptable educational opportunity for all children, should the federal government step in and help out? By and large, the answer thus far has been no; a qualified no, but still no.

To be sure, the Land Ordinances of 1785 and 1787 and other grants gave millions of acres of land to the states for education; the Morrill Act of 1862 helped establish land-grant colleges; the Smith-Lever Act of 1914 supported agricultural and home-economics instruction; the Smith-Hughes Act of 1917 aided vocational education in high schools.

Emergency aid was given in the 1930's and the National Youth Administration and Civilian Conservation Corps helped youth in the depression; a bill was passed to provide aid for federally impacted school districts; the GI Bill of Rights helped millions of veterans of World War II and the war in Korea to get an education; and the National Defense Education Act of 1958 gave loans to students and supported specific programs in foreign-language training, science, guidance, and audiovisual methods.

But up to the present, the idea of federal-state partnership in public-school support has not been squarely faced by the federal government. For nearly a hundred years a whole series of bills had been introduced in Congress to achieve this purpose. Beginning with the Hoar bill, Perce bill, and Burnside bill of the 1870's and the several Blair bills in the 1880's, Republicans were the chief advocates of federal aid, but Democrats of the South were afraid that the federal government was trying to punish them and impose Northern ideas upon them.

In the decade between 1950 and 1960 it was the liberal Democrats from the North and West who tried to achieve federal aid, but were thwarted by economy-minded Republicans and by some Southern Democrats who feared federal imposition of integrated schools upon the South. Throughout the century many Roman Catholic leaders opposed federal aid unless it would help parochial as well as public schools.

The race issue, the religious issue, and the economy issue successfully blocked federal aid for decades. After the close of the Civil War, it was touch and go for a while whether federal action would result in equal educational opportunity for Negroes in the South.

The Fourteenth Amendment (1866) guaranteed "equal protection of the laws" to all citizens, but the federal education bills failed and the Civil Rights Act of 1875 was declared unconstitutional. The Southern states proceeded to set up segregated school systems, one system for Negroes and one for whites. The United States Supreme Court decision in *Plessy* v. *Ferguson* (1896) was taken to mean that separate school systems were permissible provided they had equal facilities.

In the 1940's a whole series of court cases began the process of gaining access for Negroes to the public institutions of the South—first to the universities and then to the schools. The historic decisions headed by the Brown case of May 17, 1954, reversed the "separate but equal" doctrine of Plessy and declared that segregated schools were inherently unequal even if each had "equal" amounts of money spent on it.

In the following years, case after case was taken to court to require boards of education to admit Negroes to the public schools, on an unsegregated basis.

Violence, often instigated by outside agitators, broke out in Clinton, Tennessee, and a number of other places; and federal troops were called to Little Rock, Arkansas, when the governor interfered with a federal court order to integrate the schools. Gradually, however, desegregation spread through the border states and by 1960 was being faced in the Deep South.

Some Southern governors and legislatures tried to prevent integration by legal devices. Laws were passed to close the public schools, to give public money to parents so they could send their children to segregated private schools, and even to abolish the public-school system itself.

These actions posed the most serious threat to the ideals of both republican and democratic education it was possible to pose. Does a state have the right to abolish its "fourth branch of government?" What *is* essential to a "republican form of government" (as guaranteed in the United States Constitution) if public education is not? Could the principles of a free society withstand this onslaught safely?

If the demands for private religious education and the demands for private segregated education were joined by economy demands for reducing public-school budgets, the result could be a repudiation of the public-school idea itself and a return to the "voluntary" principle of the sixteenth and seventeenth centuries in Europe: Let those have an education who can pay for it; let education be fully private. Or, alternatively: Let us divide up the public moneys among competing racial and religious groups so they can set up their own private schools; let us have many free *private* educational systems.

In either of these cases, the central idea of American education would disappear. An unlimited role for free private enterprise in education would take the place of a limited role for free public enterprise. The freedom of segmented voluntary groups to work at cross purposes would replace the freedom of the people as a whole to work through a system of public schools. The 1960's will doubtless see the struggles heightened. How will the search for freedom come out?

Just as the keynote to *quantity* in education for the century of democratic education has been "more education for more people," so the keynote to *quality* in education has been "better education for all." Each decade had its reformers who demanded better education than the schools were then offering, but there has been little agreement concerning what is "better."

Different reformers have demanded different measures at different times. As the times changed, the schools were behind the times for different reasons. Nowhere else in the world have so many people been so much concerned about education so much of the time—and almost never has everyone been satisfied.

No sooner had the elementary schools been established to start six-year-olds on the road to formal schooling than reformers began to argue that we ought to have a pre-school school called the kindergarten. So, borrowing ideas from Friedrich Froebel in Europe, we began to attach kindergartens to the public schools, beginning in the 1870's. The idea was to help children of four to six years learn by directed play activities.

By 1960 most American cities had kindergartens, and some of them had even established nursery schools for two-to-four-year-olds.

The elementary school itself was subject to recurring reforms. No sooner did it make headway in teaching the three R's to every child than someone, outside the schools or in, would urge it to broaden its curriculum: Add drawing and the arts; add geography and history; add nature study; hygiene and physical training; manual training; domestic science. And these all seemed reasonable.

The famous Swiss educator, Pestalozzi, had said so; Edward E. Sheldon, founder of the Oswego (New York) Normal School, said so; Francis W. Parker, superintendent of schools in Quincy, Massachusetts, said so. And so said a host of others, including such diverse characters as the presidents of Harvard (Charles W. Eliot) and of Columbia (Nicholas Murray Butler), publicists like Joseph Mayer Rice, social workers like Jane Addams and Lilian Wald, reformers like Jacob Riis and Walter Hines Page.

Social reformers, humanitarians, and philanthropists, especially in the cities of the 1890's, were indignant about the endless memory work that marked most schools. Schools, they said, were far too intellectualistic—they dealt almost exclusively with words and numbers that did not mean very much to the children. They felt that schools should be alive, interesting, exciting, practical and useful.

This seemed fair enough. John Dewey took up the ideas in his experimental school at the University of Chicago, and Teachers College at Columbia University applied them in its experimental Lincoln School. Eventually "progressive" schools mushroomed on the landscape, and "progressive" ideas became popular in the 1920's and 1930's. Chief among the spokesmen after John Dewey was William H. Kilpatrick at Teachers College, Columbia University.

All sorts of plans were devised to loosen up the formal curriculum and give it life and vitality—units, projects, activities, excursions and visits, handicrafts, gardens, laboratories, audio-visual aids, and much else—anything to overcome the slavish drill on the textbook or notebook. There was little doubt that the general quality of learning for most children was raised as the school added vitality and zest to the learning process.

But in the 1940's and 1950's a new set of "reformers" began to charge that the schools were too soft. Schools, they said, were just letting children play and not teaching them anything. Elementary schools were exhorted to return to the three R's and stiffen up discipline and concentrate on intellectual studies.

Many of the criticisms were overdrawn and unfair, but many had some truth in them. Progressive methods *had* been carried to an extreme by a few spokesmen and by a few teachers who assumed that all children learned better by "direct" experiences, by visits, or by physical activities than they did by reading or writing. A general tightening of school methods was evident by 1960.

Sputnik and Russian education strengthened the critics' hands. But how long would it be before "loosening" and flexibility in the curriculum would again be necessary and a new wave of progressive reform to overcome excessive academic formalism be desirable?

Meanwhile, the controversy over religion in the public schools continued. By the beginning of the twentieth century, most public schools had not only dropped sectarian religious teaching but also much of the nonsectarian religious instruction they had attempted in the early nineteenth century. In other words, although the public schools dealt with moral and spiritual values, they no longer tried to deal with religion at all; they were secular. But after World War II the demand rose again that the public schools restore some kind of religious instruction.

Some Protestants proposed that the Bible be read without comment by the teacher, but Catholics and Jews opposed this as really sectarian. It was proposed that students be given time off from regular classes to receive sectarian instruction from their own religious teachers (released time).

In 1948 the United States Supreme Court in the McCollum decision said that released-time religious instruction could not be given inside public-school buildings, but in 1952 (Zorach decision) the Supreme Court said it could be done outside schools if the public teachers did not coerce or persuade students to go to the religious classes. Neither of these decisions has satisfied many people. Some educators have proposed that public schools avoid religious instruction as such but undertake factual study about religion right along with the study of other regular school subjects, but most religious groups have been cool to this proposal. The formula for honoring religious diversity while still promoting social unity through common schools had not been satisfactorily found.

Reform movements stirred through secondary as well as elementary schools. Most revolutionary reform was the very idea of a secondary school which would accept students of the whole range of ability and try to give all a course of study suited to their abilities and their possible vocations in life.

Most other countries divide children at age eleven or twelve, send a few to academic (college-preparatory) schools, others to vocational schools, and the majority directly to work. The American high school, however, has tried to be a comprehensive school, one in which students from all walks of life would study and work and play together. This meant that many new subjects and courses have been added periodically to the high-school curriculum.

The resulting number of elective studies has worried the colleges. As early as 1893 the National Education Association tried to encourage a standardized high-school curriculum. Noteworthy were the efforts of the Committee of Ten (1893) and the Committee on College Entrance Requirements (1899).

These "reforms" stressed those academic studies which should be required for college entrance; namely, four units in foreign language, two in mathematics, two in English, one in history, and one in science. (The relative inattention to science is at least sixty years old.) It was assumed that such studies would be good for all students whether they were headed for college or not. This was fair enough at a time when seventy-five per cent of high-school graduates were going on to college.

But after 1900 the pressures of enrollment on the high schools grew stronger. By 1918 an NEA Committee formulated *The Seven Cardinal Principles of Secondary Education,* in which preparation for college was definitely less important than it had been twenty years before. Now, the high school's aims were to give attention to health, command of the fundamental processes, worth home membership, vocational preparation, citizenship, leisure-time activities, and ethical character.

This note continued to be emphasized in the 1930's and 1940's. By 1950 about thirty per cent of high-school graduates were going to college. Preparation for college had actually become a minor function of the high schools.

However, a new wave of reaction (or was it reform?) began to criticize secondary schools for permitting low academic standards, for not stimulating youth to rigorous study, for letting youth take so-called "easy" courses instead of working hard at the regular academic subjects. The success of Russian space flights and the threat of falling behind in the armament race raised fears that American high schools were not doing their jobs.

Many of the critics did not know what they were talking about, but some did. There was little doubt that many high schools could do a better job for college-bound youth than they were doing. Some high-school educators were still assuming that only a small minority of high-school graduates were headed for college. They had not noticed that by 1960 many more high-school students were expecting to go to college.

It might not be long until we would be back where we were in 1900 with 75 per cent of high-school graduates bound for college, but with this vast difference: In 1900 only 10 per cent of youth were in high school; today 90 per cent are there.

The potential enrollments called for a drastic new look at the secondary school, at both the junior-high and senior-high levels. The first thing the schools did was to give more attention to the academic subjects, especially to the foreign languages, science, and mathematics. The time was ripe, however, for a complete overhauling of the junior-high school, which was just about fifty years old and born in a very different age from that of the 1960's.

Undoubtedly the pressure of high-school graduates upon college doors would lead to even further drastic expansion of junior colleges and other two-year institutions. They too were just about half a century old and, in some ways, the epitome of the democratic movement in American education.

It was being estimated that by the decades following 1970 all students with an IQ of one hundred or over would be finishing at least a two-year college. If this proved to be true, standards of admission to some colleges would go up and in others they were bound to go down.

Finally, the upward push of the educational surge left its unmistakable mark on the four-year colleges and universities. In the 1870's most institutions of higher education were relatively small undergraduate colleges. Their curriculums were still largely devoted to the liberal arts of Greek and Latin, mathematics, and philosophy; and these courses were all required of all students.

In a relatively short time, however, new studies, like the modern languages, English, modern history and the social sciences, modern science, and the fine arts found a place in the curriculum. Students had to be given a choice because they could not possibly study all these subjects in four years. So the elective system was instituted.

Meanwhile, graduate study began to change the whole character of higher education. When Johns Hopkins University opened its doors in 1876, it helped to set the pattern for graduate schools devoted to the advancement of knowledge and research in the entire range of the arts and sciences. Professional schools of medicine, law, education, engineering, agriculture, business administration, and the like began to flourish.

This meant that universities were now devoted to direct professional preparation for an even larger number of vocations rather than for just a few. Some liberal-arts colleges tried to maintain their nonvocational and nonprofessional character, but most were not able or did not care to do so. The democratic surge was too strong.

In the 1920's and 1930's a number of experimental colleges tried to grapple with the overcrowded curriculum and to design new patterns of liberal education. Bennington, University of Wisconsin, Sarah Lawrence, Bard, University of Minnesota were among them.

Critics arose, such as Robert Hutchins and Alexander Meiklejohn, to call for preservation of the liberal-arts college free from professionalism and vocationalism. They were struggling against the tide. Nevertheless, undergraduate colleges did institute a wide variety of programs which, in one way or another, tried to assure that all students would have some acquaintance with the humanities, the social sciences, the sciences and mathematics, and the fine arts. Whatever a liberal education or a general education was supposed to be, it was to deal with these fields of knowledge.

Much criticism was directed at the professional schools for not giving enough attention to the liberal arts. They began to give heed. As the 1960's opened, considerable ferment was evident in medical schools, business schools, engineering schools, and schools of education.

It seemed likely that the teachers college, as a separate institution devoted exclusively to the training of teachers, would disappear. Normal schools had become teachers colleges, and now teachers colleges were becoming state colleges and even state universities. These changes were signs on the road of the march of democratic education.

Higher education was no longer confined to the few nor to the upper classes of wealth or privilege. It was on the way to becoming financially free, as secondary and elementary education had become before it. The opportunity was great.

The question was whether all this educational activity could measure up to the intellectual and moral demands of a free society in the modern world. If individuals used the vast resources of American higher education simply to further their own interests, this was one kind of small freedom all right, but in the long run would it serve the cause of the free society? How to enable American education to serve the cause of the larger freedoms was the paramount question. The answer to this question cannot be rigged. The fate of the nation rides upon it.

At the heart of the answer to the fateful question is the scholarship, the wisdom, the vitality and the freedom of American teachers. If teachers are weak, timorous, or poorly trained, the American idea of education has little chance of success. If powerful or selfish groups demand that teachers conform to *their* ways of thinking or to *their* beliefs, education will be a narrow little thing. And our history here is not too reassuring.

Orthodoxy of belief in colonial days was a prime requirement for teaching. Oaths of loyalty to the crown and to the doctrines of the church were familiar trappings of colonial rule. The American Revolution in its turn demanded that teachers be faithful to the Revolution rather than to the crown; and, similarly, Congress exacted loyalty oaths to the Union in the Reconstruction Period after the Civil War.

Conformity of economic belief, faith in private business enterprise, and opposition to any radical movements were expected of teachers in the nineteenth century. State laws required special loyalty oaths from teachers as early as the 1920's, and as late as 1958 the National Defense Education Act required such oaths from students applying for federal loans.

After World Wars I and II, thirty states passed laws requiring teachers to sign special loyalty oaths. Other laws (notably the Feinberg Law of 1949 in New York State) were passed to hunt down and dismiss teachers suspected of belonging to subversive organizations. Many patriotic organizations served as self-appointed censors of school textbooks and complained about outspoken teachers.

The frantic search for communist teachers and others suspected vaguely of "leftist" leaning was fired up by McCarthyism and the wave of legislative investigations that swept the country in the early 1950's.

As a result, a cloud of timidity, suspicion, and fear settled down upon the schools and colleges in what *The New York Times* called "a subtle, creeping paralysis of freedom of thought." Classroom teachers and school administrators tended to avoid acts or ideas that might "cause any trouble" or arouse any criticism.

This general atmosphere of caution and anxiety affecting millions of students did infinitely more damage to the cause of freedom in education than the handful of communist teachers could possibly do. Fortunately, the most active "Red hunts" have now passed, but their revival is an ever-present danger, especially if teachers and students are fearful or are indifferent to the importance of freedom in education.

The first defenses of freedom in education are strong professional organizations of teachers like the American Association of University Professors and the National Education Association. If they do their jobs, they will insist upon high-quality training for teachers, upon fearless and competent scholarship in the classroom, and upon freedom to seek the truth in research and in the publication of findings. They will defend those qualified teachers who come under attack.

The ultimate defenses of freedom in education, however, are the people themselves who will realize that education's main function is to free the minds of the younger generation and to equip them as free citizens and free persons.

The schools and colleges must therefore generate a spirit of intellectual, political, and personal freedom throughout the land. To do this, they must in turn have a genuine measure of self-government resting upon the competent scholarship of the teachers.

The most distinctive mark of a free society is that it specifically delegates to its educational institutions the task of constant study and criticism of the free society itself. No other kind of society dares to permit such a thing. No other kind of society prevents its government from endangering the liberties of the people and at the same time entrusts the government with the obligation to guarantee the rights of the people against attack by powerful groups or individuals in the community.

Just as a free government guarantees the freedom of the press, of association, of religion, and of trial by jury, so must a free government guarantee the freedom of teaching and learning.

A free society knows that its surest foundation rests upon the liberal education of the people—a liberal education available freely and equally to all, beginning with the earliest stages of the elementary school, extending to the highest reaches of the university, and limited only by considerations of talent.

As the fourth century of American history reaches its mid-point and as the second century of the American Republic draws to a close, the search for freedom in American education has just well begun. That is why the story of American education must continue to be, in the future even more than in the past, the unflagging search for freedom.

ROBERT MIDDLEKAUFF | **Education in Colonial America**

When an American colonist discussed a "public school," he was not talking about the institution familiar to us since the nineteenth century; usually he simply meant a school open to anyone who wished to attend. The chances were that the school was privately owned and financed. The designation "public" was given to distinguish it from a school catering exclusively to a special group—usually a religious sect.

Indeed, the modern idea of "public education," implying a state-owned system of schools, supported by taxation, and administered by officials chosen by the community, which compels attendance of all children within a certain age group and which carefully separates itself from the educational efforts of private groups, did not exist in the colonial period. To be sure, the state sometimes participated in organizing and financing schools, but its role (outside of New England) was small. Instead, several other agencies assumed the burdens of education; chief among them were the family, apprenticeship, and private schools of various sorts.

Of these institutions early in the colonial period, the family carried the greatest burden. In the primitive conditions of settlement, other agencies did not exist. Parents had to give their children education—if any was to be given. Frequently, of course, children went untutored or picked up rudimentary vocational training while they were working.[1]

The family continued to be an important center of training even after colonial society developed. For colonial parents, like their English forefathers, frequently placed their children with other families for rearing and training. They had good reasons for doing so: some did not trust

[1] Bernard Bailyn, *Education in the Forming of American Society* (Chapel Hill: University of North Carolina Press, 1960), pp. 15–16.

From *Current History* (July 1961), pp. 5–8, 14. Reprinted by permission.

themselves to discipline their own children vigorously enough; others, wishing to see their children acquire certain skills, apprenticed them to masters capable of providing the appropriate knowledge.[2]

Throughout most of the colonial period, indentures, as the apprentice agreements were called, usually enjoined the master to see that his charge was taught the essentials of the Christian religion and to read and write. Apprenticeship, of course, was never simply an educational instrument. A master taking on a young boy or girl expected his charge to work as well as to learn. The indenture always provided that the apprentice would obey and serve his master for a specified time, usually seven years or until the apprentice reached twenty-one. The instruction a boy received was always in return for this service. Sometimes apprenticeship proved to be only an agency of work, as masters refused to teach their boys. In such cases, the apprentice's only protection was his parents—or the local courts.

Schools in the first years of settlement were scarce in all the colonies. Scattered settlement and scant resources discouraged attempts to maintain schools continuously. Thus in the first years education in schools was largely a temporary, even sporadic affair.

Education in the South

If education in the first years of settlement was much alike in all the colonies, it took on regional characteristics as colonial society matured. In the southern colonies—Virginia, the Carolinas, Maryland and later Georgia—where population always remained scattered on farms and plantations, geography prevented a neat structure of schools. Yet children were educated. A wealthy planter sent his sons to England to sit in one of the great grammar schools, or brought a tutor to the plantations, where he lived with the family. Smaller planters and farmers, especially in Virginia, sometimes combined their resources to build a "field school"—a building in a tobacco field, hence the name—and to hire a teacher to instruct the children living nearby. Boarding schools usually established by an ambitious college graduate or itinerant schoolmaster appeared late in the colonial period and were usually found only in the larger villages like Williamsburg or Charles Town.[3]

Tutors, field schools, boarding schools, were all maintained without any reference to public authorities. This was not true of most of the endowed schools of the southern colonies. Founded through the generosity of private donors, these schools were usually managed by county

[2] E. S. Morgan, *The Puritan Family* (Boston: 1956), pp. 37–38; and *Virginians At Home* (Williamsburg–New York: Holt, Rinehart and Winston, 1952), p. 23.
[3] Morgan, *op. cit.*, pp. 8–32.

or parish officials—or a combination of both. Such officers found a place for the school's meeting, hired its master, and supervised its operation.

The most renowned of these institutions were the Symmes and Eaton schools. Both were founded around the middle of the seventeenth century from bequests of Virginians. Both were controlled by a board of trustees composed from county and parish officers. Symmes school secured incorporation in 1753; Eaton in 1759. During at least a part of its history each offered instruction in the classical languages as well as in reading, writing and arithmetic.[4]

Altogether nine such schools in Virginia survived at least a part of the colonial period. All in all, they were not of great importance for they took root in only seven parishes; eighty-three parishes had none.[5] In the colonial South only the grammar school at the College of William and Mary consistently received public funds.

The Middle Colonies

The southern colonies were not unique; contributions from public treasuries in the middle colonies—New York, Pennsylvania, Delaware, New Jersey—rarely were given. Even Philadelphia and New York, large cities in the eighteenth century by English standards, did not direct municipal revenues into education.

An energetic and self-conscious denominationalism supplied Philadelphia with schools. First on the scene, the Society of Friends established elementary schools and a single grammar school shortly after Pennsylvania was settled. William Penn gave his encouragement by bestowing a charter on the grammar school in 1701. The Friends apparently needed no official endorsement, and throughout the colonial period they gave the schools vigorous support through private subscriptions and legacies.[6]

Other religious groups as eager as the Friends to preserve their identity and to perpetuate themselves maintained schools in Philadelphia. An Anglican parish school was begun in 1698, and the Society for the Propagation of the Gospel supported a charity school for poor children for most of the period before the Revolution. The Lutheran church opened a classical school around the middle of the eighteenth century, and the Baptists followed with the same type in 1755; the Moravians—never a rich group—began an elementary school in 1745.[7]

Besides these efforts—and probably equally important—were the nu-

[4] G. F. Wells, *Parish Education in Colonial Virginia* (New York, 1923), pp. 32–39.
[5] *Ibid.*, p. 48.
[6] Carl Bridenbaugh, *Cities in the Wilderness* (New York: Knopf, 1955), pp. 123–24, 283; and *Cities in Revolt* (New York: Knopf, 1955), p. 174.
[7] Bridenbaugh, *Cities in the Wilderness, op. cit.*, p. 284; *Cities in Revolt, op. cit.*, p. 174.

merous private school masters of Philadelphia. The average private master displayed a variety of skills to Philadelphians. If his newspaper advertisements accurately stated his qualifications, he could teach everything from arithmetic to astronomy—including Latin and Greek, rhetoric, oratory, logic, navigation, surveying, bookkeeping, higher mathematics and natural science. His offerings were necessarily broad; he had to attract students since their tuition provided his sole means of support.[8]

New York, the other city of the middle colonies, could not match Philadelphia's denominational offerings. Still, its religious groups were important agencies of education. Under the Dutch in the first half of the seventeenth century, the Reformed Church maintained a school. After the English took over the colony in 1664, the church, in an attempt to hold its children to the old ways and to the old language, opened several more. Though English culture eventually washed out the results, these attempts helped preserve Dutch homogeneity for years. As in Philadelphia the Society for the Propagation of the Gospel also proved active, sponsoring charity schools for children of the poor.[9]

New York could also boast numerous private schools in the eighteenth century with masters, judging from their claims in the newspapers, no less talented than those of Philadelphia. But on the whole, education was neglected in New York. Perhaps the most auspicious development of the pre-Revolutionary period was the opening of a grammar school by the newly-founded Kings College in 1762. The college and its school promised to renew interest in education beyond the elementary level.[10]

Small towns and villages in the middle colonies lagged badly in education. A few parish schools struggled along in several; private masters taught reading, writing and arithmetic and occasionally vocational subjects like surveying; apprenticeship supplied most of the skilled crafts. If a boy desired advanced training in the languages or higher mathematics, he had to travel to New York or Philadelphia. By the late colonial period apparently there were many boys who sought such instruction, for the city schools were filled with students from the country.

The New England Area

This brief treatment of the southern and middle colonies suggests, perhaps, that a variety of agencies—each for its own purposes—promoted education. In New England a number of the same forces appeared: the Society for the Propagation of the Gospel sent out masters instructed to bring the dissenters back to the true faith; Baptists, Quakers and other religious groups strove to maintain schools purveying learning and their

[8] Bridenbaugh, *Cities in the Wilderness,* pp. 447–48.
[9] *Ibid.,* pp. 123–26, 287.
[10] *Ibid.,* p. 287; *Cities in Revolt,* p. 174.

versions of Christianity; and in large towns and cities, private masters giving classical and vocational training flourished. Although this was in the familiar colonial pattern, New England, in education as in much else, departed from the familiar. The state made the difference by entering the field of education in Massachusetts, Connecticut, New Hampshire, and (before it merged with Massachusetts) in Plymouth.

New England was settled by Puritans who, unlike some of the radical sects they left behind in England, valued education. The Puritans came to the New World imbued with a sense of mission. They had left the Old World to complete the Protestant Reformation, to demonstrate that they held the true conception of church polity and religious doctrine. The success of their task depended in large measure, they were convinced, on an educated community. Hence they wished to erect a system of schools equal to the task.

They wasted no time getting started. Six years after the Great Migration of the faithful began in 1630, the Massachusetts General Court set Harvard College on its distinguished road. Erecting and financing schools proved a difficult task (as did financing the college for that matter) and after a period in which private contributions were relied upon, the General Court of Massachusetts decided to compel towns to assume the burden.

Towns of at least 50 families, it decreed in 1647, must maintain a reading and writing master, and those of at least 100 families, a grammar master—as one who taught Latin and Greek was often called. Responsibility for enforcement of the law was placed with the county courts which were empowered to fine offending communities.[11]

With the exception of Rhode Island, the other New England colonies followed the Massachusetts example, though requirements and enforcement varied from one to another.

The statutes compelled local authorities to provide education; they did not force parents to send their children. Nor did the laws require communities to support their schools from taxes; finance was left entirely to the community's discretion.

Under the laws a pattern of control and finance appeared among New England villages. In its meeting—the most important institution of local government—the town handled the school in about the same way it did any public business. This was a fact of enormous importance, for, so located, the school could not avoid the impact of local politics and of public financial pressures.

Though the town meeting formulated school policy, it depended upon a committee (chosen in the meeting) or the selectmen (the most impor-

[11] S. E. Morison, *The Intellectual Life of Colonial New England* (New York: New York University Press, 1956), pp. 65–78.

tant officials chosen by the meeting) to carry it out. School committees and selectmen were usually the best men available—men who had education and political experience.

Committee functions varied little from town to town. Usually the committee hired the schoolmasters, found a place for the school to meet if a regular building was lacking, and handled the finances of the school. In most towns how the committee went about hiring a master was its own business, though it did have to satisfy the meeting. In Massachusetts a statute added another requirement: the local minister with one of his brethren, or any two neighboring ministers together, were supposed to approve the schoolmaster before he was hired. Though evidence is lacking, towns seem to have observed this statute. Only rarely did cases of noncompliance get into the county courts.[12]

School Expenses

As local taxes on polls and property provided most of the money for ordinary expenses, so also they provided school expenses. Only in Connecticut could towns look to the provincial government for consistent financial help. Connecticut towns received an annual contribution out of provincial taxes, but few, if any, found this subsidy large enough to meet the expenses of their schools.

In every New England colony, there were towns which could rely on public lands for part of their school expenses. Donated by individuals, the colony, or set aside by the towns themselves, these lands could be rented or sold. Shrewdly invested, the income from such lands could often relieve the taxpayers of a large portion of school charges.

One other source of finance for schools existed— the parents of boys who attended. They could be assessed tuition for every child they sent to school and until the middle of the eighteenth century they occasionally were. In Watertown, Massachusetts, in 1700, for example, six pence a week was collected for each Latin scholar, four pence for a "writer," and three for a "reader."[13] Few towns required tuition payments but many insisted that parents provide firewood in the winter. Parents also purchased paper, pens and schoolbooks for their children.

Town growth intensified financial problems and created new difficulties. As its once compact population increased and spread out, a village saw its single school become inadequate. Far from the original settlement, children could not attend the once centrally located school. Nothing, of course, prevented a town from providing a second more accessible

[12] This paragraph is based on an examination of manuscript court and town records.

[13] *Watertown Records* (6 vols., Watertown, 1894–1906), II, 132.

school—nothing except money. To soften the clamor for education that arose from remote areas, many towns decided to uproot their schools and send them out on the road. The school might "go round with the Sun" as it did in Duxbury, Massachusetts, for many years, meeting successively in the four quarters of the town for three months at a time.[14]

Putting the school on the move had the obvious disadvantage of spreading learning very thin. A boy who had attended the school for nine or ten months out of a year when it was located in one place might only be able to attend the moving school the three of four months that it was near his house. If he was determined he might follow the school as it traveled from one spot to the next. But this was such a difficult and expensive process that probably few boys did it.

If many towns sent their schools into outlying sections, an equal number divided themselves into districts and established a school in each. Usually citizens in each district elected a committee charged with responsibility for hiring a master and providing a place for the school to meet. The authority of the district, and its committee, rarely included more important matters. Towns continued to hold taxing powers and understandably enough were reluctant to share them. Every town allocated annually a portion of its revenues to districts on the basis of their populations. Such divisions were often contested by jealous districts, but on the whole the system worked well.

The success of the system left Rhode Islanders unimpressed, and their legislature steadfastly refused to establish educational standards for its towns. The results for the colony's intellectual life were obvious: in the seventeenth century only one Rhode Island boy attended college. In the next century more traveled to Harvard and Yale but no college took shape in Rhode Island itself until just before the Revolution.[15]

Yet there were publicly-supported schools in Rhode Island, even a few which offered instruction in Latin and Greek. But most of these schools were in towns which had been transferred from Massachusetts to Rhode Island on the settlement of a boundary dispute in 1747. Thoroughly imbued with the educational tradition of Massachusetts, they probably never considered dropping their schools in removal from the Bay Colony's jurisdiction.

For the most part, Rhode Islanders relied upon private sources for the support of schools. Often this means failed them; and their schools compared to those of the neighboring colonies, enjoyed a precarious existence.

Rhode Island's educational history obviously parallels much of that of the southern and middle colonies, where no public commitment to edu-

[14] *Records of Duxbury, Mass.* (Plymouth, 1893), p. 320.
[15] Morison, *The Intellectual Life of Colonial New England,* p. 70.

cation existed and no private source of support was ever entirely reliable. In no colony did one group monopolize education. Rather, variety in support, in sponsors, in state participation, and in the forms institutions assumed characterized colonial education. Inevitably educational development followed an uneven course.

It did because it was an expression of a colonial society, which was altering at an uneven pace. Education itself, of course, was a force in this process of change. As it helped shape colonial society, so also was it shaped. What emerged by the end of the colonial period was a peculiar blend of public and private, classical and vocational, religious and secular. Modern "public education" had not yet been conceived.

RUSH WELTER | **The Common School: Three Views**

The first significant group of American writers to criticize republican theories of education as undemocratic and to condemn republican educational achievements as inadequate were the self-styled "working men" and "mechanics" of Pennsylvania, New York, and New England. These spokesmen for the lower middle and working classes elaborated a theory of democratic education that was to become the most characteristic social theory of the age. Their numbers were few and their direct political influence was slight, but they first spelled out the educational perspective in which several generations of American democrats would see their society and their politics.

The Doctrines of the Workingmen's Parties

The causes of the early workingmen's movement were both social and economic: skilled craftsmen and petty entrepreneurs sensed that the comfortable handicraft society in which they had grown up was threatened by such developments as factory production and industrial capitalism. "We are fast approaching those extremes of wealth and extravagance on the one hand, and ignorance, poverty, and wretchedness on the other," said the Philadelphia *Mechanics' Free Press* in 1830, "which will eventually terminate in those unnatural and oppressive distinctions which

From *Popular Education and Democratic Thought in America* (New York: Columbia University Press, 1962), pp. 45–50, 56–57, 97–101, 105–109. Reprinted by permission.

exist in the corrupt governments of the old world."[1] Acting on this premise they set out to destroy the engines of corporate wealth—banks, chartered monopolies of all kinds, an antiquated legal system—and to protect their own kind against the hazards of debt and bankruptcy. They were conservative republicans, in the sense that they thought of themselves as finding ways to perpetuate the social patterns of an agrarian democracy. But they were also radical democrats. They did not propose to stand idly by and be overwhelmed by what they identified as "aristocratic" economic and social innovations.

Inasmuch as most workingmen already possessed the suffrage, the characteristic vehicle of their early agitation was political parties formed for the purpose. Their willingness to go into politics attracted in turn a miscellaneous group of political adventurers, some of whom were neither workingmen by trade nor democrats by temperament. Yet the confusions that these adventurers introduced into the workingmen's parties should not blind us to the doctrines the parties voiced. Their great target was special privilege, which they thought that state legislatures could abolish simply by refusing to incorporate banks and turnpikes and other economic enterprises. But they also insisted that the same legislatures must establish public schools in order to secure the blessings of education to all who wanted it.

Their belief in public education was as much a product of antimonopoly sentiment as was their attempt to restrict legislative incorporation. In the fall of 1830, for example, the workingmen of New York City, assembled to nominate candidates for state office, declared that public education was their preeminent political measure, on the grounds that "unless this safeguard of liberty is secured, and by the enlightening of the mass, the axe of knowledge is laid at the root of aristocracy, there is effected, as it were, nothing. The best labours are lost, and the success of the present is ever hazarded in the future." Likewise, Boston workingmen formed a political organization in 1830 which proposed most of the egalitarian reforms that characterized the movement everywhere and which held: "5. That the establishment of a liberal system of education, attainable by all, should be among the first efforts of every lawgiver who desires the continuance of our national independence," and "6. That provision ought to be made by law for the more extensive diffusion of knowledge, particularly in the elements of those sciences which pertain to mechanical employments, and to the politics of our common country."[2]

[1] John Commons, *History of Labour in the United States,* Vol. I (New York: The Macmillan Company, 1951), p. 192.

[2] As quoted by Commons, *History of Labour, I,* 283, from the *Working Man's Advocate* for September 18, 1830; resolutions adopted at a meeting of "Working Men, Mechanics, and others friendly to their interests," Commons, ed., *Documentary History,* V, 188.

Nor would the workingmen be content with a mere extension of existing educational institutions. Indeed, their restlessness led them to repudiate as "aristocratic" the very educational innovations that had constituted the outstanding achievements of the republican era. Particularly in Pennsylvania, they mounted an exaggerated attack upon the granting of state funds to "colleges and universities . . . exclusively for the benefit of the wealthy." "Funds thus expended," a committee of Philadelphia working men argued, "may serve to engender an aristocracy of talent, and place knowledge, the chief element of power, in the hands of the privileged few; but can never secure the common prosperity of a nation nor confer intellectual as well as political equality on a people." Because they treated educational privilege as a source of political privilege, moreover, the workingmen demanded identical privileges for all. "The original element of despotism," the committee's statement continued, "is a monopoly of talent, which consigns the multitude to comparative ignorance, and secures the balance of knowledge on the side of the rich and the rulers. If then the healthy existence of a free government be, as the committee believe, rooted in the will of the American people, it follows as a necessary consequence . . . that this monopoly should be broken up, and that the means of equal knowledge (the only security for equal liberty) should be rendered, by legal provision, the common property of all classes." Workingmen's groups everywhere joined in the demand for equal treatment and the abrogation of a class-oriented education, and in New York as well as Philadelphia they were loud in their criticisms of the educational establishment introduced by the founding fathers.[3]

Thus antimonopoly sentiment and the fear of "aristocratic" innovations led workingmen to demand an effective system of public schools in place of the inadequate institutions of the previous generation. But we cannot understand their educational faith in its full significance if we treat it simply as a logical extension of their opposition to monopoly. The workingmen's belief in public education entered so largely into their diagnosis of contemporary evils that we must also trace the specific responsibilities they assigned to public education as a vehicle of democratic reform.

In the first place, they clearly believed that education would secure the political authority of the people, who might otherwise be led astray from their true objectives. One of the earliest manifestoes of the Philadelphia workingmen's movement articulates this assumption.

It is true [it observed in the spring of 1827] in this favored nation we enjoy the inestimable blessing of "universal suffrage," and constituting as we every-

[3] "Report of the Joint Committees of the City and County of Philadelphia," Commons, ed., *Documentary History,* V, 98, 98–99; Hugins, *Jacksonian Democracy and the Working Class,* pp. 132–34; and see "Address and Resolutions of the Conference Committee of the Wards," Commons, ed., *Documentary History,* V, 158.

where do, a very great majority, we *have the power* to choose our own legislators, but . . . this blessing . . . can be of no further benefit to us than as we possess sufficient *knowledge* to make a proper use of it. It will be an instrument of unlimited good to the great mass of the people when they shall possess that degree of intelligence which will enable them to direct it *for their own benefit;* but at present this very blessing is suffered, through our want of information, to be directed against our prosperity and welfare by individuals whose interest is at variance with ours.[4]

In these terms, public education had a twofold political purpose. On the one hand, it would bring about urgent social reforms by alerting the victims of inequality to the machinations of the aristocracy and the misrepresentations of the politicians. On the other hand, it would also protect established democratic principles against political and social evils that had not yet materialized. It seemed, that is, a political engine of extraordinary promise, which would serve both radical and conservative democratic purposes, immediately and in the distant future.[5]

Nevertheless, we must not infer that the workingmen contemplated a truly positive or constructive use for political education. In their eyes political knowledge was useful, not because it supported the exercise of governmental authority, but because it provided an intellectual resource against authority. Although the advocates of democratic education thought that it would inform the suffrage and instruct potential legislators, they hoped that in the long run it would cause state governments to cease tampering with the economy.

By contrast, the workingmen visualized education in its social and economic aspects as a major instrument of public policy. Nor was the role they assigned it in the society and the economy accidental. Skeptical of contemporary governments, and resolved to eliminate "aristocratic" influences from the economy, they proposed to employ education to destroy adventitious social distinctions and to ensure every man an equal opportunity for prosperity. They would educate to abolish class distinctions, to guarantee social and economic equality, to preserve an open society in which merit would find its appropriate reward.

For this reason the early "unions" strove to establish mechanics' institutes and reading rooms and libraries where aspiring young men might both broaden their intellectual horizons and improve their command of their crafts. Even more characteristically, they demanded common schools in which children of every social class might mingle as equals, and where

[4] As quoted by Commons, *History of Labour, I,* 186, from *Mechanics' Free Press,* June 21, 1828.

[5] See in particular the "Circular to the Working Men of the City and County of Philadelphia," as quoted by Commons, *History of Labour, I,* 227–28; "Address of the Working Men's Political Association of the Northern Liberties" (June 30, 1829), as quoted *ibid., I,* 192; and the discussion in *ibid., I,* 227–332 *passim.*

all might acquire the elements of education that would be indispensable to them in later life. From our point of view, elementary schooling could never have been an adequate vehicle for the hopes of the workingmen; but from the point of view of the workingmen, who found themselves deprived of formal education, nothing short of universal common schooling could overcome contemporary evils and redeem contemporary society. Their theory of society led directly to public schools.[6]

In the social and economic realm, therefore, the single compelling reform the workingmen proposed was a reform in education itself, while in the realm of politics education was to be either the chief instrument of reform (the original weapon against aristocracy and despotism) or one of several crucial instruments. In either case, workingmen assumed with remarkable unanimity that once public education had been achieved it would eradicate obstacles to democracy and maintain equality and prosperity. Looking back we may see in their pressure for educational innovations a dawning recognition that in an industrial society talent will not rise without some assistance from the state, but we see too much. Rather, the thought of the early workingmen implied, educational innovation was to be a substitute for other kinds of legislation.

Here, indeed, was the fundamental proposition that gave point to the workingmen's demands for public schools: effective universal education depends upon legislation, but when it has been achieved it will make unnecessary other forms of legislative activity. So far as domestic policy was concerned, the workingmen were advocates of laissez-faire liberalism who proposed to support and extend liberty by means of popular education. Hence their attack on "monopoly" was both destructive and constructive. Attacking existing legislation, they repudiated the traditional authority of government to shape economic development through selective incorporation and other forms of public encouragement to private enterprise. But in attacking existing educational institutions they insisted upon a most generous public provision for the welfare of the democracy. They defined democratic public policy in terms of anarchy with a schoolmaster. . . .

Like the workingmen's agitation of the 1820s, the agitation of the 1830s ultimately focused in education. Moreover, it embraced democratic rather than republican concepts of the diffusion of knowledge: education must be formal, public, and equal—not an uncertain mixture of formal and informal institutions, public and private responsibilities, "aristocratic" and pauper training. The nature of the educational commitment workingmen and reformers expressed during both the 1820s and the 1830s takes on added significance if we apply to it the same analytical scheme

[6] See especially Commons, *History of Labour, I,* 169–332 *passim* and the works cited in note 2.

that we employed in evaluating colonial and republican commitments to popular education. Those commitments, we remember, were instrumental, hierarchical, authority-oriented, and limited in scope. By contrast, although the workingmen advocated public schools for clearly instrumental reasons, in other respects their educational doctrine constituted a stunning departure from republican precedent.

In the first place, the workingmen obviously repudiated a hierarchically oriented education. Not only did they denounce private schools and colleges for their "aristocratic" pretensions, but they also focused their constructive efforts on building up a genuinely democratic educational system. It is true that they made relatively little effort to extend this democracy to higher levels of education, but only because they were sure that elementary schooling would serve their political and social ends.

By the same token, their definition of the relationship between authority and education drastically modified the traditional sense of that relationship. On the one hand, their theory called for a popular education that would abridge—not enhance—the authority of established leaders of the society. They proposed both to eliminate encroachments on popular liberty and to protect the electorate against new political impositions. On the other hand, in educating that electorate against contemporary evils, they also proposed to make schools serve a new authority, that of the people. Whereas republican educational institutions had been intended to serve the *needs* of the people, democratic institutions were much more likely to respond to their *wants.* Common schools were only the first of many educational innovations that democratic authority would produce. . . .

The Professional Educational Reformer: Horace Mann

Clearly, religious agitation during the 1830s and 1840s helped to produce a theory of education that lent support to, even if it did not stem from, the democratic commitment to limiting the scope of government. One outgrowth of this agitation was Emerson's Transcendentalism, which broke completely with orthodox traditions in social theory and repudiated every influence that one man might attempt to exercise over another. Another outgrowth, however, was Horace Mann's work as an educational reformer. According to Emerson, writing in his journal in 1839, Mann was "full of the modern gloomy view of our democratical institutions, and hence the inference to the importance of schools."[7] But

[7] Ralph Waldo Emerson, entry for September 14, 1839, *Journals of Ralph Waldo Emerson* (Edward W. Emerson and Waldo E. Forbes, eds.) (Boston: Houghton Mifflin, 1909–1914), V, 250.

Emerson's criticism really missed the point: Mann was also the country's leading pedagogical reformer, and he became one of the country's leading social theorists. If his philosophy fell far short of Emerson's Transcendentalism, it nevertheless did much to make American education an agency of liberal democracy.

As a Unitarian, Mann was predisposed to visualize the education of children more hopefully than many of his contemporaries. Most of his *Ninth Report* (1845) as secretary of the Board of Education of Massachusetts was devoted to explaining methods of classroom instruction that would cultivate the native abilities and natural goodness of common school pupils, and his other writings consistently urged teachers and school committees to adopt liberal pedagogical methods in place of the tyrannical methods employed in the past. Although Mann demanded over and over again that the common schools inculcate morality, he treated moral education as a consequence of good teaching, and he blamed bad teaching for contemporary threats to the moral order of society. Furthermore, stressing the proposition that knowledge is power for good or evil according to the moral framework in which it is presented, Mann also insisted that the common schools practice self-government. "He who has been a serf until the day before he is twenty-one years of age," he wrote in 1845, "cannot be an independent citizen the day after; and it makes no difference whether he has been a serf in Austria or in America. As the fitting apprenticeship for despotism consists in being trained to despotism, so the fitting apprenticeship for self-government consists in being trained to self-government." In every way Mann represented educational reform as a pressing necessity of democratic government.[8]

Yet despite his theological and pedagogical liberalism Mann was far from being an uncritical advocate of democracy. It is clear in his writings that he regretted the materialism and the craving for personal success that marked the age, and equally clear that he conceived of popular education as a vehicle carrying not only morality but truth itself to those who might otherwise neglect them. Thus, he complained in his valedictory *Twelfth Report* (1848) that "education has never yet been brought to bear with one-hundredth part of its potential force upon the natures of children, and, through them, upon the character of men and of the race," and he insisted that a nondenominational Christianity must be inculcated in order to overcome the "moral oscillation" to which all human beings are susceptible. In most important respects he accepted the conservative fears and the conservative injunctions that spokesmen for orthodox Calvinism subscribed to.[9]

[8] Horace Mann, "Report for 1845," *Life and Works, IV,* 1–104, 37. Mann's social and educational philosophy are ably discussed in Merle Curti, *Social Ideas of American Educators* (Paterson, N.J.: Littlefield-Adams, 1960), Ch. 3.

[9] Mann, "Report for 1848," *Life and Works, op. cit.,* 287, 292.

Like many other advocates of educational reform, that is, Mann thought in terms that were socially conservative yet pedagogically liberal. When he examined the Prussian educational system in his *Seventh Report,* for example, he praised its efficiency in instructing the whole population, but he was also sensitive to its pedagogical innovations because they stimulated intelligence and the ability to think. Conservative though he was in discussing American institutions, moreover, Mann criticized the Prussian monarchy for depriving its subjects of an opportunity to exercise their intellectual and moral faculties in elections, legislation, the conduct of public affairs, or the practice of religious freedom. He also predicted that a well-educated people would ultimately demand the right of self-government, and he pleaded with the king to liberalize his government rather than precipitate a revolution.[10]

Mann's plea may well have been disingenuous, intended to confirm American institutions rather than to challenge Prussian practices. But it lent support to a striking statement of his educational theory. Mann went on to argue that the lower classes throughout the rest of Europe were poverty-ridden, burdened with militarism, deprived of genuine religious freedom, and brutalized and ignorant because "vested interests" prevented their education. By contrast, the United States was exempt from most European evils; but in its indifference to education and to educational reform it had failed to eliminate vice and pauperism and ignorance and the political evils that threatened American liberty. By this means Mann identified hostility to educational reform in America with hostility to education in Europe. More than this, he offered American conservatives the strongest possible reason for adopting liberal principles in education. He believed that all men have a natural right to education, which European nations ignored; but quite apart from natural rights his argument in the *Seventh Report* also suggested that when popular education has been initiated it cannot be stifled and must therefore be carried to its logical extreme. In Mann's analysis, democratic education demanded educational reform.[11]

Although Mann was wont to emphasize the conservative and preservative character of public schooling, moreover, in his final report he spelled out a theory of progress grounded upon the widest possible diffusion of education and popular liberty. Now he emphasized not the hazards to which even the United States might be subject but the opportunities "intellectual education" offered for encouraging universal prosperity and removing class distinctions. On the one hand, he differentiated American social theory from European doctrine: "According to the European the-

[10] Mann, "Report for 1843," *ibid., III,* 287–379, especially pp. 335–344, 365–369, 372–379.

[11] *Ibid., III,* 402–417.

ory, men are divided into classes,—some to toil and earn, others to seize and enjoy. According to the Massachusetts theory, all are to have an equal chance for earning, and equal security in the enjoyment of what they earn." On the other hand, he insisted that Massachusetts as well as Europe was threatened by industrial feudalism, and he urged that

> Now, surely nothing but universal education can counterwork this tendency to the domination of capital and the servility of labor. If one class possesses all the wealth and the education, while the residue of society is ignorant and poor, it matters not by what name the relation between them may be called: the latter, in fact and in truth, will be the servile dependents and subjects of the former. But, if education be equably diffused, it will draw property after it by the strongest of all attractions; for such a thing never did happen, and never can happen as that an intelligent and practical body of men should be permanently poor.[12]

In 1848, that is, he accepted virtually the same diagnosis of contemporary social evils that workingmen had first voiced, and he proposed virtually the same cure.

The one major point in democratic criticism of the existing social order that Mann refused to accept was the charge that some men are poor because other men are rich. Rather than seek to divide established wealth, he argued, men should recognize the extraordinary resources education offers for creating new wealth.[13] Here was a conservative argument that might justify maintaining every other detail of the status quo on the grounds of what education would bring in the future. But it was a conservative doctrine that reflected contemporary radical sentiments. Like most Democratic liberals, Mann anticipated an almost infinite human progress, guaranteed by free institutions and supported by public schools. If he was a conservative social theorist he was also an extreme advocate of liberty and education.

Mann was unusual among professional educational reformers in that his interest in the extension and improvement of public education led him increasingly to adopt liberal democratic sentiments where other reformers often remained explicitly and exclusively conservative in their social thought. Nevertheless, his career as an educational reformer, which converted him from an advocate of improved standards of instruction and school facilities to an avowed proponent of democracy, foreshadowed a development that affected educational reform throughout the country. Once the possibilities of educational reform had been recognized, in a society which prided itself on its free institutions, it could not help but serve democratic rather than conservative purposes. . . .

[12] Mann, "Report for 1848," *ibid., IV*, 245–267, 246, 250–251.
[13] *Ibid., IV*, 251–265.

Religious Intransigence

The gravest obstacle to the development of an effective common school system throughout the United States, therefore, was neither urban taxpayers' parsimony nor rural complacency but religious intransigence. During the 1830s and 1840s prominent spokesmen for most of the Protestant sects, and for the Catholic Church as well, insisted that sectarian religious training was indispensable to the maintenance of public morality. In 1845, for example, a committee of the Presbyterian Synod of New Jersey attacked public schooling on the grounds that "the race of irreligious and infidel youth, such as may be expected to issue from public schools, *deteriorating more and more,* with the revolving years will not be fit to sustain our free institutions." In their place it proposed to establish Presbyterian parochial schools, which the General Assembly of the church initiated in 1847. By the same token, during the late 1830s a group of religious conservatives led by Frederick Packard, secretary to the American Sunday School Union, accused Horace Mann and the Massachusetts Board of Education of conspiring to drive the Bible and religion itself out of the public schools. The fact that Mann and most of the board were Unitarians added zeal to the attack, but fundamentally the controversy arose because Mann wished to restore moral instruction to the schools wihout imposing the kind of teaching that would offend against individual conscience. He proposed to teach a nonsectarian Protestantism, which his opponents condemned both because it resembled Unitarianism and because it abandoned sectarian principles.[14]

Yet the most significant fact about the controversy in Massachusetts was the way in which it was resolved in favor of Mann. So long as devout men of various sects identified Mann's nondenominational morality with his Unitarianism, they could ally themselves against him despite their own religious differences. But as soon as spokesmen for religious training in the schools revealed themselves as in effect advocates of

[14] J. J. Janeway, *Report to the Synod of New Jersey on the Subject of Parochial Schools,* as quoted by Sherrill, *Presbyterian Parochial Schools,* p. 14, which see *passim;* Culver, *Horace Mann and Religion in the Schools,* Chs. 5–6.

The issue between Packard and Mann arose in the first place because Mann was authorized to recommend books for district school libraries. Technically, therefore, the controversy that ensued over sectarian teaching in the schools was irrelevant. The Massachusetts legislature had banned sectarian textbooks from the common schools long before the Board of Education came into being, and in any event Packard was a resident of Pennsylvania whose interest in Massachusetts stemmed from the fact that the American Sunday School Union wished to force its unsalable library upon an indifferent New England. But the very way in which a major controversy built up in spite of these circumstances indicates how important it was to the success of the common school awakening that the alignments and emotions it generated find some common ground.

established religion the alliance was doomed. Thus the Universalist journal that had pressed the attack against Mann in 1838 for proposing to teach religion in the schools lined up behind him in 1839 and denounced Packard on the same grounds. After two attempts to destroy the Board of Education had failed in the legislature, it was out of danger. What happened was dramatized in the shifting opinion of the Universalists. Men who had every reason to disagree bitterly in religion agreed to disagree in such a fashion as to preserve the common schools which sustained their common social order.[15]

Nevertheless, although Mann and the Board of Education survived the attack on their principles, and although what happened in Massachusetts was duplicated elsewhere in less dramatic form, the politics of religious dissidence were hardly sufficient to convert die-hard advocates of sectarian instruction into enthusiastic supporters of nondenominational public education. The chief vehicle of this conversion was probably the nativist crusade of 1830–1860, which attracted support from both political and religious conservatives.[16]

Two phenomena made Protestant bigotry especially significant in our educational history. One was the fact that when orthodox Protestants were confronted with a demand for public aid to Catholic schools, even the most dedicated sponsors of religious training usually opted for nondenominational common schools as a lesser evil. Significantly, when Governor Seward proposed to subsidize the Catholic schools of New York City, the state legislature responded by depriving the Protestant Public School Society of its subsidy and by barring state aid to religious education. Between 1844 and 1860, moreover, nine northern and midwestern states prohibited state aid by constitutional enactment: New Jersey, Wisconsin, Michigan, Ohio, Indiana, Massachusetts, Iowa, Minnesota, and Kansas. Protestants were obviously more eager to bar aid to Catholic schools than to make sure that public education was inoffensive to Catholics (during the 1850s the Maine supreme court and the Massachusetts legislature required reading of the King James Bible as a part of school exercises), but their very zeal to limit Catholicism taught them the virtues of undifferentiated Protestantism.[17]

Furthermore, the terms in which some of the most vigorous Protestant bigots mounted their attack on the Catholic Church also served to reinforce the prevailing American commitment to nonsectarian moral and intellectual instruction. In his famous *Plea for the West* (1835), for

[15] Raymond Culver, *Horace Mann and Religion in the Common Schools* (New Haven: Yale University Press, 1929), pp. 105–109.

[16] See especially Chs. 4–7 and 11 of Billington, *The Protestant Crusade,* which stresses the religious aspect of nativist hostility to immigrants.

[17] Lawrence, Cremin, *The American Common School: An Historic Conception* (New York: Columbia University Press, 1951), pp. 172–75; Beale, *History of Freedom of Teaching,* pp. 93–104.

example, the Reverend Lyman Beecher urged New England Protestants to interest themselves in western education on the ground that "the great experiment is now making, and from its extent and rapid filling up is making in the West, whether the perpetuity of our republican institutions can be reconciled with universal suffrage. Without the education of the head and heart of the nation, they cannot be; and the question to be decided is, can the nation, or the vast balance power of it be so imbued with intelligence and virtue, as to bring out, in laws and their administration, a perpetual self-preserving energy?" While this phase of his argument reflected little more than a traditional eastern exhortation to educate the West, the book as a whole described "the conflict which is to decide the destiny of the West" in terms of "a conflict of institutions for the education of her sons, for purposes of superstition, or evangelical light; of despotism, or liberty." Although Beecher was soliciting aid for Lane Seminary and other sectarian academies, in its broader reaches his argument had the effect of placing common schools in the balance against Catholic parochial schools.[18]

Indeed, the only significant point of educational controversy between nativist agitators and the sponsors of nonsectarian instruction in the public schools was the extent to which the latter were willing to go in removing the King James Bible from the schools in order to make them acceptable to Roman Catholic pupils and their parents. In 1844 a convention of Ohio Presbyterians and Congregationalists declared bluntly that "the liberty to *worship* God according to the dictates of conscience, conceded to our citizens by the Constitution, cannot, by any principle of legitimate interpretation, be construed into a right to embarrass the municipal authorities of this Christian and Protestant nation in the ordering of their district schools." *The Sons of the Sires,* an anonymous prospectus of the nativist American party, adopted the same attitude in 1855: "Our revolutionary sires held that the Bible, the sabbath, and the common schools, were the strong bulwarks of our national freedom and prosperity. Whatever denominational distinction may exist, the nation cannot live and prosper without the Bible and the sabbath." Anti-Catholic sentiment remained powerful until the Civil War, and it helped to prevent the development of a common school system that Catholics as well as Protestants might attend, but in other respects it lent strength to the movement for universal popular education in nondenominational public schools.[19]

Conservative Protestants themselves recognized the change that had taken place in their thinking. Horace Bushnell expressed it in classic

[18] Beecher, *A Plea for the West,* pp. 42, 12.
[19] The convention declaration as quoted by Beale, *History of Freedom of Teaching, op. cit.,* p. 101; [Anspach], *The Sons of the Sires,* p. 50.

terms in 1853: "We can not have Puritan common schools—these are gone already—we can not have Protestant common schools, or those which are distinctly so; but we can have common schools, and these we must agree to have and maintain, till the last or latest day of our liberties. These are American, as our liberties themselves are American, and whoever requires of us, whether directly or by implication, to give them up, requires what is more than our bond promises, and what is, in fact, a real affront to our name and birthright as a people."[20] For reasons that must always be an embarrassment to Americans who truly respect religious idiosyncrasy, orthodox Protestants ultimately adopted the nonsectarian public school as the fundamental guarantee of democratic liberties.

It is important in the history of American thought, moreover, that writers like Beecher and Bushnell, who were conservative in their social philosophy and who regretted the passing of the religious establishment of their youth, should have been led by religious bias to sanction nondenominational instruction at public expense. They were not like Channing, whose religious liberalism forced him to share contemporary democratic principles, nor even like Wayland, whose economic dogmas had much the same effect, but unmistakable conservatives who turned voluntarily to the same educational institutions that contemporary democrats and educational innovators had originally sponsored. The educational awakening in the United States was never a device conservative die-hards invented so much as a liberal development they acquiesced in on substantially the terms in which it had been proposed. . . .

LAWRENCE A. CREMIN | ***The Revolution in American Secondary Education, 1893–1918***

The quarter-century between 1893 and 1918 was an extraordinarily creative one in American educational history. Within its confines are rooted many ideas and outlooks which have since become basic in pedagogical theory and practice. For no other reason than this, the period would be worthy of serious critical review. Sharpening educational controversies since World War II, however, have rendered such a review absolutely indispensable, for it is increasingly clear that several of the most hotly debated issues in recent educational discussion stem directly from decisions made during that momentous era.

[20] Bushnell, "Common Schools," p. 5.

From *Teachers College Record, 56:*295–308 (1955), Teachers College, Columbia University, N.Y. Reprinted by permission.

Nowhere is the case better illustrated than in the realm of secondary education, where all of the great contemporary battles seem to revolve around ideas which first gained currency during the years in question. At the beginning of the period stands the Report of the Committee of Ten,[1] a statement which summed up with impressive coherence the best of the generation which had preceded it. The end of the period is marked by the Report of the Commission on the Reorganization of Secondary Education,[2] a statement which literally ushered in a whole new age. In the contrast between the two lies a key to the pedagogical revolution which brought the modern American high school into existence.

The heart of this revolution was a shift in the conception of the school, of what could be and should be its primary goals and responsibilities. And it is this above all, perhaps, that makes this revolution important to the present. Americans today may well have entered upon another period in which just such a redefinition will take place. Given this, an understanding of this revolution and of the social and intellectual forces which occasioned it is essential, and it is to this end that the present initial study has been undertaken.

Committee of Ten Report

It was only natural that the National Educational Association in the early 1890's would turn its attention to the program of the secondary schools. Enrollments had already taken the upward turn that presaged a doubling of the high school population every ten years thereafter, and curricula, reflecting this trend, were rapidly expanding.[3] Discussions among the educators and laymen alike revealed conflicts of purpose and confusions of aim. One could quickly enough gain agreement that the goal of the high school was "preparation for life"; but, like agreements on "motherhood" and "sin," what this meant in practice was not entirely clear. True, growing numbers of high school students were not going on to college, but whether this meant adjustments in program was a moot issue. True, too, the colleges themselves differed so fundamentally in their conceptions of higher education that even the proper lines of college preparation were by no means clearly defined. By and large, each

[1] United States Bureau of Education, *Report of the Committee on Secondary School Studies Appointed at the Meeting of the National Educational Association, July 9, 1892* (Washington, D.C.: Government Printing Office, 1892). Hereafter cited as *Committee of Ten Report.*

[2] United States Bureau of Education, *Cardinal Principles of Secondary Education. A Report of the Commission on the Reorganization of Secondary Education Appointed by the National Education Association* (Washington, D.C.: Government Printing Office, 1918). Hereafter cited as *Cardinal Principles.*

[3] See John Elbert Stout, *The Development of High School Curricula in the North Central States from 1860 to 1918* (Chicago: University of Chicago Press, 1921), as an illustration.

high school devised its own approaches to program-making, and the ensuing diversity quickly came to pose one of the most serious educational problems of the nineties.

In an effort to attack the situation in fundamental terms, the NEA appointed a committee—one which from the vantage point of 1955 seems entirely appropriate to the character both of the association and of the secondary school as then conceived. It included five college presidents, a college professor, three secondary school principals, and the United States Commissioner of Education. The committee was charged with planning a series of national conferences, each devoted to one of the principal subjects of the secondary school curriculum. Representatives of both secondary and higher education would participate in the deliberation and report to the Committee, who would then take any action deemed appropriate. The several conferences were held in the winter of 1892–93, and the Committee's final action came in the form of a report tendered a year later.

The report itself is a model of clarity and, in spite of criticism to the contrary in the years since its publication, entirely self-consistent. While the total document deserves careful analysis, its conception of the secondary school is here all-important. The secondary school is viewed as an institution designed to prepare a small segment of American youth "for the duties of life" by improving their intellectual abilities. The Committee saw absolutely no conflict between this conception and that of the high school as a college-preparatory institution, for the task of improving intellectual abilities centered squarely in the studies of the college. True, the studies were made equivalent, thus reconciling the long debate over the respective merits of languages and the classics versus the natural and social sciences. And this was in and of itself an impressive step forward. But the Committee was interested primarily in improving intellectual ability by disciplining the mind; and for this purpose, all of the principal subjects might do. "They would all be taught consecutively and thoroughly, and would all be carried on in the same spirit; they would all be used for training the powers of observation, memory, expression, and reasoning; and they would all be good to that end, although differing among themselves in quality and substance."[4]

In sum, to teach a young person to think was to teach him to think, whether he strengthened his mind on the materials of languages, the humanities, or the sciences. And so to strengthen the mind was the best possible preparation for life. Close articulation between secondary school and college in pursuit of this goal was, in the Committee's mind, all to the good. Indeed, the Committee strongly believed such articulation "advantageous alike for the schools, the colleges, and the country."[5]

[4] *Committee of Ten Report,* p. 52.
[5] *Ibid.,* p. 53.

Although most graduates of secondary school were not destined for college, the secondary school was to remain, as it had been for centuries, a downward extension of the college. In the words of the day, it was to be truly the university of the people.

Some Changing Demands on the School, 1893–1918

The acceptance given the Committee of Ten Report was indeed overwhelming, and within a decade after its publication most American secondary schools had moved into line behind its proposals. Yet, in this very same period, political, economic, and social changes of the first magnitude were beginning to occasion new demands on the school—demands destined profoundly to alter the outlook of 1893. These changes were myriad, and only a few of them can be discussed here. They provide important leads in understanding the enormous pedagogical shift which occurred.

Industrialism

The Civil War had been at heart a struggle between alternative ways of life: the decentralized agricultural way of the South and the centralized industrial way of the North. Not only the victory of the North, but the character of the War itself, had contributed significantly to what Louis Hacker has called the triumph of industrial capitalism. By 1890, the die of an industrial nation had been cast, for the value added to products by manufacturing already exceeded the value of agricultural products. Thirty years later, not only had the number of persons engaged in manufacturing surpassed the number in agriculture, but the gross value of American manufactures had already far outrun that of any other nation.

The changes wrought by this technological revolution influenced every dimension of American life. With the "closing" of the frontier in the 1890's, the youth of America were looking to industry and the city for opportunities which had formerly inhered in westward migration. Urbanization continued, and by 1920 well over half the population lived in the cities. Moreover, American life in general—and urban life in particular—began to display a growing complexity which demanded ever higher levels of social and economic skill. Working in a factory, negotiating public transportation, buying and selling on credit, understanding intricate political organization—all necessitated abilities on the part of the average citizen which had simply not been called for in earlier days.

Then, too, the very changes which were ushering in these new demands were simultaneously destroying the foundation of the informal social agencies which had formerly borne much of the educational load. The well-knit agrarian home, within which had been organized and concentrated the productive energies of the whole family, was giving way to the industrial home from which family members scattered daily, each to his respective place of employment. Similarly, the rural neighborhood, with its network of face-to-face and stable relationships, was giving way to urban neighborhoods characterized by impersonality and transcience.[6] All too often, within the newer milieu, the young were left to their own devices and soon became prey to the unwholesome influence of unsupervised peer groups. The streets were a powerful school, and their pedagogical fare of thrill and excitement was well-nigh irresistible.

It is little wonder that political, social, and educational leaders began to look to the public schools for constructive approaches to these problems. The public schools were the public's schools, and as such they were in theory institutions obliged to serve the public's needs. To the schools gradually fell a conglomeration of educational responsibilities formerly borne by family and neighborhood and traditionally deemed appropriate to them. As early as 1896, Nicholas Murray Butler argued that the public education of a great democratic people "has other aims to fulfill than the extension of scientific knowledge and the development of literary culture. It must prepare for intelligent citizenship."[7] And his conception of citizenship was of the broadest scope, embracing social as well as political responsibilities. Growing demands from industry and labor pressed for trade, commercial, and agricultural instruction in the schools. From charitable organizations like New York City's Industrial Education Association came efforts to obtain domestic and family training for the children of working-class parents. Slowly, but almost inevitably, these demands logically converged on a position destined to enjoy growing currency as the twentieth century wore on: that the boundaries of the school are the boundaries of life, and that no fundamental activity of life is therefore irrelevant to the classroom.[8] In their earnest desire to fill the widening educational breach caused by the transformation of home and neighborhood, the public schools assumed tasks of a prodigious order.

Immigration

These same decades which saw the growth of American industry also witnessed a gradual but unerring shift in the character of American immigration. Before 1880, most immigrants had come from northwestern Europe, particularly England, Ireland, Germany and Scandinavia. Except

[6] Dewey elaborated this theme with considerable insight in "The School and Social Progress," *The School and Society* (Chicago: University of Chicago Press, 1899). See also, Ellwood P. Cubberley, *Changing Conceptions of Education* (Boston: Houghton Mifflin, 1909).

[7] Nicholas Murray Butler, "Democracy and Education," National Educational Association, *Proceedings and Addresses,* 1896, p. 91.

[8] For an illustration of the way in which the idea evolved in practice, see Randolph S. Bourne, *The Gary Schools* (Boston: Houghton Mifflin, 1916).

for the Irish, they had generally pushed inland, settling the rich, fertile territories of the middle Atlantic, midwestern, and northwestern states. During the 1880's, however, the percentage of immigrants from southern and eastern Europe increased sharply, presaging the vast numbers from these areas who were to come between 1890 and 1920.

Apart from nationality, the "new" immigrants were substantially different from their predecessors. They tended to remain in eastern cities rather than move to western agricultural areas. Differing markedly among themselves in religion, language, and custom, they seemed far more than earlier comers to settle in self-contained urban neighborhoods which perpetuated the life of the old world. As one immigrant from Roumania reminisced about his arrival in New York: ". . . my problem was to fit myself in with the people of Vaslui and Roumania, my erstwhile fellow-townsmen and my fellow-countrymen. It was not America in the large sense, but the East Side Ghetto that upset all my calculations, reversed all my values, and set my head swimming."[9]

To the contemporary American reviewing the history of these immigrants it is striking to note, first, how quickly the public school became the primary link between the immigrant neighborhood and the wider American culture; and, second, the apparent unawareness on the part of most public-school authorities before 1914 of the magnitude of the immigrant education problem. Very often the public school in a heterogeneous urban neighborhood was the one place where the foreign-born might become conversant with American language, attitudes, beliefs, and customs. And yet, as late as 1910 many a school seeking to serve the immigrant made little special provision for him and persisted in having husky laborers repeat puerile nonsense from outdated children's readers.[10]

While widespread national consciousness of "Americanization" was really occasioned by World War I, there is evidence in the decade immediately preceding the War that educators and social workers alike were beginning really to confront the problem. By that time, the social settlement movement was in its second decade, and the heart of the settlement idea—namely, the effort to bring about social improvement through family and community education—was deemed increasingly suitable for the

[9] Marcus Ravage, *An American in the Making* (New York: Harper and Brothers, 1917), p. 61.

[10] The survey of the Cleveland public schools in 1916 found immigrant men twenty-five to thirty years of age busily copying, "I am a yellow bird. I can sing. I can fly. I can sing to you." See Herbert Adolphus Miller, *The School and the Immigrant* (Cleveland: The Cleveland Foundation, 1916), pp. 91 ff., and Frank V. Thompson, *Schooling of the Immigrant* (New York: Harper and Brothers, 1920). The problem was by no means confined to adult evening classes. By 1911, in the public schools of 37 large American cities, 57.5 per cent of the children were of foreign-born parentage. See *The Children of the Immigrants in the Schools*. Abstract of the Immigration Commission Report (Washington, D.C.: Government Printing Office, 1911).

school. This meant that the school would be ultimately concerned with the total lives of individuals, rather than restrictively or even primarily with things intellectual. Indeed, it meant that each school would eventually itself become a social settlement dedicated to the improvement of community life in all its manifold dimensions.[11]

While there was little agreement on the meaning of Americanization,[12] essays in educational journals and elsewhere revealed growing concern with school-community relations, with the necessity of inducting foreign-born adults and children alike into worthy and responsible community membership, and with the need for fostering a sense of community among heterogeneous immigrant groups. Once again, this could mean nothing less than the school's taking on educational functions classically assigned to home and neighborhood. Immigrant parents, unable by the very nature of their situation to inculcate in their children *American* values and habits, slowly—sometimes reluctantly—relinquished parental functions to the school in their effort to close no avenue of social advancement. And when the divided allegiances of World War I raised to the forefront the question of immigrant loyalty, the pressure on the school to Americanize with renewed vigor and effectiveness achieved nationwide proportions.[13]

Progressivism

Related to the economic and social transformations of the period were spirited demands for political reform. Most such efforts represented attempts to realize in the new industrial context Lincoln's great principle of government by, of, and for the people. The exploitation of resources and labor for personal gain, the increasingly unequal distribution of wealth, the untold personal misery occasioned by the new industrialism, the deplorable corruption in politics, all came in for sharp criticism by crusading humanitarians and for ever so gradual amelioration through reform legislation.

In social thought, this was the era of the muckrakers and their shocking exposés; and of Jane Addams and Lillian Wald, Jacob Riis and Judge Ben Lindsey. Politically, progressivism's banner was carried by William

[11] The data for these propositions are taken from a Ph.D. dissertation in progress at Teachers College, by Morris I. Berger, entitled "The Immigrant, the Social Settlement, and the Public School." See also Alan M. Thomas, Jr., "American Education and the Immigrant," *Teachers College Record,* Vol. 55, No. 5 (February 1954), pp. 253–267.

[12] See Isaac B. Berkson, *Theories of Americanization* (New York: Bureau of Publications Teachers College, Columbia University. Contributions to Education, No. 109, 1920).

[13] The pressure was a prime factor in the passage of a law in Oregon making attendance of children between the ages of eight and sixteen at a public school mandatory. The law was ruled unconstitutional in 1925 by the United States Supreme Court in *Pierce* v. *Society of Sisters,* 268 U.S. 510.

Jennings Bryan, Robert LaFollette, Theodore Roosevelt, and Woodrow Wilson. The "square deal" and the "new freedom" continued into the twentieth century the spirit of protest that had flowed from the Jacksonians through the Populists. In the context of big industrialism, humanitarianism remained an intensifying theme.

In educational thought, the new progressivism manifested itself in the cry that universal schooling was not enough, that a certain *kind* of schooling was foundational to democracy. As early as 1891, when he delivered his lectures on pedagogy at a teachers' retreat of the New York Chautauqua, Francis W. Parker treated at length the problem of "democracy and education," arguing that every school should be an "embryonic democracy" wherein children's rights would be protected, children's freedoms preserved, and children's natural gifts built upon. In the distinctively American idea of a common public school embracing the children of all classes, nationalities, and sects, Parker saw the essential foundation of a democratic education.[14]

While a growing number of educators gave attention to such themes, especially after the turn of the century, no one gave the problem more searching or more penetrating treatment than John Dewey. In a number of shorter writings, but particularly in *Democracy and Education* (1916), Dewey carefully analyzed the fundamental conditions of democracy and then sought educational arrangements which would nurture and support these conditions. "Since education is a social process," he argued, "and there are many kinds of societies, a criterion for educational criticism and construction implies a *particular* social ideal." Based on this, Dewey continued:

> A society which makes provision for participation in its good of all its members on equal terms and which secures flexible readjustment of all its institutions through interaction of the different forms of associated life is in so far democratic. Such a society must have a type of education which gives individuals a personal interest in social relationships and control, and the habits of mind which secure social changes without introducing disorder.[15]

Given these initial propositions, Dewey proceeded to explore what educational aims, what conceptions of interest, thinking, knowledge, and vocation, and what organization of studies could best contribute to the support and advancement of democracy. His work was a classic insofar as it cast the problem in fundamental terms and provided an internally consistent set of conceptual tools for dealing with it. And inasmuch as the

[14] Francis W. Parker, *Talks on Pedagogics* (New York: Kellogg, 1894), Ch. 16.
[15] John Dewey, *Democracy and Education* (New York: The Macmillan Company, 1916), p. 115.

problem was itself inherent in the century-old effort to build a public school that would undergird American values and institutions, the influence of Dewey's position was inestimable.

Some Changing Conceptions of the School, 1893–1918

An expanding industrialism, a changing immigration, and a vigorous democracy exerted fundamental new demands on American schools between 1893 and 1918. Equally important in the evolving pedagogy of the era, however, were changes in the conception of the school itself—of its relationship to society and to the individuals who attended it. Once again, only a few among many possible themes can here be discussed in the effort to understand the emergence of a fundamentally new educational outlook.

Dynamic sociology

Forty-five years after Comte first coined the term, "sociology," and thereby set the new social science on the course of its phenomenal development, Lester Frank Ward published the volume that marked the beginning of American sociology. Ward's book, entitled *Dynamic Sociology*, provided systematic "scientific" treatment of a theme which had been central in American thought since the founding of the Republic: namely, that man, through his rational powers, could master the laws of nature and thereby achieve for himself a life of goodness and plenty on this earth. Ralph Gabriel has called Ward "the St. Augustine of the American cult of science." More than any other individual, Gabriel argues, "Ward formulated the basic pattern of the American concept of the planned society."[16]

Ward's thesis was an engaging one. Nature, he maintained, was essentially wasteful. Man, possessed of the power to comprehend nature's laws, could eliminate this waste, and could thereby seek to create a new order consequent upon worthy human purposes.

> The office of mind is to direct society into unobstructed channels, to enable these social forces to continue in free play, to prevent them from being neutralized by collision with obstacles in their path. In a word, mind has for its function in civilization to preserve the dynamic and prevent the statical condition of the social forces. . . . Just as it is not psychological force which propels the water wheel on the piston . . . but merely the forces of gravity and gaseous expansion compelled by mechanical power under the guidance of intelligence to operate for the benefit of man, so it is not mind which moves the civilization

[16] Ralph Henry Gabriel, *The Course of American Democratic Thought* (New York: Ronald Press, 1940), p. 204.

of the world, but only the great and never-ceasing forces of society, which but for the guidance of mind would rush blindly on into a thousand entanglements with rival forces, and assume that position of statical equilibrium which represents social stagnation.[17]

The thesis very obviously bestowed a tremendously important role on education. For Ward, education was the basis of all progress in the extent to which it equipped leaders to lead and equipped average men to understand and support their leadership. Therefore, to supply universal education was a primary function of any beneficent state administered in the interest of its citizens.[18]

While Ward himself never wrote extensively on education, his point of view profoundly influenced Albion Small, who in 1892 became head of the first American department of sociology at the University of Chicago. Small, who quickly became identified in professional circles as an educational sociologist, was unalterably committed to an orientation which saw the school not only as closely related to community life but also as capable of substantially modifying the course of community life. Through the work of Small and of a growing number of his students who went out to fill top posts in American education, the ideas of dynamic sociology were firmly injected into pedagogical thought; and the conceptual basis was laid for a school which might exert profoundly important influence on the future of American society.

The natural child

If a conception of the school-society relationship is central in any pedagogical orientation, equally important is a conception of the child and his relation to pedagogical processes. The foundations of the view that gained prominence after 1890 dated all the way back to the seventeenth century Moravian clergyman, Johann Amos Comenius. Comenius had argued in *The Great Didactic* and other writings that certain natural laws govern the development of human beings, that these can be scientifically determined, and that knowledge of these laws is the only sound basis for pedagogical theory and practice. The child, observing thus the laws of nature, is good rather than evil, conceived in hope rather than in sin.

The long succession of writings through which similar ideas found their way into twentieth century thought is the content of any standard work in educational history. Suffice it here to say that through the works

[17] Lester F. Ward, *Dynamic Sociology* (New York: Appleton-Century, 1883), pp. 698–699.

[18] Some of Ward's educational ideas are in his *Glimpses of the Cosmos* (New York: G. P. Putnam's Sons, 1913–1918).

of Jean Jacques Rousseau and Johann Heinrich Pestalozzi they became generally familiar to nineteenth-century educational leaders. While Horace Mann and others had advanced them well before the Civil War,[19] it was largely through the work of Edward Sheldon and Francis W. Parker after 1870 that they really began to achieve prominence. By 1891, Parker could proclaim with optimistic gusto: "The spontaneous tendencies of the child are the records of unborn divinity; we are here, my fellow teachers . . . to understand these tendencies and continue them in all these directions, following nature";[20] and his words instilled a virtually messianic ardor in the teachers who heard them.

The man who provided such ideas with truly "scientific" underpinnings was G. Stanley Hall. Having studied experimental psychology in Germany, Hall established one of the first psychological laboratories in the United States at Johns Hopkins University in 1882. He soon began to concentrate his energies on the unexplored field of child development, and when he assumed the presidency of Clark University in 1889, that institution quickly became a leading center for research and writing in this area.

Hall's first major contribution to receive widespread notice was *The Contents of Children's Minds on Entering School* (1891),[21] a monograph with an implied plea for tailoring the program of the introductory grades more effectively to what children actually knew on entering them. In advancing his material, Hall was proposing something far more radical than the thesis that subject matter might be taught more efficiently if the results of child study were used. Rather, he was arguing that the content of the curriculum itself could be determined from the data of child development.

That this is so is evident from his essay, "The Ideal School as Based on Child Study," published ten years later in *The Forum*.[22] One can assume that it reached a highly literate and influential audience, both lay and professional. Here his key concept concerned the difference between the *scholiocentric* and the *pedocentric* school. The former, in Hall's view of the dominant ideal of Western education throughout its history, fitted the child to the school; the latter, in Hall's view the only defensible ideal for a republic, fitted the school to the child. "The guardians of the young," he argued, "should strive first of all to keep out of nature's way,

[19] Will S. Monroe, *History of the Pestalozzian Movement in the United States* (Syracuse, New York: Bardeen, 1907).

[20] Parker, *op. cit.*, pp. 23–24.

[21] G. Stanley Hall, "The Contents of Children's Minds on Entering School," *Pedagogical Seminary*, Vol. I (1891), pp. 139–173.

[22] G. Stanley Hall, "The Ideal School as Based on Child Study," *The Forum*, Vol. XXXII (1901–1902), pp. 24–39.

and to prevent harm, and should merit the proud title of defenders of the happiness and rights of children. They should feel profoundly that childhood, as it comes fresh from the hand of God, is not corrupt, but illustrates the survival of the most consummate thing in the world; they should be convinced that there is nothing else so worthy of love, reverence, and service as the body and soul of the growing child."[23] Thus did Hall build upon the *laissez-faire* pedagogy first advanced in *Emile*, the idea of a child-centered school whose curriculum would be principally determined by data on the nature, growth, and development of children.

Hall's position, particularly when later bolstered by his monumental *Adolescence*, paved the way for a fundamental shift in the meaning of equal opportunity at the secondary level. Formerly, when the content and purpose of the secondary school had been fairly well defined, equal opportunity meant the right of all who might profit from secondary education as so defined to enjoy its benefits. Now, the "given" of the equation was no longer the school with its content and purposes, but the children with their backgrounds and needs. Equal opportunity now meant simply the right of all who came to be offered something of value, and it was the school's obligation to offer it. The magnitude of this shift cannot be overestimated; it was truly Copernican in character. And tied as it was to the fortunes of the child-study movement, it gained vast popularity during the first decade of the twentieth century.[24]

Activist psychology

Another intellectual development of the first importance lay in the beginnings of educational psychology. Spearheaded at Chicago by John Dewey's early papers before the National Herbart Society and at Teachers College, Columbia, by Edward L. Thorndike's numerous research papers following upon *Animal Intelligence* (1898), the movement to found teaching on a new science of learning made rapid headway.

A number of fundamental ideas undergirded the new psychology. Those associated with Thorndike's connectionism conceived of an original nature in each individual which would be changed as selections were made from among possible responses and "stamped in" according to the laws of readiness, exercise, and effect. The psychology was *activist* insofar as it sought data in observable behavior rather than in some "stream of consciousness" posited by the experimenter and tapped by way of introspection. Its dynamic lay in the operation of rewards and punishments. ". . . practice without zeal," argued Thorndike in a now-classic state-

[23] *Ibid.*, pp. 24–25.

[24] Cubberley as early as 1909 was complaining about the "monopoly" of child study in the field of education. *Op. cit.*, pp. 54–55.

ment, "—with equal comfort at success and failure—does *not* make perfect, and the nervous system grows *away* from the modes in which it is *exercised with resulting discomfort.*"[25]

Insofar as connectionism also argued that the original natures of individual men and women are not exact duplicates, and that different individuals learn at different rates, it made the problem of individual differences a central one for padagogy.[26] Finally, insofar as connectionist psychology tended to be molecular rather than molar, it denied the possibility of transfer of training except in the case of "identical elements." It therefore refuted the theory of mental discipline. While Thorndike himself was not willing to move from complete generalism to complete specialism on the basis of his researches, some of his readers were; and as early as 1913, he criticized certain "careless thinkers" for rushing "from the belief in totally general training to the belief that training is totally specialized."[27]

While Dewey's functionalism was, like connectionism, an activist psychology, it made far more of the purposeful act as the basis of education. In the doctrine of interest lay the beginning of the modern movement to make motivation central in learning theory;[28] and while it was perhaps not until Woodworth published *Dynamic Psychology* (1918) that the idea of drive achieved genuine currency, the discussions of interest at the turn of the century were enormously influential. Indeed, in criticizing the Herbartian doctrine of interest as primarily the end point of education, Dewey probably paved the way for the psychology of motivation to a considerable degree.

That connectionism and functionalism could be synthesized into a single pedagogical outlook is well illustrated in the publication of William Heard Kilpatrick's article, *The Project Method,* in 1918.[29] Using the concept of wholehearted, purposeful activity as his unifying theme, Kilpatrick was able to embrace in the project idea major insights from both psychologies. His article achieved wide circulation, and in a short while "the project" had captured the attention of the profession. For many in the field who had read neither Thorndike nor Dewey, the article became a highly effective vehicle for translating the new Psychology into educational terms, and for developing its meaning in practice.

25 Edward L. Thorndike, *The Psychology of Learning* (New York: Bureau of Publications, Teachers College, Columbia University, 1913), p. 22.

26 See Edward L. Thorndike, *Mental Work and Fatigue and Individual Differences and Their Causes* (New York: Bureau of Publications, Teachers College, Columbia University, 1914), Part II, *passim.*

27 Thorndike, *The Psychology of Learning*, p. 365.

28 John Dewey, "Interest as Related to Will," in National Herbart Society, *Second Supplement to the Herbart Year Book for 1895* (Bloomington, Illinois: 1896), pp. 209–255.

29 William Heard Kilpatrick, *The Project Method* (New York: Bureau of Publications, Teachers College, Columbia University), 1918.

The New Pedagogy and the Cardinal Principles

"The great men of a great epoch," wrote Charles Summer in 1906, "are those who have understood new currents in the mores." A study of some of the outstanding writings in education—particularly secondary education—between 1893 and 1918 reveals a widespread and growing sensitivity to the forces described above.[30] Indeed, there seems ample evidence that by the time of World War I, awareness of the new currents and of their educational concomitants was fairly common among educational leaders. Such awareness was in evidence at the major graduate centers offering doctoral work in education; it was present too in the growing list of textbooks on secondary education which appeared as courses, and students in this area multiplied.[31] In sum, the ideas discussed above were both familiar and gaining in acceptance when the NEA in 1913 appointed another committee destined to produce another landmark in American pedagogy. This was the Commission on the Reorganization of Secondary Education.

The Commission was originally conceived as a central body to embrace, coordinate, and review the work of a number of previously organized groups already dealing with various facets of the secondary program. Among these were a dozen NEA committees appointed in 1912 and 1913, each one for the purpose of studying the reorganization of a single high school subject. Also included was the NEA's Committee on the Articulation of High School and College, whose recommendations in 1911 had initially occasioned the appointment of the above-mentioned groups. The chairmen of all of these committees, together with ten "members at large," were designated a "reviewing committee" of the Commission, and given the task of preparing a final report.

When the final appointments to this "reviewing committee" had been made, the contrast with the Committee of Ten was striking. While the 1893 group had been dominated by people from higher education, the new committee was far more representative of secondary school person-

30 Extensive evidence in support of this proposition may be gleaned from the addresses and proceedings of the NEA during these years, particularly the Department of Secondary Education. Publications of the United States Bureau of Education will serve a similar function.

31 Excellent examples are John Franklin Brown, *The American High School* (New York: The Macmillan Company, 1909); Charles De Garmo, *Principles of Secondary Education* (New York: The Macmillan Company, 1907); Alexander Inglis, *Principles of Secondary Education* (Boston: Houghton Mifflin, 1918); Paul Monroe (ed.), *Principles of Secondary Education* (New York: The Macmillan Company, 1914); and David Snedden, *Problems of Secondary Education* (Boston: Houghton Mifflin, 1917).

nel and college and university professors of education. Of the twenty-seven members on the final roster, ten were directly associated with the public schools, nine were from schools or departments of education, four were from higher education, three were from the United States Bureau of Education, and one was from the YMCA. One might naturally expect such a group to be far more concerned with the high school as an integral institution with its own distinctive aims than simply as a handmaiden of the college; and such was indeed the case.[32]

The Commission's report, entitled *Cardinal Principles of Secondary Education,* was five years in the making and, like the Committee of Ten Report before it, is worthy of careful and critical study. The conception of the secondary school therein clearly reflects the several new currents of educational thought which were increasingly gaining adherence. The purpose of democratic education is to "develop in each individual the knowledge, interests, ideals, habits, and powers whereby he will find his place and use that place to shape both himself and society toward ever nobler ends." To give this proposition meaning, it is necessary to analyze the life activities of the average individual in a democratic society. The results of such analysis yield seven primary educational objectives: health, command of fundamental processes, worthy home membership, vocation, citizenship, worthy use of leisure, and ethical character. These being deemed the central aims of education at all levels—elementary, secondary, and higher—the specific task of the secondary school is to seek to realize them in the lives of *all* children approximately twelve to eighteen years of age. How can the secondary school do this? By so reorganizing the offering in each of the subject areas and by so arranging the activities of the school that growth on the part of individual students in health, command of fundamental processes, and so forth will be facilitated.

The report is clear about a number of other things. It explicitly assumes that the vast social changes inherent in industrialism and the findings of the new psychology must be taken into account. It assumes, too, that marked changes in the secondary school population "can no longer be safely ignored." Granting the ethnic diversity of the American people, it argues that "the school is one agency that may be controlled definitely and consciously by our democracy for the purpose of unifying its people." Further, and of the greatest importance, the report maintains that secondary education should be for all, that it should be closely articulated with elementary schooling as part of a continuous educational

[32] The differences in orientation between the two groups are insightfully analyzed in a report of the Committee on the Teaching Profession of the American Academy of Arts and Sciences entitled "On the Conflict between the 'Liberal Arts' and the 'Schools of Education,'" *The ACLS Newsletter,* Vol. V, No. 2, pp. 17–38.

experience in the life of every child, that entry into the secondary school should be governed by age rather than by academic accomplishment, and that the colleges should modify their entrance requirements to enable graduates of such secondary schools freely to attend.

> . . . the secondary school should admit all pupils who would derive greater benefit from the secondary than from the elementary school. With the demand of democratic society for extended liberal and vocational education for an ever-increasing number of persons, the higher institutions of learning, taken as a whole, are under a similar obligation with reference to those whose needs are no longer met by the secondary school and are disposed to continue their education.[33]

Such is the report's radical departure from tradition; it clearly espouses the new conception of equal educational opportunity inherent in G. Stanley Hall's "pedocentric" school.

Finally, the report comes out squarely in favor of the comprehensive high school, embracing all curricula in one unified organization, as "the standard type of secondary school in the United States." A school so organized is seen as the only agency which can extend upward the essential meaning of the common public school: the idea of unity with diversity and diversity within unity. In offering the opportunity to specialize within the context of a single school, the comprehensive school becomes "the prototype of a democracy in which various groups must have a degree of self-consciousness as groups and yet be federated into a larger whole through the recognition of common interests and ideals."[34] Life in such a school, the report contends, "is a natural and valuable preparation for life in a democracy."

In the contrast of these ideas with those of the Committee of Ten most assuredly lies a pedagogical revolution. From an institution conceived for the few, the high school became an institution conceived for all. From an adjunct to the college, the high school became the pivotal point in the public school system, one which carried forward objectives yet unfinished by the elementary school and opened new vistas leading on to the college. And from an institution restrictively concerned with the intellectual, the high school became an agency with no less a goal than the progressive amelioration of every individual and social need. Such was the grand design of this Commission, one which, in weaving a multitude of new and pressing demands into an integral view of the school, was able to face squarely toward the future and thereby to usher in a whole new age in American secondary education.

[33] *Cardinal Principles*, p. 20.
[34] *Ibid.*, p. 26.

A Postscript

"The school," wrote Dewey in 1896, "is fundamentally an institution erected by society to do a certain specific work." Few generalizations are more patently supported by the study of American educational history. From the very earliest period in which the American people sensed their uniqueness, the principal theme of their educational history has been the search for a school which in its scope, program, organization, and administration might best support and advance their most cherished ideals.[35] This was true of the period in which the great state systems of public education were founded; and it has been equally true of the period since that time. The theme was undoubtedly the *leitmotif* of the years between 1893 and 1918.

Stated simply, the contribution of the Commission on the Reorganization of Secondary Education was to redefine the role of the secondary school. To the extent that in so doing the Commission was able to grasp certain new and highly significant social and intellectual forces in American life, its redefinition became a lever for needed change and reform. The effects of the *Cardinal Principles* have been legion. Indeed, it does not seem amiss to argue that most of the important and influential movements in the field since 1918 have simply been footnotes to the classic itself. While cogent criticisms over the years have called for refinements, further denotations and extensions of the *Cardinal Principles,*[36] the statement has for close to four decades provided the orientation and terminologies for the development of secondary education.

During the current period of educational reappraisal, these facts are of the highest import.[37] There seems every indication that the secondary school, as the pivotal point in the public school system, will be a focus for discussion by citizens and educators for some years to come. As in the period between 1893 and 1918, new social and intellectual currents are calling for new educational outlooks. The great immigrations are over. Industrialism is entering upon a new era of automation and atomic energy. The United States has assumed a leadership position in a world whose centers of power are rapidly shifting. Technology has made possible the creation of vast new educational media, and new social agencies have arisen to administer them. Researches in psychology are giving new

[35] See Educational Policies Commission, *Public Education and the Future of America* (Washington, D.C.: National Education Association, 1955).

[36] Of the wealth of material that has come forth, one of the most perceptive critiques is George S. Counts's *Secondary Education and Industrialism* (Cambridge, Mass.: Harvard University Press, 1929).

[37] For a discussion of the reappraisal, see Lawrence A. Cremin, "Public Education and the Future of America," *NEA Journal* (January 1955), pp. 9–10.

meaning to concepts like instinct, learning, personality, and transfer of training; while the rapid progress of anthropology has profoundly altered classical theories of human development. These and other sweeping changes may well call for a new view of secondary education as different from the *Cardinal Principles* as were the *Cardinal Principles* from the ideas of the Committee of Ten.

Such fundamental reappraisals are extraordinarily difficult and strenuous. They proceed unplanfully, and engender conflict, skepticism, and doubt. Early responses almost always include the call for conservatism and reaction, for the comfort of the habitual is ever engaging. And yet the promise of such reappraisal is the abiding faith of the democrat. Perhaps the best one can do is to take heart from successes of the past and hope that as the citizenry and the profession journey into uncharted pedagogical seas, a vision of the high school will emerge which both profits from the wisdom of prior generations and yet boldly reaches toward new goals. Such must be the hope of all who continue to believe in the "publicness" of American public education.

JANE ADDAMS | *The Immigrant in the Primary Schools*

The following paper is given with great diffidence. The writer has never been a teacher, nor even a close observer, in primary schools. She only had unusual opportunities for seeing the children of immigrants during and after the period of their short school life. She submits some of the observations and reflections which have come to her concerning the great mass of those children who never get beyond the primary grades, in the hope that they may prove suggestive to the educators present. The observations are confined to the children of the Italian colony lying directly east of Hull House, in the nineteenth ward of Chicago, although what is said concerning them might be applied, with certain modifications, to the children of Chicago's large Bohemian and Polish colonies.

For the purpose of this paper it will be best to treat of the school as a social institution, within which a certain concentration of social interests takes place, for the purpose of producing certain social results. This is certainly legitimate, if we take Dr. Dewey's statement that "the school selects,

From "Foreign-Born Children in the Primary Grades," by Jane Addams in *Journal of Proceedings and Addresses, National Educational Association* (Chicago, 1897), pp. 104–112. Reprinted by permission of the National Education Association, Washington, D.C.

and presents in an organized manner, influences and instruments which may expedite and facilitate the socializing of the individual." Certainly, after the child leaves school his experiences consist of his participation in the social life in the various groups of which he is a member, or with which he comes in contact.

Whatever may be our ultimate conception of education, and however much we may differ in definition, as doubtless the members of this convention do widely differ, we shall probably agree that the ultimate aim is to modify the character and conduct of the individual, and to harmonize and adjust his activities; that even the primary school should aim to give the child's own experience a social value; and that this aim too often fails of success in the brief sojourn of the child of the foreign peasant in the public school.

The members of the nineteenth ward Italian colony are largely from south Italy, Calabrian and Sicilian peasants, or Neapolitans, from the workingmen's quarters of that city. They have come to America with a distinct aim of earning money, and finding more room for the energies of themselves and their children. In almost all cases they mean to go back again, simply because their imaginations cannot picture a continuous life away from the old surroundings. Their experiences in Italy have been that of simple, out-door activity, and the ideas they have have come directly to them from their struggle with nature, such a hand-to-hand struggle as takes place when each man gets his living largely through his own cultivation of the soil, with tools simply fashioned by his own hands. The women, as in all primitive life, have had more diversified activities than the men. They have cooked, spun, and knitted, in addition to their almost equal work in the fields. Very few of the peasant men or women can either read or write. They are devoted to their children, strong in their family feeling to remote relationships, and clannish in their community life.

The entire family has been upheaved, and is striving to adjust itself to its new surroundings. The men work for the most part on railroad extensions through the summer, under the direction of a *padrone*, who finds the work for them, regulates the amount of their wages, and supplies them with food. The first effect of immigration upon the women is that of idleness. They, of course, no longer work in the fields, nor milk the goats, nor pick up fagots. The mother of the family buys all the clothing not only already spun and woven, but made up into garments of a cut and fashion beyond her powers. It is, indeed, the most economical thing for her to do. Her house cleaning and cooking are of the simplest; the bread is usually baked outside of the house, and the macaroni bought prepared for boiling. All of those outdoor and domestic activities, which she would naturally have handed on to her daughters, have slipped away from her. The domestic arts are gone, with all their absorbing interests for the children, their educational value and incentive to activity. A household in a tenement receives almost no raw material. For the hundreds of children who have never seen wheat grow there are dozens who have never seen bread baked. The occasional washings and scrubbings are associated only with discomfort. The child of these families receives constantly many stimuli of most exciting sort from his city street life, but he has little or no opportunity to use his energies in domestic manufacture, or, indeed, constructively, in any direction. No activity is supplied to take the place of that which, in Italy, he would naturally have found in his own home, and no new union is made for him with wholesome life.

Italian parents count upon the fact that their children learn the English language and American customs before they themselves do, and act not only as interpreters of the language about them, but as buffers between them and Chicago, and this results in a certain, almost pathetic dependence of the family upon the child. When a member of the family, therefore, first goes to school, the event is fraught with much significance to all the others. The family has no social life in any structural form, and can supply none to the child. If he receives it in the school, and gives it to his family, the school would thus become the connector with the organized society about them.

It is the children aged six, eight, and ten who go to school, entering, of course, the primary grades. If a boy is twelve or thirteen on his arrival in America, his parents see in him a wage-earning factor, and the girl of the same age is already looking toward her marriage.

Let us take one of these boys, who has learned in his six or eight years to speak his native language, and to feel himself strongly identified with the fortunes of his family.

Whatever interest has come to the minds of his ancestors has come through the use of their hands in the open air; and open air and activity of body have been the inevitable accompaniments of all their experiences. Yet the first thing that the boy must do when he reaches school is to sit still, at least part of the time, and he must learn to listen to what is said to him, with all the perplexity of listening to a foreign tongue. He does not find this very stimulating, and is slow to respond to the more subtle incentives of the schoolroom. The peasant child is perfectly indifferent to showing off and making a good recitation. He leaves all that to his schoolfellows who are more sophisticated and who are equipped with better English. It is not the purpose of this paper to describe the child's life in school, which the audience knows so much better than the writer, but she ventures to assert that if the little Italian lad were supplied, then and there, with tangible and resistance-offering material upon which to exercise his muscle, he would go bravely to work, and he would probably be ready later to use the symbol of letters and numbers to record and describe what he had done; and might even be incited to the exertion of reading to find out what other people had done. Too often the teacher's conception of her duty is to transform him into an American of a somewhat snug and comfortable type, and she insists that the boy's powers must at once be developed in an abstract direction, quite ignoring the fact that his parents have had to do only with tangible things. She has little idea of the development of Italian life. Her outlook is national and not racial, and she fails, therefore, not only in knowledge of, but also in respect for, the child and his parents. She quite honestly estimates the child upon an American basis. The contempt for the experiences and languages of their parents which foreign children sometimes exhibit, and which is most damaging to their moral as well as intellectual life, is doubtless due in part to the overestimation which the school places upon speaking and reading in English. This cutting into his family loyalty takes away one of the most conspicuous and valuable traits of the Italian child.

His parents are not specially concerned in keeping him in school, and will not hold him there against his inclination, until his own interest shall do it for him. Their experience does not point to the good American tradition that it is the educated man who finally succeeds. The richest man on Ewing Street can neither read nor write—even Italian. His cunning and acquisitiveness, combined with the credulity and ignorance of his countrymen, have slowly brought about his large fortune.

The child himself may feel the stirring of a vague ambition to go on until he is as the other children are; but he is not popular with his schoolfellows, and he sadly feels the lack of dramatic interest. Even the pictures and objects presented to him, as well as the language, are strange.

If we admit that in education, it is necessary to begin with the experiences which the child already has, through his spontaneous and social activity, then the city street begins this education for him in a more natural way than does the school.

The south Italian peasant comes from a life of picking olives and oranges, and he easily sends his children out to pick up coal from railroad tracks or wood from buildings which have been burned down. Unfortunately, this process leads by easy transition to petty thieving. It is easy to go from the coal on the railroad track to the coal and wood which stand before the dealer's shop; from the potatoes which have rolled from a rumbling wagon to the vegetables displayed by the grocer. This is apt to be the record of the boy who responds constantly to the stimuli and temptations of the street, although in the beginning his search for bits of food and fuel was prompted by the best of motives. The outlets offered to such a boy by the public school have failed to attract him, and as a truant he accepts this ignoble use of his inherited faculty. For the dynamic force which the boy has within himself, the spirit of adventure and restless activity, many unfortunate outlets are constantly offered.

The school, of course, has to compete with a great deal from the outside in addition to the distractions of the neighborhood. Nothing is more fascinating than that mysterious "down town," whither the boy longs to go to sell papers and black boots; to attend theaters, and, if possible, to stay all night, on the pretense of waiting for the early edition of the great dailies. If a boy is once thoroughly caught in these excitements, nothing can save him from overstimulation, and consequent debility and worthlessness, but a vigorous application of a compulsory-education law, with a truant school; which, indeed, should have forestalled the possibility of his ever thus being caught.

It is a disgrace to us that we allow so many Italian boys thus to waste their health in premature, exciting activity; and their mentality in mere cunning, which later leaves them dissolute and worthless men, with no habits of regular work and a distaste for its dullness.

These boys are not of criminal descent, nor vagrant heritage. On the contrary, their parents have been temperate, laborious, and painstaking, living for many generations on one piece of ground.

Had these boys been made to feel their place in the school community; had they been caught by its fascinations of marching and singing together as a distinct corps; had they felt the charm of manipulating actual material, they might have been spared this erratic development. Mark Crawford, for many years the able superintendent of the Chicago House of Corrections, has said that in looking over the records of that institution he found that 21,000 boys under seventeen years of age who had been sent there under sentence less than eighty were schoolboys. . . .

Leaving the child who does not stay in school, let us now consider the child who does faithfully remain until he reaches the age of factory work, which is, fortunately, in the most advanced of our factory states, fourteen years. Has anything been done up to this time, has even a beginning been made, to give him a consciousness of his social value? Has the outcome of the processes to which he has been subjected adapted him to deal more effectively and in a more vital manner with his present life?

Industrial history in itself is an interesting thing, and the story of the long struggle of man in his attempts to bring natural forces under human control could be made most dramatic and graphic. The shops and factories all about him contain vivid and striking examples of the high development of the simple tools which his father still uses, and of the lessening expenditure of human energy. He is certainly cut off from nature, but he might be made to see nature as the background and material for the human activity which now surrounds him. Giotto portrayed the applied arts and industries in a series of such marvelous beauty and interest that every boy who passed the Shepherd's Tower longed to take his place in the industrial service of the citizens of Florence. We, on the contrary, have succeeded in keeping our factories, so far as the workers in them are concerned, totally detached from that life which means culture and growth.

No attempt is made to give a boy, who, we know, will certainly have to go into one of them, any insight into their historic significance, or to connect them in any intelligible way with the past and future. He has absolutely no consciousness of his social value, and his activities become inevitably perfectly mechanical. Most of the children who are thus put to work go on in their slavish life without seeing whither it tends, and with no reflections upon it. The brightest ones among them, however, gradually learn that they belong to a class which does the necessary work of life, and that there is another class which tends to absorb the product of that work.

May we not charge it to the public school that it has given to this child no knowledge of the social meaning of his work? Is it not possible that, if the proper estimate of education had been there; if all the children had been taught to use equally and to honor equally both their heads and hands; if they had been made even dimly to apprehend that for an individual to obtain the greatest control of himself for the performance of social service, and to realize within himself the value of the social service which he is performing, is to obtain the fullness of life—the hateful feeling of class distinction could never have grown up in any of them? It would then be of little moment to himself or to others whether the boy finally served the commonwealth in the factory or in the legislature.

But nothing in this larger view of life has reached our peasant's son. He finds himself in the drudgery of a factory, senselessly manipulating unrelated material, using his hands for unknown ends, and his head not at all. Owing to the fact that during his years in school he has used his head mostly, and his hands very little, nothing bewilders him so much as the suggestion that the school was intended as a preparation for his work in life. He would be equally amazed to find that his school was supposed to fill his mind with beautiful images and powers of thought, so that he might be able to do this dull mechanical work, and still live a real life outside of it. . . .

Foreign-born children have all the drudgery of learning to listen to, and read and write an alien tongue; and many never get beyond this first drudgery. I have interrogated dozens of these children who have left school from the third, fourth, and fifth grades, and I have met very few who ever read for pleasure. I have in mind an Italian boy whose arithmetic was connected with real life, while his reading was not. He is the son of a harnessmaker who, although he can neither read nor write, kept his little shop, and slowly made money. The great ambition of his life was that his son Angelo should be enough of a scholar to keep his books and to read him the daily papers; for he had a notion that the latter told you when and how to buy leather to the best advantage. Angelo was kept steadily at school until he was in the fifth grade. He used to come every evening to Hull House for help in his arithmetic, bringing with him slips of paper on which was written the amount of his father's sales during the day. His father himself could not add, but remembered accurately what he had charged for each thing he had disposed of. Before Angelo left school he read fairly well from the Fifth Reader. Five years have passed since then, and, although he keeps the accounts of the shop in which he had a vivid interest from the first, he has almost wholly forgotten how to read. He occasionally picks up a paper and attempts to read it to gratify his father, but he reads it badly and much dislikes the proceeding.

There is one fixed habit, however, which the boy carries away from school with him to the factory. Having the next grade continually before him as an object of attainment results in the feeling that his work is merely provisional, and that its sole use is to get him ready for other things. This tentative attitude takes the last bit of social stimulus out of his factory work, and he pursues it merely as a necessity. His last chance for a realization of social consciousness is gone.

From one point of view the school itself is an epitome of the competitive system, almost of the factory system. Certain standards are held up and worked for; and, even in the school, the child does little work with real joy and spontaneity. The pleasure which comes from creative effort, the thrill of production, is only occasional, and not the sustaining motive which keeps it going. The child in school often contracts the habit of expecting to do his work in certain hours, and to take his pleasure in certain other hours; quite in the same spirit as he later earns his money by ten hours of dull factory work, and spends it in three hours of lurid and unprofitable pleasure in the evening. Both in the school and the factory his work has been dull and growing duller, and his pleasure must constantly grow more stimulating. Only occasionally, in either place, has he had a glimpse of the real joy of doing a thing for its own sake. . . .

If the army of school children who enter the factories every year possessed thoroughly vitalized faculties, they might do much to lighten this incubus of dull factory work which presses so heavily upon so large a number of our fellow-citizens. Has our commercialism been so strong that our schools have become insensibly commercialized, rather than that our industrial life has felt the broadening and illuminating effect of the schools?

The boy in the primary grades has really been used as material to be prepared for the grammar grades. Unconsciously his training, so far as it has been vocational at all, has been in the direction of clerical work. Is it possible that the business men, whom we have so long courted and worshiped in America, have really been dictating the curriculum of our public schools, in spite of the conventions of educators and the suggestions of university professors? The businessman has, of course, not said to himself: "I will have the public school train office boys and clerks for me, so that I may have them cheap"; but he has thought, and sometimes said: "Teach the children to write legibly, and to figure accurately and quickly; to acquire habits of punctuality and order; to be prompt to obey, and not question why; and you will fit them to make their way in the world as I have made mine."

Has the workingman been silent as to what he desires for his children, and allowed the businessman to decide for him there as he has allowed the politician to manage his municipal affairs? Or has the workingman suffered from our universal optimism, and really believed that his children would never need to go into industrial life at all, but that his sons would all become bankers and merchants?

Certain it is that no sufficient study has been made of the child who enters into industrial life early, and remains there permanently, to give him some set-off to its monotony and dullness; some historic significance of the part he is taking in the life of the commonwealth; some conception of the dignity of labor, which is sometimes mentioned to him, but never demonstrated. We have a curious notion, in spite of all our realism, that it is not possible for the mass of mankind to have interests and experiences of themselves which are worth anything. We transmit to the children of working people our own skepticism regarding the possibility of finding any joy or profit in their work. We practically incite them to get out of it as soon as possible.

I am quite sure that no one can possibly mistake this paper as a plea for trade schools, or as a desire to fit the boy for any given industry. Such a specializing would indeed be stupid when our industrial methods are developing and changing, almost day by day. But it does contend that life, as seen from the standpoint of the handworker, should not be emptied of all social consciousness and value, and that the school could make the boy infinitely more flexible and alive than he is now to the materials and forces of nature which, in spite of all man's activities, are unchangeable.

We do not wish to hold the school responsible for what should be charged up to the industrial system, but we may certainly ask that our schools shall not feed and perpetuate the baser features and motives of that system.

The isolation of the school from life—its failure to make life of more interest, and show it in its larger aspects—the mere equipping of the children with the tools of reading and writing, without giving them an absorbing interest concerning which they wish to read and write, certainly tends to defeat the very purpose of education. . . .

LAWRENCE A. CREMIN | ***John Dewey and the Progressive-Education Movement, 1915–1952***

John Dewey had a story—it must have been a favorite of his—about "a man who was somewhat sensitive to the movements of things about him. He had a certain appreciation of what things were passing away and dying and of what things were being born and growing. And on the strength of that response he foretold some of the things that were going to happen in the future. When he was seventy years old the people gave him a birthday party and they gave him credit for bringing to pass the things he had foreseen might come to pass."[1] With characteristic modesty, Dewey told the story autobiographically, using it to describe his own place in the history of American life and thought. And granted the genuinely seminal character of his contribution, there was a measure of truth to his disclaimer.

Consider, for example, Dewey's relation to the early progressive-education movement; it provides an excellent case in point. We know that the movement arose during the 1890's as a many-sided protest against pedagogical narrowness and inequity. It was essentially pluralistic, often self-contradictory, and always related to broader currents of social and political progressivism. In the universities it appeared as part of a spirited revolt against formalism in philosophy, psychology, and the social sciences. In the cities it emerged as one facet of a larger program of social alleviation and municipal reform. Among farmers, it became the crux of a moderate, liberal alternative to radical agrarianism.

It was at the same time the "social education" demanded by urban settlement workers, the "schooling for country life" demanded by rural publicists, the vocational training demanded by businessmen's associations and labor unions alike, and the new techniques of instruction demanded by *avant garde* pedagogues. Like progressivism writ large, it compounded a fascinating congeries of seemingly disparate elements: the romanticism of G. Stanley Hall and the realism of Jacob Riis, the scientism of Joseph Mayer Rice and the reformism of Jane Addams. Its keynote was diversity, of protest, of protestor, of proposal, and of pro-

[1] *John Dewey: The Man and His Philosophy* (Cambridge, Massachusetts: Harvard University Press, 1930), p. 174.

Reprinted from *School Review,* Vol. 67, No. 2 (Summer 1959), pp. 160–171, by permission of The University of Chicago Press.

ponent; it was a diversity destined to leave its ineradicable mark on a half-century of educational reform.[2]

There were, needless to say, numerous attempts to portray this remarkable movement in its early decades; but nowhere is its extraordinary diversity more intelligently documented than in Dewey's volume *Schools of To-Morrow,* published in 1915 in collaboration with his daughter Evelyn.[3] Over the years, Dewey's continuing interest in pedagogical theory, his widely publicized work at the Laboratory School he and Mrs. Dewey had founded in 1896, his reputation as a tough-minded analyst of pedagogical schemes, and his unfailing support of progressive causes had combined to make him increasingly an acknowledged spokesman of the progressive-education movement. *Schools of To-Morrow* did much to secure this image of him in the public mind. Within ten years the book had gone through fourteen printings, unusual for any book, unheard-of for a book about education.

Written neither as a textbook nor as dogmatic exposition of "the new," the volume is designed "to show what actually happens when schools start out to put into practice, each in its own way, some of the theories that have been pointed to as the soundest and best ever since Plato" [3: "Preface"]. More than anything, the Dewey of *Schools of To-Morrow* is the man "sensitive to the movement of things about him." The reader is treated to a fascinating collection of glimpses—into Marietta Johnson's Organic School at Fairhope, Alabama, Junius Meriam's experimental school at the University of Missouri, the Francis Parker School in Chicago, Caroline Pratt's Play School in New York, the Kindergarten at Teachers College, Columbia University, and certain public schools of Gary, Chicago, and Indianapolis. In each instance, the guiding educational theory is given and the techniques by which the theory is put into practice are described. The approach is essentially journalistic; Dewey's enterprise is to elucidate rather than to praise or criticize.

Yet there is a very special kind of reporting here, one that bears closer examination. Richard Hofstadter has observed that the Progressive mind was typically a journalistic mind, and that its characteristic contribution was that of a socially responsible reporter-reformer.[4] Certainly this was Dewey's central contribution in *Schools of To-Morrow.* For in addition to the who, the what, the when, and the where, Dewey gives us a succession of social whys that quickly transform a seemingly un-

[2] See my essay "The Progressive Movement in American Education: A Reappraisal," *Harvard Educational Review,* XXVII (Fall 1957), 251–270.

[3] John Dewey and Evelyn Dewey, *Schools of To-Morrow* (New York: E. P. Dutton & Co., 1915).

[4] Richard Hofstadter, *The Age of Reform* (New York: Alfred A. Knopf, 1955), p. 185.

related agglomeration of pedagogical experiments into the several facets of a genuine social movement.

Merely as a record of what progressive education actually was and what it meant to Dewey *circa* 1915, the book is invaluable. The text abounds in vivid descriptions of the physical education, the nature studies, the manual work, the industrial training, and the innumerable "socialized activities" in the schools of tomorrow. There is exciting talk of more freedom for children, of greater attention to individual growth and development, of a new unity between education and life, of a more meaningful school curriculum, of a vast democratizing of culture and learning. Nowhere is the faith and optimism of the progressive-education movement more dramatically conveyed.

Moreover, as the analysis proceeds, Dewey's powers as a "socially responsible reporter-reformer" are soon apparent. He points enthusiastically to the concern with initiative, originality, and resourcefulness in the new pedagogy, deeming these qualities central to the life of a free society. He commends the breadth of the new school programs, their attention to health, citizenship, and vocation, arguing that such breadth is not only a necessary adaptation to industrialism but an effort to realize for the first time in history the democratic commitment to equal educational opportunity. He sees the new emphasis on "learning by doing" as a device par excellence to narrow the gap between school and life; and closeness to life is required "if the pupil is to understand the facts which the teacher wishes him to learn; if his knowledge is to be real, not verbal; if his education is to furnish standards of judgment and comparison" [3:294]. Even more important, perhaps, a school close to life sends into society men and women "intelligent in the pursuit of the activities in which they engage" [3:249]. People educated in this way are inevitably agents of constructive social change, and the schools which educate them are thereby intimately bound to the larger cause of reform [3:226–227]. Indeed, it is this very tie that makes progressive education progressive!

Actually, the dialectic between Dewey the observer and Dewey the reformer is probably the most intriguing thing about the volume.[5] On the one hand, we know that many of the pedagogical experiments he describes grew up quite independently of his own theorizing.[6] On the other hand, we recognize much in *Schools of To-Morrow* that exemplifies the very things he himself was urging in pamphlets going back at least

[5] Actually, Evelyn Dewey visited the several schools and wrote the descriptive chapters of the volume; but no pun is intended by the phrase—*Dewey the observer*. The larger design of the book—both descriptive and analytical—is obviously the elder Dewey's.

[6] One need only check some of the independent accounts, for example, Marietta Johnson, *Thirty Years with an Idea* (unpublished manuscript in the library of Teachers College, Columbia University, 1939), or Caroline Pratt, *I Learn from Children* (New York: Simon and Schuster, 1948).

twenty years.[7] The only way to handle the two Deweys, it seems, is to return to his own disclaimer, that he really was "the man sensitive to the movement of things about him" and to the thesis that his most seminal contribution was to develop a body of pedagogical theory which could encompass the terrific diversity of the progressive-education movement. It is no coincidence that *Democracy and Education* came a year later and wove the diverse strands of a quarter-century of educational protest and innovation into an integral theory.[8] The later work has since overshadowed *Schools of To-Morrow,* but the two ought not to be read apart. One is as much the classic of the early progressive-education movement as the other. Their genius was to express a pedagogical age. For their very existence, the movement was infused with larger meaning and hence could never be the same again.

World War I marks a great divide in the history of progressive education. Merely the founding of the Progressive Education Association in 1919 would have changed the movement significantly, since what had formerly been a rather loosely defined revolt against academic formalism now gained a vigorous organizational voice.[9] But there were deeper changes, in the image of progressivism itself, that were bound to influence the course and meaning of educational reform.

Malcolm Cowley, in his delightful reminiscence of the twenties, *Exile's Return,* describes these changes well. He notes insightfully that intellectual protest in prewar years had mingled two quite different sorts of revolt: bohemianism and radicalism. The one was essentially an individual revolt against puritan restraint; the other, primarily a social revolt against the evils of capitalism. World War I, he argues, brought a parting of the ways. People were suddenly forced to decide what kinds of rebels they were. If they were merely rebels against puritanism, they could exist safely in Mr. Wilson's world; if they were radicals, they had no place in it.[10]

[7] The ideas of *My Pedagogic Creed* (New York: E. L. Kellogg & Co., 1897), *The School and Society* (Chicago: University of Chicago Press, 1899), *The Child and the Curriculum* (Chicago: University of Chicago Press, 1902), and "The School as Social Center" (published in the National Education Association *Proceedings* for 1902) are particularly apparent. See Melvin C. Baker, *Foundations of John Dewey's Educational Theory* (New York: King's Crown Press, 1955) for an analysis of Dewey's pedagogical ideas prior to 1904.

[8] John Dewey, *Democracy and Education* (New York: Macmillan, 1916).

[9] The organization was founded by a young reformist educator named Stanwood Cobb, who had come under the influence of Marietta Johnson. Dewey refused a number of early invitations to associate himself with the group, but later served as its honorary president. The best account of the Association's first years is given in Robert Holmes Beck, "American Progressive Education, 1875–1930" (unpublished Ph.D. thesis, Yale University, 1942).

[10] Malcolm Cowley, *Exile's Return* (New York: W. W. Norton & Co., 1934), Ch. 2. Henry F. May contends that the shift toward what Cowley calls bohemianism actually began well before the War. See "The Rebellion of the Intellectuals, 1912–1917," *American Quarterly,* VIII (Summer 1956), 114–126.

Cowley's analysis provides a key to one of the important intellectual shifts of the twenties. With the end of the War, radicalism seemed no longer in fashion among the *avant garde,* particularly the artists and literati who flocked to the Greenwich Villages of New York, Chicago, and San Francisco. It did not die; it was merely eclipsed by a polyglot system of ideas which combined the doctrines of self-expression, liberty, and psychological adjustment into a confident, iconoclastic individualism that fought the constraints of Babbitry and the discipline of social reform as well. And just as prewar progressivism had given rise to a new educational outlook, one which cast the school as a lever of social change, so this postwar protest developed its own characteristic pedagogical argument: the notion that each individual has uniquely creative potentialities, and that a school in which children are encouraged freely to develop these potentialities is the best guarantee of a larger society truly devoted to human worth and excellence.

Now those who had read *Schools of To-Morrow* must certainly have recognized this essentially Rousseauan stance; it had been at the heart of several of the schools Dewey had described. Yet readers who had troubled to follow Dewey's argument to the end, and who had accepted his analysis incorporating Rousseau's insights into a larger social reformism, must have noted a curious difference of emphasis here.[11] For just as radicalism seemed eclipsed in the broader protests of the twenties, so it seemed to disappear from the progressive pedagogy of the decade.[12] For all intents and purposes, the *avant garde* pedagogues expanded one part of what progressive education had formerly meant into its total meaning.

Nowhere is this transformation more clearly documented than in the characteristic exegesis of progressive education during the twenties, *The Child-Centered School.*[13] Written by Harold Rugg and Ann Shumaker in 1928, the volume attempts for the movement in its time what *Schools of To-Morrow* had done a decade earlier. Its pages teem with pedagogical experiments illustrating the new articles of pedagogical faith: freedom, child interest, pupil initiative, creative self-expression, and personality development. And just as Dewey had seen a central connection with democracy as the crux of the earlier movement, so Rugg and Shumaker saw the relationship with the creative revolution of the twenties as the essential meaning of this one. To grasp the significance of the child-centered

[11] The incorporation is most clearly evident in Chapter 12 of *Schools of To-Morrow.* See also Dewey's comments on Rousseau in Chapter 7 and 9 of *Democracy and Education.*

[12] Radicalism even tended to disappear from the pedagogical formulations of many political radicals. See, for example, Agnes de Lima, *Our Enemy the Child* (New York: New Republic, 1925), Ch. 12.

[13] Harold Rugg and Ann Shumaker, *The Child-Centered School* (Yonkers-on-Hudson, New York: World Book Co., 1928).

schools, they urged, one had to comprehend the historic battle of the artist against the standardization, the superficiality, and the commercialism of industrial civilization. The key to the creative revolution of the twenties was the triumph of self-expression, in art and in education as well. Hence, in creative self-expression they found the quintessential meaning of the progressive-education movement.

Dewey, of course, was not unaware of the continuing ferment in pedagogical circles. His interest in education persisted, but as the decade progressed he became less and less the sensitive observer and interpreter of the progressive-education movement and increasingly its critic. As early as 1926, for example, he attacked the studied lack of adult guidance in the *avant garde* schools with a sharpness uncommon in his writing. "Such a method," he observed, "is really stupid. For it attempts the impossible, which is always stupid; and it misconceives the conditions of independent thinking" [14:37]. Freedom, he counselled, is not something given at birth; nor is it bred of planlessness. It is something to be achieved, to be systematically wrought out in co-operation with experienced teachers, knowledgeable in their own traditions. Baby, Dewey insisted, does not know best![14]

Two years later, the same year *The Child-Centered School* appeared, Dewey used the occasion of a major address before the Progressive Education Association to reiterate his point. "Progressive schools," he noted, "set store by individuality, and sometimes it seems to be thought that orderly organization of subject-matter is hostile to the needs of students in their individual character. But individuality is something developing and to be continuously attained, not something given all at once and ready-made" [15:201]. Far from being hostile to the principle of individuality, he continued, some systematic organization of activities and subject matter is the only means for actually achieving individuality; and teachers, by virtue of their richer and fuller experience, have not only the right but the high obligation to assist students in the enterprise.[15]

His strictures were not heeded, and in 1930 he leveled them even more vigorously in the concluding essay of a *New Republic* series evaluating a decade of progressive education.[16] The formalism and isolation of the conventional schoolroom had *literally* cried out for reform, he recalled. But the point of the progressive revolt had been not to rid the school of subject matter, but rather to build a new subject matter, as well or-

[14] His essay, originally published in the *Journal of the Barnes Foundation*, is reprinted in John Dewey *et al., Art and Education,* pp. 32–40.

[15] John Dewey, "Progressive Education and the Science of Education," *Progressive Education,* V (July-August-September 1928), 197–204.

[16] John Dewey, "How Much Freedom in New Schools?" *New Republic,* LXIII (July 9, 1930), 204–206. The decade to which the *New Republic* refers is, of course, 1919–1929. The implication, that progressive education really began with the founding of the Progressive Education Association, is oft-repeated but erroneous.

ganized as the old but having a more intimate relation to the experience of students. "The relative failure to accomplish this result indicates the one-sidedness of the idea of the 'child-centered' school" [16:205].

Then Dewey went on to a more pervasive criticism. Progressive schools, he conceded, had been most successful in furthering creativity in the arts. But this accomplishment, however much it contributed to private sensibilities, had hardly met either the social or the aesthetic needs of a democratic-industrial society. A truly progressive education, he concluded, "requires a searching study of society and its moving forces. That the traditional schools have almost wholly evaded consideration of the social potentialities of education is no reason why progressive schools should continue the evasion, even though it be sugared over with aesthetic refinements. The time ought to come when no one will be judged to be an educated man or woman who does not have insight into the basic forces of industrial and urban civilization. Only schools which take the lead in bringing about this kind of education can claim to be progressive in any socially significant sense" [16:206].

Dewey's comments seemed particularly *à propos* in the summer of 1930. Already the depression which was to envelop the nation and become the central fact of the thirties was very much in evidence. Breadlines were common in the industrial cities, and women could be seen raking through community refuse heaps as soon as garbage trucks departed. Suddenly radicalism was no longer passé; it was bohemianism that appeared a little out of date.[17] Socially conscious notions of progressive education, disparaged by the *avante garde* of the twenties as "social efficiency," were now very much to the point.[18]

It should be no surprise that Dewey's formulation of the meaning of progressivism in education came once again to the fore. Early in 1932 he accepted membership on a yearbook commission of the National Society of College Teachers of Education dedicated to producing a statement of philosophy of education appropriate to the times. The volume which emerged, *The Educational Frontier,* is, like *The Child-Centered School,* the characteristic progressivist statement of its decade. And while its formulations are essentially collaborative, Dewey's own views are clearly discernible in two chapters he wrote jointly with his student, John L. Childs.[19]

[17] Cowley's "Epilogue" in the 1951 reissue of *Exile's Return* is an interesting commentary on this point.

[18] The common cry was that Dewey had been too much the rationalist to develop an adequate theory of creativity. See, for example, *The Child-Centered School,* pp. 4, 324–325.

[19] William H. Kilpatrick (ed.), *The Educational Frontier* (New York: Appleton-Century, 1933). Dewey actually wrote Chapters 2 and 9, though as joint efforts with Childs. See also "The Crucial Role of Intelligence," *Social Frontier,* I (February 1935), 9–10.

The Dewey of these chapters is now the vigorous proponent. His plea is for an educational program conceived in the broadest terms, one which has "definite reference to the needs and issues which mark and divide our domestic, economic, and political life in the generation of which we are a part" [19:36]. As with his educational outlook from the beginning, his call is for a school close to life, one that will send into society people able to understand it, to live intelligently as part of it, and to change it to suit their visions of the better life. Once again, he sees changes through education as "correlative and interactive" with changes through politics. "No social modification, slight or revolutionary, can endure except as it enters into the action of a people through their desires and purposes. This introduction and perpetuation are effected by education" [19:318].

Dewey held essentially to this position throughout the stormy thirties. To George Counts's provocative question "Dare the school build a new social order?" Dewey replied that in an industrial society with its multiplicity of political and educative agencies, the school could never be the main determinant of political, intellectual, or moral change.[20] "Nevertheless," he continued, "while the school is not a sufficient condition, it is a necessary condition of *forming the understanding and the dispositions* that are required to maintain a genuinely changed social order."[21] It would be revolution enough, Dewey once told an NEA audience, were educators to begin to recognize the fact of social change and to act upon that recognition in the schools.[22]

Dewey steadfastly opposed indoctrination in the form of the inculcation of fixed social beliefs. But he did contend that for schools to be progressive, teachers would have to select the newer scientific, technological, and cultural forces producing changes in the old order, estimate their outcomes if given free play, and see what could be done to make the schools their ally.[23] To some, of course, this was as crass a form of indoctrination as any; and Dewey was criticized on the one hand by those who insisted that his notions would cast the school into an indefensible presentism at the expense of traditional values and verities, and

[20] See George S. Counts, *Dare the School Build a New Social Order?* (New York: John Day Company, 1932). The tension between bohemianism and radicalism within the progressive-education movement is dramatically portrayed by Counts in an address in 1932 to the Progressive Education Association, "Dare Progressive Education Be Progressive?" *Progressive Education,* IX (April 1932), 257–263.

[21] John Dewey, "Education and Social Change," *Social Frontier,* III (May 1937), 235–238. Italics mine. See also "Can Education Share in Social Reconstruction?" *Social Frontier,* I (October 1934), 11–12.

[22] John Dewey, "Education for a Changing Social Order," National Education Association *Proceedings,* 1934, pp. 744–752.

[23] John Dewey, "Education and Social Change," *op. cit.,* and "Education, Democracy, and Socialized Economy," *Social Frontier,* V (December 1938), 71–72. The latter article deals with an exchange between John L. Childs and Boyd H. Bode in the previous issue of *Social Frontier.*

on the other by those in the progressive camp who maintained that any social guidance by adults was really an unwarranted form of imposition.

Dewey replied to both groups in what was destined to be his most important pedagogical work of the thirties, *Experience and Education.* The volume is really a restatement of aspects of his educational outlook in the context of the criticisms, distortions, and misunderstandings which had grown up over two decades. There is little fundamentally new, except perhaps the tone. Progressive educators, he suggests, should begin to think "in terms of Education itself rather than in terms of some 'ism about education, even such an 'ism as 'progressivism.' For in spite of itself any movement that thinks and acts in terms of an 'ism becomes so involved in reaction against other 'isms that it is unwittingly controlled by them. For it then forms its principles by reaction against them instead of by a comprehensive constructive survey of actual needs, problems, and possibilities."[24] By 1938, Dewey the sensitive observer could already note, probably with a measure of sadness, that the movement was devoting too much of its energy to internecine ideological conflict and too little, perhaps, to the advancement of its own cause.

Frederic Lilge, in a perceptive essay he recently published in a volume honoring Robert Ulich, contends that Dewey's pedagogical progressivism embodies a fundamental inconsistency which Dewey never really resolves.[25] A theory which seems to harmonize the school with the larger social environment, Lilge argues, and which casts the school as a lever of reform, inevitably faces a twofold difficulty: first in determining which social goals to serve in the school; and second, in deciding whether or not to embark on an ever broader program of political reform outside the school. Thus, "Dewey was confronted by two equally repellent alternatives: pursuing his basic aim of adjusting the schools to the social environment, he could integrate them with institutions and practices whose underlying values he rejected; or he could attempt to withdraw them from being thus corrupted, but at the cost of sacrificing that closeness to actual life which it was one of the main aims of his educational philosophy to establish" [25:29]. Lilge contends that Dewey accepted neither, and that the thirties saw him and a number of influential followers increasingly thrust into a clearly political program of reform, both via the schools and outside them. Their manifesto was Counts's pamphlet, *Dare the School Build a New Social Order;* their statement of educational principles was *The Educational Frontier;* their intellectual organ was

[24] John Dewey, *Experience and Education* (New York: The Macmillan Company, 1938), pp. vi–vii.

[25] Frederic Lilge, "Politics and the Philosophy of Education," in *Liberal Traditions in Education,* George Z. F. Bereday (ed.) (Cambridge, Mass.: Graduate School of Education, Harvard University, 1958), pp. 27–49.

the *Social Frontier,* a journal which appeared regularly in the decade following 1934.

Now Lilge himself grants that his analysis is far more relevant to some of Dewey's disciples than to Dewey himself. Even so, some clarification is needed. For to pose the dilemma in the first place is to misread the relationship between progressive education and progressivism writ large, particularly as Dewey perceived it. Dewey had no illusions about the school changing society on its own; that educational and political reform would have to go hand in hand was the progressive view from the beginning.[26] Nor did the notion of adjusting the school to society imply that the school would have to accommodate itself to all institutions and practices. Dewey wanted schools to use the stuff of reality to educate men and women intelligent about reality. His notion of adjustment was an adjustment *of* conditions, not *to* them, a remaking of existing conditions, not a mere remaking of self and individual to fit into them.[27] And as for the corrupting influence of life itself, Dewey was no visionary; the problem for him was not to build *the perfect society* but *a better society.* To this he thought a school that educated for intelligence about reality could make a unique contribution.

Dewey restated these faiths in the introductory essay he wrote for Elsie Clapp's 1952 volume, *The Use of Resources in Education;* it is probably his last major statement on education.[28] Once again, he returns to the role of sensitive observer. "In the course of more than half a century of participation in the theory and practice of education," he writes, "I have witnessed many successes and many failures in what is popularly known as 'progressive education,' but is also known as 'the new education,' 'modern education,' and so on." He sees the triumph of the movement in the changed life-conditions of the American classroom, in a greater awareness of the needs of the growing human being, in the warmer personal relations between teachers and students. But as with all reform victories, he sees attendant dangers. No education is progressive, he warns, unless it is making progress. And he observes somewhat poignantly that in schools and colleges across the country, progressive education has been converted into a set of fixed rules and procedures "to be applied to educational problems externally, the way mustard plasters, for example, are applied." If this ossification continues, he fears progressive education will end up guilty of the very formalism it sought to correct, a formalism "fit for the foundations of a totalitarian society and,

[26] Dewey makes the point on page 226 of *Schools of To-Morrow* and in Article V of *My Pedagogic Creed.*

[27] This is a central point in view of contemporary attacks on Dewey. See *The Educational Frontier,* p. 312.

[28] Elsie Ripley Clapp, *The Use of Resources in Education* (New York: Harper & Row, 1952), pp. vii–xi.

for the same reason, fit to subvert, pervert and destroy the foundations of a democratic society."

"For the creation of democratic society," he concludes, "we need an educational system where the process of moral-intellectual development is in practice as well as in theory a cooperative transaction of inquiry engaged in by free, independent human beings who treat ideas and the heritage of the past as means and methods for the further enrichments of life, quantitatively and qualitatively, who use the good attained for the discovery and establishment of something better." Dewey's sentence is involved, complex, and overly long; but it embodies the essence of the movement as he saw it. Those who would understand progressive education would do well to ponder it, as would those who set out to build today's schools of tomorrow.

RICHARD HOFSTADTER | **Democracy and Anti-Intellectualism in America**

American education today is in the midst of a great crisis, the general outlines of which I believe we can all recognize. About the first part of this crisis, its financial aspect, I shall have nothing to say. A second part of it comes from outside education, in the shape of tremendous pressures to conform, for we live in a society in which the most dynamic force is provided by a small group of politicians who seek to base careers upon the policing of opinion. About the problems of freedom and conformity, I will speak briefly. The third part of this crisis, which concerns me most, is internal, it is less dramatic and perceptible than the others and it has been going on for a longer time. It stems from an inner failure of nerve, for it is nothing less than the growing loss of confidence among educators in the importance and value of the life of the mind, a capitulation within the educational world—indeed, in many quarters an eager capitulation—to the non-intellectual or anti-intellectual criteria that many forces in our society wish to impose upon education and which we might well consider it the bounden duty of educators to resist. It is about this that I wish primarily to speak: and I hope to suggest some relations between this species of educational failure and our popular democracy.

Since I am speaking about education and intellectualism, I want to make it entirely clear that I do not make the mistake of identifying higher education in general with intellectualism. Quite the contrary; I

From *The Michigan Alumnus Quarterly Review, LIX*, 21 (August 8, 1953), pp. 281–295. Reprinted by permission.

propose to emphasize the extent to which anti-intellectualism is rampant within the educational community. But it is also probably true that in America the greater part of the leadership of those who can be called intellectuals lives and works in academic communities. And if higher education can be said to be under fire today, it can be said with greater certainty that the distinctively intellectual part of the educational community is the part that stands to lose most.

The crisis in higher education is also a crisis in the history of the intelligentsia. Today, everywhere in America, intellectuals are on the defensive. They have been identified with the now-defeated inheritance of the New Deal and the Fair Deal. That this identification should have been made is ironical, because the New Deal itself, for all its Brain Trusters, had its own streak of anti-intellectualism. But it has also been unfair: the intellectuals are never given credit for the successes of the New Deal, but they have had to take the blame for everything that has been charged up to the Democratic administrations of the past twenty years—with so-called creeping socialism, with the war, with the alleged failure at Yalta, even with treason. In the Eisenhower-Stevenson presidential campaign a political leader who embodied the kind of traits that the intellectual would most like to see in our national leadership found the support of the intellectuals of slight value in overcoming the disadvantages of his party and his hour. During that campaign the nation also found the epithet for the intellectuals that it has so long wanted—"egg-heads."

Do not imagine, however, that the intellectual is going into permanent eclipse. He always has his day posthumously, for the very men who are most forward in proclaiming their dislike of living intellectuals are the most abject followers of the dead ones. They may not like contemporary intellectuals but they are often quite hypnotized by the intellectual leavings of Adam Smith or Herbert Spencer, or Edmund Burke, or Thomas Aquinas, or similar gods of the past. They have restored an old slogan of the frontiersman with a new meaning and a new object: "The only good intellectual is a dead intellectual."

What Is an Intellectual?

But what is an intellectual, really? This is a problem of definition that I found, when I came to it, far more elusive than I had anticipated. A great deal of what might be called the journeyman's work of our culture —the work of engineers, physicians, newspapermen, and indeed of most professors—does not strike me as distinctively intellectual, although it is certainly work based in an important sense on ideas. The distinction that we must recognize, then, is one originally made by Max Weber between living *for* ideas and living *off* ideas. The intellectual lives for ideas; the journeyman lives off them. The engineer or the physician—I don't mean here to be invidious—needs to have a pretty considerable capital stock in frozen ideas to do his work; but they serve for him a purely instrumental purpose: he lives off them, not for them. Of course he may also be, in his private role and his personal ways of thought, an intellectual but it is not necessary for him to be one in order to work at his profession. There is in fact no profession which demands that one be an intellectual. There do seem to be vocations, however, which almost demand that one be an anti-intellectual, in which those who live off ideas seem to have an implacable hatred for those who live for them. The marginal intellectual workers and the unfrocked intellectuals who work in journalism, advertising, and mass communication are the bitterest and most powerful among those who work at such vocations.

It will help, too, to make the further distinction between living for ideas and living for *an idea.* History is full of cases of great men with good minds, a capacity to deal with abstractions, and a desire to make systems of them—all qualities we associate with the intellectual. But when, as it has in many of them, this concern with ideas, no matter how dedicated and sincere, reduces in the end to the ingenious use of them for a central preconception, however grand, then I think we have very little intellectualism and a great deal of something else. A good historical illustration is that of Lenin, who, as his more theoretical works show, had in him a powerful element of intellectuality; but this intellectuality was rendered thin by his all-absorbing concern with certain very limiting political values. His book on philosophy, *Materialism and Empirio-Criticism,* a shrill work and an extremely depressing one to read, makes it altogether clear that the politician in him swallowed up the intellectual. I choose the illustration of Lenin because it helps me to make another point that seems unfortunately necessary because of the present tendency to identify intellectuals with subversives. That point is that the idea of a party line and political messianism is inherently inconsistent with intellectualism, and those few intellectuals who have in some way survived that tension are few, pitiable, and on the whole sterile.

The journeyman of ideas, and the janizary who makes a somewhat complicated but highly instrumental use of ideas, provide us with two illustrations of people who work with ideas but are not precisely intellectuals, as I understand the term. What, then, are the differences between the men who work with ideas but are *not* intellectuals and the men who work with ideas and *are* intellectuals?

Two things, that seem in fact to be mutually at odds, mark off the intellectual from the journeyman of ideas; one is playfulness, the other is piety.

Certainly the intellectual, if he is nothing else, is one who relishes *the play of the mind* for its own sake, for whom it is one of the major ends of life. The intellectual has a full quotient of what Veblen called "idle curiosity." His mind, instead of falling to rest when it has provided him with his girl and his automobile and his dinner, becomes even more active. Indeed if we had to define him in physiological terms, we might define him as the creature whose mind is *most* likely to be active after dinner.

I speak of playfulness too because of the peculiar nature of the relationship, in the intellectual's mind, between ideas and practicality. To the journeyman of ideas the be-all and end-all of ideas lies in their practical efficacy. Now the intellectual, by contrast, is not necessarily impractical; I can think of some intellectuals like Thomas Jefferson and Robert Owen and John Maynard Keynes who have been eminently practical, and I consider the notion that the intellectual is inherently impractical to be one of the most contemptible of the delusions with which the anti-intellectual quiets his envy—the intellectual is not impractical but primarily concerned with a quality of ideas that does not depend upon their practicality. He neither reveres nor disdains practical consequences; for him they are either marginal or irrelevant. And when he does talk about the practicality of the "relevance" of ideas, the kind of practicality that he is concerned with is itself somewhat different from the practicality of building a bridge, curing a disease, or making a profit—it is practical relevant to spiritual values themselves.

The best illustration of the intellectual's view of the purely practical that has recently come to my attention is the reaction of Clerk Maxwell, the great nineteenth-century mathematician and theoretical physicist, to the invention of the telephone. Maxwell was asked to give a lecture on the workings of this wonderful new instrument, which he began by saying how difficult it was to believe, when the word first came from America, that such a thing had actually been devised. But then, he said, "when at last this little instrument appeared, consisting, as it does, of parts, every one of which is familiar to us, and capable of being put together by an amateur, the disappointment arising from its humble appearance was only partially relieved on finding that it was really able to talk." Perhaps, then this regrettable appearance of simplicity might be redeemed by the presence somewhere of "recondite physical principles, the study of which might worthily occupy an hour's time of an academic audience." But no; Maxwell had not met a single person who could not understand the physical processes involved, and even the science reporters for the daily press had almost got it right! The thing was a disappointing bore; it was not recondite, it was not profound, it was not complex, it was not *intellectually* new.

To be sure, what this illustration suggests is not merely that the telephone disappointed Maxwell as a pure scientist and an intellectual, but that the strain of intellectuality in him was not as broadly developed as it might have been. The telephone might well excite not merely the commercial imagination but the historical imagination. But my point is, after all, not that Maxwell was a universal intellectual, but that he was displaying the attitude of the intellectual in his particular sphere of interest.

The second element in intellectualism is its religious strain, the note of piety. What I mean by this is simply that for the intellectual the whole world of moral values becomes attached to ideas and to the life dedicated to ideas. The life given over to the search for truth takes on for him a primary moral significance. Intellectualism, although hardly confined to doubters, is often the sole piety of the skeptic. A few years ago a distinguished sociologist asked me to read a brief manuscript which he had written primarily for students planning to go on to advanced work in his field, the purpose of which was to illustrate various ways in which the life of the mind might be cultivated. The essay had about it a little too much of the how-to-do books, and my friend abandoned it. But the nub of the matter from the standpoint of our present problem was that I found myself to be reading a piece of devotional literature, comparable perhaps to Cotton Mather's *Essays To Do Good* or Richard Steele's *The Tradesman's Calling.* My friend was trying to communicate his sense of dedication to the life of ideas, which he conceived much in the fashion of the old Protestant writers as a *calling.* To work is to pray. Yes, and for this kind of man, to think—really to think—is to pray. What he knows best, when he is at his best, is the pursuit of truth; but *easy* truths bore him. What he is certain of becomes unsatisfactory always; the meaning of his intellectual life lies in the quest for new uncertainties.

In a bygone day when men lived even more by dogma than they do now, there were two kinds of men whose special office it was to seek for and utter the truth; and they symbolize these two sides of the intellectual's nature. One was the angelic doctor, the learned schoolman, the conserver of old orthodoxies but also the maker of the new, and the prodder at the outer limits of received truths. The other was the jester, the professional fool, who had license to say on occasion for the purposes of amusement and release those things that bordered on *lèse majesté* and could not be uttered by others who were accounted serious men.

The fool and the schoolman are very far apart. No doubt you will ask whether there is not a contradiction between these two qualities of the intellectual, piety and playfulness. Certainly there is great tension between them; human beings are tissues of contradictions, and the life even of the intellectual is not logic, to borrow from Holmes, but experience. If you will think of the intellectuals you know, some will occur to you in whom the note of playfulness seems stronger, others who are predominantly pious. But I believe that in all intellectuals who have any stability as intellectuals—and that includes the angelic doctors of the middle ages—each of these characteristics is at some point qualified by the other.

Perhaps the tensile strength of the intellectual can be gauged by his ability to maintain a fair equipoise between these aspects of himself. At one end of the scale, an excess of playfulness leads to triviality, to dilettantism, to cynicism, to the failure of all sustained creative effort. At the other, an excess of piety leads to fanaticism, to messianism, to ways of life that may be morally magnificent or morally mean, but in either case are not quite the ways of intellectualism. It is of the essence of the intellectual that he strikes a balance.

The widespread distrust of intellectuals in America reflects a tendency to depreciate their playfulness and distrust their piety. Ours is a society in which every form of play seems to be accepted by the majority except the play of the mind. It does not need to be explained to most people in America why sports, sex, liquor, gambling, motoring, and gourmandizing are all more or less legitimate forms of amusement for those who happen to find them amusing. The only forms of *mental* play that are similarly accepted and understood are those that do not involve the particular kinds of critical intelligence that are called into play by intellectualism; I refer, of course, to such highly cerebral amusements as bridge, chess, and the various forms of the crossword puzzle. I suppose that those who are inclined to find economic explanations will point out that the play of the mind, being the only kind that has not been susceptible to commercialization, has not been able to rally the support of a vested interest. I believe, however, that a large part of our common neglect of the humanities is attributable to the absence of a traditional and accepted leisure class which looks upon this kind of personal cultivation as a natural goal of life. The idea of leisured intellectual exercise, not put to the service of some external end, has been offensive to mass democracy. One of the best signs of this is the rhetoric adopted by college presidents and others who appeal to the public for support for education. Always these appeals tell how much education does for citizenship, science, technology, morals or religion. Rarely do they point to the glories or pleasures of the human mind as an end in itself.

Just as the truly religious man is always a misfit in a secular society, so it is the piety of the intellectual that makes the greatest difficulties for him. Playfulness may be disdained or misunderstood, but it is not usually thought to be dangerous. Piety is another matter, for it is almost certain in the end to challenge something. It is the piety of the intellectual that puts iron into his nonconformism, if he happens to be a nonconformist. It is his piety that will make him, if anything does, a serious moral force in society. In our day the pressures operating against boldness in thought, as well as the sheer bureaucratization of intellectual life, bear hardest against the elements of piety in the intellectual. The temptation is very strong for some intellectuals to suppress the note of piety in themselves, to turn increasingly to the playful and generally more esoteric aspects of their work, to give up the office of spiritual leadership. Such self-suppression is psychologically and morally dangerous, and cannot be indulged in without paying a serious price. It does not become the intellectual, it is much too false to an important part of him, to give in altogether to playfulness and play the fool to the powerful. The jester had his prerogatives, to be sure, but we should also remember that he was usually a slave.

Democracy and Intellectualism

I have attempted thus far to define and elucidate intellectualism. Let me now explain what I mean by democracy when I say that in an important sense higher education and democracy have often been at odds. I do not mean by democracy simply the indispensable formal essentials of our society—constitutionalism, government by discussion, guarantees for the civil liberties of political minorities. These I neither challenge nor criticize; and I am sure that free higher education cannot in our time stand without them. But I do mean to criticize something that relates to the spirit of our politics, something that for lack of a better term I will call populistic democracy. Populistic democracy is neither progressive nor conservative, although it is in a perverse way equalitarian. Populistic democracy is the meeting ground, in fact, of the extreme left and the extreme right. It is government by or through the mass man, disguised behind the mask of an easy sentimentalization of the folk. It is the idea that anything done in the name of the people is *ipso facto* legitimate, even if the same act done in the name of a vested interest would be considered outrageous. It is the idea that a dozen postcards to a congressman from the wildest cranks should be given the same weight as a dozen reasoned letters from sober citizens. Transferred to the field of education, which is our concern, it is the idea that a university ought to cater to the needs of anybody who comes out of or pretends to represent the folk, whether or not he has any real need for or interest in the use of ideas. Put in terms of the state university, it is the idea than any graduate of the public high school should be accepted as a freshman no matter how dismal his prospects are as a student. Put in broader terms, it is the idea that any of the wants, real or fancied, of a mass society, should be absolute imperatives to its system of higher education.

We Americans are noted for our faith in both democracy and education. It has been our assumption that democracy and education, both being good, must be closely related and mutually reinforcing. We should have, it is argued, as much education and as much democracy as possible. It is also assumed that education serves democracy, and one of the most common shibboleths in our educational literature is the slogan "education for democracy." It is characteristically American that very few of us trouble to inquire whether democracy serves education. Whether it does indeed do so as fully and unambiguously as we might consider desirable is the question I insist we must face.

That there is any necessary relation between a vital system of higher education and a democratic society, one may readily deny on the basis of historical evidence. Two of the greatest periods in university history, that of the thirteenth and fourteenth centuries and that of the German universities in the nineteenth century, occurred in societies that were not notably democratic. In our own experience, I do not believe it incorrect to say that the great age of American university development from 1870 to 1910 was for the most part an age of political and economic oligarchy; and also that our finest universities and small colleges, by and large, have been those started and endowed by rich men and patronized chiefly by the upper classes.

All this does not mean, of course, that there is any necessary antagonism between democracy and higher education. Presumably there is no inherent or universally necessary opposition between a political democracy and a vital, respected, intellectually rich and alert university system. But I do wish to point out that there has been a historically persistent tension between our popular democracy and intellectualism that has been very sadly felt in the sphere of university and college life. The problem of how democracy and education can best serve and complement each other—as we would all, no doubt, like them to do—has not been nearly as constructively attacked as it might be for the simple reason that it has not often enough been candidly faced.

Long ago Tocqueville saw that the democratic culture that had emerged in the United States had brought with it pressures that were seriously hostile to the free use of the mind. He found that the democratic and equalitarian impulse had weakened the ability of the individual to resist the pressure of the opinion of the mass:

> The fact that the political laws of the Americans are such that the majority rules the community with sovereign sway, materially increases the power which that majority naturally exercises over the mind. For nothing is more customary in man than to recognise superior wisdom in the person of his oppressor. . . . The intellectual dominion of the greater number would probably be less absolute among a democratic people governed by a king than in the sphere of a pure democracy, but it will always be extremely absolute; and by whatever political laws men are governed in the ages of equality, it may be foreseen that faith in public opinion may become a species of religion there, and the majority its ministering prophet.
>
> Thus intellectual authority will be different, but it will not be diminished; and far from thinking that it will disappear, I augur that it may readily acquire too much preponderance and confine the action of private judgment within narrower limits than are suited either to the greatness or the happiness of the human race. In the principle of equality I very clearly discern two tendencies;

the one leading the mind of every man to untried thoughts, the other inclined to prohibit him from thinking at all. And I perceive how, under the dominion of certain laws, democracy would extinguish that liberty of mind to which a democratic social condition is favourable; so that, after having broken all the bondage once imposed on it by ranks or by men, the human mind would be closely fettered to the general will of the greatest number.

Tocqueville found that in his time the most absolute monarchs in Europe were unable to prevent certain heretical notions from circulating through their dominions and even in their courts:

Such is not the case in America; as long as the majority is still undecided, discussion is carried on; but as soon as its decision is irrevocably pronounced, a submissive silence is observed, and the friends, as well as the opponents of the measure unite in assenting to its propriety. The reason for this is perfectly clear: no monarch is so absolute as to combine all the powers of society in his own hands, and to conquer all opposition with the energy of a majority which is invested with the right of making and of executing the laws. . . .

I know no country in which there is so little true independence of mind and freedom of discussion as in America. In any constitutional state in Europe every sort of religious and political theory may be advocated and propagated abroad; for there is no country in Europe so subdued by any single authority as not to contain citizens who are ready to protect the man who raises his voice in the cause of truth from the consequences of his hardihood. If he is unfortunate enough to live under an absolute government, the people is upon his side; if he inhabits a free country, he may find a shelter behind the authority of the throne, if he requires one. The aristocratic part of society supports him in some countries and the democracy in others. But in a nation where democratic institutions exist, organized like those of the United States, there is but one sole authority, one single element of strength and of success, with nothing beyond it.

While I do believe that Tocqueville was exaggerating the case of the United States in 1835, he pointed to the heart of the problem of majority tyranny over the soul. It is a problem that has grown still more acute in our own age, an age of mass communications and the mass man; for now the tyranny of the majority can be spread uniformly over the surface of a great nation otherwise well suited by size and diversity to a multiplicity of opinions, and it can be to some degree forged and manipulated from a few centers. If there were any horrors in that spontaneous, grass-roots variety of popular tyranny, as Tocqueville saw it, they must be greatly compounded by the artificial and centralized means of manipulation that the communications technology of our time has made possible.

But has there been substantial historical evidence in the development of American higher education for the validity of Tocqueville's fear of mass tyranny? I believe there is certainly enough evidence to warrant a reconsideration of our views of the relation between democracy and university culture. I propose to argue that while populistic democracy has been on the side of many educational improvements and reforms, it has often been aligned as sharply with forces tending to constrain freedom in higher education and to lower its devotion to intellectual goals.

Democracy and Education

There may have been some popular upsurges in our history that have been auspicious for intellectualism in general, and for higher education in particular; but the popular movements that have been notable for their failure to understand the place of learning in our culture, or even on occasion for their hostility to it, are quite numerous. One of the first, the Great Awakening of the mid-eighteenth century, was notable for its hostility to a free and liberal-minded theological education such as was emerging in the older colleges; and while the Awakening must be in the end credited for enlarging the number of colleges, the goal sought at first in these enterprises was not an enhancement of the sphere of free learning but simply the creation of schools that would teach the right brand of theology. Jeffersonian democracy was not, on the whole, what I call populistic—at least not in its leadership. Its most constructive work in education, the founding of a liberal university in Virginia, was the work of aristocratic leadership. Jacksonian democracy, whatever its benefits in other areas, was identified with a widespread deterioration in the standards of professional education, masquerading under the ideology that easier access to these privileged areas of life must be made available to the people.

The founding of early state universities was badly hampered by popular hostility to advanced education that was held to be of use chiefly to the aristocrats, who, in fact, usually provided the basic impetus to the cultivation of the higher learning, whether in state-founded or private institutions. The movement that destroyed the old classical curriculum and made American universities, especially our state universities, the nurseries of all kinds of subintellectual practical skills of less than university grade was in its impetus very largely a popular movement; and while many of the consequences of that movement must be set to its credit as compensations, the undercurrent of vocationalism and anti-intellectualism was undeniable. Our history books tell us—to come toward our own time—that during the Populist-Bryan period the university professors who failed to accept the gold-standard economics of the well-to-do classes were often victims of outrageous interference; they do not usually trouble to tell us that when the Populists captured Kansas they raised hob with the University of Kansas in much the same way that they complained of so bitterly when the shoe was on the other foot. One of the most genuinely popular, and I believe democratic, political leaders in our history was William Jennings Bryan; and the sort of respect he showed for science and academic freedom is familiar to you all. His concept of the rights of the dissenting teacher reduces to his famous comment: "A man cannot demand a salary for saying what his employers do not want said."

My aim in stressing these facts is not to cast discredit upon popular democracy, whose merit in our whole scheme of things must be weighed by taking into account all its achievements as well as its deficiencies; I am simply trying to suggest that many of us have in the past made a mystique of the masses and have tended too much to attribute all the villainy in our world to the machinations of vested interests. I find it rather suggestive that the sole ruling group in our history that could be called a vested intellectual interest of any considerable power—I refer, of course, to the early Puritan clergy—has suffered the fate of being scandalously libelled by our "liberal" historians who have written in the tradition of V. L. Parrington.

Why this persistent tension between popular democracy and free higher learning? Obviously it is to some degree an aspect of social striving: a college education is a privilege that has not been open to all. While it can open up otherwise unavailable opportunities to the children of the less favored classes, it can also confirm the privileges of the upper classes by adding to those social, political, and economic advantages which are theirs by birth and family, the advantages of a superior education. Much of the early opposition to state universities was based precisely upon this argument. Why tax the poor, it was repeatedly asked, to educate the sons of the rich? No doubt there is such an element of resentment on the part of the lower classes for the privileges and attainments of the upper classes. But this, to my mind, will not get us very far in explaining why the United States in particular has been a happy hunting ground for anti-intellectualism. Class divisions exist in all western societies. Moreover, of all western nations, the United States has given by far the greatest proportion of its total population an opportunity to have a college education. In our more than 1700 colleges, for instance, we offer higher education, or a reasonable facsimile thereof, to about ten times as large a portion of our population as is done in the British Isles. Moreover, while we have always had our class stratification, class lines have been less sharp in the United States, and mobility between classes somewhat easier, than in European countries. By the showing of these facts, the United States should, in accordance with the class envy theory, have much less resentment of higher education as a source of privilege than any other country on the globe.

The evidence is all to the contrary, and this is enough to give us pause. It remains to be explained why, in a culture that seems to value education very highly, that has provided an enormous apparatus for the collegiate education of its youth, the genuine intellectual content of higher education is so little esteemed, why the teacher in general and the college professor in particular has so much less social status than he does almost anywhere else. I believe that the problem of status is, indeed, quite crucial, but that the situation cannot be explained in terms of broad assertions about the envy of manual for intellectual labor, the poor for the well-to-do, or the middle classes for the leisure classes. We must look to some of the unique factors of American historical development for our answers.

From the beginning the American people were confronted with rich resources, an immense task of continental settlement, and a shortage of labor. Their culture thus came to set a premium on practical achievement, the manipulation of material reality, and quick decision. It did not encourage reflection or a respect for the ultimate and irreducible disagreements of life. On the contrary, it suggested that it was to everyone's interest to arrive at a quick consensus, general enough to get the work done, that any disagreement on details was, in the light of the rich potentialities of organized work, unimportant. The American still sets a very high premium on such a consensus; he implicitly approaches broad intellectual and philosophical problems with that model of prompt decision in mind. "What can we agree on?" he wants to know. The wonderful persistence of irreducible differences of opinion, of the plurality of human dreams and perspectives, the exchange or contemplation of differences as an exercise in mutual understanding—all these are likely to be dark mysteries to him. He makes an ideology of normality; he asks not "What am I?" but "What is customary and proper to be around here?" He *thinks* he is an individualist because he does truly and genuinely resent any rude coercive efforts to make him conform, but he cannot realize that he spends half his time trying to figure out how he can conform "spontaneously." One of the most appalling things in American life is the failure of those who prate most about individualism to develop any understanding of individuality. The loudest hosannas to individualism are sung by grim, regimented choruses.

The effects of our chronic shortage of labor have also struck quite directly at the teaching profession from grammar schools to graduate schools. Our historic abundance of land and other resources has continually beckoned to the inadequate resources of our labor power. The consequences of this for other areas of life than education have often been noted. Our agriculture, for instance, was dedicated from the outset to extensive and wasteful cultivation and rapid mechanization rather than to intensive and careful cultivation and farming as a settled way of life. Too little has been said about a similar trend in our educational history. I think we have cultivated man wastefully and mechanically too. The teaching of our young, for instance, has been all too regularly left over to those whose imaginations and energies were not absorbed—or not yet absorbed—in the more exciting and lucrative life of physical and economic conquest, or to those who for one reason or another were altogether incapable of entering upon it. Ichabod Crane was, I suppose, the archetype of the American schoolmaster—the timid misfit, the amiable failure, the man who was scared out of town; and when Brom Bones chased him that terrible night through Sleepy Hollow and frightened him almost to death with a pumpkin, he was passing upon him the characteristic comment of the American philistine upon the American teacher. If the teacher was not Ichabod Crane, then it was the lonely spinster, driven by desperation to take up teaching when all else failed. If not the spinster, it was the young man who was merely marking time, supporting himself before launching upon a more permanent career in business or some really serious profession. "The men teachers," wrote an observer of early Massachusetts schools—mind you, even Massachusetts schools—

> may be divided into three classes: (1) Those who think teaching is easier and possibly a little more remunerative than common labor. (2) Those who are acquiring, or have acquired, a good education, and who take up teaching as a temporary employment, either to earn money for pressing necessities or to give themselves time to choose deliberately a regular profession. (3) Those who, conscious of weakness, despair of distinction or even the means of subsistence by other means. . . . They are often very young, they are constantly changing their employment, and consequently can have but little experience; and what is worse than all, they have never had any direct preparation for their profession. . . . No standard of attainments is fixed . . . so that any one *keeps school*, which is a very different thing from *teaching school*, who wishes to do it, and can persuade by herself or her friends, a small district to employ her. And this is not a very difficult matter, especially when the remuneration for the employment is so very trifling. . . . If a young man be moral enough to keep out of State prison, he will find no difficulty in getting approbation for a schoolmaster.

An exaggeration? Possibly. But in 1930–31, even after much had been done to improve standards of teacher training in the United States, the National Survey of the Education of Teachers showed that American teacher education, although only slightly inferior to that of England, was drastically inferior to that of France, Germany and the Scandinavian countries. The teacher of a high school in the continental countries was found to be a much superior person, attracted by the relatively high social position, higher salaries, and advanced professional morale. And while I have been speaking here of the teaching profession below the university grade, most of what I have said will apply almost as well to

American colleges down at least to the last three decades of the nineteenth century.

Let us look for a moment at those old colleges and the situation of their faculties. One of the first things that any observer of American higher education is struck by is the fact that the American professoriat is the only profession in the United States that is governed by laymen. Outside the continent of North America university faculties are nowhere governed, as they are here, by lay boards of trustees. Of course it is not easy to say whether the American professor lacks status because he is not self-governing or whether he has failed to get self-government in part because he lacks status. Genetically, however, it is not too difficult to explain how the curse of absentee government came to afflict American education. American colleges were called into existence before the community had the full means to support them amply, and indeed before there was a body of learned men professionally given to teaching. The great independent, self-governing universities of the middle ages, which established the pattern for early modern university government, came into existence only where there were well-established bodies of students and masters; they took their political form from the guild model of corporate self-control and the church's model of independence from the power of the state. The American colleges were founded in a Protestant milieu, which, no longer accepting the principles of hierarchy and corporate independence, had introduced lay government of churches. From this to lay government of colleges was a natural step, made the more natural by the fact that the greater part of the teaching personnel in early American colleges, for over a century and a half, consisted of young tutors, recent graduates, who were merely waiting and studying preparatory to entering the ministry. These men usually had no permanent interest in teaching as a profession, no permanent stake in its welfare. And they were considered by the philanthropic non-teachers who founded the college to be too young and too transient to be entrusted with the task of governing the colleges and managing their resources. Hence governmental powers were kept in the hands of trustees. The only working member of the college who held the full stature of a master of university learning was the president who, in the absence of the trustees, took over a larger and larger share of the task of determining college policy. Hence to this day the only person in the American community who enjoys a measure of prestige and respect comparable to that enjoyed by the university professor in most countries of Europe is our college or university president. Needless to say, with the development of the modern university, a great deal of the power to govern academic affairs has informally passed into the hands of faculties. But in almost all cases, such powers are delegated and may be legally retaken on any issue at any time by trustees. While few American university professors would argue for full self-government at this date, the legal inability of the American academic community to govern itself in matters bearing on academic freedom and tenure is a major disability in its struggle against the external forces of anti-intellectualism.

It may also be said in passing that the historic lack of prestige within the American academic community has tended to feed on itself. I am sure that no man anywhere whose primary desire is for a large share of the material goods of life enters the teaching profession with the idea that it will supply them with any abundance. He enters it because of other inducements: because he wants to pursue knowledge, because he values leisure (he will be lucky if he gets it), because he likes the idea of living in an academic community, or because of the prestige of the office. But American academic life, having so little prestige to offer, has failed to recruit a very large percentage of its professorial personnel from the upper classes, as does the professoriat in England or on the continent. The American college professor is characteristically drawn from the lower middle classes. I hope you will not imagine that I am being snobbish when I argue that this has been a signal disadvantage both to the freedom and the intellectualism of the academic community. Logan Wilson, in his study of *The Academic Man* in the United States, has pointed out that the recruit from the lower middle classes often comes from a background of cultural poverty in which, of necessity, the view taken of most things has to be profoundly affected by their material efficacy. I should also add that a man who comes from a well-established family with secure connections, and has perhaps in addition some personal resources to draw on, can confront the problems of free expression with far greater boldness than the man who feels that he must cling to his academic job at all costs. I have been impressed, in studying the development of a certain measure of liberalism in the American colleges of the eighteenth century, by the important role played by men who came to academic life from secure positions of social prestige, either in great commercial families or the ministry. One of the boldest men in early academic life was Professor John Winthrop, the great Harvard astronomer, and no little part of his boldness rested upon the security derived from the fact that he was, after all, a Winthrop in Massachusetts.

The low prestige of the professor in America was matched by the low prestige of the college itself. At the end of the eighteenth century and the beginning of the nineteenth, as the American population broke through the Allegheny mountains and began to spread across the continent, a process of educational fragmentation began which still profoundly afflicts our educational system. Every sect of Protestants wanted to have a little college to service every part of a great country. Localities thought that a community college would be good for local development. Parents welcomed the opportunity to educate their sons near at home in small schools whose annual tuition was often not much larger than the cost of transportation to a distant and perhaps more formidable seat of learning. They were advised, too, that the country college was socially democratic and that it protected their offspring from the corrupting atmosphere of great cities. This passion for breaking up the educational system into small units destroyed much of the potential strength and prestige of the old college. Where English colleges had clustered at a few university centers, American colleges were strewn across three thousand miles of continent. Innumerable colleges failed because they were so flimsily launched. Many that survived were much too tiny to maintain decent teaching staffs and adequate educational standards. It became a commonplace among serious educators before the Civil War that the American college was not, in the terms of international educational standards, a college at all, but a closer equivalent to the German gymnasium, the French lycée, the English public school.

After a time the old college became the butt of a great deal of criticism. It was, of course, devoted chiefly to the inherited classical curriculum, featuring Latin, Greek, and mathematics. This kind of schooling was increasingly held to be unadapted to the needs of American business, technology, and agriculture. It was held, and quite correctly, to be too limited and rigid to be adequate to the growing fund of human knowledge. Between the educational reformers, who were dissatisfied with the low level of work that the existing colleges were unable to transcend, and the practical reformers, who wanted to make American higher education work for the community in a clearer and more easily definable way, a curiously mixed transformation was finally effected in the last half of the nineteenth century. Universities, both state and private, were at last reared on adequate foundations; graduate and professional schools were created; schools of agriculture and engineering were founded; the curriculum was broadened; and the elective system was introduced.

Within only a few decades a curriculum system that had been too tight and too rigid was made too loose and too sprawling. All kinds of practical skills that had neither professional nor intellectual stature—no matter how necessary they might be to the community—were taught, or presumed to be taught, at universities. The president of a great state university was proud to say: "The state universities hold that there is no intellectual service too undignified for them to perform." Vast numbers of students without notable intellectual interests or skills flocked to the colleges and universities, availed themselves freely of the multitude of elective courses with little or no intellectual content, and passed out into the world with padded degrees. Much of the information thus inculcated may be thought to have no place in any system of formal education. A still larger part belongs to purely technical and mechanical education of the sort that can be properly taught in formal education but is not elsewhere considered proper to a university—the sort of thing that on the continent of Europe is to be found among the offerings of the German *technische Hochschule* and its many counterparts in other countries.

The Cost of Anti-Intellectualism

Now all this has taken place at serious cost to intellectualism. It is possible, of course, to argue that the professor of some field of pure learning is not interfered with in the pursuit of his work simply because his colleague in the school of agriculture is busy teaching farmers how to raise healthy pigs. Theoretically, no; but those who are familiar with the problems of university administration and finance know that these things have a way of pulling against or tripping over each other; and that when all kinds of skills of various levels are jumbled together and taught in one institution, the hierarchy of values that places intellectual accomplishment at the top, as one would expect to do in a university, is somehow broken and destroyed. Thus the universities, that we might have expected to stand as solid barriers against the undercurrents of American anti-intellectualism, have actually intensified the push of the stream. How they could have resisted it, I do not honestly know. For one thing, our system of higher education is, unlike all the other systems in the world, a system of mass education, that today enrolls about 3,000,000 people. In a way, that is a preposterous figure, and I suppose it is altogether unreasonable to expect that students in such numbers will all get anything that could be called a common liberal education. All kinds of things pass for a college education in this country and will no doubt continue to do so for a long time to come. The difficulty is that we now have an educational system which rarely produces educators who will themselves dare to defend an education wholeheartedly directed to the goal of increasing intellectual power. The famous report of the President's Commission on Higher Education published in 1948—a report prepared by a representative group of American educators and laymen interested in education—had this to say on the subject:

> We shall be denying educational opportunity to many young people as long as we maintain the present orientation of higher education toward verbal skills and intellectual interest. Many young people have abilities of a different kind, and they cannot receive "education commensurate with their native capacities" in colleges and universities that recognize only one kind of educable intelligence.
>
> Traditionally the colleges have sifted out as their special clientele persons

possessing verbal aptitudes and a capacity for grasping abstractions. But many other aptitudes—such as social sensitivity and versatility, artistic ability, motor skill and dexterity, and mechanical aptitude and ingenuity—also should be cultivated in a society depending, as ours does, on the minute division of labor and at the same time upon the orchestration of an enormous variety of talents.

I can think of no more shameful capitulation than this to the canons of anti-intellectualism: a group of educators urging that our de-intellectualized colleges become still more de-intellectualized by giving up their alleged preoccupation with "verbal aptitudes" and "a capacity for grasping abstractions"—that is, the power to think and to express thought—for a motley batch of skills which, however valuable, one does not have to go to college to learn; for "social sensitivity" that no doubt includes ballroom dancing and parlor games; for "motor skill and dexterity" that must clearly mean athletics if it does not mean the ability to wash dishes without dropping them; and for "mechanical aptitude and ingenuity" that may very well mean the ability to drive and repair an automobile. Worthy skills every single one of them, and no doubt a necessary part of our life; but why they have to be acquired in something that calls itself a college or university the Commission, whose business was supposed to be with *higher* education, did not take the trouble to explain. No doubt its members did not feel themselves to be on the defensive, for they were expressing the dominant point of view in American society.

What is it, I think we may properly ask, that brings our nation's educators to such depressing disavowals of the fundamentally intellectual purposes of education? Much the same thing, I believe, that has them cringing before the onslaughts of politicians who are beyond the pale of moral decency—and that is the lack of a self-confident dedication to the life of the mind. What the root of that failure of self-confidence is, no one really knows; but I venture to suggest that it has a great deal to do with our false piety for populistic democracy, our sense of guilt at daring to suggest that there is anything wrong with the mob, even when a large part of it has obviously been whipped up by demagogues to a state of frantic suspicion of everything it does not care to understand. I think it would help us all morally, even if it would do nothing else, to face the fact that the very idea of intellectualism implies an elite of some kind—not, to be sure, a ruthless elite with special privileges or powers, but simply a group of people who have interests not shared by everyone in the community and whose very special interest is in freedom. Not everyone really wants to belong to that elite. But the primary fact is that this elite must maintain a certain spiritual autonomy in defining its own standards. I am not optimistic enough to believe that in any calculable future the rest of society can be brought to recognize that intellectuals have their own rights and interests, not special rights or privileged interests, but of the same sort that any other group has. What the intellectual community can do is what any group of sensible people will do whose values are under attack—and that is not to try to find some plausible reason for abandoning those values because they are not shared by the majority; and not to try to convince themselves that they really agree with the majority after all—but to show cohesion and firmness under fire, until the point has been reached when it is no longer profitable to encroach upon them.

This world will never be governed by intellectuals—it may rest assured. But *we* must be assured, too, that intellectuals will not be altogether governed by this world, that they maintain their piety, their longstanding allegiance to the world of spiritual values to which they should belong. Otherwise there will be no intellectuals, at least not above ground. And societies in which the intellectuals have been driven underground, as we have had occasion to see in our own time, are societies in which even the anti-intellectuals are unhappy.

DAVID B. TYACK | *Growing Up Black: The Education of the Negro*

Shortly after the Civil War, General O. O. Howard visited a school for freedmen in South Carolina and asked the children what message he should take to their friends in the North. "Massa," said a little Negro boy, "tell 'em we is rising." Ex-slaves, young and old, men and women, flocked to study the alphabet and spelling book and Bible in old plantation sheds or at town streetcorners. The first generation of emancipated Negroes trusted that education would lead them to a promised land of opportunity, a hope soon shattered for a people disenfranchised, economically suppressed, socially barred by rigid rules of caste, and frequently subjected to humiliation or terror.

By contrast, first generation immigrants often feared the common school as a wedge between them and their children. But public education often led the second or third generation out of the ghetto into the mainstream of American life. Though often chauvinistic and intolerant in spirit, the common school did open opportunities to the children of the foreign born and helped to make one nation from many people. But with the Negro the tale was otherwise. The failure of Negro education is

Reprinted by permission of the publisher, from David B. Tyack, *Turning Points in American Educational History* (Waltham, Mass.: Blaisdell Publishing Company, 1967).

interwoven with the story of the larger failure of American society to make emancipation real.

Slavery was the "congenital defect" of the American republic. Slaves began their long journey in the dank jungles of Africa, wrenched from tribal folkways, chained to victims in front and in back, marched along trails where they saw skeletons of others who had fallen on the way. Perhaps a third of the victims died during the terrors of the Atlantic crossing. On small ships they were stacked like spoons, fed pulpy horsebeans, stifled and parched under the blasting sun, and seasick and cold in winter storms. Systematically Africans were robbed of identity. Owners changed their names—a matter of great symbolic importance in many tribal cultures—and tried to eradicate their language and customs. When "broken in" and ready to be sold as plantation hands, they entered an institutional form of slavery which was harsher in its impact on personality and family structure than servitude in ancient times or in South America.

Slavery had not taken firm root in the English-speaking world prior to the importation of Negroes to the American colonies. Hence it lacked the legal and religious safeguards which cushioned its severities elsewhere. Alexis de Tocqueville observed that "the only means by which the ancients maintained slavery were fetters and death; the Americans of the South of the Union have discovered more intellectual securities for the duration of their power. They have employed their despotism and their violence against the human mind. In antiquity precautions were taken to prevent the slave from breaking his chains; at the present day measures are adopted to deprive him even of the desire for freedom." Once slavery had been regarded as a misfortune which could happen to anyone, but southern apologists argued that it was the only fit condition for an inferior and dependent race. In South America, Spanish and Portuguese legal and ecclesiastical tradition assured some checks on the power of masters: slaves had to be married in church; families could not be separated; and owners had to provide religious instruction.

But in the United States, as Stanley Elkins has pointed out, slavery was a closed system. Enjoying almost absolute power, the slaveowners took steps to fulfil their own prophecies: by trying to reduce the slave to a faceless and dependent child they created the shiftless, ignorant, amiable "Sambo" of the American stereotype. Marriage of slaves had no legal status; in many states it was against the law to teach a Negro to read; and a slave had no rights save those his master chose to give him. In short, the master owned the slave's mind as well as his labor. Legally the slave had no more identity than other forms of live property. Whether slaveowners treated slaves well or poorly—whether Negroes ate good food, had comfortable cabins, worked reasonable hours—is irrelevant to the issue Tocqueville raised: the institution of slavery was designed to liquidate independence and perpetuate dependence. Slaves sometimes openly rebelled; sometimes engaged in mild sabotage; but the role they were forced to play made deep inroads on their sense of identity and worth. "I've been a boy long enough," remarked a seventy-two year old man in Selma in 1964.

Slavery devastated family structure. The Negro father was not responsible for supporting his children nor could he protect his mate against miscegenation. At any time families might be broken up for sale. At auction slaves were described in terms normally reserved for brood mares and studs. The instability of the slave family and the childlike dependence enforced by masters proved exceedingly difficult to change after emancipation.

The experience of the emancipated slave, then, must be set against this dark background. Freedmen were puzzled as well as joyful; what did freedom mean? Certain changes had great symbolic value. Now they might move about, change their names, engage in politics, learn to read. The most available model of the free citizen was the white master, whose distinguishing characteristics seemed to be his aversion to manual labor, his classical education, and his political activism. "During the whole of the Reconstruction period," wrote the Negro leader Booker T. Washington, "two ideas were constantly agitating the minds of the coloured people, or, at least, the minds of a large part of the race. One of these was the craze for Greek and Latin learning, and the other was a desire to hold office. . . . There was a . . . feeling that a knowledge, however little, of the Greek and Latin languages would make one a very superior human being, something bordering almost on the supernatural."

Observers both friendly and hostile to the ex-slaves agreed that the emancipated Negroes passionately desired education. Sharing their hopes were a band of Yankee schoolteachers who came South from the old abolitionist strongholds to teach the Negro the meaning of freedom. Many of these teachers saw their work as the continuation of the war: "We might withdraw our swords, but we should send spelling books and Bibles to the front. The military might has been disbanded, but the missionaries should organize." They shared a sense of absolute righteousness, a belief that the South was the land of Satan, and Southerners sinners all—the whites, that is. "What a magnificent revenge Massachusetts has now . . . upon South Carolina," said one teacher. "Oh for an hour of the wizard's cunning, to evolve the spirit of Calhoun from the trance of death, and show him the thronging thousands of the people he despised as brutes, crowding around the school-house doors." One of the widely used readers was *The Freedmen's Book,* a selection edited by an abolitionist which included a speech by William Lloyd Garrison, a eulogy of the Haitian revolutionary Toussaint L'Ouverture, and other laudatory accounts of slave revolts. One excerpt declared that when southern whites want to sell goods to Negroes, "they will no longer call you Jack or Joe; they will begin to think that you are *Mr.* John Black and *Mr.* Joseph Brown."

The Southerners, their currency and banking ruined, their capital in slaves gone, their railroads destroyed, their wharves rotting, much of their land lying in swaths of devastation, their army defeated, had left "one inestimable privilege" which the Yankees couldn't take away: "to hate 'em. I git up at half-past four in the morning and sit up till twelve at night, to hate 'em." And hate them they did, making the life of the Yankee schoolteachers as miserable as possible. The teachers were of the martyr breed, willing to endure the slings of outraged Southerners, but many of them became discouraged because the Negroes did not live up to their exaggerated hopes. Still these missionaries did help to build anew the individuality of Negroes eroded by generations of slavery, and helped them to interpret and take advantage of their freedom.

Wilbur Cash, in his study of *The Mind of the South*, sketches the impact of the "Yankee schoolma'am" on the southern whites: "Generally horsefaced, bespectacled, and spare of frame, she was, of course, no proper intellectual, but . . . the South, with its vague standards in these matters, accepted her as such. It . . . read in the evils springing abundantly from her meddlesome stupidity categorical proof that Northern 'theory' was *in toto* altogether mad. And so she served as a distinct power in bringing Southern fear and hate to explicit focus in the purely ideological field—in setting up as definite a resistance to Yankee thought as to Yankee deeds."

After the first wave of northern interest in the ex-slave displayed by the Federal Freedmen's Bureau and various religious and charitable associations, a number of northern foundations continued to pour money into southern education. Following the precedent set by the Peabody Fund, northern philanthropists accepted the southern view that public education had to be segregated. Sometimes the agents of the foundations accepted without question the common view that Negro schools should be not only separate but also unequal; one agreed to pay less to teachers in Negro schools, explaining that "it did not cost so much to operate a Negro school as it did a white school." But in a time when the southern states were starving the Negro schools, the donations of the General Education Board, the Julius Rosenwald fund, and other large foundations raised the pitifully low level of preparation of teachers, paid for demonstration teachers and model schools, encouraged construction of decent schoolhouses by giving matching grants, and paid for agents who were educational circuit riders in the southern educational awakening.

During the nineteenth century and well into the twentieth, Negro education was primarily a branch of southern education, and subject to all the general handicaps of that region in addition to the special handicaps imposed by the racial caste system. Southern education generally trailed far behind the national average, reflecting the South's poor tax base, its thinly spread population, its high ratio of children to adults. Over 4,000,000 of the nation's 4,442,000 Negroes lived in the South in 1860; the proportion was about the same in 1890. Not until the large-scale northward migrations of the Negro in the twentieth century—especially as a result of the two world wars—did a substantial percentage of American Negroes come to live outside the South.

Public education in the South essentially began during the days of Reconstruction. Before the Civil War the common school took only meager root in a few southern states, but in the period from 1867 to 1877 state after state wrote extensive educational provisions into their constitutions. They voted generous support for schools, provided centralized supervision, and created schools for Negroes as well as whites. Two states—South Carolina and Louisiana—developed integrated school systems, but these lasted only a short while. Negro members of Reconstruction legislatures argued that integrated schools were their right under the Fourteenth Amendment and their guarantee that the schooling would in fact be equal. But in most southern states the public schools were segregated, even under Reconstruction legislatures.

Segregated schooling compounded the high cost of educating a rural population. When southern whites regained control of state affairs in 1877, conservatives cut back school expenditures sharply. By 1880, in comparison with 1871, the length of the school term dropped 20 per cent and outlays for schools fell 40 per cent. Opposition to Negro education grew virulent: why should whites pay for the education of Negroes, who paid few taxes, asked the retrenchers? Southern leaders devised a number of ways of disinheriting the Negro educationally, just as they displayed ingenuity in disenfranchising him. In 1874 the agent of the Peabody Fund told a group of South Carolina Negroes not to worry that separate schools would be unequal; but in 1932, after a long history of fiscal sabotage, one county in that state spent $8 on each Negro student in the public schools and $178 for each white.

Following the lead of the United States Congress in providing for Negro schools in the District of Columbia, some states allotted tax money to Negro schools only in proportion to receipts from Negro taxpayers. In the black belt counties of the deep South money from the public school funds was distributed on a per capita basis which included whites as well as Negroes, but in the apportionment of funds within the county the officials saw to it that the white schools received the lion's share. In one Mississippi county, to take an extreme example, each Negro child received $.18 to every $25 allotted to each white child (this in a county in which there were 974 white children and 4,016 Negro children enrolled). Poor whites from the "white" counties of Mississippi objected to the education of Negroes in general and the per capita distribution of the school fund in particular. Governor James Vardaman of Mississippi argued that any money spent on the education of Negroes was wasted and a "robbery of the white man. . . . You take it from the toiling white men and women, you rob the white child of the advantages it would afford him, and you spend it upon the negro in an effort to make of the negro what God Almighty never intended should be made, and which men cannot accomplish. . . ."

In the drive to economize on the education of Negroes, and to evade constitutional provisions concerning equal education of the races, states developed "certification" laws which enabled them to pay Negro teachers half as much as white. Another way to save money was to have large classes: for example, the average class size in southern Negro schools in 1912–13, was sixty-seven. As Booker T. Washington lamented, standards for selecting teachers for Negro schools were abysmal; as late as 1930 more than one-third of the Negro teachers in fifteen southern states had not completed high school. The majority of school buildings were miserable shacks, the books and equipment ante-diluvian. In 1931 in the South as a whole the average figures spent on white students in the public schools were $45.63 in comparison with $14.95 for Negro. And besides having poor teachers and squalid classrooms, the Negro child bore the yoke of inferiority which Richard Wright has described in his vivid account of his school days in *Black Boy*.

The Negro was the man farthest down. White supremacists were determined to keep him there. In many counties of the Georgia and Mississippi black belts not more than one Negro in one hundred owned the land he worked. In the South as a whole three-fourths of Negro farmers were sharecroppers or tenants. In a relatively good year for cotton prices —1881—*monthly* farm wages ran from $4 to $15. Increasingly Negroes were barred from the crafts and trades they had learned as slaves and were relegated to the hardest and dirtiest work in cities and towns.

One would suppose that the "free labor" of the share cropper or road crew was the economic mudsill, but such was not the case: below even the poorest worker lay the horror of the convict labor gang. For trivial offenses or trumped-up charges a Negro might be sentenced to work for five years under the lash. Contractors turned convict labor into private profit in a system whose closest parallel is the Nazi or Soviet labor camp. Crowded beyond endurance at night in filthy rolling pens or log stockades, infested with vermin, bereft of medical care, whipped into working at a frenzied pace in mines and in turpentine camps, on roads and construction jobs, the convicts died at rates sometimes reaching 25 per cent annually.

Even after white Southerners had regained control of their governments, many conservatives believed that the disenfranchisement of the

Negro was "a political impossibility under any circumstances short of revolution." As late as 1890 the Superintendent of Public Instruction in Mississippi declared that Southerners "have no fears of serious or general trouble growing out of the act of negro suffrage, if not interfered with by a low class of political agitators." But by the end of the century disenfranchisement of the Negro was in sight in almost all the South. Although the South had never welcomed the Negro as a voter—and had tried to exclude him by the persuasion of groups like the Ku Klux Klan and the Pale Faces—only when the Negro became a pawn in party struggles between whites, did both Populists and Bourbons conclude that the Negro must lose the vote. In a series of state constitutional conventions Southerners passed regulations which struck at Negro suffrage: the poll tax, requiring voters to "understand" the constitution (as interpreted by discriminating registrars); and the "grandfather clause," exempting from property and literacy tests those citizens—and their sons and grandsons—who were entitled to vote on January 1, 1867 (a new version of the divine right of kings, complained one Negro). The provisions effectively excluded most Negroes. In 1897, 130,344 Negroes were registered in Louisiana; under the New Constitution only 5,320 were registered in 1900.

In the southern constitutional conventions delegates revealed a depth of hatred and fear toward the Negro which alarmed moderates. Ex-Governor Oates declared in the Alabama convention that "now, when the negro is doing no harm, why, people want to kill him and wipe him from the face of the earth." A Negrophobic fever swept the South and other parts of the nation. In the decade from 1889 to 1899 there was an average of 187 lynchings a year. Race riots raged through both northern and southern cities in the first decade of the twentieth century. In Springfield, Illinois, mobs seized control of the city, terrorizing and killing Negroes, crying "Lincoln freed you, we'll show you where you belong." The rankest form of anti-Negro literature—books like *The Clansman* and *The Negro a Beast*—found a ready audience. The older paternalistic stereotype was sometimes expressed—paeans to the happy "little fellow coming down the street . . . with a piece of watermelon in one hand and a set of cane quills from the swamp tied together with a string, in the other, blowing 'Boogoo Eyes' "—but distrust came to replace the intimacy which the old plantation system sometimes afforded. Moderates in the South bowed to the white supremacists; the North, having largely abandoned the Negro in the Compromise of 1877 which concluded Reconstruction, was embarked with the South on imperialistic adventures in the Spanish-American war, with its own jargon of Anglo-Saxon superiority. Thus racism had an open field.

One result was the legal codification of the social caste system, a movement partially underway when ratified by the United States Supreme

Court in 1896 in the case of *Plessy v. Ferguson.* Homer Plessy, one-eighth Negro, protested that the Fourteenth Amendment forbade legislation of the state of Louisiana requiring racial segregation on railroad cars. The Court replied that the Amendment "in the nature of things . . . could not have been intended to abolish distinctions based on color . . . or a commingling of the two races upon terms unsatisfactory to either." Fortified by the Court's "separate but equal" doctrine, southern states passed a plethora of detailed caste laws. In 1898 a South Carolina newspaper tried to stem the Jim Crow tide by ridicule: "If there must be Jim Crow cars on the railroads, there should be Jim Crow cars on the street railways. Also on all passenger boats. . . . If there are to be Jim Crow cars, moreover, there should be Jim Crow waiting saloons at all stations, and Jim Crow eating houses. . . . There should be Jim Crow sections of the jury box, and a separate Jim Crow dock and witness stand in every court—and a Jim Crow Bible for colored witnesses to kiss." The tragedy was that this *reductio ad absurdum,* with the exception of the witness stand, became cold fact.

During this nadir of Negro rights in the United States an ex-slave, Booker T. Washington, became the chief spokesman for his people. Thwarted on every hand, his early hopes to rise through education dashed, the southern Negro learned from Washington a gospel of industrial education, of patient endurance of wrong, of thrift and cleanliness. In a famous speech to white Southerners in 1895, later labeled "the Atlanta Compromise," Washington declared that "the agitation of questions of social equality is the extremist folly." "In all things that are purely social we can be as separate as the five fingers," he said, "yet one as the hand in all things essential to mutual progress." Negroes needed farms and wages, not opera tickets.

Washington believed that social equality was an impractical goal—however desirable it might be in the long run—and he was a pragmatist above all. Recognizing that the Negro needed just about everything, he believed it wisest to start with the improvements least threatening to the dominant whites: the training of the hand and heart. It is perhaps not coincidental that the white supremacist James Vardaman was also fond of talking about educating the Negro's hand and heart. So permeated was Washington's school, Tuskeegee Institute, with the ethic of manual work that a faculty member was rebuked for carrying too many books under his arm—it might give wealthy visitors the wrong idea, he was told. Actually, many of the trades taught at Tuskeegee were anachronistic in an industrial age. Washington's emphasis on middle-class virtues made him a parent-surrogate and patron of the black bourgeoisie. Without irony Washington could announce: "I have watched carefully the influence of the tooth-brush, and I am convinced that there are few single agencies of civilization that are more far-reaching."

As a moderate, Washington pleased neither the white supremacists nor the integrationists. An Alabamian foe of Washington's portrayed him as "a rattler with his mouth open and his fangs ready, a rattler who has control of nearly all the other snakes, especially of his color and of his pedigree." Some Negroes, like W. E. B. duBois, on the other hand, blamed him for accepting the caste system, for neglecting the Negro's intellect, and for being the puppet of the white power structure. Washington was neither rattler nor puppet, of course. But he was indeed a compromiser. In a reply to a man who claimed that education could not solve the race problem because Negroes were inherently inferior, Washington could actually commend his opponent's "sincere and kindly spirit." In the ugly racist climate of the turn of the century, in the midst of lynchings and rigid Jim Crowism, when white liberals had all but abandoned the Negro, Washington's compromising stance was perhaps the most rational and effective one. A self-made man if anyone was—for he went from a slave's cabin to a meal in the White House with President Theodore Roosevelt—he worshipped success and was a Philistine. But set in his time and place, he deserves to be recognized as a man of limited though beneficent vision and great energy and good will, neither lionized as in his day nor vilified as in recent years by those who see him as an Uncle Tom.

One answer which Washington might have given to the Mississippian who claimed that education could not solve the race problem was that the southern Negro, in the mass, had never really been educated. Denied political power, economically and socially suppressed, the Negro was entitled, said a candid educator, only to "have the crumbs that fall from the white man's table." What this policy meant in practice was explained by a Negro boy in Chicago who was six years behind his grade level. His teacher in the South had been the town iceman: "He didn't come to school until he was through totin' ice around. Then if anyone wanted ice they comed after him. He wasn't learning me anything so I quit."

From such schools as these came the Negroes who emigrated to the cities of the North in the great internal migrations of the twentieth century. To the promised land they went, to North Philadelphia, to South Chicago, to Harlem. Within the decade 1910–1920 the Negro population of Chicago doubled, reaching 109,000. The labor shortages of World War I brought similar growth elsewhere. In the northern cities Negroes escaped legalized Jim Crowism but entered a world in many ways as trying as the one they had left. Locked into ghettoes by residential segregation, they often paid exorbitant rents for hovels or single tenement rooms furnished with a light bulb, sink, and bed. In these crowded communities malnutrition, disease, crime, and vice abounded. Mutual fear and hatred of white and Negro did not stop at the Mason-Dixon line. In 1919 in city after city of the North and West racial violence broke out. On

July 27, 1919, in Chicago a Negro swam offshore near a beach the whites had reserved for themselves, was stoned, and drowned, touching off a riot which lasted for thirteen days and resulted in 38 killed, 537 wounded, and over 1,000 people homeless.

In a study of *The Negro in Chicago*, probing the causes of the 1919 riot, the Commission on Race Relations found that the public school was one of the few places where white and Negro children could come to know one another. Despite some prejudice on the part of teachers and students, the school seemed to offer hope of bridging the chasm of racism. But as the influx of Negroes grew and northern attitudes hardened, contacts between the races in most schools declined, either through isolation by housing, by gerrymandering of school boundaries, or by state or local policy requiring segregation. A reporter studying race relations in the North in 1907 wrote that the white "people one ordinarily meets don't know anything about the Negro, don't discuss him, and don't care about him." The Negro seemed invisible and nameless.

Foreign immigrants in urban ghettoes often had a social cohesiveness and pride created by strong family, church and ethnic ties. They could see members of their group succeed in moving up the American economic and social ladder. Negroes, on the other hand, inherited from slavery a weak, matriarchical family structure which further disintegrated under the impact of urban life. They saw that economic opportunities in white America were restricted for Negroes. The white child saw all around him models for emulation, in his textbooks, in newspapers, in his everyday life. In a society which coveted success the Negro child bore the scar of knowing that even if he acquired skill and knowledge he might have to dig ditches and carry trays. A New York school principal said early in the century that "the saddest thing that faces me in my work is the small opportunity for a coloured boy or girl to find proper employment." He told of talking with a typical bright student asking for his working papers:

'Well, my boy, you want to work, do you? What are you going to do?' 'I'm going to be a door-boy, sir.' 'Well, you will get $2.50 or $3 a week, but after a while that will not be enough; what then?' After a moment's pause he will reply: 'I should like to be an office boy.' 'Well, what next?' A moment's silence, and 'I should try to get a position as bell-boy.' 'Well, then, what next?' A rather contemplative mood, and then, 'I should like to climb to the position of head bell-boy.' He has now arrived at the top; further than this he sees no hope. He must face the bald fact that he must enter business as a boy and wind up as a boy.

While economic opportunities improved as Negro communities developed their own business and professional class, and new jobs opened in the white world considerably during World War II, school segregation continued to belie the basic premises of the common school. As late as

1951 twenty-one states and the District of Columbia either compelled or permitted by law the separate education of the races. In that year, Linda Brown, an eight-year-old Negro girl in Topeka, Kansas, had to cross the railroad tracks and take a bus twenty-one blocks to a segregated school because she could not attend the white school five blocks away. Her father instituted a case which found its way to the Supreme Court and transformed American history.

In the years immediately preceding the 1954 *Brown* decision the Supreme Court had slowly whittled down the doctrine of "separate but equal" enshrined since 1896. In a series of cases involving graduate education the Court had denied that admitting Negroes to segregated law schools or giving them out-of-state scholarships granted them equal education. In the Brown case, however, the Court went well beyond these precedents by ruling that separate education was "inherently unequal." Employing psychological and sociological evidence on the effects of segregation and pointing to the crucial role of the school in modern society, the Court concluded that "segregation is a denial of the equal protection of the laws." In a subsequent opinion the following year the Court, recognizing the formidable difficulties in implementing the decision, left with the District Courts the duty of enforcing compliance "with all deliberate speed."

Though most communities of the border states and the District of Columbia readily obeyed the decision, the deep South resisted bitterly. Whether in open defiance—as at Little Rock, Arkansas, and the University of Mississippi—or through tactics of evasion and delay, the old Confederate States slowed integration to a snail's pace. But gradually through court orders and the denial of federal funds to discriminatory school systems the will of the highest court in the land and the federal government have begun to be felt.

In the 1960's national attention in the Negro revolution has also focused on the school systems of northern cities. In the 1961 case of *Taylor v. Board of Education of New Rochelle* the New York Federal Court of Appeals upheld a lower court decision that the New Rochelle School Board had unconstitutionally gerrymandered school district boundaries to perpetuate a segregated school. In other communities, in which no intent to segregate was apparent, schools in the North were often entirely Negro because of a residential segregation which isolated both the Negro neighborhood schools of the inner city and the white neighborhood schools of the periphery.

Unavoidably, much of the burden of bringing the Negro more fully into the mainstream of American society, of providing him with genuine equality of opportunity, has fallen on the public schools. In concert with other social agencies the schools are being asked to alleviate racial isolation and distrust created by residential segregation and mutual stereotypes and antipathies; to provide the basic intellectual and emotional background lacking in many disadvantaged children; and to give white and Negro children alike a sense of their intertwined history and destiny. Only as it makes progress in this arduous task can the *common* school fulfill its promise.

DAVID B. TYACK | *Catholic Power, Black Power, and the Schools*

The parents and leaders in the ghetto grew angry. It was time to protest. For years their children had read textbooks in which their people were ignored or scorned. Teachers often regarded them as outsiders and inferiors, really beyond the mainstream of American aspiration and achievement. Influential citizens and redneck workers talked darkly about the guerrilla warfare being plotted in the ghettoes. On both sides of the ghetto walls rhetoric escalated. Fearing riots and violent reprisals, moderate spokesmen in the ghetto warned against processions of their people on downtown streets.[1] But the ghetto folk were angry: by the thousands they withdrew their children and boycotted the schools; it was time, men said, that the ghetto began to learn the uses of *power.* They knew that a political backlash impended, but their cause was just.

Black power? No, Catholic power, and the time was a century ago. Systematically the Protestant majority was assaulting the faith of Catholics through the "non-sectarian" religious instruction offered in public schools which Catholics, as taxpayers, were forced to support. In Boston, in 1859, a teacher beat a Catholic child for a half-hour for refusing to repeat the King James version of the Ten Commandments. Taking the case to court, his irate father was told by the judge that his rights were not violated. "What different excitement would have convulsed the 'Athens of America' if the boy had been a Negro," exclaimed *The Catholic Telegraph.*[2]

Humanitarians were willing to extol the virtues of the Negro, to defend him from oppression; but who would speak for the rights of the despised Catholic? In schoolbook stereotypes, authors portrayed the Roman Church

[1] James O'Connor, "Anti-Catholic Prejudice," *American Catholic Quarterly Review,* 1:18–19 (January, 1876).

[2] Daniel Reilly, *The School Controversey, 1890–1893* (Washington, D.C.: Catholic University of America Press, 1943), pp. 18–19.

as a corrupt machine dependent on the sale of indulgences; as an inquisitorial and repressive institution; as an ambitious, covert, and sinister force in government.[3] Less respectable bigots delighted in telling about pregnant nuns, an American papal army, and even a clerical plot to capture boys and grind them into tasty sausages; mobs, poisoned by such propaganda, took to the streets to persecute Catholics. Leaders all over the nation claimed that America was a Protestant land and that Catholics —a large proportion of them immigrants—were a pernicious and foreign element which had to be homogenized or else denied full citizenship.[4]

The schools were a focal point of conflict. In the relatively homogeneous Protestant America of the era before large Catholic immigration, Protestants had agreed to call a truce in their sectarian quarrels at the schoolhouse door and to teach in the common school an evangelical consensus they called "non-sectarian": to read the King James Bible without comment, letting it "speak for itself" as Horace Mann said. For Catholics, of course, this was hardly non-sectarian, and the influence of Protestant teachers and textbooks further undermined their religion. Boldly, many Protestant ministers, schoolmen, and politicians argued that the majority had a *right* to dictate religious instruction, and since the Catholics were a minority, they had to capitulate.[5]

Catholics could not accept this second class citizenship nor this violation of their religious rights. In city after city they withdrew their children and boycotted the schools. They took their grievances to court but usually gained little satisfaction. Here and there they managed to persuade Protestant allies of the justice of their case.[6] One of these, Samuel Spear, ridiculed the opinion that " 'These Catholics who are making so much disturbance about the public schools, being largely of foreign birth, are mere interlopers.' "

This is simply an appeal to anti-Catholic prejudice, as anti-American as it is bigoted and ignorant. It may be well to remember that our Protestant ancestors were all of them a set of interlopers. The Puritans were interlopers. The whole people of the United States, with the exception of the Indians, are either interlopers or the descendants of interlopers. A great and powerful nation started

[3] Sister Marie Fell, *The Foundations of Nativism in American Textbooks, 1783–1860* (Washington, D.C.: Catholic University of America Press, 1941), *passim.*

[4] Ray Billington, *The Protestant Crusade, 1800–1860: A Study of the Origins of American Nativism* (New York: Macmillan Company, 1938), ch. xiv.

[5] David Tyack, "The Kingdom of God and the Common School: Protestant Ministers and the Educational Awakening in the West," *Harvard Educational Review,* 36:447–469 (Fall, 1966); and Tyack, "Onward Christian Soldiers: Religion in the Common School, 1870–1900," in forthcoming book edited by Paul Nash, *History and Education* (New York: Random House, 1968).

[6] Daniel Dorchester, *Romanism versus the Public School System* (New York: Phillips & Hunt, 1888), pp. 47, 97.

with interloping, and interloping has been one of the elements of its rapid increase.[7]

But court cases, voluntary persuasion, and boycotts did not win justice for the Catholic cause. Increasingly, Catholics realized that only through gaining political leverage and through building their own institutions would they achieve the respect and autonomy they deserved. This quest for Catholic power aroused as much consternation then as the demand for Negro power today. When Catholics sought successfully to eject the Protestant Bible from the common school, Protestants thought that they were attacking the very basis of American institutions. When they demanded the removal of biased textbooks, citizens and school officials thought Catholics were trying to control the curriculum.[8] Politicians saw a Jesuit plot in the desire of Catholics to win public support for their parochial schools, and President Grant predicted that the forces of "superstition" might precipitate a new civil war. Republicans attempted to capitalize on this Protestant backlash until the boomerang of the "Rum, Romanism, and Rebellion" speech helped them to lose the election of 1884.[9]

The quest for Catholic power became successful. Catholics quickly expanded their parochial school system, consolidated political power, especially in the cities, and in the twentieth century began to move, *on their own terms,* into the American mainstream. Aided by strong leaders in a vigorous hierarchy, proud of their religious and ethnic traditions, growing by immigration and natural increase from one per cent of the population in 1790 to seventeen in 1907, they helped to transform a Protestant America into a pluralistic America.

In retrospect one sees how much Catholics gained from being white in white America, even though in 1859 they thought that a Negro child would have fared better in Boston. Today the differences between Black Power and Catholic Power are more salient than the similarities. Catholic Power stemmed partly from efforts by the Protestant majority to *force* Romanists to become assimilated; Black Power has reflected white *refusal* to permit Negroes to enter the American mainstream. While Catholics fought "integration," Negroes often sought it unsuccessfully. Some Protestants tried to compel Catholics to attend the common school, but Negroes usually had to attend schools segregated by law or custom. Catholic Power has changed its character as Americans have become more tolerant of differences and dissent expressed in religious terms; Black

[7] Samuel Spear, *Religion and the State, Or the Bible and the Public Schools* (New York: Dodd, Mead & Co., 1876), p. 371.

[8] Billington, *op. cit.,* ch. vi; Dorchester, *op. cit.,* pp. 85, 115 ff.

[9] John Higham, *Strangers in the Land: Patterns of American Nativism, 1860–1925* (New York: Atheneum, 1966), pp. 28–29.

Power reveals a continuing pattern of bigotry about differences of race.

By and large, Negroes have lacked the strong hierarchy and leadership provided by the Church, the proud ethnic traditions (despite recent interest in African culture), and the comparatively strong family and national ties of the Catholic immigrants. Carried to America by force, ineradicably marked by color, with folkways and personality shattered by slavery, Negroes have faced discrimination far more severe than that experienced by Catholics even in the worst periods of oppression. The call for Black Power has resulted mostly from anger, despair, and desperation.

Still, in its more constructive forms, the doctrine of Black Power stems from frustrations and aims at goals similar to those of the advocates of Catholic Power. It is one of the ironies of history that so many of the descendants of the pioneers of Catholic Power should find the search for Black Power so incomprehensible and so threatening.

JOHN H. FISCHER | ***Realities of Education in Our Time***

When George Counts asked in 1932, "Dare the schools build a new social order?" the response could hardly have been called resounding. Whatever it was the country needed in those Depression days, not many expected to find it in the schools.

Two wars, a technological revolution, and a massive social upheaval have put a different face upon the matter. No longer is education the optional affair it was a generation ago. Almost overnight the people of America have discovered that what they have so long and so casually been saying about education is actually true. The easy rhetoric about the nation's reliance on its schools has become an uneasy reality. Every hope modern man entertains, every competence he needs, every effort he makes to cope with the problems that beset him ultimately requires some form of learning.

The unfinished business now facing the school is enough to take the measure of the best institutions and the best men, but the prospect need not intimidate us. To be sure, many of our problems are unprecedented, but so were the ones our predecessors faced. In 1870, the high schools of the United States enrolled 80,000 students. Had the teachers and school boards of that day been told that in less than a century there would be

16,000,000 high school students, they could have been forgiven for calling the prediction absurd and the task impossible. But the unimaginable has become a fact and yesterday's impossibility today's routine. While the population of the country increased five times, attendance in the secondary schools grew two-hundred-fold.

More recent accomplishments are hardly less impressive. In the nineteen fifties we were deploring the unreadiness of the colleges to receive the burden that was clearly foreshadowed by the post-war birth rate. As we became aware of the need and sensed its urgency, we found ways to meet it. Today the colleges are accommodating twice the number of students they enrolled in the early fifties, and the expansion continues. New community colleges are appearing at the rate of one a week. Many institutions are establishing supplementary programs for students who heretofore would rarely have thought of going to college or found a welcome there if they had.

Nor have the gains been only quantitative. Although the quality of the curriculum in many schools still leaves much to be desired, the improvements of the last decade are quite remarkable. Advancement has come so rapidly and on so broad a front in secondary schools that the very college faculties that led the earlier criticism of the schools now find themselves under heavy pressure to improve their own offerings.

Despite numerous reasons for satisfaction and the many schools that give us proper cause for pride, there is nonetheless a widely shared sense of uneasiness about the schools. It is a feeling rather different from the atmosphere of the nineteen fifties. The main complaint then was that academic standards were too low and the performance of students, particularly the able ones, below what should have been expected of them. Our concerns today center more on the shortcomings of the school system as a system. The specific questions being asked are both more fundamental and more complex than those of a few years ago:

Why is it so difficult to bring about changes in the schools?

How can parents, particularly in large cities, have a more effective voice in school affairs?

What role should teachers have in policy making?

What part should the schools play in new efforts to combat poverty and deprivation?

What is the appropriate relationship of the school to other public and private agencies that influence the development of the individual and the shaping of the culture?

To deal with these queries we must begin by re-examining the assumptions on which our school system is constructed. The mechanism we are employing for present tasks was designed long ago and for quite different work. The prototype institution of our system was the single-room schoolhouse devised to shelter children from six to fourteen years of age who could reach it on foot from their homes. The curriculum promised simple but adequate preparation for the requirements of a simple, rural, and intellectually undemanding culture. Given the existing circumstances, the only, hence the best, agency for establishing, governing and evaluating the performance of such a school was a group of local citizens. It was unimaginable that the information or wisdom to render policy decisions would not be available within the district the school was meant to serve. And that district was a circle whose radius was the distance a six year-old could cover in an hour's walk.

The first notion of optimum district size, and the initial concept of the neighborhood school it embodied, has changed a good deal in the last ten or fifteen decades. For half a century the one-room schoolhouse has been disappearing at the rate of 3000 a year and for reasons both clear and persuasive. Better physical facilities, more varied and flexible curricula, well-trained teachers, and expert supervision have been accepted as more consequential in the education of children than the benefits of smaller units and more closely held control.

Yet, despite the success of these reforms, the view that the school's tasks are best determined within the local district, and that locally made policy decisions are inherently and invariably superior, persists as a fundamental assumption. To question that belief is, for many Americans, tantamount to disputing the validity of the Declaration of Independence. The heart of much of the difficulty we now face in formulating school policy is the need to distinguish and to interrelate the rights of the individual and the conditions requisite to maintaining a community of free men.

We are reluctant to face the truth that the nature of our communities and the forces that affect them have changed much more rapidly than our readiness to recognize the changes or to respond to them. This is not the first time in human experience that preoccupation with old assumptions has diverted attention from new facts, but the nostalgia and inertia we exhibit regarding the operation of schools differ sharply from our attitude toward other institutions.

In the world of free business enterprise, for example, our behavior is strikingly different. The great-grandson of the farmer who built the one-room schoolhouse in the corner of his pasture would consider ridiculous any suggestion that his operations should be controlled wholly by what happens in his county. He buys his supplies and sells his crops in a nationwide market. His cooperative spans the continent and much of the information he uses every day comes from commodity exchanges or experiment stations thousands of miles away.

The counterpart of the local miller or distiller who took his ancestor's grain is now a corporation of widely diversified interests which finances the country. Its directors would consider incompetent, if not insane, any executive who thought that a particular plant should be subject entirely to the control of local residents or its policies based only on local needs. The company adapts its advertising to local circumstances, but its advertisements are planned and placed by agencies with nationwide perspective. And the chairman of the board enjoys the highest esteem for his vigorous devotion to the American way of life.

The point, of course, is that we would not expect a business to prosper today unless it reflected in its operations the breadth of the social and economic world in which it lives and to which it must respond. Far from resisting the widening of that world, the corporation that thrives welcomes the chance and finds in it greater resources, more attractive incentives, and both the opportunity and the stimulus to continuous innovation and renovation.

In the management of schools, response to the wider world has been at best reluctant and not infrequently recalcitrant. Many a town that has waged an aggressive campaign to acquire a local branch of a national corporation has had to be dragged, kicking and screaming, into consolidation with a high school two miles down the road.

In proposing that our schools might be improved by relying somewhat less on practices devised to meet nineteenth-century circumstances, I am by no means suggesting that reliance on local initiative and responsibility be abandoned. What I do argue is that we should examine questions of educational strategy and policy with enough objectivity and rationality to determine in what respects they are actually local in character and when local action might be expected to yield the best results. There are problems and circumstances in which a locally centered approach is not only more appropriate but probably superior to any other.

It is no less true of education, however, than of other major enterprises that the interconnectedness of modern life gives rise to conditions and needs that affect simultaneously and in similar ways the lives of people in all parts of the country. The artificial and often meaningless boundaries that separate school districts bear less and less relation socially, economically, or geographically to the problems with which they must deal.

Young people have to acquire facility in mathematics and science not because their town considers science important or because a nearby university has installed a cyclotron, but because of the character of the twentieth century. The times impose that goal as an inescapable imperative and local preference cannot modify that fact. Nor do most school districts possess the capability to analyze the need or to design a curriculum to meet it.

The school must help its students to acquire a reasonable working knowledge of many more cultures and countries than their own, but, again, not because a local curriculum committee happens to think well of the idea. No citizen who lacks such knowledge can hope even to be aware of many of the major issues of the modern world, much less react to them constructively. Any school that ignores that requirement neglects its students and reduces the prospect for democracy.

In the difficult dilemmas of race relations, no school system is morally free to ignore its broader duty. The inequities that beset the country have sprung from roots in the history of every state, and every community shares the obligation to confront the consequences. Dealing with so urgent a national problem calls for more than pious dedication to the sanctity of local option.

The time has come to stop quibbling about ancient prerogatives and to abandon outmoded preconceptions. The progress of all free institutions and particularly of democratic government, school government included, will continue to depend upon the work of creative and courageous individuals and minorities; but efforts to serve the common good should not be circumscribed by petty preference nor restricted by the limitations of narrow localism.

The most relevant index for appraising the schools of any community is not the number of its policies that were written by local officials. A better gauge is the degree to which its children are enabled to make the most of their capacities; to acquire the knowledge and skills the world requires of them; and to find, on terms of genuine equality, the opportunity and the incentive to lead lives of dignity and accomplishment.

John Dewey summarized it well: "What the best and wisest parent desires for his own child, that must the community want for all its children. Any other ideal is narrow and unlovely; acted upon, it will destroy democracy."

The school community is no longer what it was in 1899 when those lines were written and certainly not what it was in 1830—or even 1930. In many respects, the community is now the country. If our mechanisms for releasing and managing the energies of education are to be relevant to the times and the country we live in now, they had better be constructed upon the facts we face, not the assumptions we have inherited.

Another assumption that we are reappraising and beginning to reject is the idea of the school as a sequence of sieves through which only the ablest and most deserving minority can hope to survive to the top. This assumption is being replaced by the view that the public school is obliged to do the most and the best it can for every child, regardless of the quality or quantity of his talent; that it is the school's responsibility to find ways to teach all its pupils rather than only those who happen to respond to its traditional procedures.

At the same time school people and the psychologists who advise them are discovering more and more reason to question the customary tests of children's ability. Every day the evidence becomes more impressive that the differences children display in school are due more to their experiences and less to their heredity than we have ever before been willing to believe. We are finding it less easy to be certain about the categories to which we assign children and the labels we put on them. The old clichés about the children who "have it" and those who don't are turning out in many cases to be cruel mistakes. Too often it has been the school people who didn't "have it." What we have lacked has been the faith and the ingenuity to discover children's potentialities and the skill to encourage their development.

Benjamin Bloom estimates that whether a child grows up in a culturally abundant environment or in a deprived one can make a difference of twenty points in his I.Q. That figure happens to come pretty close to the difference in average I.Q. between slum schools and good suburban districts. The question is unavoidable: How much of the retardation in slum schools is due to the nature of the children and how much to the circumstances, including the schools, in which they grow up?

Another thing we know is that a child's future is very strongly influenced by what happens to him before he is six years old. There is good evidence that fifty percent of the variation in intelligence at the age of seventeen is predictable by age four, and another thirty percent by age eight. There is nothing new about the general notion that bending the young twig inclines the tree, but the documentation is new. And so are the implications for action that, if taken wisely and in time, might enable literally millions of children to live more productive and satisfying lives than they will if we continue only our present efforts. To fail to establish as quickly as possible suitable programs for three-, four-, and five-year-olds will be to deny those children opportunities they should have and can be given; and to saddle the rest of the community for years to come with the financial and social consequences of *our* shortsightedness.

We assume and state as a cardinal principle of our way of life that this is an open society. Every one of us, we insist, is entitled to as good a chance as his neighbor. But if we are honest we must ask what real hope there is for maintaining a genuinely open society if our communities and our schools continue to become more and more stratified. For it is a fact that in significant ways the problem of segregation is worsening.

Twelve years after the Brown decision, nine out of every ten Negro students are in schools in which the majority, and often all, of the pupils are Negroes while the vast majority of white students attend schools that are almost wholly white. This is no regional problem, but a national one and many of the most serious situations are in northern cities. In a sample of seventy-five typical urban school systems, the United States Civil Rights Commission found that in 1965–66, seventy-five per cent of the Negro children were in schools where ninety per cent or more of their schoolmates were of their own race. A whole school generation after 1954 the fundamental problem of racial isolation in schools still plagues the nation and in many places is growing worse. In St. Louis, in 1954, 27,000 Negroes were enrolled in segregated schools. In 1965, 52,000 were in schools enrolling ninety per cent to 100 per cent Negro students. In Milwaukee, in 1950, 1,300 Negroes were enrolled in such schools; in 1965 the number was 14,000.

Such situations are easy to describe, but hard to correct. In the twenty-four largest metropolitan areas, which contain over half of the urban population of the country, virtually the entire increase in white population between 1940 and 1960 was accounted for by suburban growth. The central cities lost a million and a half white residents and gained two million Negroes. The separation of the relatively advantaged and the relatively disadvantaged by political boundaries and school district lines is one of the glaring facts of our time.

The modern city, in point of fact, is not the central city alone, but the entire metropolitan area. Yet we continue to separate our urban communities into enclaves that divide our people from each other along lines of class, caste, and color. Although it is inconceivable that any of these subdivisions could possibly exist independently, we continue to behave as though they could. The truth is that each part of the urban complex is a member of the others, and that all are mutually interdependent. Why can we not bring ourselves to see and to admit that in the long run it cannot be well for any of us until it is well for all?

Would it not make sense to begin joint metropolitan cooperation among our school systems? The common school, in which Horace Mann saw the best hope of democracy, could again in our time become "the great equalizer of the conditions of men,—the balance wheel of the social machinery." But this is not likely to happen so long as we tolerate the separation of racial and social groups which now characterizes so many of our communities and our schools.

To correct this condition ways must be devised to bring children of different backgrounds to school together. In most metropolitan areas this means that city and suburban pupils must share the same classrooms. The most promising device yet proposed for accomplishing this purpose is the metropolitan school park. The park would be a large campus on which would be located enough schools, of whatever size desired, to accommodate children from a large segment of the city and the adjacent suburbs. The district served by such a park can be thought of as a pie slice of the central city and surrounding suburbia, the park located on the edge of the city and drawing children from both directions. A ring of school parks encircling the city could furnish a setting for education at a level of quality that most of our children have never even imagined, much less experienced. Each park could be so governed as to give both city and suburban parents a wholly new range of opportunities to participate in school affairs.

At one stroke, if we could but muster the resolution to do it, we could equalize educational opportunities for thousands of children, end the stranglehold of administrative centralization, combine the cultural and economic resources of the city and the suburbs, and take a giant stride toward rational metropolitan co-operation.

Obviously such action would require radical changes in our customary approaches to school problems. New structures for policy making, administration and finance would be needed. Local governments, state authorities, and federal agencies would all be involved. Large scale and long range community planning commitments would be required. In brief, we would have to attack our educational problems on a strategic, rather than a tactical level. But it should by now be clear that education has become so important in the life of this country, and of every community in it, that small-scale tinkering with existing machinery, or the mere multiplication of present weaknesses cannot meet the needs of the times.

No one scheme can produce a panacea, no single reform will save us. But of one thing we can be certain: The grievous human problems that now plague our people will not solve themselves. They will respond only to far-sighted, resolute, and bold action. That action will have to be conceived on a scale commensurate with the conditions to be corrected, and it must be undertaken with the vigor that we reserve for our most important tasks.

Selected References

BAILYN, BERNARD. *Education in the Forming of American Society: Needs and Opportunities for Study*. Chapel Hill: University of North Carolina Press, 1960.

BIDWELL, CHARLES. "The Moral Significance of the Common School," *History of Education Quarterly* (Fall 1966), pp. 50–91.

BRUBACHER, JOHN S. *A History of the Problems of Education*, 2nd. ed. New York: McGraw-Hill Company, 1966.

BUTTS, R. FREEMAN. "Civilization-Building and the Modernization Process: A Framework for the Reinterpretation of the History of Education," *History of Education Quarterly* (Summer 1967), pp. 147–181.

CREMIN, LAWRENCE A. *The Transformation of the School: Progressivism in American Education, 1876–1957*. New York: Alfred A. Knopf, 1961.

GOOD, H. G. *A History of American Education*, 2nd ed. New York: The Macmillan Company, 1964.

GREENE, MAXINE. "The Professional Significance of the History of Education," *History of Education Quarterly* (Summer 1967), pp. 182–190.

HOFSTADTER, RICHARD. *Anti-Intellectualism in American Life*. New York: Alfred A. Knopf, 1963.

JONES, HOWARD MUMFORD. *O Strange New World: American Culture, the Formative Years*. New York: Viking Press, 1964.

KRUG, EDWARD A. *Salient Dates in American Education*. New York: Harper and Row, 1966.

PERKINSON, HENRY J. *The Imperfect Panacea: American Faith in Education, 1865–1965*. New York: Random House, 1968.

POWER, EDWARD J., *Main Currents in the History of Education*. New York: McGraw-Hill Company, 1963.

SANDS, LESTER B., and RICHARD E. GROSS. *The History of Education Chart: A Time-Line of Scope and Perspective*. Cleveland: World Publishing Company, 1967.

SEIFMAN, ELI. "Education or Emigration: The Schism Within the African Colonization Movement, 1865–75," *History of Education Quarterly* (Spring 1967), pp. 36–57.

SMITH, WILSON. "The Teacher in Puritan Culture," *Harvard Educational Review* (Fall 1966), pp. 394–411.

TOPPIN, EDGAR A. "Walter White and the Atlanta NAACP's Fight for Equal Schools," *History of Education Quarterly* (Spring 1967), pp. 3–21.

TYACK, DAVID B. *Turning Points in American Educational History.* Waltham, Mass.: Blaisdell Publishing Co., 1967.

WELTER, RUSH. *Popular Education and Democratic Thought in America.* New York: Columbia University Press, 1962.

WIGGINS, GLADYS A. *Education and Nationalism: An Historical Interpretation of American Education.* New York: McGraw-Hill Company, 1962.

WOODWARD, C. VANN. *The Comparative Approach to American History.* New York: Basic Books, 1968.

SECTION III | *Aims and Purposes of American Education*

IT IS FITTING that the study of education should deal with an inquiry into its aims and purposes by philosophers because philosophical reflection has its roots in educational concerns. From Plato through Herbart and Dewey runs the line of inquiry into one of man's most important ventures. The common goals, beliefs, and aspirations of a society and the aims and purposes of the schools it sets up imply an underlying system of values. One of the jobs of the philosopher is to ask fundamental questions regarding these values and to force a continuous examination of them. This examination provides the opportunity for a continuing dialogue regarding the ends and means of education.

Those engaged professionally in education are obligated to analyze and to evaluate their fundamental commitments guiding their daily activities. Such a task is indeed difficult, yet what alternative ways of operating are available? What happens when teachers give little or no thought to the ends that should be shaping their actions? William H. Burton describes the result.

> Uncounted thousands of teachers proceed everyday without objectives, without anything remotely approximating an objective. They attempt only to cover the text, to follow the course of study, to go through the motions of teaching. Teachers without clear objectives cannot be other than incompetent.[1]

The reader is asked to think about the aims of education from two points of view: first, the values chosen by certain groups in his society; second,

[1] William H. Burton, *The Guidance of Learning Activities*, 3d ed. (New York: Appleton-Century-Crofts, 1962), pp. 126–127.

his own functioning as a prospective teacher in his society. The readings represent significant statements of alternate aims and purposes of education that should help the reader to evaluate his own position and to rethink his own values.

In the first selection, Whitehead covers at least four of the aims of education that are also treated in later selections. The vocational, moral, and "cultured gentlemen" purposes receive his endorsement; mental discipline or the "training of compartments of the mind" comes off badly. Two of the phrases used by Whitehead in this essay have become quite famous and are often quoted: the first is his denunciation of "inert ideas," and the second is "You may not divide the seamless coat of learning." Students may want to analyze these concepts in the light of Whitehead's views of knowledge and learning.

In Maritain's essay the student will find the Catholic philosophy of education. There is considerable agreement among Catholic educators about the philosophical bases of education, and these are analyzed with great clarity by Maritain. This selection is offered here because the Thomist views have exerted and are still exerting a considerable influence on the thinking of our Western civilization in general and upon education in particular.

Hutchins' work in higher education and as a critic of public education is widely known. As a classical humanist he has advocated a return to the liberal arts curriculum that has its roots in the Greek educational philosophy. According to Hutchins the aim of education should be the same for all men, that is, everywhere and always, in every mode of society and in every condition of life. This means that the ends of education are absolute and universal. It will benefit the student to discuss Hutchins' philosophy in the light of Maritain's point of view.

Dewey has been called the greatest educational philosopher since Plato. Whether or not this is true, his numerous books and articles have had profound influence on education, not only in America but throughout the globe. In order to understand the aims of American education and how they have evolved, it is desirable to consider the nature and function of aims. For this purpose, a statement by Dewey has been included here. In these articles, attention should be given to the main points of the analysis—that is, to the nature, the function, and the criteria of good aims—and to the nature and structure of the subject matter.

Professor Brameld is associated with the school of thought that visualizes the school as the agency most responsible for the reconstruction of society. Professor Brameld in the article included in this section stresses the fact that such behavioral sciences as cultural anthropology and psychiatry offer new bases for organization of subject matter, processes of teaching and learning, and formulation of purposes for school and society.

Terms such as *other directed, organization man,* and *mass communication* have come into our language to reflect the direction our society is taking. Van Cleve Morris decries the loss of the private personal life. He sees the task of education as the development of the individual who must recognize his conditions of existence and should be helped to develop values for himself.

In the concluding article of this section, "Education's 'Romantic' Critics," Peter Schrag finds that new critics—Edgar Z. Friedenberg, Paul Goodman, Jules Henry, John Holt, and others—are not concerned with developing a consistent voice or a systematic program of educational philosophy and practice. They attack established practices and conventional assumptions, and at the same time maintain that "if education does not deal with the humanity of children, it does not deal with anything."

The wide range of ideas in these readings concerning the nature of man or the purposes of education, capped by an attack on the traditional philosophical approach, should leave the reader with many unanswered questions. His questions, and those offered in the following paragraph, should lead him on to deeper analysis and more questions, avoiding crystallization of thought and attitude at a point far too early in his development as a student in the demanding discipline of education.

Some questions that should help the reader in his examination of writings on educational aims and purposes are: What is the nature of society and of the individual and the role of the school? What value system underlies each author's aims for education? How do differing conceptions of educating, teaching, and learning affect the role of the school in a society? How have these varying points of view forced an examination of previously held personal beliefs? In what manner do these conceptual frameworks support or conflict with the historical assumptions upon which the American educational system is based? What unique contribution has each author made to a more sophisticated concept of the nature of education?

ALFRED NORTH WHITEHEAD | **The Aims of Education**

Culture is activity of thought, and receptiveness to beauty and humane feeling. Scraps of information have nothing to do with it. A merely well-informed man is the most useless bore on God's earth. What we should aim at producing is men who possess both culture and expert knowledge in some special direction. Their expert knowledge will give them the ground to start from, and their culture will lead them as deep as philosophy and as high as art. We have to remember that the valuable intellectual development is self-development, and that it mostly takes place between the ages of sixteen and thirty. As to training, the most important part is given by mothers before the age of twelve. A saying due to Archbishop Temple illustrates my meaning. Surprise was expressed at the success in after-life of a man, who as a boy at Rugby had been somewhat undistinguished. He answered, "It is not what they are at eighteen, it is what they become afterwards that matters."

In training a child to activity of thought, above all things we must beware of what I will call "inert ideas"—that is to say, ideas that are merely received into the mind without being utilised, or tested, or thrown into fresh combinations.

In the history of education, the most striking phenomenon is that schools of learning, which at one epoch are alive with a ferment of genius, in a succeeding generation exhibit merely pedantry and routine. The reason is, that they are overladen with inert ideas. Education with inert ideas is not only useless: it is, above all things, harmful—*Corruptio optimi, pessima.* Except at rare intervals of intellectual ferment, education in the past has been radically infected with inert ideas. That is the reason why uneducated clever women, who have seen much of the world, are in middle life so much the most cultured part of the community. They have been saved from this horrible burden of inert ideas. Every intellectual revolution which has ever stirred humanity into greatness has been a passionate protest against inert ideas. Then, alas, with pathetic ignorance of human psychology, it has proceeded by some educational scheme to bind humanity afresh with inert ideas of its own fashioning.

Let us now ask how in our system of education we are to guard against this mental dryrot. We enunciate two educational commandments, "Do not teach too many subjects," and again, "What you teach, teach thoroughly."

The result of teaching small parts of a large number of subjects is the passive reception of disconnected ideas, not illumined with any spark of vitality. Let the main ideas which are introduced into a child's education be few and important, and let them be thrown into every combination possible. The child should make them his own, and should understand their application here and now in the circumstances of his actual life. From the very beginning of his education, the child should experience the joy of discovery. The discovery which he has to make, is that general ideas give an understanding of that stream of events which pours through his life, which is his life. By understanding I mean more than a mere logical analysis, though that is included. I mean "understanding" in the sense in which it is used in the French proverb, "To understand all, is to forgive all." Pedants sneer at an education which is useful. But if education is not useful, what is it? Is it a talent, to be hidden away in a napkin? Of course, education should be useful, whatever your aim in life. It was useful to Saint Augustine and it was useful to Napoleon. It is useful, because understanding is useful.

I pass lightly over that understanding which should be given by the literary side of education. Nor do I wish to be supposed to pronounce on the relative merits of a classical or a modern curriculum. I would only remark that the understanding which we want is an understanding of an insistent present. The only use of a knowledge of the past is to equip us for the present. No more deadly harm can be done to young minds than by depreciation of the present. The present contains all that there is. It is holy ground; for it is the past, and it is the future. At the same time it must be observed that an age is no less past if it existed two hundred years ago than if it existed two thousand years ago. Do not be deceived by the pedantry of dates. The ages of Shakespeare and of Molière are nc less past than are the ages of Sophocles and of Virgil. The communion of saints is a great and inspiring assemblage, but it has only one possible hall of meeting, and that is, the present; and the mere lapse of time through which any particular group of saints must travel to reach that meeting-place, makes very little difference.

Passing now to the scientific and logical side of education, we remember that here also ideas which are not utilised are positively harmful. By utilising an idea, I mean relating it to that stream, compounded of sense perceptions, feelings, hopes, desires, and of mental activities adjusting thought to thought, which forms our life. I can imagine a set of beings which might fortify their souls by passively reviewing disconnected ideas.

Humanity is not built that way—except perhaps some editors of newspapers.

In scientific training, the first thing to do with an idea is to prove it. But allow me for one moment to extend the meaning of "prove"; I mean—to prove its worth. Now an idea is not worth much unless the propositions in which it is embodied are true. Accordingly an essential part of the proof of an idea is the proof, either by experiment or by logic, of the truth of the propositions. But it is not essential that this proof of the truth should constitute the first introduction to the idea. After all, its assertion by the authority of respectable teachers is sufficient evidence to begin with. In our first contact with a set of propositions, we commence by appreciating their importance. That is what we all do in after-life. We do not attempt, in the strict sense, to prove or to disprove anything, unless its importance makes it worthy of that honour. These two processes of proof, in the narrow sense, and of appreciation, do not require a rigid separation in time. Both can be proceeded with nearly concurrently. But in so far as either process must have the priority, it should be that of appreciation by use.

Furthermore, we should not endeavour to use propositions in isolation. Emphatically I do not mean, a neat little set of experiments to illustrate Proposition I and then the proof of Proposition I, a neat little set of experiments to illustrate Proposition II and then the proof of Proposition II, and so on to the end of the book. Nothing could be more boring. Interrelated truths are utilised *en bloc,* and the various propositions are employed in any order, and with any reiteration. Choose some important applications of your theoretical subject; and study them concurrently with the systematic theoretical exposition. Keep the theoretical exposition short and simple, but let it be strict and rigid so far as it goes. It should not be too long for it to be easily known with thoroughness and accuracy. The consequences of a plethora of half-digested theoretical knowledge are deplorable. Also the theory should not be muddled up with the practice. The child should have no doubt when it is proving and when it is utilising. My point is that what is proved should be utilised, and that what is utilised should—so far as is practicable—be proved. I am far from asserting that proof and utilisation are the same thing.

At this point of my discourse, I can most directly carry forward my argument in the outward form of a digression. We are only just realising that the art and science of education require a genius and a study of their own; and that this genius and this science are more than a bare knowledge of some branch of science or of literature. This truth was partially perceived in the past generation; and headmasters, somewhat crudely, were apt to supersede learning in their colleagues by requiring left-hand bowling and a taste for football. But culture is more than cricket, and more than football, and more than extent of knowledge.

Education is the acquisition of the art of the utilisation of knowledge. This is an art very difficult to impart. Whenever a text-book is written of real educational worth, you may be quite certain that some reviewer will say that it will be difficult to teach from it. Of course it will be difficult to teach from it. If it were easy, the book ought to be burned; for it cannot be educational. In education, as elsewhere, the broad primrose path leads to a nasty place. This evil path is represented by a book or a set of lectures which will practically enable the student to learn by heart all the questions likely to be asked at the next external examination. And I may say in passing that no educational system is possible unless every question directly asked of a pupil at any examination is either framed or modified by the actual teacher of that pupil in that subject. The external assessor may report on the curriculum or on the performance of the pupils, but never should be allowed to ask the pupil a question which has not been strictly supervised by the actual teacher, or at least inspired by a long conference with him. There are a few exceptions to this rule, but they are exceptions, and could easily be allowed for under the general rule.

We now return to my previous point, that theoretical ideas should always find important applications within the pupil's curriculum. This is not an easy doctrine to apply, but a very hard one. It contains within itself the problem of keeping knowledge alive, of preventing it from becoming inert, which is the central problem of all education.

The best procedure will depend on several factors, none of which can be neglected, namely, the genius of the teacher, the intellectual type of the pupils, their prospects in life, the opportunities offered by the immediate surroundings of the school, and allied factors of this sort. It is for this reason that the uniform external examination is so deadly. We do not denounce it because we are cranks, and like denouncing established things. We are not so childish. Also, of course, such examinations have their use in testing slackness. Our reason of dislike is very definite and very practical. It kills the best part of culture. When you analyse in the light of experience the central task of education, you find that its successful accomplishment depends on a delicate adjustment of many variable factors. The reason is that we are dealing with human minds, and not with dead matter. The evocation of curiosity, of judgment, of the power of mastering a complicated tangle of circumstances, the use of theory in giving foresight in special cases—all these powers are not to be imparted by a set rule embodied in one schedule of examination subjects.

I appeal to you, as practical teachers. With good discipline, it is always possible to pump into the minds of a class a certain quantity of inert knowledge. You take a textbook and make them learn it. So far, so good. The child then knows how to solve a quadratic equation. But what is the point of teaching a child to solve a quadratic equation? There is a traditional answer to this question. It runs thus: The mind is an instrument, you first sharpen it, and then use it; the acquisition of the power of solving a quadratic equation is part of the process of sharpening the mind. Now there is just enough truth in this answer to have made it live through the ages. But for all its half-truth, it embodies a radical error which bids fair to stifle the genius of the modern world. I do not know who was first responsible for this analogy of the mind to a dead instrument. For aught I know, it may have been one of the seven wise men of Greece, or a committee of the whole lot of them. Whoever was the originator, there can be no doubt of the authority which it has acquired by the continuous approval bestowed upon it by eminent persons. But whatever its weight of authority, whatever the high approval which it can quote, I have no hesitation in denouncing it as one of the most fatal, erroneous, and dangerous conceptions ever introduced into the theory of education. The mind is never passive; it is a perpetual activity, delicate, receptive, responsive to stimulus. You cannot postpone its life until you have sharpened it. Whatever interest attaches to your subject-matter must be evoked here and now; whatever powers you are strengthening in the pupil, must be exercised here and now; whatever possibilities of mental life your teaching should impart, must be exhibited here and now. That is the golden rule to education, and a very difficult rule to follow.

The difficulty is just this: the apprehension of general ideas, intellectual habits of mind, and pleasurable interest in mental achievement can be evoked by no form of words, however accurately adjusted. All practical teachers know that education is a patient process of mastery of details, minute by minute, hour by hour, day by day. There is no royal road to learning through an airy path of brilliant generalisations. There is a proverb about the difficulty of seeing the wood because of the trees. That difficulty is exactly the point which I am enforcing. The problem of education is to make the pupil see the wood by means of the trees.

The solution which I am urging, is to eradicate the fatal disconnection of subjects which kills the vitality of our modern curriculum. There is only one subject-matter for education, and that is Life in all its manifestations. Instead of this single unity, we offer children—Algebra, from which nothing follows; Geometry, from which nothing follows; Science, from which nothing follows; History, from which nothing follows; a Couple of Languages, never mastered; and lastly, most dreary of all, Literature, represented by plays of Shakespeare, with philological notes and short analyses of plot and character to be in substance committed to memory. Can such a list be said to represent Life, as it is known in the midst of the living of it? The best that can be said of it is, that it is a rapid table of contents which a deity might run over in his mind while he was thinking of creating a world, and had not yet determined how to put it together.

Let us now return to quadratic equations. We still have on hand the unanswered question, "Why should children be taught their solution?" Unless quadratic equations fit into a connected curriculum, of course there is no reason to teach anything about them. Furthermore, extensive as should be the place of mathematics in a complete culture, I am a little doubtful whether for many types of boys algebraic solutions of quadratic equations do not lie on the specialist side of mathematics. I may here remind you that as yet I have not said anything of the psychology or the content of the specialism, which is so necessary a part of an ideal education. But all that is an evasion of our real question, and I merely state it in order to avoid being misunderstood in my answer.

Quadratic equations are part of algebra, and algebra is the intellectual instrument which has been created for rendering clear the quantitative aspects of the world. There is no getting out of it. Through and through the world is infected with quantity. To talk sense, is to talk in quantities. It is no use saying that the nation is large,—How large? It is no use saying that radium is scarce,—How scarce? You cannot evade quantity. You may fly to poetry and to music, and quantity and number will face you in your rhythms and your octaves. Elegant intellects which despise the theory of quantity, are but half developed. They are more to be pitied than blamed. The scraps of gibberish, which in their school-days were taught to them in the name of algebra, deserve some contempt.

This question of the degeneration of algebra into gibberish, both in word and in fact, affords a pathetic instance of the uselessness of reforming educational schedules without a clear conception of the attributes which you wish to evoke in the living minds of the children. A few years ago there was an outcry that school algebra was in need of reform, but there was a general agreement that graphs would put everything right. So all sorts of things were extruded, and graphs were introduced. So far as I can see, with no sort of idea behind them, but just graphs. Now every examination paper has one or two questions on graphs. Personally, I am an enthusiastic adherent of graphs. But I wonder whether as yet we have gained very much. You cannot put life into any schedule of general education unless you succeed in exhibiting its relation to some essential characteristic of all intelligent or emotional perception. It is a hard saying, but it is true; and I do not see how to make it any easier. In making these little formal alterations you are beaten by the very nature of things. You are pitted against too skillful an adversary, who will see to it that the pea is always under the other thimble.

Reformation must begin at the other end. First, you must make up your mind as to those quantitative aspects of the world which are simple enough to be introduced into general education; then a schedule of algebra should be framed which will about find its exemplification in these applications. We need not fear for our pet graphs, they will be there in plenty when we once begin to treat algebra as a serious means of studying the world. Some of the simplest applications will be found in the quantities which occur in the simplest study of society. The curves of history are more vivid and more informing than the dry catalogues of names and dates which comprise the greater part of that arid school study. What purpose is effected by a catalogue of undistinguished kings and queens? Tom, Dick, or Harry, they are all dead. General resurrections are failures, and are better postponed. The quantitative flux of the forces of modern society is capable of very simple exhibition. Meanwhile, the idea of the variable, of the function, of rate of change, of equations and their solution, of elimination, are being studied as an abstract science for their own sake. Not, of course, in the pompous phrases with which I am alluding to them here, but with that iteration of simple special cases proper to teaching.

If this course be followed, the route from Chaucer to the Black Death, from the Black Death to modern Labour troubles, will connect the tales of the mediæval pilgrims with the abstract science of algebra, both yielding diverse aspects of that single theme, Life. I know what most of you are thinking at this point. It is that the exact course which I have sketched out is not the particular one which you would have chosen, or even see how to work. I quite agree. I am not claiming that I could do it myself. But your objection is the precise reason why a common external examination system is fatal to education. The process of exhibiting the applications of knowledge must, for its success, essentially depend on the character of the pupils and the genius of the teacher. Of course I have left out the easiest applications with which most of us are more at home, I mean the quantitative sides of sciences, such as mechanics and physics.

Again, in the same connection we plot the statistics of social phenomena against the time. We then eliminate the time between suitable pairs. We can speculate how far we have exhibited a real causal connection, or how far a mere temporal coincidence. We notice that we might have plotted against the time one set of statistics for one country and another set for another country, and thus, with suitable choice of subjects, have obtained graphs which certainly exhibited mere coincidence. Also other graphs exhibit obvious causal connections. We wonder how to discriminate. And so are drawn on as far as we will.

But in considering this description, I must beg you to remember what I have been insisting on above. In the first place, one train of thought will not suit all groups of children. For example, I should expect that artisan children will want something more concrete and, in a sense, swifter than I have set down here. Perhaps I am wrong, but that is what I should guess. In the second place, I am not contemplating one beautiful lecture stimulating, once and for all, an admiring class. That is not the way in which education proceeds. No; all the time the pupils are hard at work solving examples, drawing graphs, and making experiments, until they have a thorough hold on the whole subject. I am describing the interspersed explanations, the directions which should be given to their thoughts. The pupils have got to be made to feel that they are studying something, and are not merely executing intellectual minuets.

Finally, if you are teaching pupils for some general examination, the problem of sound teaching is greatly complicated. Have you ever noticed the zig-zag moulding round a Norman arch? The ancient work is beautiful, the modern work is hideous. The reason is, that the modern work is done to exact measure, the ancient work is varied according to the idiosyncrasy of the workman. Here it is crowded, and there it is expanded. Now the essence of getting pupils through examinations is to give equal weight to all parts of the schedule. But mankind is naturally specialist. One man sees a whole subject, where another can find only a few detached examples. I know that it seems contradictory to allow for specialism in a curriculum especially designed for a broad culture. Without contradictions the world would be simpler, and perhaps duller. But I am certain that in education wherever you exclude specialism you destroy life.

We now come to the other great branch of a general mathematical education, namely Geometry. The same principles apply. The theoretical part should be clear-cut, rigid, short, and important. Every proposition not absolutely necessary to exhibit the main connection of ideas should be cut out, but the great fundamental ideas should be all there. No omission of concepts, such as those of Similarity and Proportion. We must remember that, owing to the aid rendered by the visual presence of a figure, Geometry is a field of unequalled excellence for the exercise of the deductive faculties of reasoning. Then, of course, there follows Geometrical Drawing, with its training for the hand and eye.

But, like Algebra, Geometry and Geometrical Drawing must be extended beyond the mere circle of geometrical ideas. In an industrial neighborhood, machinery and workshop practice form the appropriate extension. For example, in the London Polytechnics this has been achieved with conspicuous success. For many secondary schools I suggest that surveying and maps are the natural applications. In particular, plane-table surveying should lead pupils to a vivid apprehension of the immediate application of geometric truths. Simple drawing apparatus, a surveyor's chain, and a surveyor's compass, should enable the pupils to rise from the survey and mensuration of a field to the construction of the map of a small district. The best education is to be found in gaining the utmost information from the simplest apparatus. The provision of elaborate instruments is greatly to be deprecated. To have constructed the map of a small district, to have considered its roads, its contours, its geology, its climate, its relation to other districts, the effects on the status of its inhabitants, will teach more history and geography than any knowledge of Perkin Warbeck or of Behren's Straits. I mean not a nebulous lecture on the subject, but a serious investigation in which the real facts are definitely ascertained by the aid of accurate theoretical knowledge. A typical mathematical problem should be: Survey such and such a field, draw a plan of it to such and such a scale, and find the area. It would be quite a good procedure to impart the necessary geometrical propositions without their proofs. Then, concurrently in the same term, the proofs of the propositions would be learnt while the survey was being made.

Fortunately, the specialist side of education presents an easier problem than does the provision of a general culture. For this there are many reasons. One is that many of the principles of procedure to be observed are the same in both cases, and it is unnecessary to recapitulate. Another reason is that specialist training takes place—or should take place—at a more advanced stage of the pupil's course, and thus there is easier material to work upon. But undoubtedly the chief reason is that the specialist study is normally a study of peculiar interest to the student. He is studying it because, for some reason, he wants to know it. This makes all the difference. The general culture is designed to foster an activity of mind; the specialist course utilises this activity. But it does not do to lay too much stress on these neat antitheses. As we have already seen, in the general course foci of special interest will arise; and similarly in the special study, the external connections of the subject drag thought outwards.

Again, there is not one course of study which merely gives general culture, and another which gives special knowledge. The subjects pursued for the sake of a general education are special subjects specially studied; and, on the other hand, one of the ways of encouraging general mental activity is to foster a special devotion. You may not divide the seamless coat of learning. What education has to impart is an intimate sense for the power of ideas, for the beauty of ideas, and for the structure of ideas, together with a particular body of knowledge which has peculiar reference to the life of the being possessing it.

The appreciation of the structure of ideas is that side of a cultured mind which can only grow under the influence of a special study. I mean that eye for the whole chessboard, for the bearing of one set of ideas on another. Nothing but a special study can give any appreciation for the exact formulation of general ideas, for their relations when formulated, for their service in the comprehension of life. A mind so disciplined should be both more abstract and more concrete. It has been trained in the comprehension of abstract thought and in the analysis of facts.

Finally, there should grow the most austere of all mental qualities; I mean the sense for style. It is an æsthetic sense, based on admiration for the direct attainment of a foreseen end, simply and without waste. Style in art, style in literature, style in science, style in logic, style in practical execution have fundamentally the same æsthetic qualities, namely, attainment and restraint. The love of a subject in itself and for itself, where it is not the sleepy pleasure of pacing a mental quarter-deck, is the love of style as manifested in that study.

Here we are brought back to the position from which we started, the utility of education. Style, in its finest sense, is the last acquirement of the educated mind; it is also the most useful. It pervades the whole being. The administrator with a sense for style hates waste; the engineer with a sense for style economises his material; the artisan with a sense for style prefers good work. Style is the ultimate morality of mind.

But above style, and above knowledge, there is something, a vague shape like fate above the Greek gods. That something is Power. Style is the fashioning of power, the restraining of power. But, after all, the power of attainment of the desired end is fundamental. The first thing is to get there. Do not bother about your style, but solve your problem, justify the ways of God to man, administer your province, or do whatever else is set before you.

Where, then, does style help? In this, with style the end is attained without side issues, without raising undesirable inflammations. With style you attain your end and nothing but your end. With style the effect of your activity is calculable, and foresight is the last gift of gods to men. With style your power is increased, for your mind is not distracted with irrelevancies, and you are more likely to attain your object. Now style is the exclusive privilege of the expert. Whoever heard of the style of an amateur painter, of the style of an amateur poet? Style is always the product of specialist study, the peculiar contribution of specialism to culture.

English education in its present phase suffers from a lack of definite aim, and from an external machinery which kills its vitality. Hitherto in this address I have been considering the aims which should govern education. In this respect England halts between two opinions. It has not decided whether to produce amateurs or experts. The profound change in the world which the nineteenth century has produced is that the growth of knowledge has given foresight. The amateur is essentially a man with appreciation and with immense versatility in mastering a given routine. But he lacks the foresight which comes from special knowledge. The object of this address is to suggest how to produce the expert without loss of the essential virtues of the amateur. The machinery of our secondary education is rigid where it should be yielding, and lax where it should be rigid. Every school is bound on pain of extinction to train its boys for a small set of definite examinations. No headmaster has a free hand to develop his general education or his specialist studies in accordance with the opportunities of his school, which are created by its staff, its environment, its class of boys, and its endowments. I suggest that no system of external tests which aims primarily at examining individual scholars can result in anything but educational waste.

Primarily it is the schools and not the scholars which should be inspected. Each school should grant its own leaving certificates, based on its own curriculum. The standards of these schools should be sampled and corrected. But the first requisite for educational reform is the school as a unit, with its approved curriculum based on its own needs, and evolved by its own staff. If we fail to secure that, we simply fall from one formalism into another, from one dung-hill of inert ideas into another.

In stating that the school is the true educational unit in any national system for the safeguarding of efficiency, I have conceived the alternative system as being the external examination of the individual scholar. But every Scylla is faced by its Charybdis—or, in more homely language, there is a ditch on both sides of the road. It will be equally fatal to education if we fall into the hands of a supervising department which is under the impression that it can divide all schools into two or three rigid categories, each type being forced to adopt a rigid curriculum. When I say that the school is the educational unit, I mean exactly what I say, no larger unit, no smaller unit. Each school must have the claim to be considered in relation to its special circumstances. The classifying of schools for some purposes is necessary. But no absolutely rigid curriculum, not modified by its own staff, should be permissible. Exactly the same principles apply, with the proper modifications, to universities and to technical colleges.

When one considers in its length and in its breadth the importance of this question of the education of a nation's young, the broken lives, the defeated hopes, the national failures, which result from the frivolous inertia with which it is treated, it is difficult to restrain within oneself a savage rage. In the conditions of modern life the rule is absolute, the race which does not value trained intelligence is doomed. Not all your heroism, not all your social charm, not all your wit, not all your victories on land or at sea, can move back the finger of fate. Today we maintain ourselves. Tomorrow science will have moved forward yet one more step, and there will be no appeal from the judgment which will then be pronounced on the uneducated.

We can be content with no less than the old summary of educational ideal which has been current at any time from the dawn of our civilisation. The essence of education is that it be religious.

Pray, what is religious education?

A religious education is an education which inculcates duty and reverence. Duty arises from our potential control over the course of events. Where attainable knowledge could have changed the issue, ignorance has the guilt of vice. And the foundation of reverence is this perception, that the present holds within itself the complete sum of existence, backwards and forwards, that whole amplitude of time, which is eternity.

JACQUES MARITAIN | *Educational Aims and Values*

The Aims of Education

Concerning philosophical principles

The primary aim of education in the broadest sense of this word is to "form a man" or rather to help a child of man attain his full formation or his completeness as a man. The other aims (to convey the heritage of culture of a given area of civilization, to prepare for life in society and for good citizenship, and to secure mental equipment required for implementing a particular function in the social whole, for performing family responsibilities, and for making a living) are corollaries and essential but secondary aims. (Parenthetically, it must be observed that education in the broad sense of the word continues during the entire life-time of every one of us. The school system is only a *partial* and *inchoative* agency with respect to the task of education. Moreover, because it deals essentially with that which can be taught, it refers to the education and formation of intelligence more than of the will.)

It is clear that the primary aim is determined by human nature. The question "What is man?" is the unavoidable preamble to any philosophy of education. It has two implications: first, a philosophic or "ontological" implication, dealing with human nature in its essential being; second, a scientific or "empiriological" implication, dealing with human nature in the phenomenal characteristics that lie open to our modern sciences of observation and measurement. These two implications are in no way incompatible; they complement each other.

With respect to both the mind and the body, science, and especially empirical psychology, provides us with invaluable and ever growing information, by which our practical approach to the child and the youth must profit. But, by itself, it can neither primarily found nor primarily guide education, for education needs primarily to know what man *is*—what are the constitutive principles of his being, what is his place and value in the world, what is his destiny. This has to do with the philosoph-

From "Thomist Views on Education," *NSSE Yearbook, 1955*, Vol. 54, Part 2, pp. 62–72. Reprinted by permission of the author and the National Society for the Study of Education, Chicago, Ill.

ical knowledge of man—including additional data which relate to his existential condition.

The Thomist idea of man coincides with the Greek, Jewish, and Christian idea: man as an animal endowed with reason, whose supreme dignity is in the intellect; and man as a free individual in personal relation with God, whose supreme righteousness consists in voluntarily obeying the law of God; and man as a sinful and wounded creature called to divine life and to the freedom of grace, whose supreme perfection consists in love.

At the same time Thomist philosophy lays stress on the basic psychosomatic unity of the human being (one single substance composed of matter and a spiritual "form" or entelechy)—thus affording us with a philosophical key for a sound interpretation of great modern discoveries in neurology and psychiatry. Also, it lays stress on the notion of human personality. Man is a person, who holds himself in hand by his intelligence and his will. He does not exist merely as a physical being. There is in him a richer and nobler existence: He has spiritual superexistence, through knowledge and love. He is thus, in some way, a whole, and not merely a part; he is a universe unto himself, a microcosm in which the great universe can be encompassed through knowledge. Through love he can give himself freely to beings who are to him, as it were, other selves; and for this relationship no equivalent can be found in the physical world.

Man evolves in history. Yet his nature as such, his place and value in the cosmos, his dignity, rights, and aspirations as a person, and his destiny do not change. Consequently, the secondary aims of education have to be adjusted to changing conditions in successive historical periods; but as concerns the primary aim, as well as the intrinsic domination it exercises on the secondary aims, it is sheer illusion to speak of a ceaseless reconstruction of the aims of education.

Concerning practical application

Human nature does not change, but our knowledge of it may be philosophically warped or inadequate. Moreover, this knowledge steadily progresses in the field of the factual and empiriological sciences.

The philosophical knowledge of man which reigned as a rule in the last three centuries was basically Cartesian, and Thomist philosophy is strongly opposed both to Cartesian dualism and to the idealist and narrowly rationalistic bias it made prevalent in education. On the other hand, while shifting toward a philosophical outlook which is equally warped, but in the opposite way (the empiricist, positivist, or materialist bias), our epoch witnesses outstanding progress in the experimental sciences of man.

Accordingly I would say that both in its reaction against Cartesian rationalism and its heedfulness of the achievements of modern psychology, progressive education provides us with invaluable improvements. Our understanding of the realities connected with the aims of education has become truer and deeper. For example, due attention has been paid to the unconscious, the instincts, the nonrational elements in the psyche of the child. At the same time, educational techniques are in a process of continual broadening and enriching, so that it is right to speak of a ceaseless reconstruction of the *means* of education, so long as such reconstruction does not indulge in errors deriving from pseudophilosophical extrapolation, like the overemphasis on sex and sexual complexes due to cheap psychology and spurious Freudianism, or the "cultural epoch" theory of G. Stanley Hall with free rein to be given to the instincts of the child coming to civilization through savagery. The greatest attention must be paid in this connection to Piaget's experiments and similar researches and to renewals in the educational approach, such as those advocated by Montessori.

The Hierarchy of Values

Concerning philosophical principles

There is no unity or integration without a stable hierarchy of values. Now in the true hierarchy of values, according to Thomist philosophy, knowledge and love of what is above time are superior to, and embrace and quicken, knowledge and love of what is within time. Charity, which loves God and embraces all men in this very love, is the supreme virtue. In the intellectual realm, wisdom, which knows things eternal and creates order and unity in the mind, is superior to science or to knowledge through particular causes; and the speculative intellect, which knows for the sake of knowing, comes before the practical intellect, which knows for the sake of action. In such a hierarchy of values, what is infravalent is not sacrificed to, but kept alive by, what is supravalent, because everything is appendent to faith in truth. Aristotle was right in sensing that contemplation is in itself better than action and more fitted to what is the most spiritual in man, but Aristotelian contemplation was purely intellectual and theoretical, while Christian contemplation, being rooted in love, superabounds in action.

Education obviously does not have to make of the child or the youth a scientist, a sage, and a contemplative. Yet, if the word "contemplation" is taken in its original and simplest sense (to contemplate is simply to *see* and to enjoy seeing), leaving aside its highest—metaphysical or religious—connotations, it must be said that knowledge is contemplative in nature, and that education, in its final and highest achievements, tends to develop the contemplative capacity of the human mind. It does so neither in order to have the mind come to a stop in the act of knowing and contemplating, nor in order to make knowledge and contemplation subservient to action, but in order that once man has reached a stage where the harmony of his inner energies has been brought to full completion, his action on the world and on the human community, and his creative power at the service of his fellow-men, may overflow from his contemplative contact with reality—both with the visible and invisible realities in the midst of which he lives and moves.

While dealing with the first steps in man's formation, education must itself be aware of the genuine hierarchy of intellectual values, be guided by such awareness in its task of preparation, preserve in the youth the natural germs of what is best in the life of the mind, and equip them with the beginnings of those disciplines of knowledge which matter most to man. It is a pity to see so many young people bewildered by highly developed and specialized, but chaotic, instruction about anything whatever in the field of particular sciences and miserably ignorant of everything that concerns God and the deepest realities in man and the world. What we are faced with, in this regard, is a kind of regular frustration—by adults and the general organization of teaching—of certain of the most vital needs and aspirations, and even of the basic rights, of intellectual nature in young persons.

Concerning practical application

One of the vices of the sort of education described in the Lynds' *Middletown*[1] was not only to treat the child as a piece of inert matter to be moulded from the outside but also to try to make him into a reduction or imitation of an adult, a kind of perfect manufactured intellectual dwarf. Hence, the prevalence of a merely theoretical and abstract formation, in accordance with an ideal of the adult man himself which, by the most confusing abuse of language, is often described as "contemplative," though it has nothing to do with genuine contemplative virtues, and refers in actual fact to that particular selfishness of the mind which comes about when intelligence is both separated from things—occupied only with handling and moving ideas and words—and separated from the emotional and affective tonus of life. This ideal was in its heyday during the seventeenth and eighteenth centuries. It was far removed from the Aristotelian one; it originated, philosophically, in Cartesian rationalism and, socially, in a trend, among the elite, toward a kind of lofty Epicurean freedom. According to it, the enviable condition of the man of leisure was to sit down before the spectacle of the achievements of the human mind and to taste the pleasure of "general ideas" without engaging either his heart or his intellect in the reality of things.

[1] Robert S. Lynd and Helen M. Lynd, *Middletown: A Study of Contemporary American Culture* (New York: Harcourt, Brace, 1929).

Out of gear as it may have been, the pragmatist protest against such an attitude was sound in its origin. Concern for action and practical life was to be rehabilitated in education. The misfortune was that the true hierarchy of values was broken at the same time. We have to integrate many views of pragmatism and progressive education—but at their appropriate place, which is secondary, and as regards especially the ways and means of education—in a nonpragmatist conception intent on the organic order of knowledge and directed toward wisdom.

As I pointed out, the order of human virtues come to completion demands that practical action on the world and on the human community superabound from contemplation of truth, which means not only contemplation in its purest forms but, more generally, intellectual grasping of reality and enjoyment of knowledge for its own sake. But in the educational process, what we have to do with is not human life as come to perfection; it is the very first beginnings of the lifelong movement toward such an ultimate stage. Then the perspective is reversed. Action must come first—and concern for application, practical significance, and the impact of the things which are taught on man's existence—not for action itself as final end, but in order to awaken progressively the child and the youth to seek and perceive truth for the sake of truth, to exercise their power to think, and to sense the joy of intellection. *From praxis to knowledge,* this is the normal method of education, especially in its first steps.

Educational Process

The remarks I just made about action must be qualified on a particular point: If it is a question of the atmosphere of the classroom, contemplation, in a sense, and especially as regards young children, should come first; in Montessorian classes, which obey the two fundamental rules of *silence* and *personal effort,* the behavior of children changes completely; they move as they work, but with no agitation, and become so concentrated and so absorbed in their task that the visitor in these noiseless classrooms is surprised to have the impression of a monastic climate. Miss Hélène Lubienska de Lenval observes that these children simply reveal, in an appropriate environment, the contemplative capacity peculiar to early childhood (ages two to eight). They are contemplative, as she puts it, "in the sense that they are capable of steadily fixing their attention by absorbing themselves in a disinterested admiration with no verbal manifestation (the latter will arise in due time after a long silent maturation). This contemplation seems akin to poetic inspiration." And because "it comes about most often before objects that represent dimensions and numbers," she calls it "Pythagorean contemplation."[2] This contemplative faculty of the child is ephemeral, it disappears at the moment when discursive thought replaces intuitive thought. But something of it remains, for those who once enjoyed it show remarkable powers of attention in later years.

If we pass now to the question of learning by way of solving problems, I would say that this method of learning is normally a way to truth-grasping or "contemplative" learning, just as *praxis* is a way to knowledge. It is a normal auxiliary means, destined to sustain personal initiative and interest, and to prevent contemplative learning from degenerating into passivity and inert docility. For there is no contemplative learning if it does not respond to and stimulate a searching effort of the mind, an anxiety to know. Truth, in education, can be betrayed in two ways: either by substituting mechanical drill, and skill in solving difficulties, for the *élan* toward knowledge; or by putting the intellect of the student to sleep in ready-made formulas, which he accepts and memorizes without engaging his own self in the grasping of what they supposedly convey to him. Genuine contemplative or truth-grasping learning fails in its very nature if it does not develop in the youth both critical activity and a kind of thirst and anguish whose reward will be the very joy of perceiving truth.

But, in this section on the educational process, the point I should like especially to consider is the relationship between adults and youth.

In the educational task, adult people do not have to impose coercion on children, with a kind of paternalism or rather imperialism of the grown-ups, in order to impress their own image upon the child as upon a bit of clay. But what this service requires from them is, first, love and, then, authority—I mean genuine authority, not arbitrary power—intellectual authority to teach and moral authority to be respected and listened to. For the child is entitled to expect from them what he needs: to be positively guided and to learn what he is ignorant of.

What do adults essentially owe to youth in the educational task? First of all, what corresponds to the primary aim of education, that is, both truth to be known at the various degrees of the scale of knowledge and the capacity to think and make a personal judgment, to be developed, equipped, and firmly established; then, what corresponds to the secondary aims of education, especially the heritage of a given culture, to be conveyed.

Now, if we consider the way in which adults perform their task with respect to youth, in practice and actual existence, it seems that more often than not children are victims of the grown-ups rather than the beneficiaries of their good services. Hence, progressive education might

[2] Hélène Lubienska de Lenval, "La Contemplation Silencieuse chez les Enfants," *Nova et Vetera* (Fribourg, Switzerland, July–September 1951).

be described as expressing a kind of revolt against the reign of adults. This would have been all for the good if youth had not been made, once again, a victim, this time not of the selfish domination of the world of the grown-ups, but of the illusions and irresponsibility of well-intentioned adults, who rightly insist on the freedom of the child—but what kind of freedom? Too often freedom from any rule or freedom to do as the child pleases, instead of genuine freedom for the child to develop as a man and genuine progress toward autonomy.

A twofold crucial problem arises when the educational task has to be performed in a changing world of knowledge and a changing world of culture and social conditions.

As concerns the social changes in the contemporary world, teachers have neither to make the school into a stronghold of the established order nor to make it into a weapon to change society. The dilemma could not be solved if the primary aim and function of education were defined in relation to society and social work. In reality they are defined in relation to intelligence. Then the dilemma is transcended because teachers must be concerned, above all, with helping minds to become articulate, free, and autonomous. It is neither for conservative nor for revolutionary purposes but for the general purpose of teaching how to think, that they have to foster in the pupils the principles of the democratic charter.

As concerns our changing world of knowledge, the answer is simple in itself: *vetera novis augere;* all new gains and discoveries should be used, not to shatter and reject what has been acquired by the past, but to augment it: a work of integration, not of destruction. This, however, is easier said than done. For it presupposes that the mind of the adults, especially the teachers, is not itself in a state of division and anarchy, and that the adults are in possession of what they have to communicate, namely, wisdom and integrated knowledge. Not to speak of exceptionally remarkable achievements in interdepartmental co-operation like the "Committee on Social Thought" in the University of Chicago, one possible remedy for the lack of integration in the minds of teachers themselves would be, in my opinion, the development, on a large scale, of study clubs and seminars in which teachers belonging to various disciplines and departments would meet together, on a voluntary basis, and discuss basic problems which are relevant to the unity of knowledge and which have an impact on a variety of fields, as well as controversial issues that are raised by contemporary research and creative activity. I am convinced that it would thus be possible for fresh and quickening blood to circulate in the campuses. But such initiative could obviously start and succeed only if teachers had the necessary free time, that is to say, if they were not faced with overburdened schedules and a much too heavy number of teaching hours—one of the most serious impediments to the progress of the present educational system. It is preposterous to ask people who lead an enslaved life to perform a task of liberation, which the educational task is by essence.

Education and the Individual

Concerning philosophical principles

Among the many questions which can be discussed under this heading, the one I shall point out is the essential question: Who is the "principal agent" in the educational process?

The teacher exercises a real causal power on the mind of the pupil, but in the manner in which a doctor acts to heal his patient: by assisting nature and co-operating with it. Education, like medicine, is *ars co-operativa naturae*. The contention of Thomist philosophy is that in both cases nature (the vital energies of nature in the patient, the intellectual energies of nature in the pupil) is the principal agent, on whose own activity the process primarily depends. The *principal agent* in the educational process is not the teacher, but the student.[3]

Concerning practical application

This basic truth was forgotten or disregarded by the advocates of education by the rod. Here we have the fundamental vice of the "Middletown" conception of the school. Into whatever exaggeration it may have fallen, progressive education has had the merit of putting the forgotten truth in question in the foreground. The "principal agent" is not able to give himself what he does not have. He would lead himself astray if he acted at random. He must be taught and guided: But the main thing in this teaching process is that his natural and spontaneous activity be always respected and his power of insight and judgment always fostered, so that at each step he may master the subject matter in which he is instructed. In this perspective, what matters most is to develop in the child the "intuitivity" of the mind and its spiritual discriminating and creative energies. The educational venture is a ceaseless appeal to intelligence and free will in the young person.

The most precious gift in an educator is a sort of sacred and loving attention to the child's mysterious identity, which is a hidden thing that no techniques can reach. Encouragement is as fundamentally necessary as humiliation is harmful. But what must be specially stressed is the fact that the teacher has to center the acquisition of knowledge and solid formation of the mind on the freeing of the learner's intuitive power.

The liberation of which I am speaking depends essentially, moreover, on the free adhesion of the mind to the objective reality to be seen:

[3] *Cf.* Thomas Aquinas, *Sum. theol.*, I, q. 117, a. 1; *Contra Gent.*, Bk. II, Chap. lxxv; *De Verit.*, q. 11, a. 1.

Let us never deceive or rebuke the thirst for seeing in youth's intelligence! The freeing of the intuitive power is achieved in the soul through the object grasped, the intelligible grasping toward which this power naturally tends. The germ of insight starts within a preconscious intellectual cloud, arising from experience, imagination, and a kind of spiritual feeling, but it is from the outset a tending toward an object to be grasped. And to the extent that this tendency is set free and the intellect becomes accustomed to grasping, seeing, expressing the objects toward which it tends, to that very extent its intuitive power is liberated and strengthened.[4]

In asking a youth to read a book, let us get him to undertake a real spiritual adventure and meet and struggle with the internal world of a given man, instead of glancing over a collection of bits of thought and dead opinions, looked upon from without and with sheer indifference, according to the horrible custom of so many victims of what they call "being informed." Perhaps with such methods the curriculum will lose a little in scope, which will be all to the good.[5]

ROBERT MAYNARD HUTCHINS | **The Basis of Education**

The obvious failures of the doctrines of adaptation, immediate needs, social reform, and of the doctrine that we need no doctrine at all may suggest to us that we require a better definition of education. Let us concede that every society must have some system that attempts to adapt the young to their social and political environment. If the society is bad, in the sense, for example, in which the Nazi state was bad, the system will aim at the same bad ends. To the extent that it makes men bad in order that they may be tractable subjects of a bad state, the system may help to achieve the social ideals of the society. It may be what the society wants; it may even be what the society needs, if it is to perpetuate its form and accomplish its aims. In pragmatic terms, in terms of success in the society, it may be a "good" system.

But it seems to me clearer to say that, though it may be a system of training, or instruction, or adaptation, or meeting immediate needs, it is not a system of education. It seems clearer to say that the purpose of education is to improve men. Any system that tries to make them bad is

[4] Jacques Maritain, *Education at the Crossroads* (New Haven, Conn.: Yale University Press, 1943), p. 44.
[5] *Ibid.*, pp. 44–45.

---

not education, but something else. If, for example, democracy is the best form of society, a system that adapts the young to it will be an educational system. If despotism is a bad form of society, a system that adapts the young to it will not be an educational system, and the better it succeeds in adapting them the less educational it will be.

Every man has a function as a man. The function of a citizen or a subject may vary from society to society, and the system of training, or adaptation, or instruction, or meeting immediate needs may vary with it. But the function of a man as man is the same in every age and in every society, since it results from his nature as a man. The aim of an educational system is the same in every age and in every society where such a system can exist: it is to improve man as man.

If we are going to talk about improving men and societies, we have to believe that there is some difference between good and bad. This difference must not be, as the positivists think it is, merely conventional. We cannot tell this difference by any examination of the effectiveness of a given program as the pragmatists propose; the time required to estimate these effects is usually too long and the complexity of society is always too great for us to say that the consequences of a given program are altogether clear. We cannot discover the difference between good and bad by going to the laboratory, for men and societies are not laboratory animals. If we believe that there is no truth, there is no knowledge, and there are no values except those which are validated by laboratory experiment, we cannot talk about the improvement of men and societies, for we can have no standard of judging anything that takes place among men or in societies.

Society is to be improved, not by forcing a program of social reform down its throat, through the schools or otherwise, but by the improvement of the individuals who compose it. As Plato said, "Governments reflect human nature. States are not made out of stone or wood, but out of the characters of their citizens: these turn the scale and draw everything after them." The individual is the heart of society.

To talk about making men better we must have some idea of what men are, because if we have none, we can have no idea of what is good or bad for them. If men are brutes like other animals, then there is no reason why they should not be treated like brutes by anybody who can gain power over them. And there is no reason why they should not be trained as brutes are trained. A sound philosophy in general suggests that men are rational, moral, and spiritual beings and that the improvement of men means the fullest development of their rational, moral, and spiritual powers. All men have these powers, and all men should develop them to the fullest extent.

Man is by nature free, and he is by nature social. To use his freedom rightly he needs discipline. To live in society he needs the moral virtues.

Good moral and intellectual habits are required for the fullest development of the nature of man.

To develop fully as a social, political animal man needs participation in his own government. A benevolent despotism will not do. You cannot expect the slave to show the virtues of the free man unless you first set him free. Only democracy, in which all men rule and are ruled in turn for the good life of the whole community, can be an absolutely good form of government.

The community rests on the social nature of men. It requires communication among its members. They do not have to agree with one another; but they must be able to understand one another. And their philosophy in general must supply them with a common purpose and a common concept of man and society adequate to hold the community together. Civilization is the deliberate pursuit of a common ideal. The good society is not just a society we happen to like or to be used to. It is a community of good men.

Education deals with the development of the intellectual powers of men. Their moral and spiritual powers are the sphere of the family and the church. All three agencies must work in harmony; for, though a man has three aspects, he is still one man. But the schools cannot take over the role of the family and the church without promoting the atrophy of those institutions and failing in the task that is proper to the schools.

We cannot talk about the intellectual powers of men, though we can talk about training them, or amusing them, or adapting them, and meeting their immediate needs, unless our philosophy in general tells us that there is knowledge and that there is a difference between true and false. We must believe, too, that there are other means of obtaining knowledge than scientific experimentation. If knowledge can be sought only in the laboratory, many fields in which we thought we had knowledge will offer us nothing but opinion or superstition, and we shall be forced to conclude that we cannot know anything about the most important aspects of man and society. If we are to set about developing the intellectual powers of men through having them acquire knowledge of the most important subjects, we have to begin with the proposition that experimentation and empirical data will be of only limited use to us, contrary to the convictions of many American social scientists, and that philosophy, history, literature, and art give us knowledge, and significant knowledge, on the most significant issues.

If the object of education is the improvement of men, then any system of education that is without values is a contradiction in terms. A system that seeks bad values is bad. A system that denies the existence of values denies the possibility of education. Relativism, scientism, skepticism, and anti-intellectualism, the four horsemen of the philosophical apocalypse, have produced that chaos in education which will end in the disintegration of the West.

The prime object of education is to know what is good for man. It is to know the goods in their order. There is a hierarchy of values. The task of education is to help us understand it, establish it, and live by it. This Aristotle had in mind when he said: "It is not the possessions but the desires of men that must be equalized, and this is impossible unless they have a sufficient education according to the nature of things."

Such an education is far removed from the triviality of that produced by the doctrines of adaptation, of immediate needs, of social reform, or of the doctrine of no doctrine at all. Such an education will not adapt the young to a bad environment, but it will encourage them to make it good. It will not overlook immediate needs, but it will place these needs in their proper relationship to more distant, less tangible, and more important goods. It will be the only effective means of reforming society.

This is the education appropriate to free men. It is liberal education. If all men are to be free, all men must have this education. It makes no difference how they are to earn their living or what their special interests or aptitudes may be. They can learn to make a living, and they can develop their special interests and aptitudes, after they have laid the foundation of free and responsible manhood through liberal education. It will not do to say that they are incapable of such education. This claim is made by those who are too indolent or unconvinced to make the effort to give such education to the masses.

Nor will it do to say that there is not enough time to give everybody a liberal education before he becomes a specialist. In America, at least, the waste and frivolity of the educational system are so great that it would be possible through getting rid of them to give every citizen a liberal education and make him a qualified specialist, too, in less time than is now consumed in turning out uneducated specialists.

A liberal education aims to develop the powers of understanding and judgment. It is impossible that too many people can be educated in this sense, because there cannot be too many people with understanding and judgment. We hear a great deal today about the dangers that will come upon us through the frustration of educated people who have got educated in the expectation that education will get them a better job, and who then fail to get it. But surely this depends on the representations that are made to the young about what education is. If we allow them to believe that education will get them better jobs and encourage them to get educated with this end in view, they are entitled to a sense of frustration if, when they have got the education, they do not get the jobs. But, if we say that they should be educated in order to be men, and that everybody, whether he is a ditch-digger or a bank president, should have this education because he is a man, then the ditch-digger may still feel frustrated, but not because of his education.

Nor is it possible for a person to have too much liberal education, because it is impossible to have too much understanding and judgment. But it is possible to undertake too much in the name of liberal education in youth. The object of liberal education in youth is not to teach the young all they will ever need to know. It is to give them the habits, ideas, and techniques that they need to continue to educate themselves. Thus the object of formal institutional liberal education in youth is to prepare the young to educate themselves throughout their lives.

I would remind you of the impossibility of learning to understand and judge many of the most important things in youth. The judgment and understanding of practical affairs can amount to little in the absence of experience with practical affairs. Subjects that cannot be understood without experience should not be taught to those who are without experience. Or, if these subjects are taught to those who are without experience, it should be clear that these subjects can be taught only by way of introduction and that their value to the student depends on his continuing to study them as he acquires experience. The tragedy in America is that economics, ethics, politics, history, and literature are studied in youth, and seldom studied again. Therefore the graduates of American universities seldom understand them.

This pedagogical principle, that subjects requiring experience can be learned only by the experienced, leads to the conclusion that the most important branch of education is the education of adults. We sometimes seem to think of education as something like the mumps, measles, whooping-cough, or chicken-pox. If a person has had education in childhood, he need not, in fact he cannot, have it again. But the pedagogical principle that the most important things can be learned only in mature life is supported by a sound philosophy in general. Men are rational animals. They achieve their terrestrial felicity by the use of reason. And this means that they have to use it for their entire lives. To say that they should learn only in childhood would mean that they were human only in childhood.

And it would mean that they were unfit to be citizens of a republic.[1] A republic, a true *res publica,* can maintain justice, peace, freedom, and order only by the exercise of intelligence. When we speak of the consent of the governed, we mean, since men are not angels who seek the truth intuitively and do not have to learn it, that every act of assent on the part of the governed is a product of learning. A republic is really a common educational life in process. So Montesquieu said that, whereas the

[1] I owe this discussion to the suggestions of Scott Buchanan.

principle of a monarchy was honor, and the principle of a tyranny was fear, the principle of a republic was education.

Hence the ideal republic is the republic of learning. It is the utopia by which all actual political republics are measured. The goal toward which we started with the Athenians twenty-five centuries ago is an unlimited republic of learning and a world-wide political republic mutually supporting each other.

All men are capable of learning. Learning does not stop as long as a man lives, unless his learning power atrophies because he does not use it. Political freedom cannot endure unless it is accompanied by provision for the unlimited acquisition of knowledge. Truth is not long retained in human affairs without continual learning and relearning. Peace is unlikely unless there are continuous, unlimited opportunities for learning and unless men continuously avail themselves of them. The world of law and justice for which we yearn, the world-wide political republic, cannot be realized without the world-wide republic of learning. The civilization we seek will be achieved when all men are citizens of the world republic of law and justice and of the republic of learning all their lives long.

JOHN DEWEY | *Aims in Education*

I. The Nature of an Aim

The account of education given in our earlier chapters virtually anticipated the results reached in a discussion of the purport of education in a democratic community. For it assumed that the aim of education is to enable individuals to continue their education—or that the object and reward of learning is continued capacity for growth. Now this idea cannot be applied to *all* the members of a society except where intercourse of man with man is mutual, and except where there is adequate provision for the reconstruction of social habits and institutions by means of wide stimulation arising from equitably distributed interests. And this means a democratic society. In our search for aims in education, we are not concerned, therefore, with finding an end outside of the educative process to which education is subordinate. Our whole conception forbids. We are rather concerned with the contrast which exists when aims belong within the process in which they operate and when they are set up from without. And the latter state of affairs must obtain when social relationships are not equitably balanced. For in that case, some portions of the whole social group will find their aims determined by an external dictation; their aims will not arise from the free growth of their own experience, and their nominal aims will be means to more ulterior ends of others rather than truly their own.

Our first question is to define the nature of an aim so far as it falls within an activity, instead of being furnished from without. We approach the definition by a contrast of mere *results* with *ends.* Any exhibition of energy has results. The wind blows about the sands of the desert; the position of the grains is changed. Here is a result, an effect, but not an *end.* For there is nothing in the outcome which completes or fulfills what went before it. There is mere spatial redistribution. One state of affairs is just as good as any other. Consequently there is no basis upon which to select an earlier state of affairs as a beginning, a later as an end, and to consider what intervenes as a process of transformation and realization.

Consider for example the activities of bees in contrast with the changes in the sands when the wind blows them about. The result of the bees' actions may be called ends not because they are designed or consciously intended, but because they are true terminations or completions of what has preceded. When the bees gather pollen and make wax and build cells, each step prepares the way for the next. When cells are built, the queen lays eggs in them; when eggs are laid, they are sealed and bees brood them and keep them at a temperature required to hatch them. When they are hatched, bees feed the young till they can take care of themselves. Now we are so familiar with such facts, that we are apt to dismiss them on the ground that life and instinct are a kind of miraculous thing anyway. Thus we fail to note what the essential characteristic of the event is; namely, the significance of the temporal place and order of each element; the way each prior event leads into its successor while the successor takes up what is furnished and utilizes it for some other stage, until we arrive at the end, which, as it were, summarizes and finishes off the process.

Since aims relate always to results, the first thing to look to when it is a question of aims, is whether the work assigned possesses intrinsic continuity. Or is it a mere serial aggregate of acts, first doing one thing and then another? To talk about an educational aim when approximately each act of a pupil is dictated by the teacher, when the only order in the sequence of his acts is that which comes from the assignment of lessons and the giving of directions by another, is to talk nonsense. It is equally fatal to an aim to permit capricious or discontinuous action in the name of spontaneous self-expression. An aim implies an orderly and ordered activity, one in which the order consists in the progressive completing of a process. Given an activity having a time span and cumulative growth within the time succession, an aim means foresight in advance of the end or possible termination. If bees anticipated the consequences of their activity, if they perceived their end in imaginative foresight, they would have the primary element in an aim. Hence it is nonsense to talk about the aim of education—or any other undertaking—where conditions do not permit of foresight of results, and do not stimulate a person to look ahead to see what the outcome of a given activity is to be.

In the next place the aim as a foreseen end gives direction to the activity; it is not an idle view of a mere spectator, but influences the steps taken to reach the end. The foresight functions in three ways. In the first place, it involves careful observation of the given conditions to see what are the means available for reaching the end, and to discover the hindrances in the way. In the second place, it suggests the proper order or sequence in the use of means. It facilitates an economical selection and arrangement. In the third place, it makes choice of alternatives possible. If we can predict the outcome of acting this way or that, we can then compare the value of the two courses of action; we can pass judgment upon their relative desirability. If we know that stagnant water breeds mosquitoes and that they are likely to carry disease, we can, disliking that anticipated result, take steps to avert it. Since we do not anticipate results as mere intellectual onlookers, but as persons concerned in the outcome, we are partakers in the process which produces the result. We intervene to bring about this result or that.

Of course these three points are closely connected with one another. We can definitely foresee results only as we make careful scrutiny of present conditions, and the importance of the outcome supplies the motive for observations. The more adequate our observations, the more varied is the scene of conditions and obstructions that presents itself, and the more numerous are the alternatives between which choice may be made. In turn, the more numerous the recognized possibilities of the situation, or alternatives of action, the more meaning does the chosen activity possess, and the more flexibly controllable is it. Where only a single outcome has been thought of, the mind has nothing else to think of; the meaning attaching to the act is limited. One only steams ahead toward the mark. Sometimes such a narrow course may be effective. But if unexpected difficulties offer themselves, one has not as many resources at command as if he had chosen the same line of action after a broader survey of the possibilities of the field. He cannot make needed readjustments readily.

The net conclusion is that acting with an aim is all one with acting intelligently. To foresee a terminus of an act is to have a basis upon which to observe, to select, and to order objects and our own capacities. To do these things means to have a mind—for mind is precisely intentional purposeful activity controlled by perception of facts and their relationships to one another. To have a mind to do a thing is to foresee a future possibility; it is to have a plan for its accomplishment; it is to note the means which make the plan capable of execution and the obstructions in the way—or, if it is really a *mind* to do the thing and not a vague aspiration—it is to have a plan which takes account of resources and difficulties. Mind is capacity to refer present conditions to future results, and future consequences to present conditions. And these traits are just what is meant by having an aim or a purpose. A man is stupid or blind or unintelligent—lacking in mind—just in the degree in which in any activity he does not know what he is about, namely, the probable consequences of his acts. A man is imperfectly intelligent when he contents himself with looser guesses about the outcome than is needful, just taking a chance with his luck, or when he forms plans apart from study of the actual conditions, including his own capacities. Such relative absence of mind means to make our feelings the measure of what is to happen. To be intelligent we must "stop, look, listen" in making the plan of an activity.

To identify acting with an aim and intelligent activity is enough to show its value—its function in experience. We are only too given to making an entity out of the abstract noun *consciousness.* We forget that it comes from the adjective *conscious.* To be conscious is to be aware of what we are about; conscious signifies the deliberate, observant, planning traits of activity. Consciousness is nothing which we have which gazes idly on the scene around one or which has impressions made upon it by physical things; it is a name for the purposeful quality of an activity, for the fact that it is directed by an aim. Put the other way about, to have an aim is to act with meaning, not like an automatic machine; it is to *mean* to do something and to perceive the meaning of things in the light of that intent.

II. The Criteria of Good Aims

We may apply the results of our discussion to a consideration of the criteria involved in a correct establishing of aims. (1) The aim set up must be an outgrowth of existing conditions. It must be based upon a consideration of what is already going on; upon the resources and difficulties of the situation. Theories about the proper end of our activities—educational and moral theories—often violate this principle. They assume ends lying *outside* our activities; ends foreign to the concrete make-up of the situation; ends which issue from some outside source. Then the problem is to bring our activities to bear upon the realization of these externally supplied ends. They are something for which we *ought* to act. In any case such "aims" limit intelligence; they are not the expression of mind in foresight, observation, and choice of the better among alternative possibilities. They limit intelligence because, given ready-made, they must be imposed by some authority external to intelligence, leaving to the latter nothing but a mechanical choice of means.

(2) We have spoken as if aims could be completely formed prior to the attempt to realize them. This impression must now be qualified. The aim as it first emerges is a mere tentative sketch. The act of striving to realize it tests its worth. If it suffices to direct activity successfully, nothing more is required, since its whole function is to set a mark in advance; and at times a mere hint may suffice. But usually—at least in complicated situations—acting upon it brings to light conditions which had been overlooked. This calls for revision of the original aim; it has to be added to and subtracted from. An aim must, then, be *flexible;* it must be capable of alteration to meet circumstances. An end established externally to the process of action is always rigid. Being inserted or imposed from without, it is not supposed to have a working relationship to the concrete conditions of the situation. What happens in the course of action neither confirms, refutes, nor alters it. Such an end can only be insisted upon. The failure that results from its lack of adaptation is attributed simply to the perverseness of conditions, not to the fact that the end is not reasonable under the circumstances. The value of a legitimate aim, on the contrary, lies in the fact that we can use it to change conditions. It is a method for dealing with conditions so as to effect desirable alterations in them. A farmer who should passively accept things just as he finds them would make as great a mistake as he who framed his plans in complete disregard of what soil, climate, etc., permit. One of the evils of an abstract or remote external aim in education is that its very inapplicability in practice is likely to react into a haphazard snatching at immediate conditions. A good aim surveys the present state of experience of pupils, and forming a tentative plan of treatment, keeps the plan constantly in view and yet modifies it as conditions develop. The aim, in short, is experimental, and hence constantly growing as it is tested in action.

(3) The aim must always represent a freeing of activities. The term *end in view* is suggestive, for it puts before the mind the termination or conclusion of some process. The only way in which we can define an activity is by putting before ourselves the objects in which it terminates—as one's aim in shooting is the target. But we must remember that the *object* is only a mark or sign by which the mind specifies the *activity* one desires to carry out. Strictly speaking, not the target but *hitting* the target is the end in view; one *takes* aim by means of the target, but also by the sight on the gun. The different objects which are thought of are means of *directing* the activity. Thus one aims at, say, a rabbit; what he wants is to shoot straight: a certain kind of activity. Or, if it is the rabbit he wants, it is not rabbit apart from his activity, but as a factor

in activity; he wants to eat the rabbit, or to show it as evidence of his marksmanship—he wants to do something with it. The doing with the thing, not the thing in isolation, is his end. The object is but a phase of the active end—continuing the activity successfully. This is what is meant by the phrase, used above, "freeing activity."

In contrast with fulfilling some process in order that activity may go on, stands the static character of an end which is imposed from without the activity. It is always conceived of as fixed; it is *something* to be attained and possessed. When one has such a notion, activity is a mere unavoidable means to something else; it is not significant or important on its own account. As compared with the end it is but a necessary evil; something which must be gone through before one can reach the object which is alone worth while. In other words, the external idea of the aim leads to a separation of means from end, while an end which grows up within an activity as plan for its direction is always both ends and means, the distinction being only one of convenience. Every means is a temporary end until we have attained it. Every end becomes a means of carrying activity further as soon as it is achieved. We call it end when it marks off the future direction of the activity in which we are engaged; means when it marks off the present direction. Every divorce of end from means diminishes by that much the significance of the activity and tends to reduce it to a drudgery from which one would escape if he could. A farmer has to use plants and animals to carry on his farming activities. It certainly makes a great difference to his life whether he is fond of them, or whether he regards them merely as means which he has to employ to get something else in which alone he is interested. In the former case, his entire course of activity is significant; each phase of it has its own value. He has the experience of realizing his end at every stage; the postponed aim, or end in view, being merely a sight ahead by which to keep his activity going fully and freely. For if he does not look ahead, he is more likely to find himself blocked. The aim is definitely a *means* of action as is any other portion of an activity.

III. Applications in Education

There is nothing peculiar about educational aims. They are just like aims in any directed occupation. The educator, like the farmer, has certain things to do, certain resources with which to do, and certain obstacles with which to contend. The conditions with which the farmer deals, whether as obstacles or resources, have their own structure and operation independently of any purpose of his. Seeds sprout, rain falls, the sun shines, insects devour, blight comes, the seasons change. His aim is simply to utilize these various conditions; to make his activities and their energies work together, instead of against one another. It would be absurd if the farmer set up a purpose of farming, without any reference to these conditions of soil, climate, characteristic of plant growth, etc. His purpose is simply a foresight of the consequences of his energies connected with those of the things about him, a foresight used to direct his movements from day to day. Foresight of possible consequences leads to more careful and extensive observation of the nature and performances of the things he had to do with, and to laying out a plan—that is, of a certain order in the acts to be performed.

It is the same with the educator, whether parent or teacher. It is as absurd for the latter to set up their "own" aims as the proper objects of the growth of the children as it would be for the farmer to set up an ideal of farming irrespective of conditions. Aims mean acceptance of responsibility for the observations, anticipations, and arrangements required in carrying on a function—whether farming or educating. Any aim is of value so far as it assists observation, choice, and planning in carrying on activity from moment to moment and hour to hour; if it gets in the way of the individual's own common sense (as it will surely do if imposed from without or accepted on authority) it does harm.

And it is well to remind ourselves that education as such has no aims. Only persons, parents, and teachers, etc., have aims, not an abstract idea like education. And consequently their purposes are indefinitely varied, differing with different children, changing as children grow and with the growth of experience on the part of the one who teaches. Even the most valid aims which can be put in words will, as words, do more harm than good unless one recognizes that they are not aims, but rather suggestions to educators as to how to observe, how to look ahead, and how to choose in liberating and directing the energies of the concrete situations in which they find themselves. As a recent writer has said: "To lead this boy to read Scott's novels instead of the old Sleuth's stories; to teach this girl to sew; to root out the habit of bullying from John's make up; to prepare this class to study medicine—these are samples of the millions of aims we have actually before us in the concrete work of education."

Bearing these qualifications in mind, we shall proceed to state some of the characteristics found in all good educational aims. (1) An educational aim must be founded upon the intrinsic activities and needs (including original instincts and acquired habits) of the given individual to be educated. The tendency of such an aim as preparation is, as we have seen, to omit existing powers, and find the aim in some remote accomplishment or responsibility. In general, there is a disposition to take considerations which are dear to the hearts of adults and set them up as ends irrespective of the capacities of those educated. There is also an inclination to propound aims which are so uniform as to neglect the specific powers and requirements of an individual, forgetting that all learning is something which happens to be an individual at a given time and place. The larger range of perception of the adult is of great value in observing the abilities and weaknesses of the young, in deciding what they may amount to. Thus the artistic capacities of the adult exhibit what certain tendencies of the child are capable of; if we did not have the adult achievements we should be without assurance as to the significance of the drawing, reproducing, modeling, coloring activities of childhood. So if it were not for adult language, we should not be able to see the import of the babbling impulses of infancy. But it is one thing to use adult accomplishments as a context in which to place and survey the doings of childhood and youth; it is quite another to set them up as a fixed aim without regard to the concrete activities of those educated.

(2) An aim must be capable of translation into a method of coöperating with the activities of those undergoing instruction. It must suggest the kind of environment needed to liberate and to organize *their* capacities. Unless it lends itself to the construction of specific procedures, and unless these procedures test, correct, and amplify the aims, the latter is worthless. Instead of helping the specific task of teaching, it prevents the use of ordinary judgment in observing and sizing up the situation. It operates to exclude recognition of everything except what squares up with the fixed end in view. Every rigid aim just because it is rigidly given seems to render it unnecessary to give careful attention to concrete conditions. Since it *must* apply anyhow, what is the use of noting details which do not count?

The vice of externally imposed ends has deep roots. Teachers receive them from superior authorities; these authorities accept them from what is current in community. The teachers impose them upon children. As a first consequence, the intelligence of the teacher is not free; it is confined to receiving the aims laid down from above. Too rarely is the individual teacher so free from the dictation of authoritative supervisor, textbook on methods, prescribed course of study, etc., that he can let his mind come to close quarters with the pupil's mind and the subject matter. This distrust of the teacher's experience is then reflected in lack of confidence in the responses of pupils. The latter receive their aims through a double or treble external imposition, and are constantly confused by the conflict between the aims which are natural to their own experience at the time and those in which they are taught to acquiesce. Until the democratic criterion of the intrinsic significance of every growing experience is recognized, we shall be intellectually confused by the demand for adaptation to external aims.

(3) Educators have to be on their guard against ends that are alleged to be general and ultimate. Every activity, however specific, is, of course, general in its ramified connections, for it leads out indefinitely into other things. So far as a general idea makes us more alive to these connections,

it cannot be too general. But *general* also means *abstract*, or detached from all specific context. And such abstractness means remoteness, and throws us back, once more, upon teaching and learning as mere means of getting ready for an end disconnected from the means. That education is literally and all the time its own reward means that no alleged study of discipline is educative unless it is worth while in its own immediate having. A truly general aim broadens the outlook; it stimulates one to take more consequences (connections) into account. This means a wider and more flexible observation of means. The more interacting forces, for example, the farmer takes into account, the more varied will be his immediate resources. He will see a greater number of possible starting places, and a greater number of ways of getting at what he want to do. The fuller one's conception of possible future achievements, the less his present activity is tied down to a small number of alternatives. If one knew enough, one could start almost anywhere and sustain his activities continuously and fruitfully.

Understanding then the term *general* or *comprehensive aim* simply in the sense of a broad survey of the field of present activities, we shall take up some of the larger ends which have currency in the educational theories of the day, and consider what light they throw upon the immediate concrete and diversified aims which are always the educator's real concern. We premise (as indeed immediately follows from what has been said) that there is no need of making a choice among them or regarding them as competitors. When we come to act in a tangible way we have to select or choose a particular act at a particular time, but any number of comprehensive ends may exist without competition. Since they mean simply different ways of looking at the same scene. One cannot climb a number of different mountains simultaneously, but the views had when different mountains are ascended supplement one another: they do not set up incompatible, competing worlds. Or, putting the matter in a slightly different way, one statement of an end may suggest certain questions and observations, and another statement another set of questions, calling for other observations. Then the more general ends we have, the better. One statement will emphasize what another slurs over. What a plurality of hypotheses does for the scientific investigator, a plurality of stated aims may do for the instructor.

Summary

An aim denotes the result of any natural process brought to consciousness and made a factor in determining present observation and choice of ways of acting. It signifies that an activity has become intelligent. Specifically it means foresight of the alternative consequences attendant upon acting in a given situation in different ways, and the use of what is anticipated to direct observation and experiment. A true aim is thus opposed at every point to an aim which is imposed upon a process of action from without. The latter is fixed and rigid; it is not a stimulus to intelligence in the given situation, but is an externally dictated order to do such and such things. Instead of connecting directly with present activities, it is remote, divorced from the means by which it is to be reached. Instead of suggesting a freer and better balanced activity, it is a limit set to activity. In education, the currency of these externally imposed aims is responsible for the emphasis put upon the notion of preparation for a remote future and for rendering the work of both teacher and pupil mechanical and slavish.

JOHN DEWEY | *The Nature of Subject Matter*

Subject Matter of Educator and of Learner

. . . The educator's part in the enterprise of education is to furnish the environment which stimulates responses and directs the learner's course. In last analysis, *all* that the educator can do is modify stimuli so that response will as surely as is possible result in the formation of desirable intellectual and emotional dispositions. Obviously studies or the subject matter of the curriculum have intimately to do with this business of supplying an environment. The other point is the necessity of a social environment to give meaning to habits formed. In what we have termed informal education, subject matter is carried directly in the matrix of social intercourse. It is what the persons with whom an individual associates do and say. This fact gives a clew to the understanding of the subject matter of formal or deliberate instruction. A connecting link is found in the stories, traditions, songs, and liturgies which accompany the doings and rites of a primitive social group. They represent the stock of meanings which have been precipitated out of previous experience, which are so prized by the group as to be identified with their conception of their own collective life. Not being obviously a part of the skill exhibited in the daily occupations of eating, hunting, making war and peace, constructing rugs, pottery, and baskets, etc., they are consciously impressed upon the young; often, as in the initiation ceremonies, with intense emotional fervor. Even more pains are consciously taken to perpetuate the myths, legends, and sacred verbal formulae of the group than to transmit the directly useful customs of the group just because they cannot be picked up, as the latter can be in the ordinary processes of association.

As the social group grows more complex, involving a greater number of acquired skills which are dependent, either in fact or in the belief of the group, upon standard ideas deposited from past experience, the content of social life gets more definitely formulated for purposes of instruction. As we have previously noted, probably the chief motive for consciously dwelling upon the group life, extracting the meanings which are regarded as most important and systematizing them in a coherent arrangement, is just the need of instructing the young so as to perpetuate group life. Once started on this road of selection, formulation, and organization, no definite limit exists. The invention of writing and of printing gives the operation an immense impetus. Finally, the bonds which connect the subject matter of school study with the habits and ideals of the social group are disguised and covered up. The ties are so loosened that it often appears as if there were none; as if subject matter existed simply as knowledge on its own independent behoof, and as if study were the mere act of mastering it for its own sake, irrespective of any social values. Since it is highly important for practical reasons to counteract this tendency the chief purposes of our theoretical discussion are to make clear the connection which is so readily lost from sight, and to show in some detail the social content and function of the chief constituents of the course of study.

The points need to be considered from the standpoint of instructor and of student. To the former, the significance of a knowledge of subject matter, going far beyond the present knowledge of pupils, is to supply definite standards and to reveal to him the possibilities of the crude activities of the immature. (*i*) The material of school studies translates into concrete and detailed terms the meanings of current social life which it is desirable to transmit. It puts clearly before the instructor the essential ingredients of the culture to be perpetuated, in such an organized form as to protect him from the haphazard efforts he would be likely to indulge in if the meanings had not been standardized. (*ii*) A knowledge of the ideas which have been achieved in the past as the outcome of activity places the educator in a position to perceive the meaning of the seeming impulsive and aimless reactions of the young, and to provide the stimuli needed to direct them so that they will amount to something. The more the educator knows of music the more he can perceive the possibilities of the inchoate musical impulses of a child. Organized subject matter represents the ripe fruitage of experiences like theirs, experiences involving the same world, and powers and needs similar to theirs. It does not represent perfection or infallible wisdom; but it is the best at command to further new experiences which may, in some respects at least, surpass the achievements embodied in existing knowledge and works of art.

From the standpoint of the educator, in other words, the various studies represent working resources, available capital. Their remoteness from the experience of the young is not, however, seeming; it is real. The subject matter of the learner is not, therefore, it cannot be, identical with the formulated, the crystallized, and systematized subject matter of the adult; the material as found in books and in works of art, etc. The latter represents the *possibilities* of the former; not its existing state. It enters directly into the activities of the expert and the educator, not into that of the beginner, the learner. Failure to bear in mind the difference in subject matter from the respective standpoints of teacher and student is responsible for most of the mistakes made in the use of texts and other expressions of preëxistent knowledge.

The need for a knowledge of the constitution and functions, in the concrete, of human nature is great just because the teacher's attitude to subject matter is so different from that of the pupil. The teacher presents in actuality what the pupil represents only in *posse*. That is, the teacher already knows the things which the student is only learning. Hence the problem of the two is radically unlike. When engaged in the direct act of teaching, the instructor needs to have subject matter at his fingers' ends; his attention should be upon the attitude and response of the pupil. To understand the latter in its interplay with subject matter is his task, while the pupil's mind, naturally, should be not on itself but on the topic in hand. Or to state the same point in a somewhat different manner: the teacher should be occupied not with subject matter in itself but in its interaction with the pupil's present needs and capacities. Hence simple scholarship is not enough. In fact, there are certain features of scholarship or mastered subject matter—taken by itself—which get in the way of effective teaching *unless* the instructor's habitual attitude is one of concern with its interplay in the pupil's own experience. In the first place, his knowledge extends indefinitely beyond the range of the pupil's acquaintance. It involves principles which are beyond the immature pupil's understanding and interest. In and of itself, it may no more represent the living world of the pupil's experience than the astronomer's knowledge of Mars represents a baby's acquaintance with the room in which he stays. In the second place, the method of organization of the material of achieved scholarship differs from that of the beginner. It is not true that the experience of the young is unorganized—that it consists of isolated scraps. But it is organized in connection with direct practical centers of interest. The child's home is, for example, the organizing center of his geographical knowledge. His own movements about the locality, his journeys abroad, the tales of his friends, give the ties which hold his items of information together. But the geography of the geographer, of the one who has already developed the implications of these smaller experiences, is organized on the basis of the relationship which the various facts bear to one another—not the relations which they bear to his house, bodily movements, and friends. To the one who is learned, subject matter is extensive, accurately defined, and logically interrelated. To the one who is learning, it is fluid, partial, and connected through his personal occupations.[1] The problem of teaching is to keep the experience of the student moving in the direction of what the expert already knows. Hence the need that the teacher know both subject matter and the characteristic needs and capacities of the student.

THEODORE BRAMELD | *Imperatives for a Reconstructed Philosophy of Education*

Recently an invitation came to me, as it did to others, that was unusual not only in itself but because of its signers. I was asked to comment for the impending 10th Anniversary Conference of the New Lincoln School on this kind of question: "What should American education become in the next ten years?" The signers were William H. Kilpatrick, Jerrold Zacharias, Arthur Bestor, and Robert M. Hutchins. Almost anyone would be intrigued by such an invitation: could it mean that leaders representing such extremely diverse educational views as Kilpatrick and Hutchins were actually going to listen carefully to one another? My reply provides the framework for this article.

Addressing myself to Dr. Kilpatrick, I wrote as follows:

> Your desire to include the views of people of very different educational outlooks is most commendable and surely much needed in a time of extraordinary concern. . . . As you know, my own philosophic position in education is quite unorthodox and differs at rather crucial points not only from your own but particularly from that of Dr. Bestor and Dr. Hutchins whose names accompany your own. . . . I assume that, since you have written me, you wish to have my viewpoint heard along with others.
>
> . . . The challenge of the sputnik has not only aroused the American people from their educational lethargy as few if any events have done, but it has

[1] Since the learned man should also still be a learner, it will be understood that these contrasts are relative, not absolute. But in the earlier stages of learning at least they are practically all-important.

From *School and Society*, Vol. 87, No. 2145 (January 17, 1959), pp. 18–20. Reprinted by permission of the publisher.

since demonstrated the appalling confusion among us as to the functions and purposes of education in our democracy. Even more appalling, if that is possible, is the evidence that exceedingly powerful voices in America—exemplified by *Life* and *Time*—oversimplify and prejudge the issues. The editorial in the March 31st [1958] issue of *Life*, reprinted in *Time, The New York Times,* and elsewhere, so outrageously falsified these issues that the Philosophy of Education Society in its annual meeting, Indianapolis, April 2, 1958, unanimously went on record in condemnation of such "irresponsible" journalism. The President of the Society, incidentally, was Father R. J. Henle, S.J., and many members are in disagreement with the philosophy of John Dewey, which was especially under attack in the editorial.

And yet, in one respect, the thesis of the *Life* editorial represents the attitudes of millions of so-called, self-appointed "authorities" on American education. This thesis is, of course, that education must ultimately choose between two points of view—the one, represented by the progressivism of Dewey and his disciples; the other, represented by the kind of neoconservatism which *Life* itself espouses and which, typified by the writings of such earnest persons as Professor Bestor, has the support of all those forces in the culture that identify education with traditional forms of learning and classical subject matters.

. . . This kind of either-or choice is quite as false as is the kind of pseudosyntheses and patchwork proposals exemplified in the equally earnest writings of Professor Paul Woodring. There is, I submit, a radically different approach to the problem which we shall have to give consideration if we are not to be deluded indefinitely by oversimplifications and fuzzy or nostalgic thinking. This approach is based upon at least two fundamental premises.

The first premise is that we live today in one of the greatest periods of crisis in human history. Granting that all history consists of recurrent crises, this one is unprecedented in several ways, the most monstrous of which is the fact that man has achieved the capacity to destroy civilization over night. America, living as it does in an aura of deceptive prosperity and complacency, refuses thus far to admit this fact with any real conviction. In many other parts of the world, however, the masses of people are very deeply concerned—so deeply that, as anyone knows who follows world events, our own country is looked upon with more and more skepticism, less and less as the great democratic vanguard which it once was.

The second premise is that, just as the physical sciences have recently passed through a revolution which was, indeed, partly responsible for the crisis itself, so today the behavioral sciences . . . are rapidly entering upon a revolution of their own. This revolution is already awakening those familiar with it to the realization that mankind is now approaching the opportunity to achieve a world civilization of abundance, health, and humane capacity that is as life-affirming and promising as the crisis symbolized by sputniks and hydrogen bombs is life-denying and dreadful.

The kind of education needed in America must, I submit, be reconstructed upon these two premises. It can become an education that inspires young people to adventure and creation and yet is at diametrically opposite poles from its one real opponent—the totalitarian education of the communist orbit.

Instead of being based upon outmoded conceptions of learning and discipline, such as are at bottom endorsed by the neoconservative forces, it can utilize the richest resources of the behavioral sciences and a theory of unified man which those resources elucidate. The superficial arguments of the pro-science versus the pro-humanities groups are overarched in the same way as are those between the so-called educationists and academicians.

Teacher training, for example, would of course be reorganized once such a conception took hold. Of course it is cluttered with busy work, with overemphasis upon method, and with all sorts of absurdities. But so, too, would the liberal-arts program of the typical high school and college require reorganization—characterized as it often is with a chaos of unrelated courses, bad teaching, and unmotivated learning. Neither teacher training nor liberal arts can be called satisfactory because neither is governed by a philosophy of education and culture suitable to a world in crisis. And neither is satisfactory because neither is aware (except vaguely at most) that a revolution in the behavioral sciences, which is breaking down old classifications and opening new vistas of human potentiality, is already well under way.

I cannot now indicate in any detail what this conception would mean for the curriculum, for standards of scholarship, for school administration, or for the profession of teaching; I can only suggest that it does mean a completely new look at all of them. The question of how to move from the high level of generalization to the concrete level of practice is, however, answerable in one way here. There is pressing need for new forms of educational experimentation —new designs in the form of testable hypotheses. . . . The time has come to initiate audacious, imaginative pilot projects based upon the conception I have tried to indicate. Teachers and students alike would enter into them with an excitement that could be contagious, and that could affect education not only throughout America but throughout other countries that are attuned to the crisis of our time and await our leadership again.

The remaining paragraphs spell out a little further the implications of the above statement.

The first premise—that we live in an age of crisis—is supportable in a great many ways besides the one selected for mention. Granting that destruction by nuclear war is the most horrifying fear of our time, only a little less horrifying are the insidious disintegrations threatened by radioactive fallouts. Add to these the record of two bloody intercontinental wars within a quarter-century, the rise of a mighty totalitarian system that already jeopardizes America's position as the foremost industrial power, and now the looming conquest of space with its portents of evil as well as good. For any educational system not to give these events priority, for it not to provide every possible opportunity to diagnose their causes and to consider how the growing generation may cope with them while time remains, is for that system to shirk its most urgent responsibility.

Although certain other viewpoints besides the one I support would agree on the fact of major crisis, no other derives from it similar educational imperatives. The most crucial of these rest upon the second major premise—the revolution occurring in the behavioral sciences. This revolution requires education to re-examine its whole conventional structure and to consider new ways of (1) ordering its subject matters, (2) engaging in the processes by which they are taught and learned, and (3) formulating the purposes of school and society.

None of these imperatives would have been practicably realizable before the emergence of such young sciences as cultural anthropology and psychiatry, or the interrelating of these with such older ones as economics, sociology, and history. None of them depends upon metaphysical or otherwise speculative doctrines of the classical philosophies. All of them, while open to a great deal of further clarification and verification, are potentially demonstrable and defensible in the same way that all science is demonstrable and defensible.

Let me try now to illustrate each of the three imperatives in educational terms.

1. Up to this time, the structure of the typical school and college curriculum has been largely a jumble of discrete subject matters that, for the average student, have little or no meaningful relations to one another—languages, mathematics, social science, natural science, and others—each of which is often again subdivided into further discrete units. The behavioral sciences are now demonstrating that, as far at least as all the areas having to do with biopsychological experience are concerned, these divisions and subdivisions are less and less tenable. Concepts such as organism, connoting relationships between parts as much as the parts related, are replacing the older atomistic concepts. Human life, individually and culturally, is increasingly seen in terms of patterns and configurations.

Programs of general or integrated education, recognizing that something must be done to give meaningful unity to the curriculum structure, have sometimes been tangentially affected by this interdisciplinary view of human behavior. Unfortunately, however, they also have been plagued by the same confusions in theory and practice that are chronic to other educational programs. Some general educationists, for example, take their cue from the physical sciences; others, from neo-scholasticism or like doctrines. Few as yet regard the tasks and goals of human beings as the first and most important concern of vital education in an age such as our, or, for that matter, in any age.

This is not to say that the physical sciences, any more than the humanities, should be neglected by the needed new framework. It does mean that they are encompassed by it. A theory of unified man, both derived from and contributing to our experimental knowledge of human behavior in its multiple perspectives, not only should integrate all other fields of knowledge; it should provide them with a fresh and potent significance.

2. The required rebuilding of teaching and learning processes is heralded by a great body of recent behavioral research, only a fraction of which has begun to permeate educational practice. Perhaps the one point where permeation has occurred at all fruitfully thus far is in the methodology of "group dynamics." Yet, even here, as so commonly happens in educational circles, it has acquired more often the earmarks of a superficial fad than of a profound process dependent upon a widening range of discoveries about the "fields of force" that constitute the interactions of human beings in their multiple roles.

Even more promising is the "culture-and-personality" frontier. Here anthropologists and psychologists are joining hands. And they are demonstrating that learning, for example, involves polaristic dimensions of inner and outer experience, some of it quite unconscious, that have been almost totally neglected by the orthodox formulations still underlying classroom routines.

Again, the problem of how to enlist education in the processes of institutional change so that it functions, not merely to transmit but to modify and reconstruct outmoded arrangements, can now be attacked with the aid of substantial knowledge. The concept of crisis itself exemplifies this opportunity. Citing outstanding authorities in the behavioral sciences, I have pointed out elsewhere that

> There is no good reason, except timidity or irresponsibility, that prevents high schools and colleges from encouraging young people to analyze both the meaning of crisis theoretically and its manifestations overtly. Leaders ought accordingly to clarify their orientation here: they ought to face the issue of whether education is to be regarded as capable of sharing importantly in the control and resolution of crises, or as a pawn of overpowering material or spiritual forces beyond control and resolution.[1]

3. The shaping of new purposes for education and culture is also becoming feasible in a way that could hardly have been conceived even three or four decades ago. In other words, the behavioral sciences are beginning to prove, really for the first time in history, that it is possible to formulate human goals not for sentimental, romantic, mystical, or similarly arbitrary reasons, but on the basis of what we are learning about cross-cultural and even universal values. Though studies in this difficult field have moved only a little way, they have moved far enough so that it is already becoming plausible both to describe these values objectively and to demonstrate that most human beings prefer them to alternative values.

Freedom is an example. By analyzing drives and motivations, by deter-

[1] "Cultural Foundations of Education—An Interdisciplinary Exploration" (New York: Harper, 1957), p. 153.

mining what human beings in many different cultures most deeply need and want, freedom both as fact and norm undergoes something of a metamorphosis of meaning. Yet it preserves the rich kernel of significance intuited by Jefferson and other geniuses of a pre-scientific age.

This way of constructing educational purposes rests, too, upon an expanding inventory of research evidence. Human resources for a happy life on earth are infinitely greater than we have ever dreamed possible—resources that we have hardly begun to tap because we are so often blinded by conflict, ignorance, and fear. A truly goal-centered education could contribute more than any other agency to displacing these destructive forces by scientifically ascertainable and testable hopes for the future of mankind.

To what extent is educational theory presently concerned with the kind of imperatives that I have indicated? I regret to say: very little, indeed. The only recent books that, in my judgment, help (each in a different way) are three: *The Ideal and the Community—A Philosophy of Education*, by I. B. Berkson;[2] *Philosophy of Education for Our Time*, by Frederick Mayer;[3] and *Philosophy and Education*, edited by Israel Scheffler.[4]

It is difficult, however, to feel that the dominant neo-conservative mood of the moment is anything more than passing. The single most encouraging fact about the behavioral sciences as they are now swiftly developing (I have been able, of course, to reveal only a few glimpses) is that they offer so little comfort to those of such a timid if not defeatist mood and so much support to those who continue deeply to believe in the need of a philosophy and program appropriate to our revolutionary age.

[2] (New York: Harper, 1958.)
[3] (New York: Odyssey, 1958.)
[4] (Boston: Allyn and Bacon, 1958.)

VAN CLEVE MORRIS | ***Existentialism and the Education of Twentieth-Century Man***

As philosophies go, existentialism may be said to be something of a "special case." Born of crisis in Europe, it has found tough going in a sensate, indulgent, and philosophically self-satisfied America. Imported into the United States it has had to buck not only the well known mass-man, conformist patterns of contemporary life, but also the more sophisti-

From *Educational Theory*, Vol. 4, No. 4 (October 1954), pp. 247–258. Reprinted by permission of the author and publisher.

cated notion that Dewey's Experimentalism is all America needs in the way of ideological rationale. Signs are posted: "New philosophies (especially gloomy ones)—Keep Out!"

Existentialism therefore enjoys only the most precarious of reputations today. Many people, even intellectuals who should know better, have the vague feeling that it is a kind of mystical and somewhat illicit poetry which is concocted in an apparently nihilist atmosphere on the Parisian Left Bank by intense characters who wear little beards. The Italian philosopher Guido de Ruggiero, for example, calls it "metaphysical pornography."

Or perhaps, as *Life* magazine seems to make it out, it is a form of lower-classlessness resembling a morally negativistic "country club," what you might call a super-Bohemian offshoot of the Greenwich Village variety of institutionalized Bohemianism, made up of individuals who are avant-avant-garde, wear dirty T-shirts, live in San Francisco, make a studied effort to look "beat," and get written about by Jack Kerouac.

I don't know that it matters too much whether these people are or are not Existentialists. What quite obviously does matter, however, is that sober and thoughtful attention be given to the authentic message of Existentialism and what this message has to say about the management of the educative process. To achieve the necessary sobriety, this paper means to turn from these spectacular, semi-licit images the public mind has developed concerning this outlook, and to address itself directly to the central position of Existentialist thinkers.

What does Existentialism say? It comes as something of a surprise to many people that it is not so complicated and esoteric as they had thought. The focal problem resides within every one of us and it is relatively simple to describe. Every human being lives out his every day with a monstrous paradox he cannot resolve. In the first place, you must take the position that you are the most important being in the world. There is no other possible platform from which to view life. You are the center of everything, the focal headquarters for all that you experience. And you always place a higher valuation on your continuing existence than of any other being in the world. Heroic suicides to the contrary notwithstanding, every individual's conscious selfhood exerts a continuing existential judgment in its own favor. That is to say, we assign to our selves—without any help from Christian doctrine or democratic preachments about the worth of the individual—we assign to our own selves, I say, an *absolute* value and an ultimate worth.

On the other hand, each of us knows that, when you come right down to it, we count for absolutely nothing. The universe does not require our perpetual existence—our mortality proves it. Nor does it take any kind of stand, pro or con, on our longevity. Concerning our existence, the cosmos, in the idiom of our time, "couldn't care less."

Now this, to the Existentialist, is the central predicament of human existence, the contradiction of absolute worth and absolute worthlessness in our being. And it is this predicament which prompts such ugly language in Existentialist writings as "anguish," "despair," "homelessness," and "nausea." For any thoughtful person, if he does not turn away from this predicament, cannot experience anything else.

Now it is true that we have invented all sorts of palliatives for this malaise. The classical humanists invented a set of Platonic Ideas to whose understanding man was in a sense privy. Human exclusiveness in the Rationalists' Club gave us a feeling of rank in the natural order. The Medievalists and, of course, others throughout human time gave us religions, and Gods, and transcendental love to convince us that we really counted for something. And modern man has found that society—other people—can, in a secular kind of way, provide the support for an existence that continuously borders on the impossible. Worth, dignity, value, i.e., really counting as a self, are all now to be found, if one wants to, in the social collective.

The appeal to other people—the modern approach—turns out to be far more powerful than most of us suppose. David Riesman, sociologist now with Harvard, has added a new word and concept to our language, i.e., *otherdirectedness.* His analysis and documentation of this new character trait in America in *The Lonely Crowd* was masterful and convincing. But there now come along more detailed findings to document the awful power of these "others."

For instance, Elaine Bell, a psychologist, has found a decided preference for "groups" as against "individualist" hobbies, careers, and life objectives in a group of high school and college students.[1]

At Purdue University, Prof. H. H. Remmers has been studying adolescents for seventeen years. His most recent work indicates that high school youngsters almost always look to see what others think before saying or doing anything. Questioned concerning their problems and desires, these youngsters give as their most frequent response: "Want people to like me more." In a kind of scholarly despair, Remmers concludes: "As a nation we seem to have a syndrome characterized by atrophy of the will, hypertrophy of the ego and dystrophy of the intellectual musculature."[2]

Perhaps the most grotesque, Frankensteinish psychological experiment was conducted at the Laboratory of Social Relations at Harvard University. In this study it was found possible to induce a subject to tell downright lies in order to find acceptance in a group. As the reporter of this fascinating study summed it up: "That we have found the tendency to

[1] Reported in David Riesman, "Psychological Types and National Character," *American Quarterly* (Winter 1953), pp. 340–1.

[2] H. H. Remmers and D. H. Radler, "Teenage Attitudes," *Scientific American* (June 1958), p. 26.

conformity in our society so strong that reasonably intelligent and well-meaning young people are willing to call white black is a matter of concern. It raises questions about our ways of education and about the values that guide our conduct."[3]

It is plain to see that in our own time we look to other people to provide the sustenance we all need to be certain that we count for something in this life. But the point is, getting back to our problem, that, while we have historically concocted various nostrums for our "sickness unto death," we have not in any way treated the disease; we have only received the symptoms with psychological analgesics. And the distressing irony of it all is that as we find our sense of worth today in social togetherness, we mistake the consequent glow we get for real health. Like the dope addict who relies on a daily dose of heroin, we get the same boot from a daily dose of other people. In this special kind of euphoria, we say with the addict, "we're really livin'!"

Of course, this is not "really livin' " at all; it is just the opposite—it is to be only partially alive. To want the nearness of other people in our lives is to choose a pleasant numbness to the predicament we are in—the predicament of ultimate lost-ness within the paradox described earlier. As with heroin, when we bury ourselves in the social collective we purchase a subtraction from pain at the cost of a paralysis of the will. And to become habituated to it, that is, to crave and hunger for the company of others and to turn gregariousness itself into a moral value (as we have done in modern America), is to testify to the dangerously advanced stage of our situation. Modern man is in a kind of somnambulant torpor in which he has rendered the world more comfortable and hospitable than it really is by inoculating himself against its most distressing attribute, namely, its total indifference to man.

It is for this reason that modern man is not easily convinced that he is sick. He strides about his globe in scientific splendor, matter in one hand, energy in the other, proclaiming his conquest of the elements. But once back home from the campaign, he hasn't the faintest idea of what to do with all his technological plunder. He is lost under a pile of his own war medals.

Now what does all this imagery really mean? To the Existentialist it means simply that the paradox cannot be solved in this way, that to pass from paradox to palliative, to relieve our psychic pain with artificial narcotics, is to pass from aliveness to numbness in this exciting adventure called human life. It means that once we recognize the nature of our predicament, once we see that the full exercise of the spontaneous human self is the avenue to authenticity as a person, and what is more, once we

[3] Solomon Asch, "Opinions and Social Pressure," *Scientific American* (November 1955), p. 34.

discover we are really up to it, we will forget about palliatives and pain killers and return to the place where we belong—the stadium of human choice where men can establish their sense of worth, where they can pronounce their value to the cosmos through the very lives they choose to lead.

It is something of a shock to realize that one has a human life all his own, that he can render this life and its works unto any God he chooses, that he can lay it upon the altar of any value he selects. None of us is quite prepared for this recognition; it is, so to speak, too much for us. The ones who come closest to understanding what this means are perhaps the Zen Buddhists. In Zen (which comes from the Japanese word meaning to sit and meditate) there is a primary attention to the nature of the human will. If you reflect for a moment on the fact of one human life completely within your charge, you will recognize the enormous region of decision open to you to make this life say to the cosmos what you want it to say. The totality of your will is so complete that it can even end this life, truncating the message this life is delivering to the cosmos. Thus, the will has domain over everything—except one thing: its origin. To put it more simply, the willing self had no jurisdiction over its own creation. It just found itself in existence. And when the self awakens to this, awakens to the recognition that it is now responsible for a life for which it was not initially responsible, we can see the emergence of the self-same predicament of the Existentialists.

For this is what the Existentialists mean by the priority of existence, indeed why they call themselves Existentialists. The customary view, both in popular language and in classical philosophy, is that the Idea or essence of Man preceded the creation or existence of Man, in quite the same way that the idea of a Cadillac emerges in the designer's mind before the factory hands put one together. The popular conception of God is that of the Supreme Designer or Idea Man. The Existentialists turn this around to say that, while Cadillacs may happen this way, man did not. Man arrived without a plan. He awakened to his existence and is now forced, by virtue of his will, to shape his own design. In short, man wakes up to find himself here; he then sets about the task of declaring his own nature, in establishing the Idea of Man. Hence, existence comes before essence.

I do not think this idea is altogether ridiculous. It is reenacted in a microcosmic way by every one of us in our own lives. We grow up from infancy into childhood quite oblivious of our own selves. We eat, we sleep, we play, we learn; but we are really not in charge of our own lives. This is because we are not really aware that we exist. Then some time around the early teens, there comes a moment—which I shall call the "Existential Moment"—when suddenly we clasp ourselves and exclaim, "It's me, me! I'm a person. I'm here!" We may possibly regress at times, especially when under punitive treatment by our parents, to the view that "Well, I didn't ask to be born!" Which, of course, is quite right. But it is no longer relevant; it is perhaps the most ridiculous irrelevancy a person can utter. For the fact of the matter is that whether you asked to be born or not, here you are, present in the world, committed to responsibility for your own life.

Thus, in Existentialism there is an absolute inevitability about the human predicament. We are placed, whether we like it or not, into a circumstance of choice and responsibility. Even were we to choose not to choose, this would still be a choice, still a signal to indicate what we wished our life to say in our behalf. And what is more, there would be no escaping our responsibility for choosing not to choose. There is no escape back to moral infancy once you have passed the Existential Moment.

The world that opens out to us after we pass this critical point is a baffling and difficult place to inhabit. Tillich speaks of it as essentially an "encounter with meaninglessness." He does so not with any sign of deprecation or despair, for we must always remember that a world of meaninglessness, that is, a world that does not have meaning already woven into and embedded in it, is a world which, in a manner of speaking, is "on our side." That is, it presents possibilities without exacting the reciprocal tribute of human compliance. If there is no *a priori* meaning to it—and this is the way Existentialism looks at the world—then we can creatively assign meaning to it. We are on our own. And it is not too early to suggest that boys and girls, as they grow up and go to school, might better be inducted into this kind of open-ended world than into the ready-built, card-house worlds our traditional educational programs would have them know.

For the open-ended world, the world of all possibilities and no compliances (except those that we impose upon ourselves) is the most exciting kind of world one can hope to live in. It is difficult, to be sure, and the challenges it presents may daunt the more flimsy and fragile among us, leading to the malaise of anguish, homesickness, and nausea of which we have spoken. But this is not so much a rebuke of the world as it is a critique of the half-men who populate the earth and require all kinds of protection from the metaphysical elements. They are huddling together in their air-conditioned huts—their enclosed orthodoxies and their insulated societies—where all is relatively peaceful and serene, convincing each other of their essential preciousness as human beings in the total scheme of things. These people are, of course, entitled to their own air-conditioning; but they cannot claim full human stature, in Existentialist terms, until they realize that the world, the real world of men, is outside in the cold and heat of brute circumstance.

Albert Camus has written vividly of this world, of the strangeness of it, of the sense of rebellion we feel at attempts to screen it out and filter it down to make it less strange and less real. As one of his commentators has so aptly said, "The work of Albert Camus is of the kind that requires us to be worthy of it."[4]

To be worthy of an author is to be worthy of the kind of existence he describes. It is to be worthy of the role that human beings have been cast in, the role of ultimate moral choice. I think, in a way, that, for all their self-conscious rebellion, the so-called San Francisco Group are testing to see if they are worthy of this kind of world. They have chosen to move out of the air-conditioned moral system of upper-middle-class America, where split-levels, station wagons, and togetherness have become indiscriminate badges of the amorphous elite. They have ripped to shreds, voluntarily, their protective canopy of orthodox values: working for a living, striving to get ahead, purchasing amusement in prepared packages on television and at the drive-in. They have instead nihilistically turned away from this and struck out on their own, in some kind of unpiloted search for meaning in modern life.

What they will find no one can know. But they are quite certainly living a fuller kind of life than the rest of us as we plod through day after day making only those motions and uttering only those thoughts which have been thoroughly roadtested for acceptability. I do not mean to say that their life is necessarily any higher, only that it is fuller in the sense of involvement in moral choice. There is nothing essentially superior about being an odd-ball. Professional odd-balls—what I have referred to elsewhere as "card-carrying Bohemians"—have no more Existentialist rank than anyone else. But whoever involves himself in problems of moral judgment, whoever deliberately inserts himself into situations requiring human decision, he is the one for whom the Existentialist will hold a place in whatever might be an Existentialist's heaven.

This is so for the simple reason that an individual cannot be expected to take charge of his own life, to fashion in the living of his life a statement of what he thinks his life is all about, if he refuses to involve himself in moral decision. There is no more chance for him to do this than there if for Mickey Mantle to hit 6- home runs next year by sitting out every other game to keep his strikeout total down. If we mean to assert our humanity, it can only be done in the thick of the human predicament, not in some comfortable isolation booth of social convention. And it is precisely because modern man has chosen the isolation booth, in preference to the bracing but admittedly difficult moral weather outside, that Existentialism becomes so relevant today.

The paradox of the human self, if confronted seriously, no doubt stirs up every metaphysical anguish imaginable; but one thing is certain—it

[4] Albert Maquet, *Albert Camus: The Invincible Summer* (trans. from French by H. Briffault) (New York, G. Braziller, 1958), p. vii.

cannot be resolved lying down. The only proper posture to assume in the face of this paradox is to live our lives *as if* what we do and say shall be added up somewhere as our contribution to the definition of Man. We need assume neither that we count for everything nor that we count for nothing in this world; the only imperative is that we recognize that what we *do* count for will be determined by what we "say" with our own individual lives. And to this, we must accept total involvement in the moral situation of man, total entanglement in the net of choice which is the only world the self can truly inhabit.

Now what can all of this bizarre language have to do with educating boys and girls; what, to be specific, would an Existentialist program of education be like? To answer this question, we must refer briefly to the popular meaning of education in modern, civilized society. We are told on good authority that the school is above all a *social* institution, that its principal function in modern life is to recreate in each individual the beliefs, outlooks, behaviors, and preferences of the society which it serves. To do this effectively and efficiently we in America have insisted via compulsory attendance laws that all of our youngsters participate in this activity. To assert that we have socialized the educational process in this country is to utter the most fatuous of understatements; we have taken John Dewey at his word and turned education into the crowning paradigm of corporate group life.

Now this is all very good and there is nothing particularly pernicious or monstrous about it. But it does tend to blur the image we have of the developing individual. The school is not just a social institution; it is also an "individual" institution, i.e., an institution for individuals. Indeed it is somewhat of an irony, pointed out some years ago by Professor Boyd Bode, that while so-called progressive education pretended to give so much new prominence to the individual in its educational doctrine, it wound up burying him in group dynamics in the socialized learning process. We are now called upon to extricate the poor fellow from the crushing overload of social controls that he takes on in school and to find again that the school is a school for individual selves quite as much as it is a school for social integration.

What this means is simply that the school must direct its attention to the release of the human self, to the involvement of the child in personal decision and moral judgment to a far greater degree than he knows at present. He is too tangled up in group controls, as the Harvard experiment vividly shows, to learn much about what and who he is. He is too enmeshed in peer-group response to discover that he is there himself as one of the peers.

We thought when we secularized the school that we had driven orthodoxy and narrowness out of the educational process. The great historical joke, however, is that while we have successfully driven sectarian, religious orthodoxies out of the school we have simultaneously driven the school into the waiting arms of another kind of orthodoxy, i.e., the tyranny of middle class society. The task now is to perform another bit of social surgery to separate at least a part of the youngster's school life from the moral tyranny of the community.

To take a concrete example, consider the matter of privacy and quiet reflection. How much opportunity is there in a typical school in America for a youngster to sit still and quiet and go over the personal choices he must make that day? I venture to say that it would be difficult to locate a minute and a half in a typical schoolboy's day for this kind of activity. We have elevated gregariousness to the status of a moral commitment for today's youth. It is now suspicious behavior to declare that one wants to be alone. Privacy has declined both as a behavior trait and as a worthwhile thing in our lives; it is a new and embarrassed form of immorality to separate one's self from other people, to reflect quietly on what one is doing, to locate where one is in the rolling ocean of social experience. The great doctrine of "shared experience," so novel and exciting when John Dewey first announced it, has flooded down over the social landscape as if it were a moral law, and it has flushed us all out into the public open where we can no longer call our private selves our own.

This, to the Existentialist, is the tragedy of modern Western life, and the super-tragedy is that American public education is presently designed to aggravate instead of rectify this sorry predicament. The first task, then, of any Existentialist program would be to provide for more private experience for the child while he learns in school. It is noteworthy, it seems to me, that there are tell-tale signs of this in the field of art.[5] In this portion of the school program, at both the elementary and secondary levels, there is a real and genuine interest in allowing the individual youngster to look at his world and to say with his hands what he sees, without prior compliance with so-called artistic laws of form, balance, and line. It is altogether possible that Existentialism will establish its first beachhead in education in the field of the arts.

But the provision of private experience in the program of the school is not all, simply because it is not enough. What one does with his privacy, what content he puts into his reflection is the vital statistic of learning. And the Existentialist educator is necessarily interested in having the youngster fill his quiet moments with the personal judgments he must make concerning his own life. That is to say, his reflections should contain the subject matter of moral choice. If the Humanists wish to fill the mind with the content of our intellectual past and if the Experimentalists wish to develop trained intelligence through the solving of problems,

[5] See V. C. Morris and I. L. de Francesco, "Modern Art and the Modern School," *The Clearing House* (October 1957), pp. 67–71.

certainly there should be a little time in the school day for awakening the moral powers of young people to get them to ask who they are and what they are doing around here.

This might be done, I think, in a number of ways. Reference was made above to the so-called Existential Moment in each of our lives. That this moment comes after we have been going to school for six or eight years is a fact of enormous significance, it seems to me, for elementary education. During these half dozen years we do not, I say, know who we are; we do not even know *that* we are. We are not yet existentially awake. But once we come awake, perhaps around the sixth or seventh grade, the elementary school should seize upon every opportunity to present moral problems to the youngster—at the level of his understanding—to provide small beginnings for the long, slow climb to moral maturity. Preferably these problems should be the kind that have no answer, such as "What would you do if you knew everything?" or "Is it ever right to kill a man?" At the very least they should open up the moral sphere to youngsters to introduce them to the most difficult sector of the world they inhabit. Moreover, if some of the anecdotes I hear are accurate, there is a genuine appetite for moral problems in the child of the age here considered.

Somewhat later in his schooling, a youngster should be given a more systematic exposure to the ethical questions of life. Perhaps he might be asked to imagine himself in complete charge of another individual, capable of making him do anything, experience anything, desire anything, know anything. What, for the assignment, would be his plan of life for this individual? Then when this assignment was complete, the teacher could ask the student to compare this program with what plans he has for himself.

From this point forward, into college and beyond, the individual should be constantly provoked to expand upon this plan for his developing self, checking here, amending there, but always mindful of the control he has over his own single life, the precious offering he is to contribute to the developing Idea of Man. We should all, I suppose, wish that we had more than one life to work on; there are so many mistakes. But one is all we are allotted. Nathan Hale, if he had been a little more metaphysical with his heroism, might just as well have said "I regret I have but one life to give to Man."

I should suppose from all of this that the school in the Existentialist frame would become a more metaphysical kind of place than it is at present. This should not frighten anybody. I am only suggesting that the ultimate questions of life and destiny should have some place in the educative program along with all the penultimate and lower-order questions which currently claim the student's entire attention. And ultimate questions are the kind which force us to ask ourselves whether our inner sense of worth is to gain recognition somewhere beyond this existence.

If we could somehow simply awaken boys and girls to the "need for ultimate recognition," to the idea that the universe does not respond obligingly to this need, and that when all is said and done we ourselves are the authors of the response this need must have through our own lives and works, then we should be on our way to a newer and, I think, higher kind of meaning in the education of the young.

PETER SCHRAG | *Education's "Romantic" Critics*

In the free-for-all of educational commentary, where the half life of ideas is pitifully short, the ashes of fallen gods often materialize in the bodies of new critics. Jefferson and Rousseau returned in the form of John Dewey, Pestalozzi in the work of Maria Montessori, and now Dewey is re-emerging in what is probably the most significant body of educational criticism since World War II. What makes this criticism significant, however, is not its debt to the master, but its irreverent freshness, and, more often than not, its radical refusal to accept the terms of the increasingly sterile debates of the past twenty years.

The new critics—Edgar Z. Friedenberg, Paul Goodman, Jules Henry, John Holt, and others—are far too independent and cantankerous to develop a consistent voice or anything that could be considered a program, but their common defense of children and adolescents and their fundamental attacks on established practices have given them a place apart from the conventional critics. They have been attacked as anti-intellectuals and hailed as saviors. But for the most part the established leadership of American education has simply ignored them.

In many respects the new critics are more interested in the processes of growing up, in learning and experience, than they are in the formalities of educational programs, the design of curricula, or the planning of administrative conveniences. They share with Dewey a faith in the healthy capabilities of children and with Rousseau a belief that "everything is good as it comes from the hands of the creator; everything degenerates in the hands of man." Holt writes that "nobody is born stupid," that "we encourage children to act stupidly." In their common view, a hostile society and its educational system cripple and destroy the processes of learning, the dignity of youth, and the natural instincts of curiosity and self-realization, and they regard schools particularly as coercive instruments designed to enforce conformity and deny self-esteem. Their tone is often that of the radical left, but the values are conservative, upholding the virtues of honest, meaningful work, of community and family, and of civil human relationships. Some of this criticism—and notably Goodman's—contains a sense of loss and a feeling that somewhere in the past the world offered opportunities to the young man—that there is no longer any "man's work" to do. To Goodman, the society now looks on the young not as individuals but as part of some "national purpose," making them "an exploited and an outcast class."

Although the new critics are all teachers, and are all affiliated with American education, they belong to no establishment, nor even to a single kind of institution. Spiritually—and often physically—they are itinerants. Their home, if they have one at all, is the liberal weekly or monthly, the campus lecture platform (often at the invitation of students), and occasionally the scholarly journal. Friedenberg is a sociologist now teaching at the University of California at Davis, Goodman a humanist and novelist who has become a kind of academic traveler, Henry an anthropologist at Washington University (St. Louis), and Holt a teacher in a private secondary school. Nevertheless they share common attitudes derived from their belief that contemporary society and its educational system are hostile to the processes of learning and maturation. Goodman's books—*Growing Up Absurd* (1956), *The Community of Scholars* (1962), and *Compulsory Mis-education* (1964)—Friedenberg's *The Vanishing Adolescent* (1959) and *Coming of Age in America* (1965), and Henry's *Culture Against Man* (1963) are variations on the theme of alienation, empty conformity, and middle-class repression. Holt, in *How Children Fail,* is primarily concerned with the strategies teachers and students employ in the classroom—the way students learn to beat the system without learning to understand mathematics or science or history; Friedenberg is preeminently a sociologist of adolescence; Goodman the voice of the alienated college student and the elder statesman of the New Left. But their works overlap and intersect. They are all reports on the emptiness of the adult world and on the way teachers, guidance counselors, parents, and administrators seduce and coerce children into self-denial, how they teach them games of evasion, and how they deprive them of their desires for honest confrontations with the adult world.

Friedenberg writes in *The Vanishing Adolescent:*

> Adolescent growth can and should lead to a completely human adulthood; defined as a stable sense of self, it could lead nowhere else. . . . Youngsters who do not achieve this stability [are], in a sense, victims of cruelty, misfortune, or social pathology. . . . But they are also the products of what, in

our society, is normal growth; of growth that is consistently distorted so as to lead to the outcome society actually expects, and under ordinary circumstances, rewards. . . .

Subjective intensity, disciplined but not repressed, lies at the heart of integrity, of artistic creativity, and of adolescence. It seems to me in the last analysis, that *this* is what terrifies the contemporary middle-class adult most. Any individual through whom subjective intensity may intrude into the processes of bureaucratic equilibrium is extremely threatening to our society.

The argument is that adults fear adolescents, fear their unrepressed instincts and their honest questions—sexual and otherwise—because the adults themselves are too involved in conflicting commitments and ambiguous moral situations. Indeed, Friedenberg says, contemporary American society simply cannot tolerate the natural humanity of the young. It must therefore confuse and twist it, leaving an accumulation of pathology in its wake. To Goodman, dropouts, delinquents, and college beatniks are all victims of the same process, and have all refused to accept the terms of organized society and the empty rat race (his phrase) which it imposes. Here, as in other ideas, Goodman and Friedenberg borrow a great deal from David Riesman and Erik Erikson, who were among the first to explore the paths of contemporary alienation and conformity. What they add to these ideas, however, is not simply popularization or the optimistic view of human nature derived from Rousseau and Dewey, but also their observations of the demands and denials which schools and teachers inflict on the young. They are not interested in test scores, rates of college admission, and other ordinary means of evaluation. But they have gone to the classroom and the campus and have chosen to look at things that most teachers and administrators have never seen. They have become adept at analyzing the sociological and pedagogical games that schools and teachers play with their students, how they teach children to pretend and prevaricate. In *How Children Fail*, Holt concludes:

We have only to convince ourselves that a lie will be "better" for the children than the truth, and we will lie. We don't always need even that excuse; we often lie only for our own convenience. . . .

We present ourselves to children as if we were gods, all-knowing, all-powerful, always rational, always just, always right. This is worse than any lie we could tell about ourselves. . . . As we are not honest with them, so we won't let children be honest with us. . . . We require them to take part in the fiction that school is a wonderful place and that they love every minute of it. They learn early that not to like school or the teacher is *verboten*, not to be said, not to be even thought.

For Goodman, the whole process of conventional education is brainwashing:

The components are a uniform world-view, the absence of any viable alternative, confusion about the relevance of one's own experience and feelings, and a chronic anxiety, so that one clings to the one world-view as the only security. This *is* brainwashing.

Holt and Jules Henry advance the argument further with their contention that the whole educational process is obsessed with fear. "In order not to fail," says Henry in *Culture Against Man,* "most students are willing to believe anything and not to care whether what they are told is true or false. Thus one becomes absurd through being afraid; but paradoxically, only by remaining absurd can one feel free from fear." When Holt and Henry write that schools teach children to be stupid, they are describing a system that sacrifices curiosity and intelligence to the cause of order and simplicity in classroom management. To cite Henry again: "An intellectually creative child may fail, for example, in social studies, simply because he cannot understand the stupidities he is taught to believe as 'fact.' He may even end up agreeing with his teachers that he is 'stupid' in social studies. Learning in social studies is, to no small extent . . . learning to be stupid. The child with a socially creative imagination will not be encouraged to play among new social systems, values, and relationships; nor is there much likelihood of it, if for no other reason than that the social studies teachers will perceive such a child as a poor student."

Friedenberg, who sees conventional education in highly sophisticated terms, and who is considerably less prone to polemics than most of the others, describes the school—especially the high school—as a great engine functioning to obfuscate the human instincts and moral quests of the young. The school is more interested in good public relations, administrative convenience, and political peace than it is in the growth of its students. Thus, instead of confronting the problems of students directly, it denies or evades them, teaching its students that "they can only win esteem by how they look and behave, not for what they are. . . ." He continues:

> It is more firmly convinced than ever that its job is to teach youngsters to respond to other people's expectations. While it emphasizes the expression of personality, it conveys to the student that personality should be built on certain standard plans, superficially varied according to taste, and that expression should consist of a fairly continuously emitted code signal by which other persons can recognize what they want when they see it. If they don't want it, there must be something wrong with either the personality or the signal, and it must be changed.

In such a system even the rebelliousness of the lower-class youngster is quickly crushed:

These youngsters are handy with their fists and worse; but they are helpless in the meshes of middle-class administrative procedure and are rapidly neutralized and eliminated by it. . . . They quickly learn that the most terrifying creatures are those whose bite passes unnoticed at the time and later swells, festers, and paralyzes; they cannot defend themselves against the covert, lingering hostility of teachers and school administrators.

The school, in brief, becomes a production plant turning out shoddy goods for the dime-store trade; its teachers are not professionals but petty civil srevants; and guidance counselors, far from helping, generally operate as the agents of a "Ministry of Adjustment." The school denies students the right to go to the john without a pass, the privilege of determining how they will cut their hair or wear their clothes, even the honor of direct personal punishment:

What has been violated is not so much freedom as dignity. I do not mean simply that somebody has been unnecessarily rude—quite the opposite. Assaults on dignity are usually very friendly and well meaning—that is part of the strategy. But the action taken has been basically contemptuous of students, negligent of their real characteristics as human beings and indifferent to their needs and feelings as individuals. In the blandest possible way, they have been pushed around. They have been pitted against one another in strategically organized committees, seduced with litlte awards of leadership and contributions to school life; taught gamey old political tricks for ensuring the triumph of good government; playfully spanked for displaying undue and unreasonable ardor. If this is not enough, playfulness abruptly ceases and is replaced by pious sorrow that heedless young people are ruining their chances with their record in school. The record is being very carefully kept.

The arguments of the new critics take them into territory in which most other educational commentators fear to tread. By recognizing schools and colleges as agents of a society that is seriously maladjusted to human purposes, if not altogether sick, they attack the institutions not because they fail the purposes of the order, but because they are too successful. Goodman and Friedenberg are both critics of the leveling effect of a middle-class motivated and operated system of education that denies true distinction by pretending it doesn't exist, and they conclude by questioning the system itself. Goodman assigns the ultimate responsibility to a bureaucratic, warfare-oriented state that demands recruits to help make it function; Friedenberg places it in the insecurity of the lower middle class which staffs the schools and remains their chief influence. But both see the consequences in the same light and, independently, they arrive at similar recommendations.

Because the schools are destructive not only of genuine learning and academic quality, but also of personal dignity, they serve only the goals of an unhealthy social order and not the human purposes toward which education is presumably directed. Would it therefore not be better to abandon compulsory public education altogether in favor of a far more diversified set of voluntary opportunities ranging from apprentice trade programs to high quality boarding schools for rich and poor students? Would it not be preferable to make all education voluntary, for—in Goodman's words—"no growth to freedom occurs except by intrinsic motivation"? In urging these arguments Goodman and Friedenberg raise issues that not long ago would have been considered undiscussible. To question the validity of the American system of democratic education was like spitting on the flag, and any individual caught suggesting that it be broken up was immediately stripped of his credentials as a responsible critic.

Because of their inescapable radicalism and their assault on the absurdity of the conditions of growing up, Goodman, Holt, and the others have pejoratively been dubbed romantics (i.e., soft-headed). If the society has to be reconstituted before education can become a viable human enterprise, or if the school system has to be torn apart, then the whole argument can be labeled as the work of a collection of dreamers. But what was unthinkable a few years ago has started to look only visionary in 1967. The obvious educational failures of the past few years, the crash programs of compensatory education, the Head Starts, the dropout centers, the Job Corps programs already indicate that, at least when it comes to its most obvious problems, the society may be ready to go beyond the traditional program of the public schools to avert total catastrophe. It has become clear, moreover, that the demonstrations at Berkeley and elsewhere reflect serious discontent among undergraduates with the way conventional academic institutions—and the society beyond—have treated their students. Goodman has in great measure, become the spokesman of the alienated and the rebellious, and he has become a sort of roving prophet for the independent students who are establishing free universities and similar para-academic organizations. Thus the pejorative description of Goodman and others as romantics has required at least the qualification that the size of their student following makes mandatory.

But the sobriquet "romantic" nevertheless holds true in Goodman's sentimental regard for the relations and significance of a community of citizens that ceased to exist with the passing of the nineteenth-century village and a community of scholars not seen since the Middle Ages. Where will we find the kind of productive employment that qualifies as "man's work?" How will we control the power of contemporary technology without the bureaucracies to manage it? How will we operate successful universities of independent scholars without administrators, president, and trustees? It is, after all, very difficult to construct a Boeing 707 in one's basement; Goodman, in some of his campus talks, has spoken about apprenticing young men to small printers (where, like Ben Franklin, they can learn a trade and simultaneously become literate), but where are the small printers, and what can one learn on a hand press that will be useful on a high speed, automated machine that can turn out 30,000 impressions in an hour? Goodman himself acknowledges that his liberalism has taken him fairly close to the radical Right, but the sentimental regard for the virtues of an agrarian society that he shares with some of the people who call themselves conservatives is no more relevant when it comes from him than when it originates with Barry Goldwater.

It is Goodman's apparent unwillingness to come to terms with the demands of the technological culture that has earned him and some of his philosophical brothers the label "anti-intellectual." His chief villains—men like James B. Conant—are people who see education as training ground for the demands that this culture makes: They accept those demands while Goodman appears reluctant to have anything to do with them. But the charge confuses the issue because it rides roughshod over Goodman's sense that the mind is being harnessed to organizational demands like a computer, instead of being left unfettered to work out the development of civilized possibilities. What is not clear is how that is possible *before* the social managers have learned to operate and control the technological and bureaucratic structures with which we all have to live. In the world of the romantics, the ideal adolescent is a Huck Finn type—independent, candid, unabashed, lighting out for the territories. But the irony of Huck's declaration—Mark Twain's intended irony—is that there are no territories left, that you have to make it right here, in a world already made.

More important, perhaps, than any weakness in the diagnosis is the vagueness of the remedy. The strength of the new critics lies in their ability to see the educational process as part of a coherent system that involves not only the schools but the general demands of the social order. But if the whole society is sick, where do you find the lever and fulcrum to move it? While Goodman has accurately identified the ailments of the alienated students, his message, in their mouths, has as often as not become no more than an agonized wail. To act at all in such a situation is to deny the universal hopelessness of the whole thing and to trade your alienation for commitment, thereby denying the premise on which you act. And what of the committed—students who do have programs and who generally hold the philosophical esteem of the new critics? They, after all, are also products of the educational system. The social activists of Students for a Democratic Society, the Peace Corps volunteers, the campus rebels—they all attended the schools and colleges that Friedenberg, Holt, Henry, and Goodman have so effectively described. The irony of the romanticism in the message of people like Goodman is that students may be able to play the game of rebellion just as effectively as they play the game of acquiescence; frustrated creativity can be thrown up to a demanding teacher just as easily as resignation, and chaotic incoherence can be disguised in the garb of self-expression.

Friedenberg acknowledges that the students may be more implicated in the process—not as victims, but as protagonists—than he had supposed when he wrote *The Vanishing Adolescent* in the late Fifties. The book, he says, "pictures the young as engaged in a gallant, if hopeless struggle with the timidity and corruption of the adult world, usually in the person of school officials; it would have been more accurate to picture American youth rather as already deeply implicated in the deeds and values of their culture. Mostly they go along with it and sincerely believe that in doing so they are putting down troublemakers and serving the best interests of their community." What this argument represents, clearly, is a realization that even the kids are not free of original sin—an understanding of the ubiquity of the problem. It suggests that children also can be nasty little rascals, and that some of those finky juveniles scrambling up the ladder of success aren't doing it just because somebody else is pushing. This is what makes Friedenberg a more sophisticated writer than those of his fellows who see the whole business as a conspiracy of the old against the young.

The observations of the new critics take them to what is essentially an elitist position. They are, ultimately, critics of the techniques and attitudes that the liberals and progressives worked out thirty years ago. What they attack is what democratic education *turned out to be*. The criticism is directed not at John Dewey or at Jefferson but at the corruptions established in their name. It tends to uphold, instead, the principles of distinction and privilege. There can be no genuine civility—and clearly no community—where human relations are based solely on anonymous contracts formed between people having no identity other than the presumed equality of the marketplace and the voting booth. *Human* relations can be derived only from a recognition of distinctions.

The case is, in some measure, the case of Jeffersonian democracy against Jacksonian egalitarianism, a case which values the human relations that distinctions support. Goodman describes how the student liberties at the University of Virginia, which had been meant by Jefferson to be gentlemanly and revolutionary, "have come to be a tight little code, prohibiting walking on the lawn and regulating the nuances of getting drunk. . . ." Dewey's notion to train people through actual experience, to learn by doing, was entirely perverted. "The conservatives and the businessmen cried out and the program was toned down. The practical training and community democracy, whose purpose was to live scientifically and change society was changed into 'socially useful' subjects and a psychology of 'belonging.'"

Using different terms, Holt and Friedenberg describe the perversion as the substitution—under corrupted Deweyan impulses—of manipulation for coercion. "The would-be progressives thought," says Holt, "that there were good ways and bad ways to coerce children (the bad ones, mean, harsh, cruel; the good ones, gentle, persuasive, subtle, kindly), and that if they avoided the bad and stuck to the good they would do no harm." Because the traditional school dealt with masses of children, says Henry, it could only manage by reducing them all to a common definition. Thus it created, in his words, "the essential nightmare" which had to be dreamed to provide the fears necessary to drive people from failure to success. The modern school is a response to this nightmare, providing fun and impulse release, and a bland emptiness in place of the traditional obsessions. Thus contemporary educators are unable to understand that "a vital democracy can be the product of a disciplined and intelligent population only; that disorder and laxity are poison to democracy."

Friedenberg is far more sympathetic to the elitist pretensions of college fraternities, for example, than to the middle-class liberals who would make them accessible to all; and he respects the aristocratic orientations of prep schools far more than the bland management of the typical middle-class public high school. "I am not seeking to eliminate privilege, but to create it and distribute it more intelligently," he writes in *Coming of Age in America.* "I am not trying to be fair, or to identify and reward the most deserving, but to find educational means for sponsoring and nurturing more trustworthy and humane people than those among whom our lives now seem destined to be spent, and spent utterly." This is a worthy cause, but it is also a risky one. For thousands of years, people have struggled against those who claimed to be more trustworthy and humane, and who oppressed others in the name of culture and civility.

But that is not to disparage either the wish or the possibilities that it may produce. The fact that the schools reflect perfectly the society that produced them is not necessarily justification for the perpetual maintenance of either. The vague oppressiveness of the order demands not less diversification, not fewer distinctions, but more: It is only when the distinctions and the diversification exist that any genuine humanity is possible. Almost every sympathetic critic concedes that what went wrong with Jefferson and Dewey was not the ideal but the execution: to be a democrat and to believe in individual fulfillment is the very antithesis of being a leveling apostle of homogenization. And if the failures of the Deweyan utopia ought to teach the advocates of new utopias some humility there is no reason why the corruptions and degradations of our status-conscious technological wonderland should be immune from the commentary they deserve.

If nothing else, people like Friedenberg have raised the level of the current discourse from its programmatic, managerial plateau to a level in which individual human beings are restored to the argument. The passions that followed Sputnik and the college panic divided us between those who wanted to make education a more efficient training instrument for the Cold War and middle-management, and those who resisted because the pap of life adjustment was more comfortable than intellectual rigor. The new critics have reminded us—sometimes, albeit, with too much wail—that relevant education has little to do with either, and that if it does not deal with the humanity of its students, it is not dealing with anything.

Selected References

Aiken, H. D., *et al. Philosophy and Educational Development.* Boston: Houghton Mifflin Company, 1966.

Barzun, Jacques. *The House of Intellect.* New York: Harper and Row, 1959.

Belth, Marc. *Education As a Discipline.* Boston: Allyn & Bacon, 1965.

Brameld, Theodore. *Toward a Reconstructed Philosophy of Education.* New York: Dryden Press, 1956.

Brumbaugh, R. S., and N. M. Lawrence. *Philosophers on Education: Six Essays on the Foundations of Western Thought.* Boston: Houghton Mifflin Company, 1963.

Bruner, Jerome. *The Process of Education.* Cambridge, Mass.: Harvard University Press, 1960.

Childs, John L. *American Pragmatism and Education.* New York: Holt, Rinehart & Winston, 1956.

Dewey, John. *Democracy and Education.* New York: The Macmillan Company, 1916.

Hook, Sidney. *Education for Modern Man: A New Perspective.* New York: Alfred A. Knopf, 1963.

Hutchins, Robert Maynard. *The Conflict of Education in a Democratic Society.* New York: Harper and Row, 1953.

Maritain, Jacques. *Education at the Crossroads.* New Haven, Conn.: Yale University Press, 1943.

Morrish, Ivor. *Disciplines of Education.* London: George Allen & Unwin, 1967.

Niblett, W. R. *Education and the Modern Mind.* London: Faber & Faber, 1962.

O'Connor, D. J. *An Introduction to the Philosophy of Education.* New York: The Philosophical Library, 1957.

Peters, R. S. *Ethics and Education.* London: George Allen & Unwin, 1966.

Phenix, Philip. *Philosophy of Education.* New York: Holt, Rinehart & Winston, 1958.

Reid, L. A. *Philosophy of Education.* London: Wm. Heinemann, 1962.

Scheffler, Israel. *Philosophy and Education: Modern Readings.* Boston: Allyn & Bacon, 1958.

Smith, B. Othanel, and R. H. Ennis. *Language and Concepts of Education.* Chicago: Rand McNally & Company, 1961.

Walton, John, and J. L. Kuethe. *The Discipline of Education.* Madison: University of Wisconsin Press, 1963.

SECTION IV | *Directions of Curriculum Development*

THE TERM CURRICULUM is applied to those ideas and experiences chosen by the school for use by and with students for the achievement of established goals. Traditionally, the curriculum is viewed as a number of subjects to be mastered by the learner. In contrast, a large group of curriculum workers consider the curriculum to consist of all the experiences that the learner has under the guidance of the school. Between these two extremes lie a number of alternatives, some of which are explored in this section.

At this point in our national life, curriculum has become the focus of attention and action for two new "communities," segments of the black population and groups of students in the high schools, colleges, and universities. Terms such as "black curriculum" and "curriculum for relevance" represent only two of the many challenges to the traditional practices of our schools. The new demands for "relevance" are ironic since relevance has been and will continue to be a major concern of curriculum workers.

What is taught in the schools and how it is taught must be continually examined and evaluated on the basis of aims and purposes, available sources of knowledge and experience, and the utilization of time, space, talent, and technological innovation. Subjects or experiences simply added to the present curriculum or replacing other subjects and experiences on a piecemeal basis, in response to varying, often conflicting pressures, simply create confusion. Once purposes are set, curriculum must be developed on the basis of clear, comprehensive theories of learning, teaching, and knowledge.

In "The Structure of Knowledge," Professor Arno Bellack of Columbia's Teachers College, explores the relationships that should be sought among teaching fields that comprise the curriculum. He suggests that those concerned with curriculum concentrate on these aspects: interdisciplinary approaches to specific problems, the relationships that exist among major fields of endeavor as between science and the humanities, and the mutual dependency existing between organized knowledge and human affairs. Harvard's noted psychologist, Jerome S. Bruner, delineates four areas pertinent to curriculum construction in "Needed: A Theory of Instruction." To his continued devotion to structure of knowledge approach to curriculum development, Bruner adds three other important considerations that cannot be ignored: the matter of sequence in curriculum planning, the consideration of the child's predisposition to learn, and a reevaluation of the concept of reward and punishment.

William Van Til could well serve as a model for those who demand relevancy. In his article "The Key Word Is Relevance," he illustrates the damaging effects of irrelevant curriculum and then discusses some comprehensive approaches to curriculum changes. He favors content change as superior to manipulation of an existing curriculum in the face of great change. He asks not for a curriculum biased in one direction or the other, not for "anything they want," but content that has meaning for the group intended. In his provocatively titled "Live Students and Dead Education," Oscar Handlin, Pulitzer Prize winning historian, traces the reasons for the gap between the needs of students and the program of the high school. He notes that the high school is still geared to the preparation for college of a small, select group while the population to be served is actually all of the young people with many different needs. Professor Handlin poses two major tasks for the high school: the development of the ability to communicate and familiarity with the quantitative techniques of science and technology. A different kind of focus is offered by E. Paul Torrance on the basis of his intensive investigation and experimentation. In "Uniqueness and Creativeness: The School's Role," Professor Torrance explores the ways in which schools should develop content for the nurturing of creativeness in the student.

If curriculum content has been slow to change in view of changing needs and understandings, what can be said about the organization of the school? Most schools operate in much the same way now as they did fifty years ago. One teacher for one class of thirty or forty for one period of time, three or five times weekly, is still the basic approach despite radical changes in technology and theories of learning and school organization. A pioneering study of advanced approaches was carried on a decade ago by J. Lloyd Trump under the auspices of the National Association of Secondary School Principals. It inspired much of the work being done today in the areas of flexible scheduling, grouping for instruction, team teaching, and radical changes of school plants and equipment. In "Organization of Instruction," Trump dismisses the traditional teacher-student ratio and develops a three-phase approach to utilization of student and teacher resources. Large group instruction and individual study will each take 40 per cent of the student's time while small group instruction will take 20 per cent. It is easy to see from this one phase that Trump's challenges are profound as well as wide-ranging. Investigation of intra-school organization is being complemented by a reevaluation of the total educational "ladder." Stanley G. Sanders offers an alternative to the Junior High School which was itself an attempt to better serve a particular age group. Earlier physical, mental, and emotional maturity of youngsters seems to suggest the shifting of present-day ninth graders into the high school and a middle or intermediate school to serve children in the intermediate grades. Professor Sanders reminds us that no one approach is the final answer; school organization must be responsive to change in the children served by the schools. The single piece of equipment with the most awesome potential for education is the computer. Ignorance of its possibilities and limitations has led to a sense of threat among some teachers including a fear of replacement. Patrick Suppes of Stanford University explains some of the uses of the computer, stressing the ways in which it can relieve the teacher of many routine tasks. He then answers simply and directly the questions most often raised by teachers. Following Trump's lead, Dean Robert J. Schaefer of Teachers College, Columbia University explores the organization of students and teachers for radically different purposes. In "The School as a Center for Inquiry" Dean Schaefer advocates a change in schools from dispensers of information to centers for the production of better education through the study of their own educative processes.

What will the curriculum be like in the future? John I. Goodlad of U.C.L.A. offers his views in "Directions of Curriculum Change" and a brief passage on "Schools of Tomorrow." Noting the shifting of emphasis over each generation, Professor Goodlad predicts a gradual transition from our present discipline-centered curriculum to a humanistic curriculum by the end of the century. Beyond that he sees great technological support and much flexibility in the utilization of the learner's time. But, Professor Goodlad reminds us, the questions of aims and purposes will still be waiting for new investigation and debate. In their "Forecast for the Seventies" the Shanes of Indiana University predict a change in emphasis from upper to lower education with the gradual disintegration of grade levels and the ascendancy of the individual child as the major focus of educational effort. They offer quick glances at two intriguing notions—biochemical and psychological mediation of learning. The future in education as in all fields seems no longer a distant spot on time's horizons. We are entering it now.

ARNO A. BELLACK | **The Structure of Knowledge and the Structure of the Curriculum**

During the current period of curriculum reform, most of the debate hinges on an old and familiar question: "What shall the schools teach?" This is a perennial question, one that apparently every generation has to solve over again for itself in the light of changing conditions and changing needs. And it is a question that can be answered only by reference to one's view of the nature of knowledge, for by universal agreement knowledge is the stock-in-trade of the school. Few would deny that the fields of organized inquiry are significant aspects of our culture that the school is uniquely equipped to introduce to students.

But there is also general agreement that the school's responsibility extends beyond teaching the organized fields of learning and inquiry; the school must also serve a multitude of ends and needs created by our society and our culture. At different times in the history of our schools widely different views have been held regarding the way in which knowledge should be organized and taught to meet these ends and needs. The traditionalists, for example, taught the time-honored subjects as anthologies of separate topics, with the hope that the bits and pieces of information would somehow or other turn out to be useful in the lives of their students. History became a recital of "one damned thing after another" (the phrase is Toynbee's), civics turned out to be a collection of miscellaneous information about government, and geography was nothing more than a catalogue of facts about places scattered over the globe.

Convinced that this kind of teaching would not prepare students to face the increasingly complex problems of their society, the progressive reformers of the 1930's and '40's proposed a new curriculum—one centered on the personal and social problems of youth and drawing on the academic disciplines as they became relevant to the problems under study. The disciplines were viewed as reservoirs from which facts and ideas could be drawn as needed; emphasis was on the *practical* ordering of knowledge with reference to problems to be solved.

Contemporary efforts to redefine the role of knowledge in the curriculum place emphasis on the *logical* order inherent in knowledge itself, on the structure of concepts and principles of inquiry that characterize the

From *A Reassessment of the Curriculum,* Dwayne Huebner, ed. Reprinted by permission of the Bureau of Publications, Teachers College, Columbia University, N.Y.

various fields of learning. Whereas formerly factual and descriptive content was stressed, now the emphasis is on basic concepts and methods which scholars use as intellectual tools to analyze and order their data.

Several claims are made for teaching the fundamental structures of the disciplines, two of which are of central importance and are worth considering here. The first is that understanding of fundamental ideas is the main road to adequate transfer of training. Professor Bruner, who is largely responsible for introducing the concept of structure into educational discourse, observes that

> . . . knowledge is a model we construct to give meaning and structure to regularities in experience. The organizing ideas of any body of knowledge are inventions for rendering experience economical and connected. We invent concepts such as force in physics, the bond in chemistry, motives in psychology, styles in literature as means to the end of comprehension. . . . The power of great organizing concepts is in large part that they permit us to understand and sometimes to predict or change the world in which we live. But their power lies also in the fact that ideas provide instruments for experience.

Therefore, he contends, "the structure of knowledge—its connectedness and its derivations that make one idea follow another—is the proper emphasis in education."[1]

The second important claim for emphasis on structure is that by constantly re-examining material taught in the schools for its fundamental patterns of organization, the schools will be able to narrow the gap between "advanced" knowledge and "elementary" knowledge. Since scholars at the forefront of their disciplines are able to make the greatest contribution to the substantive reorganization of their fields, current curriculum projects place great emphasis on the participation of university researches in continuing revision of the program of studies. Scholars in the various disciplines and their professional organizations have in recent years made proposals for revamping the curriculum in elementary and secondary schools—first in mathematics, physics, chemistry, and biology; then in English; and recently and belatedly in economics, geography, anthropology, and history.

The focus of attention in each of these projects is an individual discipline. Little or no attention is given to the relationships of the individual fields to each other or to the program of studies within which they must find their place. National committees in the fields of chemistry, physics, and biology have proceeded independently of each other. The projects in economics, geography, and anthropology are unrelated to one another or to the other social sciences. Only in mathematics has there

[1] Jerome Bruner, *On Knowing* (Cambridge, Mass.: Harvard University Press, 1962), p. 120.

been a disposition to view the field as a whole, but this is a reflection of developments within the discipline of mathematics at the highest levels of scholarship.

The situation developing in the elementary and secondary schools thus begins to reflect, at least to some degree, the state of affairs in the universities with respect to the development and organization of knowledge, which Professor John Randall has described in this way:

> As reflected in the microcosm of the modern university, the world of knowledge has today become radically plural. It is a world of many different knowledges, pursued in varied ways to diverse ends. These many inquiries are normally carried on with little thought for their relations to each other. The student of John Donne's poetry, the student of the structure of the atom—each gives little enough attention to what the others are doing, and none at all to any total picture of anything. Each has his own goals, his own methods, his own language for talking about what he is doing and what he has discovered. Each seems happiest when left to his own devices, glad indeed if he can keep others from treading on his toes. Each is convinced that what he himself is doing is worth while. But none has too much respect for the others, though he is willing enough to tolerate them. They have all little understanding of each other's pursuits—what they are trying to do, how they are doing it, and what they really mean when they talk about it.[2]

I emphasize this pluralism in the academic world not to deplore it but to call attention to the problem that it presents for those who are concerned with the organization of the entire curriculum. For the curriculum builder is concerned not only with the structures of the individual disciplines, but also with the structure of the instructional program within which the fields of knowledge find their place. The problem can be very simply stated, if not easily solved: What general structure of the curriculum can be developed so that autonomy of the parts does not result in anarchy in the program as a whole? This is the question I propose to discuss briefly here.

When one looks beyond the structure of the individual disciplines and asks about the structure of the curriculum, attention is focused on *relationships* among the various fields that comprise the program of studies. For just as relationships among ideas is at the heart of the concept of structure as applied to the individual disciplines, so relationships among the disciplines is at the heart of the notion of structure as applied to the curriculum as a whole.

The mathematics teacher, the science teacher, the music teacher, and so on through the list of specialized functionaries in the school—each tends typically to interpret the entire program of the school through his

[2] John H. Randall, Jr., "The World to be Unified," in Lewis Leary (ed.), *The Unity of Knowledge* (Garden City, N.Y., Doubleday and Company, 1955), p. 63.

own specialized teaching field. This is probably inevitable, and it would not be undesirable except for one stubborn fact: each of the specialized aspects of the program deals with human beings, and since human beings are not infinitely plastic in adapting to particular situations, it follows that what goes on at one place in the system sets limiting conditions for the accomplishments of purposes elsewhere in the system. Hence the importance of giving attention not only to connections between ideas in an individual field, but also to relationships among the fields of knowledge included in the curriculum.

There are many ways in which one can conceive of these inter-connections. I should like to focus attention on three types of relationships that obtain (or *ought* to obtain) among the teaching fields that comprise the curriculum:

1. *Relationships among cognate or allied disciplines that deal with similar problems or phenomena.* Here I have in mind, for example, relations among the social sciences, whose common objective is to describe and explain the social and cultural behavior of man; and connections among the natural sciences, whose common aim is to describe and explain physical and biological phenomena.

2. *Relationships among the broad areas of knowledge—the sciences and mathematics on the one hand, and the humanities on the other.* Call to mind the problem raised by C. P. Snow in his *The Two Cultures and the Scientific Revolution,* the great gulf that lies between the literary world and the scientific world. Snow insists that the only way to close the gap between the two cultures is by rethinking our education.

3. *Relationships of knowledge to human affairs.* Given the current emphasis on the role of organized knowledge in the curriculum, we do well to remind ourselves that the goal of general education is not to train students as specialists in mathematics, geography, biology, or whatever other subjects they might study. Rather, the goal is to make available to students the intellectual and æsthetic resources of their culture in such a way that they become guides for intelligent action and help students create meaning and order out of the complex world in which they find themselves.

Let us briefly examine these three types of relationships.

I. Relationships Among Allied Disciplines

According to long and honorable tradition, knowledge is grouped for pedagogical purposes in four major categories—the natural sciences, the social sciences, mathematics, and the humanities (the latter an omnibus term that includes art, literature, philosophy, and music). These broad groupings of organized disciplines are generally recognized as basic cultural interests of our society which constitute both the resources and the obligations of the schools. Each major field represents distinctive methods and conceptual schemes in which the world and man are viewed from quite different vantage points. Instruction in these areas has as its primary goal equipping students with key concepts and methods that inform and sustain intelligent choice in human affairs.

Although the four major areas of knowledge are generally recognized as important components of the curriculum, they are not currently used as the context or framework for curriculum building. Instead, as we have already noted, recent curriculum projects have focused attention on individual disciplines without concern for their relationships to allied fields. Thus the economists, the geographers, and the anthropologists have proceeded independently of each other, as have the biologists, chemists, and physicists. To be sure, economists suggest ways in which economic ideas can be taught in history; and anthropologists show how some of their generalizations can be woven into courses in geography. This is all to the good; it even seems to suggest that integration of a limited variety might be appropriate for teaching purposes. But scant attention is given to building a curriculum design within which the individual fields might find their place.

It is my contention that this approach has certain inherent shortcomings and that we would do well to shift the context for curriculum planning from the individual disciplines, as is now the vogue, to the broad groupings of knowledge represented by the natural sciences, the social sciences, mathematics, and the humanities. Let us briefly consider some of the problems involved in curriculum building in the social sciences to show why this proposed shift is desirable and necessary.

The social sciences—economics, social psychology, political science, sociology, anthropology, geography, and history—are all seeking explanations of the same phenomenon, man's social life. This common goal is what makes it reasonable to group them together as the *social* sciences. All of them have grown out of man's attempt to interpret, understand, and control the social environment. But each field formulates its own questions about this subject matter and develops its own system of concepts to guide its research. The economist is preoccupied with the concept of scarcity, the political scientist with the concepts of power and authority, the anthropologist with the notion of culture, and the sociologist with social functions and social systems. Each science is thus abstract, dealing with only certain facets of actual social relationships and institutions—facets that do not permit of physical separation but only of analytical separation.

Man's social life as it is actually lived is therefore far more complex than the limited image of it reflected in the concepts and generalizations of any one of the social disciplines. It follows then, as Professor Kingsley

Davis has suggested, that "in so far as the prediction of actual events is concerned, the various social sciences are mutually interdependent, because only by combining their various points of view can anything approaching a complete anticipation of future occurrences be achieved."[3] Policies that are proposed and actions that are taken to deal with problems in social affairs are of necessity interdisciplinary, for concrete social reality is not mirrored in the findings of any one discipline.

Now this is a matter of central importance to those whose job it is to plan and organize the social studies curriculum. To focus exclusive attention on certain aspects of the social world as seen through the eyes of one or two of the social sciences is to give students a myopic vision of man's social behavior and his institutions. To shape children's conceptions of the social world through exclusive emphasis on the language of the economist, for example, to the exclusion of the language of the sociologist, political scientist, anthropologist, and historian is to determine that they shall interpret human affairs principally in terms which the economist uses to view reality—in terms of supply, demand, scarcity, production, and consumption.

Students must be helped to see the limitations as well as the uses of a single discipline in interpreting events as they actually occur. And for anything approaching a comprehensive view of man's functioning in society, the specialized perspectives of all the social sciences are needed. Curriculum builders in the social studies have the enormously difficult job of providing a place in their programs for all the social sciences, each of which contributes its distinctive perspective on human institutions and human behavior.

It is clear that such a program can be developed only on the basis of collaboration among the various social sciences. Such collaboration does not presuppose a "unified social science" as the basis for planning the elementary and secondary school curriculum. Quite the opposite is the case. For the social disciplines today are characterized by a plurality of methods and conceptual schemes developed by social scientists to deal with problems within their individual spheres. Instead of a unity of method or a single universe of discourse, we find a vast confederation of separate areas of study. Modes of thinking and analysis differ from field to field, and even from problem to problem within the same field. In time, a Bacon of the sciences that bear on the social and cultural behavior of man may emerge, but that time is not yet.

At the same time, in spite of increasing specialization and internal differentiation, there are interconnections among the social sciences that curriculum planning for the schools should take into account. For example, the various social sciences borrow rather handily from each other

[3] *Human Society* (New York: The Macmillan Company, 1948), p. 8.

when it comes to both concepts and methods. Historians make use of concepts from all the other social sciences. Political scientists interested in political socialization get their methods from behavioral scientists and seem in many respects more closely related to sociologists and social psychologists than to fellow political scientists. Certain anthropologists have utilized the Freudian view of human development in analyzing patterns of various cultures. Geographers make extensive use of the perspectives of history and concepts developed by all the behavioral sciences.

Furthermore, we find not only interchange of concepts and methods but growing collaboration among specialists. For example, studies of the nature and function of "authority" are now undertaken jointly by political scientists and sociologists, and there have been recent studies conducted by economists in collaboration with anthropologists to determine whether certain economic theories hold for different types of economic systems. The convergence of social scientists upon the same problems has given rise to what Professor Robert Merton calls "interdisciplines," such as social biology, political sociology, and sociological history.

The picture that emerges from this cursory review of the current state of affairs in the social sciences is one of great diversity. Given this mosaic of disciplines and interdisciplines, each characterized by multiple conceptual schemes and methods, the curriculum builder is faced with the problem of developing structures for teaching that relate the social sciences to each other in meaningful ways and avoid undue fragmentation of knowledge.

What has been said about the social sciences applies in principle to the natural sciences, mathematics, and the humanities. The significant point is that there is a need for a broader context for curriculum planning than the separate disciplines, and the broad fields of knowledge furnish a useful framework for this purpose. I am not calling for indiscriminate scrambling of superficial knowledge. Indeed, at this point we would do well to suspend judgment as to when in the school program teaching should be organized around the individual disciplines, and when around the broad groupings of the disciplines. In all likelihood, different patterns of organization will be found to be appropriate for different levels of the school program. Dewey's notion of the "progressive organization of knowledge," long ignored by most of his interpreters, might serve as a guiding hypothesis in planning the sequence of the program through the elementary and secondary school years.

In sum, scholars in the natural sciences, the social sciences, mathematics, and the humanities should now be invited to join in the search for new structures for teaching—structures that respect the integrity of the individual fields and at the same time help these fields find their place in a pattern of studies that provides a substantial measure of coherence and relatedness for the program as a whole.

II. Relationships Among Broad Fields of Knowledge

There is not only the question of relationships among disciplines that deal with similar problems or phenomena, but also the question of the relationships among the broad areas of knowledge—the sciences and mathematics on the one hand, and the humanities on the other. The growing separation and lack of effective communication between the arts and sciences have been widely noted and greatly deplored. C. P. Snow's analysis of this situation in terms of the two cultures of the literary intellectuals and the scientists is well known to all of us. That this state of affairs should somehow be remedied is the theme of many earnest discussions. The upshot of the discussion is usually that there is one way out of all this: it is, as Snow suggests, by rethinking our education.

But how shall the school go about bridging the gulf between the literary and aesthetic and the scientific studies? It seems reasonable to inquire first of all if human knowledge in its many dimensions forms a recognized unity within which the fields of inquiry and creativity fall neatly into place. Is there a sense in which all knowledge is one, with the arts and the sciences having a place in a unity of fundamental principles or basic methods of inquiry?

The progressives, taking their cue from Dewey, found for themselves such a unity in the "scientific method" (or the "method of intelligence," as it was frequently labeled) that was assumed to characterize all types of rational, intelligent activity in academic pursuits and in artistic and practical affairs as well. The problem-solving method came to be viewed as the basic ingredient in programs of general education.

But by no means is there agreement among scientists that there is a single all-encompassing set of procedures, even in the natural sciences, as assumed by those who talk about *the* scientific method. There seems to be little warrant for assuming that there is one overarching method sufficiently flexible and inclusive to deal with problems in the various scientific fields, to say nothing of the arts, crafts, and applied areas. Indeed, as we have already noted, the intellectual world today is characterized by a plurality of methods and conceptual schemes developed by the disciplines to deal with problems within their individual spheres. Analysis of the various disciplines reveals a wide range of organizations and intellectual methods associated with them. Instead of a unity of method or a single universe of discourse, we are confronted with a vast confederation of separate areas of study. Modes of analysis differ from field to field, and even from problem to problem within the same field.

The heterogeneous character of the intellectual resources that are a part of the culture is a fact of major significance for the curriculum builder. We would do well frankly to recognize this and make a place in our programs for the variety of logical orders that characterize the fields of knowledge on which we draw in building the curriculum.

But what then of the relationships among the various fields of creativity and inquiry? Is it perhaps possible, in spite of the variety of logical orders characteristic of knowledge in its various branches, to identify the principal kinds of cognitive operations or modes of thinking that characterize man's intellectual activities?

A proposal to facilitate students' insight into relationships among the various fields of knowledge by introducing them to the "principal modes of intellectual activity" comes from Professor Peterson of Oxford University. In making suggestions for the reform of secondary education in Britain, Peterson urges educators to stop thinking of general education in terms of "general knowledge":

> It is not a sign that a man lacks general education if he does not know the date of The Treaty of Utrecht, the latitude of Singapore, the formula for nitroglycerine or the author of the *Four Quartets.* It does denote a lack of general education if he cares nothing for any of the arts, confuses a moral judgment with an aesthetic judgment, interprets the actions of Asian political leaders in terms of nineteenth century English parliamentarianism or believes that the existence of God has been scientifically disproved.[4]

Peterson urges therefore that the British secondary schools devise programs of general education not in terms of wide general knowledge, but in terms of development in the main modes of intellectual activity, of which he identifies four: the logical (or the analytic), the empirical, the moral, the aesthetic. These different modes of thought are associated with different uses of language. For example, the empirical mode has to do with statements about the world based on our experience of it. The analytic mode has to do with statements that do not describe the world of fact, but rather tell us how the meanings of symbols are related to one another logically. (A definition is a special case of analytic sentences.) The moral and the aesthetic modes are concerned with statements of preferences, evaluations, and judgments of the good and the evil, the beautiful and the ugly, the desirable and the undesirable.

Any one discipline gives opportunity for the development of more than one mode of thought, and each mode can be developed through more than one of the disciplines. For example, literature can contribute to the development of both moral and aesthetic judgment. Mathematics and philosophy both contribute to the development of the analytic mode. History has probably the widest range of any discipline, for the historian em-

[4] Oxford University Department of Education, *Arts and Sciences Sides in the Sixth Form* (Abingdon-Berkshire: The Abbey Press, 1960), p. 13.

ploys all four modes in constructing his comprehensive interpretation of what happened in the past.

If students are to gain understanding of the similarities and differences among the fields of knowledge, the different modes of mental activity must be made explicit to them:

> They must have time and guidance in which to see that what is a proof in the Mathematics they pursue on Tuesday is not the same kind of thing as a proof in History, which follows on Wednesday; that the truth of George Eliot or Joseph Conrad is not the same thing as the truths of Mendel or Max Planck; and yet that there are similarities as well as differences.[5]

Peterson accordingly suggests that in addition to giving attention to these varying modes of thought in the subject fields, the secondary program include a special course in which these ways of thinking are the object of study. One important aspect of such teaching has to do with ways in which these modes of thought are verified. Verification is particularly significant in that it is the guide to meaning of the various types of thought. For example, empirical statements are verified by tests conducted in terms of experience, whereas moral statements are verified by reference to criteria or principles of judgment. On the other hand, analytic statements depend for their truth on an agreed upon set of rules, and follow logically from accepted definitions.

Thus far I have suggested that in structuring the curriculum with due regard for the relationships among the fields of knowledge we view knowledge from two complementary perspectives. In the first, emphasis is on the conceptual schemes and methods of inquiry associated with the broad fields of knowledge, the natural sciences, the social sciences, mathematics, and the humanities. In the second, attention is focused on modes of thought—the analytic, the empirical, the aesthetic, and the moral—that transcend the boundaries of the individual fields. These two views thus represent mutually reinforcing conceptions of knowledge that serve well as the basis for curriculum planning.

Professor Toulmin has coined two terms that might be helpful in clarifying the relationships between these two views of knowledge. He distinguishes between "participant's language" and "onlooker's language."[6] Participant's language is the language used by members of a professional group or discipline as they carry on their work in their specialized field. Hence we talk today about the language of science, the language of psychology, the language of mathematics, and even the language of education. In the context of our discussion, participant's language has to do

[5] Ibid., p. 18.

[6] S. Toulmin, *Philosophy of Science* (London: Hutchinson University Library, 1953), p. 13.

with the language systems that are the distinguishing characteristics of the various disciplined areas of study such as the sciences, mathematics, and the humanities.

Now if we want to examine or talk about the language we use in any one of these fields, we must use another level of discourse. We must, in Toulmin's terms, use onlooker's language. For example, it was suggested that students need help in understanding that a proof in mathematics is not the same as a proof in science or that the "truth" of a scientist is not the same as the "truth" of the poet or novelist. To make these comparisons and contrasts we need a language system that enables us to look at these various areas of study from the outside, as it were. The principal modes of thought—the analytic, the empirical, the moral, and the aesthetic—furnish us with language tools that are useful for this purpose. Hence their importance in teaching.

III. Relationships of Knowledge to Human Affairs

That the schools ought to provide students with the means for intelligent action is not a new or controversial idea. When, however, it comes to deciding what to teach and how to teach to accomplish this goal, we find marked differences of opinion.

Is it sufficient in general education, for example, to have students learn how to think like physicists, historians, or economists? I think not. For the economist *as* economist (to mention just one field) is in no position to prescribe courses of action regarding the host of public policy issues we face, and questions of public policy and decision loom large in general education. To be sure, economics does provide us with a body of theory that is essential in examining the probable consequences of alternative economic policies, and a good many of these analytical tools ought to become part of the intellectual equipment of all students. Economists are able to tell us what the probable consequences will be if the supply of money is increased, or if the interest rates are lowered; but they cannot *as* economists tell us whether or not we ought to take either of these two courses of action. Decisions regarding these alternative courses of action involve technical economic analysis *and* weighing of values.

It is therefore clear that both values and economic theory are involved in deciding courses of action in economic affairs, and both must find their place in social studies teaching. Here the different modes of thought come prominently into play. Technical economic analysis involves the empirical mode of thinking (that is, it is concerned with matters of fact and theory), while considering alternative values involves the moral mode (that is, it is concerned with criteria of what is desirable or undesirable). The teacher's job is to help students learn to make these necessary distinctions, so that they recognize when questions of fact and analysis are under consideration and when questions of value are at stake.[7] This would of course hold as well for instruction in fields of study other than economics.

Thus far we have been talking about problems associated with a single field. But problems in the world of human affairs do not come neatly labeled "historical," "economic," or "political." They come as decisions to be made and force us to call upon all we know and make us wish we knew more. It was concern for broad cultural and moral questions that go beyond the boundaries of any one discipline that led the progressives to urge that students have the opportunity to deal with them in all their complexity. They proposed a new curriculum, one centered on the problems of youth and broad social issues and drawing upon the academic disciplines as they become relevant to the problems under study. This idea became the hallmark of progressivism in curriculum building. It gained wide acceptance among educators and found expression in many influential statements of policy and opinion during the 1920's, '30's, and '40's. Attempted applications of this viewpoint were made in courses labeled core, common learnings, and the like.

Difficulties in this approach soon became apparent, not the least of which was the students' lack of first-hand acquaintance with the disciplines that were the source of the concepts and ideas essential to structuring problems under study. Without adequate understanding of the various fields of knowledge, students had no way of knowing which fields were relevant to problems of concern to them. Indeed, without knowledge of the organized fields it was difficult for them to ask the kinds of questions about their problems that the various disciplines could help them answer.

Giving students an opportunity to grapple with broad social and cultural problems was basically a promising innovation. But at the same time one is forced to recognize that problem solving on such a broad base cannot be pursued successfully without growing understanding of the fields of knowledge on which the problem solver must draw.

Recognizing then the value in systematic study of the fields of knowledge and the importance of developing competence in dealing with problems and issues that are broader than those of any one field, the question arises of why opportunities for both types of activities should not be included in the program for all students. One might envision a general education program that would include basic instruction in the major fields defined earlier in this paper (the natural sciences, the physical sciences, mathematics, and the humanities), together with a coordinating seminar in which students deal with problems "in the round" and in which special

[7] See *Economic Education in the Schools,* Report of the National Task Force or Economic Education, 1961.

effort is made to show the intimate relationships between the fields of study as concepts from those fields are brought to bear on these problems. Such a seminar would also furnish excellent opportunities to help students become aware of the different modes of thought and various types of language usage involved in dealing with problematic situations and the necessity for making clear distinctions among them.

This is not a new proposal. I am here dusting off an old idea first set forth in the 1956 ASCD Yearbook, *What Shall the High Schools Teach?* In making this suggestion, we were much influenced by Dewey's contention that

> The aim of education should be to secure a balanced interaction of the two types of mental attitude (the practical and the theoretical), having sufficient regard to the disposition of the individual not to hamper and cripple whatever powers are naturally strong in him. The narrowness of individuals of strong concrete bent needs to be liberalized. Every opportunity that occurs within practical activities for developing curiosity and susceptibility to intellectual problems should be seized. Violence is not done to natural disposition; rather, the latter is broadened. Otherwise, the concrete becomes narrow and deadening. As regards the smaller number of those who have a taste for abstract, purely intellectual topics, pains should be taken to multiply opportunities and demands for the application of ideas, for translating symbolic truths into terms of everyday and social life. Every human being has both capabilities, and every individual will be more effective and happier if both powers are developed in easy and close interaction with each other.[8]

Let it be recognized that the difficulties in building a curriculum that takes account of the relationships among the various fields of inquiry and creativity are overwhelming. The greatest difficulty is that the job involves the collaboration of specialists—in the various disciplines, in curriculum development, and in teaching. In such collaborative efforts it would seem that curriculum specialists, concerned as they are with the instructional program as a whole, have a crucial role to play. But in all frankness it must be recognized that they do not play a central crucial role in curriculum revision projects now underway. Whether they will be able to do so in the future is another matter. And I suspect that whether they will indeed make the contribution one might reasonably expect them to make will depend, first of all, on their ability to work effectively with representatives of the various fields of knowledge to identify important relationships among these fields and to fashion programs of instruction that take due account of these relationships and connections; and secondly, on their ability to build curricula that help students see the relevance of the intellectual resources of the culture for their own lives

[8] *How We Think* (Boston: D.C. Heath and Co., 1933), pp. 228–229.

as productive workers, as citizens, and as individuals. For as Professor Bestor, who scarcely qualifies as an advocate of education for life adjustment, has reminded us, "The basic argument of the intellectual disciplines in education is not that they lift a man's spirits above the world, but that they equip his mind to enter the world and perform its tasks."[9]

[9] *Educational Wastelands* (Urbana, Ill.: University of Illinois Press, 1953), p. 15.

JEROME S. BRUNER | *Needed: A Theory of Instruction*

Over the past several years it has become increasingly clear to me, as to any thinking person today, that both psychology and the field of curriculum design itself suffer jointly from the lack of a theory of instruction. Such a theory of instruction would indeed be interesting just for its own sake, for purely theoretical reasons. There cannot be, for example, a theory of development which leaves somehow to chance the question of the way in which societies pace and structure the experiences with which children come in contact; and to talk about the nature of development without talking about the way in which society does and can structure the sequence, is to be as intellectually foolish as it is to be morally irresponsible. So even if one were seeking only a better theory about the nature of man, one would indeed want a theory of instruction as one of the instruments by which one understood man and how he was shaped by his fellow man.

Yet we also realize that a theory of instruction is about as practical a thing as one could possibly have to guide one in the process of passing on the knowledge, the skills, the point of view, and the heart of a culture. Let us, then, see whether we can set forth some possible theorems that might go into a theory of instruction.

What do we mean by a theory of instruction? I found myself beginning this exercise by putting down theorems that tried to separate what we might mean by a theory of instruction from other kinds of theories that have been current. The first thought that occurred to me is that in its very nature a theory of instruction is *prescriptive* and not *descriptive*. Such a theory has the aim of producing particular ends and producing them in ways that we speak of as optimal. It is not a description of what has happened when learning has taken place—it is something which is normative, which gives you something to shoot at and which, in the end,

From *Educational Leadership,* Vol. 20, No. 8 (May 1963), pp. 523–532.

must state something about what you do when you put instruction together in the form of courses. Now, this is not a very surprising thing, yet I am struck by the fact that many persons in the field of education have assumed that we could depend on other kinds of theories than the theory of instruction to guide us in this kind of enterprise. For example, I find that the dependence upon learning theory among educators is as touching as it is shocking. The fact of the matter is that the learning theory is not a theory of instruction; it is a theory that describes what takes place while learning is going on and after learning has taken place.

There is no clear-cut way in which one can derive wisdom, or indeed implication, from learning theory that will guide him in the constructing of a curriculum. When I say a theory of instruction is prescriptive, I mean it is *before the fact*. It is before learning has taken place and not while and after learning has taken place. Let me give you an example of the kind of difficulty you get into when you assume that you can use the slender reed of learning theory to lean on. Take, for example, the case of programed instruction.

There is in the current doctrine (I will call it) of programed instruction the idea that somehow you should take small steps, that each increment should be a small step. Now, this idea is derived willy-nilly from a theory of learning which states that learning is incremental and goes in small steps. Nowhere in the evidence upon which such a theory is based —and it is only partial evidence—nowhere is there anything that says that simply because learning takes place in small steps the *environment* should be arranged in small steps. And so we set up a curriculum that also has small steps. In doing so we fail to take sight of the fact that, indeed, organisms from vertebrate on up through the highest primate, man, operate by taking large packets of information and breaking these down into their own bite size and that unless they have the opportunity to do that, learning may become stereotyped. At least it is a worthy hypothesis about instruction.

A theory of instruction must concern itself with the relationship between how things are presented and how they are learned. Though I myself have worked hard and long in the vineyard of learning theory, I can do no better than to start by warning the reader away from it. Learning theory is not a theory of instruction. It describes what happened. A theory of instruction is a guide to what to do in order to achieve certain objectives. Unfortunately, we shall have to start pretty nearly at the beginning, for there is very little literature to guide us in this subtle enterprise.

What shall a theory of instruction be about? I would propose that there are four aspects of such a theory. First, a theory of instruction should concern itself with the factors that predispose a child to learn effectively; and there are many such factors that predispose. These are factors which, on the whole, precede the child's entry into our scholastic care. These factors relate to his earliest childhood and indeed one might say that we should provide some theorems for a theory of toys, and for a theory of family, and for a theory of stimulation, because the thing that comes to mind here is the question of what kind of stimulation ought a child to have before he is faced with this formidable thing we call a schoolroom and a teacher. What sorts of identification might he best form? How shall we bring his linguistic level up to a point where he is able to handle things symbolically? I shall not treat further these predispositions because what I want to do after this introduction of the different aspects of the theory is to go back and have a look at each one of these in detail, so let me pass on now to a second aspect of a theory of instruction.

It should concern itself with the optimal structuring of knowledge. By this, I mean that for any body of knowledge there is a minimal set of propositions, or statements, or images from which one can best generate the rest of what exists within that field. For example, from the conservation theorems plus a little more, a great deal of physics can be reconstructed. This is the "guts" of physics.

Now, I think when we speak of the optimal structuring of knowledge, we probably have three things in mind about this set of underlying propositions. They should have the power of simplifying the diversity of information within the field, somehow rendering the particular redundant, making it clear that this case is just a sub-case of something else, that one fact is not the same as every other fact. I speak of this power of simplification as the economy of a structure. Secondly, such a structure would enable you to generate new propositions, to go beyond the information given. This I would speak of as the productiveness of a structure. And finally, there is another aspect to the structure of knowledge which has to do with the extent to which it increases the manipulability of knowledge. It is classically the case, for example, that when you put something into words it now becomes possible for you to take that thing which before you only intuited in some rough way and to subject it to the combinings and recombinings that are made possible by the transformative powers of language. And this I want to speak of as the power of a structure. In thinking of structure, then, we shall want to consider economy, productiveness, and power. All of these things are relative to a learner. It does not do to say simply that because physics has great economy, great productiveness, and great power as practiced by a Feinman or a Purcell, that therefore you have children ape those distinguished scientists. You take the child where you find him and give him the structure that is economical, productive, and powerful for him and that allows him to grow.

A third aspect of a theory of instruction deals with the optimal sequence that is required for learning. In what order do we present things?

If you are presenting the Napoleonic period, where do you start? If you would give a sense of the sixteenth century, do you begin with the fact that mercantile prices and prosperity were going up at a booming rate, whereas the rents that were got by the landlords were not going up because there were long-term leases? You might. If you want to produce drama, you would. But, we will return to that because there is a question of how to give the learner a place from which to take off, something upon which to build. What order to do it? What exercises do you give him to strengthen the sinews of his own thinking? What type of representation do you use? How much particular? How much generality?

Finally, a fourth aspect of a theory of instruction should concern itself with the nature and pacing of rewards and punishments and successes and failures.

To sum up then, a theory of instruction should be constructed around four problems: predispositions, structures, sequences, and consequences. What can we say about the factors that predispose a student to be a learner? Let us begin with the following simple proposition: that in order to learn or to solve problems, it is necessary that alternatives be explored and that you cannot have effective learning or problem solving without the learner's having the courage and the skill to explore alternative ways of dealing with a problem.

It seems that if you take this as the first proposition concerning predisposition, there are three things that immediately can be said. First, that if this is the case, learning in the presence of a teacher, or a tutor, or an instructor should somehow minimize the risks and the severity of the consequence that follows upon exploration of alternatives. It should be less risk for a child to explore alternatives in the presence of a teacher, than without one present. It is obvious that, at the level of coping with nature in the raw, the child searching for food on his own would stand more risk of eating toadstools and poisoning himself, and thereby bringing exploration to a close.

Yet there are other less obvious things that have to do with the closing down of the exploration of alternatives. A teacher or parent can instill the fear of being a fool. That can surely paralyze the will to explore alternatives, for the moment an unreasonable alternative is made to seem like a foolish one, the inner freedom to explore is limited by the requirements of face saving. The encouragement of exploration of alternatives requires some practical minimization of the severity of consequences following exploration.

It seems to me, further, that one of the ways in which a sense of alternatives to be explored can be opened, is to increase the informativeness of error. To increase the informativeness of error essentially involves making clear to the child what produced a failure. One of the major functions of a teacher is to lead the child to a sense of why he failed. I do not mean why he failed in terms of a characterological analysis; I mean in terms of the nature of what it is that he is doing. If you can somehow make the child aware that his attempted answer is not so much a wrong answer, as an answer to another problem, and then get him back on the track, it becomes possible for the child to reduce the confusion that is produced by picking a wrong alternative. One of the things that, I believe, keeps us from exploring alternatives is precisely the confusion of making the wrong choice.

Still another goad to the exploration of alternatives is through the encouragement of "subversiveness." I mean that you must subvert all of the earlier established constraints against the exploration of alternatives. This kind of subversiveness has to do with a healthy skepticism toward holy cows, prefabricated doctrines, and stuffed shirtliness. Let there be no question or doubt that is "not nice to express." The moment you as teachers lose your role as subversives in this respect, you are doing the child an injustice and yourself an injustice as a teacher. I want to rescue the word "subversion" from the wrong senses to which it has been put in recent years.

When we think about predispositions to learn, we have to bear in mind that the very relationship that we have with our pupils is a privileged relationship involving authority and direction; that is to say, the exchange is uneven. We know; they do not. Since that is the case, it becomes very necessary for us not to use this implicit authoritative relationship as a means of using our own office as a way of establishing truth and falsity. It is so easy in the mind of the impressionable child to equate truth with Miss Smith!

The nature of learning in a school situation requires at least a dyadic relation; at least two people are involved, and usually many more than two. This obvious point requires that there be some set of minimal social skills that a child brings with him to a learning situation. We do not know much about the nature of these social skills that are required for an exchange of information. The act of exchanging information mutually, or even of accepting information and working on it until you make it your own, is not well understood. In addition to minimum social skills, there are elementary intellectual skills that are necessary for a first encounter with school learning. We "know" this, but we do little either to investigate these elementary skills or to devise ways of strengthening them. I am thinking principally of linguistic skills. Where a child has been socially underprivileged in his early years, it may be necessary for example to look squarely at the situation and say: This child, before he can go on in these subjects, simply needs more linguistic training or all of our words will be just mere wind going by his ears. I do not mean vocabulary, but, rather, the development of the full transformative power of language which our linguists are only now beginning to understand.

It is necessary for the beginning child to have certain kinds of manipulative and almost intuitive geometric skills. We have started studies of children on the borders of the Sahara in the interior of Senegal. We are struck at the difference in the behavior of American children and children in the African bush who do not have toys with mechanical or geometrical constraint to play with. We take it for granted that our children can deal with geometrical forms, put them together and take them apart, yet the fact of the matter is that it should not be taken for granted. The experience of manipulating materials gives our children a stock of images and geometric transformations that permit them to work geometrically and mechanically in a way that our African subjects cannot. These elementary forms of intellectual skills are essential. Is there more that we can do that we are not doing?

My last point before passing on to the topic of structure in learning has to do with attitudes toward the use of mind. These are predisposing factors of an enormously important kind. For example, we know that these vary to some extent, speaking sociologically, by class, by ethnic group, by culture. There is no question, for example, that in terms of social class, very frequently you will find in the lowest social class an attitude toward life that is governed by the concept of luck. This means that there is really nothing you can do by your own efforts, that things happen to a considerable extent by luck. The business of applying the mind, the idea that man has a chance if he will use his mind, is an attitude which is not frequently present and which has to be created. This is an extremely difficult thing to do and I hope no one asks me how do you do it, because I do not know. Yet it is quite clear that we must use the most intelligent opportunism we can muster, to do anything we can to get the idea started that by the use of mind one can increase effectiveness or any other desired state. We also know that different ethnic groups have different attitudes toward the use of mind, and again, I do not think we take full advantage of this. The Muslim-African culture, for example, has an attitude toward the use of mind that it should be used principally for grasping the word that has been passed on. This is not the kind of use of mind that makes for what might be called a very active, vigorous mind.

Now let us turn to the question of the structure of knowledge, its economy, productiveness, and power as related to the capacities of a learner. The first point relates to theorem in the theory of computation proposed by Turing. Turing proposed that any problem that can be solved can be solved by simpler means. That is the theorem. Out of this theorem has come the technology of computing machines. What it says —and it says this only for so-called well-defined problems with unique solutions—is that however complicated the problem, we can break it down into a set of simpler elementary operations and finally end up with operations as simple as: make a mark, move a mark, take the mark out, put the mark back, etc. These elementary operations are then combined into sub-routines that are more complex and then these are combined, etc. The machine succeeds in being practically interesting because it can run off so many of these operations in so short a time. Turing's theorem has a certain relevance to the structure of knowledge; it, in a sense, is another way of stating what by now I am afraid has become an old saw: that any subject can be taught to anybody at any age in some form that is honest. There is always some way in which complicated problems can be reduced to simpler form, simple and step-by-step enough for a child to grasp.

Now, to move ahead one step, I believe it can be said that knowledge about anything can, generally speaking, be represented in three ways, three parallel systems of processing information. One of these is what I call the enactive representation of knowledge. How do you tie a running bowline? You will reply that you can't quite say it or draw it, but that you will show me by tieing one. Try to tell somebody how to ride a bicycle, or ski. It is knowing by doing. It is the way in which the young child on a seesaw "knows" Newton's Law of Moments. He knows that in order to balance two children on the other side he has to get farther out on his side, and this is the Law of Moments, but known enactively. Only with time do children free themselves from this tendency to equate things with the actions directed toward them. We never free ourselves from it completely. Let me, now speak of ikonic representation. If somebody says to me, for example, "What's a square?" I might say, "Well, a square is a set of sets such that the number of elements in each set is equal to the number of sets." This is a good definition of a square, formalistically. Yet the fact of the matter is that there is another way of representing a square, by an image. It isn't a square, it's an image of a square, and it's a useful image—we can start with it. Many of the things we use in representing knowledge have this ikonic property. I use the word "ikonic" because I do not really mean a kind of imitation of nature. Let us not run down the importance of these useful images. They have limits, these representing pictures.

Finally, a third way in which knowledge can get represented is symbolically. By this I mean in words or in those more powerful versions of words, powerful in one way in any case, mathematical symbols. I think you can turn around the Chinese proverb to the effect that one picture is worth a thousand words. For certain purposes one word is worth a thousand pictures. For example, draw a picture of "implosion"; and yet the idea of implosion as such was one of the basic notions that led to the idea of thermonuclear fusion. Implosion is the concept that results from the application of a contrast transformation on the more familiar concept of explosion. The word was so important that it was classified as top secret during the war. It is this capacity to put things into a symbol system with rules for manipulating, for decomposing and recomposing and transforming and turning symbols on their heads that makes it possible to explore things not present, not picturable, and indeed not in existence.

Now the three modes of representation do not disappear as we grow older; quite to the contrary, they remain with us forever. When we speak of the application of Turing's theorem to the question of structuring of knowledge, it is in reference to the representation forms we have been discussing. Early in life and also early in our mastery of a subject we may have to represent things in terms of what we do with them—in much the same way as a child "knows about" balance beams by knowing what to do on a seesaw. We may then emerge with an image of it, however nonrigorous the image may be. Then and only then can language and symbol systems be applied with some degree of likelihood that their reference will be understood. I do not think I can say anything more important than that. You create a structure, not by starting off with the highest brow symbolic version, but by giving it in the muscles, then in imagery and then giving it in language, with its tools for manipulation. The basic task is to orchestrate the three kinds of representations so that we can lead the child from doing, to imaging what he has done, and finally to symbolization.

Usually in a college catalog when a course is listed it will say something about a "prerequisite." Let me urge that any topic also has internal prerequisites in addition to the things that you are supposed to have mastered beforehand. The internal prerequisites may indeed be just precisely the easier modes of representation that get one to a less rigorous, more imageful or enactive grasp of a subject before it gets converted either into ordinary or mathematical language. The way you get ahead with learning is to translate an idea into those non-rigorous forms that can be understood. Then one can, with their aid, become more precise and powerful. In mathematics such techniques are called "heuristics." Their use often constitutes a prerequisite to grasping a subject in its full depth. This is most of what is meant when we speak of "spiral curriculum."

With respect to the sequence in which material is presented, different sequences are obviously needed to achieve different objectives. The idea of one right sequence is a myth. You have to be quite clear about what kind of learning you are trying to produce before you can specify what is a good sequence for presenting it. There are sequences that can be described for the production of parrots. We use them all the time. But there is also a sequence that is particularly interesting in that it seems to increase the likelihood that knowledge will be converted into a structure that is economical, productive and powerful—and therefore transferable. It is worth pausing over.

I would like to suggest that if you wanted to do this, the first thing that you might do is to try leading the child to grasp a structure by induction from particular instances. You would give him lots of particular instances and let him recognize their underlying regularity. If you want the child to transfer his learning to new situations you had better give him some practice in transfer while he is learning.

The second thing you might try is the use of contrast in your sequence. The fish will be the last to discover water. Economy of representation often makes it necessary for the child to see the contrasting case. Often concepts are structured in terms of contrast and can only be fully understood in terms of them. To grasp the meaning of commutativity in arithmetic—that $3 \cdot 4 = 4 \cdot 3$—often may require that we recognize the noncommutative case of ordinary language—that for quantifiers, for example, "very much" is not equal to "much very" or as a little girl once put it "black shoe" isn't "shoe black."

Third, if one wants a sequence that is going to produce powerful learning, avoid premature symbolization. Do not give them that word to parrot before they know what it is about either by manipulation or in images. Ask yourselves how much you understand about simultaneous equations.

Fourth, you might try to give the child practice at both leaping and plodding. Let him go by small steps. Then let him take great leaps, huge guesses. Without guessing he is deprived of his rights as a mind. We cannot get all of the evidence. It is often by guessing that we become aware of what we know.

Another question related to sequence has to do with what I would call "revisiting." Rarely is everything learned about anything in one encounter. Yet we seem to be so impelled to cover, to get through the Elizabethan Period, and on through such-and-such period that we forget the obvious point—that the pot is rarely licked clean at one swipe. Perhaps we would do well to take music listening as a model. It is not simply a matter of mastering this subject, or even of converting it into more powerful form. Rather, revisit means an opportunity of connecting what we have learned now with what else we know. Why is such an obvious point so often ignored?

Now the question of pacing reward and punishment for success and failure. First distinguish two states. One is success and failure; the other one is reward and punishment. By success and failure, I mean the end state that is inherent in a task. The problem is solved or not solved or close to solved. By reward and punishment, I mean something quite different. It relates to the consequences that follow upon success and failure—prizes, scoldings, gold stars, etc.

It is often the case that emphasis upon reward and punishment, under the control of an outside agent such as a teacher or parent, diverts attention away from success and failure. In effect, this may take the learning initiative away from the child and give it to the person dispensing the rewards and punishments. This will be the more likely if the learner is not able to determine the basis of success and failure. One of the great problems in teaching, which usually starts with the teacher being very supportive, is to give the rewarding function back to the learner and the task. Perhaps we can do this by rewarding good errors so that the child becomes aware of the process of problem solving as worthy as well as the fruits of successful outcome. In any case, I wish to mention these matters to suggest that old dogmas about the role of "reinforcement" can be looked at afresh. The independent problem solver is one who rewards and punishes himself by judging the adequacy of his efforts. Equip him with the tools for thinking and let him be his own man.

I should warn you, in conclusion, to beware of the likes of us. We do not have a tested theory of instruction to offer you. What is quite plain is that one is needed and I would propose that we work together in its forging.

I warn you for a good reason. Educators are a curiously doctrinal or ideological kind of people. You are given to slogans and fight and bleed in their behalf. You have looked to psychology for help and have often been misled into accepting mere hypotheses as the proven word. It is partly because it is so hard to test the adequacy of ideas in an educational setting.

Now we are living through a great revolution in education. Our survival may depend on its successful outcome—our survival as the human race. I know no group in our society more devoted to the common weal than our educators. In this era of new curricula, new teaching arrangements, new automated devices, your best rudder is a healthy sense of experimentation backed by a skepticism toward educational slogans.

If we are to move toward a serviceable and sturdy theory of instruction —and I think we are—then your greatest contribution will be a willingness to give new ideas a try and full candor in expressing your reactions to how things worked. The prospect is strenuous, but gains to be won are enormous.

WILLIAM VAN TIL | *The Key Word Is Relevance*

Let us begin with an admission: Some of the content we teach in American schools is not as relevant as it might be to the lives of the young people we teach, to the society in which they are growing up, or to the clarification of democratic values.

Some illustrations are obvious. For instance, one of the many Puerto Rican schools I visited during a New York University survey of education in Puerto Rico was in a village high in the mountains of the interior. The villagers were very poor and afflicted with the problems that go with poverty—poor nutrition, inefficient agriculture, dilapidated housing, bad health, and the rest.

Only a handful of young people of the village and the surrounding countryside ever enrolled in any kind of educational institution beyond high school. Yet, what were the young people studying in the secondary school in this little mountain village? In a social studies class, they were memorizing lists of products of South American countries. Their mathematics work had no relationship to the problems they might encounter in the school shop or at home or elsewhere. In an English class, students were reading eighteenth and nineteenth century British novels: At the time of my visit one class was dissecting *Ivanhoe*. (This mountain school and community, I hasten to say, was not typical; many other Puerto Rican schools were more relevant to learners, society, and values, and many other communities had higher living standards.)

Recognizing the lack of relevance in education in an exotic, faraway setting is easy. Such was the case when I visited a home economics class in a town of mud hovels in Iran: The girls were making scrapbooks of pictures (clipped from very old magazines) that portrayed the clothes and foods of prosperous Americans and Europeans.

The closer to home we get, however, the harder it becomes for a teacher to recognize irrelevance. Take Doris Smith and Harry Jones, for instance. She teaches in the suburbs in the Midwestern United States; he, in the slums of a West Coast city. Both of them would quickly recognize the lack of meaning in the two faraway examples cited. Yet, both might have difficulty recognizing that they have their own problems in making the content of their classes meaningful to some students.

Doris Smith teaches social studies in an affluent suburb that is among the first places where new national projects and proposals are tried. A genuine innovator, she uses a variety of methods and materials with versatility. She uses simulation techniques, for example, and has just completed an academic game with her eleventh graders. The game deals with economics; the players adopt roles and the ones who make the most money are the winners.

Margaret, one of Miss Smith's better students, went through the motions of the game but was fundamentally uninvolved. Why? Because, like Benjamin in *The Graduate,* Margaret had painfully learned from the lives of her parents and their friends that affluence did not necessarily result in a good life. Why, wondered Margaret, were teachers blind to what was most relevant to young people? For instance, why didn't the teacher see that the most important thing about this game would be to examine the materialistic goals which were taken for granted as desirable?

During follow-up discussions, Miss Smith raised questions with the class about the strategy of moves made during the game. Margaret's responses were correct but unrelated to her concern for values.

Harry Jones teaches language arts in an intermediate school in a slum neighborhood. Though Mr. Jones is white and most of his students are black, racial differences have not been a barrier to mutual liking and respect. The class is now reading a selection in a new anthology which is quite appropriate to the level of the students' reading abilities. Mr. Jones notices that Jess isn't reading the assigned selection, but instead is simply leafing through the pages. It isn't as though I'd asked the class to read dull, difficult material simply because it's supposed to be an English classic, Harry thinks. I guess Jess just doesn't care.

Jess is thinking: I can't find black men in this book. Where's the brothers? This is Whitey's book. How can a good guy like Mr. Jones be so dumb? Not for me, baby.

"What are you doing, Jess?" asks Harry. "Just looking'," says Jess.

Good teachers though they are, even Miss Smith and Mr. Jones sometimes attempt to teach content that is unrelated to the lives of learners. Some teachers have even greater difficulty in achieving relevance than do methodologically skilled Doris and well-liked Harry. Classes do exist in your community and mine in which an uninterrupted academic content bores young people. Classes do exist where subject matter is quite unrelated to the dilemmas and struggles and aspirations of many prospective learners.

The teacher who realizes that his content of instruction isn't meaningful has two viable alternatives. He can change his content from the irrelevant to the relevant. Or, if he cannot change the required content, he can teach it in such a way as to give it relevance.

Yes, a third possibility does exist. One can continue with the meaningless content, break his heart trying to teach, and achieve very little.

A teacher does not need extensive instruction in educational psychology to realize that his teaching must be connected with the student's background, drives, and life if any learning is to take place. Experience soon teaches a teacher this axiom.

The obvious and sensible thing to do is to replace the irrelevant with the relevant through changing the content. Remember, for instance, the poverty-stricken Puerto Rican mountain village in which the students were memorizing products, being taught mathematics without application, and reading *Ivanhoe*. Here was a setting characterized by a host of problems in the areas of health, sanitation, housing, nutrition, safety, use of resources, production, and consumption. Here were Puerto Rican youngsters who would face bewildering life problems including those presented by the continuing restless migration from the rural ways of the *barrio* to the urbanized ways of San Juan; from the hospitable island of their birth to the impersonal, tenement-lined canyons of New York City, with its strange folkways and less-than-warm welcome to those regarded as "foreigners."

Reality could be introduced into their education. In social studies, students might well learn of the real problems of the village, the island, the mainland. In mathematics, they might see a relationship between mathematics and the problems they encounter in school shop and in their homes. In English classes, students might well acquire the bilinguality they need by reading English-language newspapers and magazines, as well as books of fiction and nonfiction by Puerto Rican and mainland Americans, plus a sampling of British authors. Fortunately, the better Puerto Rican schools do introduce such realities into their programs.

In mainland America, too, the obvious and sensible approach is to change the content if it is not germane. Most educators will readily grant that a teacher must begin at the actual level of accomplishment of those who are to be educated—not to stay there but begin there. Most will grant that pitching the learning at an unreachable level is an exercise in futility. But additionally we must recognize the vital importance of selecting suitable content.

The curriculum should be made more relevant to the lives of the children and youth for whom the curriculum exists. Through their reading materials, for example, city children must often meet people like themselves, rather than always encounter the legendary Dick and Jane and Spot of suburban life. The world of the city must itself become part of the subject matter if young city dwellers are to improve human relations, develop citizenship, widen horizons, and meet the problems of urban living. In Harry Jones's class, and those of his colleagues, surely the contributions of Negro-Americans should be an integral part of the American literature curriculum for both Negroes and whites.

Nor are the suburbs exempt from the blight of irrelevance. Though some suburban young people have an economic head start in life, they, too, are sometimes cheated. When communities are bland and homogenized and indifferent to reality, the young are sometimes cheated of the opportunity to know people of varied races, religions, nationality backgrounds, and social classes.

When high school students are regarded as college fodder, they are sometimes cheated of sufficient experience in home economics, music, fine arts, and industrial arts. When the only god worshipped is academic success in formal learning, students are sometimes cheated of the opportunity to explore seriously their allegiances to values, their relationships to the adult world, their ways of finding satisfaction, and their participation in political action and social change.

"But," a teacher may say, "I cannot change the required content to make it relevant. I am not a board of regents or a local board of education or a curriculum bigwig attached to the central office staff." He may add, "I am just a humble teacher, a prisoner of the syllabus, the required textbook, and the system in which I am caught. Deviation is not permitted. THEY would not allow it."

Maybe so, but I doubt it. Before the teacher resigns himself to a prisoner's life, he might wish to reexamine his chains. Perhaps they are not as strong as he assumes.

In today's world, more and more educators and laymen are realizing that not all of the answers to the problem of curriculum are in. Since the early 1960's, increasing numbers of educators have attempted to develop curriculums that are more important to the culturally disadvantaged or, in a plainer phrase, the poor.

Now recognition is growing that we are far from having achieved the best of all possible worlds with respect to the education of the economically advantaged. In 1969, still more educators will be looking for curriculums appropriate for young people from affluent backgrounds. Paradoxically, today's disenchanted young people, including democratic activists and serious and sensitive students as well as hippies and nihilists and revolutionaries, stem mostly from the middle and upper classes.

Possibly the chains of established content are not as binding as assumed. Teacher power grows. In a time of teacher shortage, few need stay as teachers in repressive atmospheres, for some administrators are seeking change-minded teachers.

In those cases where, through a variety of circumstances, the chains do prove real and teachers simply must use some prescribed content which is not as relevant as they would wish it to be, how can they make their work more meaningful?

Rather than making fundamental changes in the content, some teachers use the second alternative mentioned and adapt the content to make it more relevant. Illustrations are legion: In literature, teaching *Julius Caesar* in relationship to contemporary dictatorships; in history, preparing and contrasting attitudes toward past American wars with present attitudes on war in Viet Nam; in biology, relating the study of human blood to false claims and misleading mythologies as to blood differences between races; in modern languages, teaching the culture as part of the culture's language; in language arts, stressing those readings in anthologies which have most meaning to the particular learners. Miss Smith, for instance, could have discussed with the class the value assumptions behind the economic game that was the required content.

Some readers may ask for the prescription good teachers use for adaptation of content. There isn't any. Sorry about that. If there were a single sovereign remedy, it would have been discovered long ago. The good teacher uses his intelligence in relating the required content to the world of the learner. Good teachers have been doing so for a long time; adaptation is no revolutionary doctrine.

In making content more relevant, there is no substitute for knowing the social realities which characterize the environment of the student. There is no substitute for knowing the learner as an individual. There is no substitute for having a philosophy which gives direction to the educational enterprise. So armed, one can relate much of the content to the learner, the class, the school, and the community.

OSCAR HANDLIN | ***Live Students and Dead Education: Why the High School Must Be Revived***

More money will help. But it will not itself solve the problem. American schools, particularly the high schools, are entering a prolonged crisis, obscured by the debate over the ways and means of financing them. However the funds will be raised, we shall have to reconsider the function of secondary education if we wish to spare our children the chaos that now threatens them in the most vulnerable years of their lives.

From *The Atlantic* (September 1961), pp. 29–34. Reprinted by permission of Collins-Knowlton-Wing, Inc.

The evidence is clear. The number of high school students is larger than ever before, and it will continue to increase for years to come. In this group are boys and girls of types that did not formerly ascend to this level of instruction; it will be dangerous to neglect their needs and interests. Above all, the high schools operate in a new social context, of which they must take account. These developments pose a challenge so serious that we can disregard it only at our peril.

The federal census conveniently tabulates the population by age groups and projects its size into the future. The number of Americans aged fifteen to nineteen grew from slightly more than eleven million in 1955 to well over twelve million in 1958. At that point we began to feel the effects of the post-war baby boom. The size of the group grew more rapidly. In 1965 it will amount to more than seventeen million; in 1970, to well over nineteen million. There is no guesswork to these estimates; these children are already born and on their way toward adolescence. They will enormously expand the pool from which the high school population of the future will be drawn.

An ever-larger percentage of the eligible age group will demand and receive a secondary education. Almost twice as large a proportion of entering students will receive high school diplomas in 1961 as were able to do so twenty years ago. More than 90 per cent of the boys and girls over five and under eighteen are now enrolled in some school; before long *almost all of them will be.* The high school population has already soared under these pressures. From six and a half million in 1950, it has risen to over ten million in 1961.

One can anticipate an even larger increase in the decade ahead, for the high birth rate and the rising level of expectations throughout American society show no signs of subsiding. In addition, the dominant economic trends of our period literally drive young people into the schools.

There is nothing else for them to do. The range of unskilled jobs open to youths of under eighteen years of age is steadily shrinking. The decline of the family farm and mechanization and automation of industry continually reduce the number of places for which they can qualify. The talk of a thirty-hour week to spread employment reflects the desire to limit the size of the labor force, a situation not likely to make attractive openings for the very young. The number of white-collar jobs has grown, but these jobs generally require a high school diploma. As the long process of formal education becomes the universal norm, the thing to do, those who lack education suffer increasingly and are compelled to adhere to the general pattern. All the ways up now lead through the high school, and only the misfits or the children of the very poor and underprivileged are pushed into the narrowing range of employments from which there is no exit. It is not in the least likely that these trends will be reversed in the future.

The high school cannot meet the challenge of the oncoming tide of new students simply by increasing its existing facilities. The high school was an institution developed for a rather select student body, and this much larger aggregate will not fit into its established forms.

The Total Student Body

Our students vary greatly in intelligence; as many are below as are above average. The problems of the high school change radically as it begins to serve a clientele unselected as to ability.

The situation of the talented boys and girls is clear-cut. The old curriculum was made for them; the road ahead to college and the professional schools is open; and a good deal of attention is already being devoted to them. They will have to learn to avoid being dragged down by the average of the mass about them. But success in doing so is one of the tests of their ability.

The high school has had less experience in dealing with those who, lacking competence or motivation, are euphemistically called the "academically untalented." The traditional course of study is above their grasp, and the careers open to them are by no means clear. Yet the untalented will comprise a rising percentage of the total student body. They cannot be thrown into a labor market which has no room for them, but the imperatives of a democratic society demand that they have their chance. Formerly, it was possible to shut them off into various vocational educational programs. Rarely did these programs reflect a positive comprehension of the students they served; all too often they aimed simply to get the less able out of the way of the more able. Characteristically, they absorbed the underprivileged, who lacked the opportunity to develop their ability. It was no coincidence, for instance, that Georgia in 1958 had three times as many students enrolled in such programs as did Massachusetts.

In any case, the old forms of vocational education will be even less useful in the future than in the past; the very same economic changes that drive more students into the schools also undervalue the handicraft skills that can be taught there. These vocational programs are therefore growing at a far lower rate than are other sectors of secondary education.

A large part of the high school population consequently finds itself enmeshed in an institution that has little relevance to present or future needs. These boys and girls have drifted on into the ninth grade because it follows after the eighth. They are told to study subjects they cannot grasp and to acquire skills they may never use. Only athletics, marching bands, and their own social life rescue them from total boredom.

And they are adolescents! Growing into maturity, they feel the need to test their powers and assert their individuality. Lacking recognized means for doing so, confined to a round of purposeless tasks, some become utterly apathetic. Others divert their vitality into the rebellion of juvenile delinquency.

The secondary school must adjust to meet the needs of all these young people. In the 1960s, either it will prepare or it will fail to prepare them for citizenship and for careers.

The Nineteenth-Century Pattern

There is no simple formula for reshaping the structure of an institution that prepares some of its students for college and others for trades, and that is also intended to equip all of them with the ability to vote, to drive cars, to make friends, and to take a useful part in life. The high school must now become something more than the bridge between the elementary school and the college, a function which hitherto shaped its development.

The American high school took its present form in the last two decades of the nineteenth century. Until then, there had been no organization whatever to secondary education in the United States. Side by side there existed public and private academies and a multitude of high, trade, and finishing schools of various sorts, each with its individually fashioned curriculum. Most of the students terminated their education at this level, for it was not yet necessary to go further to enter upon an apprenticeship in business or the professions. Only a small minority went on to college.

There was no consistent pattern to the preparation of that minority. Requirements for college admission differed, and rarely did colleges insist upon the completion of a secondary school course. Students entered when they could prove that they were ready, by passing an entrance examination to the satisfaction of the faculty of the college to which they applied. And those examinations varied in scope as well as in difficulty.

The multiplication in the number of both colleges and secondary schools after 1870 created confusion and generated controversy between the two groups of educators. The schools demanded that the colleges guarantee admission to their graduates. The colleges insisted that the schools devote themselves primarily to instruction prerequisite to their own offerings. Yet the ability of the schools to do so was complicated by the fact that the colleges were changing under the impetus of the new scientific scholarship.

The virtual anarchy of the 1880s induced the National Educational Association to appoint a distinguished committee of ten to look into the secondary school curriculum, under the chairmanship of President

Charles W. Eliot of Harvard. The committee drew together the best minds in American education, and its report, published in 1893, presented an incisive and penetrating analysis of secondary education in the United States. Although not all the changes it recommended were adopted, it did set a formalized pattern that very quickly dominated instruction at this level and helped to establish the basic features of the high school as we know it. This was to be an intermediate school with a term four years in duration between elementary and collegiate instruction. It was to be secular and primarily public in its control. Most important of all, the committee recommended that the curriculum be standardized in terms of units of instruction, so that the students could be uniformly evaluated for the purposes of college admission.

The members of the committee had approached their task in no parochial spirit. They were acutely aware that not every high school student would cross the bridge into college and that the schools had to meet the needs of the whole society and not simply those of a selected portion of it. Yet, precisely in that respect, public education had failed.

The function of the high school was to transmit to the student the guides that would help him pass safely by the distractions of popular fads in tastes and ideas. The college preparatory subjects presented to him a body of knowledge, organized in subject units, that every educated man had to know. Familiarity with that body of knowledge was expected to impart to each youth a set of standards that he could thereafter accept as good and right. The educated man would know what he ought to enjoy in literature, art, and music; what was proper in economics and politics; and what was just and decent in personal relationships. He could measure every problem by the criteria of the defined culture acquired in the high school, not as well as if he had gone on to college, but in the same way.

Although that culture was detached and apart from life, it nevertheless prepared the student for most contingencies. Through science he acquired practice in classification and induction; with the logic absorbed from mathematics he was endowed with the methods of right reasoning. History and the classics taught him how to draw analogies from experience; and from literature and art he acquired taste and discrimination. Thus armed, he was ready to sally forth from the bastion of the school to do battle with life.

The concealed premise of this assumption was that knowledge of any subject was to be acquired not for its intrinsic value but as a means toward some more general purpose. The farmer or the businessman who wondered why his taxes should go to support instruction in Latin or geometry or history was told that these courses were to be studied not merely because they were worth knowing for their own sakes but because of the mental discipline involved in learning them.

Confusion in the Curriculum

The disastrous consequences of this point of view emerged in the next quarter century. As the high school absorbed an increasing part of the population, the pressure for accommodating new interests mounted, and the conception of indirect training proved infinitely extensible. Since no subject was worthy of attention in itself, but primarily as a means of mental training, the way was open for the intrusion of many new subjects. If music was to be studied because it gave our heterogeneous population "the feeling for order and symmetry," and literature because it "will keep us pure and keep us strong," then why not basketball, which developed a sense of discipline and a respect for law?

The teachers in the entrenched academic course continued to argue the peculiar merits of their own subjects. But they could not demonstrate, to the satisfaction of parents and school boards, that Greek and Latin were indeed more valuable instruments of mental discipline than French or home economics.

The confusion in the curriculum grew worse after World War I, when new psychological investigations shook the confidence of educators in the theory of the transfer of learning. Now it appeared that the training acquired in one subject did not carry over automatically to another. The power of reasoning acquired in physics did not add to a man's ability to make judgments in politics; the sense of harmony gained in music did not contribute to neighborliness. The result was the dissipation of any effort to select some subjects as more worthy of inclusion in the high school curriculum than others. The core of academic courses retained their prestige because they led to college; any worthy boy or girl would take them. The other students were left to judge unaided what would be most immediately useful to them. But so long as culture was compartmentalized in blocks of subject matter, there could be no effort to put it within the reach of students not destined for college.

The idea of education as adjustment to life, which emerged from the work of John Dewey and his followers, useful as that was, did not fill the void. Indeed, one of the weaknesses of the Dewey approach, in breaking down established disciplines, was to strengthen the impression that all things were equally worthy of being taught.

The high school therefore lacked the ability to adjust to new pressures, other than through adding new courses. On the one hand, the community demanded that it assume more functions; on the other, the contracting labor market thrust larger numbers of the untalented into the high school. As long as the only standard of judgment was that of immediate utility, the case for drivers' education or etiquette was as plausible as that for history or geometry. To add a new subject, it was only necessary to appease the guardians of the old ones by leaving their cultural domain untouched.

Any effort at reconstruction must recognize the crucial situation of the high school in the enlarging American social structure. It cannot be simply, or even primarily, the first stage in preparation for a career, as the Continental European secondary school is. In our society, careers are not chosen at the age of eleven; few boys and girls know what they will do even at graduation. Indeed, a majority of our college students have not yet made up their minds at the end of their freshman year. And experience indicates that the gains of our type of procedure, time-consuming though it be, far outweigh the losses.

The high school must remain an undifferentiated institution through which the whole population will pass. It must focus its attention not on the preparation of one segment or another of its student body, but on the development in all of it of the core of habits, ideas, and assumptions that will make them, to the best of their abilities, creative citizens. In doing so, it will also, but incidentally, provide them with a basis for selecting their future vocations, as they learn to know the world about them and as they come to test their own abilities and aptitudes.

To understand what such an institution can best teach, it is necessary to expose two pervasive errors in recent American thought about education.

Every dabbler in curriculums begins with the assumption that what is taught is learned. To require a course is to spread the knowledge of its contents; therefore, it remains only to be decided what should be required. Nothing could be further from the truth. Few subjects are as much taught as American history; in most states it is doled out repetitively in the fifth and eight grades of elementary school and again in the last year of high school. Yet a national survey by the New York *Times* some years ago showed the abysmal ignorance that was the product of all this teaching. In fact, every college course of which I know begins from the beginning and takes for granted no previous knowledge of the subject. More than two decades of experience with the best-trained students in the country have convinced me that it would make no difference whatever if they had never studied American history before they came to college.

The rate at which knowledge fades after the final quiz in mathematics or languages is fully as rapid. It means little how many students take three years of French; what matters is how few will ever thereafter look into a French book. What is taught simply cannot be equated with what is learned and retained.

Nor is it true that what is not taught will not be learned. I pass by the men like Benjamin Franklin, who learned six languages, something about prose style, and a good deal of science without being taught; they were, perhaps, exceptions. I come rather to the lad who cannot remember the date of the Spanish-American War or the meaning of "sixteen to one," but who can name the pitchers in each game of the World Series of 1948 and can reel off batting averages by the yard. These had significance to him, while dates and monetary ratios did not. When we wish to do so, we learn without teachers, and, sometimes, despite them.

To recognize that not everything that ought to be learned can or should be taught by the school is to set the problem of its curriculum within manageable terms. Any renewed effort, after the fashion of the Committee of Ten, to define a body of knowledge that every educated man ought to have is futile and needless. By what criteria can we tell the boys and girls who enter high school next year to take French and Latin rather than German and Russian, Medieval rather than Oriental history, physics rather than chemistry? The world of information that reaches from antiquity to the present is so complex that such simple evaluations are impossible. The high school cannot endow its students with everything they ought to know. It can only equip them to get what they need as they come to recognize the need for it.

The Two Fundamentals

Given its place in American society and the character of its students, the high school must focus on two tasks: It ought to impart to its students the ability to communicate and to be communicated with; and it ought to introduce them to the quantitative techniques on which modern science, and technology rest. If it succeeds in these tasks, it will give its graduates the equipment for future learning.

Reading, writing, and arithmetic have, of course, long been elements of the traditional curriculum. Unfortunately, their function has been so frequently misunderstood by teachers as to make instruction in them almost totally ineffective. When the class creeps through *Ivanhoe* at the rate of eight pages a day, it is not learning to read; when it parses sentences or memorizes the rules for the use of indefinite pronouns, it is not learning to write; and when it acquires facility in problem-solving, it is not learning the nature of mathematics.

The prevailing pattern of instruction has emphasized drill in rules and diligence in the performance of ritual exercises at the expense of understanding the content. The teachers have been dominated by the assumption that the student, good, bad, or indifferent, must first learn to make bricks before he can be allowed to see the outlines of the building. Alas, the meaningless monotony of brickmaking destroys in all but a few any desire to see the building.

The incorrigible optimist within me nevertheless insists that the high school can perform these tasks. The processes of comprehension, expression, and measurement can be made real and meaningful—even pleasurable—to adolescents at every level of ability. Nor would it take a major revolution to do so, only a decisive clarification of purpose.

Certainly the high school has available the means of enabling its pupils to acquire through reading some familiarity with the important conceptions of our culture, and through practice in writing and speaking the ability to express themselves clearly.

The classics occupy a central place in such training. These are the great works of human intelligence which, whether produced in Palestine, Greece, Rome, Italy, England, or the United States, have demonstrated the capacity for being understood over long periods of time and in a variety of places. Acquaintanceship with them introduces the student to the significant common ideas of our civilization. But before they can be used, the classics must be rescued from the classicists.

I know not how many Gauls Caesar slaughtered. But I know that he has killed the interest of three generations of Americans in the classics. More than sixty years ago, the consultants to the Committee of Ten demonstrated that the *Gallic Wars* belonged in the library, not in the classroom. "The book is altogether too difficult for beginners; it is too exclusively military in content to be generally interesting; its vocabulary is too largely restricted, from the nature of the subject, to marches, sieges, and battles to afford the best introduction to subsequent reading; and, finally, it touches human life at too few points to be morally helpful and significant." Yet, of the glory that was Greece and Rome, this is what the high school student first encounters. And for many it is all.

The stubborn attachment of the classicists to Caesar is due to more than inertia, profound though that may be. It springs also from an underlying insistence that the ultimate purpose of their teaching is to produce scholarly masters of an elegant Latin style. For the same reason, *Beowulf* has been set as an impenetrable barrier in the way to a love of English literature by those who believe that nothing can be accomplished in this sphere without beginning with the Anglo-Saxon.

If, however, the function of the classics be recognized as that of offering the American adolescent a glimpse of the seminal ideas of our culture, quite different texts can be held forth to him. Any boy or girl can read some Aristophanes or Thucydides or Livy or Chaucer or Dickens with interest. Inclusive lists are of no importance, for these books should be the beginning, rather than the sum, of their reading. And that reading should be in the available good English translations. No translation is, of course, the equivalent of the original. But the question is not whether *The Clouds* should be read in Greek or in English; the question is whether it should be read in English or not at all. And there is more likelihood that a few students will be drawn to study the language through knowing its literature than that any will be drawn to the literature through drill in the language.

The Common Attributes

Reading is one prerequisite of learning to write; the other is actual practice in writing, and this the high school offers hardly at all. Year after year, the colleges face a dismal encounter with freshmen who may have composed a few three-hundred word papers, or, more likely, have in all their studies written nothing whatever. No amount of exercise in word definition or grammar can take the place of the regular and frequent experience of setting words meaningfully on paper.

Finally, the disappearance of what a century ago was known as rhetoric has had deplorable effects in the broken sentences and indirect, ambiguous phraseology characteristic of American speech. Training in the tricks of elocution and debate is no substitute for practice, as a normal part of the teaching of the language, in the habits of clear and forceful oral expression.

The content of instruction in reading, writing, and speaking can readily be adjusted to the varying levels of student ability. The untalented will command a smaller vocabulary; they will absorb a narrower range of meanings from stories; they will apprehend myths and metaphors more readily than abstract symbols or logical connections. But whatever they learn will be of immense use in establishing a means of communication with the rest of the society in which they live.

I write with less confidence and less knowledge of what is wrong with the teaching of mathematics. But that something is wrong seems certain. The last sixty years have witnessed revolutionary changes in fundamental conceptions, yet the standard sequence of algebra, plane geometry, intermediate algebra, trigonometry, advanced algebra, and solid geometry, until just a few years ago, remained anchored in a pre-Newtonian universe. Most young people who are excellent at problem-solving and make perfect scores on the mathematical achievement test do not begin to understand what modern mathematics is about until they are well into their college careers. What have the vast majority who never go beyond plane geometry got?

The high school teaching of mathematics seems to reflect the same concentration upon rules and exercises that blights the study of language. It needs an analogous shift in emphasis that will introduce all students, at different levels of competence, to the concepts of quantity and space they will encounter throughout their lives. That task ought not to be left to popularizations, which in their wide sales show the genuine public interest in the subject.

If the high school can supply a solid groundwork of training in the use of language and of mathematics, the rest of its curriculum need not be so rigidly specified. Let it recognize the variety of students who meet within its halls. Let it offer what courses in languages, art, music, history, science, bookkeeping, machine-shop practice, personal behavior, and athletics its size, budget, and location dictate. Let the students move where interest and ability draw them. Above all, let it occupy the boys and girls in activities relevant to their present needs and to a future in which leisure may be as prominent a part of life as work.

There need be no fear either that talents will be wasted or that students will lack exposure to important aspects of our culture. The lad who is unwillingly forced into a course in American history or physics will not learn anything of value, and his presence will impede the learning of those who are interested. Let him have instead his course in French or family relations. If he has really learned to read, he will someday see the relevance of American history to his own life and find available the means of knowing what he should about it. And if he has a solid foundation in mathematics and shows a desire to study physics in college, he will not be at a great disadvantage in doing so.

Nor will society suffer, in consequence, a shrinkage in the supply of historians or physicists. Our colleges manage to produce geologists and astronomers and philosophers without advance preparation at the secondary level. They can do the same in every sphere of scholarship.

As for the untalented, they will pass these four critical years sharing the social and communal experiences of their fellows. They will not be excluded from the realm of culture by their failure to go on to college, but will catch glimpses of it commensurate with their ability. Just as the peasant and Saint Thomas apprehended the awe of the cathedral, although in different ways, or as Emerson and the farmer spoke of progress, so our own culture can be grasped at different levels. And the high school is its critical teaching mechanism.

We may thus hope to imbue these young people with a sense of community that will make their future work worth while. We cannot restore the small-town carpenter or tinkerer of the past, who took pride in his handiwork. But we can endow the mechanics and factory hands of the future with enough awareness of the world in which they live to give them a sense of the value of their labor and of its relation to others. And that same awareness outside the job will help them lead useful lives as parents and citizens.

The illusion of the Committee of Ten that culture can be defined in frozen units of essential subject matter which will train the mind of every student has too long deceived us. A large percentage of our boys and girls will resist the efforts of the school to stuff culture into them. It does not matter. They will make good citizens, businessmen, and parents despite the lack of Latin or history, if they can grow through the difficult years of adolescence, learning by experience to relate themselves to the world about them.

What is important is that the high school do well what it can do. It serves a democratic society at a point in the lives of its young people when their future is still vague and undefined. It can do no more, but it must do no less, then to endow them, to the limits of their abilities, with the common attributes of our culture.

E. PAUL TORRANCE | Uniqueness and Creativeness: The School's Role

Throughout the history of education, in a diversity of ways men have asked, "Should the school assume more responsibility than it now does for the identification and cultivation of uniqueness and creativeness in and among its pupils?" Usually, the answer has been a very definite "No." Creative individuals have almost always had serious difficulty in surviving in the schools of their day.

Many rationalizations have been offered for the negative answer. Some people say, "There is no way of identifying a creative individual." Others say, "It is not possible to cultivate creativity in a person; if a child has a spark of creativity, it will come out no matter what you do." Still others argue, "We already have too many creative individuals; we need obedient, disciplined people who can follow orders and be loyal citizens." These very same people have, of course, held to the dreams of an educational system that would help each person in our society develop his potentialities.

One could almost dichotomize learning theories, educational methods, and teaching procedures into those that emphasize the receptiveness of the human mind and those that emphasize the self-acting, creative nature of the human mind. A failure to recognize that there are vast individual differences in receptive and self-acting tendencies has generally resulted in confusion when the validity of these two opposing views (as represented by learning theories, teaching methods, etc.) has been subjected to experimental tests. In actual practice, methods emphasizing the receptiveness of the human mind have generally "won out."

From *Educational Leadership,* 24(6):493–96; March 1967. Reprinted with permission of the Association for Supervision and Curriculum Development and E. Paul Torrance.

To many educators these methods are appealing because they do not seem to require continued creative energy to apply them. The results are fairly predictable, promising the educator greater control of the behavior of children and young people. Such methods are thus less threatening to the educator. Some advocates of these methods for all children recognize a body of knowledge that shows that different children have different ways or styles of learning. They argue that we cannot afford financially to apply such knowledge, that it would accentuate individual differences, and that this would be dangerous.

One of the tragic consequences of this point of view is that certain types of children and young people simply do not learn when taught according to the stimulus-response psychology that emphasizes the receptivity of the mind. Forcing them to learn in ways unnatural for them and incompatible with their best abilities and preferred ways of learning robs them of much of their human dignity and a chance to achieve their potentialities.

Some observers have concluded quite erroneously that there has been a "creativity boom" in American education. I have simply been unable to see any of the evidences of such a "boom." I know of no rigorous observational study of classroom behavior that gives much evidence of attempts to identify and acknowledge creative potentialities or to facilitate creative functioning and development. In workshops and institutes on creative ways of teaching, I have found many of the essential skills absent from the behavior repertoire of teachers at all levels.

However, I have encountered thousands of teachers who are trying to develop some of these skills and are experimenting successfully with creative ways of teaching. I have encountered several hundred principals and supervisors who want to help teachers acquire the requisite skills. I am asked what the research efforts of the past ten years have contributed to help them in this task. Most briefly, I shall list what I regard as some of the most important implications of this research for educational practice.

1. "Creativity" Not Mystical

For ages, educators have been preoccupied with the personal-mystery concepts of the creative process. The development of instruments to assess the mental abilities involved in creative thinking and the personal qualities required for creative achievement[1]; the designing of sequences of guided learning experiences[2] and the production of instructional materials

[1] E. P. Torrance, *Torrance Tests of Creative Thinking: Norms-Technical Manual. Research Edition.* (Princeton, N.J.; Personnel Press, 1966).

[2] E. P. Torrance, and R. Gupta, *Development and Evaluation of Recorded Programmed Experiences in Creative Thinking in the Fourth Grade.* (Minneapolis: Bureau of Educational Research, University of Minnesota, 1964).

to facilitate creative development and functioning in the classroom[3,4]; and experimentation with teaching methods designed to facilitate creative development and functioning[5] have done much to take "creativity" out of the realm of the mystical. Whenever any aspect of human behavior is removed from the realm of mystery, educational practice is affected.

2. *A Definition Operationalized*

In my research and developmental work, I have maintained that creative thinking occurs when a person responds constructively to a situation that calls for non-habitual behavior, solutions for which the behaver has no learned response. I have been concerned primarily with creativity among school children, in classrooms, and among teachers. I have chosen, therefore, to define creativity as a process whereby one becomes aware of problems, difficulties, gaps in information, and disharmonies for which he has no learned solution; searches for clues in the situation and existing knowledge, formulates hypotheses, tests them, modifies and retests them; and communicates the results.

If one accepts this definition, he can then ask what mental abilities or kinds of mental functioning are brought into play in the process; what personal qualities facilitate the process; what kinds of teaching methods, classroom procedures, and instructional materials will facilitate the process. The definition can also be used to guide evaluations of the products that result from the process. The process can be replicated in classrooms at all levels of education. Since any skill must be practiced to be developed, it seems reasonable that classroom activities that replicate the process will contribute to creative development.

3. *Assessment Instruments*

A variety of assessment instruments attempting to operationalize the above definition have been developed. After nine years of development one achievement in this area is the publication of a research edition of alternate forms of both verbal and figural batteries of tests of creative thinking. The technical-norms manual for these batteries offers a variety of test-retest reliability, interscorer reliability, and validity information.

Progress has also been made on the development of measures of crea-

[3] B. F. Cunnington, and E. P. Torrance, *Imagi/Craft-Materials* (10 albums and teacher guides) (Boston: Ginn and Co., 1965).

[4] R. E. Myers, and E. P. Torrance, *Can You Imagine?; Invitations to Thinking and Doing; Invitations to Speaking and Writing Creatively* (Pupil ideabooks and teacher guides) (Boston: Ginn and Co., 1965).

[5] E. P. Torrance, *Rewarding Creative Behavior: Experiments in Classroom Creativity* (Englewood Cliffs, N.J.: Prentice-Hall, Inc., 1965).

tive motivation, preferences for learning in creative ways, and procedures for helping teachers identify creative potentialities.

Whatever the limitations of these tests might be, they can help educators become aware of potentialities that might otherwise go unnoticed. These instruments may also provide models for developing measures of subject matter achievement, and sequences of learning experiences that provide experience in creative thinking.

4. *Not Necessary to Leave to Chance*

The work of my associates and me, Crutchfield and his associates[6] and dozens of others has demonstrated that creative functioning and development among school children can be facilitated by deliberate methods, sequences of guided experiences. Instructional materials developed through these projects give classroom teachers some ready-made helps which, if used intelligently, contribute to creative development. This, of course, is in keeping with a general conclusion of Alfred Binet[7] in 1909 that intelligence consists of all of the little functions of discrimination, observation, retention, imagination, and the like and that all of these functions are susceptible to development through education.

5. *Continuity of Development*

For many years, investigators have found that drops in creative functioning and participation in creative activities occur at about age five, the fourth grade, and seventh grade. It was generally assumed that these drops or discontinuities were inevitable and healthy aspects of development. My associates and I have been unwilling to accept this assumption.

In a series of studies, we have shown that these discontinuities do not occur under teachers who deliberately build upon skills already acquired and make use of activities that give opportunities for the practice of the creative thinking abilities and creative personality characteristics. Comparative developmental curves in several different cultures have shown that the shape of the developmental curves differs from country to country and that drops tend not to occur in cultures that have been described as continuous. We have also shown that intelligent use of well-prepared instructional materials makes the influence of the school strong enough to offset the effects of cultural discontinuities.[8]

[6] R. S. Crutchfield, "Creative Thinking in Children: Its Teaching and Testing." In O. G. Brim, Jr., R. S. Crutchfield, and W. H. Holtzman. *Intelligence: Perspectives 1965.* (New York: Harcourt, Brace & World, Inc., 1966, p. 33–64).

[7] A. Binet, *Les Idées Modernes sur les Enfants* (Paris: E. Flamarion, 1909).

[8] E. P. Torrance, and R. Gupta, *op. cit.*

6. Children Learn in Different Ways

To me, the most exciting insight that has come from creativity research is that different kinds of children learn best when given a chance to learn in ways best suited to their motivations and abilities. Whenever teachers change their ways of teaching in significant ways, a different group of learners become the stars or high achievers. In another source, I have summarized some of the evidence for this conclusion.[9] This conclusion has far-reaching implications for educating a larger number of people to a higher level and for achieving a higher level of human dignity and mental health in our society.

In conclusion, many critics have equated creative ways of learning with progressive education, permissiveness, and lack of discipline. A careful examination of the methods and materials that have been developed and evaluated reveals that such a conclusion is grossly in error.

The most sensitive and alert kind of guidance and direction is required. Although there are moments of play, the most rigorous kinds of discipline are required. Learning in creative ways requires expensive energies and emphasizes the self-acting rather than the receptive nature of the mind. The importance of the informed mind and the acquisition of authentic information are central themes.

The creative mind wants to know, digs deeper, gets into deep water, and encounters closed doors. It makes and corrects mistakes, builds sand castles, cuts holes to see through, "sings in its own key," and "has a ball." To fail to recognize this complexity reflects a misunderstanding of the creative process and the educational practices necessary to identify, acknowledge and develop creative potentialities through education.

[9] E. P. Torrance, "Different Ways of Learning for Different Kinds of Children." In E. P. Torrance and R. D. Storm, eds., *Mental Health and Achievement* (New York: John Wiley & Sons, Inc., 1965), pp. 253–62.

J. LLOYD TRUMP | *Organization of Instruction*

The secondary school of the future will not have standard classes of 25 to 35 students meeting five days a week on inflexible schedules. Both the size of the groups and the length of the classes will vary from day to

From *Images of the Future: A New Approach to the Secondary School* by J. Lloyd Trump (Urbana, Ill.: National Association of Secondary-School Principals, NEA, 1959). Reprinted by permission.

day. Methods of teaching, student groupings, and teacher and pupil activities will adjust to the purposes and content of instruction.

No longer will one teacher endeavor to be in charge of all of a class's activities in one subject. Instead teaching will be organized to be more efficient and effective.

Some aspects of learning will be presented by specially qualified teachers to relatively large groups of students. This, in turn, will provide more opportunities for students to explore ideas in small discussion groups. Although some classes will be much larger, paradoxically the student will assume more individual responsibility for learning.

The school will be organized around three kinds of activities: large-group instruction; individual study; small-group discussion.

LARGE-GROUP INSTRUCTION

Large-group instruction will include a number of activities carried out in groups of 100 or more students. (Of course, limited enrollments in some courses may reduce that figure.) Instruction and discussions will be conducted by teachers who are particularly competent, who have more adequate time to prepare, and who will utilize the best possible instructional aids.

The following activities will be undertaken before these large groups:

Introduction	New topics, units, and concepts are introduced and placed in relation to other knowledge. Purposes are presented. Preparation for learning is developed.
Motivation	Reasons for study are understood. Interest is stimulated. Students are assisted in self-analysis of present knowledge.
Explanation	Understanding of terms and concepts is further developed. Questions by students and teachers are raised and answered.
Exploration	Identification of the range of possible learning activties is provided. Interests are amplified. Problems to be solved by students are considered.
Planning	Decisions are made regarding learning activities. Methods of study are planned.
Group Study	What has been learned is shared by use of buzz-sessions, panels, and other group techniques. Drill, memorization, problem solving, and organization devices are practiced.
Enrichment	Content not readily available to students is introduced.
Generalization	Understandings and appreciations are developed. Concepts that can be transferred to other situations are summarized.

Evaluation Knowledge, appreciations, skills, and generalizations are measured prior to study, during study, and at the conclusion of the activity. A variety of evaluative techniques are utilized.

These large-group activities will occupy about 40 per cent of the students' time. The amount of time spent in large groups will vary according to subjects, at different stages within a subject, and in accordance with student interest and maturity.

Individual study

Students will engage in *study* activities as individuals, or in groups of two or three, with a minimum of constant supervision. Teachers and other staff personal will serve more as consultants than task masters. Conferences between students and instructors will be held whenever necessary to clarify goals, content, and personal problems. Students will read, listen to records and tapes, view, question, experiment, examine, consider evidence, analyze, investigate, think, write, create, memorize, record, make, visit, and self-appraise. These activities will take place in project and materials centers, museums, workshops, libraries, and laboratories, in and outside the school.

Study activities will require students progressively to take more responsibility for self-direction. The amount of time will vary according to subject and student maturity. On an average it will be about 40 per cent of their time.

Small-group discussion

Small groups of 12 to 15 students and a teacher will pit mind against mind to sharpen understanding. They will examine terms and concepts, solve problems, and reach areas of agreement and disagreement. At the same time they will learn about getting along together. This is primarily a student activity with the teacher sitting in as counselor, consultant, and evaluator. The *discussion* activities will occupy about 20 per cent of the students' time.

A New Concept

Experimentation will determine how education can best be divided among *large-group instruction, individual study,* and *small-group discussion.* Decisions will be made concerning relative times to be spent, sequences, and the most appropriate learning activities and resources. The decisions will take into account the differences among individuals, groups, and subjects. This will bring forth a variety of study patterns.

No longer will one teacher have the responsibility of teaching all of a subject to a group of 25 students meeting as a class five days a week.

There will be frequent regroupings of students in order to cope with the differences in abilities, interests, and needs. Flexibility of grouping will be a key characteristic. Individuals will not necessarily be placed in a single group for an entire year, nor for a semester.

The class of 25 to 35—so frequently found in today's schools, and often highly esteemed—will have no regular place in the secondary school of tomorrow. A class of 25 is unnecessarily small for *large-group instruction* activities. Not only is the size financially uneconomical, but also it means deadening repetition for teachers who must go over the same materials for several sections. Moreover, because classes are limited to 25 to 35 students, present teaching schedules usually require a teacher to conduct 25 (or more) classes a week. With a teacher's other activities, this leaves insufficient time for preparing instruction, developing imaginative teaching materials, counseling individual students, evaluating students, and keeping professionally up to date.

Today's class of 25 to 35 is too large for effective *study*. Freedom of movement, independent creative activity, and development of student responsibility for learning are difficult in a group of this size.

The class of 25 to 35 is also too large for successful *discussion*. Research in group process indicates that a group cannot be larger than 12 to 15 if there is to be effective participation of all its members.

Curriculum and Class Schedules

The general education required of *all* citizens in this democratic society will be determined carefully. In addition, students will follow specialized studies. The students will have demonstrated that their specialized goals are desirable for sound reasons and that they have the ability to achieve them. The rationalized organization of instruction already described, as well as an extended school day and year, will provide more time for specialized interests.

Much more emphasis will be placed on training students to check their own progress. Students will be able to make more immediate self-appraisals, using a variety of machines and self-marking tests, instead of waiting for teachers to grade their work. Obviously, there also will be independent evaluation by the faculty, but this will occupy a less important position than it does now. Teachers will have more time to plan and conduct evaluations that will be helpful to students in showing progress toward achieving *all* the purposes of instruction rather than merely the possession of facts, the principal area of evaluation at present.

The school will do less scheduling of students in 40- to 55-minute class periods. A student absorbed in work on a project will more frequently not have to stop when a bell rings at the end of a relatively short period. He will be able to continue his work instead of going on to something perhaps quite unrelated which often seems less interesting and less important. Possibly no bells will ring in the school of the future.

Today's school schedules students tightly so that they go from one class or study hall to another, six or more periods a day, with the same periods repeated five days a week. Students now spend about six hours a week on each of five subjects. These six hours per subject usually involve attending a daily 50- to 55-minute class session, plus approximately 20 minutes of work daily in study hall or at home. In the case of 40-minute class sessions, students are expected to do about 30 to 35 minutes of outside preparation. This means that students spend some 30 hours a week in school, not including time at extraclass activities, or in the homeroom.

The school of the future will schedule students in class groups an average of only 18 hours a week, instead of the present 30 hours. Twelve of the 18 hours will be spent in *large-group instruction* (100 or more students) and six will be spent in *small-group discussions* (12 to 15 students). In addition to these 18 hours, the average student will be scheduled for about 12 hours a week in *individual study*. Most students will continue to spend about 30 hours a week on their regular subjects, as they do now, but it also will be possible for them to spend more.

Students who do not have out-of-school jobs or heavy activity schedules often will spend as much as 20 or 24 hours weekly, instead of the average 12 hours, in *individual study*. The number of hours and locations of independent study will vary with the needs and the capacities of individual students. Using recommendations of teachers and counselors, individual schedules will be worked out by electronic devices. Although there will be flexibility in scheduling, the school will continue to know where its students are and what they are doing. Students will have adult supervision as needed.

The 12 hours a week spent in *large-group instruction* will be divided among the subject areas as seems desirable. Experience and judgment will determine how many hours yearly are desirable in such fields as mathematics, science, foreign language, history, English, physical education, music, practical arts, or general education. Similarly, experience will determine the optimum length of time, the frequency, and in what portion of the school these large groups should be scheduled. The same policies will apply to scheduling the six hours a week of small *discussion* groups. Some of these periods will be 20 to 30 minutes, others will be longer.

An underlying purpose of the school will be to develop ability to study, think, and solve problems, in contrast to today's emphasis on memorizing facts. In large groups, small-group discussions, and individual study, the emphasis will be put on the goal of helping the student develop the ability to solve problems on his own.

The Instructional Staff

The school of the future's instructional staff will include the following kinds of personnel:

PROFESSIONAL TEACHERS: { TEACHER SPECIALISTS / GENERAL TEACHERS }

INSTRUCTION ASSISTANTS

CLERKS

GENERAL AIDES

COMMUNITY CONSULTANTS

STAFF SPECIALISTS

Teacher specialists will include experienced teachers who demonstrate career interests and abilities. They will possess a master's degree as a minimum and many will have considerable training beyond that. They will be responsible for overseeing all the instruction in a given subject.

These specialists will teach subject matter for which they are particularly well qualified, usually to relatively large groups of students. At times they will serve as consultants to individuals and groups of students working in and outside the school and will assist with extraclass activities. Most of these teachers will be specialists in the use of such teaching aids as television, tape recordings, projectors, students' self-appraisal devices, and the like, although some may be particularly effective in working with smaller groups of students. They will continue to encourage pupils to share in planning instruction in order to sharpen incentive. They will be even more competent than now in one or more subjects. The *teacher specialists* will have general charge of evaluating student achievement.

General teachers will be qualified, certificated persons with less experience. Or perhaps they do not plan to continue in the profession on a long-term basis. This group would also include those whose family responsibilities or other interests prevent their giving full-time, uninterrupted service. These teachers will participate primarily as observers and consultants in discussion groups.

The assignment of *general teachers* to such small groups does not imply any lack of importance in this type of activity, but it recognizes that small-group discussions require less daily preparation by the teacher. At times, these teachers will also assist in individual student counseling and with the evaluation of the student's progress. These teachers will work with the *teacher specialists* so that all phases of school work may be coordinated. Like the specialists, they will be especially competent in a subject area.

All professional teachers will not find themselves by interest or function as either *teacher specialists* or *general teachers*. An example might be a teacher whose other responsibilities do not permit his devoting as much time as a career teacher spends, but who has some special ability. Flexible schedules will permit these teachers to serve in functions accepted by both of the kinds of professional teachers described. Thus, teachers' individual differences in abilities, interests, physical energy, and available time will be recognized in ways that are impossible today when uniformity characterizes staff assignments.

There will be one professional teacher for each 40 students in the school.

Instruction assistants, a group of technicians carefully selected on the bases of training and experience to do specific parts of the teaching job, will aid the professional staff. This group will work at activities higher on the professional scale than those assigned to clerks, but different from those assumed by professional teachers. The *instruction assistant* will carry out such services as reading and evaluating *some* English themes, science reports, social studies essays, mathematics exercises, and other types of student papers. They will evaluate and criticize some of the student work in art, mechanical drawing, and other phases of creative and practical arts. When they are particularly competent, they will instruct.

The assistants will confer with individual students about their work and report to teachers about its quality. They will serve as laboratory, library, and materials center assistants and supervisors both during regular school hours and at other times when facilities are open to students. They will take over most of such laboratory activities as behind-the-wheel driving instruction. Supervision of some in- and out-of-school projects in agriculture, homemaking, and other vocational fields will be handled by this group. The assistants will supervise the practice of certain music groups, help in the supervision of field trips, and check the progress of students working on projects in the community or in local business and industry.

These *instruction assistants* are likely to be part-time workers, serving the school about 10 to 20 hours weekly. Although most of them will be housewives, there will also be men who do not have to spend more than 30 to 40 hours per week at other jobs. Most of them will be college graduates. All will have the necessary minimum training to perform their assignments.

College and high school students will provide another source of assistants. While care must be taken not to make too many demands on the time of these carefully selected students, many of them will profit from part-time teaching assistantships. They can provide valuable services. The experience will be most profitable to those who hope to become teachers and to those actually in teacher training institutions. However, these assistantships may stimulate the interest of others and contribute toward recruiting them into the profession.

The number of hours a week of instruction assistants' services will be about 20 times the number of professional teachers in the school.

Clerks will do routine duties which are part of the instructional program. Ordinarily they will be high school graduates with reasonable competence in typewriting and ability to check materials and prepare reports. They will also grade objective tests, keep records, copy materials, operate duplicators, handle supplies, and perform similar duties.

The number of hours a week of clerical services for teachers will be about 10 times the number of professional teachers in the school.

General Aides will supervise students in such large areas as the school grounds, cafeteria, corridors, auditoriums, and large meeting rooms. They will assist at school performances. These aides will be adults with a minimum of a high school education and preferably with some work beyond high school. Their training need not include typing or other clerical skills. Unlike the *instruction assistants,* they will not need to have competence in specific subjects. However, many of the aides might serve as sponsors for some extraclass activities when they have the interest and the abilities to do so. This group will be trained for the specific tasks assigned to them.

The number of hours a week their services will be available will be about five times the number of professional teachers in the school.

Community Consultants will be members of the community who will be used in specific assignments where they are better qualified than any available teacher. For example, a physician might answer questions on puberty, a world traveler on geography, or an atomic scientist on peacetime uses of nuclear energy. Such persons will usually volunteer their services. On occasion it may be desirable to employ an outstanding person for a number of appearances on a systematic basis. In this case the consultant would receive payment. Their contributions ordinarily will be taped, filmed, or recorded in some way for future use. These specialists in their fields will be employed from lists developed by the schools to supplement the services of the professional staff.

Staff Specialists, mainly professional workers, will provide services such as guidance, research, health, and aid to exceptional children, much as in today's schools. No doubt some of these specialized staff activities will be expanded and others added as the program develops.

. . . In a school with 400 students, or for each 400 students in a larger school, the instructional staff will be composed of 10 professional teachers

—full time; instruction assistants—200 hours a week; clerical assistants—100 hours a week; general aides—50 hours a week; and community consultants and staff specialists as needed.

This would contrast with today's school which requires approximately 16 full-time professional teachers for each 400 students. Each of these teachers must teach five classes a day plus supervising study halls and fulfilling other assignments. Staff specialists may be available from a central office. But clerical help for the teacher is usually only available when a clerk in the principal's office has some free time and is willing to lend a hand. This is an irregular situation over which the teacher has no control.

STANLEY G. SANDERS | ***Challenge of the Middle School***

Rapid acceptance of the junior high school has occurred within the life span of present leaders of our profession. This movement was led by men who were respected and have become revered. For the past two or three decades, school officials, in the vast majority, have accepted this as the preferred grade organization.

Within the past two or three years, small but significant numbers of school districts have been investigating and organizing intermediate schools, middle schools, or junior high schools with grades other than the accepted seven through nine. They have adopted their new patterns, not as second best substitutes for the junior high school, but as something better, something designed to overcome observed weaknesses of the older organization.

The junior high school was adopted during a period when much lip service was given to the scientific approach. One might assume, therefore, that its acceptance came as a result of convincing research. Such was not the case. A number of early studies attempted to compare academic achievement of groups of students from the new junior high schools with that of comparable groups from traditional eight-year elementary schools. Although a few of the studies showed superior achievement by students from the traditional schools, and even fewer found superior achievement by students of the new junior high schools, the most typical finding was "no significant difference." Junior high school proponents began to take satisfaction from the fact that their students did "as well" on tests of "fundamentals" while spending substantially less time on the study of them.

More subjective evaluations did show that the new junior high schools seemed to have more advantageous effects upon the development of students and were deemed preferable by majorities of teachers, administrators, parents, and pupils.

Factors Influencing Acceptance of the Junior High School

In the nineteenth century the eight-grade elementary school and the four-year secondary school had become the dominant pattern. In the 1890s, President Charles W. Eliot of Harvard criticized that existing arrangement as being wasteful of time. Other leaders, particularly those who served on a series of national committees to study the problem, supported his contention that six years was long enough for provision of the elementary education. By about 1910, schools began to be formed which adopted the six-year secondary plan, but which dealt in a practical way with the extreme age range between grades seven and twelve by putting half the grades in a junior high school and half in a senior high school. At the same time, shocking studies of dropouts called attention to the need for programs which better met the needs of many youngsters in grades seven through nine. A change in the handling of these students was hastened after publication of Hall's classic *Adolescence,*[1] which looked upon the young adolescent as a "new breed" passing through a period of ferment and upheaval. Changes in educational philosophy, under the leadership of Dewey, demanded reform and reaction against the traditional school, and adoption of the junior high school became a "thing to do," a dramatic and progressive way to demonstrate a determination to eliminate the weaknesses of the schools of the past.

Some observers have interpreted the growth of the junior high school as merely an expedient solution to a housing problem. It has been common for districts to change the grade alignment of the schools when enrollments in the existing grades have outgrown the buildings, or when the buildings have become obsolete. However, a need for new buildings does not necessarily require a new grade combination. Officials of a school district have some choice between alternative solutions to their housing problems.

Proponents of the junior high school were influenced by factors which were many, varied, complex, and interrelated. However, all of these factors and conditions were based on, or reinforced by, one dominant and continuing theme—the desire to provide a better education to students in the period of transition between childhood and youth.

[1] G. Stanley Hall, *Adolescence,* Vols. I and II (New York: D. Appleton & Co., 1904).

Challenges by Other Grade Combinations

The 7-8-9 junior high school has been challenged by various individuals who maintained that other grade combinations were equally or more desirable. Table I summarizes the various reorganized grade plans which have received support.

In 1965, two publications called national attention to a growing interest in the "middle" or "intermediate" school.[3] These schools, by definition, include one or more grades from the elementary school (below grade seven) and one or more grades previously found in the junior high school. It is not uncommon for districts to begin considering the 4-4-4 plan because of the symmetry of the equitable distribution of grades into three divisions. However, in many cases it is decided that fifth graders do not fit into the more advanced school, so that a majority of these schools are composed of grades six, seven, and eight.

There has been no complete, official survey to show the prevalence of schools of this type. Cuff reported on a survey which included returns from all states, but some of which were described as being "unofficial,"

Table I. Organization Plans Other Than 8–4 and 6–3–3[2]

Organization Patterns	*Years Advocated*	*Advocates and Occurrence*
6–6	About 1900 by early reorganization committees	Always common in smaller communities as a substitute for 6–3–3
7–5	Existed in early 1900s.	Prevalent in the South where seven-year elementary schools were common
6–2–4	Late 1800's	Constantly common through the years
6–4–4	1940's	Leading advocate—Koos. Much recommended, seldom adopted
4–4–4	1950's	Leading advocate—Woodring. Receiving more attention in the 1960's
5–3–4	1950's	Most common in Texas and some cities of the Northeast. Now receiving support as more than an expedient

[2] Stanley G. Sanders, *Differences in Mental and Educational Development from Grades Six Through Nine and Implication for Junior High School Organization* (Iowa City: The University of Iowa, 1960, unpublished doctoral dissertation), p. 68.

[3] Judith Murphy, *Middle Schools* (New York: Educational Facilities Laboratories, 1965), and "Middle Schools," *Educational Research Service Circular,* No. 3, 1965 (Published by the American Association of School Administrators and the Research Division of the National Education Association).

"probably incomplete," or "indefinite." For the purpose of that survey, a middle school was defined as including grades six and seven and not extending below grade four or above grade eight. He found 499 middle schools in 446 public school districts in 29 states, during the school year 1965–66.[4]

Some of these schools adopted their particular grade patterns because of unique enrollment and housing problems. Most claim that their decisions also were influenced by the possibility of offering to children in grades five and/or six certain special programs, facilities, and faculties usually available only in the junior high school. Implicit in this recommendation is the assumption that this generation's fifth or sixth graders are *ready* for experiences similar to those which were deemed appropriate only at the seventh-grade level in the past.

The Ninth-Grade Problem

Most of those who have adopted the middle school plan also are seeking solutions to some problems involved with having the ninth grade in the junior high school.

Rigid state and college requirements have demanded four years of "Carnegie Credits" for admission to college or in some instances for high school graduation. Vocational education programs which are supported by federal aid have traditionally been four-year programs, beginning with ninth grade. These factors have limited the ability of school officials to provide flexible programs of study for the ninth grade. Once the program has allocated staff, facilities, and time to the ninth grade, schedules for seventh and eighth grades are automatically structured and limited in many schools. In other schools this problem has been met by planning one type of program for the seventh and eighth grade years and a distinctly different one for the ninth grade, even though all three are supposed to comprise one unified school. "For all practical purposes we frequently find that the ninth grade is attached to our building for quarters and rations only."[5] In their extensive study of the Carnegie Unit and its effects, Tompkins and Gaumnitz found it to be used more extensively and to be emphasized more restrictively in the East and South and less in the North Central and Northwest regions.[6] It is interesting to note that the middle school is appearing more frequently in the former two regions, where the problem of ninth-grade credits has been less satisfactorily solved.

[4] William A. Cuff, "Middle Schools on the March," *The Bulletin of the National Association of Secondary School Principals,* 51:316:82–83 (February, 1967).

[5] Alvin Howard, "Which Grades in Junior High School?" *The Clearing House,* 33:7:405 (March, 1959).

[6] Ellworth Tompkins and Walter Gaumnitz, "The Carnegie Unit: Its Origin, Status and Trends," *NAASP Bulletin,* 48:288:19 (January, 1964).

Proponents of the junior high school stressed as one of its chief advantages the separation of ninth graders from older students in the senior high school. The freshmen obviously lacked the development and interests which patterned the social and extracurricular activities of the high school. However, today's youngsters, for better or worse, are far more precocious and sophisticated in these areas than were those of past generations. School officials and parent groups have battled, often in vain, against the tendency for the junior high school to become a little high school. If the school ignored the demand of the ninth-grade students for evening activities, dating, and wider contacts through interscholastic activities, large numbers of the more mature students turned to non-school related groups having less stringent controls. School activities, and consequently the school itself, tended to be viewed as juvenile, "square," "out"! Often school administrators and parents surrendered to the demands of these more mature students and allowed more advanced activities to develop; activities which then aroused opposition because they were inappropriate for a majority of seventh- and eighth-graders. In some cases, behavior problems in the ninth grade have been so severe as to occasion demand for its separation from the earlier grades. *Newsweek* described this issue as considered by a special panel recommending a new organization for New York City.

> "Middle school students," said the report, "would begin their exposure to secondary education earlier, yet not be subjected to the undesirable peer models provided by so many ninth graders." This was a polite way of calling attention to the extraordinary discipline problems that prevail in many of New York's junior highs.[7]

Obviously, it may be undesirable for ninth-graders to be closely associated with more mature eleventh- and twelfth-graders. The administrative staff of one school district has recommended a four-year high school, but with arrangements for appropriate distinctions between the ninth and tenth grades, on the one hand, and the eleventh and twelfth grades, on the other hand. These arrangements would, in effect, call for a school-within-a-school organization.[8]

Changing Developmental Patterns of Children and Youth

Junior high schools were organized in order to meet the peculiar needs of youngsters in the age range where they must make the transition from childhood to adolescence. The needs and characteristics of this group

[7] "Remaking the City Schools," *Newsweek*, 63:21:100 (May 25, 1964).

[8] Administrative and Supervisory Staffs, *A Plan for Reorganization of the Clear Creek Schools* (League City, Texas: Clear Creek Independent School District, 1965 [mimeographed]).

differ from those of children in the lower elementary grades and also from those of adolescents in the senior high school. For the past two generations educators have operated on the premise that the young people in grades seven, eight, and nine constituted this transitional group. Assuming that the decisions to combine these particular grades were wise decisions, the question now arises as to whether or not the conditions which made this desirable at the time remain unchanged in this generation. There is evidence to indicate that the youngsters in these grades today differ from the children who comprised the same grades one and two generations ago. They differ in chronological age. They differ in physical growth and development, as children not only are bigger and heavier today, but they mature at earlier ages. They certainly differ strikingly in social development. It is also very possible that they differ in mental development. Publishers of standardized tests have found that their national norms must be revised every three or four years, if they are to be appropriate for students enrolled in our improved educational programs. It is possible that today's sixth-graders are equivalent to yesterday's seventh-graders in age, size, physical maturity, and social development, and also in intellectual development, and that today's eighth-graders are similarly equivalent to yesterday's ninth graders.

Two recent research projects have attempted to compare the appropriateness of the middle or intermediate school containing grades six, seven, and eight with that of the junior high school containing grades seven, eight, and nine. Each of the two studies was based upon the premise that, while many factors will influence the determination of the graded organization of schools, serious consideration should be given to the characteristics and needs of the children or youth who would make up the student bodies of the schools. Each then sought to determine which group, grades six through eight, or grades seven through nine, constituted a more compatible or more homogeneous group.

In 1963, Dacus completed a study which compared the social maturity, emotional maturity, physical maturity, and opposite-sex choices of students in the respective grades, selecting his sample from one school district. In attempting to identify the more compatible group, Dacus obtained measures of the four characteristics, and then examined the significance of differences between measures of central tendency for successive grades. He found that ninth-graders were more similar to tenth-graders in the characteristics measured than they were to eighth-graders. Also, sixth-grade subjects were slightly more similar to seventh-graders than they were to fifth-graders, but this finding was influenced almost entirely by measurements of the female half of the sample. It should be pointed out that differences were comparatively slight, and that the author was very cautious in the conclusions which he drew from the findings. Furthermore, it must be remembered that the study was based upon subjects from a single school district, and that there was no evidence that the findings would be the same in other districts.[9]

Another study attempted to determine whether there was greater intellectual homogeneity within a student body composed of grades seven through nine or one composed of grades six through eight. The raw score distribution for the original nationally representative norming samples were reconstructed for three intelligence or academic aptitude tests, four achievement test batteries, and one reading survey test. The nine batteries, with their various subtests, provided forty-nine measures of various aspects of mental ability or educational achievement. For each of the forty-nine measures, variances for the two grade combinations were compared to see which was the larger. The primary finding was that differences in variances were too small to be deemed educationally significant, and that one grade combination could not be considered inferior to the other in this respect. Where differences in mental or educational development did exist, they tended to favor slightly the grade combination six through eight as being more homogeneous than grades seven through nine. Not surprisingly, variances between grades were shown to be much smaller than variances within grades, showing that no combination of grades can remove the need to provide for very substantial differences in intellectual development within each grade.[10]

Tradition and the Proponents of the Junior High School

In 1932, Spaulding, Frederick, and Koos carried out an extensive national survey of secondary education designed to determine "the existing forms of American secondary school organization with the greatest promise." After analyzing data from representative schools having different major types of organization, they identified certain characteristics which were likely to promote an effective organization. Among these desirable characteristics was "adoption of grade combinations which free the school from a traditional pattern."[11] In the early 1930's the junior high school composed of grades seven through nine was a combination which departed from the traditional. Today, the junior high school is no longer

[9] W. Pence Dacus, *A Study of the Grade Organizational Structure of the Junior High School as Measured by Social Maturity, Emotional Maturity, Physical Maturity and Opposite-Sex Choices* (Houston, Texas: University of Houston, 1963, unpublished Ed.D. dissertation); also Dacus, *A Grade Structure for the Early Adolescent Years* (Houston, Texas: Bureau of Educational Research and Services, University of Houston, 1963).

[10] Sanders, *op. cit.*

[11] F. T. Spaulding, O. I. Frederick, and L. V. Koos, *The Reorganization of Secondary Education,* National Survey of Secondary Education Monograph No. 5, U.S. Office of Education Bulletin No. 17, 1932.

an innovation. In fact, the junior high school is no longer a departure from the traditional. It is the traditional.

Most of today's educational leaders "grew up" during a period when forward-looking innovators led the movement away from the traditional organizational pattern and toward the adoption of junior high schools as an improvement upon the previous educational program. During that period, opposition to the junior high school amounted to opposition to improvement. Failure to respect the new institution amounted to lack of respect for its proponents. It is natural for many of today's educators to be defensive when this revered institution, which bears the label "modern," is attacked or when its basic form is questioned.

However, the early proponents themselves might well be leading the reexamination of the structure if they were alive and active today. Certainly they would not object to the questioning of the existing pattern merely because it is "approved."

It is doubtful if the most extensive study of the characteristics of pre-adolescents or early adolescents could ever result in unanimous agreement that one combination of grades is inherently superior for all schools. However, failure to examine their development and blind acceptance of one pattern could result in programs which are inappropriate in many, many schools.

PATRICK SUPPES | ***The Teacher and Computer-Assisted Instruction***

Educators have shown increasing interest in the use of computers for classroom teaching, especially during the last year or two, and they have raised a number of fundamental questions that need analysis and discussion. The purpose of this article is to acquaint the reader with some of the ways that computers can be used for instruction, and to answer, at least briefly, some of the questions that are frequently asked about computer-assisted teaching.

Some of the most important questions are: How can the computer help in individualizing instruction? How might it change the teacher's role? How will computer-assisted instruction change teacher-administrator relationships? Will it lead to impersonality and regimentation in the classroom? How can teachers play a part in planning and using computers for instructional purposes?

Let us begin by looking at a student seated at a console or station that is connected by a telephone line to a central computer. The console will usually contain a typewriter keyboard that the student can use to "talk to" the computer and a television screen that can display written messages as well as drawings, equations, and other graphic material. In many cases, the student will also have a "light pen," which he can use to select answers to the problems shown on the screen; he can even erase or change the images that appear. The computer talks to the student through a pair of earphones or a loudspeaker, thus providing him with the verbal communication necessary for effective learning, particularly when new concepts are being presented.

The central computer, which controls the presentation of information and evaluates the students' responses, need not be in the school but can be located at a central point in the school district. Because of its great operating speed, one large computer can serve many students, and a number of students can "time-share" the computer simultaneously.

Computer-assisted instruction is possible with only one console per classroom, which would be shared by many students during the school day. In a more expensive and elaborate arrangement, a classroom would have a large number of consoles, and each student could spend considerable time—as much as an hour and a half a day—at the console. It is important to emphasize, however, that in either arrangement the student would still be spending most of his time in the regular class setting, directly under teacher supervision.

Recent research indicates that students at all age levels come to feel at home with this sort of equipment and are quite willing to make its use a part of their daily school experience.

The student and the computer program may interact at three distinct levels, each of which comprises a particular system of instruction. (This use of the word *system* also corresponds to its use in the computer industry).

Individualized Drill-and-Practice Systems. This kind of interaction between the student and the computer program is meant to supplement the regular teaching process. After the teacher has introduced new concepts and ideas in the standard fashion, the computer provides regular review and practice of basic concepts and skills. In elementary school mathematics, for example, each student would receive 15 or 20 exercises a day. These would be automatically presented, evaluated, and scored by the computer program without any effort by the classroom teacher.

In addition, these exercises can be presented to the student on an individualized basis, with the brighter children receiving harder-than-average exercises, and the slower children receiving easier problems. One important aspect of this individualization should be emphasized: In the drill-and-practice computer system, a student need not be placed on a track at the start of school in the fall and held there the entire year. At the beginning of each new concept block—whether in mathematics or in language arts—a student can be "recalibrated" if the results indicate that he is now capable of handling more advanced material.

Drill-and-practice work is particularly suitable for the skill subjects that make up a good part of our curriculum. Elementary mathematics, reading, and aspects of the language arts, such as spelling, elementary science, and beginning work in a foreign language, benefit from standardized and regularly presented drill-and-practice exercises.

Tutorial Systems. In contrast to the individualized drill-and-practice systems, tutorial systems take over the main responsibility for helping the student to understand a concept and develop skill in using it. Basic concepts, such as addition or subtraction of numbers, can be introduced by the computer program in such systems. The aim is to approximate the interaction a patient tutor would have with an individual student.

In the tutorial programs in reading and elementary mathematics that we have been working with at Stanford University for the past three years, we have tried hard to avoid having slower children experience any initial failures. On the other hand, the program has enough flexibility to avoid boring the brighter children with too many repetitive exercises. As soon as the child shows that he has a clear understanding of a concept by successfully working a number of exercises, he is immediately introduced to a new concept and new exercises.

Dialogue Systems. Dialogue systems are computer programs and consoles that enable the student to conduct a genuine dialogue with the computer. It will be some years before we are able to implement dialogue systems in classrooms, because a number of technical problems remain unsolved. One problem is the difficulty of devising a computer that can "understand" oral communication, especially that of young children. We would like to have a computer that would respond to questions. To attain this interaction, the computer would have to recognize the speech of the student and to comprehend the meaning of the question. It will be some time before a computer is developed that will be able to do either of these with any efficiency and economy.

Dialogue systems have been mentioned here in order to give readers an idea of the depth of interaction we ultimately hope for. Drill-and-practice systems and tutorial systems, on the other hand, are already in operation on an experimental basis and will no doubt find an increasing application throughout the country in the next few years.

Effective programs of computer-assisted instruction now exist for elementary school mathematics, parts of language arts programs (particularly reading and spelling), and various topics in mathematics and science at the secondary and university levels. The programs have been developed primarily at universities, the following of which are currently the main centers of activity: Stanford, Illinois, Michigan, Texas, Pennsylvania State, Pittsburgh, Florida State, and the Los Angeles campus and the Irvine campus of the University of California.

Let us now look at some of the most frequently asked questions about computer-assisted instruction:

What role can computers play in individualizing instruction? The theme of individualized instruction has been prominent in American education for over 50 years. Psychologists have shown that individuals differ in their abilities, their rates of learning, and often even in their general approaches to learning. Unfortunately, the cost of providing individualized instruction that adapts to these differences is prohibitive if it depends on the use of professional teachers. For example, consider what it would cost to reduce present classroom size to four or five students per teacher.

The computer offers perhaps the most practical hope for a program of individualized instruction under the supervision of a single teacher in a classroom of 25 to 35 students. The basis for this practical hope is the rapid operation of the computer, which enables it to deal on an individual basis with a number of students simultaneously and thus lowers the cost per student of the computer.

How will the computer change the teacher's role? Drill-and-practice systems will modify the teacher's role only slightly. What they will do is relieve teachers of some of the burden of preparing and correcting large numbers of individualized drill-and-practice exercises in basic concepts and skills and of recording grades.

The teacher will be more significantly affected by tutorial systems. Let us consider a concrete example: teaching addition and subtraction of fractions at the fourth grade level. The computer will provide the basic ideas and the procedure of how to add and subtract the fractions. The program will probably be written so that if a student does not understand the basic concepts on first presentation he will receive a second and possibly even a third exposure to them.

The new role of the teacher will be to work individually with all students on whatever problems and questions they may have in assessing and handling the new concepts. Tutorial systems allow teachers greater opportunity for personal interaction with students.

How will computer-assisted instruction affect teacher-administrator relationships? Teachers and administrators should be able to develop even closer relations in a setting where computers are used to aid instruction. The information-gathering capacity of the computer enables administrators to have a much more detailed profile and up-to-date picture of the strengths and weaknesses of each area of curriculum. As they develop skill in interpreting and using the vast amount of information about students provided by the computer, administrators and teachers should be able to work together more effectively for improvements in curriculum.

Is there a danger that the computer will impose a rigid and impersonal regime on the classroom and even replace teachers? Contrary to popular opinion, the computer's most important potential is to make learning and teaching *more* an individual affair rather than *less* so. Students will be less subject to regimentation and moving in lockstep because computer programs will offer highly individualized instruction. In our own work at Stanford, for example, we estimate that the brightest student and the slowest student going through our tutorial program in fourth-grade mathematics have an overlap of not more than 25 per cent in actual curriculum.

The computer program is neither personal nor impersonal. The affect and feeling of the program will depend on the skill and perceptivity of those responsible for constructing it.

There seems to be little reason to think that computers will ever replace teachers or reduce the number of teachers needed. The thrust of computer-assisted instruction is to raise the quality of education in this country, not to reduce its cost. In any sort of computer-assisted instructional system used in classrooms in the near future, teachers will continue dealing with children on an individual basis and doing most of the things they are now doing during most of the school day with only slight changes.

Finally, we emphasize once again that no one expects that students will spend most of their school hours at consoles hooked up to computers. They will work at consoles no more than 20 to 30 per cent of the time. All teachers everywhere recognize the help that books give them in teaching students. The day is coming when computers will receive the same recognition. Teachers will look on computers as a new and powerful tool for helping them to teach their students more effectively.

ROBERT J. SCHAEFER | *The School as a Center of Inquiry*

The primary job of the school is to teach—to provide instruction in the various skills and subjects deemed crucial for the young. Society has not expected the school to be systematically reflective about its work—to serve as a center of inquiry into teaching—for the simple reason that

From *Perspectives on Education,* Fall 1967, pp. 9–16. Reprinted by permission of Teachers College, Columbia University and Robert J. Schaefer.

there has seemed nothing of great complexity in the instructional task, few problems in teaching which demand serious investigation. Educational reform, therefore, has historically focused upon modifying the curriculum or raising the standards for admission into teaching.

The truth, however, is that we can no longer afford to conceive of the schools simply as distribution centers for dispensing cultural orientations, information, and knowledge developed by other social units. The complexities of teaching and learning in formal classrooms have become so formidable and the intellectual demands upon the system so enormous that the school must be much more than a place of instruction. It must also be a center of inquiry—a producer as well as a transmitter of knowledge.

By a school organized as a center of inquiry, I imply an institution characterized by a pervasive search for meaning and rationality in its work. Fundamentally, such a school requires that teachers be freed to inquire into the nature of what and how they are teaching. Discovering new knowledge about the instructional process is the distinctive contribution which the lower schools might possibly be expected to provide. As every teacher knows, however, pedagogical strategies cannot be meaningfully separated from content, and there also must be continuing opportunity for the teacher to inquire into the substance of what is being taught. Finally, no school can be reflective about its work or serious in its commitment to learning if students are not similarly encouraged to seek rational purpose in their own studies.

Toward a School That Inquires

It is wholly within our command to make schools more intellectually exciting institutions—places not only where youngsters are pressured to learn a little of what is known, but also where adults investigate matters not yet understood. All that might be required to create schools which serve as centers of inquiry may be beyond our present ability to specify, but the main outlines seem clear enough. At least we could start with the following program.

Frank admission of modest accomplishment

Crucial to any change would be school administrators of sufficient security of tenure, or perhaps simply of sufficient courage, to admit publicly that the school is ordinarily only modestly successful.

To cease behaving as if all that was required was more of the same —the kind of facilities, learning materials, and instructional routines which we have comfortably and unaggressively deemed sufficient— would provide a notable beginning. For educators to drop the essentially buck-passing assertion that the heart of the problem is society's unwillingness to pay for "better" teachers would be an even more desirable improvement. The first obstacle to be overcome, therefore, if any school is to become a center of inquiry, is the fear of revealing how little we know. But such an ill-kept secret cannot be closeted indefinitely, and continued public concern about education will undoubtedly make it more dangerous for educators to feign wisdom than to demand a search for knowledge. Such a demand, once widely enunciated, might easily gain impressive momentum.

Drastic reduction of teaching loads

The university professor ordinarily carries a formal teaching load of six to nine hours per week, and he complains that too large a fraction of his remaining time is consumed in preparing for the ordeal. Why do deans and university trustees hold such markedly different expectations than those held by superintendents and boards of education? An important part of the answer, of course, is that professors presumably devote major energies to original research in a particular field, but it is also relevant that a different conception of the teaching task obtains. It is assumed, and not simply piously, that a college course must be illuminated by a scholarship which ranges far beyond the limits of any set of texts or outside readings and by a continuous reexamination of appropriate sources and interpretations. If society were to take seriously the job of teaching in the lower schools and, particularly, if teachers were to be encouraged to inquire into the substance of what they are teaching, or into the nature of the students with whom they work, or into the learning process itself, it is apparent that a teaching load of more than twelve to fifteen hours per week could not be condoned.

There is a beginning tendency, although more often discussed than actually used, to relieve the professional teacher of many routines by the appointment of para-professionals to serve as clerical assistants, to correct papers, and to file the numerous forms and reports a school requires. There is a veritable revolution on the way, in the use of automated devices which youngsters can employ on their own and which may relieve the teacher of the aversive role of drillmaster. But these changes have not yet been fully incorporated into school practice, and their effect upon the teaching role is as yet undetermined.

Concurrent reduction of student class time

In American secondary schools the dreadful legacy of the Carnegie unit and the dreary persistence of the assign-study-recite method of instruction inhibit intellectual pleasure for both teachers and students. Both notions preclude the development of the school as a center of inquiry. If pupils are to inquire into the substance of what they study, we "have to remember," with Whitehead, "that the valuable intellectual development is self-development."[1]

What is the mysterious difference between the senior in high school and the freshman in college, that the latter may stretch his mind in libraries, museums, and laboratories as well as when he listens to instructors? If it be feared that many high school students are not sufficiently disciplined for self-directed learning, then surely we should recognize that some schools may require other types of personnel in addition to teachers. Certainly, however, teachers need not be forever confused with supervisors of study halls or petty officials in places of incarceration.

In the elementary school the mystique of the self-contained, and therefore unrelieved, classroom has excluded teachers, during their working hours at least, from the adult world. Such deprivation may meet some psychological need of children—although I gravely doubt it—but it has most assuredly prevented teachers from systematically inquiring into the rationality of their craft.

Deliberate nurturing of "colleague authority"

The system of executive authority which characterizes American education—hierarchical flow from the top down, from the superintendent's office through the supervisory staff to the worker-teacher—has deep roots in our history. I am strongly convinced, however, that present circumstances have drastically altered the need for hierarchical control. The number of teachers who do not hold a bachelor's degree grows smaller each year. The quality of the initial preparation in the teaching field steadily improves. A great many teachers are far better educated—particularly in their teaching specialty but often also in their general liberal preparation—than the supervisors under whose "guidance" they presumably work. Teaching is increasingly perceived as affording a lifelong rather than a fleeting career. Most importantly, teaching is now attracting an ever-larger fraction of exceptionally able and well-motivated young people. Some of our best college graduates seek positions, not in industry, but, in their own terms, where the action is. If it isn't in education, it could be.

Under present circumstances, vigorous, alive, intelligent, and socially committed young people often find the schools lonely and intellectually barren places. The social norm which prevails is to treat one's fellow teachers, new or experienced, in a friendly but nonintervening manner. There are few opportunities for serious discussion, and the lack of a developed, specialized vocabulary and meaningful sets of pedagogical concepts makes the professional communication which does occur nebulous and imprecise. Teacher-education programs rarely prepare teachers

[1] Alfred North Whitehead, *The Aims of Education* (New York: The New American Library, 1929), p. 13.

for powerful and continuous professional association, but ordinarily aspire only to readying the neophyte for the here-and-now demands of the job.

For really able and dedicated young people this physical and intellectual isolation can be intolerable. The need for productive colleagueship becomes especially acute when one realizes how much exciting work could be tackled. Studies of particular pupil populations, production of specialized curricular materials, the development of particular pedagogical strategies, experimental efforts to translate unduly complex content into terms appropriate to an elementary or secondary school youngster, and the development of nonverbal approaches to learning are only suggestive of the range of activities in which teachers might be engaged.

Concurrent reduction of executive authority

In the university, administrators are not, as J. Douglas Brown has observed, "simply passive servants arranging things to make life simple for great minds."[2] Neither, on the other hand, do deans and presidents unilaterally arrive at all the decisions which must be reached in the development and nurturing of a faculty. There are large areas of colleague authority, areas in which administrators only participate in their role as colleagues rather than control by virtue of their hierarchical position. Determining the nature and development of curriculum, establishing grading and admission standards, and judging the competence of representatives of particular disciplines and professional specialties are all familiar examples of such shared responsibility.

In the university "the creative scholar tends to resist the judgments, standards, and criticisms of others unless he respects their previous contributions. This leads to a more or less conscious discounting of advice from any authority based on hierarchical status alone, whether in the university, industry, or government. As all presidents and deans well know, there are strict limits to their authority once a faculty member attains tenure."[3]

In the schools, too, the most creative teachers are frequently disdainful of authority based upon assigned position in the hierarchy rather than upon demonstrated expertness as a scholar-teacher. But there is a fundamental difference. The university administrator ordinarily feels a profound respect for productive scholarship. He gladly pays the small tuition of reduced authority and prestige because he fully realizes that no generalist-administrator can presume to make final judgments on matters central to a specialized discipline. In the schools, however, there is little tradition of colleague authority, and the administrator rarely believes that his judgments should be questioned by mere underlings.

[2] J. Douglas Brown, "Development of Creative Teacher-Scholars," *Daedalus* (Summer 1965), p. 623.

[3] *Ibid.*

In many systems, particularly in the larger and more bureaucratically organized cities, teachers have begun to rebel against a subordinate role and have turned to unionization as a collective means of protecting the individual teacher against the worst abuses of arbitrary superordinate authority. Administrators who wish to retain some shared association in the instructional efforts of a school—and not only as managers who sit on the other side of the bargaining table—must learn to forgo some of their traditional prerogatives. Teachers have become too well educated and too sophisticated to accept permanent assignment as mere drones, slaving under the so-called instructional leadership of hierarchically appointed others.

If there is to be fruitful inquiry in the schools, however, administrators can perform no higher function than to facilitate it. To do so will require the deliberate and self-conscious reduction of executive authority and the nurturing of free scholar-teachers. But it may very well be that such a voluntary dispersing of power remains the only viable means for administrators to retain any actual leadership in educational affairs. The only alternative may be a monolithic education industry—packages of texts, teaching programs, and computer-based courses supplied by IBM or Time Inc. and passively dispensed by teacher-clerks.

Encouragement of skepticism toward administrative tinkering

In any corporate structure in which power is held by a relative few, it is possible to make seemingly sweeping changes by administrative manipulation. We can introduce in schools a Lancastarian system, a dual-progress plan, or team teaching, for example, and give the appearance to the outside world that something vital and revolutionary has occurred. Such an impression may or may not be justified. To the degree that an organizational change adds powerful new ingredients, and does not simply afford a rearrangement of the same old parts, it may be significant. To the extent that team teaching encourages collegial association, provides expanded opportunities for investigation and experimentation, and adds para-professionals to free career teachers for basic intellectual work, it can, of course, make important differences. If, however, it merely imposes an added hierarchy of subadministrators, without at the same time affording new intellectual outlets for teachers, it can become an essentially trivial innovation.

If teaching is to consist of routinely overseeing the flow of information and materials, a more refined division of labor among instructors probably does not matter too much. What bothers me most about such gross organizational rearrangements is their tendency to divert our attention from concerns which merit higher priority. Our overarching problem is our relative ignorance of how to attract more youngsters to the life of the mind. Our basic job is to inquire into the problem. We can best recruit and maintain able young people in teaching, not by decreeing new status and organizational roles, but by creating conditions which assure the chance for the continuing development of teaching power.

JOHN I. GOODLAD | **Directions of Curriculum Change**

We are in a period of tumultuous and perhaps unprecedented educational activity, but not all of it has reached into elementary and secondary schools. In fact, one often gets the almost eerie impression of huge clouds of educational reform drifting back and forth from coast to coast, and only occasionally touching down to blanket an actual educational installation.

Of all the recent changes, what is commonly referred to as the current curriculum reform movement is and has been the most influential. It has reached into thousands of classrooms all across this land and abroad. The movement is fifteen years old, if one takes the work of the University of Illinois Committee on School Mathematics, launched in 1951, as the beginning. Since it did not get into high gear until late in 1957, however, intense activity dates back only a decade.

The movement is discipline-centered, the ends and means of schooling being derived from the academic subject. Some educators claim that this cycle of *discipline-centered curriculum* reform is over. I doubt it, although it may have reached its peak in the sense that new thrusts are emerging, new outlines are taking shape. For the next several years, however, educators' concern will focus more and more on the *total curriculum*, rather than on bits and pieces of it.

If all goes well, this second cycle of curriculum development, just emerging, will plateau out in perhaps ten or fifteen years. If so, what will be the third cycle of curriculum change in the second half of the twentieth century?

I believe it will be what one might call the *humanistic curriculum* and that it may become significantly evident by 1990 or 2000.

Before discussing these three cycles of curriculum development, let me emphasize that they are not discrete. Further, they are not new. They merely represent the periodic, cyclical reappearance of some persistent themes in formal education: concern for organized subject matter, concern for the learner's total educational diet, and concern for man himself.

Discipline-Centered Curriculum. In the present era of curriculum development, the curriculum builders are physicists, mathematicians, and historians, many of whom seek to organize their field around primary structural elements of the discipline: concepts, key ideas, principles, and modes of inquiry.

The assumption is that understanding these elements (rather than merely possessing facts) enables the student to attack unfamiliar problems and to grasp intuitively the relationship of new phenomena not previously encountered to phenomena already experienced. Teachers are encouraged to let students discover meanings for themselves.

The current curriculum reform movement is not simply a return to the three R's. Nor is it a repudiation of John Dewey or progressive education. Quite the contrary on both counts.

Many concerns of progressive education—emphasis on principles rather than facts, on learning through problem solving rather than by precept, and on individual differences, for example—are stressed and extended by some of today's curriculum builders. But the emphasis, until very recently, has been almost exclusively on the discipline as a separate entity in the curriculum: not science but biology, chemistry, and physics; not social studies but history, geography, and economics.

The separate-subject approach creates few immediately visible problems for the secondary school, where teachers have been prepared in a major field and supporting disciplines. It does create problems for the elementary school, however.

First, in all but a very few states, teachers are prepared as generalists rather than as subject-matter specialists. Second, difficult choices have to be made because there is a limit to the number of disciplines that can be taught within the time available. Third, if secondary education involves teaching the basic structures and root concepts of the academic disciplines, what approach does that leave for the elementary curriculum?

Problems of this sort caused some hesitation in undertaking curriculum revision at the elementary school level with assumptions that had sufficed for the secondary school. Some re-examination was called for and some fresh approaches are beginning to emerge. For example, although four current, major efforts to reorganize the elementary school science curriculum differ markedly in their emphases, not one is committed to developing each science field separately.

The first cycle of current curriculum reform, initiated at the secondary school level, has not been experimental; it has been one of refining some initial assumptions. The second cycle, just beginning, focuses on the elementary school, questions earlier assumptions, is likely to be experimental, and will probably initiate a fresh round of curriculum revision for the high school.

It must be remembered that the impetus, planning, and financial support for the type of subject-centered curriculum revision currently taking place come from outside the state and local school districts legally responsible for precollegiate public education in the United States.

The curriculum products of the Physical Science Study Committee, the School Mathematics Study Group, the Chemical Bond Approach Project, and so on, carry both ends and means of schooling into the classroom. It would be reassuring, perhaps, to believe that school districts, after careful appraisal of these materials, decided to use the products of one curriculum study group rather than another because they clearly served better those aims of education to which the districts are committed. But this is rarely the case.

Few state departments of education and few school districts have devoted serious attention to determining in any precise way what their schools are for and what objectives are to be achieved. We cling stubbornly to the notion of local control of education while allowing remote and impersonal curriculum planners to make the most important decisions of schooling.

We should be acutely aware of the decisions we are delegating and to whom. Developing this awareness and developing our stance toward it are curricular agenda items for tomorrow.

Total Curriculum. Now that the curriculum has had an injection of revitalized substance and syntax, it requires balance: balance between the learner and his material and balance among subjects.

Curriculum planners need (a) more precise objectives, (b) criteria for all kinds of choices and decisions, and (c) operational models of what happens when differing data and differing sets of values are used in making these decisions. These are pursuits for this emerging second cycle of curriculum development.

While the current curriculum reform movement has filled in some gaps and righted some deficiencies, it has also spawned some excesses and shortcomings which now must be remedied. In particular, the separate-subject approach to curriculum organization has proved troublesome.

Those subjects traditionally in the high school program, and especially those seen as closely related to national welfare (mathematics, biology, chemistry, physics, and foreign languages) have received added strength. But those previously receiving little or no attention, such as law, psychology, political science, and anthropology—fields which have both changed and expanded rapidly in recent years—now have an even more difficult time in finding a toehold.

Add to this the fact that curriculum reformers in the well-established fields want extra periods for some subjects, that the position of the arts is tenuous, and that we are uncertain about the role of the secondary school in vocational education, and formidable problems emerge.

The problems of an elementary school curriculum organized around discrete disciplines are no less troublesome, as we have seen. The search for the beginings of truly fundamental concepts and for ways of introducing them effectively to the very young has proved baffling. Equally baffling has been the selection of subjects to be included. Which of the many natural and social sciences, for example, should be chosen among all those available?

One possible solution for the choice problem is to select and teach key ideas from a broad realm of knowledge, irrespective of the subjects to which these ideas most closely belong. In the social studies, for example, topics may be selected which give attention to fundamental concepts, such as supply and demand (economics), due process (law), consent of the governed (political science), cultural evolution (anthropology), and so on, without identifying each subject and giving it a place in the curriculum.

Another possibility for taking care of the plethora of subjects struggling for recognition in the curriculum is to identify intellectual processes common to several related disciplines and to teach for them, again without providing a place for all the disciplines represented in a realm of knowledge.

This is a significant aspect of *Science—A Process Approach* for the elementary school, sponsored by the American Association for the Advancement of Science, which is organized around such desired behaviors as observation, classification, recognition and use of these space-time relations, recognition and use of numbers and number relations, measurement, communication, inference, and prediction.

The criticism of both approaches is that they sacrifice the ways of viewing and thinking about organized knowledge that constitute the very essence of the current discipline-centered curriculum reform. But change is by definition a shift from what exists. And so a new generation of change-agents appears, seeking to correct the excesses in what exists. Tension results. Out of this tension, a new cycle is born.

Unfortunately, these proposals for correcting an excess of subject matter in the curriculum throw us into the classical either-or curriculum dilemma in which we seem unable to have our cake and eat it, too. Exploding knowledge suggests the need for breadth, but power to deal significantly with any aspect of the knowledge explosion demands depth. And so we have cyclical dominance of first one and then the other.

There is a way out of this dilemma, I think, though we have been patently reluctant to follow it.

Let us assume, first, that there is enough wisdom on each side of the long-standing breadth-depth argument to warrant substantial recognition for both. (We alternate at intervals from thought and practice emphasizing breadth to thought and practice emphasizing depth. *Since the latter position is firmly in the saddle at present,* it follows, then, that there will soon be a change to a fresh emphasis on general education.)

Let us assume, second, that virtually all of our young people will complete high school. Let us think, therefore, of precollegiate education in the full sweep from nursery school or kindergarten through the secondary school. And let us remember, too, that children and youth go through distinct phases of development, determined by both biological and environmental factors, even though this development is irregular and markedly different from individual to individual.

Should we not think and plan, therefore, for successive, sequential phases of schooling, each with unique and distinctive functions as well as common school functions and each geared as much as possible to successive phases of human development and societal expectation?

Thus, the early childhood phase might devote itself over a period of two or three years to the development of awareness, self-confidence, and habits of thought; a subsequent phase of three or four years to fundamental skills of speaking, reading, and writing; a later phase to significant ideas and modes of thought irrespective of subjects represented; and a still later phase to the various academic disciplines. The phases would overlap each other, so that a student might be in more than one at once, according to the irregularity of his growth, but he would miss none.

This "phases" concept of schooling would enable each individual to have experience in all the various curriculum emphases by completion of high school. This is in marked contrast to traditional processes of curriculum cycles in which an individual completely skips a curricular emphasis simply because it happens to be out of fashion while he is attending school.

Our continuing curriculum sin is that we vacillate from excess to excess, indiscriminately applying what is currently fashionable in curriculum thought to the whole of formal education, from nursery school through college. What we need is a thorough appraisal of functions thought to be appropriate for each successive phase of schooling, translation of these functions into specific educational objectives, and allocation of human and material resources specifically pertinent to attainment of these objectives.

These are tasks for state and local school systems, aided by the research and development centers and regional laboratories now made possible by actions of the 88th and 89th Congress. There are, however, no models for this work. Local school districts lack the resources for the development of comprehensive curriculum design. State departments of education are not staffed for the job, and appear to be not at all clear on their leadership role. In my opinion, with few exceptions, the curriculum staffs of colleges and universities are very weak.

The time has come to develop cooperative approaches to curriculum study and improvement which will bring together research, facilities and techniques for field testing, and machinery for implementation across the whole length and breadth of the curriculum. Anticipating the need for these approaches, the NEA Project on Instruction recommended the creation of regional centers to study the curriculum as a whole. It appears that we are to have several such centers in addition to NEA's Center for the Study of Instruction (the Project's successor).

Subject-by-subject curriculum reform is an important, never-ending enterprise and must continue. By its very nature, however, it cannot resolve the comprehensive issues of the total curriculum. I am anticipating, therefore, a decade or two of emphasis on the total curriculum, with a resurgence of interest in general education. Regrettably, this emphasis is likely to be overemphasis and what is conceived to be good is likely to be perceived as good for all levels of schooling.

I am not really hopeful that my proposal for sequential phases of schooling will gain much currency. But I am hopeful that this next cycle will profit from what we have learned, that it will not repudiate the past fifteen years.

Dare we hope that the decade of curriculum change immediately ahead of us will see an end to the subject-learner dichotomy? Are we to see, at long last, some operational curriculum models linking the substance and syntax of subject matter and the cognitive styles of learners? These would be achievements worth being alive to see. But even the heroic efforts necessary to their accomplishment will not give us, by the end of the century, the humanistic curriculum promised at its beginning.

Humanistic Curriculum. Webster defines humanism as "a way of life centered upon human interests or values." Only within a humanistic conception of education and a humanistic conception and conduct of the whole of schooling can a humanistic curriculum center upon human interests and values. Perhaps I can best sharpen what I mean by a brief discussion of what humanistic education is not.

First, we do not yet value education for the right reasons. The central force in our striving for more formal education is our expectation that it helps in the acquisition of worldly goods and in gaining access to certain circles of power and influence. The school mirrors this expectation. Nowhere is this observation more clearly substantiated than in our marking practices. This system of rewards and punishments, which is extraneous —and probably deleterious—to learning, is based on society's materialistic conception of education.

We are becoming acutely aware of the material consequences of lack of success in the system of rewards and punishments, but we have given little thought to the possibility that complete adjustment to and success in the system may have alarming human consequences.

Second, we have too little faith in man's ability to find worthy interests and to do good work in the absence of coercion. Consequently, we hasten to initiate others into our own interests, especially if these persons are young and we are responsible for their welfare. When they balk before this narrow range of alternatives, we exercise restraints and impose punishments. What should be a happy, shared pursuit becomes negative, punitive, and a source of conflict.

(This lack of faith carries over into the conduct of schooling. University personnel hesitate scarcely a moment at treating elementary and secondary school teachers in ways that they would never tolerate for themselves: Take, for example, the belittling attitude of collegiate curriculum reformers who announce that they are trying to produce "teacher proof" materials.)

Large segments of our educational enterprise simply do not provide a way of life centered upon the interests and values of their clients. In fact, many schools do not regard their students as clients and thus fail to reach them in any deep and meaningful way. Perhaps we shall regard students' time as valuable only when we pay them to go to school, as some economists seriously propose we do.

Despite the difficulties, however, a humanistic conception of education always manages to stay with us, to enjoy continuing reinterpretation, and to attract its spokesmen. Such a conception sets as its goal the development of each individual's potential, fosters school programs centered on man, takes teachers and teaching seriously, and values each student simply because he is a human being.

Substantial fruition of the humanistic curriculum by the year 2000 will depend in large measure on how well we have learned and are learning some important lessons.

The first lesson grows out of the period in American education immediately preceding the current curriculum reform movement. Shocked by the human devastation of World War II, we sponsored sweeping child study programs centered on the value of each individual. Because we defined curriculum as broadly as life itself, we failed to influence significantly the content of learning. Did this failure teach us, in the words of Bruno Bettelheim, that "love is not enough?"

Recent curriculum reforms were motivated more by a cold war of the intellect than by a hot war of blood and bone. With a much narrower definition of curriculum, reformers changed the *content* of learning and placed new *things* of instruction in the classroom.

This curriculum reform has been far more influential than any of the recent innovations. But there has been overconfidence in the power of the materials accompanied by the belief, during recent years, that teachers either could be prepared quickly to use them or that they could not defeat the intent of the materials, anyway. This is an erroneous assumption as witnessed by the number of teachers who unwittingly destroy the intent of the new inductive curriculums by teaching large segments of them deductively.

The second lesson, then, is that the well-designed learning package, like love, is not enough.

The third lesson, closely related, is that knowledge reconstructed so as to make it comprehensible "in some intellectually honest form to any child at any stage of development" is not a humanized curriculum. As Cremin points out so well, this principle (stated by Bruner) clears the air of a lot of nonsense about readiness, but it merely liberates us to determine what ought to be taught at any given stage.

More important, to paraphrase Bettelheim once again, it liberates us to move on to the real question of what kind of persons they should be. We now have some hope of conceiving a humanistic curriculum because, at long last, we address ourselves to a truly human question.

The fourth lesson is that ideas, to make any real difference, must find their way through the political structure. We have striking evidence of what can happen when education—conceived in recent years as an instrument of national welfare—receives vigorous political support.

Clearly, government can enhance mightily a comprehensive commitment of home and school to a conception of education. Further, it can and does shape this commitment and will continue to shape it. The fundamental curricular concern is, What *kind* of commitment is likely to be shaped and supported? I am hopeful that it will be toward a humanistic conception of education. In the last eight years, there has been a truly remarkable shift in emphasis in the individual-and-society interplay as represented by federal pronouncements and enactments.

The School of Tomorrow

When we try to envision the school of tomorrow, we must not be limited by our concept of the school of today. Education is not a static process, and the school of today cannot be considered a sacred or unchangeable institution. After all, every decision governing schools was at one time or another made by man. At the time the decisions governing today's schools were made, fewer data were available.

The men who made those decisions were no brighter than schoolmen today, and they were less well-educated. Therefore, it behooves us to reexamine every decision about schooling: size of building and whether we

From NEA *Journal* (February 1968), pp 50–51. Reprinted by permission.

want one at all, numbers of teachers and whether we need a fully certificated teacher for every 28.5 children, whether the library is to be one that houses real books or computerized microfiche. (A fully automated library with no books but only microfiche is now out of the realm of science fiction into the actuality of college and university planning in the United States.)

We must not continue to assume that tomorrow's school will have X number of qualified teachers for Y number of children or that we will construct a school building large enough for all of the children to be housed. There is no reason at all why we could not employ half the usual quota of fully qualified teachers, using the balance of our money for part-time specialists and a host of instructional aids. And there is no reason at all why we could not plan an educational program that requires a school building only half the usual size, with the balance of the money going for trips, special projects, and individualized activities supervised by the staff or even programed by a computer.

A school is not necessary to teaching and learning. We do not need a school to guide children and youth in grasping their culture. And, certainly, we do not need a school to teach the fundamentals of reading, writing, and arithmetic. But we do need a formal process of instruction with the most able members of our society giving their time to it in planning and programing instructional materials, in computerizing varied programs for learning, and in interacting with other humans in the delightful business of learning from one another.

The computer, which we must legitimatize for learning and teaching in an imminent era, probably will contribute significantly in a still later era to the demise of what we now call school. We shall regard this as undesirable only if we lack faith in the ability of man to fashion a better world.

In viewing learning and teaching for the year 2000 and beyond, it is easier to predict what will *not* be than what will be. A prescribed age for starting school will be meaningless. The computer console with an array of devices for stimuli and feedback will be as natural for the child of the twenty-first century as television is for today's two-year-old. Teaching and learning will not be marked by a standard 9 to 3 day, or a standard September to June year, or a year for a grade of carefully packaged material. The child's age will not be a criterion for determining what he is to learn.

Will learning be any less because there will be no periods, no Carnegie units, no bells, no jostling of pupils from class to class? I think not. The student will be free to concentrate exclusively on a given field for weeks or months or to divide his time among several fields. The variability and comprehensiveness of programed learning sequences will be such that the student, unaided by human teachers, will control a significant portion of his curriculum.

Clearly, the role of teachers will change markedly. Hundreds of hours of their time will go into what will occupy each student for an hour or two. But because thousands or even millions of students might eventually select this hour, the teachers' preparation time will be well spent. And the quality of education will be vastly improved.

School as we now know it—whether egg crate or flexible space—will have been replaced by a diversified learning environment including homes, parks, public buildings, museums, and guidance centers. It is quite conceivable that each community will have a learning center and that homes will contain electronic consoles connected to it. This learning center will provide not only a computer-controlled videotape, microfiche, and record library, but also access to state and national educational television networks. It is even possible that advanced technology will return the family to center stage as the basic learning unit.

The most controversial issues of the twenty-first century will pertain to the ends and means of modifying human behavior and who shall determine them. The first educational question will not be "What knowledge is of most worth?" but "What kinds of human beings do we wish to produce?" The possibilities defy our imagination.

The nerve cells of the brain, far more than muscles or any other organs, are highly sensitive to small electric currents, to a variety of chemicals, and to changes in blood supply. Sedatives, barbituates, tranquilizers, and various psychedelics provide powerful ways of controlling behavior by direct action on the brain. Similarly, we can manipulate behavior by applying electric currents to regions of the brain. Experiments are now under way with drugs and brain extracts designed to enhance learning or memory.

Aldous Huxley long ago introduced us to the possibilities of genetic selectivity through the availability of sperm and ovum banks. The means of drastically altering the course of human development through artificial insemination, chemical treatment, and electric manipulation are with us. We are already tampering with human evolution. The possibilities for further doing so will be enormously enhanced and refined as we move into the twenty-first century.

We of the teaching profession have tended to get bogged down in the narrow details of our calling, in details pertaining primarily to means: buildings, classrooms, textbooks, and so on. We have seldom gone beyond these trivialities to recognition of the fact that education and teaching are much bigger than schools. Schools are only a convenient means to more important ends, means that may no longer be relevant several decades from now.

As individual leaders, we must assert by our very competence that we know how to manage the means. Our constituencies lose faith in our competence when we hesitate, falter, and in desperation turn to the community for guidance in technique. But the charge to the organized profession is a much larger one. We must raise the level of the dialogue to the truly significant questions of educational ends, and we must be as diligent as our lay citizens in laying bare instructional deficiencies in the pursuit of these ends.

As to ends, let me put them as questions to ask about the educational enterprise:

1. To what extent are our young people coming into possession of their culture?
2. To what extent is each child being provided with unique opportunities to develop his potentialities to the maximum?
3. To what extent is each child developing a deep sense of personal worth, the sense of selfhood that is a prerequisite for self-transcendence?
4. To what extent are our people developing universal values, values that transcend all men in all times and in all places?

A fifth question is the most important, challenging, and frightening of all, now that men possess such manipulative powers: *What kinds of human beings do we wish to produce?* As a citizen and an educator, I cherish the right to participate in the dialogue about it.

HAROLD G. AND JUNE GRANT SHANE |
Forecast for the Seventies

During the last five years, there has been a marked increase in long- and short-range speculation regarding possible educational futures that may lie before us in the remaining years of the twentieth century. For the past three years, we have studied approximately 400 published and unpublished articles and books in which such conjectures and projections occur.

These current writings clearly indicate that education and schools, as they exist today, will change drastically during the 1970's and will be modified almost beyond recognition by the end of the century. The paragraphs that follow summarize some of the more important developments that could occur in the next decade and propose some of the new roles in which the teacher is likely to be cast. In conclusion, we give thought to the question: For what kind of world should children who will live most of their lives in the twenty-first century be prepared? Here, then, as many scholars see it, are some of the possible designs of educational futures in the seventies.

Education will reverse its traditional pattern of expenditure. From the beginning, more money has been spent per student in higher education, with secondary education coming in a strong second and elementary education, a poor third. Preschool and kindergarten programs have not even been in the race for funds. But now, major support for early childhood education seems highly probable because of our belated recognition that we have spent literally billions at the upper-age ranges to compensate for what we did not do at the two- to seven-year age levels.

Now priorities for education of the youngest will bring to public education nonschool preschools, minischools, and a preprimary continuum. As nonschool preschool programs begin to operate, educators will assume a formal responsibility for children when they reach the age of two. We will work with parents of young children both directly and through educational TV programs for young mothers. And we will offer such services as medical-dental examinations and follow-up, early identification of the handicapped and deprived, attacks on nutritional needs, and —of major importance—early referral to cooperating social agencies for treatment of psychobehavioral problems.

New programs for two-year-olds will involve the coordination of community resources, under school auspices, to equalize educational opportunity for these children before cultural deprivation makes inroads on their social and mental health.

The minischool, as envisioned here, is one that provides a program of carefully designed experiences for the three-year-old—experiences deliberately devised to increase the sensory input from which the children derive their intelligence. Each minischool presumably would enroll six or eight children under a qualified paraprofessional. A professionally prepared childhood environmental specialist would directly supervise clusters of approximately six minischools.

We will probably build these small schools into housing projects, make them part of new schoolhouse construction, or open them in improvised space in convenient buildings.

The preprimary continuum is a new creation intended to replace contemporary kindergartens for the four- and five-year-old. This program presupposes that the young learner will spend from one year to four years preparing himself to perform effectively in a subsequent primary continuum, the segment of education now usually labeled grades one through three. The preprimary interval should sharply reduce the problems of widely varied experience and social adjustment encountered by children who are arbitrarily enrolled in grade one at age six regardless of their previous cultural environment.

Major environmental mediation for two- to six-year-olds, as described above, will permit schools to abandon the current transitional concept of nongrading. In the coming decade, a seamless primary, middle-school, and secondary continuum of coordinated learning experiences will begin to replace the nongraded programs of the sixties.

Here, progress and the time spent on a given topic will become completely individual matters, as one emergent design for learning serves all ages. The intellectually advantaged child, for instance, might spend only two years in the primary or intermediate continuum, accomplishing what most children would accomplish in three or four years.

In this personalized educational continuum, the question of how to group children will no longer be relevant. The child will simply work with others in ephemeral groupings during whatever time certain shared learning experiences happen to coincide.

Admission age quibbles, too, will become irrelevant after several years of minischool and preprimary experience. There is no need to group children for first grade at the magic age of six, since they would be phased into their primary school year at any time from age four at one extreme to age eight at the other.

Promotion problems will also vanish, since in a continuum of learning there are no specific points at which a student passes or fails; he merely moves ahead at his own pace. Grade cards are likewise destined to disappear: Evaluation of progress will be continuous, and a progress report can be made in a parent conference whenever pupil performance analysis is in order.

The school will provide more learning experiences that parallel or accompany conventional academic content. The creative and enjoyable will begin to vie strongly with the utilitarian and academic dimensions of education. Such paracurricular ventures as educational travel, school camping, informal dramatics (including sociodrama), enlarged intramural sports programs that stress mass participation, and engaging youth in useful service to the community are due to increase in frequency and extent.

Biochemical and psychological mediation of learning is likely to increase. New drama will play on the educational stage as drugs are introduced experimentally to improve in the learner such qualities as personality, concentration, and memory. The application of biochemical research findings, heretofore centered in infra-human subjects, such as fish, could be a source of conspicuous controversy when children become the objects of experimentation.

Enrichment of the school environment in the seventies—especially in the ghetto—to "create" what we now measure as intelligence by improving experiential input also will become more accepted. Few are likely to make an issue of efforts to improve educational opportunities for the deprived child. However, there could be a tinderbox quality to the introduction of mandatory foster homes and "boarding schools" for children between the ages of two and three whose home environment was felt to have a malignant influence. Decisions of the 1970's in these areas could have far-reaching social consequences. Although it is repugnant to permit a child's surroundings to harm him, there is no clear social precedent for removing a child from his home because it lacks the sensory input needed to build normal intelligence and, therefore, in effect condemns him to a lifetime of unskilled labor.

The next decade will see new approaches to "educational disaster areas." Most of America's large cities, and some suburban and rural sections, contain a central core that can only be described in this way. Damage surrounding this core decreases from severe, to extensive, to moderate, to negligible.

Up to now, perhaps, we may have spent too much energy and money on just the worst schools of these central cores. In such neighborhoods, we cannot create a decent educational opportunity until the *total* social setting is rehabilitated. In the early 1970's, we may find it both more efficient and more educationally sound to direct our attention initially to improving those areas and schools where educational damage is moderate to extensive rather than drastic. For such areas, immediate attention may prevent their deteriorating in the near future into severe disaster areas. Once the deterioration in these outer ring schools is reversed, greater educational resources will become available to help us close in on the ghetto schools where damage is severe or total.

It would be unthinkable to ignore the children who live in our worst educational disaster areas until we can mobilize the greater forces needed to bring these schools up to necessary standards of excellence. Therefore, until inner cities regain their socioeconomic and educational health, we often will transport their children to outlying areas. In the next decade, this will involve a rapid buildup of facilities in these areas both in terms of enlarging existing schools and of creating new types of learning environments. Removing children from inner-city problem areas has the added merit of stimulating them through contacts with children from other social groups.

Later in the seventies, the elementary school changes will cause the junior and senior high schools to modify their programs. Their curriculums will presumably become more challenging and interesting. Wider age ranges, increased pupil interchange within and between schools, and individualized programs built around new instructional media will inevitably influence emerging secondary school organization.

In the late 1970's or early 1980's, it is not unlikely that students will graduate from high school with knowledge and social insight equal or superior to that of the person who earned a bachelor's degree in the 1960's.

On entering college, these students will be ready to begin postbaccalaureate studies, and our undergraduate college programs *in their present forms* will be unnecessary.

If this seems farfetched, bear in mind that the young person pictured here will have had the benefit of carefully developed learning opportunities in a skillfully mediated milieu since he was two or three years old.

During the next 10 years, business will participate in education to a greater extent. Although many of their activities are neither widely known nor generally understood, major corporations are already contracting to tackle pollution, teach marketable skills to the deprived, administer police protection, reclaim slums, and manage civic governments.

John Kenneth Galbraith has noted that the modern corporation already has the power to shape society. Frank Keppel commented recently that the revival of U.S. metropolitan schools depends as much on the action of leaders of finance and commerce as it does on educators. And Hazel Henderson commented last summer in the *Harvard Business Review* that industry's expansion into such areas as housing, education, and dropout training is probably the best way to handle our central needs if suitable performance standards and general specifications are properly controlled.

The growth of a cooperative business-and-education relationship will be of great portent in the seventies as corporations both expand the production activities of the education industry and assume more management and control responsibilities.

The roles and responsibilities of teachers will alter throughout the next decade. Future-think suggests that between 1970 and 1980 a number of new assignments and specialties will materialize if present trends continue.

For one thing, the basic role of the teacher will change noticeably. Ten years hence it should be more accurate to term him a "learning clinician." This title is intended to convey the idea that schools are becoming "clinics" whose purpose is to provide individualized psychosocial "treatment" for the student, thus increasing his value both to himself and to society.

In the school of the future, senior learning clinicians will be responsible for coordinating the services needed for approximately 200 to 300 children. In different instructional units (an evolution of the "team" concept) we will find paraprofessionals, teaching interns, and other learning clinicians with complementary backgrounds. Some will be well-informed in counseling, others in media, engineering, languages, evaluation, systems analysis, simulation, game theory, and individual-need analysis.

But on the whole, the learning clinician will probably not be appreciably more specialized in subject matter disciplines than he was in the 1960's except for being more skilled in using educational technology. He will do more *coordinating* and *directing* of individual inquiry and will engage in less 1968-style group instruction. He will be highly concerned with providing and maintaining an effective environment, skilled in interpersonal transactions, and able to work with persons of different ages and learning styles.

Ten years from now, faculties will include:

1. *Culture analysts,* who make use of our growing insights into how a subculture shapes the learning style and behavior of its members.

2. *Media specialists,* who tailor-make local educational aids, who evaluate hardware and software and their use, and who are adept in the information sciences of automated-information storage and retrieval, and computer programing.

3. *Information-input specialists,* who make a career of keeping faculty and administration aware of implications for education in broad social, economic, and political trends.

4. *Curriculum-input specialists,* who from day to day make necessary corrections and additions to memory bank tapes on which individualized instructional materials are stored.

5. *Biochemical therapist/pharmacists,* whose services increase as biochemical therapy and memory improvement chemicals are introduced more widely.

6. *Early childhood specialists,* who work in the nonschool preschool and minischool programs and in the preprimary continuum.

7. *Developmental specialists,* who determine the groups in which children and youth work and who make recommendations regarding ways of improving pupil learning.

8. *Community-contact personnel,* who specialize in maintaining good communication, in reducing misunderstanding or abrasions, and in placing into the life of the community the increased contributions that the schools of the 1970's will be making.

As educators turn a speculative eye on the next decade, they must seek to answer a question that most of them have hesitated to face. For what kind of world should we strive to prepare children and youth who will spend most of their lives in the next century? We say this question is crucial because educational policy decisions in the 1970's will not only anticipate tomorrow, they probably will help to *create* it.

Recent publications in the physical, natural, and social sciences suggest emerging changes in society that seem likely to characterize the world of 2000 A.D. A number of future-think writers agree that unless unforeseen catastrophes intervene, such developments as the following are probable:

The individual's personal freedom and responsibility will be greater.
The IQ of the average child will be 125, perhaps 135.
Cultures throughout the world will be more standardized because of the impact of mass media and increased mobility.
Access to more information will carry us toward an international consensus as to what is desirable in family life, art, recreation, education, diet, economic policies, and government.
Cruelty will be more vigorously rejected and methodically eliminated.
Leaders will be those who are the most able, regardless of their racial origins, religious beliefs, family backgrounds, or lack of great wealth.
The worldwide status and influence of the female will greatly increase.
Differences in wealth and ownership between haves and have-nots will narrow.
Through the mediation of trends, society will begin to design or give direction to the future so that the years ahead will better serve human welfare.

The changes described above will open many more doors for educational leadership. During the coming decade, however, education must do more than just lengthen its stride to keep pace with trends and innovations. We must bring social perception and long-range vision to the task of designing and planning schools that can help bring about the best of many possible tomorrows.

Selected References

Association for Supervision and Curriculum Development. *Humanizing Education: The Person in the Process.* Washington, D.C.: The Association, 1967.

BEGGS, DAVID W. III, and EDWARD G. BUFFIE (eds.). *Nongraded Schools in Action.* Bloomington: Indiana University Press, 1967.

BELLACK, ARNO A., *et al. The Language of the Classroom.* New York: Teachers College Press, 1967.

BRUNER, JEROME S. *Toward a Theory of Instruction.* New York: W. W. Norton & Company, 1968.

College Entrance Examination Board. *The Challenge of Curricular Change.* New York: The Board, 1966.

DOLL, RONALD C. *Curriculum Improvement: Decision Making and Process.* Boston: Allyn & Bacon, 1964.

EICHORN, DONALD E. *The Middle School.* New York: Center for Applied Research in Education, 1966.

ELAM, STANLEY (ed.). *Education and the Structure of Knowledge.* Chicago: Rand McNally & Company, 1964.

FANTINI, MARIO, and GERALD WEINSTEIN. *Making Urban Schools Work.* New York: Holt, Rinehart & Winston, 1968.

FORD, G. W., and LAWRENCE PUGNO (eds.). *The Structure of Knowledge and the Curriculum.* Chicago: Rand McNally & Company, 1964.

GOODLAD, JOHN I., *et al. The Changing School Curriculum.* New York: Fund for the Advancement of Education, 1966.

GWYNN, J. MINOR, and JOHN B. CHASE, JR. *Curriculum Principles and Social Trends,* 4th ed. New York: The Macmillan Company, 1969.

HIRSCH, WERNER Z., *et al. Inventing Education for the Future.* San Francisco: Chandler Publishing Company, 1967.

HYMAN, RONALD T. (ed.). *Teaching: Vantage Point for Study.* New York: J. B. Lippincott, 1968.

KINDRED, LESLIE W., *et al. The Intermediate Schools.* Englewood Cliffs, N.J.: Prentice-Hall, 1968.

KING, ARTHUR R., and JOHN A. BROWNELL. *The Curriculum and the Disciplines of Knowledge.* New York: John Wiley & Sons, 1966.

MANLOVE, DONALD C., and DAVID W. BEGGS, III. *Flexible Scheduling.* Bloomington: Indiana University Press, 1965.

MICHAEL, WILLIAM B. (ed.). *Teaching for Creative Endeavor.* Bloomington: Indiana University Press, 1968.

National Society for the Study of Education. *Programmed Instruction* (66th Yearbook, Part II). Chicago: University of Chicago Press, 1967.

———. *Vocational Education* (64th Yearbook, Part I). Chicago: University of Chicago Press, 1965.

Oettinger, A. G. "Myths of Educational Technology," *Saturday Review* (May 18, 1968), pp. 76–77.

Parker, J. Cecil, and Louis J. Rubin. *Process As Content: Curriculum Design and the Application of Knowledge.* Chicago: Rand McNally & Company, 1966.

Swenson, Gardner, and Donald Keys. *Providing for Flexibility in Scheduling and Instruction.* Englewood Cliffs, N.J.: Prentice-Hall, 1966.

Trump, J. Lloyd, and Delmas F. Miller. *Secondary School Curriculum Improvement.* Boston: Allyn & Bacon, 1968.

SECTION V | *Persistent Problems and Current Concerns*

THE SCHOOL HAS BECOME such a vital focus for many of the diverse patterns of change and conflict of the larger society that in essence it serves as a microcosm of current developments. Advocates of conflicting interests use the schools to promote particular loyalties and specific values. Pressure for greater minority representation is opposed by demands for segregated facilities; local control is opposed by those who believe the state and federal governments should have a larger role; power for policy decisions among all elements—parents, students, teachers, school administrators—is opposed by those who believe that "professionals" should retain authority for decision making; the determination of "relevance" by the consumers of education, the students, is opposed by those who feel adult consideration of what is taught should prevail. Clearly, the problems and concerns facing the nation's schools today represent the area "where the action is." To help clarify the complex interrelationships of current developments, the editors have enlarged the scope and organizational format of this section for the second edition by grouping articles under three major sub-headings. While these new divisions should be of assistance in understanding issues of the current controversy, the reader needs be mindful of the fact that such splendid isolation is rarely encountered in actual practice.

"Youth in Transition" represents a rational investigation into youth's demands and challenges, an area which frequently generates emotional excesses. "Teachers in Transition" probes the underlying bases for much of today's teacher unrest. By far the greatest share of attention in this section is devoted to the school as a primary social institution. In essence, most of the articles in "Schools in Transition" raise crucial questions about the role of public education in a democracy. Is public education relevant to today's youth? Can the public school meet the continuing complex demands that a technological society imposes upon its members? Are the only alternatives open those represented by the polarized positions of a Paul Goodman who would do away with the system of public education as we know it or of a Charles E. Martin who sees the enlightened leadership of the schools providing the basis for a truly integrated, multiracial society?

Youth in Transition

THE POSTWAR GENERATION, those who were in schools and colleges throughout the 1950's and the early part of the 1960's, was the cause of great concern to educators, parents, and laymen because of its evident listlessness and apathetic attitudes. Their sole interest, so it seemed to adults, was for the attainment of a good, secure, well-paying job that would allow them to enjoy the new leisure created by the technological genius of America. Youth were willing to conform in order to "get ahead." Paul Goodman sums up this attitude: "Students will 'do' Bronx Science in order to 'make' M.I.T. and will 'do' M.I.T. in order to 'make' Westinghouse. . . ."

During the mid-sixties and beyond, however, growing numbers of youth had initiated an activist attack on many injustices of established institutions in society with an unexpected suddenness that startled and alarmed unprepared adults. Some youth demonstrated their resentment of their elders ("don't trust anyone over thirty") by withdrawing into communal groups to show their scorn of material possessions so highly prized in America; others sought to escape from society and themselves by the use of drugs and narcotics; others became political activists challenging almost every facet of social, economic, and political life. The impression here would be false if one were to suggest that all youth were involved in rejecting the establishment or that these three modes of behavior were the only discernible patterns of rebellion.

As the authors in the following articles point out, perhaps a majority of young people, albeit an ever-dwindling majority, sought objectives which society looked upon favorably. A growing awareness of an alienation with adult society—that a wide divergence exists between the professed beliefs and values of adults and their actions—is increasingly evident even among those who are relatively passive. The triviality of life that frequently characterizes the world of adults is heightened by a growing adherence to a "cult of youth."

The adult members of this cult, who lack the ability or the willingness to provide direction, models, or guidance for the young, adopt in an indiscriminate, wholesale fashion the ideas and values (or lack of them) of youth themselves. This adult worship at the shrine of youth is expressed in many patterns—in the commercial exploitation of the adolescent market for monetary gain, in a misunderstood "permissiveness" that caters to youthful desires, in attempts of adults to relive their youth or to realize their ambitions in the lives of their children, or in a simple belief that "if you can't beat them, join them."

This adult fawning is interpreted by youth as a sign of weakness (a feeling they themselves are experiencing) that breeds distrust of the adult society as a whole. Alienation is further increased. What most youth want, and what they want adult society to assist them in achieving, is not exploitation, but the development of some sense of their own worth; not worship, but the achievement of some measure of self-esteem; not to have adults join their society, but to have adult guidance in helping them create some conception of their own identity.*

Social critic Paul Goodman believes that it is precisely the absence of any meaningful adult guidance for youth that has brought the schools today to the status of a "universal trap." His sweeping criticism of the schools extends over a wide range of diverse groups, from slow learners who frequently drop out of school to youth of superior academic ability who are "conned" by teachers and administrators. All are being cheated. Goodman's caustic query, "Is schooling good for them, or much good for anybody?" may cause angry retorts from "the establishment," but it deserves serious consideration if schools are in earnest about reexamining their responsibility to contemporary youth.

Youth's refusal to accept the existing patterns of life, former United States Supreme Court Justice Abe Fortas maintains, is the common element in the revolt of the youth generation. Activists in this group, however, represent only a minority of present-day youth. Whatever their cause, disaffected youth strike out with the righteous zeal of a missionary against the ills of society, and, because their motives are "pure," they bitterly resent being punished for actions which violate the law. Yet, Fortas believes the law should be used to oppose violence after persuasion has failed.

Goodman's defense of youth is answered by Spencer Brown, headmaster at New York's Fieldston School, who feels that adult behavior toward young people strongly resembles the tactics of appeasement. In the so-called war between the generations, Brown pleads for some sort of balance that would recognize that good and bad qualities are found in all age groups. Not all virtue resides in the young, nor does the lack of virtue reside exclusively with those "over thirty." Youth are not exploited in any greater degree than are adults. Nothing constructive, con-

* Harold Full, *Controversy in American Education: An Anthology of Crucial Issues* (New York: The Macmillan Company, 1967), pp. 173–174.

cludes Brown, can be gained from charges and countercharges. What is needed, especially among the younger generation, is the development of three "senses"—a sense of balance, a sense of humor, and common sense. Unless balance is achieved in our daily intercourse, we are in danger of nourishing serious social discord in American society. Historian Arthur Schlesinger, Jr. examines factors currently feeding the growth of primitive emotions that explode in acts of hatred and violence. Our only recourse is a greater loyalty to a life of reason characterized by discipline and restraint. It is the academic community that must safeguard this reasoned approach. What disturbs Schlesinger, however, is that it is the intellectuals, young and old, who demonstrate a growing cynicism about democratic institutions and processes. They treat the Bill of Rights as an oppressive document designed to resist social change. These ideas advocated by Marcuse are based on "the belief that it is *necessary* and *right,* as a matter of principle, to suppress views with which one disagrees and to howl down those who utter such views." This dangerous doctrine, increasingly evident in examples of forcible take-overs of public buildings and in the presentation of "non-negotiable" demands, celebrates violence and intolerance. The editors regard Schlesinger's exposé of Marcuse's philosophical point of view, which sows the seeds of death for rational democracy, as one of the most important articles in this anthology.

Perhaps only a few student activists on college campuses are aware of the views of Marcuse. Eight hypotheses that do seem to motivate college youth are thoughtfully examined by S. L. Halleck, professor of psychiatry at the University of Wisconsin. While this essay is directed primarily to young people in college, the hypotheses hold much value and insight for the growing unrest among adolescents below the college level. This important essay poses a basic question with which all, not solely the young, must reckon in our highly complex technological society—"how can progress and change be controlled without allowing these forces to control us."

PAUL GOODMAN | *The Universal Trap*

The dropouts are importantly victims of poverty, cultural deprivation, race prejudice, family and emotional troubles, and neighborhood uprooting. This Conference will surely thoroughly explore these background conditions, will suggest ingenious expedients to counteract them, and will—I guess much less thoroughly and ingeniously—look to remedying them. There are, however, other questions: Where are the dropouts *from?* Is the schooling good for them or much good for anybody? Since there are difficulties with the present arrangements for growing up, might not some better arrangements be found? Unless we lay stress on these other questions, our Conference can well be an evil one—at best a smoke screen for the real troubles of youth, at worst social engineering for the crew that have power in the world. Certainly in the discussions of this subject which I have read, there has been an appalling lack of the philosophical and Enlightenment ideas that *cannot* be omitted from education, for youth *are* the future.

Education is a natural community function and goes on anyway, since the young grow up on the old, toward their activities, and into their institutions; and the old foster, train, exploit, and abuse the young. Formal schooling is a reasonable auxiliary of the inevitable process. Nevertheless it by no means follows that the complicated artifact of our school system has much to do with education, and certainly not with good education. If it presumes to be compulsory, then it must prove that it does not do more harm than good—both to persons and society as a whole.

Let us keep in mind the ways in which big school systems have nothing to do with education at all. The New York system turns over $700 million annually. It is a vast vested interest, and it is very probable that —like much of our economy and almost all of our political structure (of which the public schools are a part)—it goes on for its own sake. In doing so, it keeps thousands busy, wastes wealth, crushes life, and preempts the space in which something interesting could go on. Notoriously, the school system is a gigantic market for textbook manufacturers and building contractors. Further, its fundamental design is ancient, yet has

This article first published in *The School Dropout,* Daniel Schreiber (ed.), Washington, D.C., National Education Association, Project: School Dropouts 1964. Reprinted by permission.

not been altered although its present operation is altogether different in scale and must be in meaning. For example, in 1900, high school graduates were 6 per cent of the 17-year-olds, and 4 per cent went to college. In 1961, nearly 61 per cent are graduates; and of these, nearly 60 per cent are bound for something called college. Likewise, there is a difference between a few hours' attendance in school intermitted in life on a farm or in a city with plenty of small jobs and schooling that is a child's only adult contact. Thus, a perhaps outmoded institution has become almost the only available way of growing up. And this pre-empting has occurred not only in extent but also in meaning. Just as our American society as a whole is more and more tightly organized, so its school system is more and more regimented as a part of that organization, with little leeway of its own. Unfortunately, that organization of society is mindlessly drifting toward catastrophe. In the organizational plan, the schools play a noneducational and an educational role. The noneducational role is very important: in the tender grades, the schools are a baby-sitting service during a period of collapse of the old type of family and of great neighborhood mobility; in the junior high and high school grades, they are an arm of the police, providing cops and concentration camps paid for in the budget under the heading "Board of Education." The educational role is, increasingly, to provide apprentice training for corporations and the War Department and to train the young—as New York's Commissioner of Education, James Allen, said (in the Worley case)—"to handle constructively their problems of adjustment to authority."

There is no doubt that the school system has been, and continues to be, a powerful force for the democratizing of our great and mixed population. But we must be careful to keep reassessing it when it becomes a universal trap and democracy begins to look like regimentation.

Let us spend a page on the history of the compulsory nature of the system. When, in *The Child, the Parent, and the State,* James Conant[1] refers to the possible incompatibility between "individual development" and "national needs," it is a watershed in American philosophy of education and puts us back to the ideology of Imperial Germany, or on a par with contemporary Russia. When Jefferson and Madison conceived of compulsory schooling, such an incompatibility would have been unthinkable. They were in the climate of the Enlightenment, were strongly influenced by Congregational (town-meeting) ideas, and were of course makers of a revolution. To them "citizen" meant society maker, not one adjusted to society; and it is clear that they regarded themselves and their friends as citizens existentially, so to speak. To make society was

[1] James B. Conant, *The Child, the Parent, and the State* (Cambridge, Mass.: Harvard University Press, 1959), 211 pp.

their breath of life. (In my opinion, the majority of Americans at that time were less citizens in this sense, and nearer to small-community anarchists and guerrillas.) Obviously such conceptions are worlds removed from, and diametrically opposed to, our present political reality, where the ground rules, and indeed the game, are predetermined. For Jefferson, *people had to be taught in order to multiply the sources of initiative.* And the curriculum that those of good parts were to learn was corresponding: a technological natural philosophy, in order to make inventions and produce useful goods; and the social study of history, in order to make constitutional innovations and be fired to defend freedom. What are the compelling reasons compelling everybody to know how to know what goes on? To keep the economy expanding, to choose between indistinguishable Democrats and Republicans, and to understand the official press and TV. Planning and decision making are lodged in the top managers; rarely, and at most, the electorate serves as a pressure group.

Scientifically, the urban mass exists only as consumers. (As serious education, let us note, under these circumstances of powerfulness and non-involvement there is not much way to learn anything, and not much is learned.)

Another great impulse for compulsory education came from the new industrialism and urbanism, especially during the three or four decades after the Civil War, a time also of great immigration. Here the curricular demands were more modest: in the grades, literacy and arithmetic; in the colleges, professional skills to man the expanding economy. But again, no one would have spoken of an incompatibility between "individual development" and "national needs," for it was considered to be an open society, abounding in opportunity. And indeed there was an endless proliferation of economic and technical small enterprises—plus westward emigration and considerable imperialism in Latin America and the Far East. Typically, the novels of Horatio Alger, Jr., treat education as morally excellent as well as essential for getting ahead; and there is no doubt that the immigrants saw education-for-success as also a human value for their children. Also, the system was not an academic trap. The 94 per cent who in 1900 did not finish school had other life opportunities, including often the possibility of making a lot of money or/and of rising in politics—though not in high policy, an area which belonged to the schooled.

But again, by and large, this is not our present situation. There is plenty of social mobility; there are plenty of opportunities to rise—except for the ethnic minorities who are precisely our main concern as dropouts. But how to rise and what to rise to are increasingly rigidified, stratified, cut and dried. Most enterprise is parceled out by the feudal corporations, or by the state; and these determine the requirements and assign the statuses and salaries. Ambition with average talent meets their rules, or fails; and those without relevant talent, or with unfortunate backgrounds, cannot even survive in decent poverty. And the requirements of survival are importantly academic, or at least have come to be attained in public schools and universities. We do not have an open economy. Jobs are scarce, and the corporations and state can dictate the terms. Thus, IBM, Westinghouse, etc., swoop down on the colleges and skim off the youth who have been given what amounts to an apprenticeship at public and private expense (the private expense running upwards of $10,000). Even a department store requires a diploma or diplomas for its salespeople, not so much because of the skills they have learned but because it sets a guarantee of the character useful for sales help: punctual, obedient, and with a smooth record. And more generally, since our powers-that-be have opted for an expanding economy with a galloping "high standard of living" and since all the powers of the world are in an arms and space race, there *is* a national need for many academic graduates specifically trained. Such a need is irrelevant to citizenly initiative, the progress of an open society, or personal happiness.

Thus, education becomes equivalent to regimentation. The schools become a universal trap. Those not in the schools fall outside of society altogether.

These schools are *not* geared to "middle class values," a misleading use of words which has become common. The schools less and less represent *any* human values, but simply adjustment to a mechanism.

In the face of the increasing failure of the schools with the poor urban mass, there has developed a line of criticism—e.g., Oscar Lewis, Patricia Sexton, Frank Riessman, and Edgar Friedenberg—asserting that there is a "culture of poverty" that the "middle class" schools do not fit, but which has its own virtues of spontaneity, sociality, animality, etc. The implication is that the "middle class," for all its virtues, is obsessional, prejudiced, prudish. Pedagogically, this insight is indispensable: we must try to reach a child in terms of his background, his habits, and the language he understands. But if taken to be more than technical, it is disastrous. For our philosophic aim must be to get each one out of his isolated class and into the one humanity. Prudence and responsibility are not middle class virtues but human virtues; and spontaneity and sexuality are not powers of the simple but of human health. (One has the impression that our critics are looking not to a human community but to a future in which the obsessionals will take care of the impulsives.)

In fact, some of the most important strengths that have historically belonged to the middle class are flouted by the schools: independence, initiative, scrupulous honesty, earnestness, utility, thoroughness, respect for disinterested scholarship and science. Rather than bourgeois, our schools are petty bourgeois, bureaucratic, gradgrind-practical, and *nouveau riche* climbing; and added to these, last but not least, they exude a cynicism, in the upper grades and colleges, that belongs to rotten aristocrats and racketeers.

Naturally, however, the youth of the poor and of the middle class respond differently to the school trap. Many poor youth, herded into a situation that does not fit their disposition, for which they are unprepared by their background, and which does not interest them, simply develop a reactive stupidity very different from their behavior on the street or ball field. They drop behind, play truant, and as soon as possible drop out. If the school situation is immediately useless and damaging to them, their response must be said to be life preservative. They thereby somewhat diminish their chances of a decent living and of being effective citizens. We must remember that the usual propaganda—that schooling is a road to high salaries—is, for most of these poor youth, a lie; and the increase in security is arguably not worth the torture involved, for we allow almost nobody actually to starve.

Certainly the reasonable social policy would be not to have these youth in school, but to educate them otherwise and provide opportunity for a decent future in some other way. It would be wise to have a conference on *this* issue, omitting the notion of dropout altogether. At present, our society does not know how to cope with these youth, and really isn't interested. I fear that most of the concern for the dropouts is because they are a nuisance and a threat and can't be socialized by the existing machinery. Ethically, therefore, I am dubious about the attempts of James Coleman, or even Dan Schreiber, to use methods and bait which are not beautiful in themselves and which sometimes come to conning and cajoling these young people by adolescent tricks and prizes rather than treating them earnestly as persons. Very different is the aspect of the Higher Horizons Program as reopening hope for a future that is really worthwhile and desirable. This is to take the young seriously and to be their champion.

But numerically far more important than these overt dropouts at 16 are the children who conform to schooling between the ages of 6 to 16 or 20, but who drop out internally through daydreaming—their days wasted, their liberty caged and scheduled, their desires inhibited, their imagination and aspiration lost. There are many such in the middle class, from backgrounds that have not been so horrendous as to foment overt rebellion—where there is some interest in books and arts; where the youth is seduced by the prospect of money and status, but even more where he is terrified to jeopardize the only pattern of life he knows.

It is in the schools and from the mass media, rather than at home or from their friends, that the mass of our citizens in all classes learn that life is inevitably routine and phony, depersonalized, venally graded, and bureaucratized; that it is best to toe the mark and shut up; that there is no place for spontaneity, open sexuality, free spirit. Trained in the schools, they go on to the same quality of jobs, culture, politics. This *is* education, bad education—socializing to the national norm, regimenting to the national needs.

The educational psychology of it is elementary. Our society and its school trap first deprive the young of objective human opportunities, including virtues that belonged to the middle class. As I put it in *Growing Up Absurd*—

> With all the tidying up of background conditions that you please our abundant society is at present simply deficient in many of the most elementary objective opportunities that could make growing up possible. It is lacking in enough man's work. It is lacking in honest public speech and people are not taken seriously. It is lacking in the opportunity to be useful. It thwarts aptitude and creates stupidity. It corrupts ingenuous patriotism. It corrupts the fine arts. It shackles science. It dampens animal ardor. It discourages the religious convictions of Justification and Vocation and it dims the sense that there is a Creation. It has no honor. It has no community.[2]

But once frustrated in these things, and sometimes punished for dumbly trying for them, it is a short step to resignation. And since the resigned must have something, it is another short step to narcissism and cynicism or spite. Let us examine realistically three or four aspects of the school that is dropped out *from.*

There is a widespread anxiety about teaching reading. And indeed, reading deficiency is an accumulating disadvantage that results in painful inferiority, truancy, and dropout. Reading is crucial—by the standards of the school and because of the kinds of success that schooling leads to. Yet there is something phony here. What does *reading* mean today? We cannot say that, as humanities or science, the reading matter of the great majority is in any way superior to the movies or TV that the illiterate can share. Certainly many people would be better off without most of this mass culture, including the reading matter. And why should most people *bother* to learn to read seriously? In the decision making of our society, serious literacy is of no practical importance whatever. It is as powerless as it is rare. Anyway, those who achieve it do not do so by the route of "Run, Spot, Run" to *Silas Marner,* but by their own explorations.

It is claimed that without universal literacy our economy and technology could not operate. I doubt that this is true for many unskilled and many craft and mechanical jobs. Unlike the expanding industrialism mentioned above—or the present situation in the underdeveloped regions of Africa, Asia, and Latin America—the automated future that we face in the United States will have no need for workers. In my opinion, it is

[2] Paul Goodman, *Growing Up Absurd* (New York: Random House, 1961), p. 12.

rather the kind of urbanism, politics, and buying and selling that we have that has put a premium on literacy; and, in my opinion, these are of dubious human value. Since I do not think that an indefinitely expanding economy is the right use of modern technology, I am unimpressed by the need for artificial demand fomented by advertising. Also, I am hostile to the common denominator produced by the mass media.

In the present dispensation, we would be as well off if it were socially acceptable for large numbers not to read. It would be harder to regiment people. There would be more folk culture. Serious letters would benefit if society were less swamped by trash, lies, and bland verbiage. Much suffering of inferiority would be obviated. And conceivably, *more people might become genuinely literate if it were understood that reading is a useful art with a proper subject matter, imagination and truth—not "communication" of top down decisions and bad norms.*

The young rightly resist animal constraint. But, at least in New York, most teachers—and many principals who visit their classes—operate as if Progressive Education had not proved the case for noise and freedom of bodily motion. Of course, the classes are too large to cope with without "discipline." Then make them smaller; or don't wonder if children escape out of the cage, either into truancy or baffled daydream. Here is a case: an architect replacing a Harlem school is forbidden by the Board to spend money on sound-proofing the classrooms even though the wise principal has declared it to be a must for the therapy of the pent-up and resentful children. Resentment—pent-up hostility—is a major cause of reactive stupidity; yet there is usually an absolute discouragement of any overt expression of resentment, or even of normal anger or aggression.

Again, one has to be blind not to see that the dissidence from school is importantly sexual, especially from the onset of puberty. Theoretically, the junior high school was introduced precisely to fit this change of life, yet astoundingly it is sexless. My own view, for what it's worth, is that sexuality is lovely, that there cannot be too much of it, that it is self-limiting if it is satisfactory, and that satisfaction diminishes tension and clears the mind for attention and learning. Therefore sexual expression should be approved in and out of season, also in school, and where necessary made the subject of instruction. But whether or not this view is ideal, it is at present the only practical one. Our society has so developed that sexual drives cannot be kept out of consciousness (in repression). Then there is no alternative, to avoid distortion and preoccupation, except to raise the discharge to the level of the tension. When, on so crucial an issue, the schools act 100 years out of date, they are crucially irrelevant.

But let me mention a further aspect of inhibition of the motoric, the sexual, and the angry. There is now public alarm about children's physical unfitness. The President's Committee ludicrously proposes a standard of three chin-ups, etc.; schools institute some calisthenics and proudly record the improvement in meeting the standard. But no program is instituted to unblock the muscles tensed by inhibition—the fear of expression, the fear of body contact, and the fear of nakedness. Physical training teachers do not try to free the bodies of the children to weep, shout, reach in love, strive with determination, strike in anger, and dance in rhythm. The children are supposed, somehow, to manifest grace, agility, and strength as if they were not unitary organisms. Is this realistic? Of course, if a teacher used eurythmics and physical therapy to unblock feeling, there would be an outcry from the churches, some parents, and the yellow press that fattens on pornography and murder. The officials would cower, the teacher would be fired. Instead, the children are sacrificed—or drop out.

The schools are supposed to educate for the satisfaction of life and for leisure. Again, let us try to be realistic. For most people, I think that a candid self-examination will show that their most absorbing, long, and satisfactory hours are spent in things like friendly competitive sports, friendly gambling, love making and sex, earnest or argumentative conversation, dedicated political activity, solitary study and reading, contemplation of nature and the cosmos, art working, music, and religion. Now none of these requires the use of many commodities. Indeed, elaborate arrangements and equipment take the life out of them. Friends use one another as resources; and God, nature, and creativity are free. The media of fine arts are cheap stuff. Health, luck, and a simple heart are the only requirements for good sex. Good food requires taking pains more than spending money.

On the other hand, it is the necessity of a profitable economy, with high employment and expanding by reinvestment, to *increase* the number of commodities consumed, and therefore to prevent, curtail, or debauch the profound satisfactions of life; that is, to see to it that a "high standard of living" is a bad, wasteful, and unsatisfactory, but titillating, standard of living. In our present political and economic dispensation, an advanced technology *cannot* be humane.

What is the moral for our purposes? Can it be denied that in some respects the dropouts make a wiser choice than many who go to school, not to get real goods but to get money? Their choice of the "immediate" is not altogether impulsive and neurotic. The bother is that in our present culture they are so nagged by inferiority, exclusion, and despair of the future that they cannot much enjoy their leisure. Because they know little, they are deprived of many profound satisfactions; being afraid of exposing themselves, they just hang around. And our urban social arrangements—for example, rent—have made it impossible for anybody to be decently poor on a "low" standard.

Untold damage is done to children simply by the size and standardization of the big system. Suppose a class size of 20 is good for some purpose: it does not follow that 35 is better than nothing. Rather, it is likely to be positively harmful for the children who have ceased to be persons, and it destroys the teacher. A teacher with a 10-year-old class reading at 7-year level will have to use the content as well as the vocabulary of *Dick and Jane* since that is the textbook bought by the hundred thousand. The experience of a wise principal is that the most essential part of his job is to know every child's name and be an available godfather. Yet the city will build the school for 2,000. The chief part of learning is in the community of scholars, where classwork and social life cohere; yet social engineers like Dr. Conant will, for putative efficiencies, centralize the high schools.

A program—for example, to prevent dropout—will be, by an attentive teacher, exquisitely tailored to the children he works with; he will have a success. Therefore his program must be standardized (watered down) in 75 schools—otherwise it cannot be financed. But here is an unbeatable anecdote: An architect is employed to replace a dilapidated school but is forbidden to consult the principal and teachers of the school as to their needs, since his building must conform to uniform plans at headquarters (the plants are a generation out of date). Being a functionalist, the architect demurs, and it requires an *ad hoc* assembly of all the superintendents to write a special contract!

Presumably all the standardization, etc., is administratively necessary, but then it is also necessary for bruised children to quit. Our society makes a persistent error in metaphysics. Production techniques which apply to commodities, to administrative and logistics techniques, to armies and banks have *no relevance whatever to* the personal relations of teaching and learning and to the community relations of educating the young. When they are applied, what the young learn is not the lesson but a reaction to the Procrustean bed.

As a loyal academic, I must make a further observation. Mainly to provide apprentices, as I have said, there is at present a strong pressure to gear the "better" elementary schools to the colleges and universities. This is the great current reform, genre of Rickover. But what if the top of the ladder is corrupt and corrupts the lower grades? On visits to 50 colleges everywhere in the country, I have been appalled at how rarely the subjects are studied in a right academic spirit, for their truth and beauty and as part of humane international culture. Rather, the students are given, and seek, a narrow expertise aimed at licenses and salary. They are indoctrinated with a national thoughtlessness that is not even chauvinistic. Administrators sacrifice the community of scholars to aggrandizement and subsidized research.

Conversely, there is almost never conveyed the sense in which learning is truly practical, enlightening experience, initiating and giving courage for change, reforming the state, deepening personal and social peace. On the contrary, there is a professional cynicism and the resigned conviction that Nothing Can Be Done. This is Yale. If this is the University, how can we hope for aspiring scholarship in the elementary schools? On the contrary, everything will be grading, conformist "citizenship," and getting ahead—not in the subject but up the ladder. Students will "do" Bronx Science in order to "make" MIT, and they will "do" MIT in order to "make" Westinghouse, and they will "do" Westinghouse in order to "make" jail. The improvement of "academic" standards is a sell, and the bright boys and girls are being had. Some of them know it and balk.

The compulsory system has become a universal trap, and it is no good. Very many, and perhaps most, of the youth—both underprivileged and middle class—might be better off if the system did not exist, even if they then had no formal schooling at all. But what would become of them? For very many—both underprivileged and middle class—their homes are worse than the schools, and the streets are worse in another way. Our urban and suburban environments are precisely not cities or communities where adults attend to the young and educate to a viable life. Also, perhaps especially in the case of the overt dropouts, the state of their body and soul is such that we must give them some refuge and remedy—whether it be called school, youth work, work camp, or settlement house.

This is not the place for a long list of practical proposals to make the schools worth attending. However, it is relevant to offer a few ideas toward the main subject we have been discussing—the system as a compulsory trap. In principle, when a law begins to do more harm than good, the best policy is to alleviate it. I would suggest the following experiments:

1. Have "no school at all" for a few classes. These children should be selected from tolerable, through not necessarily cultured, homes. They should be numerous enough and neighborly enough to be a society for one another. Will they learn the rudiments anyway? The experiment could not harm them, since there is evidence (Sloan Wayland) that normal children can make up the first six or seven school years with a few months of good teaching.

2. Largely dispense with the school building for a few classes, and use the city itself as a school—the streets, cafeterias, stores, movies, museums, parks, and factories. Such a class should probably not exceed 10 children for 1 pedagogue. The idea (an Athenian one) is not dissimilar to Youth gang work, though not employing delinquents nor playing to the gang ideology.

3. Along the same lines, but both outside and inside the school, use appropriate adults of the community—such as the druggist, the storekeeper, the mechanic—as the proper educators of the young into the grown-up world. By this means, it would be possible to overcome the

separation of the young from the grown-up world in our urban life and to diminish the omnivorous authority of the school. This experience would be useful and animating for the adults. (We have begun a volunteer program along these lines in New York City.)

4. Make class attendance not compulsory (A. S. Neill). If the teachers are good, absence should soon be eliminated. The reason for the compulsory law is to get the children from the parents, but it must not be a trap for the children. A modification might be permission to spend a week or a month in any worthwhile enterprise or environment (Frank Brown).

5. Decentralize the school into small units of perhaps 100—in clubhouses—combining play, social activity, discussion, and formal teaching. Special events could bring together the many small units to a common auditorium or gymnasium so as to give the sense of the greater community.

6. For a couple of months of the school year, send children to farms to take part in the farm life, perhaps two or three children to a farmer. This would serve to give the farmer cash, as part of a generally desirable program to redress the urban-rural ratio to something nearer to 70–30.

Above all, apply these or any other proposals to particular individuals or small groups, without the obligation of uniformity. There is a case for uniform standards of achivement, but they *cannot* be reached by uniform techniques. The claim that standardization of procedure is more efficient, less costly, or alone administratively practical is usually false. Particular inventiveness requires thought, but thought does not cost money. And the more the authority to initiate is delegated to many, the wiser and freer we will be.

ABE FORTAS | The Revolt of Youth

The revolt of the young people, on and off the campus, is a fairly new phenomenon for this country. Our young people have been submissive, hedonistic, and practical-minded. Their idealism has been largely confined to dreams, poetry, and abstractions. Even in the depths of the Depression, relatively few of them were activists. They have accepted the leadership of their elders, not uncritically, but passively. Their revolt has usually taken the form of social misbehavior, not of political activism.

Until the generation of John F. Kennedy, their participation in practical politics was marked by acceptance of "Junior" status: The Junior Chamber of Commerce, the Young Democrats, etc. Only a few years ago, in

President Eisenhower's administration, many of us despaired because the college generation was so passive, so docile, and so uninvolved. It was apparently uninterested in anything that was not safe, conventional, and serviceable in practical terms.

Now this has drastically changed. Young people have suddenly taken on distinctive character and quality. They are not merely junior size editions of their elders. They have become a positive, differentiated factor in American life. They are no longer predictably proceeding in a straight line behind their parents and grandparents, preparing to receive the torch from their elders to run the next lap in the old relay race.

This refusal to accept the existing pattern of life and thought merely because it exists is, I think, the common element in the revolt of the youth-generation. I do not suggest that most of this age group are active, conscious participants in the revolt. A sharp change in the philosophy of life of a generation is always the work of a few, although it may influence the destiny of all. Probably a majority of today's young people are going about their lives with little discernible difference between their basic actions and those of their parents' generation. But the existence of a special, independent outlook and orientation of the youth-generation is an article of faith to which most of them subscribe. Even though it is ill-defined, hazy in outline, and uncertain in context, the revolt profoundly affects the lives of all of them—even of those who do not participate in the new activities.

This refusal to accept the domination of the past—the insistence upon this generation's right and duty to make its own life-decisions—has produced both count-me-outs and count-me-ins. It has produced the hippies, the psychedelic addicts, and the flower-children. It has also produced other young people, not so picturesque in their appearance or habits, who have quietly divorced themselves from the mainstream of life. These are the count-me-outs who decline to join in the agony and activity of their time, or in its customary preoccupations. They are immersed in the warm fluid of me-ness. They reject a world which they regard as crass and callous.

On the other hand, there are the activists, the militants, who are passionately devoted to the cause of the Negroes and the poor, and to promoting student domination of university management, and to such causes as opposition to the war in Vietnam and to the draft. They participate vigorously in the life around them to advance those causes. These are the count-me-ins. They have ideas, programs, convictions, energy, and initiative. Some of them were significant participants in the freedom rides and marches and the early struggle to end discrimination against Negroes. They organize and participate in mass activities to achieve their objectives, and to defeat governmental and university actions which they oppose.

Many reasons have contributed to the youth revolt: the affluence of our society and the resulting removal of the pressure to prepare oneself for economic survival; the deterioration of the family unit; the increasing involvement of universities and their faculties with non-teaching interests; the disruptive shock of the atom bomb, which gave a new uncertainty and instability to life; the prospect that their lives will be interrupted by compulsory military service; the opposition to the war in Vietnam; the shock of discovering that our national pride and progress concealed the misery and degradation in which Negroes and the poor were living; disillusionment with the standards of the older generation; the new awareness of the wretched state of most of the world's people which came in with the end of colonialism; and the example of Negroes in this country and of the people of Africa and Asia, who by individual and group effort, courage and organization have fought and sometimes won heroic battles.

Most of all, the revolt has found impetus, reason, and outlet in the opposition to the war in Vietnam and to the draft. Many of the younger generation, as well as some of their elders (justifiably or not) have come to regard this as a war of a small people against oppression by a vast power, as a struggle for national unity, or as a purely civil war in which our country is "brutally" participating. This has reinforced the natural and familiar opposition of many young men to military service, and especially to compulsory military service. In the minds of these young people, the draft is bad enough; but to be drafted to fight a war which they are led to believe is disreputable, is intolerable.

The disaffection of youth is expressed by a great variety of activities, ranging from the amusingly juvenile to formidable, threatening assaults upon the institutions of our society. It is difficult for the young people who are moved to passionate action by these factors to resign themselves to the idea that they may be punished if their actions violate the law. They *know* they are right. They are certain that their motives are pure. And they do not accept the proposition that there is any virtue in obedience to authority. They are not broken to society's bridle.

Negroes and poor people are more likely than the young to have experienced conflict with law and police. They are more likely to accept the fact that transgression of the rules carries with it the penalty of punishment. They may not like the consequences, but they do not react with the sense of injustice that the campus "radical" feels. He knows that he is both righteous and right. Generally, his background is middle-class and "respectable." It is impossible for him really to visualize a confrontation between himself and the power of the law. He cannot really see himself as a "criminal," even if he starts a scuffle with the police, destroys property, or assaults persons engaged in recruiting for the armed forces or war industries.

But the rules apply to him as well as to the Negroes and the indigent.

The college youth who is protesting against the college administration or the war in Vietnam or the draft has, of course, the full scope of First Amendment rights. He is entitled to the full protection of the state and the courts in the exercise of speech and symbolic speech, however hostile. But he is not entitled to immunity if he directly and willfully incites violence or insists upon deliberately disrupting the work or movement of others.

A university may choose to refrain from complaining to the police if students disrupt classes by physical violence, or destroy university property, or manhandle recruiters for the armed services or for industries making war materials. If it does not take action itself or summon police assistance, the police are not likely to take the initiative on the campus. But if it lodges a complaint, the governing legal principles in this country are not essentially different from those applicable off campus.

Campus and university facilities are public facilities; but public use does not authorize either the general public or the university faculty and students to use them in a way which subverts their purpose and prevents their intended use by others. The public character of a university does not grant to individuals a license to engage in activities which disrupt the activities to which those facilities are dedicated.

I know of no legal principle which protects students on campus from the consequences of activities which would be violations of law if undertaken elsewhere. This is the law; but we are now confronted with a problem which is not solved by mechanical application of the criminal law: the problem of readjusting campus life to the new attitudes and demands, and of coping with the disaffections which afflict so many students.

Here again, perhaps it is a beginning to separate student activities which are nonviolent from those which involve assault or damage to persons or property. Where the law violation is nonviolent or technical (such as blocking entrance to a campus building, or even orderly occupancy of a university facility), there may be sense in patient forbearance despite the wrong that the action involves. But violent activities, in my judgment, should be regarded and treated as intolerable. Punishment of on-campus violence involves risks. Particularly in respect to the youth generation, it should be undertaken only after all efforts to persuade, patiently applied, have been exhausted. But the toleration of violence involves, I think, even greater risks, not only of present damage and injury but of erosion of the base of an ordered society. The point, I think, is not whether the aggressor should be halted and punished, but how; and it is here that moderation, consideration, and sympathetic understanding should play their part.

I do not know how profound in intensity or how lasting the current youth revolt may be. It may presage a new and welcome era of idealism in the nation. It may forecast the development of greater maturity and independence of outlook among our young people, and this may be productive of much good. It may even bring about the development of increased maturity in the educational and living rules of our colleges. In any event, it presents a challenge to the older generations as well as to youth to reconsider the goals of our society and its values, and urgently to reappraise the distribution of function and responsibility among the generations.

SPENCER BROWN | ***We Can't Appease the Younger Generation***

The war of the generations has been going on a long time, and it is unlikely that anything really new can be contributed to it. But I should like to say a word on behalf of the elderly, remembering, of course, that whatever I say is suspect as reactionary, fuddy-duddy or dead.

We have spend a good deal of time in the last few decades trying to understand young people. It is no surprise when a conservative educator, someone perhaps like Jacques Barzun of Columbia or Douglas Bush of Harvard, tells us to pay no attention to what young people say; or to give them a standard curriculum—back to the three R's.

But it is high time for someone not committed to a rigid curriculum, for an admirer of Freud and Dewey, for one who has voted against conservative candidates in every election since 1932, for someone who rejoices in the march of modern science and is not the least interested in turning back the clock—for such a one to ask for understanding of the adult world and to argue against victory by the young in their warfare with the old.

Thus, I wish to examine the fairly common claim that today's younger generation—the young people in the last years of high school and in college—are uniquely miserable, uniquely persecuted and uniquely virtuous. In examining that claim and determining what we elderly people should answer to it, I ask that we examine our own vocabulary, our thinking and our moral nerve. I ask that in addition to patience, which we have already shown in overwhelming abundance, we learn balance, common sense and humor.

At the outset we may well remember Logan Pearsall Smith's remark: "The denunciation of the young is a necessary part of the hygiene of

From *The New York Times Magazine* (November 27, 1966).

elderly people, and greatly assists the circulation of their blood." But let us permit the elderly another word from the same essayist: "Uncultivated minds are not full of wild flowers, like uncultivated fields. Villainous weeds grow in them, and they are the haunt of toads." Having thus demonstrated our balance, we may proceed.

Much of our difficulty stems from our habits of talk. At one extreme we rejoice in being apocalyptic: we say that history is a race between education and catastrophe. But this race is no 100-yard or 100-year dash; if it were, catastrophe would have won long ago since education has not yet come up with a complete solution to any major problem. The race must be at least a marathon. Or we say, as did a group of reporters interviewing Robert Frost on television, that this is the worst or most dangerous or most difficult time man has ever lived through. They kept trying to badger the octogenarian poet into saying what they wanted him to say; but at last he succeeded in outshouting them and making himself heard: "Yes, yes, yes, it's a terribly difficult time for a man to try to save his soul—about as difficult as it always has been."

Or at the other extreme, we speak gobbledygook sociologese-psychologese. We say that our young people are undergoing an identity crisis and think of them as alienated and suffering from anonymity. We remark that they are "acting out" their problems. We sympathize with their rebellion, for they have much to rebel against. We admire their courage when they "speak out" against their exploitation. And even when we are uneasy over what they are doing, we are glad that at least they are actively protesting, and not behaving passively. We do not question their motives.

Phrases like these, I am convinced, corrupt our thinking. They suggest that these troubles are new, whereas they are as old as the human race. They change their form with each generation, sometimes oftener, since the best thing about youthful fads is the rapidity with which they age and disappear. But our cant phrases, suggesting unprecedented gravity, deprive us of our sense of humor and perspective. "Growing pains" is an older phrase—half-mocking, half-tolerant—quite as useful as "identity crisis," since it suggested the recurring nature of the phenomenon. Youth has been lonely for centuries. What has "alienation" got that differentiates it from old-fashioned loneliness? And youth generally "acts out" its problems by raising hell, which is hardly a modern monopoly.

That youth has very real grievances, no sane man can doubt. Yet, just as surely, no sane man should subscribe to the statements of those grievances that we read in the press. As one example, there is the frequent assertion by Paul Goodman that college students are the most exploited class in our society; recently, he told a group of Rutgers freshmen that society had "dragooned" them into college. It is hard to take such things seriously: Mr. Goodman is merely working the old Shavian trick of taking an obvious truth and stating the opposite, to promote an uproar. College students are one of the most favored groups in our society, perhaps the most favored.

It may be that college students are miserable. At the same time, though, they are the largest leisure class in America. In comparison with the tiny numbers of immensely wealthy adults, they are more numerous and fairly wealthy. They are our mass consumers of culture, the advanced guard of the great owning and managerial orders into which they will move at graduation, when they lose their leisure. Far from being exploited, they ride on the backs of all of us, and they sometimes use spurs.

True, the college student is usually not allowed free access to liquor; his sex life is often uncertain. His future, though rosy and assured in general, is unknown in detail and perhaps therefore frightening. He may debate whether it is more miserable to be young and unrealistically ambitious and therefore anxious about success or to be young and realistically unambitious and reconciled to anonymity.

Many have described these troubles, but few have done it better than Robinson Jeffers:

> Age has infirmities
> Not few, but youth is all one fever.

In short, the exploitation of youth is by its own ambitions, its own contradictions, its own hopeless passions, its own destructive violence—and certainly not, in middle-class America, by society's intervention and destruction. To equate the "exploitation of youth" with the exploitation of the Negro in Mississippi, as the Berkeley mutineers did, is a type of insanity. It reminds me of what E. B. White said about a certain kind of mad poet: he takes leave of his reason deliberately, as a commuter might of his wife.

Doubtless one concern is with the draft, which does cramp youth and freedom. But whatever the inequities of the draft, most campus objections come from those who disapprove of the Vietnam war. And the reasonably well-to-do and reasonably astute collegians have so far found ways to beat the system, though often at the cost of becoming perpetual graduate students. There is some resentment at not being allowed to drop out freely—but no matter how horrible Harvard is, it is still preferable to Vietnam.

It is true, also, that the student is under pressure. Prof. Seymour M. Lipset, in a speech at Brandeis recently, reported on a survey he made of the ambitions and problems of students and noted that pressures on students have increased drastically. Their greatest problem, he said, is getting into a first-rate college and later into a high-ranking graduate school. "Some reactions to this pressure include getting off the treadmill, becoming beatniks and radicals, particularly among graduate students," Professor Lipset declared. But he added that the vast majority of students merely studied harder.

Is the pressure intolerable? Obviously not. If it were, the activists on the campus (such of them as are not nonstudents) would all flunk out. College students have always had time to lead double and triple lives; they still do. They are certainly better off than the 9-to-5 jobholder.

As for worries, students today are considerably better off than their parents were, though they work harder than their parents ever did in college. The parents of today's students, plagued all through school by money worries, looked forward to a world of unemployment or, later, to a war of considerably larger size than the current phase of the cold war. Today's students, and younger faculty members, have never known a time when the country was not affluent. Indeed, in a romantic or nostalgic effort to regain the raptures of unemployment, the modern activist will drop out of his prosperity—like the activist students' idol, Bob Dylan, who "created his own Depression" by bumming about the countryside.

Nevertheless, for most such dropouts-as-a-social-class the poverty is play-poverty. They can always write home for money. They make their own Depression, yet they insist also on an expensive hi-fi or electric guitar or wig or sports car or motorcycle or airplane tickets or drugs. These, they suggest, are what society owes them because society is hypocritical.

Society's hypocrisy is the great weapon in the hands of youth in the war with age. The older generation is bad, youth says, and only youth can be relied on to act with pure motives. From that notion stems the moral arrogance so noticeable in the pronouncements of youth leaders. For example, a high school editorial writer, protesting a school regulation, says that opposition to the rule is "a peaceful method of rebellion by a generation that has watched its parents solve problems by atomic bombs, napalm, civil rights murders, and genocide."

Though such a statement ought to be astonishing in the venom of its phrasing, it did not seem astonishing to any elderly person with whom I discussed it. I generally got a reply such as, "Well, it's true that the older generation has made a mess of things." Apparently the arrogance of moral superiority has become impudence too vast to be visible.

I imagine that the younger generation would become indignant—and properly so—if an elderly editorial writer said that youth solves problems by pouring kerosene over pathetic Bowery derelicts and igniting them, desecrating Jewish graves, breaking up peaceful meetings, filling the jails and hospitals with addicts, and murdering a President. Yet such a description would be no more venomous and misleading than their description of us.

The reaction of the elderly liberal (the elderly conservative merely gobbles like an angry turkey) is generally to turn away in silent shame when youth makes one of its monstrous general accusations. We must have lost our moral nerve if we cannot say, at least to ourselves, that such accusation comes with poor grace from a generation saved by its parents from Dachau and Belsen; a generation saved from physical destruction in World War II and political destruction in the cold war; a generation in which the diseases that slowly killed Schubert and Keats (those flowers of youthful genius) can be cured in a couple of weeks.

Instead, the young say, with Omar Khayyam, the poet of all poets of youth,

> Ah Love! Could you and I with Him conspire,
> To grasp this Sorry Scheme of Things entire,
> Would we not shatter it to bits—and then
> Re-mould it nearer to the Heart's Desire!

We oldsters have seen some master shatterers and remolders in our time—Mussolini, Stalin, Hitler, Castro, Mao. Hence, we have a right to be at least skeptical when some youngster advocates shattering as the essence of morality and the good life. But we are tempted to grin and put our hands over our ears rather than argue at the top of our lungs.

What I am really concerned about is the addled pates of the older generation. We don't believe the incredible generalizations that youth makes about age, and we should have the grace not to pretend we believe them. We also don't have to believe the generalizations youth makes about youth. Professor Lipset found that the great majority of college students support the Vietnam war and are notably "more bellicose" than their elders. He added that though students are more permissive about sexual norms, Kinsey researchers find sexual behavior has not changed significantly in 30 years. In short, the Vietnik-beatnik image that some youth would have us accept about all youth is simply not so.

I recently asked a highly intelligent young man about alienation and loneliness. He said that young people felt alienated from society. I pressed him about loneliness, adducing for comparison the loneliness of a number of fictional heroes that we both knew. He said, "Oh, it's not that any more; it's mass alienation. When you're all alienated together, you're not really lonely."

I asked another young man if he felt alienated. He said, "Nope." Was he undergoing a crisis of identity? Nope. This lad already has a direction: he is headed for medicine. And, by and large, the youngsters who are going to be our scientists and mathematicians do not seem rootless and alienated. Perhaps because they feel the future belongs to them, they have built-in sanity valves.

But it is not only they; the vast majority of young people are Men At Work. They have their enormous sorrows and world-weariness and hopeless love affairs. But in general they expect to be successful, and they see that the world has plenty of room for them to be successful in. As if these virtues were not enough, there are the virtues that belong peculiarly to the last 10 or 15 years—the altruism that shows itself, above all, in the Peace Corps.

Should we then conclude that we clearly have no cause to concern ourselves with the troubles of this younger generation? Not altogether, for there is a small but significant portion of that generation at open war with society—or with the older generation.

The aim of militant youth in this war is to force us into either of two untenable positions: conservatism—the old-hat, the fuddy-duddy, Colonel Blimp; or radicalism—growing with the youngsters, trying to outdo them in the art of appearing youthful and up-to-date, longing for the joys of playing left-wing in the good old Depression college days.

A political analogy is not far-fetched. The task of combating Communism is too often relegated to the reactionary and the lunatic right. The liberal, who should know the most and fight the most intelligently, pussyfoots. When he does what he calls Speaking Out, he deals a blow to the right and a lovetap to the left. Similarly, the young are denounced from conservative pulpits and platforms. But when the liberal educator Speaks Out, he usually delivers a blow to the old and a lovetap to the young. Even when the young have done something everyone is ashamed of, he tells us their motives are good.

About a year ago I was asked by the father of a former student if I would attest to the good character of his son, who was about to be fined for his part in one of the Berkeley uproars. I am afraid I rather shocked the good man by saying: "Sure, he's a good boy, none better, but it was a damn fool thing to do." The father expected me to admire him for getting tossed into the paddy wagon in a foolish demonstration. We seem to have forgotten that not everything a good boy does is good. The father, wishing me to attest to his son's good character, did not wish me to object to his son's bad—or stupid—action. But if I did object to the action, what was the point of my character endorsement?

In the old days, we might forgive the boy but not the action. If he raised hell, we might laugh, or secretly envy him, but we did not stultify ourselves by condoning his act. Today, if he breaks a window, for example, under the notion of the total nobility of human motives we search for some principle of which window-breaking is an understandable manifestation.

When we tell youngsters that whatever they do is forgiven (in fact, approved in advance), we are telling them that their motives don't matter either. This is to make all youngsters as anonymous as a company of angels. Many young people resent their anonymity; nevertheless, by our abdication of moral judgment we are making them more anonymous. The crisis of identity, if it does exist in any form different from the personal crises of the past, must therefore reside in this absence of moral judgment. If anything goes, then I am no better than the worst, a youth tells himself. Since, like everybody else, I am perfectly virtuous, I am nobody.

This assumption of noble motivation is simply the argument of the natural depravity of man turned upside down. If we assume the depravity of man, we don't have to observe or understand the young—just beat the old Adam out of them. And if we believe in man's total virtue, we don't observe or understand him either; we forgive him without looking at him. Thus, youth has come to expect institutions such as our courts and our universities to have built-in forgiveness. Thus they have arrogated to themselves that sense of moral superiority which no human being has a right to. Thus, they raise hell.

In short, we have been had.

We have been had by a number of adults who have gained cheap approbation from young people by turning traitor, not to their class, since this is not a class struggle, but to their own wisdom. They have persuaded us, or loudly assumed, that left-wing activism is altruistic, but that right-wing extremism is the product of "the authoritarian personality" and neurosis. They have used academic freedom as a sort of Yalu River, behind which they are immune to attack but from which they are free to sally forth and attack anything else, including their own school or college.

In so doing they have done evil twice. They have hurt the adult world by their feckless policies and reckless tactics. And they have hurt the young by teaching them, not that good ends excuse bad means, but that bad means are a good end in themselves; that mere action is somehow mysteriously virtuous; that anger is wisdom.

They have hurt the young also by depriving them of their youth—of the opportunity to be different, private and naughty, rather than anonymously and monotonously violent; of the opportunity to make mistakes and suffer consequences; that is, of the opportunity to learn.

All of us, I think, and not only the professional camp followers of youth's army, have spent too much time flattering our children. As teachers, we abdicate the role of teacher. As parents, we abdicate the role of parent. We wish to be colleagues and brothers and sisters, forgetting that the difference in age makes us look awkward. In the meantime we are tolerated, at best, by the young and, at worst, used.

Youth is more likely to condemn us than to love us for such disrespect of ourselves, this refusal to take them seriously enough to tell them what we really think—or rather, what we ought to think as a result of our experience. If youth, looking at parents and teachers, sees no wisdom beyond what youth has learned, we should not blame youth for disregarding us.

In the war between the generations the elderly can often outmaneuver the young, but this is a poor way of doing business since the young can spend all their time thinking up tricks and the old have work to do. If we play for time, hoping they will grow up, they *will* grow up—but not as quickly as if we refuse to play their games. If we try only to outwit and wait, a new generation will take their place, trained by them and not by us.

The aim of the elderly should not be to try to win the war. Our aim should be to win our opponents to our side and make use of their energy. Our aim is to uphold society from attacks on it by young or old. Our aim is to improve society, not to destroy it in the transparently unlikely hope of making it better by making it worse. Our aim is to deny the validity of the war.

We cannot win, and society can only lose, if we alternate old-fashioned repression with new-fashioned appeasement. There are probably just as many wicked young people as wicked old people, and just as many virtuous people in both camps. Our young people have a right to look to us for balance, common sense and a sense of humor. With these unspectacular but indispensable qualities we can call off the war and proceed with the job of education.

ARTHUR SCHLESINGER, JR. | *Existential Politics and the Cult of Violence*

The world today is asking a terrible question—a question which every citizen of this republic should be putting to himself: What sort of people are we, we Americans?

And the answer which much of the world is bound to return is that we are today the most frightening people on this planet.

We are a frightening people because for three years we have been

From *The Crisis of Confidence* by Arthur Schlesinger, Jr. Reprinted with the permission of Houghton Mifflin Company.

devastating a small country on the other side of the world in a war which bears no rational relationship to our national security or our national interest.

We are a frightening people because we have already in this decade murdered the two of our citizens who stood preeminently before the world as the embodiments of American idealism—and because last night we tried to murder a third.

We are a frightening people because the atrocities we commit trouble so little our official self-righteousness, our invincible conviction of our moral infallibility.

The ghastly things we do to our own people, the ghastly things we do to other people—these must at last compel us to look searchingly at ourselves and our society before hatred and violence rush us on to more evil and finally tear our nation apart.

We can not take the easy course and blame everyone but ourselves for the things we do.

We can not blame the epidemic of murder at home on deranged and solitary individuals separate from the rest of us. For these individuals are plainly weak and suggestible men, stamped by our society with a birthright of hatred and a compulsion toward violence.

We can not blame our epidemic of murder abroad on the wickedness of those who will not conform to our views of how they should behave and how they should live. For the zeal with which we have pursued an irrational war—a war which makes no sense in the traditional terms of foreign policy—suggests the internal impulses of hatred and violence demanding outlet and shaping our foreign policy to their ends.

We must recognize that the evil is in us, that it springs from some dark, intolerable tension in our history and our institutions. It is almost as if a primal curse had been fixed on our nation, perhaps when we first began the practice of killing and enslaving those whom we deemed our inferiors because their skin was another color. We are a violent people with a violent history, and the instinct for violence has seeped into the bloodstream of our national life.

We are also, at our best, a generous and idealistic people. Our great leaders—Lincoln most of all—have perceived both the instinct for hatred and violence and the moral necessity of transcending hatred and violence if we are going to have any sort of rational and decent society. They have realized how fragile the membranes of civilization are, stretched so thin over a nation so disparate in its composition, so tense in its interior relationships, so cunningly enmeshed in underground fears and antagonisms, so entrapped by history in the ethos of violence.

Now, as our nation grows more centralized our energy more concentrated, our inner tensions more desperate, our frustrations in our own land and in the world more embittered, we can no longer regard hatred and violence as accidents and aberrations, as nightmares which will pass away when we awake. We must see them as organic in our national past; we must confront them; we must uncover the roots of hatred and violence and, through self-knowledge, move toward self-control. And we must exert every effort in the meantime to protect and strengthen the membranes of civility against the impulses of destruction.

In this effort, I would suggest, a special responsibility lies on our intellectual community. For one can expect primitive emotions on the part of those who roughly occupy the right wing of our national politics. But the intellectual community should be the particular custodian of the life of reason. It should be the particular champion of discipline and restraint. It should be the particular enemy of hatred and violence.

Little is more dismaying than the way in which some, a few, in the intellectual community have rejected the life of reason, have succumbed to the national susceptibility for hatred and violence, have, indeed, begun themselves to exalt hatred and violence as if primitivism in emotion constituted a higher morality.

I do not suggest that such intellectuals are responsible for the atrocities committed at home and abroad. I do suggest that they have contributed to the atmosphere in which hatred and violence are not only tolerated but prized. I do suggest that they are reinforcing the assault on civility and hastening the decomposition of the American social process.

Some wonder, no doubt, whether that social process is worth saving. But the alternative to process is anarchy, where those who dispose of the means of violence win out; and the intellectual community has never disposed of the means of violence. Our process, with all its defects, is a process of change—a process of peaceful change—on which all decency and rationality depend.

Let me make it clear that I am not talking about the student uprisings of recent weeks. I have no question that on balance the world stands to gain from student protest. No doubt such protest has on occasion led to excess. But it is already a shameful state of affairs when excess proves the only way of attracting the attention of complacent administrations and indifferent faculties to the problems and perplexities of the coming generation.

The causes of student insurgency vary from college to college, and from country to country. It would seem likely that the primary incitement in our own nation has been the war in Vietnam—a war which has tempted our government into its course of appalling and insensate destruction, a war which, through the draft, has demanded that young Americans kill and die where they can see no rational relationship between personal sacrifice and national interest. But the cause is also more than the Vietnam war. For that war has come for many to pre-figure a larger incomprehensibility, a larger absurdity, even a larger wickedness, in our official society. For some it has come to seem, not an aberration, but the inevitable result of the irremediable corruption of the American system.

I cannot share the belief that there was something foreordained and ineluctable about the war in Vietnam—that the nature of American society would have compelled any set of men in Washington to pursue the same course of folly. This really seems determinist nonsense. One can still understand, though, why the contradictions of our society weigh so heavily on the young—the contradictions between the righteousness of a Secretary of State and the ruthlessness of a B-52; between the notion that violence is fine against simple folk ten thousand miles away and shocking against injustice in our own land; between the equality demanded by our constitutional structure and the equality denied by our social structure; even between the accepted habits of one generation and the emerging habits of the next, as when a parent tipsy on his fourth martini begins a tirade against marijuana.

The very weight of these contradictions produced a rush of despair about libertarian democracy itself. By libertarian democracy I mean simply the system in which the rule of the majority at any given time rests on the guarantee of the right of minorities to convert themselves into new majorities. Such a system assumes political action to be in its essence a rational process—that is, a deliberate choice of means to achieve desired ends. As a rational process, libertarian democracy requires the widest possible freedom of discussion and debate; and this implies, of course, a considerable indulgence of wrongheadedness and imbecility along the way.

This has been the American theory, as laid down, for example, in the Constitution and the Bill of Rights. And, in the course of our national history, libertarian democracy has led to many useful results. It has also led to many frustrations. It has left problems unsolved, wrongs unredressed, and sinners unpunished. It cannot be relied upon to produce rapid and conclusive change. The very insistence on reasonableness and due process has seemed at times a pretext for inaction and therefore a mask for injustice. This has been particularly the case in recent years. From the moment we started bombing North Vietnam in February, 1965, our government appeared rigidly and sanctimoniously unresponsive to reasoned criticism of its course. Increasingly persuaded that change was impossible within the constitutional order, people started to turn to civil disobedience, emotional agitation, and even violent protest. A sense began to arise that libertarian democracy itself was impotent in the new world of economic, military, and intellectual corporatism. One saw a growing conviction, especially among the young, that party politics were a facade and a fake. One saw a growing cynicism about democratic institutions, a growing defection from the democratic process. In due course, the spreading sense of the impotence of libertarian democracy generated a creed systematically and candidly opposed to libertarian democracy.

The new creed has two parts. The first part is an attempt to clear away what its theorists regard as the noxious rubbish of the Bill of Rights. The new creed thus perceives the First Amendment as the keystone, not of liberty, but of a wicked apparatus of tolerance employed by an oppressive social order to resist basic change. I do not wish to do this new doctrine an injustice, so I will state in the words of its leading advocate—that is, Herbert Marcuse—the belief that it is *necessary* and *right,* as a matter of principle, to suppress views with which one disagrees and to howl down those who utter such views.

Marcuse begins with the proposition that contemporary society, in his idiom, is defined by "the passing of the historical forces which, at the preceding stage of society, seemed to represent the possibility of new forms of existence." In other words, contemporary society has absorbed and abolished the historic means of social revolution. It has learned the secret of "containing social change—qualitative change which would establish essentially different institutions, a new direction of the productive process, new modes of human existence."

The strategy by which contemporary society achieves these results, Marcuse argues, is through a system of indoctrination and manipulation made possible by an ingenious and despicable combination of welfarism and tolerance. Capitalism, in short, buys off potential opponents by offering a measure of apparent economic security and personal freedom. Marcuse regards this as a terrible state of affairs. As he sees it, any improvement in the condition of the powerless and the oppressed only plays into the hands of the rulers—and is therefore to be regretted. And the evil device of tolerance renders "the traditional ways and means of protest ineffective—perhaps even dangerous because they preserve the illusion of popular sovereignty."

Tolerance is evil because it dissipates the force of protest. It is also evil because it permits the promulgation of evil ideas. Therefore, Marcuse suggests, the way to revive the possibilities of social change is to strike at the root of the evil. He is candid about his repudiation of the Bill of Rights.

> The traditional criterion of clear and present danger seems no longer adequate to a stage where the whole society is in the situation of the theater audience when somebody cries: "fire." . . . The whole post-fascist period is one of clear and present danger. Consequently, true pacification requires the withdrawal of tolerance before the deed, at the stage of communication in word, print, and picture. . . . Certain things cannot be said, certain ideas cannot be expressed, certain policies cannot be proposed, certain behavior cannot be permitted without making tolerance an instrument for the continuation of servitude.

And he is specific about what he would forbid. His program, as he states it,

> would include the withdrawal of toleration of speech and assembly from groups and movements which promote aggressive policies, armament, chauvinism, discrimination on the grounds of race and religion, or which oppose the extension of public services, medical care, etc. Moreover, the restoration of freedom of thought may necessitate new and rigid restrictions on teachings and practices in the educational institutions.

Marcuse's call for the forcible suppression of false ideas is, I have suggested, only the first part of the new creed. Nor is such an assault on the Bill of Rights new, even for radicals. The Stalinists of the Thirties, for example, had no compunction in arguing in much the same way that civil freedom should be denied those who resist the Stalinist truth. What particularly distinguishes the New Left of the Sixties from previous American radicalisms is the second part of its creed—and here not the summons to revolution, which again is familiar, but the refusal to state revolutionary goals except in the most abstract and empty language. To put it more precisely, what distinguishes the New Left is not only its unwillingness to define what it aims for after the revolution but its belief that such reticence is a virtue.

In its positive side, the new creed becomes, so to speak, a kind of existentialism in politics—a primitive kind, no doubt, but still rooted in some manner in the existential perception that man dwells in an absurd universe and defines himself through his choices. In extreme cases, this perception may lead to *voyages au bout de la nuit:* As Nietzsche said, "Nihilism represents the ultimate logical conclusion of our great values and ideals—because we must experience nihilism before we can find out what value these 'values' really had." In its serious form, existentialism can lead to an immense and intense sense of individual responsibility as every man realizes that only he can provide his own escape from the enveloping nothingness around him. In its vulgar form, however, with which we are dealing here, existential politics becomes the notion that we must feel and act before we think; it is the illusion that the experience of feeling and action will produce the insight and the policy.

Existential politics in this form springs much more from Sorel than from Kierkegaard. Sorel, you will recall, drew a distinction between myths, which, he said, were "not descriptions of things, but expressions of a determination to act," and utopias, which were intellectual products, the work of theorists who "seek to establish a model to which they can compare existing society." Sorel regarded utopias—that is, rational programs—as contemptible. The myth must be the basis of action; the myth would produce the revolution, which would then produce its own program; and "the myth," Sorel emphasized, "must be judged as a means of acting on the present; any attempt to discuss how far it can be taken literally as future history is devoid of sense." So, in the footsteps of Sorel, the New Leftists believe in the omnipotence of the deed and the irrelevance of the goal. The political process is no longer seen as the deliberate choice of means to move toward a desired end. Where libertarian democracy had ideally demanded means consistent with the end, and where the Stalinist left of the Thirties contended that the end justified the means, the New Left propounds a different doctrine: that the means create the end.

Let us not ignore the attractions of the existential approach. After all, there are many absurdities in our world. Our country has never undertaken any thing more absurd in its history than the Vietnam war. After all, a man does make himself by his decisions. After all, our conventional liberalism is to a discouraging degree a liberalism of promises and excuses. After all, social renewal can only come from personal commitment.

All these things help explain, I think, the appeal of the new creed. Yet this creed contains so much in the way of fakery and fallacy—to put it bluntly, it is so preposterous and so depraved—that I do not see how it can be long entertained by any serious democrat.

Let us look first at the negative part: the demand for the forcible suppression of false ideas. This immediately raises a self-evident question: How is one to tell which ideas are admissible and which are to be suppressed? "In the interplay of theory and practice," Marcuse replies, "true and false solutions become distinguishable. . . . Freedom is liberation, a specific historical process in theory and practice, and as such it has its right and wrong, its truth and falsehood." But who is to make this determination? What agency is the repository of final judgment on truth and falsehood? Here, alas, Marcuse lets us down, except to introduce hopelessly vague standards, as, for example, that "what is *not* conducive to a free and rational society, what impedes and distorts the possibilities of its creation" should be forbidden; in the end, he places his confidence in what he mystically calls "the democratic educational dictatorship of free men."

This is not very satisfactory; so let us pursue the question a step further. I suppose that the new creed does not expect to make such judgments through a man. But, if not through a man, these judgments must be made through a mechanism, which means through men. Such a mechanism would plainly have to have an extraordinary degree of power. What assurance can there ever be that this power would be used disinterestedly—that is, for the good and the true, should there ever be a means of defining the good and the true—rather than in the interests of the men operating the mechanism? What will this mechanism become—

what have such mechanisms ever become—but a means for the suppression of all criticism of the manipulators of the mechanism? So the mechanism, in the end, rests on an assumption of human infallibility.

But the assumption of human infallibility has never been justified in the long and varied history of mankind. It implies the rule of those whom Mr. Dooley long ago defined as men who do what they think "th' Lord wud do if He only knew the facts of th' case"—and Mr. Dooley was defining a fanatic. Jefferson in his First Inaugural made a relevant comment:

> Sometimes it is said that man cannot be trusted with the government of himself. Can he, then, be trusted with the government of others? Or have we found angels in the form of kings to govern him? Let history answer this question.

History has answered the question: Man has never found angels in the form of kings, or even of philosopher-kings, to govern him. And, if he should, "the unfortunate thing," Pascal said, "is that he who would act the angel acts the brute."

Not only do men who claim infallibilty in politics do far more evil than good, but the systematic suppression of supposedly false ideas would deeply constrict and impoverish human knowledge and understanding. "There is no error so crooked," Tupper said, "but it hath in it some lines of truth." Or, as Norman Mailer recently put it, "Sometimes a profound idea is buried in a particularly ugly notion." Human creativity takes a marvelous and sinister diversity of forms. How dare anyone assume the right to censor and deny the unlimited freedom of human expression? "I tolerate with the utmost latitude the right of others to differ from me in opinion without imputing to them criminality," wrote Jefferson. "I know too well the weakness and uncertainty of human reason to wonder at its different result."

The demand for the forcible suppression of "false" ideas would be an enormously effective way of calling a halt to human progress. Nor does the other half of the new creed make any more sense: that is, the conviction that one should feel and act first and think later, that the means create the end. The kind of action supremely required to strike through the mask of official society, we are told, is violence. Without violence, official society, in its present sophisticated condition, will calmly co-opt and emasculate the opposition. Only violence will force official society to drop the amiable mask of tolerance and reveal its inner viciousness. More than this, violence becomes a means of social and individual redemption. As Franz Fanon has written, "Violence is a cleaning force. It frees the native from his inferiority complex and from his despair and inaction; it makes him fearless and restores his self-respect. . . . Violence alone, violence committed by the people, violence organized and educated by its leaders, makes it possible for the masses to understand social truths."

This is hardly, of course, a new doctrine. Others in this century have propagated the cult of the deed. It was, after all, Mussolini who used to distinguish between "a violence that liberates and a violence that enslaves . . . a violence that is moral and a violence that is immoral." And it was Hitler who wrote, "The very first essential for success is a perpetually constant and regular employment of violence." It is perfectly obvious why Mussolini and Hitler favored violence: It is because violence, by abolishing the procedures and civilities of society, opens the way for those who are most successful in the use of force. I do not know about the situation in developing countries; there violence in certain contexts may have the benign effects claimed by Fanon. But surely little is more pathetic than the view that violence in American society will benefit the left. A limited amount of violence may stimulate the process of democratic change; but, if the left, through the cult of the deed, helps create an atmosphere which destroys the process of democracy itself, the only beneficiaries will be those on the right.

The new creed, with its dismissal of free discussion and its conviction that violence will mystically generate policy and program, represents an assault on rationality in politics—an assault based on the ultimate proposition that rights and wrongs in public affairs are so absolute and so easily ascertainable that opposition can be legitimately destroyed. This assault on the Bill of Rights and on libertarian democracy is in my judgment wrong, because no one is infallible. It is stupid, because the beneficiaries of this view will not be the idealists of the left but the brutalists of the right. It is dangerous because it represents a reversion to and rationalization of the strain of hatred and violence in our own national tradition: the politics of lynch law against the politics of Lincoln. It is a vote for the worst against the best in our political ethos.

The new creed above all overlooks the fact of human frailty. "Men are not flattered," wrote Lincoln, "by being shown that there has been a difference of purpose between the Almighty and them." Yet men are not gods. That is why absolutism always fails in human society. Democracy requires consent—it insists, that is, that a majority of the electorate be persuaded that one course is preferable to another. If men or mechanisms were infallible, there would be no need for persuasion. But, because they are not, the discipline of consent is indispensable to civilized society. The discipline of consent means that policies must triumph not through divine right or through a "democratic educational dictatorship" but through making sense to a majority of the people; and the condition of bringing a majority along is the best guarantee that policies relate, not to personal fantasy or personal power, but to the greatest good of the greatest number.

This discussion of the new creed may seem irrelevant to the pragmatic insurgencies of our society. And, indeed, so long as these insurgencies remain pragmatic—that is, related to specific issues and specific injustices—they represent a desperately needed pressure against the established complacencies of a self-righteous nation. Yet the new creed exists; it has received serious, if not convincing, formulation; it has won support because of the spreading sense in recent years of the impotence of libertarian democracy; and it has created among some of the young a mystical passion for revolutionary upheaval.

I have said that the new creed will only weaken democracy against its enemies. I would say further that it underestimates the power of rational democracy—that is, the power of the people, in one way or another, to modify the system and alter its course. We have had, I noted earlier, a season of despair about our democracy. But those whom despair led on to desperation underestimated the capacity of public opinion eventually to catch on to what is happening, even in fairly controlled and manipulated societies, and to demand a change in things. This has happened even in authoritarian states, like France. It has happened even in Communist states, like Czechoslovakia. And it has happened in our own country.

Here the democratic process has turned out to be more effective than its critics had supposed. The rebellion against libertarian democracy gathered momentum, we have noted, because of the obstinate and righteous determination of our government to pursue a policy of military escalation in Vietnam. Yet in the last six months the democratic process, working in its own inscrutable way, has forced the President to abandon—for a moment, at least—the escalation policy; it has forced him to begin serious peace talks; it has forced him to withdraw from the presidential contest. These are not inconsiderable accomplishments.

I do not contend that the process works swiftly. Obviously, if President Johnson had given his March 31 speech a year earlier, many Americans and Vietnamese now dead might be alive; and the evidence against the escalation policy was just as strong on March 31, 1967, as it was on March 31, 1968. Nor do I contend that the process works surely. There is no guarantee against the re-escalation of the war. Nor is there any guarantee, given the irresponsibility of the romantic left, against the election of a President committed to continue the persons and policies against which the rebellion began. Nor, alas, is there any guarantee against the resurgence of violence, bloodshed, and murder. Yet, with all its tardiness and inconclusiveness, democracy in America continues to show a certain vitality and efficacy. "The sober, second thought of the people," as Martin Van Buren said years ago, "is never wrong, and always efficient." At any rate, it is wiser in the long run than the certitudes of the absolutists.

Nietzsche once wrote, "Gaze not too deeply into the abyss, lest the abyss gaze into you." Those who claim to be bearers of absolute truth are men who have gazed too deeply into the abyss. They have committed what Hawthorne called the Unpardonable Sin—the sin of self-pride, which destroys discrimination, enslaves people, breeds fanaticism and violence, and concludes in madness and catastrophe. It is sad when the derelicts of our society surrender to the Unpardonable Sin; it is despicable when our intellectuals exemplify it. Let us strike out against the concrete and particular evils of our time. But let us not yield to that awful despair which dissolves all distinctions in thought and action and rushes us on to the politics of apocalypse. In the long run, any sane society must rest on freedom and reason. If we abandon this, we abandon everything.

If we are to survive as a nation, we must resist our inbred impulse to violence, not capitulate to it, not celebrate it. We must resist our inbred impulse to intolerance. We must resist our inbred impulse to absolutism. As we identify these impulses, as we strive against them wherever they appear—whether in the gutter press or in the abstractions of intellectuals—we create a chance of defying the winds of unreason. But we cannot suppose that this problem will solve itself. We must, indeed, define ourselves by our choices, but do so by making the choices which respect human reason and human dignity—the choices which acknowledge and nourish the human capacity for mutual respect and affection.

S. L. HALLECK | *Hypotheses of Student Unrest*

Students can no longer be taken for granted. It does not matter that a great majority of students remain largely content, conservative, and apathetic. A determined minority of restless college students has forced us to examine and sometimes change institutions, rules, and values which were once considered inviolate.

The most significant aspects of student unrest can be described as follows:

1. Some students reject the political and economic status quo and are

making vigorous attempts to change the structure of our society. These are the student activists.

2. Some students reject the values of their society as well as the values of their own past and are developing a style of life which is contradictory to the Western ethics of hard work, self-denial, success, and responsibility. These students sometimes participate in efforts to change the society, but for the most part they are withdrawn and passive. They can be described as alienated.

3. Both activist and alienated students tend to come from affluent middle- or upper-class homes. They are sensitive and perceptive individuals. They are also highly intelligent.

4. Both activist and alienated students have difficulty in relating to the adult generation. They are articulate, irreverent, humorless, and relentless in their contempt for what they view as adult hypocrisy. Such youth are highly peer-oriented. They turn to one another rather than their parents when shaping their belief systems or when seeking emotional support.

5. Alienated students and, to a lesser extent, activist students find it difficult to sustain goal-directed activity. Their capacity to organize for any kind of action is limited. They often fail at work or school. Even their political efforts seem highly disorganized.

6. Alienated students live at the edge of despair. Although they seem at times to be enjoying life, there is always a sense of foreboding about them. Often they become depressed and suicidal. Activist students are more emotionally stable but are also prone to deep feelings of hopelessness and self-pity.

There is no dearth of explanations of the above phenomena. Some explanations seem to be based on opinions which support the prejudices of differing political viewpoints. Others are more scientific and are presented with analytic objectivity. No hypothesis thus far advanced can be considered a sufficient explanation of student unrest. At best, each is only a partial explanation which sheds only a small light upon highly complex phenomena.

Certain propositions often made about students are not hypotheses but are value judgments. The unsupported statement that the behavior of our restless youth represents a healthy and sensible response to the corruptions of our world is exhortative rather than explanatory. Such a position is embraced by those who are discontent with the status quo and wish to emphasize and exploit student restlessness as a phenomenon that justifies their own grievances. Similarly, unsupported statements that students are more emotionally disturbed than they had used to be have no explanatory value. Implying that students act as they do because they are mentally ill serves to demean their behavior by casting doubts upon the validity of the messages which that behavior is designed to communicate.

A more interesting proposition concerning student unrest is that it is neither new nor exceptional. Precedents can be cited which suggest that there were times in our history when students were even more restless than they are now. Periods of unrest do seem to run in cycles, and it is conceivable that we happen to be in an active phase of a predictable cycle. This proposition is reassuring to those who look forward to a quiet future. Its weakness, however, is that it assumes that those forces which make for cyclical behavior will remain relatively constant. My own opinion is that the world is changing so rapidly that using historical precedents to predict future behavior is a risky business. We can deplore student unrest or we can welcome it, but we cannot ignore it or simply wait for it to go away.

The Critical Hypothesis. Those who are critical of student activism and alienation are most likely to seek its causes in factors which they believe have created a moral weakness in our youth. They believe students are restless because they lack discipline, values, or purpose. These deficiencies are believed to originate within the disturbed family, particularly that family which has been influenced by affluence, liberal thinking, and modern psychological notions of child rearing. While these hypotheses may also appeal to those who are sympathetic toward students, they are primarily critical in the sense that they imply that something is wrong with those students who protest or withdraw.

The Permissiveness Hypothesis. Perhaps the commonest explanation of student unrest is that it is the result of too much permissiveness in rearing children. The proponents of this view argue that some parents have, through painstaking efforts to avoid creating neuroses in their children, abdicated their responsibility to teach and discipline their children. In so doing they have reared a generation of spoiled, greedy youth who are unable to tolerate the slightest frustration without showing an angry or infantile response.

Although the permissiveness hypothesis has been used in the most crude manner to berate and deplore the behavior of youth, it cannot be lightly dismissed. There is considerable evidence that activist and alienated students are members of well-educated families, deeply committed to liberal doctrines. In such homes children are given unusual freedom to criticize, debate, and question. Restless students also have frequently attended primary and secondary schools dedicated to the ideal of progressive education, schools which in their efforts to maximize freedom and creativity seek to minimize discipline and frustration.

It can, of course, be argued that children raised in permissive homes will be better citizens than those raised in stricter homes. Restless students do seem to be more open to ideas, more involved with social issues, and more flexible than their peers. The critics, however, can point to other characteristics of restless students which seem to be related to their permissive upbringing, and which are not so healthy. The response of such students to discipline, for example, is in no useful sense adaptive. Arbitrary regulations enrage them. Even rational forms of discipline, such as the need to master basic concepts before moving on to more abstract ideas, bother them. Restless students also react inappropriately when their demands are not immediately accepted. They are prone at such moments to protest violently, to give up and withdraw, or to wrap themselves in a cloak of despair. Much of their abrasiveness and much of their ineffectiveness can be explained by their uncompromising demands for immediate gratification. This inability to tolerate frustration or delay must be considered a weakness or defect.

The Non-Responsibility Hypothesis. Many who are concerned about the dangers of permissiveness also believe that our culture has been "psychologized" to an extent where youth become unwilling to assume responsibility for their own behavior. The expansion of the social and psychological sciences has confronted the public with elaborate deterministic explanations of behavior. When a behavior is totally explained, there is a tendency for people to act as though they are no longer responsible for that behavior. They confuse the theoretical issue of scientific determinism with the society's practical needs to have its citizens remain accountable for their own actions.

When the sociologist documents the impact of poverty and discrimination upon Negro youth, he is conducting a logical and scientific exercise. The subjects of his research, however, are tempted to utilize his findings to support an individual and collective feeling of responsibility. The Negro adolescent who participates in a riot, for example, might say, "How could I do otherwise? I am moved by forces over which I have no control." Psychological explanations are also utilized to avoid accountability. It is becoming more common to hear criminals say, "I should not be held responsible for what I have done because I am neurotic or mentally ill."

Psychiatry, particularly Freudian psychiatry, has been maligned as a critical agent in producing a climate of non-responsibility. While there is nothing in the theoretical doctrines of psychoanalysis which favors abdicating personal responsibility, it does seem that the psychiatrist's ability to expand and legitimize the mental illness role has had an impact on the manner in which people view the question of responsibility. Behavior once considered bad is now considered sick. Sickness implies that one cannot help himself or that one is not responsible for his actions. The proponents of the non-responsibility hypothesis would argue that by expanding the sick role to include forms of behavior that were once considered in terms of good or bad, the healing professions have helped to create a social climate in which more people manage to avoid accountability for their actions. Youth growing up in such a society are tempted to behave in a pleasure-seeking, antisocial, and irresponsible manner. Many feel that this is exactly what restless students are doing.

The evidence that activist and alienated youth are deeply influenced by a climate of irresponsibility is inconclusive. Some activist students are often impressively willing to hold themselves accountable for their actions. On the other hand, most alienated students are not. They tend to seek medical or psychiatric excuses from their obligations at the first sign of stress. They also have a discouraging tendency to break laws and to insist that their own personal needs and problems are such that they should not be held accountable for these actions. It is almost as if they say, "Because the world is so bad and because it has treated me so badly, I cannot be blamed for my actions. There is no point in holding me accountable for things which I cannot help doing anyway."

The Affluence Hypothesis. A third hypothesis which appeals to critics of student unrest is based on the alleged hazards of growing up in an affluent society. It is sometimes argued that affluence which is unearned, and which is unaccompanied by a tradition of service and commitment, creates a sense of restlessness, boredom, and meaninglessness in our youth. The child raised in an affluent society has difficulty finding useful goals. He does not learn to use work or creativity as a means of mastering some aspect of the world. He, therefore, according to this argument, is trapped in a never-ending search for new diversions and new freedoms which sooner or later begin to feel sterile and ungratifying.

It does seem likely that man is less likely to be troubled if he is distracted by some monumental task which dominates his life goals. In a relatively poor society, the very need for survival creates a structured and seemingly purposeful life. In an affluent society, man has the time and freedom to contemplate the meaning of his existence. Many restless students do come from affluent homes and many have decided that their lives are devoid of meaning. Sometimes it seems that their provocative behavior is designed primarily to invent new struggles and even imaginary hardships which will free them from their lethargy and help them atone for their guilt over "having it so good."

The affluence hypothesis has certain undertones of criticism directed towards the parents of restless students. Affluence, after all, does not always produce protest or indolence. Traditionally, many of our most useful public servants have been products of wealthy homes. The critics of student unrest would reserve their harshest barbs for those newly affluent parents who have themselves become so caught up in materialistic, pleasure-seeking life that they have failed to meet their responsibility of teaching children the kinds of values which would lend meaning to a young person's existence.

The Family-Pathology Hypothesis. A number of explanations of student unrest focus upon the disturbed family. According to these hypotheses, activist and alienated students behave as they do because they are responding to an unresolved conflict within the family unit. It is usually suggested that the restless student has been subjected to too much pressure by his parents or is "acting out" a need of his parents. A more general approach to the problem focuses upon a family structure in which the father is a weak or shadowy figure. This approach emphasizes the breakdown in authority of the paternal figure, the confusion of sexual roles in our society, and the break with tradition which such confusion produces.

The evidence for the existence of a high degree of pathology in the families of restless students is inconclusive. Sociological studies of students and their families do not support any family-pathology hypothesis. In fact, such studies suggest that activist students, at least, come from rather stable families.

Psychiatrists, on the other hand, find some evidence of serious familial conflict in most of the families of restless students they treat. It must be emphasized, however, that the psychiatrist deals with only a small proportion of such students.

If family disorganization is an important cause of student unrest, the manner in which it exerts its influence must be complex and subtle. Sociological techniques are simply too superficial to get at the complexities of the problem. The findings of psychiatrists are based on depth explorations which may be valid for some families but which cannot be generalized. Neither sociologists nor psychiatrists can provide valid answers. The most we can say is that some aspects of student restlessness may be directly related to family pathology. Certainly, it is conceivable that in today's highly charged social climate, even minimal family disturbances may be translated into highly provocative behavior.

Sympathetic Hypotheses. The next group of hypotheses put the student in a favorable light. They view him as a victim of man-made circumstances and maintain that student unrest is a legitimate and rational effort to change these circumstances. The student is viewed as either a helpless victim of a world he never created or as a hero seeking to cleanse the world of the evils of previous generations. To be useful, these hypotheses must not simply define what is wrong with the world but must suggest how various factors have made students more capable of perceiving and acting upon the injustices and irrationalities of our world.

The Two-Armed-Camps Hypothesis. This generation of students has grown in an age when the world has been divided into two large camps which compete with each other ideologically, politically, and sometimes militarily. Since the Russians launched their first satellite, the competition has also been educational. Students today are trained in a school system which emphasizes the competitive acquisition of knowledge as a source of power and stability. By the time they leave high school they are better educated than any previous generation of students, but they are also more overworked.

All of this emphasis on education and competition is not easily sustained after the student arrives at the university. By this time he is at least partially "burned out." The personal benefits of intensive studying and searching for a profitable career begin to appear less attractive in an affluent world and particularly in a world which seems to be making it increasingly difficult for a young person to become an integral part of the economic system. As the student comes to view objectively the implications of our competitiveness with communism as a never-ending phenomenon, he also begins to question the social value of his efforts. Even if he maintains enthusiasm for academic work through the undergraduate years, by the time the student reaches graduate school he increasingly asks himself whether the competitive search for knowledge is worth it. At this point he begins to view our competition with the Communist world (and sometimes competitiveness itself) as a form of mass paranoia, and he views the university as an agent of a government which contributes towards the perpetuation of the paranoid system. He reacts by protest or withdrawal.

The War-in-Vietnam Hypothesis. Although student unrest began long before the war in Vietnam ever escalated to massive proportions, there can be little doubt that in the past few years this conflict has been the major factor influencing the behavior of students. The war is particularly unpopular on our campuses. A large proportion of students, perhaps the majority, see it as a misguided effort. A significant minority see it as wholly immoral. Much of the restless behavior of students can be directly related to their efforts to do something to stop the war or to their sense of total frustration when they feel powerless to stop it.

The draft and the inequities engendered by the "S" deferment also contribute to unrest. The major issue here is fear. The average male student is plagued with fears that he will fail in school, will be drafted, and will run the risks of being killed in a conflict he may not consider vital to our interests. A second issue is guilt. The university student knows that he is spared from military service only because he is richer or smarter than someone else. While he may believe that the war is immoral, he also knows that his privileged status is immoral. When he accepts the 2S status he suffers guilt. Much of the activism on our campuses is a means of atoning for that guilt. Much of the alienation on our campuses is a means of denying the relevance of the society that created such guilt.

Students also feel some shame in not participating in those aspects of military service that might make them feel more masculine. It is rare for anyone even in peacetime to embrace military service eagerly, and a normal late-adolescent has justifiable concern with interrupting his career to face the harshness of life in the service. The unpopularity of this war gives the student a cogent reason for avoiding military service, but it does not resolve his nagging fears that he is somehow or other being cowardly or less masculine by being treated specially.

It is also true that the anti-war climate on our campuses makes the student progressively more disinclined to serve in this war the longer he remains on campus. Education breeds a dislike of violence. Furthermore, whatever romantic thoughts a young man may have about the war at the age of 18 are somewhat attenuated with a year or two of maturation. Students spend many hours arguing about the war, the draft, and means of avoiding the draft. This preoccupation creates a highly tense situation in which the student feels supported only by his peer groups. He begins to relate to subcultures which become progressively more separated from the rest of the nation and particularly from the adult generation.

The Deterioration-in-the-Quality-of-Life Hypothesis. There are many who believe that student unrest is an appropriate response to the deterioration of the quality of life in America. Overpopulation which results in crowds, traffic jams, and businesses run on the basis of mass production has taken much of the joy out of life in our towns and cities. Personal care or service is hard to find in any shop, restaurant, or hotel. People begin to feel faceless and insignificant.

Students, it can be argued, are among the first to sense the painful anonymity associated with bigness. This is a particularly serious problem on overcrowded campuses where students are generally isolated from their teachers and other adults. A sense of student-faculty intimacy or a sense of scholarly community are sorely lacking on most of our large campuses. Students find it difficult to develop a sense of identification or loyalty towards a university that they perceive as monolithic and impersonal. In their complaints that they are treated like numbers or IBM cards they strike a poignant note for all of us.

Overcrowding is only a relative thing and would not be so destructive if it were not for the manner in which we have incredibly neglected the planning and development of town and country. Our cities grow with no respect for the land. Beauty and wilderness are easy prey for the builder and contractor. Clean air and clear streams are almost a thing of the past. An adolescent who grows up in a world in which we must sit back and watch beauty fade and pollution gain comes to despair of the future.

One way of looking at student unrest is as a massive reaction to the destruction of that kind of world and way of life which their forebears enjoyed but which will be denied to them. It is not uncommon to hear a student say to an adult, "In your world life had some hope and meaning, but in the world you have left me these qualities are gone."

The Political-Hopelessness Hypothesis. Many individuals see our mass society as immutable. It has been argued that our society is so complex, our systems of checks and balances so intricate, and our interplay of pressure groups so self-equalizing that really effective change is no longer possible. Our business-oriented economy has so indoctrinated us in the role of credit-bound consumers that we are all beholden to a way of life which may not be in our best interests. An increasing number of radical students are convinced that the forces of government, industry, and education are totally interdependent and allied to one another for the purpose of warding off any reasonable attempts to change the society. They believe that a system of life has developed in our country which simply absorbs legal efforts to change our society, even protest, in a manner which ultimately preserves the status quo.[1]

Guided by the philosophy of Herbert Marcuse, many students are convinced that constructive change within our society is not possible by working through the system. They do not have any sort of vision as to what will replace the old order, but they are convinced that our society is fundamentally irrational and must be destroyed. They do not reject illegal acts or even violence as agents of destruction.

The Civil-Rights Hypothesis. The civil rights movement not only increased youth's awareness of an historical injustice which made it difficult for them to be proud of this country, but also served as a training ground for future radicals. The new campus protest began at Berkeley when students demanded the right to work freely on their own campuses on behalf of oppressed Negroes. Many campus radicals shaped their images of "the Establishment" and of unreasonable authority on the basis of their early work in the civil rights movement. Students throughout the country have developed an amazing empathy and identification with Negroes. Their commitment to the Negro cause has taught them the psychological meaning of oppression and has encouraged them to seek out and attack sources of oppression in their own lives.

Neutral Hypotheses. Some explanations of student unrest focus upon impersonal processes. The causes of unrest, according to these hypotheses, are not to be found in the actions or philosophies of other men, but are believed to reside in changes in our highly complex society which seem to create the need for new modes of psychological adaptation.

The Technology Hypothesis. Man has always lived with hope, particularly with the hope that his efforts in the present will be rewarded with gratification in the future. A certain degree of predictability in the future enables one to make commitments to goals and to other people. To the extent that we live in a society in which past, present, and future lose their interrelatedness, the power of hope to shape man's behavior is di-

[1] In this regard it is somewhat distressing to note the manner in which hippies and protesters have not only been institutionalized as part of our folklore and humor but have been exploited by the advertising industry, an institution which they initially intended to destroy.

minished. New means of adapting to the world must then be found and the manner in which people relate to one another must be profoundly altered.

Postwar America has been characterized by a massive and continuous growth of technology. Our society is one in which the conditions of everyday life are constantly changing. Moreover, the rate at which technology changes our lives is itself increasing. No one can predict what life will be like in 20 years, 10 years, or even five years. Today's knowledge, today's work skills, and today's values may be totally irrelevant to tomorrow's world. Kenneth Kenniston has described the manner in which some youth, who, when exposed to an ever-increasing rate of technological growth, come to perceive that the values of the past will be totally inappropriate for the world in which they will be adults. Moreover, they feel powerless to anticipate or direct the future. In this environment hope no longer sustains. It is adaptive to be cool, and to learn to live in the present.

What are the advantages and disadvantages of living in the present? The advantages are more or less obvious. One is more flexible, and superficially at least more comfortable. It is not necessary to delay gratification, nor need one allow himself to be tortured by the mistakes of the past nor be deluded by unrealistic hopes for the future. The disadvantages of life in the present are more subtle, yet more powerful. To live in the present one must narrow his commitments. He must travel lightly and be ready for anything. More intimate relationships are unlikely, since they cannot be sustained by reference to past experience or to promises of a better future. Passion and romantic longing must be avoided because they may breed pain or impair one's flexibility. In short, if carried to extremes, life in the present is a selfish life which is incompatible with the growth of that intimacy and passion which man has always found to be essential to a fulfilled life.

Distrust of the future and a determination to live in the present seem to be characteristic of both activist and alienated students. The student activist seeks immediate change and has difficulty in developing the patience or optimism for long-term planning. The alienated student adopts the philosophy of the hippie. Believing that the only certainty in life is change, or uncertainty itself, he adapts by "doing his own thing" and behaves as though he is responsible only to himself.

The Media Hypotheses. There are several hypotheses that attempt to relate the growth of new media, particularly television, to the troubling behavior of students. It can be argued, for example, that simply by being available to publicize the activities of protesters and hippies the media exaggerate the importance of these groups. The television camera forces all of us to take seriously forms of behavior that might have been dismissed lightly in earlier decades. Conceivably the medium may be creating a "climate of expectation" in which youth are subtly seduced into dissenting roles which may not represent their actual interests.

It is also true that many television commercials, radio ads, and most modern music are directed toward the youth market. The self-consciousness of youth is thereby heightened. Young people are made more aware of their potentialities and sometimes develop an exaggerated sense of their own power.

Another attempt to relate changing media to student unrest has been implied in the writings of Marshall McLuhan. McLuhan believes that electronic media are bringing us all closer together in a more truly communal and shared society than ever existed. Our youth who have grown up with the new media are ready for such a society. Elders who are committed to sustain the institutions of the past are not. Much of youthful rebellion can then be visualized as an effort to make older people see that the world has changed and that many of the values of the past are now irrelevant.

While McLuhan's hypothesis has some attractiveness, it does not seem as plausible as those which focus upon the psychological impact of the content of various media. Fredric Wertham believes that the massive degree of violence which young people see on television makes them more violent and less responsible. Vance Packard has argued that chronic exposure to the values implied in TV commercials could create a generation of unrealistic, demanding, and present-oriented youth.

I would like to propose my own hypothesis of student unrest based on the manner in which the media influence the character structure of youth by prematurely confronting them with the harsh truths and realities of life, as follows:

As an animal whose growth and development requires him to be dependent upon others for a long period of time, man learns to rely on others for an optimal amount of structure and order in his life. It is obvious that authority is not always benevolent or just, and yet it is true that no man can be at ease if he does not commit a part of himself to some authority, whether it be his church, his family, his government, or an ideology. Nor can one come to develop a firm sense of who he is without making such commitments. It is at least partly through experiencing limitations which are imposed by others, by respecting others, and by emulating those who are respected that one finds his own identity. The process by which one comes to terms with authority is not always deliberate or rational. Sometimes even benevolent authority relies on faith, mystique, or untruth to retain its control.

This is especially relevant to the situation of young people. The most well-meaning parents must on occasion deceive their children because they know that children would find many of the hard and cynical facts of life to be unbearable. Until recently it was possible for young people to begin to experience the world as adults know it only after they had reached adolescence. Most of the time the adolescent absorbed this new knowledge gradually and painlessly. Even when he did feel that his parents had been hypocritical or had deceived him, his awareness of their dishonesty came so gradually that his resentment and rebelliousness were restrained. Today it is different. One of the significant developments in postwar America has been the influence of mass-communication media (particularly television) which are capable of disseminating information to all age groups immediately.

Even before adolescence, television acquaints youth with the cynical facts of life at a time when such truths may be indigestible. Other media communicate knowledge so quickly now that there is little opportunity for anyone to live comfortably with myth or self-delusion. Beliefs which were once casually accepted are vigorously scrutinized. The belief that there is equality for all Americans can hardly be sustained when one has a front-row seat from which he can observe the Negro's unsuccessful struggle to maintain a decent life in this country. Blind faith in the veracity of national leaders is quickly lost when one can watch the proceedings of an organization such as the United Nations in his own living room. I have no doubt that diplomats have always lied to one another, but what is new about this world is that children can now watch them lie in living color.

The hypocrisies of the older generations have always been with us. What is new today is that it is ridiculously easy to expose them. The effect on our youth of premature emergence of truth has been to create a deep skepticism as to the validity of authority. Neither the family, the church, the law, nor any institution demands this decline in respect for authority, but in my opinion it is best understood in terms of the psychological impact of our new media.

The Reliance-on-Scientism Hypothesis. Today's restless young people have grown up in a world which has not been dominated by religious faith but which has sought many of the answers to the questions of life in science. Many of us believe that science can provide the answers to life. We ask that the speculations and opinions of the social sciences contain the same hard truths as more rigorous findings in the physical and biological sciences. In my work with students, I am often impressed to find how easily they believe or once believed in the perfectibility of man. Hostility is not seen as an innate quality of man but rather as a response to frustration. The teachings of the social psychologist that aggression is a learned phenomenon have gained prominence over Freud's more ominous warnings that aggression is innate.

This generation of students seems to have grown up with the belief that original sin in the religious sense of Thanatos in the psychoanalytic sense does not exist. (Much of this belief has been reinforced by the mode of their existence. Many are affluent and have grown up in suburban communities where, except for what they see on television, they are shielded from the tragedies of life. The realities of their own lives convince them that whatever calamities are imposed upon others are not inevitable.) Statements such as "Life is a vale of tears" or "The masses of men lead lives of quiet desperation" seem absurd to them. In their adherence to scientific rationality they also cannot accept guilt. They are convinced that in a perfectible world man should be joyful and guiltless.

When a person raised with such beliefs encounters the harsh realities of life, he has little to fall back upon. If he perceives his own aggressive tendencies, he is frightened by them and attempts to deny them. He may project his anger upon those whom he feels are frustrating him or he may simply deny that such anger exists. When he perceives the evil of others he is mortified. In his conviction that there are rational solutions to any problem, he cannot help but be intolerant of the irrationalities of those who prevent progress. In his belief that life and especially the sexual aspects of life can be enjoyed without guilt, he becomes highly disturbed when he discovers that he cannot escape his past and that a certain amount of guilt is inevitable. He even becomes plagued with additional guilt over the realization that he is guilty.

The restless student is one who has taken the message of science, rationality, and perfection literally. He is more open to action and change than were earlier generations of students. At the same time, however, he is not equipped to understand or deal with the depth of that irrationality in man which resists change and which leads man to seek his own destruction. Too often such a student finds it necessary to construct "devil" theories of history in which the existence of evil is attributed to only a few who block the progress of the many. He has sacrificed the comfort and patience which comes with the idea of accepting "original" sin.[2]

Hopefully, this review has been more than an exercise in cataloguing. By emphasizing the diversity of explanations of student unrest, I have attempted to demonstrate the intellectual futility of searching for simple explanations of a highly complex phenomenon. As citizens we may wish either to support or attack the causes which restless students have dramatized. But as scholars concerned with educating and understanding and helping students we need a more objective approach. We must recognize that there is some truth to the most critical as well as the most sympathetic hypotheses.

Some of the hypotheses suggest guidelines for action. The critical hy-

[2] Sometimes the student becomes totally overwhelmed with the irrational aspects of the world and reacts by totally abandoning his earlier beliefs. In their disillusionment some alienated students seem to be turning away from the promises of scientism and searching for solace in the most dubious form of mysticism, magic, and astrology.

potheses remind us that youth are not always as wise or powerful as we might suspect. Like adults, their actions are as much determined by personal weaknesses and selfishness as by sensitivity or idealism. While youths certainly do not need more paternalism and coddling, they still need our understanding and guidance. They can still learn much from adults who are committed to the pursuit of ideals in a climate of tolerance, compassion, and responsibility. The critical hypotheses need not be used only to berate students. If their validity is appreciated they can be helpful in freeing adults from that unreasonable guilt which impairs an honest confrontation with the issues which students have raised.

The sympathetic hypotheses emphasize the unusual degree of stress this generation of students has experienced. These hypotheses which invoke the war, overpopulation, and pollution as sources of stress forcefully remind us that student unrest is often an appropriate response to what sometimes seems to be a hopelessly troubled world. Other hypotheses raise many questions for those entrusted with the management of our universities. Does the emphasis on education as a means rather than an end have any meaning in an affluent society? Should youths be encouraged to remain in a passive role as students throughout the first third of their lives? Are there means of bringing young people into important roles in the power structure of our universiites and our social system before they reach the age of 25 or 30? Is the 2S classification anything more than a bribe which weakens the moral position of dissenting students and creates havoc upon our campuses? Should it be abolished? To what extent can we continue to depersonalize and enlarge our campuses without creating a generation of alienated youth who feel no sense of identity, no sense that they have a voice in what is done to them, and no sense of commitment to anything but their own interests?

It is my belief that the neutral hypotheses are the most intriguing and the most powerful valid explanations of student unrest. At the same time, they are the most difficult to live with optimistically. If progress itself, in the form of technology, science, or new media, is the most severe stress in the lives of our young people, then we are faced with a seemingly impossible task, namely, how to control progress and change rather than allowing these forces to control us.

Selected References

Association for Supervision and Curriculum Development. *Youth Education: Problems, Perspectives, Promises.* Washington, D.C.: The Association, 1968.

BECK, CARLTON E., *et al. Education for Relevance.* Boston: Houghton Mifflin Company, 1968.

COLEMAN, JAMES S., *et al. Equality of Educational Opportunity.* Washington, D.C.: U.S. Department of Health, Education and Welfare, 1966.

COLES, ROBERT. *Children of Crisis.* Boston: Little, Brown & Company, 1967.

DEUTSCH, MARTIN, *et al. The Disadvantaged Child.* New York: Basic Books, 1967.

FRIEDENBERG, EDGAR Z. *Coming of Age in America: Growth and Acquiescence.* New York: Vintage Books, 1967.

GOLDSTEIN, BERNARD. *Low Income Youth in Urban Areas.* New York: Holt, Rinehart & Winston, 1967.

GOODMAN, PAUL. *Compulsory Miseducation.* New York: The Horizon Press, 1964.

Harvard Educational Review Editorial Board. *Equal Educational Opportunity.* Cambridge, Mass.: Harvard University Press, 1969.

HICKERSON, NATHANIEL. *Education for Alienation.* Englewood Cliffs, N.J.: Prentice-Hall, 1966.

KENISTON, KENNETH. *Young Radicals: Notes on Committed Youth.* New York: Harcourt, Brace & World, 1968.

———. *The Uncommitted: Alienated Youth in American Society.* New York: Harcourt, Brace & World, 1965.

KOHL, HERBERT. *36 Children.* New York: New American Library, 1967.

KOZOL, JONATHAN. *Death at an Early Age.* Boston: Houghton Mifflin Company, 1967.

MILLER, HARRY L. (ed.). *Education for the Disadvantaged.* New York: The Free Press, 1967.

NORDSTROM, CARL, EDGAR Z. FRIEDENBERG, and HILLARY A. GOLD. *Society's Children: A Study of Ressentiment in the Secondary School.* New York: Random House, 1967.

RAUBINGER, FREDERICK M., and HAROLD G. ROWE (eds.). *The Individual in Education.* New York: The Macmillan Company, 1968.

ROBERTS, JOAN I. (ed.). *School Children in the Urban Slum.* New York: The Free Press, 1967.

SCHREIBER, DANIEL (ed.). *Profile of the School Dropout.* New York: Vintage Books, 1968.

"Students and Politics," *Daedalus* (Winter 1968), entire issue.

TAYLOR, HAROLD. *Students Without Teachers: The Crisis in the University.* New York: McGraw-Hill Company, 1969.

This Magazine Is About Schools. (A fresh, new periodical with realistic and off-beat articles about youth in Canadian schools. Published in Toronto.)

WINTER, GERALD D., and EUGENE M. NUSS. *The Young Adult: Identity and Awareness.* Glenview, Ill.: Scott, Foresman and Company, 1969.

Youth in Turmoil. New York: Time-Life Books, 1969.

Teachers in Transition

FOR OVER A CENTURY teachers in America have been stereotyped as docile, loyal public servants, somewhat removed from the "real" world, performing their jobs under difficult working conditions and at low pay, but "dedicated" to a noble ideal of service to children and youth. Their contribution to society was viewed as the preservation of the status quo achieved by passing on to the young that which they were taught with little variation or individual interpretation. This stereotype, rooted in beliefs borrowed from nineteenth-century rural America, persists rather widely today in all forms of mass media. Unfortunately, teachers themselves have contributed to fostering this image as they have submitted meekly to unreasonable rules and regulations governing their dress, their public and private behavior, and their participation in policy-making decisions within and without the school.

During the past decade, however, a rather remarkable change has taken place. Growing numbers of teachers are renouncing this time-worn image of themselves and their profession. Initially spurred by efforts to improve their salaries and working conditions, teachers began enlarging their demands for a greater voice in policy matters in the school and the local community. Eventually, their militancy was extended to the larger society where they became active participants in the social, economic, and political movements of the day. Although it must be granted that not even a majority of teachers presently can be considered activists, few can deny that the efforts of the minority have irreparably damaged the nineteenth-century stereotype. If teachers today cannot be classed as militant, neither can they be characterized as docile.

Underlying causes for this rapid change within the profession are found in the great social upheaval taking place in the United States and throughout the world. More specific causes are related to the general affluence of contemporary America, to the increased stress on education as a national concern during the past decade, and to the dawning realization by teachers that, as members of the largest professional group in

America, their voice on political and economic issues carries great weight. In addition, teachers have added a new dimension to their concept of professionalism; they have demonstrated a willingness to accept practices proved successful by groups of organized labor, i. e., collective bargaining and work stoppages. This acceptance of labor's key objectives can have an important influence on the future direction of professional organization. Agreement on these points can offer an opportunity for an eventual merger of the labor-oriented American Federation of Teachers representing 200,000 members with the professional-oriented National Education Association with over a million members.

Whether or not a new militancy on social issues, a new acceptance of bargaining rights, or a new organizational structure will help teachers become a more dominant force in American society will depend further, Harry S. Broudy believes, on their identification with the "craft" or "professional" aspects of their work. So long as teachers see themselves as craftsmen, they perform their tasks guided solely by trial-and-error procedures. The true professional, on the other hand, seeks constantly to observe the conditions in which an event occurs, to question its outcome, and to propose a new course of action. Uniting theory and practice in this manner requires the highest level of intellectual power, but, Broudy asserts, only when teachers are capable of this can they call themselves professionals.

James Cass and Max Birnbaum answer their own query "What makes teachers militant?" by pointing to the major cause as the teacher's growing sense of alienation from increasingly complex school bureaucracies characteristic of expanding and less cohesive communities. Their militant behavior is further influenced by what the authors identify as the "revolution of rising expectations."

Marie Syrkin looks to urban teachers for support of a school system that "offers maximum educational opportunities for all children to become integrated in the totality of American life." Failure of teachers to unite in this goal is the basis for the current urban school crisis. As she examines charges against teachers by minority groups, Syrkin admits to the accuracy of some accusations, questions others, and rejects flatly proposals of black militants for the removal of white middle-class teachers in ghetto schools. She sees this as a dangerous and oversimplified solution to a very complicated problem.

Yet criticism persists that the American public school is a racist social institution. James Baldwin, talking informally to a group of New York City teachers, explains the effect of continued racial bias in schools on the black child. His belief is that the white man's need for superiority at the expense of the black man's status is a sign of white inferiority. Teachers of black children, Baldwin asserts, must understand this warped concept of superiority if they are to counter its outcome.

HARRY S. BROUDY | *Teaching—Craft or Profession?*

I

To ask whether teaching is or should be a craft or a profession is immediately to invite the blunt counter query: What is meant by craft, profession, and teaching? Moreover, even if workable agreement on the meaning of these terms could be achieved, where is one to begin the unraveling of the sociological, economic, psychological, historical, and political threads that are so intricately woven into this problem?

Anyone who senses the complexity of these questions may well wonder whether such answers as may be forthcoming are worth the trouble of seeking them. After all, what difference does it make whether teaching is a craft or a profession? Is it not a mere quibbling over names, a quibbling that bakes no bread and fattens no salary envelopes.

Accordingly, any discussion of this topic begins perforce on an apologetic note. It needs to justify itself. It can argue, of course, that there is some virtue in thinking an issue through clearly. If careful analysis and definition help to produce this clarity, then the inquiry achieves a theoretical blessing of sorts. Further, one might argue that theoretical clarity may reveal the role of the teacher in a new light. This illumination may enable us to discern new possibilities for action in our attempt to deal with the problems of teacher recruitment and training.

With an eye to both modes of justification we may begin by asking: Who really cares whether teaching is a craft or a profession?

For the young woman intending to teach only until marriage overtakes her this cannot be a serious matter; certainly nowhere so important as the identity of the pursuer and the date of the overtaking. Here is a socio-economic factor that obscures the whole inquiry. The answer to our question now seems to depend on the accidental factor that many of our elementary and some of our secondary school teachers are young women, and that young women in our culture with few exceptions make marriage their primary career. Can a calling claim to be a profession which rather consistently is used as an economic marking of time pre-

From *The Educational Forum* (January 1956). Copyright © 1956 Kappa Delta Pi, An Honor Society in Education. Reprinted by permission.

liminary to some other career—even if that other career is as interesting and important as marriage?

It was inevitable that in the minds of the American public elementary, and to a lesser extent, secondary school teaching would become associated with the notion of unmarried women living in the parental household. Stipends for teaching, especially when teachers were in good supply, were automatically scaled to the estimated needs of single women living at home. It was noted that households with four or five breadwinners—including a teacher or two—were collectively well off, even though each breadwinner won a modest amount of bread. As a result, men or women entering the calling but not living in the parental household found themselves atypical in more ways than one, but especially in their unhappiness about teachers' salaries and teaching as a life career. To their cozily housed female colleagues—even if marriage did not supervene as anticipated—the settling down into teaching as a genteel craft was perhaps more congenial than the prospect of becoming a member of a learned profession.

Nor can the status of teaching be a serious matter to married women who use it to supplement the income of the male breadwinner. True, such women do not regard teaching as an inferior and temporary alternative to marriage, but it still remains secondary for them to the management of their homes and families. In this respect teaching is not unique; the married woman in law or medicine is faced with a similar problem of priorities.

Nevertheless, law, medicine, the other learned professions, and those types of teaching that have become more or less professionalized do not lend themselves easily to the role of playing second fiddle. Few of us care to be treated by part-time physicians or to be represented by lawyers who, if matters were economically more favorable, would never enter a courtroom.

There seems to be no great objection to this in public school teaching; indeed there are those who regard it as something of an asset that the teacher is herself a wife and mother, because she can more naturally fulfill her role *in loco parentis* to her pupils. This may be true, and the quality of her teaching may be as good or better than that of other teachers. That, however, is not the issue at the moment. The relevant point is that teachers to whom teaching is not a primary life career are not going to become excited about whether or not teaching has or can have professional status.

Our question can be only cruel and mocking to the tired, resigned, and defeated teacher of either sex, and of any age or marital status who has been hammered into routinized compliance by diverse combinations of unhappy circumstances.

It is hard to know whether to be glad or disgusted with the pity-the-poor teacher campaign currently being waged by well-meaning segments of the press, movies, radio, and television. One wonders how many teachers yearn to become Our Miss Brooks, Mr. Peepers, or even the Mr. Chips of an earlier era. It does seem as if, as a result of this campaign, school teachers are being eyed more gently and compassionately than before. It is gratifying, of course, to have the public become aware of the economic shabbiness of the school teacher, but pity is hardly the sentiment a profession or a craft cares to inspire in the body politic.

Finally, our question is not of direct concern to faculties of colleges, universities, and highly specialized schools at all levels of instruction. The preparation for such teaching is so long and expensive that it is rarely undertaken and even more rarely completed by men or women who do not intend to make a professional career of teaching.

To whom then is our question a serious one? Only to those who regard public school teaching on the elementary and secondary levels as of unsurpassed importance for our society; only to those men and women who wish to dedicate their lives to this task; who intend to make of it their primary calling, who, finally, sense that teaching the young is not wholly commensurate with fixing leaky pipes, making cabinets, or laying bricks.

II

Our first step, obviously, is to distinguish between a craft and a profession. A craft, says Webster, is an occupation, especially one calling for manual dexterity. A profession is a calling or occupation that properly involves a liberal education or its equivalent, and mental rather than manual labor. It also involves, according to the dictionary, special mental and other attainments or special discipline. A professional is one who avows or professes such special attainments and, we may add, performs them for payment of one kind or another.

Like all dictionary definitions these reflect popular and literary usage but leave something to be desired in the way of precision. In the first place, the distinction drawn between physical and mental activity is not altogether fortunate. Few, if any, callings require one type of activity to the exclusion of the other. The surgeon and the plumber alike use both their heads and their hands. Dentists frequently complain that their profession is uncommonly hard on the feet and legs. Furthermore, there is a skill element in every profession as well as in every craft. There are facile lawyers, doctors, and clergymen. There are also clumsy ones. We have all writhed, at one time or another, before a learned professor who hemmed, hawed, and harrumped his learning away in front of our very eyes and ears. Many a pupil has become a dull and hopeless one because an inept teacher lacked the skill to find and touch the nerve of his interest.

A profession, no less than a craft, eventuates in action. Action, however, is always a matter of skill, because action is always upon the particular and the specific. The surgeon dissects this particular tissue at this particular time, and not tissue in general. We teach this pupil this lesson at this time and not pupils and lessons in general. And whenever we are confronted with the specific and particular we can act upon it with more or less skill.

It is tempting to argue that a craft relies on its skill while a profession subordinates skill to knowledge and judgment. To be sure, skill is characterized by a certain automaticity that obviates the need of conscious attention and thought to the details of action. However, this is all to the good because it would be awkward to have to attend to every detail involved in the eating of lettuce, playing the piano, or making a speech. Furthermore, insofar as the professional employs skill he, no less than the craftsman, appreciates the automatic smoothness of his skillful acts.

This does not mean that the craftsman any more than the professional can dispense with knowledge and judgment. The craftsman, we shall see, has knowledge and he cannot escape the making of decisions as to how and when to use it. There are, of course, occupations that require virtually nothing more than automatic motions, but certainly these cannot be dignified by the name of craft.

Nor can we argue that professional skills require less muscular exertion and dexterity than do the craft skills. A dentist or surgeon may exert more physical energy than a typist or cabinet maker. A professor lecturing to several hundred unenthralled undergraduates probably expends more energy than an expert machinist.

To sum up, crafts and professions do not differ essentially in that one is manual and the other mental; nor in the presence or absence of skill, and not even in the amount of energy expended in the use of these skills. The difference seems to lie in another dimension, namely, in the role theory has for each, and in the degree to which both the theory and the practice are united in the worker.

A craftsman is guided by knowledge, but it is likely to be the kind of knowledge that has been gleaned from long trial-and-error experience. A carpenter makes a joint in a certain way. Why? Because that is the way good carpenters have made it for a long time. This is the way he learned to make it as an apprentice under his master carpenter, who practiced it under the eyes of his master, and so on and so on until presumably we come to Noah, who supervised one of the major building projects of Biblical antiquity and may have been the first master carpenter.

Our carpenter may defend his methods by arguing that they produce joints that work well—better than any other sort. If some hair-splitting professor persists in asking *why* this method of making a joint works better, the carpenter will probably shrug his shoulders and go on making perfectly good joints.

The professions also use this kind of empirical know-how. Drugs are administered that get good results without our medical men always knowing why or how these results are achieved. Lawyers, architects, engineers, and other professionals have tricks of the trade for which success is often the only justification. However, as professions grow in stature there also grows a body of knowledge that does provide a more valid theoretical justification, that is, a body of theory.

Medicine was a craft so long as it was confined to trial-and-error knowledge. It became a full-fledged profession when biology, chemistry, physiology, and bacteriology provided a theoretical foundation for its practice. Business for a long time was not regarded as a profession in our culture. David Harum, a fictional horse trader, typified the fact that shrewdness, energy, and persistence could guarantee success in the commercial world. They still can. David Harum might still do very well in the horse or the automobile business, but would a large corporation hire him? Is it not likely to choose a master of business administration, marketing, or finance instead? The fact seems to be that business is rapidly becoming professionalized, and on the view being argued here it is because business is basing its practice more and more on theory emanating from economics, psychology, sociology, and from not a few of the physical sciences as well.

III

All of which tempts us to hazard the generalization that whenever a calling becomes professionalized it demands that its prospective members master a body of theoretical knowledge as a prerequisite to membership. The history of the occupational status of nursing, pharmacy, veterinary medicine, retail trade, engineering, advertising, newspaper writing, and other callings can provide evidence for this generalization. As a result, the amount of formal schooling needed to qualify for a calling is a rough measure of the degree of professionalization of that calling.

Training for crafts tends to be of the apprentice type that emphasizes practice of a skill under a master. It is only when considerable theory is involved that formal schooling takes priority over apprentice training. In our time each major family of occupations can be arranged in a hierarchy based on the amount of theory prospective members need to master. Witness, for example, the variations in theory required by a surgeon, an X-ray technician, the surgical nurse, the salesman for a surgical supply house, and the attendants who keep the operating room ready for use.

Why theory as such should enhance the prestige of a calling is not obvious. Theory and theorists are not and never have been popular. Even an age that depends for its very life, not to mention its standard of motor cars and refrigerators, on theorists labels them as "eggheads" and "long-hairs," and it is hard to detect any affection beneath the contempt and mockery of these appellations.

A clue to a possible answer is the fact that ability to master theory is relatively rare. To this may be added the ancient belief that mind represents a higher order of being than do physical collocations of matter and energy. These two factors may account for the genuine albeit reluctant respect entertained by the multitude for abstract intelligence, a respect, however, that is not incompatible with fear and even hatred of the intellectual.

Accordingly, whether teaching can become a profession seems to depend, in the first instance, on whether there is or can be a body of theory to rationalize its practice.

As matters now stand, the curriculum of schools devoted to the preparation of teachers has three elements: a skill-apprenticeship element typified by practice teaching requirements, a theoretical element represented by courses in educational adaptations of psychology, sociology, philosophy, and mathematics, and a group of courses called "methods" that fall somewhere between the other two. In general, the latter are too practical to suit the theoreticians and too theoretical for the taste of the technicians. It is the first element of this curriculum that now concerns us.

In the half century recently completed "educationists" (and I use the term respectfully) worked hard and hastily to construct for the educational enterprise a theoretical skeleton strong enough to sustain the weight of its procedures and articulated enough to guide its future development. This effort was not uniformly successful. The speed with which plans and movements have flushed into popularity and paled into obscurity is more symptomatic of immature theory than of rapidly maturing theory; it betrays haste rather than progress. Consider, for example, how quickly investigative zeal has shifted from educational measurements, to developmental studies, to the present enthusiasm for group dynamics and social climates.

Much of what has been promulgated as educational theory is not so much theory as wishful thinking and uncritical commitment. For example, a theory from which commitment to providing for the infinite differences among individual pupils could logically be derived would lead into metaphysics, epistemology, ethics, and religion. Such a theory does not follow simply from the *facts* about individual differences described by the educational psychologist. From the fact that individual pupils vary in intelligence or the color of hair nothing follows as to what *ought* to be done about such differences. Yet if the average teacher or administrator were asked to give an example *par excellence* of educational theory, chances are better than ever that he would cite his laudable convictions about individual differences.

That the whole child is the concern of the school, that his interests have a presumptive importance for the curriculum, and that the school should repair the defects of home, church, government, and the attitudes of adolescents are not so much theories as commitments to certain values for which some educators, at least, would find themselves hard put to provide reasonable evidence, not to speak of scientific evidence.

One could point to other signs of education's youthfulness as an intellectual discipline, but in spite of these strictures there is a core of theory that by any standard is sound, and it has made real and lasting changes in our practice. No trained teacher, for example, today regards the timid child as the model of adjustment, nor noisiness as the most horrible of school offenses. Classroom teachers are today in much closer agreement with psychologists in their evaluation of behavior problems than were their forerunners of 25 years ago. Theory has also had an unmistakable impact on school construction, textbooks, testing, instruction and guidance. The philosophic foundations of educational beliefs are undergoing fresh, minute, and precise scrutiny, and there is reason to hope that this type of theory will gradually reduce the amount of nonsense uttered about the broader and more ultimate issues in education.

Unfortunately there is not enough sound theory to go around for the great array of education courses listed in the college catalogues. However, the remedy for this would seem to be not the abandonment of theory but rather an intensified search for it and its concentration into fewer courses. Fewer but much fatter education courses would do much to hasten the professionalization of teaching and to blunt the force of the criticisms that are so frequently and, for the most part, so unintelligently directed toward the "educationists." So much, then, for the role of theory in the professional status of teaching.

IV

The second point is that the knowledge that guides professional practice not only must have a strong theoretical component, but that it must be *in* the practitioner. There is, no doubt, a good scientific justification for the carpenter's making a joint in one way rather than another, but if he himself does not know the reason, then he may be a fine craftsman, but he is not a member of a profession. Similarly, the countless teachers who in one way or another produced a high order of learning in their pupils but who did not know why or how they produced it were excellent in their craft, but they were not practicing teaching as a profession.

For example, I recall that my eighth grade teacher had a remarkable reputation as a successful teacher. As boys approached the eighth grade they hoped to be assigned to her room because legend had it that she was not only a strict disciplinarian (a characteristic in itself of no great charm to pupils), but also a spectacularly violent one. It was said that she hurled huge dictionaries at wayward pupils, and no decent American boy would want to miss this spectacle. So far as I could discover, nobody ever saw her throw a dictionary—not even an abridged one—at any pupil, and I am certain that she never realized how much of her success was due to the expectation that she would.

Now there is something, perhaps a great deal, to be said for the notion that schoolroom craftsmen are precisely what we need these days. This argument is rarely advanced in public, but if it were, it might run something like this:

Granted there is a body of theory to guide the teaching process, it does not follow that individual classroom teachers have to master it. It will be enough if their supervisors have this theory so that they can direct the practice of the teacher. In this way the IQ requirements for teaching can remain modest, the large numbers of needed teachers can be turned out more cheaply, and finally, teachers with training limited to mastery of technical procedures will furnish a docile base for the educational line of command.

Would these hopes—especially the last one—be realized? Suppose teachers accepted the role of craftsmen. Might not their next logical step be to organize into a craft union? The greater the number of teachers, the more powerful would this union become, the less easily could it be controlled, and the higher wages would climb. Such organizing activity grieves the very people who so ardently want teaching to be a craft; oddly enough, they condemn it as being, of all things, unprofessional.

Yet forming unions was standard procedure with the learned professions in the 13th century. The terms bachelor and master together with the ceremonies of induction into these ranks were borrowed from the craft guilds. The difference between a craft and a profession is not to be sought in the way a group organizes for collective action. Carpenters without unions would not be professionals, and physicians and clergymen organized into unions would not be craftsmen. The difference lies rather in the union of theory and practice in the professional and their separation in the craftsman.

As a result of this difference there emerges an important difference in the relation of the craftsman to his employer and of the professional person to his client.

We take problems of health to the physician, problems of designing bridges and buildings to engineers and architects, and problems of sin and salvation to clergymen. We ask the professional to diagnose difficulties, appraise solutions, and to choose among them. We ask him to take total responsibility for both strategy and tactics. In other words, we ask the professional to identify himself with our goals and our welfare. From the craftsman, by contrast, we expect a standard diagnosis, correct performance of procedures, and nothing else. We hire his skill at so much an hour or so much a week just as we buy or hire any other commodity in economic exchange. A dentist, lawyer, clergyman, or engineer who quit his project or case when five o'clock struck or because the fee might not be forthcoming would arouse our indignation. But who nowadays expects a craftsman to work after the stipulated time—at regular rates—even if there is only one more wire to connect or one more square yard to paint? He may do so as a kind and sensible human being, but we no longer demand it of him as a worker.

Further, when our problems are urgent, we are willy-nilly placed in the position of a suppliant over against the professional as a benefactor. Because it will take knowledge as well as skill to solve them and because knowledge especially is not easily acquired, we cannot postpone the solutions to our problems until we have become do-it-yourself doctors, lawyers, and clergymen. In such situations it makes little sense to ask how many dollars the hour is worth in which the physician saves a life in the hospital or a lawyer saves a defendant in the courtroom. On what scale shall we calculate the value of a sermon or the deliverance of a pupil from ignorance?

It begins to dawn on us that the relation between the professional and his client is not primarily an economic one, despite its unavoidable economic aspects. There is a sense in which the client can repay the benefactor only by gratitude. In the ideal state professionals would be rewarded by *honoraria* and gratuities exclusively. Because they do not live in utopia and because human beings forget their benefactors once their distress has abated, clients have to be reminded of erstwhile benefits by bills, fees, and contracts.

Professional men could become bitter about this forgetfulness and ingratitude of the client. Yet even these pay a perverted tribute to the peculiar position of the learned professions in our social order. The public is asserting, albeit in a stupidly selfish way, that a professional service is not a commodity in economic exchange. When the citizen is reluctant to pay the doctor or the lawyer, or when he expects professional fees to be tuned to the income of the client; when he expects so much from the teacher for so little, he is ascribing to them a level of virtue to which he himself does not dream of aspiring.

The community pays its professionals only as much money as it must. Its more fundamental payments are in the coin of prestige and autonomy. The right to establish qualifications for membership and codes of conduct for its members are a group's most precious privileges, and the maturity of a profession is measured by the degree to which society allows it to regulate such matters for itself.

The claim of a profession to autonomy is based on its body of theory. It relies upon the claim of superior knowledge to which the client willingly bows. The craft can demand also autonomy and can enforce that claim by withholding its services or threatening to do so. This method of enforcing claims is not open to the professions whose duty to the client transcends even the welfare of the profession itself. It is only when the community forces a craft status on a professional group that the latter may be forced to retaliate by the collective withholding of its services. This is most likely to be the case when the professional is not self-employed.

The discussion so far should have made clear the strategic role of theory for our original question. If there is no body of theory that we can honestly call professional education, we cannot make teaching into a profession. At best it can be a craft practiced by skillful people who have a benevolent attitude towards the objects of their ministrations.

Theory demands a high order of intellect for its mastery. So long as administrators are willing to settle for mediocre intellects, teaching cannot become a profession, even if these aspirants are blessed with a great love of children. How long would medicine retain its professional standing, if admission to medical school could be achieved by candidates with low IQs but who show high promise of developing a charming bedside manner?

There are, of course, people with first-rate minds who also love children, and this is the ideal teacher candidate. However, the number of young people so endowed is small and the competition for them keen. If the public wants them in teaching it will have to raise its bids in the competition.

Without theory and a body of personnel intellectually competent to master theory, on what grounds will the teaching force claim the right to determine the qualifications for teaching? By political force possibly, but we have seen that this misses the very essence of professional autonomy, namely, that it should be based on the willing acknowledgement of superior knowledge by the layman. To assert the claim to professional autonomy for teaching without this knowledge would probably be vain and perhaps even immoral.

V

It would be unduly optimistic to believe that the professionalization of public school teaching is either imminent or even clearly foreseeable. There is a sense in which it would be more comfortable and more profitable for teaching to become an out-and-out craft. It would then have the support of other crafts in its economic struggle.

Yet there is one important factor that may prevent this alternative from becoming the inevitable solution to our problem. It is that the public is demanding from the teacher a type of service that is professional rather than craftlike. Younger parents nowadays are wise in the ways of child care and mental hygiene, and they expect teachers to be sophisticated in these branches of theory as well as competent classroom operators. Teachers today are expected to create classroom atmospheres, diagnose personality difficulties, and to take an active part in community affairs.

And this demand is being reflected in the marketplace; in the prices of land and houses as young couples want to know what kind of schools will be available for the children in the neighborhood under consideration. True, these are only a few straws in the wind, but mass movements are about as hard to stop as to start. It may be that the public is ahead of the teacher trainers in realizing that it is not hiring the teacher's skill from nine to three, but that it is asking a professionally trained group of high grade persons to devote their best energies, knowledge, and concern to developing in the young their potentialities for the good life in a complex and in many ways a frightening world.

Perhaps the greatest obstacle in the way of professionalizing the public school teacher is the image he has of himself. The weak, self-sacrificing, put-upon, and pitied school teacher is certainly not an image compatible with professional status. And the image of the impersonal, competent hired hand bargaining collectively for the best terms he can force is equally incompatible.

The new image will have to contain, first of all, the notion of the learned man, learned at least to the extent that he has traversed a course of training that had intellectual substance and required a high order of intellectual competence. It will also have the notion of dedication to the welfare of the client, that is, the learner; not to classes of pupils, but to individual human beings in predicaments from which the teacher alone is competent to help them extricate themselves. Finally, there is the notion of sacrifice and service for the community, but not the service of a servant, nor a sacrifice the consequence of timidity. Both are voluntary offerings of generous strength.

In return, the teacher has a right to ask from the community a chance and the means to live the kind of life that will exemplify for both parents and pupils what the good life can be.

It is hard enough to form such an image, let alone to translate it into actuality.

JAMES CASS AND MAX BIRNBAUM | **What Makes Teachers Militant?**

The American school teacher served notice on the public that old stereotypes have changed—kindly Mr. Chips and the meek schoolmarm are dead. On the day that schools were scheduled to open in New York City and Detroit—and in smaller districts in Michigan, Illinois, Maryland, and Kentucky—schools remained closed. Teachers were on the picket line, not in the classroom. Florida's teachers, meanwhile, were threatening to close all the schools in the state if the Governor refused to call a special session of the legislature to act on their demands for increased support for education.

To date, the growing militancy of teachers has been explained primarily in terms of the mounting competition for members and power between the small but rapidly growing American Federation of Teachers (AFT), an AFL-CIO affiliate, and the larger, professionally oriented National Education Association (NEA). It is true that in the competition for selection as teacher representative in contract negotiations, the largely urban-based AFT (146,000 members) has scored a number of notable successes in the nation's larger cities over the small-town-based NEA with its million-plus members. It is true, too, that as a result the NEA has been prodded into an unaccustomed aggressiveness in representing its members—a new stance that is virtually indistinguishable from that of its trade union competitor. But the competition between the two organizations is only one part—albeit an important part—of a complex of forces that have caused the teachers to shed their traditional middle-class behavior.

Many of the factors that have an important bearing on teacher militancy have been obscured by the emphasis on salaries in contract negotiations. The question of take-home pay is an important one, to be sure, but equally crucial for many teachers is the issue of job satisfaction.

The rewards of teaching are complex and subject to a variety of local influences. There is no doubt an element of truth in the traditional rhetoric about "love of children" and "dedication to the future of society." It seems clear, however, that there are more fundamental factors that contribute to job satisfaction. Over the years, for instance, teaching has offered a large number of capable individuals a reasonably independent professional career. It has provided a substantial degree of community status which, although often limited, was almost always present. And for an occupation dominated by women, relatively few of whom were heads of families, teaching has offered salaries that usually have been adequate —if not much more. As a larger number of men entered teaching after World War II, salaries took on added importance, but teachers also sought a stronger hand in determining their own professional fate. Therefore, in recent years there has been a growing emphasis in contract negotiations on the demand for a more influential voice in developing school policy, as well as on conditions of teaching, and the facilities available for instruction.

Once a "reasonable" salary level is reached, it appears that substantial numbers of teachers today will accept lower salaries if other job satisfactions are high. By the same token, it seems clear that when other professional rewards are lacking, the emphasis on salaries rises. What has happened in recent years is that teacher salary levels in general have risen materially—but at the same time, especially in urban areas, a number of other forces have converged on the schools that have reduced job satisfaction precipitately. It is these forces and the context in which they developed that merit more careful scrutiny.

As the crucial role of education in modern society has been more widely recognized, the schools have developed a new political potency. The National Defense Education Act of 1958 and the Elementary and Secondary Education Act of 1965 made vast new federal funds available to the schools for the first time. The level of both state and local support increased materially during the same period. New horizons for education were appearing as it was recognized as the nation's major "growth industry." Thus teachers, along with other members of society, were caught up in what has been called the revolution of rising expectations. But it soon became clear that rising expectations are not fulfilled automatically.

Many occupational groups in America have learned that it is not the justice of individual demands that wins increased salaries and higher status from society, but the economic and political power of organized groups. The nation's doctors—long the teachers' ideal professional model —demonstrated a generation or more ago the tangible returns that can be derived from a strong organization and group solidarity. But physicians constitute a relatively small, elite professional group; teaching is a mass profession. And doctors, typically, are not public employees; most schoolteachers are. Therefore, teachers had to seek elsewhere for a realistic model for professional organization and action. But the obvious examples of other public employee groups presented special problems for them.

Those groups with education equal or superior to teachers—librarians, social workers, and engineers, for instance—seldom were highly organized and, lacking the teachers' numbers or the critical nature of their function, usually received lower salaries. Those civil service groups that have developed strong organizations—police, firemen, and sanitary workers, for example—have, typically, functioned close to the center of local political power and could be counted on for a high degree of loyalty and cooperation at election time. Teachers have not. Rarely have they been willing to compromise what they considered to be their professional commitment by becoming entangled in the realities of practical politics.

Faced with the competition of other civil service groups that shared their rising expectations, and unwilling to ally themselves with the political establishment, teachers often sought, and received, the support of another major power group in the city—organized labor. For many years, nevertheless, even as they benefited from the support of labor, few teachers were willing to affiliate as union members. But it became increasingly plain that rising expectations could be satisfied only through strong organizations and direct group action. No matter how reluctant teachers might be to desert their traditional professional posture, the imperative was clear.

Given these circumstances, and lacking realistic alternatives, teachers have joined for collective action in the AFT—and, more recently, in a newly militant NEA—which could offer the power of a labor union while allowing members to retain their traditional self-image of independent professionals. Neither organization, despite the AFT's affiliation with the AFL-CIO, is solely a trade union in the traditional sense, but each can act like one when the negotiating chips are down. At other times, members and leaders can step forth as bona fide professionals.

Yet it would have been inconceivable a decade ago for the American schoolteacher, with so long a history of conformity and conservatism, to desert the professional classroom for the trade union picket line. Such action denies too directly the deeply ingrained values and attitudes of traditional middle-class behavior. So dramatic a shift in teacher attitudes was made possible only by the radical change in the etiquette of social protest that has been so visible a part of the national experience in the 1960s. The wide acceptance of civil disobedience as an appropriate means for protesting social wrongs heralded a profound change in national perspectives which were reflected in teacher attitudes.

The nonviolent action of the civil rights movement in the South during the 1950s dramatized for the public the way in which civil disobedience might be used to protest the persistence of unjust laws or the reluctance of society as a whole to take positive action to redress social inequities. During the 1960s, home television screens repeatedly carried reports of the arrest, and sometimes violent treatment, of respected national figures as they registered their rejection of social injustice. The hundreds of college students who flocked to Mississippi to work in voter registration drives in the summer of 1964 were widely applauded. And, perhaps symbolically, the most telling event occurred when the head of the United Presbyterian Church in the U.S.A., accompanied by the white-haired mother of the Back Bay governor of Massachusetts, went south to register their protest against inequality—and were arrested and jailed.

Clearly, large numbers of Americans had come to accept direct action as an appropriate means for challenging the status quo—if the cause is just. The lesson was not lost on the nation's teachers. All that remained was to translate teacher demands into social imperatives.

But the sources of teacher militancy go far deeper than merely a revolution of rising expectations and a new acceptance of direct action as a legitimate means of achieving tangible rewards when expectations are frustrated.

Teachers have always occupied an equivocal position in our society—and society has always been ambivalent about its teachers. Many individuals and agencies in the community "teach," and it has become progressively more difficult to define the unique role of the classroom teacher in an age when the mass media provide so much and such diverse kinds of information. Even more specifically, it has never been possible to establish a direct correspondence between high salaries and "good teaching"—or, more particularly, high pupil achievement. Therefore, society has felt quite comfortable in paying its respects to teachers in the loftiest rhetoric while refusing adequate support for the schools for either salaries or facilities. Americans have found both Mark Hopkins and Ichabod Crane valid representatives of the profession. And Shaw's facile dictum—"He who can, does. He who cannot, teaches"—has haunted teachers for a half century or more. Other factors, too, have conspired to reinforce society's ambivalent attitude toward the profession—and the teachers' own traditional feeling of self-doubt or—in the social psychologist's term—self-hate. As a result, teachers have been undergoing a process of progressive alienation both from the school as an institution and from the community it serves.

A major factor in the alienation of teachers has been the growing impersonality of the school as it has become larger and more highly structured. As enrollments swelled in the postwar years, education took on more and more of the features of a mass production process. Administrative and supervisory positions grew in number and importance, and the classroom teacher was progressively more removed from the central functioning of the school. It became more difficult, then, for the teacher to identify closely with the school as an institution. The problem was intensified as the management function became more complex and time-consuming, and the school principal became less the traditional senior teacher and colleague than the resident representative of absentee management.

(It appears that the recent dissolution of the Educational Policies Commission, sponsored jointly for many years by the American Association of School Administrators and the National Education Association, reflects the growing division between the interests and objectives of administrators and teachers. The NEA and AASA have always contended that the professional interests of their respective members were identical, but there are strong indications that the AFT's insistence upon the distinction between management and labor in education is more realistic—especially in the light of the growing acceptance of collective negotiations as an appropriate means for settling teacher disputes.)

Even as teachers were finding it more difficult to identify with the schools in which they taught, they were also feeling increasingly divorced from the communities served by their schools. Few grew up in the communities in which they taught, and many did not even live there. A growing number of teachers today, it appears, do not feel an integral part of the community in which they teach. In the affluent suburbs they sometimes cannot afford to live in their school's high tax district, and in the anonymity of the great city their school may serve no identifiable community or neighborhood. Therefore, the teacher's relationship to both the school and the community is changing rapidly as the sense of belonging is lost.

The alienation of teachers has been stimulated, too, by the increasing —and sometimes unrealistic—demands that have been made on the schools. Americans have always looked to education as the ultimate corrective for social ills or the means for meeting society's needs. Two or three generations ago, for instance, the schools were assigned the task of Americanizing our immigrant fathers and, at a somewhat later date, were asked to develop a pool of skilled manpower through vocational education. More recently, they have been charged with a variety of assignments from teaching the evils of alcohol to exploring the intricacies of sex education.

In the past, teachers, were expected to introduce the rising generation to the knowledge and skills that were considered appropriate for the development of competent citizens and civilized men. Some children learned more readily than others, but this was expected. Those who lacked academic talent or motivation simply disappeared from the classroom to return to the farm or to find unskilled work in the community. But today no such simple solutions to the problem of the nonlearner are possible; everyone must succeed—and the definition of success varies with the community.

In the suburbs, with a high level of education among parents, it is no longer enough to shepherd the children of the middle class through high school and into college. The revolution of rising expectations functions in many contexts, and increasing numbers of parents demand that their children be prepared to compete successfully for admission to the most selective institutions.

At the other end of the scale, in the inner city, teachers are expected to induce learning among children who are imperfectly prepared by background or experience for the discipline of classroom work. Often lacking special training for the task, the teacher may have an equally imperfect understanding of the child and his special learning problems. At the upper grades, "education" often becomes a mere exercise in custodial care, and not infrequently the teacher has reason to be physically afraid of the students. Yet, increasingly, inner-city parents and their representatives refuse to remain silent. They demand that the schools succeed in their assigned task—and charge that the teacher has failed when their children do not learn.

At the same time, education is attracting a new breed of teachers. Better educated than in the past, they are less "dedicated" and more pragmatic than their predecessors. They have a surer sense of their own professional competence, and consequently resent assignment to nonprofessional duties and have less patience with the traditional inadequacies of time, facilities, and administrative support. At home with the new etiquette of social protest and faced with the growing impersonality of the educational environment, today's teachers respond in predictable ways.

Old loyalties have crumbled, and new allegiances are emerging. Lacking the old devotion to school and community, and threatened by new demands on the schools for which neither experience nor training have prepared them, today's teachers are turning inward. It is to the group—either the trade union or the professional organization—that they look for support and security.

In *The Secular City,* Harvey Cox writes: "Urbanization means a structure of common life in which diversity and the disintegration of tradition are paramount. It means a type of impersonality in which functional relationships multiply." The massive changes in our society to which Professor Cox refers have precipitated major shifts in the values and attitudes of many individuals and groups. But few, if any, have been more fundamental or more dramatic than those of teachers. Traditional patterns of association are disintegrating, and teachers are seeking new "functional relationships" not only with administrators and school boards, but even with their staunchest supporters in the past, the parents.

The forces that have contributed to teacher alienation, and, consequently, to militancy, almost certainly are going to increase rather than diminish in the years ahead. And the virus of change is already spreading from its point of origin in the city to the suburbs and beyond. We can expect that as the forces reducing job satisfaction for many teachers increase, the demands for higher salaries will become more intense. And each time the teachers win one more bitterly fought contest for higher pay and improved working conditions, their sense of group solidarity will be increased—and their feeling of alienation from the community will grow.

Any realistic appraisal of teacher militancy today seems to indicate that we have seen only the beginning.

MARIE SYRKIN | ***Don't Flunk the Middle Class Teacher***

Educational institutions, from the elementary to the university levels, have routinely been accused of stunting the intellectual development of their charges and of thwarting the true goals of education, however these might be perceived in the pedagogic jargon of the period. Whether the emphasis was on the acquisition of skills or on the development of "the whole man," uninspired teachers, martinet administrators and irrelevant curricula have been run-of-the-mill targets of critics. Literary accounts of the formal savagery of the English public school or of the ineptness of the local equivalent of the little red school house are commonplace. James Farrell's attacks on parochial schools or Henry Roth's evocation of a wretched Jewish *heder* have become, like Shakespeare's unwilling schoolboy, part of a large body of testimony to the inadequacy of the schools and the misery of the scholars. That so many of the latter survived to bear hostile and literate witness is the only hopeful element in the litany of discontent.

Since the twenties of this century the American public school, hit by the problems of mass education on a hitherto unprecedented scale, has been at the center of the storm. When the public school veered to embrace the doctrines of progressive education, the formalists embarked on a counter-crusade; John Dewey pointed one way, Robert Hutchins another. But all sides agreed in their appraisals of the scholastic deficiencies of high school students tested in various sections of the country.

What distinguishes the current onslaught on the New York school system, as well as those of other urban centers, is not only its ferocity but the nature of the charges leveled. For the first time the public school system is being accused not of stupidity or incompetence—the traditional criticism—but of "culture genocide" directed against Negro pupils. Furthermore, this "genocide" is willed; it is the end product of a deliberate "conspiracy" to destroy the minds of black children.

This extraordinary accusation cannot be dismissed as the demagogic slogan of irresponsibles with no influence in their community. By repetition and dissemination it has acquired the respectability of usage. A conference on urban education under the chairmanship of Rhody A. McCoy, unit administrator of the Ocean Hill-Brownsville demonstration school project, issued a statement declaring, "It is no longer reasonable to expect that black people will . . . submit to a genocidal system." Robert Carson of Brooklyn CORE told an interviewer that "certain teachers have conspired to miseducate the black and Puerto Rican children," and John F. Hatchett, dismissed director of the Afro-American Student Center at New York University, wrote in his notorious article on "Anti-Black Jews" of "the cultural genocide daily practiced against my people by a group of people whose entire history should have told them no." These are but a few samples from many.

No one can sensibly dispute the fact that, whatever the reasons, the public schools have spectacularly failed in bringing masses of Negro pupils up to their grade levels in reading and other elementary skills. Because of this, the old debates as to how to educate the masses, which flourished long before the Negro influx into Northern cities, have acquired a new urgency and a completely different focus. In the past such discussions, no matter how impassioned, revolved around questions of pedagogy. Which method would provide the key? Today's argument, however, scorns theories of education. Instead of dwelling on the manifestoes of opposing schools whose principles were to be applied within an accepted frame, critics propose to scrap the frame.

In this climate of wild accusations and extreme panaceas, "cultural genocide" and "community control" have already become accepted clichés, as though the truth of the first and the desirability of the second were self-evident. Some ideas recur with sufficient regularity to have created a new educational jargon. Among these are: the public school teaches "middle-class values" and this teaching does violence to the individuality and values of the "lower-class" pupil; "middle-class" teachers are not successful because they do not understand their ghetto pupils; standard tests of achievement and ability are invariably suspect because they are not "culture free"; *de facto* segregation provides an adequate rationale for black separatism in the schools; it is more progressive to determine admission and advancement within all levels of the educational system by racial quotas than by individual merit; the civil-service system is biased because the members of some groups are "disproportionately" successful in passing examinations; and, finally, "community control" provides the remedy for these ills.

Obviously these ideas go far beyond the provision of compensatory education or equal opportunity in the usual sense. They are revolutionary in that they question two basic principles of the public school system at its best: (1) no racial, religious or class quotas for pupils or teachers, and (2) advancement on the basis of individual achievement.

One of the astonishing features of the present battle about education is the easy readiness to abandon these principles. Without viewing them as sacrosanct, ideas so fundamental to democratic education merit a serious re-evaluation before being scrapped. Enough pressure has already been generated in the Negro ghettos to initiate the restructuring of the vast New York school system according to the blueprints of Negro militants. Though such a revolution may be desirable, its full social and educational implications should be examined before it is embraced.

The school system, as Negro spokesmen never tire of declaring, has become a major instrument in the Negro struggle for equality. While the Negro parent may simply be concerned with his child's proficiency in reading, the negro militant has larger goals. His recent demand for integration "now" has changed to an insistence on black schools—a separation bound to result in rigid black and white enclaves. Such a far-reaching transformation should not be the result of frantic improvisation by a city administration eager to "keep it cool," of a harried board of education, of an alarmed teachers union, or of "community spokesmen" engaged in prodding their people to action.

Before examining the various arguments mentioned, it is well to recall that the problem of teaching black children presents in intensified form a difficulty intrinsic to the public school. As the educational ladder lengthened and widened, encouraging larger sectors of the population to climb it, educators kept discovering unforeseen stumbling blocks on its ascent. When a large proportion of those newly pouring into the high schools proved to be "not college material," vocational high schools were established.

In addition, under the sheer weight of numbers, academic high schools kept relaxing standards established at the turn of the century for a small college-oriented élite. Twenty-five years ago, as today, The New York Times, Business Week and Fortune magazine were busily reporting the results of nationwide tests indicating a woeful collapse of standards among high-school students. In July, 1943, the New York State Board of Regents reported that large numbers of high-school students were seriously deficient in basic skills.

The students referred to did not constitute a racial minority nor were they labeled "culturally underprivileged." They were for the most part white, working-class, and they found the diction and style of "Silas Marner," "Ivanhoe" or "The Tempest" incomprehensible. Teachers complained then as bitterly as now about the lack of relevance of such works to the backgrounds and attainments of their pupils. The school system adapted itself to the changed character of its clientele by a variety of devices, including the use of comics to teach the classics. Since the student body was predominantly white, no one charged a racist plot to explain scholastic deficiencies, and since many of the working-class students succeeded brilliantly and most adequately, the formula of lower- vs. middle-class was not invoked despite the obvious advantages enjoyed by children from cultivated well-to-do homes.

Today these difficulties are compounded. Negroes from the South who elide final syllables in their speech tend to transfer this pattern to written English. Classroom experiments have demonstrated how this difference in speech patterns affects the acquisition of what is called literate, let alone literary, English. Furthermore, the "cultural lag" at this stage is greater than anything previously encountered. In the forties sociologists and educators debated whether students with mean I.Q.'s of 100 could cope with an academic curriculum. (For success in college it was assumed that a minimal I.Q. of 120 was required and college admissions committees to this day look askance at a lower score.) Today nationwide tests of Negro pupils—even when administered by determined environmentalists like Otto Klineberg—indicate a mean I.Q. of 86. Regardless of the far-reaching causes, the Negro child in the immediate present enters school less equipped for the curriculum as now constituted than even the millions of "nonacademic" white children who swamped the public high schools in a floodtide of democratic enthusiasm for "higher education for all."

Are all the schools in the country engaged in "cultural genocide?" What about regional differences? In view of the extraordinary assaults on the urban school systems of the North, the victims of plots by white teachers should fare even worse than the national average. "The Coleman Report on Equality of Educational Opportunity" indicates, however, that minority achievement scores are consistently highest in the metropolitan North: "By grade 12, both white and Negro students in the South score below their counterparts—white and Negro—in the North. In addition, Southern Negroes score further below Southern whites than Northern Negroes score below Northern whites. The consequences of this pattern can be illustrated by the fact that the 12th-grade Negro in the non-metropolitan South is 0.8 standard deviation below—or, in terms of years, 1.9 behind—the Negro in the metropolitan Northeast, though at grade 1 there is no such regional difference."

What about the baleful effect of the white, middle-class teacher? The Coleman Report tells us that Negro teachers "typically" teach Negro children: "For the nation as a whole the average Negro elementary pupil attends a school in which 65 per cent of the teachers are Negro." Since better results in achievement are found in the North, where teachers are preponderantly white, this would appear to undercut the argument about the greater effectiveness of Negro teachers.

This report also informs us that three teacher characteristics which appear most to affect students achievement are the teachers' social background, their verbal ability, and the quality of their own education. The higher the teacher scores in these respects, the better the progress of her pupils. Since the three characteristics mentioned are, for obvious reasons, more readily found among white, middle-class teachers (the report indicates that over two-thirds of Negro teachers fall below the mean verbal ability scores of white teachers) the pressure for black teachers becomes difficult to defend on educational grounds. If a self-perpetuating cycle of disadvantages is to be avoided, then the teacher—white or black—scoring high in the characteristics mentioned must be sought for the minority pupil, for another conclusion reached by the report is that these teacher variables are more likely to affect the disadvantaged pupil than the white, middle-class pupil whose family educational background provides a cultural cushion.

Perhaps the most important conclusion of the Coleman Report is its assessment of the role of the school in education: it has been exaggerated. It cannot be divorced from other factors just as significant for a child's achievement. The report states unequivocally: "One implication stands out above all: that schools bring little influence to bear on a child's achievement that is independent of his family background and social context; and that this very lack of an independent effect means that the inequalities imposed on children by their home, neighborhood and peer environment are carried along to become the inequalities with which they confront adult life at the end of school."

The foregoing conclusion, based on an exhaustive series of tests seeking to establish the importance of various factors for success in school, does not exonerate society for the Negro's disadvantage on the educational ladder. On the contrary, no arraignment of the totality of causes could be more explicit; it does, however, underscore the fact that the culprit is not to be found solely or primarily in the school system.

The cultural lag resulting from generations of oppression and discrimination cannot be quickly overcome, and the modest progress achieved by remedial reading classes and other attempts at compensatory education is evidence not of the incompetence or ill will of instructors but of the existence of problems not to be exorcized by magic exposure to the teaching process. The responsibility of the school, while great, is not coextensive with that of society. The deprivations of history, environment, heredity, family background and social expectation, are in the case of many Negro children beyond the capacity of schools to make good in a spurt of "education now."

None of this relieves the public school system of the need for vital reform—but the search for remedies will not be aided by a hunt for villains. Contrary to a popular belief, the public schools have not deteriorated since the time that they were the proverbial gateway for "making it" for millions of immigrants from impoverished, non-English-speaking homes. The teachers were "middle-class" then, as they are "middle-class" now, if a college degree is indication of social class.

Viewed objectively, New York schools today offer many more opportunities for the disadvantaged than were available 30 or 40 years ago. The teachers are better trained. More money is spent per child in special schools for ghetto children than in the rest of the system. More concern is displayed for the interests of the individual child than a generation ago. No contemporary school child would unrebelliously endure the innumerable hours spent in mastering the Palmer method for good penmanship, or in the endless idiotic drawing of strawberry boxes for "perspective," or in the rigid learning by rote which children accepted as part of the dull business of going to school at a time when the reputation of the public school was at its apex.

Ironically, now when the New York public schools rate low in achievement, they are more imaginative and experimental than ever before. Nor are their results, if measured comparatively, ignominious. The Coleman Report, in evaluating regional variation in achievement, states categorically: "Consistently highest is the metropolitan North." Any sensible discussion of success or failure in given areas must bear this finding in mind.

A major argument raised by proponents of "community control" is the supposedly harmful role of the public school in fostering "middle-class values." How are these values defined? In "Education and Cultural Values," George F. Kneller comments on the public school's inculcation of "such middle-class traits as neatness, politeness, correct speech and respect for property," as well as respect for order and discipline and the value of knowledge and educational achievement. Another study of the same subject stresses the middle-class emphasis on self-denial, competence, hard work and readiness to postpone immediate gratification for further reward, in contrast to the "present-oriented" rather than "future-oriented" ghetto-dweller.

Negro and Puerto Rican educators are explicit in their rejection: "Teachers should not try to impose middle-class values on Puerto Rican children" (United Teacher, May 29, 1968); the Conference on Urban Education under the chairmanship of Rhody McCoy agreed in March that white middle-class values were detrimental to black schoolchildren.

When Negroes oppose the teaching of white middle-class values they presumably object to the presentation of the industrious WASP as an ideal image; instead, they seek to stress a native culture. This view has considerable white support as a reading of the liberal and leftist press indicates. A reviewer in The New York Review of Books, discussing "On the Outskirts of Hope," a book on the education of youth in the poverty area, criticizes the author, Helaine S. Dawson, for seeking to instill middle-class white values into her pupils so as to make it possible for them to get jobs: "It was not only the students' eating habits that she wanted to change. They had to learn to be punctual, dress conservatively, speak standard English, not to be too demonstrative physically, recognize authority."

While the reviewer, Herbert Kohl, commends Miss Dawson's manifest goodwill, he suggests that she does her students "a disservice by trying to seduce them into a life many of them are certain to find inauthentic" and that "by making conformity the price of a job Miss Dawson presented them with a severely limited perspective." Here is a less revolutionary approach to the problem of values than some, but clear in its questioning of qualities which, like proficiency in grammar, are rated on report cards.

In a plea for something that might loosely be described as cultural pluralism, one educator (Charles Calitri, "The Nature and Values of Culturally Different Youth") comments on what he calls the "Negro meta-language" and asks: "Must every American learn syntax? Must they all speak in round tones and perfect sentences? Or is there room in our world for those who will manage to communicate in less than formal ways?"

The answer to Professor Calitri is in the affirmative. There has always been room for the warmth and tang of folk idiom. Various teachers of ghetto schools have demonstrated their pupils' natural eloquence by reproducing their uncorrected compositions. In showing how vividly these pupils could describe their neighborhoods or authentic aspects of their lives, such teachers have argued that ghetto children write well if allowed to express themselves honestly instead of being put into a straitjacket of "correct" sentence structure and spelling. Anyone with teaching experience on the elementary or high-school level knows this to be true. Pedantic insistence on grammar and orthography represses the flow of consciousness.

Nevertheless, a pupil who wants to qualify as a secretary instead of a houseworker must be able to write a correct business letter. The teacher must then become a drillmaster seeking to overcome the difficulties of dialect speech and spelling patterns. And the school must decide whether such conformity is relevant to the pupil's advancement. An aspirant to a white-collar or middle-class job has to learn standard spelling and sentence structure, and a stenographer, teacher or bank clerk must be literate in the accepted sense.

The New York Urban League, in a lengthy defense of the Ocean Hill-Brownsville governing board, charges that the public schools are not teaching even "the rawest fundamentals" and that the average high-school graduate in the Negro and Puerto Rican districts "cannot read at the eighth-grade level." The Urban League blames the teachers' "failure to love their children" and their "contempt"—these white, middle-class teachers do not expect the Negro children to learn, therefore they do not learn. The Urban League is unable to prove its estimate of the teachers' emotional attitudes. "How do you document a sneer?" the framers of the statement ask. In any case, even if the charge were true, the explanation would not hold.

Admittedly, loving teachers are preferable to unloving ones. That they prove the most effective is open to doubt. Good teachers may be holy terrors and their invective readily documented, as almost everyone knows from personal experience. The belief that the teacher's "love" or some infallible pedagogic technique holds the key for teaching reading is an illusion. Children have learned to read by every conceivable method—phonetic, visual, by sentences, by syllables or by whole words. The three R's have been drilled into children with or without benefit of charts, flash-cards, or blackboards, often by untrained instructors whose sole qualification was the need to open a dame school and who never spared the rod. Between the ages of 3 and 8, depending on the child, most children get the idea regardless of teacher or method.

An example of unrealistic expectations directed at the teacher is to be found in "Death at an Early Age," by Jonathan Kozol. In addition to justified denunciations of Boston's fossilized bureaucracy and brutality in the ghetto schools, Kozol charges that the teachers lack a sensitive understanding of their pupils, many of whom are mentally retarded, delinquent, or physically disturbed. The art teacher derides a disturbed child's talent which she is unable to recognize; the English teacher demands formal correctness in spelling and will not accept "skinny," an obviously more vivid word than "thin," as an antonym for "fat," and all of them prefer well-behaved, docile children to those who present serious discipline problems.

Kozol's account of the teachers' limitations is probably accurate. The teachers he describes are ordinary, well-meaning women (Kozol complains of stupidity rather than malice) who are trying to function under exceptionally difficult circumstances. They are not psychiatrists or trained specialists for the retarded. Were they endowed with the exceptional intellectual or spiritual qualifications demanded by Kozol, they would not be schoolteachers in an elementary school. Instead, they would be highly paid psychiatric consultants or they would be composing books on what's wrong with the schools. To expect average teachers, of probably adequate or more than adequate efficiency in a normal teaching situation, to cope intelligently with the high incidence of extraordinary problems described by Kozol is asking more of the public school than it can deliver.

Those tempted to question this "common-sense" view of teacher motivation may turn to the Coleman Report, which after numerous probings and questionnaires comes up with the findings that most future teachers, *Negro as well as white,* do not want to teach in minority schools and that most teachers prefer high-ability to low-ability pupils. (One of the unfailing rewards of studying the Report is that it, like other social-science studies, so reassuringly documents the obvious.) However, the expressed preference of Negro teachers for assignments to less taxing schools indicates that the motivation of the average white teacher is not racist, merely human. A less obvious statistical finding should be quoted in this connection: "Negro students in majority-white schools with poorer teachers generally achieve better than similar Negro students in majority-Negro schools with better teachers."

All of the data point to the benefits of integration for educational progress. Though the achievements of minority pupils may be low in integrated schools, they are better than in majority-Negro schools. The reason is to be found in no racial *mystique* of "white is beautiful," but quite simply in the stimulus provided by an environment in which the achievement level of students and the expectations of teachers are higher. Yet despite this evidence, Negro leaders, basing themselves on the existence of *de facto* segregation, seek the establishment of what will prove to be autonomous black enclaves: black schools controlled by blacks.

But, granting present deficiencies in the school system, how will community control redress the balance? One significant change will be a curriculum designed to stress black culture, history, art and literature. At the same time, since proficiency in elementary skills is sought, the conventional classroom subjects will also be taught. Can this be achieved at the expense of the scorned middle-class virtues already enumerated? Will the drama of attending Malcolm X assemblies generate a greater capacity for reading, writing, and arithmetic? These are not rhetorical questions.

Any course calculated to enhance the self-confidence and sense of dignity of the black child is a gain: the humiliated and deprived must be returned a usable past. As an undergraduate at Cornell University years ago, I first encountered the trauma resulting from such a deprivation. In an ancient history course, when the professor stated that Cleopatra was white, the one, generally silent, Negro student in the class began to laugh hysterically. The uncomprehending white students waited for the paroxysm to pass, puzzled and embarrassed. Today, whatever their views on the genealogy of the Ptolemies, white students and professor would understand the nature of the wound touched by an apparently objective bit of information. We appreciate the need for knowledge of the African past and of Negro culture in the present. Courses in these areas would be intellectually and psychologically valid innovations. How about other proposals?

For anyone seeking a more concrete notion of how the curriculum might be reshaped under full community control, few blueprints are available. One such is by Herman Ferguson, a former assistant principal and now consultant to the community governing board of Intermediate School 201, who has outlined in detail what he calls "A Black Survival Curriculum." Ferguson's plan for the school day is complete. The black student enters a school adorned with the pictures of Marcus Garvey, Malcolm X, Muhammad Ali, etc. He pledges allegiance to his own red, black and green flag. His morning is devoted to military training and physical training and allied arts.

The afternoon is devoted to traditional subjects but hardly in the traditional manner. "His math problems focus on such practical matters as wind velocity, muzzle velocity and other mathematical considerations involved in firing, repairing and making weapons." Home economics stresses first aid, shop courses, gunsmithing. He also studies the history and culture of his people.

That Ferguson was suspended as assistant principal of a Queens public school, after being accused of having conspired to murder moderate Negro leaders, does not invalidate his claim to being viewed as a policymaker for black community schools. His post at I. S. 201 is proof of his influence. His curriculum, fantastic though it may seem, must be considered respectfully as a possible preview of the educational scene if Negro extremists gain control in black schools.

Will learning Swahili, mathematics via weaponry or African social studies enable Negro pupils more readily to acquire the skills in which they are now backward? There is nothing in pedagogy to suggest that a child who cannot read or spell English correctly will learn to do so by devoting energy and time to an unrelated language. Negro militants will probably answer this schoolmarmish objection by declaring that the psychic value of Swahili will more than compensate for deficiencies in English. Even should this be true, the ability to use English properly will still remain a prerequisite for advancement on a competitive basis. Ethnic or national groups who want to cultivate their linguistic and cultural heritage have generally done so as a supplement not a substitute; the study of French, Hebrew or Italian was subsidiary to the initial mastery of English.

Some Puerto Rican teachers in New York City, in addition to the usual demands for courses in Puerto Rican culture and for more Puerto Rican teachers and supervisors, are urging bilingualism—instruction in Spanish and English in New York City. Children would first be taught in Spanish, then switch to English, as late as the third grade in some plans under discussion.

The reason for this demand is the allegedly "bad education" offered by the public schools. Spanish-speaking children do poorly in classes conducted in English, hence the solution is instruction in Spanish. Had such a policy been followed in the past the public schools of the United States would not have been the melting pot for many-tongued immigrants, and neighborhood schools would have been conducted in Polish, Yiddish, Russian, Italian or any other language spoken by a given immigrant group.

Fortunately, instead of this linguistic fragmentation, newcomers were expected to acquire the language of the country as rapidly and fluently as they could. Experience has shown that whatever the accents of the parents, the children learned fast. At the same time, the home language was fostered or forgotten according to the amount of zeal shown by the parents for keeping the ethnic culture alive. This area was the privilege of the home, not the responsibility of the public school. But the separatist trend evident among the spokesmen for community control, whether they be Mexican-Americans, Puerto Ricans or French-speaking remnants in Louisiana, extends to language.

A distinction should be made between decentralization and community control, as now interpreted. Decentralization is a legitimate means to a less cumbersome school system through the creation of subdivisions more responsive to local needs and more efficiently administered than the present colossus. Its purpose is better education. Community control, on the other hand, has been candidly described by many of its proponents as the first step to forming "a separate black nation." Its purpose is social and political.

The confusion now bedeviling New York City stems from the welter of conflicting purposes. The teachers, in addition to their concern with job security and civil-service rights, have educational objectives; it is nonsensical demagoguery to contend otherwise. The Negro community has racial as well as educational goals. The average white citizen wants a good neighborhood school to which he can send his children quietly as in the past. The city administration wants peace and harmony. All groups contend vociferously that their chief aim is education.

Some of these aims are reconcilable; others are not. The kind of racist community control for which Negro militants are now pressing makes sense only if the outcome will be a "separate black nation." Barring that, the experiment as now conducted has little to recommend it educationally. The reiteration of the theme that "black is beautiful" may be useful therapy to a certain point. Beyond that—and from all reports that measure has been exceeded—it is neither psychically therapeutic nor intellectually helpful. If Negroes are to make their way in American society, their progress, like that of other ethnic or racial groups, will be judged by their acquisition of the majority culture in all its ramifications. That is what every minority which entered the main stream of American life has been obliged to do and there is no reason to assume that Negroes can be exempt.

A natural corollary of the current separatist trend is the espousal of group rather than individual rights, Previously the existence of racial or religious quotas was shamefacedly acknowledged by liberals as a failure to practice what American democracy preached. Yet, ironically, now that Negro militants propose the institution of quotas as a matter of principle, the idea is hailed by leftists and liberals as a higher concept of equality rather than deplored as retrogression to the familiar quota systems of authoritarian societies.

Many colleges throughout the country have relaxed their admissions requirements to allow for the entrance of capable minority students. These colleges have instituted compensatory courses to cope with the handicaps with which minority students come. While this is a salutary development, Negro militants scorn such palliatives. In some cities Negro and white students and teachers have raised the cry that minorities be admitted to colleges on a proportional basis. If Negroes constitute a third of a community, the students in the municipal college should be a third Negro, regardless of their qualifications. These advocates of automatic admission on ethnic grounds reduce the meaning of both equality and education to absurdity.

Nathan Hare, assistant professor of sociology at Howard University, recently stated: "Equality of opportunity is more than just the right to go to school. A colleague of mine has proposed that every Negro child be given scholarships to the Ph.D. if he so desires." Dr. Hare added: "The philosophy of black power is to bring about equality—not just equality of opportunity."

Dr. Hare's colleague who suggests a Ph.D. scholarship for every Negro pupil who applies obviously does not assume that every such pupil will meet customary educational and intellectual standards; only a small number of white students qualify for Ph.D.'s. Equality for Negroes, under this doctrine, means not the achievement of status by individuals but the conferral of group status as an act of historic justice to compensate for discrimination.

I am deliberately dwelling on extreme formulations because they highlight the nature of some demands now being voiced. While few Negro educators call for instant Ph.D.'s, most stress "relevant standards" in examinations for teachers, students and civil-service applicants. The institution of "relevant" standards may mean an intelligent attempt to develop examinations which will test knowledge and ability in terms familiar to a given social class or geographic region. But "relevant" may also become a euphemism for "lower."

While it is true that a correct definition of "chitterlings" is as relevant in judging vocabulary as a definition of "blanc-mange," a core of words, whose retention or exclusion cannot be determined by their familiarity to a given group, remains to indicate educational levels attained, and while there may be considerable flexibility in the teaching of literature and in assigning works relevant to the interests of particular students, no such flexibility is possible in setting criteria for examinations in mathematics or the exact sciences, unless proficiency in these beyond a minimal level is barred as irrelevant. The question then is relevant or irrelevant to what? How far can relevance go?

The pressure of civil-rights groups for the admission of Negro applicants who fail to meet academic entrance norms has extended to the medical schools. Such leading institutions as Columbia, New York University and Yeshiva University have enrolled Negro students of low achievement in special programs in their medical colleges. Many other colleges have followed suit. Cornell University, on the other hand, has declared unfashionably that "the Cornell University Medical College expects to continue its policy of admitting the most highly qualified students possible regardless of race, color or creed."

Again, there would be fairly general agreement on the proposition that able Negro students who suffered from inferior preparation in high school should be given special opportunities. But once admission has been complicated by other than academic considerations, it ceases to be a question of enabling a Negro student to compete on equal terms with those better prepared; in addition we must determine whether justice does not require the further adjustment of standards so that Negroes will be represented not by "token" admissions but by numbers more in accord with the size of the Negro community. The argument may well be advanced that it is more important for Negroes to have many black doctors with mediocre grades than a few who rate "A" in college. Academic excellence might reasonably be viewed as less relevant than greater self-esteem and independence, to the psychic health of the black community.

These are not negligible or unworthy considerations. Proponents of lowering the standards of medical schools for Negroes have pointed out that many parts of the world manage fairly well with what the United States would consider "inadequate" medical training, and that at the turn of the century medical standards in the United States were considerably less strict than those of today without national catastrophe.

The chief trouble with this argument is that it is only valid on the unlikely assumption that a Negro enclave, to all intents closed and self-sufficient, will be formed in the United States. In such an enclave the community could determine acceptable standards in education, medicine or engineering. It could, if so inclined, decide that the development of a quantitatively large Negro professional class was an essential first step to the creation of a qualitative élite. After a substantial number of Negro physicians, lawyers and other professionals had begun to flourish, standards would be raised. Such a process would parallel what took place in the United States where steeper medical-school requirements have been introduced each decade.

Since, however, there is small probability of the establishment of a self-contained Negro state, the Negro professional will have to compete within the total framework of American society. Unless he meets the same qualifications as whites, neither Negroes nor whites will seek his services. For this reason the present trend to reduce admission standards for Negroes cannot be uncritically hailed as belated social justice without considering whether standards for graduation should be maintained. For at what stage has opportunity been truly equalized? If a larger proportion of Negro than white students should fail, complaints about the numbers graduating, rather than the numbers admitted, will be heard. As soon as a quota system becomes a respectable educational objective, there are no logical bounds to its extension.

There is nothing new about ethnic quotas and community control. The first has been and still is the admitted mark of non-democratic societies, and the second has flourished under other names in private parochial schools, religious or cultural, and in autonomous local schools. In contradistinction to these the great new virtue of the public school was its disdain of quotas and its transcendence of special religious and ethnic interests. The establishment of an ethnic parochial school system to be financed by public means would be defensible only if it promised educational and social gains large enough to warrant a radical departure from what has been viewed as a fundamental concept of a democratic society.

Before the city, state or Federal Government undertake, contrary to previous policy, to finance an ethnic school system they should look at the results of their own research, which make it clear that a Negro or Puerto Rican parochial school system is unjustified from the point of view of educational results. And the social benefits are also dubious.

True, we are in a revolutionary situation; true, Negroes demand justice "now." And equally true, we are reaping the grim harvest of white racism. But the answer does not lie in giving formal sanction to black racism. Nor dare we forget that community control in Harlem means community control in Queens and any other district with a distinct ethnic or religious composition. While an African curriculum will be fashioned in one school, the teaching of evolution may be dropped in another in accordance with local wishes. If the governing board in one section knows best what their children need, the same holds for a governing board with other ideas. If one board can fire white teachers, another can do the same to Negro teachers. If black berets will be legitimate school headdress, so will white hoods in another locality.

No rich imagination is required to foresee to what excesses caprice and bigotry, white and black, may lead. Once uniform standards for curricula, for promotion, and for teacher hiring can be superseded by local obscurantism or self-interest, the public-school system as a progressive and unifying force has been effectively destroyed.

The answer to the needs of an ill-equipped, shifting school population, many of whose members have recently arrived from the South, lies not in the establishment of racial enclaves but in a still greater emphasis, despite their expense, on special projects such as the More Effective Schools program in New York. (In New York City the per capita cost per pupil in the 267 Special Service Schools in ghetto areas is $584 *more* per pupil than in regular schools.) At the same time, integration should be advanced through the creation of educational parks and comprehensive educational complexes wherever feasible.

Despite the demographic realities of New York City it is not dishonest double-talk to hold to integration as a goal. For the existence of the neighborhood elementary school, often with a distinct ethnic character (Jewish, Irish, etc.) never precluded ultimate integration into the totality of American society. Even if today the Jewish middle class lives in prosperous Jewish communities on Long Island, as proletarian Jews once lived clustered together in Brownsville, it is integrated into American life, though immediate neighbors and friends may all be fellow Jews. Integration means access to the opportunities of a society and acceptance by that society on terms of equality with its other constituents.

By every social index Negroes are at last entering on the road to such opportunity and acceptance. The public schools of the North, while but one factor, can be an ally in the process of preparing black youth to enter the doors that are finally opening. But at this moment we run the danger of destroying this possibility. We have become the victims of rhetoric and catch phrases. Too lightly we prattle about "ghettos" and "genocide," forgetting the terrible meaning of these terms, and obscuring realities bad enough in themselves with the smoke of false analogies. Further to confuse the real issues, we repeat uncritically the latest social science clichés about the harm to the disadvantaged of "inauthentic middle-class values."

Since these values have been defined by their critics as industry, discipline, success through achievement and the rest of the dreary Puritan catalogue, those who oppose their inculcation in the schools are caught in a vise of contradictions. On the one hand, black rage is directed at the exclusion of Negroes from the goods—in both senses—of American middle-class life. On the other hand, black power derides the qualities required for their attainment. When black Negro militants teach their youth in the style of LeRoi Jones that they are entitled to collect now as a group on the basis of America's past debt, these instructors are providing a bill which cannot be honored except through expropriation. And expropriation is not an immediate prospect. In the foreseeable future individual competence and achievement will remain the chief keys to advancement. Therefore, educators and sociologists, instead of seeking to elevate temporary deficiencies into permanent virtues, should struggle both for equality of opportunity and for the adequate preparation of Negro youth to make use of the new opportunities.

The answer to the needs of the Negro community does not lie in the creation of separate, racist enclaves. (The old neighborhood school was at least flexible and subject to uniform standards.) No rational society can be expected to support the divisive and hostile forces now developing under the guise of "local autonomy" or "community control." Only an intelligently decentralized school system—offering maximum educational opportunities, allowing for legitimate community participation on the local level, and with the overriding goal of integration into the totality of American life—offers a solution to the urban crisis.

JAMES BALDWIN | *A Talk to Teachers*

Let's begin by saying that we are living through a very dangerous time. Everyone in this room is in one way or another aware of that. We are in a revolutionary situation, no matter how unpopular that word has become in this country. The society in which we live is desperately menaced, not by Khrushchev, but from within. So any citizen of this country who figures himself as responsible—and particularly those of you who deal with the minds and hearts of young people—must be prepared to "go for broke." Or to put it another way, you must understand that in the attempt to correct so many generations of bad faith and cruelty, when it is operating not only in the classroom but in society, you will meet the most fantastic, the most brutal, and the most determined resistance. There is no point in pretending that this won't happen.

Now, since I am talking to schoolteachers and I am not a teacher myself, and in some ways am fairly easily intimidated, I beg you to let me leave that and go back to what I think to be the entire purpose of education in the first place. It would seem to me that when a child is born, if I'm the child's parent, it is my obligation and my high duty to civilize that child. Man is a social animal. He cannot exist without a society. A society, in turn, depends on certain things which everyone within that society takes for granted. Now, the crucial paradox which confronts us here is that the whole process of education occurs within a social framework and is designed to perpetuate the aims of society. Thus, for example, the boys and girls who were born during the era of the Third Reich, when educated to the purposes of the Third Reich, became barbarians. The paradox of education is precisely this—that as one begins to become conscious one begins to examine the society in which he is being educated. The purpose of education, finally, is to create in a person the ability to look at the world for himself, to make his own decisions, to say to himself this is black or this is white, to decide for himself whether there is a God in heaven or not. To ask questions of the universe, and then learn to live with those questions, is the way he achieves his own identity. But no society is really anxious to have that kind of person around. What societies really, ideally, want is a citizenry which will simply obey the rules of society. If a society succeeds in this, that society is about to perish. The obligation of anyone who thinks of himself as

From *Saturday Review Education Supplement* (December 21, 1963), pp. 42–44, 60.

responsible is to examine society and try to change it and to fight it—at no matter what risk. This is the only hope society has. This is the only way societies change.

Now, if what I have tried to sketch has any validity, it becomes thoroughly clear, at least to me, that any Negro who is born in this country and undergoes the American educational system runs the risk of becoming schizophrenic. On the one hand he is born in the shadow of the stars and stripes and he is assured it represents a nation which has never lost a war. He pledges allegiance to that flag which guarantees "liberty and justice for all." He is part of a country in which anyone can become President, and so forth. But on the other hand he is also assured by his country and his countrymen that he has never contributed anything to civilization—that his past is nothing more than a record of humiliations gladly endured. He is assured by the republic that he, his father, his mother, and his ancestors were happy, shiftless, watermelon-eating darkies who loved Mr. Charlie and Miss Ann, that the value he has as a black man is proven by one thing only—his devotion to white people. If you think I am exaggerating, examine the myths which proliferate in this country about Negroes.

Now all this enters the child's consciousness much sooner than we as adults would like to think it does. As adults, we are easily fooled because we are so anxious to be fooled. But children are very different. Children, not yet aware that it is dangerous to look too deeply at anything, look at everything, look at each other, and draw their own conclusions. They don't have the vocabulary to express what they see, and we, their elders, know how to intimidate them very easily and very soon. But a black child, looking at the world around him, though he cannot know quite what to make of it, is aware that there is a reason why his mother works so hard, why his father is always on edge. He is aware that there is some reason why, if he sits down in the front of the bus, his father or mother slaps him and drags him to the back of the bus. He is aware that there is some terrible weight on his parents' shoulders which menaces him. And it isn't long—in fact it begins when he is in school—before he discovers the shape of his oppression.

Let us say that the child is seven years old and I am his father, and I decide to take him to the zoo, or to Madison Square Garden, or to the U.N. Building, or to any of the tremendous monuments we find all over New York City, which is not Harlem. Now, where the boy lives—even if it is a housing project—is in an undesirable neighborhood. If he lives in one of those housing projects of which everyone in New York is so proud, he has at the front door, if not closer, the pimps, the whores, the junkies—in a word, the danger of life in the ghetto. And the child knows this, though he doesn't know why.

I still remember my first sight of New York. It was really another city when I was born—where I was born. We looked down over the Park Avenue streetcar tracks. It was Park Avenue, but I didn't know what Park Avenue meant *downtown.* The Park Avenue I grew up on, which is still standing, is dark and dirty. No one would dream of opening a Tiffany's on that Park Avenue, and when you go downtown you discover that you are literally in the white world. It is rich—or at least it looks rich. It is clean—because they collect garbage downtown. There are doormen. People walk about as though they owned where they were—and indeed they do. And it's a great shock. It's very hard to relate yourself to this. You don't know what it means. You know—you know instinctively—that none of this is for you. You know this before you are told. And who is it for and who is paying for it? And why isn't it for you?

Later on when you become a grocery boy or messenger and you try to enter one of those buildings a man says, "Go to the back door." Still later, if you happen by some odd chance to have a friend in one of those buildings, the man says "Where's your package?" Now this by no means is the core of the matter. What I'm trying to get at is that by this time the Negro child has had, effectively, almost all the doors of opportunity slammed in his face, and there are very few things he can do about it. He can more or less accept it with an absolutely inarticulate and dangerous rage inside—all the more dangerous because it is never expressed. It is precisely those silent people whom white people see every day of their lives—I mean your porter and your maid, who never say anything more than "Yes Sir" and "No Ma'am." They will tell you it's raining if that is what you want to hear, and they will tell you the sun is shining if *that* is what you want to hear. They really hate you—really hate you because in their eyes (and they're right) you stand between them and life. I want to come back to that in a moment. It is the most sinister of the facts, I think, which we now face.

There is something else the Negro child can do, too. Every street boy—and I was a street boy, so I know—looking at the society which has produced him, looking at the standards of that society which are not honored by anybody, looking at your churches and the government and the politicians, understands that this structure is operated for someone else's benefit—not for his. And there's no room in it for him. If he is really cunning, really ruthless, really strong—and many of us are—he becomes a kind of criminal. He becomes a kind of criminal because that's the only way he can live. Harlem and every ghetto in this city—every ghetto in this country—is full of people who live outside the law. They wouldn't dream of calling a policeman. They wouldn't, for a moment, listen to any of those professions of which we are so proud on the Fourth of July. They have turned away from this country forever and totally. They live by their wits and really long to see the day when the entire structure comes down.

The point of all this is that black men were brought here as a source of cheap labor. They were indispensable to the economy. In order to justify the fact that men were treated as though they were animals, the white republic had to brainwash itself into believing that they were, indeed, animals and *deserved* to be treated like animals. Therefore it is almost impossible for any Negro child to discover anything about his actual history. The reason is that this "animal," once he suspects his own worth, once he starts believing that he is a man, has begun to attack the entire power structure. This is why America has spent such a long time keeping the Negro in his place. What I am trying to suggest to you is that it was not an accident, it was not an act of God, it was not done by well-meaning people muddling into something which they didn't understand. It was a deliberate policy hammered into place in order to make money from black flesh. And now, in 1963, because we have never faced this fact, we are in intolerable trouble.

The Reconstruction, as I read the evidence, was a bargain between the North and South to this effect: "We've liberated them from the land—and delivered them to the bosses." When we left Mississippi to come North we did not come to freedom. We came to the bottom of the labor market, and we are still there. Even the Depression of the 1930s failed to make a dent in Negroes' relationship to white workers in the labor unions. Even today, so brainwashed is this republic that people seriously ask in what they suppose to be good faith, "What does the Negro want?" I've heard a great many asinine questions in my life, but that is perhaps the most asinine and perhaps the most insulting. But the point here is that people who ask that question, thinking that they ask it in good faith, are really the victims of this conspiracy to make Negroes believe they are less than human.

In order for me to live, I decided very early that some mistake had been made somewhere. I was not a "nigger" even though you called me one. But if I was a "nigger" in your eyes, there was something about *you*—there was something *you* needed. I had to realize when I was very young that I was none of those things I was told I was. I was not, for example, happy. I never touched a watermelon for all kinds of reasons. I have been invented by white people, and I knew enough about life by this time to understand that whatever you invent, whatever you project, is you! So where we are now is that a whole country of people believe I'm a "nigger," and I *don't,* and the battle's on! Because if I am not what I've been told I am, then it means that *you're* not what you thought *you* were *either!* And that is the crisis.

It is not really a "Negro revolution" that is upsetting this country. What is upsetting the country is a sense of its own identity. If, for example, one managed to change the curriculum in all the schools so that Negroes learned more about themselves and their real contributions to this culture, you would be liberating not only Negroes, you'd be liberating white people who know nothing about their own history. And the reason is that if you are compelled to lie about one aspect of anybody's history, you must lie about it all. If you have to lie about my real role here, if you have to pretend that I hoed all that cotton just because I loved you, then you have done something to yourself. You are mad.

Now let's go back a minute. I talked earlier about those silent people—the porter and the maid—who, as I said, don't look up at the sky if you ask them if it is raining, but look into your face. My ancestors and I were very well trained. We understood very early that this was not a Christian nation. It didn't matter what you said or how often you went to church. My father and my mother and my grandfather and my grandmother knew that Christians didn't act this way. It was as simple as that. And if that was so there was no point in dealing with white people in terms of their own moral professions, for they were not going to honor them. What one did was to turn away, smiling all the time, and tell white people what they wanted to hear. But people always accuse you of reckless talk when you say this.

All this means that there are in this country tremendous reservoirs of bitterness which have never been able to find an outlet, but may find an outlet soon. It means that well-meaning white liberals place themselves in great danger when they try to deal with Negroes as though they were missionaries. It means, in brief, that a great price is demanded to liberate all those silent people so that they can breathe for the first time and *tell* you what they think of you. And a price is demanded to liberate all those white children—some of them near forty—who have never grown up, and who never will grow up, because they have no sense of their identity.

What passes for identity in America is a series of myths about one's heroic ancestors. It's astounding to me, for example, that so many people really appear to believe that the country was founded by a band of heroes who wanted to be free. That happens not to be true. What happened was that some people left Europe because they couldn't stay there any longer and had to go someplace else to make it. That's all. They were hungry, they were poor, they were convicts. Those who were making it in England, for example, did not get on the *Mayflower.* That's how the country was settled. Not by Gary Cooper. Yet we have a whole race of people, a whole republic, who believe the myths to the point where even today they select political representatives, as far as I can tell, by how closely they resemble Gary Cooper. Now this is dangerously infantile, and it shows in every level of national life. When I was living in Europe, for example, one of the worst revelations to me was the way Americans walked around Europe buying this and buying that and insulting everybody—not even out of malice, just because they didn't know any better.

Well, that is the way they have always treated me. They weren't cruel, they just didn't know you were alive. They didn't know you had any feelings.

What I am trying to suggest here is that in the doing of all this for 100 years or more, it is the American white man who has long since lost his grip on reality. In some peculiar way, having created this myth about Negroes, and the myth about his own history, he created myths about the world so that, for example, he was astounded that some people could prefer Castro, astounded that there are people in the world who don't go into hiding when they hear the word "Communism," astounded that Communism is one of the realities of the twentieth century which we will not overcome by pretending that it does not exist. The political level in this country now, on the part of people who should know better, is abysmal.

The Bible says somewhere that where there is no vision the people perish. I don't think anyone can doubt that in this country today we are menaced—intolerably menaced—by a lack of vision.

It is inconceivable that a sovereign people should continue, as we do so abjectly, to say, "I can't do anything about it. It's the government." The government is the creation of the people. It is responsible to the people. And the people are responsible for it. No American has the right to allow the present government to say, when Negro children are being bombed and hosed and shot and beaten all over the deep South, that there is nothing we can do about it. There must have been a day in this country's life when the bombing of four children in Sunday School would have created a public uproar and endangered the life of a Governor Wallace. It happened here and there was no public uproar.

I began by saying that one of the paradoxes of education was that precisely at the point when you begin to develop a conscience, you must find yourself at war with your society. It is your responsibility to change society if you think of yourself as an educated person. And on the basis of the evidence—the moral and political evidence—one is compelled to say that this is a backward society. Now if I were a teacher in this school, or any Negro school, and I was dealing with Negro children, who were in my care only a few hours of every day and would then return to their homes and to the streets, children who have an apprehension of their future which with every hour grows grimmer and darker, I would try to teach them—I would try to make them know—that those streets, those houses, those dangers, those agonies by which they are surrounded, are criminal. I would try to make each child know that these things are the results of a criminal conspiracy to destroy him. I would teach him that if he intends to get to be a man, he must at once decide that he is stronger than this conspiracy and that he must never make his peace with it. And that one of his weapons for refusing to make his peace with it and for destroying it depends on what he decides he is worth. I would teach him that there are currently very few standards in this country which are worth a man's respect. That it is up to him to begin to change these standards for the sake of the life and the health of the country. I would suggest to him that the popular culture—as represented, for example, on television and in comic books and in movies—is based on fantasies created by very ill people, and he must be aware that these are fantasies that have nothing to do with reality. I would teach him that the press he reads is not as free as it says it is—and that he can do something about that, too. I would try to make him know that just as American history is longer, larger, more various, more beautiful, and more terrible than anything anyone has ever said about it, so is the world larger, more daring, more beautiful and more terrible, but principally larger—and that it belongs to him. I would teach him that he doesn't have to be bound by the expediences of any given Administration, any given policy, any given time—that he has the right and the necessity to examine everything. I would try to show him that one has not learned anything about Castro when one says, "He is a Communist." This is a way of *not* learning something about Castro, something about Cuba, something, in fact, about the world. I would suggest to him that he is living, at the moment, in an enormous province. America is not the world and if America is going to become a nation, she must find a way—and this child must help her to find a way—to use the tremendous potential and tremendous energy which this child represents. If this country does not find a way to use that energy, it will be destroyed by that energy.

Selected References

AMIDON, EDMUND. and ELIZABETH HUNTER. *Improving Teaching.* New York: Holt, Rinehart & Winston, 1966.

BALASSI, SYLVESTER J. *Focus on Teaching.* New York: Odyssey Press, 1968.

"Breakthroughs to Better Teaching," *Harvard Educational Review* (Winter 1963), entire issue.

BROUDY, HARRY S. "Criteria for the Professional Preparation of Teachers," *Journal of Teacher Education* (December 1965), pp. 408–415.

COMBS, ARTHUR W. *The Professional Education of Teachers: A Perceptual View of Teacher Preparation.* Boston: Allyn & Bacon, 1965.

CONANT, JAMES B. *The Education of American Teachers.* New York: McGraw-Hill Company, 1963.

LIEBERMAN, MYRON. *Education as a Profession.* Englewood Cliffs, N.J.: Prentice-Hall, 1956.

———, and MICHAEL H. MOSKOW. *Collective Negotiations for Teachers.* Chicago: Rand McNally Company, 1966.

"Methods of Evaluating Teachers," *NEA Research Bulletin* (February 1965), pp. 12–18.

MOSKOW, MICHAEL H. *Teachers and Unions.* Philadelphia: University of Pennsylvania Press, 1966.

STINNETT, T. M. *Professional Problems of Teachers,* 3rd ed. New York: The Macmillan Company, 1968.

———. *Turmoil in Teaching: A History of the Organizational Struggle for American Teachers.* New York: The Macmillan Company, 1968.

Schools in Transition

THE EDITORS consider the school as a social institution. This may imply either that the school is a society in itself, comprising a number of people together and forming a community for the purpose of realizing educative ends; or it may stress the relationship between the school and the world outside the school. The school, in that sense, is an institution having a certain sort of rapport with the larger life of society as a whole. Yet, the function of education is to anticipate and give direction to changes that are occurring day by day within society and not simply to confirm these changes. Education, in the nature of the case, has to be concerned with the future. But, if we ask ourselves what we positively know of the future, about all we can say is that it will not be like the present. The whole world is committed to the highest possible rate of technological change. The daily accomplishments of science are such as to convince us that we are eventually going to know how everything works. Then we shall be able to do anything and be able to solve everything. The first question about education we pose in this section is: How can it prepare for a future so uncertain and contingent that the main outlines of it are shrouded in the dark shadows of dubiety?

This century has been characterized as the age of the common man. This was symbolized after World War I, when various governments erected monuments not merely to heroes but also to the unknown soldier. The common man, the average man, and the little man is the outstanding hero of the century. He thrives today because of the spread of education, social legislation, greater economic opportunity, and redistribution of wealth through taxation. The common man will not tolerate being pushed around.

Exploitation of man by man is on the way out. This century has been distinguished by the most formidable advances in history, partly because the rank and file of people almost everywhere demand education as a natural right. It is no longer something doled out to the poor or reserved for the privileged. What is the meaning of education as a natural right? Does it mean that all children have the same right to an education that will enable them to achieve their growth as human beings? Does it mean that all children have the same right to the same education independently of their capacities? Do they have the same right to attend the same schools or, does it mean simply, assuming they are not subnormal, the same education for all? Soberly interpreted, democracy in education is equality of opportunity to achieve through schooling an education commensurate with one's capacities. This is America's contribution to the history of education. This requires that we grant our neighbor's children, no matter what their social background and status, the same rights and opportunities to an education we demand as parents for our own children. Anyone who accepts this principle seriously must acknowledge the great responsibility of the state as the public agency to equalize opportunities.

It appears that we have evolved what is in many respects a national system of education, and the fundamental political problem is not whether we shall have a measure of Federal control in education but how this control will be exercised and kept sufficiently responsive to the public and local communities. How to keep open public education issues to public scrutiny and criticism. The question is not whether we shall have or not have a larger amount of conscious social organization, but what kind of social organization shall we have? This question is the issue of freedom and regimentation—the question of the tension between personal liberty and initiative on the one hand, and the obvious and growing necessity on the other for a larger degree of social organization. This brings us to the final problem: education for what? schooling for what? There are those who maintain that it is the role of an educational system to pass on the cultural tradition. Yet the schools cannot do everything; there are limitations to education. Society has responsibilities that it must shoulder; it cannot leave all problems to the educational system. However we interpret the role of the educational system, it is clear that the socialization aspect of the educative process is important. The society in which American children grow up is highly diversified and complex with many groups of people having characteristically different ways of life. As the child grows older, various interpersonal and intergroup relationships broaden the scope of his participation in social life and modify his pattern of behavior. Through interaction with a wide range of social stimuli—the school, the family, the media of mass communication—his personality is molded. But, in addition to these stimuli, other forces operate to influence, directly and indirectly, the kind and quality of education he receives. Urbanization, automation, increased leisure, and social class differences are current social forces influencing today's school and shaping its transition for the future.

To analyze the implication of social class in American society, Robert J. Havighurst investigates the particular ways the quality and quantity of education of children is determined.

The school desegregation decision of the Supreme Court in 1954 transformed overnight what had been largely an academic discussion among professional educators into a public controversy that has grown in intensity each year until there is not an untouched household in the nation. What appeared originally as primarily a southern social problem has been recognized for what it was all the time—an American dilemma. Currently the focus of school controversy has shifted from rural South to urban North where the explosive problem in the ghettos ranges far beyond the inner city. Charles V. Hamilton of Harvard University seriously questions whether or not one can adequately educate black ghetto children in an integrated school system. He calls for "the involvement of more parents in the school system and the improvement of educational opportunities within the black community."

Peter Schrag goes to the heart of this issue. To him the important question, regardless of integration, is how we can make the public schools function for all children. There seem to be two elements here: one is having the community more actively involved; the other is getting the tools through which the schools can be improved. To argue that you are going to improve the education of the child just by turning the school over to the local community doesn't really meet the problem unless at the same time you are going to improve the system itself. Greater people participation, according to Schrag, is important, but with no attention to the quality of education, the eye is removed from the basic problem.

Christopher Jencks of the Graduate School of Education, Harvard University, looks at the crisis of the education of the ghetto child from a different perspective. That the black child cannot read nor write results from the fact that ghetto schools have become custodial institutions for keeping the children off the street. Jencks proposes that black nationalists follow the Catholic precedent by creating their own private schools, outside the regular public school system, but eligible for substantial tax support. This would create a sense of community solidarity and pride in the ghetto. Neil V. Sullivan examines some of the popular "myths" that act to block integration, such as, integration in the schools will lead to a decline of academic standards, to compensatory education, and to violence. He also identifies certain "gaps" that slow the process of integration—"educational gap, "cultural gap," and "behavioral gap." Charles E. Martin, Superintendent of Schools, Chattanooga, Tennessee, who comes from the deep South calls for new commitment and vigorous effort to design and effect social change and bring about genuine integration.

The United States has taken pride in the fact that the principal responsibility for operation of the schools traditionally has been delegated by the states to local districts. Yet, the basic commitment that the United States makes for education determines, in large measure, its leadership in world affairs. How can "public" education which has such a vital national function to perform be left exclusively to local districts and communities? What is the meaning of the term "public" education? John Hardin Best examines the historical changes and developments of "public education" in this country since the nineteenth century. The issue of Federal aid to private schools concerns more than the separation of church and state and involves matters other than social policy. Donald A. Erickson speaks for aid to private schools and Oscar Handlin of Harvard argues against it.

The last grouping of articles deals with the persistent problem of the place of religion in the education system. According to Wilfrid Sheed of *Commonweal,* the parochial system provides the badly needed cultural diversity in our society. It is also essential as religion continues to serve as a basis for moral values. Professor Philip H. Phenix, Teachers College, Columbia University, maintains that the public schools should teach neither a particular kind of religion nor encourage a student to be religious or nonreligious; yet he feels that the schools have an obligation to "teach religion" by helping students confront "ultimate concerns" that rise out of "common and universal human situations."

ROBERT J. HAVIGHURST | **Social Class and Education**

Introduction

As a part of the process by which a social group brings up its children to become adults, education always takes place in and for a given society. The present state and structure of the society is mirrored in its schools and reflected through the schools into the lives of its children. At the same time a society which is undergoing internal changes uses education as a means of facilitating these changes.

These two contrasting functions of education—the perpetuating and the change-promoting functions—should always be kept in mind when studying social class and education. If only one function is seen at a time, education is likely to be grossly misunderstood. For instance, the fact that children from the higher classes get better grades on the average and go further in school than children from the lower classes may lead the hasty observer to the conclusion that education perpetuates the status quo and, therefore, is "undemocratic." Yet another incautious observer may note that education is used by clever lower-class youth as a means of social climbing and, thus, is an important factor in the relatively high rate of social mobility in the United States; and he may leap to the conclusion that education contributes to instability in the social structure with a loss of the values that come from continuity and cultural tradition.

Both of these conclusions have a severely limited validity, as would be evident to an observer who saw the whole picture.

Education reflects the social-class system

The American social-class system is now generally understood to consist of three classes with subdivisions. There is a large working class, consisting of some 60 per cent of the population, most of whom work with their hands. Above this group in the social hierarchy is a substantial middle class of white-collar workers with almost 40 per cent of the popula-

From "Social-Class Influences on American Education," *NSSE Yearbook, 1960,* Part 2, pp. 120–143. Reprinted by permission of the National Society for the Study of Education, Chicago, Ill.

tion. At the top, in terms of social status, is a small upper class of 2 or 3 per cent, who have the highest social prestige and the greatest wealth.

When the middle and the working classes in the United States are subdivided, the result is the five-class system[1] which will be used in this chapter with the following percentage composition: upper, 2 per cent; upper-middle, 8 per cent; lower-middle, 30 per cent; upper-lower, 40 per cent; lower-lower, 20 per cent. This composition varies from one section of the country to another and from one city to another, but it will serve the purposes of this chapter to use these average figures for the situation in 1960.

The kind of education an American child gets depends very much on the social-class position of his family. This fact was reported by Warner[2] in the early 1930's for "Yankee City" in New England, by Hollingshead[3] in the early 1940's for "Elmtown" in the midwest, by Davie[4] in 1950 for New Haven, Connecticut, and by Havighurst and his colleagues[5] in 1958 for the midwest community of "River City." These are a few of the many studies that have documented this now familiar fact.

There was in River City in the 1950's, as there has been throughout the United States, a close relation between progress through school and the social class of a child's parents. However, there has also been a progressive increase in the amount of education obtained by children of working-class families. . . . Whereas in 1920 it was extremely rare for a student of working-class background to enter college, by 1960 the gross numbers of college students from working-class homes exceeded the numbers from the upper- and upper-middle-class homes.

Education as an Agent of Social Change

There are two types of social change. One is change within a society whose general pattern does not change. This is the type discussed in this chapter—changes within a social structure whose broad outlines are not changing. The second type is change that affects the society as a whole —its political institutions, its system of economic production, or the major elements of its social structure. The latter type of social change will not be treated in this chapter.

If even one boy from a working-class home graduates from high school

1 W. Lloyd Warner, Marcia Meeker, and Kenneth Eells, *Social Class in America* (New York: Harper & Bros., Torchbook, 1960).

2 W. Lloyd Warner, Robert J. Havighurst, and Martin B. Loeb, *Who Shall Be Educated?* (New York: Harper & Bros., 1944).

3 August B. Hollingshead, *Elmtown's Youth* (New York: John Wiley & Sons, 1949).

4 James S. Davie, "Social Class Factors and School Attendance," *Harvard Educational Review,* XXIII (1953), 175–185.

5 Robert J. Havighurst, Paul H. Bowman, Gordon P. Liddle, Charles V. Matthews, and James V. Pierce, *Growing Up in River City* (New York: John Wiley & Sons, 1961).

and college and gets a middle-class job and salary, to this extent education has contributed to change in the society. . . . There is a large and growing amount of preparation for upward social mobility through education by youth from working-class and lower-middle-class homes.

Education also prepares people for upward group mobility by giving them knowledge and skills that make them more productive as a group of manual workers or white-collar workers, and thus giving them a higher standard of living even though they stay in the social classes of their fathers.

Social-Class Policies for Education

Since the several social classes have cultures of their own which are variations of the dominant American culture, it would be expected that they might differ in their notions about the purposes and functions of education and about the methods to achieve these purposes. They certainly do differ; but they also share a common set of educational ideals.

To take the common ideals first, there is a general belief in the value of education, at least up to the end of secondary school. There is a general belief that education will lead to better jobs and higher incomes. There is a less general belief that education is a good thing, in and of itself. There is a general belief that educational opportunity should be freely available to all people.

These beliefs provide the basis in public acceptance and support for a free educational system open to all through the secondary school and widely available through the university. There is a general, or "official," ideology that favors education as a quantitative good.

Where the social classes differ is not so much in broad educational ideals as in the *means* they devote to the realization of these ideals. The middle classes are most effective in making use of education because they are "future-oriented." That is, they believe that it is worthwhile to forego present satisfactions in order to gain greater ones later. Therefore, they save money, and they devote time and energy to secondary and higher education not so much for present satisfaction as for future gain.

The typical lower-class person is more "present-oriented" than "future-oriented." He has less desire and willingness than a middle-class person to sacrifice present gains for future ones. Furthermore, his resources in terms of income are smaller, and therefore he has less real possibility of saving for investment in the future. He is less likely to encourage and assist his child to go to college, for example. This is seen in the recent survey made by Elmo Roper for the Ford Foundation on the plans of parents for college education of their children. While there was a general tendency for parents to want their children to go to college, most of the low-income parents who wanted a college education for their children had done nothing to make this a possibility by saving money for this purpose.

Another distinction between classes which bears on their educational attitudes is their attitude toward social change. Middle-class people seem to be the leaders of social change, the lower class are most resistant to it, and the upper class are selective about it. David Riesman[6] sees the middle class of today as the group which "first perceives social change, of a noncataclysmic sort: it constitutes the nervous system of society, vulnerable to news and to what is new. The middle class mans the communications and research industries including teaching. . . . it is the middle class that joins voluntary associations, such as the League of Women Voters, which devote themselves inter alia to calling attention to and disseminating the news."

Recently the middle class seems to have become more tolerant toward the lower-class attitudes and easy-going qualities with respect to child-rearing, in contrast to its former coldness and demand for early independence and achievement on the part of children. This at least is the interpretation placed by Bronfenbrenner[7] on the changes of the last thirty years in child-rearing practices, though the present writer sees the lower class as also moving toward the earlier middle-class norms in child-rearing. Perhaps there is a reduction in social-class differences in child-rearing, due to the spreading of a common culture in this area through the work of maternal and child health clinics and of pediatricians.

The middle class may be seen as the fluctuating class, open to influences from above and below in the social structure, and open also to influences from domestic and world economic conditions and from ideologies in other parts of the world. The upper class is idiosyncratic, combining a traditional conservatism with a high degree of individual variability which prevents this class from speaking with a common voice on matters of educational policy. The lower class is earthy, looking for immediate practical results from education and seeing its advantages in bread-and-butter terms.

Lower-class characteristics

Within the lower class there are variations in the extent to which a family can and will act in accord with the educational attitudes to which they give lip service. These are illustrated by the following account of the visit of a primary-grade teacher to two lower-class mothers. The first mother is trying to do her best to co-operate with the school, while the second is indifferent.

[6] David Riesman, "The Psychological Effects of Social Change," *Journal of Social Issues, XVII,* No. 1 (1961), pp. 78–92.

[7] Urie Bronfenbrenner, "Socialization and Social Class Through Time and Space," in *Readings in Social Psychology,* Maccoby, Newcomb, and Hartley (eds.) (New York: Henry Holt & Co., 1958), pp. 400–424.

I visited Mrs. Smith, who is the mother of Joan Swanson. She has five children, the oldest is about 9 or 10 years old, and she is pregnant again. The house seems a lot neater and more attractive than the house they lived in previously. They have three rooms—two small bedrooms and a kitchen; the bath is in a kind of lean-to behind the kitchen and is probably shared with other families in the building. I asked the mother how she thought Joan got along this year and she said, "Well, Joan seems to like school very well, and I think that's she's gotten along pretty well, as far as I can tell." I said that Joan had done good work in school, was reading at a pretty adequate level, and that her seat work was always neat and well done. I said that she seemed very shy and the mother said that she knew this was true, but we both agreed that she seemed reasonably happy. The mother said that her new husband, Mr. Smith, is a big improvement on Joan's father who was often extremely mean to the children and that she thought that this would help Joan.

The mother said that she hoped they would get over having lice in their hair and they wouldn't have to be bothered with that next year. She said that every child had it—it went through the family—and we talked a little bit about the methods of getting rid of them. The house seemed quite neat throughout.

In contrast, Tony Shannon's house was about as dirty as anything I have ever seen. With the exception of the new 21-inch television set, the entire living room furniture would not bring two dollars at an auction. There is a small Benjamin Franklin type wood stove in the living room with broken isinglass windows in the front, and otherwise there are only chairs and a davenport—mostly without cushions—that haven't been cleaned for twenty years or more. In the bedroom in the next room I saw some extremely tumble-down davenports and beds. There are five or six children in the family, ranging in age from about two to thirteen. Mr. Blake, who is the present father, makes $52 a week according to the mother, but they don't have any money for book rental, she said. I said I would take up the book-rental matter with the principal and would communicate with the mother further. The mother seemed quite unable to see, this time, and had trouble finding the one bare light that is in the middle of the living room. Neither the mother nor any of the children seemed to have had a bath for weeks, if not months. I told the mother that Tony was supposed to be out at the Clinic tomorrow to get glasses since he had lost one of the lenses out of his and the other is badly scratched. I told the mother that Tony could do pretty well in school, but that he didn't seem very motivated and often drifted off when he was supposed to be doing his studies. She said that's the way he's always been at home too, and she didn't seem at all concerned about it; she said if I wanted to keep him another year that was perfectly all right.

Is there a class war? American education reflects the fact that there is no class war in this society. That is, there is no explicit conflict between a militant, class-conscious labor group and an equally militant capitalist group. For this reason it is possible to have general acceptance on the verbal level, at least, of middle-class educational values and standards. Still, it would be naïve to suppose that there is no class-consciousness in America. There certainly is such a consciousness, combined with a considerable degree of hostility toward the middle class by some of the lower class who are unsuccessful by middle-class standards. This is illustrated in the following interview with Bernice Hatfield, a girl from a lower-class family who dropped out of school before she was sixteen and was married shortly afterward. The interview was made as one of a routine series on school drop-outs.

Bernice is living with her mother-in-law. I scaled a fifteen-foot muddy embankment up to this little run-down house. Apparently, there is a more accessible route from the rear. Bernice required very little explanation. I asked her how long she had been out of school.

"I quit two weeks before the end of school a year ago. I was only fifteen at the time but I talked to Mr. McCoy (principal). He said that they wouldn't come get me because I would be sixteen before fall. I just didn't take the exams. I knew I wouldn't pass anyway because I didn't do any work except in typing. I really loved typing. It seems I didn't like all of my teachers. I got kicked out of English six times. Me and the teacher couldn't get along. I don't think half the kids liked her. She talked about the same thing for about a week and you didn't learn anything. Then she would spend the whole period with one kid. I took a dislike to her the first two days. I guess I could have gotten along with her but after that I didn't try. And then I just didn't understand general math, I suppose because I don't understand arithmetic. I love it, but I don't get it. I just love fractions, but those reading problems, I could never get those all the way through school. I was really going to go all the way through Home Ec because I liked it, but then my schedule was changed so I could be in a different gym class. They said they wanted to break up a gang of us girls because we were beating all the other teams and smarting off a lot. Then I got changed to a gym class with a lot of these high-class girls, as we call them. They think they are better than everyone else. They got a lot of money. They don't like us, and we don't like them. When my class was changed, I didn't even dress for gym. So I failed that too."

"Bernice, what seems to be the rub with those high-class kids?"

"Well, they seem to look down on us kids in this neighborhood. You know, they think we are scabs. You know, those kids always hung out on the east side of the building and us kids were always on the west side. Then in class, the rich kids always had their lessons. They never came without their lessons. Then if us kids didn't have ours, and we usually didn't, they would look at us. There were only two girls, Sally Clancy and Georgia Lane, that I could get along with out of that bunch. I guess it's a good thing I quit school because whenever there was any trouble, I was in the middle of it, street fights or anything else. It seems like it has been that way all my life. My temper gets me into trouble. I slap and ask questions later. That's the way my Mother and Dad were and I guess that's the way I am."

Middle-class policies on specific educational questions

With this discussion of social-class orientations as a background, it can be expected that the dominant trends and styles in education will be sponsored by the middle class, with the lower class going along, in general, though occasionally resisting on some issue where lower-class opportunity appears to be threatened, while the upper class takes no active part in educational decisions for the public and counts on its prestige and power to guarantee satisfactory educational arrangements for its own children.

This hypothesis can be tested with respect to the principal educational emphasis of the 1950's. One of these has been the emphasis on "tough" education, with more stress on science and mathematics in the secondary school, and a heavier schedule of school and home study. The strongest proponents of this policy have been middle-class business and military men, aided by a number of university and college educators. The most vocal opponents of this policy have also been middle-class people. There has been no explicit lower-class position on the matter. The great interest in education for gifted children during the present decade has been mainly a middle-class interest, focused on providing special facilities and special treatment for gifted children, including such things as foreign language in the elementary school and college-level courses in the high school. The great majority of the children of working-class homes do not participate in such programs.

Another emphasis is on expansion in higher education. This is to the direct advantage of working-class youth, who have the greatest difficulty getting into college, but the movement is led by middle-class people who argue for it on the ground that the society needs more college-trained people. When the shortage of trained manpower is over, as it is likely to be by 1965, middle-class attitudes about expansion of higher education may change.

The issue of federal government support for education has not been resolved during the past decade, though a substantial increase in federal government support has taken place. On this issue, the working class seems to be fairly positive, through its spokesmen in organized labor. But the middle class is divided on this issue, and no basic resolution is likely to be achieved unless middle-class opinion becomes more solid in one direction or another.

Social Class and Decision-Making in Education

There are three decision-making groups with respect to education in the United States. Each of these broad groups may be examined with respect to its social-class status and the relation of its goals to its social-class composition.

Official policy-makers

Control of schools and colleges is legally vested in boards of education, boards of trustees, and boards of regents who appoint the administrators and the teachers and are responsible for the making of educational policy. There are two questions with regard to these people. What is their socioeconomic status, and do they favor their own social classes in conducting educational affairs?

With respect to the socioeconomic status of board members, the facts are established. Charters[8] reviewed the evidence for public school board members in 1953 and concluded, "that board members are recruited from among business and professional men (except in rural areas) or, in different language, from among persons in the upper-middle class of the community." There are a few apparent exceptions to this rule in communities where a "quota" of working-class men are appointed or elected to the school board.

In the field of higher education, the trustees or regents are generally upper-class or upper-middle-class men and women, the higher-status people being on boards of the higher-status institutions.

The next question is whether board members favor their own social classes in their roles as educational policy-makers. On the whole, it appears that they do not favor their own social classes in an explicit way. Seldom is there an issue in which class lines can be clearly drawn. A hypothetical issue of this sort might deal with the establishment of a free public junior college in a community where there already was a good private college which served the middle-class youth adequately but was too expensive for working class youth. In situations of this sort the board generally favors the expansion of free education. Campbell[9] studied the records of 172 school board members in twelve western cities over the period of 1931–40 and found "little or no relationship between certain social and economic factors and school board competence," as judged by a panel of professional educators who studied the voting records on educational issues.

The few cases of clear favoritism along social-class lines are as likely as not to involve representatives of the working class on the school board who favor some such practice as higher wages for janitors rather than pay increases for teachers, and such issues are not issues of educational policy.

In general, it appears that trustees and board members attempt to represent the public interest in their administration of educational policy, and this is made easier by the fact that the dominant values of the society are middle-class values, which are generally thought to be valid for the entire society. There have been very few cases of explicit conflict of interest between the middle class and any other class in the field of edu-

[8] W. W. Charters, Jr., "Social Class Analysis and the Control of Public Education," *Harvard Educational Review*, XXIII (1953), 268–283.

[9] Ronald F. Campbell, "Are School Boards Reactionary?" *Phi Delta Kappan*, XXVII (1945), 82–83, 93.

cational policy. If there were more such cases, it would be easier to answer the question whether the policy-makers favor their own social classes.

There is currently a major controversy of public education in which group interests and values are heavily engaged. This is the issue of segregated schools in the South. In this case it is primarily a matter of conflict of racial groups rather than social-class groups. Thus, the white middle and lower classes are arrayed against the Negro middle and lower classes. This conflict may be resolved in a way which will suit white middle-class people better than it suits white lower-class people. If this happens, there may be some class conflict in the South, with school boards and school teachers taking the middle-class position.

THE EDUCATIONAL PROFESSION

The members of the educational profession have a major voice in the determination of educational policy, their position being strongest in the universities. They are mostly upper-middle- and lower-middle-class people, with a few in the upper class. Do they make class-biased decisions?

In a society dominated by middle-class values and working in an institution which transmits and strengthens these social values, it is clear that the educational profession must work for the values which are characteristic of the society. There is no problem here. The problem arises, if it does arise, when the educator has to make a choice or a decision within the area of his professional competence, but which bears some relation to the social structure. For instance, in giving school grades or in making recommendations for the award of a college scholarship, does he consciously or unconsciously favor students of one or another social class? Again, in deciding on the content and method of his teaching, does he favor a curriculum which will make his students stronger competitors in the race for higher economic status, or does he favor a curriculum which strengthens students in other ways?

The answers to questions such as these certainly depend to some extent upon the educator's own social-class position and also upon his social history, as well as upon his personality and what he conceives his mission to be as an educator. In a set of case studies of teachers with various social-class backgrounds, Wattenberg[10] illustrates a variety of approaches to students and to teaching which depend upon the teacher's personality as well as on his social-class background. One upward-mobile teacher may be a hard taskmaster for lower-class pupils because she wants them to develop the attitudes and skills that will enable them to climb, while another upward-mobile teacher may be a very permissive

[10] William Wattenberg, "Social Origin and Teaching Role: Some Typical Patterns," in *The Teacher's Role in American Society,* Lindley J. Stiles (ed.) (New York: Harper & Bros., 1957), Ch. 4.

person with lower-class pupils because he knows their disadvantages and deprivations at home, and he hopes to encourage them by friendly treatment.

One social-class factor which plays a large part in educational policy today is the fact that a great many school and college teachers are upward mobile from urban lower-class and lower-middle-class families. Their own experience in the social system influences their work and attitudes as teachers. While this influence is a complex matter, depending upon personality factors in the individual as well as upon his social-class experience, there probably are some general statements about social-class background and educational policy that can be made with a fair degree of truth.

Teachers who have been upward mobile probably see education as most valuable for their students if it serves students as it has served them; that is, they are likely to favor a kind of education that has vocational-advancement value. This does not necessarily mean that such teachers will favor vocational education, as contrasted with liberal education, but they are likely to favor an approach to liberal education which has a maximal vocational-advancement value, as against a kind of "pure" liberal education that is not designed to help people get better jobs.

There is no doubt that higher education since World War II has moved away from "pure" liberal education toward greater emphasis on technology and specialization. There are several causes for this, one being rapid economic development with increasing numbers of middle-class positions requiring engineering or scientific training. But another cause may lie in the experience of so many new postwar faculty members with their own use of education as a means of social advancement.

Compared with the college and university faculty members of the period from 1900 to 1930, the new postwar faculty members consist of more children of immigrants and more children of urban working-class fathers. Their experience is quite in contrast with that of children of upper- and upper-middle-class native-born parents, who are more likely to regard education as good for its own sake and to discount the vocational emphases in the curriculum.

THE "PUBLIC INTEREST" GROUPS

Educational policies are formed by several groups who are officially or unofficially appointed to act in the public interest. Legislators are one such group, and state legislators have major responsibility for educational legislation. They generally vote so as to serve their own constituency, and if the constituency should be solidly middle class or solidly lower class, they might be expected to vote and work for middle- or for lower-class interests in education. However, there are relatively few such political constituencies, and, as has been pointed out, there is seldom a clear-cut distinction between the educational interests of one social class and those of another.

Another public interest group is the commission of laymen or educators which is appointed to study an educational problem and to make recommendations. Generally these commissions work earnestly to represent the interest of the entire society, as they conceive it. Nevertheless, their conclusions and recommendations cannot please everybody, and they often represent a particular economic or political point of view. For instance, there have been two Presidential Commissions on higher education since World War II. President Truman's Commission on Higher Education tended to take a liberal, expansionist position, while President Eisenhower's Committee on Education Beyond the High School was slightly more conservative. Both Commissions consisted of upper-middle- and upper-class people, who attempted to act in the public interest.

An example of a more definite class bias is noted in proceedings of the Commission on the Financing of Higher Education sponsored by the Association of American Universities and supported by the Rockefeller Foundation and the Carnegie Corporation. This Commissioner recommended against the use of federal government funds for the assistance of private universities and against a broad program of government-supported scholarships. This might be said to be an upper- or an upper-middle-class bias, but the Commission published as one of its staff studies a book by Byron S. Hollingshead entitled *Who Should Go to College?* which recommended a federal government scholarship program. Furthermore, the Commission set up the Council for Financial Aid to Education as a means of encouraging private business to increase its support of private higher education. Thus, the Commission acted with a sense of social responsibility within the area of its own convictions about the problem of government support to private education.

Then there are the trustees and officers of the great educational foundations, who inevitably exert an influence on educational decisions by their support or refusal to support various educational programs, experiments, and demonstrations. These people are practically always upper- or upper-middle-class persons, who attempt to act in what they regard as the interest of the entire society.

Finally there are the parent organizations and the laymen's organizations such as the National Association of Parents and Teachers, and the Citizens Committee on Public Schools. These have an upper-middle-class leadership and a middle-class membership, with rare exceptions, where working-class parents are active in local P.T.A. matters. Like the other policy-making groups, these are middle class in their educational attitudes, and they attempt to act in the general public interest, as they see it.

In general it appears that educational decisions and educational policies are made by people who intend to act in the interests of the society as a whole. They are predominantly middle- and upper-class people, and undoubtedly share the values and attitudes of those classes. They may be unaware of the existence of lower-class values and consequently fail to take them into account. But there is very little frank and conscious espousal of the interests of any one social class by the people who have the power to make decisions in education. They think of themselves as trustees for the entire society and try to serve the entire society.

Attempts to Influence Social Structure Through Education

Educational policy in the United States has as an explicit goal the maximization of economic and cultural opportunity. In so far as this goal is achieved, the society becomes more fluid, artificial barriers to social mobility are reduced, and people at the lower end of the social hierarchy share more fully in the material and cultural goods of society. On the other hand, there is a counterbalancing purpose in education which is to pass on the advantages of the parents to their children. This leads to efforts at exclusiveness through private schools and to the maintenance of social stratification in the schools. Both of these purposes exist side by side without much overt conflict under present conditions.

Maximizing economic and cultural opportunity

The broad expansion of free education results both in raising the average economic and cultural level of the society and in promoting fluidity within the social structure. Fifty years ago the general raising of the school-leaving age to sixteen was an example of this movement. During the past decade the program has been carried on through expansion of free higher education in state universities, state colleges, and community colleges. The reaffirmation of American faith in the comprehensive high school, as expressed in the Conant study,[11] is another indication of the liveliness of the ideal of maximizing opportunity through the equalizing of educational opportunity.

The recent federal government's student-loan program is another step in the direction of making higher education more available to lower-status youth. It is probably more effective than the expanded scholarship programs of the past decade, because the scholarship programs mainly aided the students with the best academic records (who were usually middle-class), and these students tended to use the scholarship funds to go to more expensive colleges. Meanwhile, the private colleges have increased their tuition rates so much that they have raised an economic barrier

[11] James B. Conant, *The American High School Today* (New York: McGraw-Hill, 1959).

which dwarfs their scholarship funds. The gains in educational opportunity during the past decade have taken place largely in the publicly supported institutions.

Another means of increasing educational opportunity and thereby increasing individual social mobility is the use of guidance procedures at the eighth or ninth grade to discover and motivate able lower-class youth to go to college. This has been promoted by the National Defense Education Act.

Increasing group mobility

Although there has been a great upward movement of the working class as a group during the present century, this has not been reflected in education that aims to promote working-class solidarity and working-class economic and cultural gains independent of the gains of other classes. Rather, education has provided both general and vocational training that has served to raise the earning power of working-class people, while the technological improvement in the arts of production has made possible a gain in real income from which the working class has profited along with the other classes.

There has been relatively little emphasis on teaching about labor unions, about working-class solidarity, about consumer economics, and consumer co-operatives. The consumer-education movement has been more a middle-class rather than a lower-class activity.

Education has not been used effectively to better the position of one social group in relation to the positions of other groups.

Efforts to preserve stratification

Private schools with high tuition fees and selective, privately supported colleges are the traditional means through which upper-class and upper-middle-class parents have attempted to confer status advantages upon their children. In varying degrees they offer the same privileges to a few lower-middle- and lower-class youth through scholarships.

A more widely prevalent method of preserving social stratification is the creation and maintenance of upper- and upper-middle-class suburbs with public schools that are 90 per cent or more middle and upper class in composition. This practice has probably increased in scope since World War II, with the great growth of metropolitan-area population.

Trends in Social Structure and Their Effects on Education

On the whole, it seems that education is more *responsive to* social forces than *responsible for* them. There are vast socioeconomic movements under way, which work to change the social structure; and education is an instrument for effecting these changes.

Growth of a technology-based-and-oriented society

American society has become urbanized and industrialized in harmony with the development of a working force which requires technological training. The number of unskilled labor jobs is decreasing rapidly, while the number of jobs requiring technical or professional training is increasing. In *The Affluent Society*, John Kenneth Galbraith writes of the "new class"—the class of people who man society's productive machinery in strategic places and who require higher education for these jobs. The "new class" includes upper-middle- and lower-middle-class people. Taking account of the growth of this group, the writer estimates that the upper-middle and lower-middle classes among the 25-34 age-group will increase from 38 per cent of the male working force in 1950 to 47 per cent in 1980.[12] At the same time, the working-class proportion will shrink comparably from 60 per cent to 52 per cent. Thus, the time is in sight when half of the population will be middle class, with corresponding middle-class educational expectations.

Rise of the common-man culture

The two largest social classes—lower-middle and upper-lower, make up 70 per cent of the population and will continue to do so. Although this group is a mixture of white-collar and blue-collar, it is becoming more homogeneous culturally, with the rising incomes of the blue-collar workers giving them approximately the same standard of living as that of the minor white-collar worker. Both groups are gaining in college entrants, and they dominate numerically both the high-school graduating class and the college-entrance group. They are in a minority in the selective colleges and universities and in the suburban high schools, but everywhere else in the field of education the "common-man" group has the weight of numbers.

The educational aspirations of the "common-man" group tend to be practical and work-oriented and will probably continue the present emphasis upon education for economic competence. However, this is a group with growing quantities of leisure and a good deal of interest in such "leisure arts" as music, travel, gardening, camping, and spectator sports. These interests are likely to be reflected in school education and also in adult education.

Elements influencing stratification in society and in education

A strong case can be made for the proposition that social forces are producing a converging society with more and more shared values, and

[12] Robert J. Havighurst, *American Higher Education in the 1960's* (Columbus: Ohio State University Press, 1960).

that education is important in bringing about such convergence. On the other hand, there are some forces that tend toward greater rigidity of the social structure and a retention, if not an actual increase, of present social-class differences.

One of these rigidity-producing forces is the middle-class birth rate. During this century and until the close of World War II, the upper-middle and lower-middle classes fell far short of reproducing themselves, thus creating vacancies in the working force with each new generation, the vacancies being filled by upward-mobile youth of lower-status families. This has been an important source of upward mobility in the United States. But since World War II, the middle-class birth rate has risen and stayed at a level high enough to replenish its numbers.

If this higher middle-class birth rate stays up, there will be relatively more middle-class youth in the next generation to compete for entrance to college and for good places in the working force, and they will have many advantages in competition with working-class youth. In such a situation guidance practices in high school and college-admission practices may come under pressure of middle-class parents to favor their children. Moreover, the present attitude of educators, which favors the promotion of opportunities for working-class youth to go to college in a period of manpower scarcity, may shift to one of encouraging boys and girls of working-class background to seek lower-status jobs which pay well for people at the level of high-school graduation.

Development of homogeneous communities

Another element making for rigidity in the social structure is the development of communities with a limited social-class range, especially in expanding metropolitan areas. It is well known that the areas of greatest population growth at present are metropolitan areas, many of which include an industrial center and its dependent suburbs. The older pattern of a population complex in a town or city, which was almost a replica of the social-class distribution of the entire society, is being replaced by communities of ten to fifty thousand which are tied loosely together into a metropolitan complex. Some of these communities are suburbs with their own local governments and school boards, while others are local community areas within large cities, with their own elementary schools feeding into a high school.

There are now three clearly marked types of homogeneous communities with corresponding school systems. One is an upper-middle- and upper-class suburb, with a very small number of lower-middle-class residents. Another is a working-class and lower-middle-class suburb, essentially of the "common-man" character, with very few lower-lower-class residents. A third is a city slum, almost solid lower class, and as much as half lower-lower. Wherever such communities exist, the school system reflects the fact, and teachers are acutely aware of it.

In the central areas of the big cities this causes acute problems, because the central city sees itself steadily becoming a grand slum as its middle- and upper-working-class residents flee to the edges of the city and beyond, to the suburbs. Thus, a great city which in 1920 was self-contained, with 20 to 25 per cent lower-lower-class residents, may in 1960 have 40 per cent lower-lower-class residents who cover great stretches of what were formerly middle-class neighborhoods.

In their efforts to halt this urban blight, the city-planners tear down old tenement buildings and erect public housing, or they spend public money on slum removal and sell the land to private developers, hoping that new middle-class residential areas will be built to restore the city to its earlier condition of balance among the social classes.

This process of urban renewal has involved the schools as a crucial factor. Middle-class parents insist upon sending their children to schools with a middle-class ethos or atmosphere, and this requires a pupil population which has more than a certain critical proportion of middle-class children. The exact size of this critical proportion is not known, and in any case it depends upon other factors such as the relative proportion of upper-lower- and lower-lower-class children and their race and nationality backgrounds. Probably the critical proportion of middle-class children is in the neighborhood of 40 per cent, if the school is to maintain itself as an attractive place for middle-class families and their children. When a school drops below this critical figure, middle-class parents begin to move out of the neighborhood or to put their children into private schools.

Urban renewal generally occurs over large enough areas to maintain an elementary-school district with an atmosphere that is satisfactory to middle-class parents and children. But it is more difficult to maintain a secondary-school district with a satisfactory social-class distribution for middle-class people in the central sections of a great city. Then, if the secondary school is not satisfactory, middle-class families move out to the city's edge and to the suburbs, making the experiment in urban renewal a failure in the small renewal areas in spite of the excellent physical condition of these areas.

Thus, the nature of population distribution in a metropolitan area is interrelated with the nature of the secondary schools of the area. To explain this more clearly, three types of secondary-school population distribution are shown in Figure 1. In this figure the social-class distribution of the school enrolment is shown, against a background of the social-class distribution of the nation's youth. If a school had an enrolment representing a cross-section of the nation, this would be shown by a straight line across the top of the figure, indicating that the enrolment contained 10 per cent upper- and upper-middle-class youth, 30 per cent lower-middle, 40 per cent upper-level, and 20 per cent lower-lower. This, however, would be a rare event, since many working-class youth drop out of school before high-school graduation, thus lowering the curve in these segments of the chart.

A typical comprehensive high school is shown in Figure 1A for a self-contained community of ten to fifty thousand, which has all social classes in it, and in roughly the same proportions as in the nation. The percentage of upper- and middle-class students in the graduating class is about 50, while in the ninth grade, before there is much dropping out, this percentage is about 40.

A high school in an upper-middle-class suburb has the distribution shown in Figure 1B, with very few students of working-class background. These are the schools which walk away with scholastic honors in national and state scholarship contests, while holding their own in athletics. Middle-class parents move to the suburbs to put their children in such schools.

Figure 1C shows the population distribution in the high school of a district of a big city which is subject to the encroachment of slums. More than half of the students are of upper-lower-class background, with lower-lower and lower-middle about evenly balanced and upper-middle-class students in a small minority. In this school it is almost impossible to maintain a college-preparatory atmosphere. However, this may be attempted by establishing a multi-track system, with a small college-preparatory group on the upper track having their own classes, home-rooms, study halls, and even assemblies. Thus they tend to become a school within a school.

Another way to meet the problem for middle-class parents of the C-type school is to enlarge the high-school district and to establish two parallel high schools, one of academic or college-preparatory type and the other of a vocational type. The academic-type school can be made selective, admitting only students with above-average school records, thus reducing the proportion of lower-class students and making the distribution more like that of Figure 1A. Something like this is being done in the secondary schools of some of the eastern cities. New York City has accomplished this with its special high schools for abler students.

Thus, the trend toward development of subcommunities within metropolitan regions which are relatively homogeneous in social class is causing some acute problems for educators, and the fate of attempts at urban renewal is largely in the laps of educators.

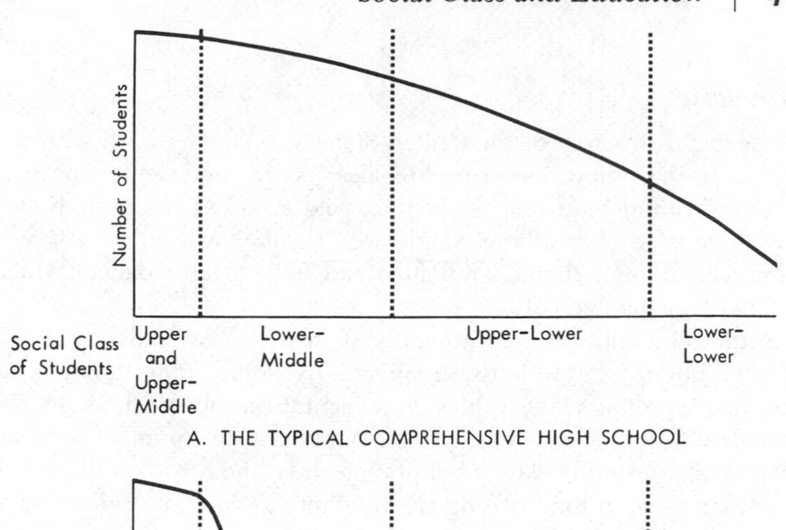

A. THE TYPICAL COMPREHENSIVE HIGH SCHOOL

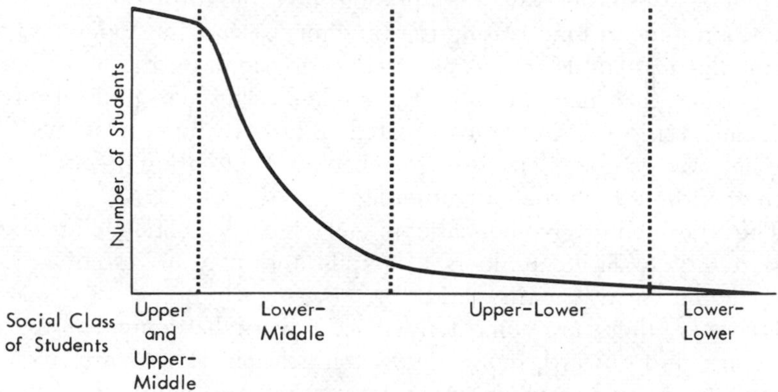

B. AN UPPER-MIDDLE-CLASS SUBURBAN HIGH SCHOOL

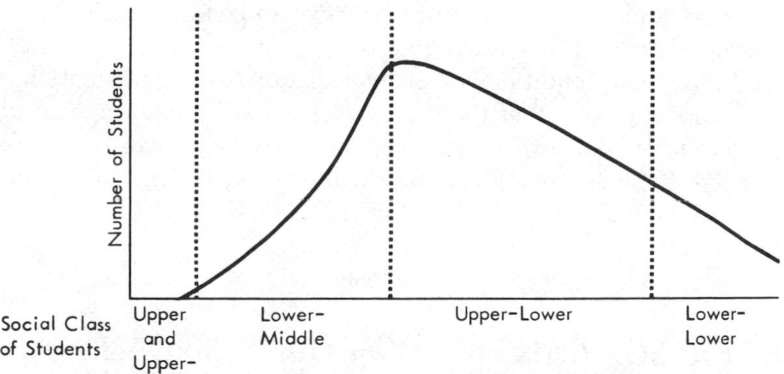

C. A CITY HIGH SCHOOL IN AN AREA WITH ENCROACHING SLUMS

Figure 1. Social-Class Distribution of Students in Three Types of Secondary Schools.

Summary

The social structure of the United States is changing in the direction of increasing the proportion of middle-class people and decreasing the proportions in the lowest reaches of the social scale. At the same time there is an expansion of middle-class ideology throughout the society, with an expansion of high school graduates and college attendance, which are middle-class characteristics.

In this situation, the educational system is run by middle-class people with middle-class standards, tempered by some understanding of the fact that working-class values and aspirations as well as habits are enough different from those of the middle class to make educational adaptations desirable. These adaptations take the form, on the one hand, of encouraging and motivating the brighter lower-class students to aspire to middle-class status by means of education and, on the other hand, of recognizing that many lower-class students will not profit from such academic fare and should be treated differently in school, with more emphasis on getting them through school and into a job or into marriage with or without high-school graduation.

Thus the schools give educational and, thereby, economic and cultural opportunity to large numbers of pupils and play an essential part in keeping the social structure fluid.

However, there are some tendencies toward hardening of the social structure and toward more rigid stratification. These are seen most sharply in the metropolitan areas. Here there are some crucial problems for educational policy-makers. They can work against the forces that make for stratification and rigidity, or they can go along with these forces, often not aware that they are doing so.

Under present conditions of economic growth and population expansion, it appears likely that the class structure will remain open and fluid, and the tendencies toward stratification and rigidity can be successfully controlled, if educators understand the social forces which are influencing the society and act wisely with respect to them.

PETER SCHRAG | *Why Our Schools Have Failed*

In the context of traditional American belief, Section 402 of the Civil Rights Act of 1964 is one of the simplest, most unambiguous directives ever issued to a government agency. It instructs the United States Commissioner of Education to carry out a survey "concerning the lack of availability of equal educational opportunities for individuals by reason of race, color, religion, or national origin in educational institutions" in the United States and its possessions. Presumably, the wording of Section 402 merely pointed toward an examination of the effects of overt racial discrimination in American schools. What it produced instead was a 737-page document that demonstrated not only the ineffectiveness of schools in overcoming the handicaps of poverty and deprivation, but also the fact that no one knows what the phrase "equal educational opportunities" means, and that, given the conditions of contemporary American society, it can have no meaning. Education in America is patently unequal, it is structured to be unequal, and it can only define its successes by its failures. On the dark side of every conception of "opportunity" lies an equal measure of exclusion and rejection.

No one needs another set of statistics to prove that American Negro children—and many others—are being miseducated, that they are behind in the elementary grades, and that they fall further behind as they move through school. In the twelfth grade more than 85 per cent of Negro children score below the average white on standardized tests of achievement, their dropout rates are higher, and their self-esteem is lower. We can dispute the validity of the tests as indicators of intelligence, but there is not the slightest doubt that if they measure educational achievement, and if they predict future success in school and college (as they do), then the children of the poor minorities in America perform well below average. What the new statistics do provide is solid evidence for the repeated assertion by civil-rights leaders and others that what children learn in school are the rules and attitudes of second-class citizenship, and that the school is a highly effective mechanism not only for advancement but for selecting people out.

Historically, "equality of educational opportunity" simply demanded that all individuals were to have access to similar resources in similar public schools: where children failed, it was because of their own limitations, their lack of ambition and intelligence, not because of the inadequacies of the schools or the society. If the schools were found to favor a particular race or economic group (as they were in many of the desegregation cases), one could rectify the inequities through application of relatively simple standards: the appropriation of equal resources to the education of children of all races, the integration of schools, or the reassignment of teachers. The definition never contemplated the difficulties children might bring from home or the fact that even the best teachers and resources, according to the conventional standards, were keyed to middle-class experience, motivation, and attitude. More important, it never contemplated genuine integration: what it presumed was that only the white middle-class society offered ideals and standards of value, and that whatever the ghetto offered, or what minority children brought with them, was to be disregarded, deflated, or denied. The traditional melting pot was stirred by Protestant hands with a white ladle.

It will be years before the sociologists and statisticians get through with the data in the government's report, "Equality of Educational Opportunity" that was prompted by Section 402. The study, headed by Professor James S. Coleman of the Johns Hopkins University, was eighteen months in the making, cost $2 million to produce, and included data on 600,000 children and 60,000 teachers in 4,000 schools. It is written, as Christopher Jencks said, "in the workmanlike prose of an Agriculture Department bulletin on fertilizer," and it is so thoroughly crammed with tables, regression coefficients, and standard deviations as to make all but the most passionate statisticians shudder. (Ultimately, it turned out, even some of the statisticians began to shudder.) Nonetheless, the Coleman Report has probably become the most influential educational study of the decade. It formed the basis of the recent report of the United States Civil Rights Commission, "Racial Isolation in the Public Schools," it provided ammunition for a federal court opinion on segregation in the Washington schools, it is the topic of conferences and seminars, it is endlessly quoted at meetings, and it became the subject of a year-long study at Harvard under the direction of Daniel P. Moynihan and Thomas Pettigrew (who also wrote the Civil Rights Commission Report). It may be a measure of the times that, where forty years ago we produced educational philosophy and ideology, we are now producing statistics.

The Coleman Report comes to two central conclusions:

(1) That the most significant determinant of educational success (as measured by standardized tests of mathematical and verbal performance) is the social and economic background of the individual student, that formal instructional inputs—which are not as unequally distributed between races as supposed—make relatively little difference, and that the social and economic composition of fellow students, not materials or libraries, is the most important in-school resource.

(2) That children from disadvantaged backgrounds (regardless of race) benefit from integration with advantaged kids (regardless of race), but that the latter are not harmed by such integration. Proper integration mixes rich and poor and produces a general social gain: the poor learn more; the performance of the rich does not go down.

The Coleman conclusions substantiate propositions that have been gaining currency in the last few years. If racial integration is pedagogically desirable, then clearly social and economic integration, and the interplay of cultural styles, are even more important. Poor blacks and whites can learn from each other, but rich and poor—under the proper conditions—can benefit even more. The Report's conclusions on the impact of teachers are not entirely clear, but they do indicate that good teachers and effective educational environments are more important to the disadvantaged than to those who have access (in the home, for example) to other resources. Even so, teachers, libraries, laboratories, and other formal inputs are not as important as fellow students.

Carried to its ultimate, the Coleman Report seems to indicate that schools make relatively little difference, except as a place where kids learn from each other, and that money spent in improving them is likely, at best, to yield marginal results. The first temptation, of course, is to dismiss that assertion as an absurdity: we take it as an article of faith that the public school has always been the great American social instrument, the device that converted the raw material of immigration into an endless stream of social success. Now, oddly enough, the school seems to be failing in the very functions on which its reputation has always been based. It does not seem to be able to bring the most indigenous and American of all "immigrants" into the mainstream or even to give them the educational qualifications that life in the mainstream requires. Given the insights of recent experience, we might now properly ask whether the school was ever as successful or important in the process of Americanization and education as the history textbooks sentimentally picture it. With the possible exception of the Jews, did the school ever become a major avenue of entry for the ethnic minorities of the urban centers? How effective was it for the Irish, the Italians, the Poles? Was it the school or the street that acculturated our immigrants? What about such Americanizing institutions as the political ward, the shop, and the small town? A half-century ago American society provided alternatives to formal education, and no one became officially distressed about dropouts and slow readers. Now the school has become *the* gatekeeper to advancement, and while it is being blamed for obvious failures, it may actually be doing better than it ever did before.

And yet, despite the accumulation of studies and statistics, we still don't know how much difference formal instruction makes, except to amplify characteristics that have already been determined somewhere else. The Coleman *conclusions* indicate that it doesn't make much difference, but here semantic problems and statistical difficulties begin to get in the way. What the Coleman group did was, in essence, to take schools with students of similar background and try to determine how much difference varying inputs seemed to make. (E.g., given two all-Negro schools, did children in the school where teachers had better training, higher degrees, for example, perform better than those in the other school?) In controlling for student background, however, Coleman and his colleagues may have underestimated the crucial fact that almost all schools are internally harmonious systems, and that where children come from disadvantaged backgrounds their teachers are also likely, in some respects, to be disadvantaged. Two economists, Samuel Bowles of Harvard and Henry M. Levin of the Brookings Institution, point out in the *Journal of Human Resources*[1] that if the methodology of the study had been reversed, so would the conclusions: that is, if Coleman had controlled for such educational inputs as teacher training, the social background of the students would have appeared to make little difference. They point out, moreover, that Coleman's Report, despite the vast sample, was unavoidably biased through the refusal of many school systems to furnish data: suburban systems were statistically over-represented while big cities, which have the most severe problems, were under-represented. The most vicious attribute of urban school systems, until recently, has not been their consistent failure with the disadvantaged, but their refusal to produce honest data on that failure. In case after case, they pretended (perhaps because of the historical definition of "equality") that, despite statistical evidence to the contrary, it was individual children, not schools, that failed. Bowles and Levin contend, moreover, that the Coleman Report's conclusions that teachers' traits (verbal facility, educational level, etc.) are relatively unimportant is not supported by the data, which suggests exactly the opposite; that the Report's data on the importance of class size are useless, and that its conclusions about the effect of integration are questionable since "the processes of residential and academic selection imply that those Negroes who attend predominantly white schools are drawn largely from higher social strata." In brief, integration is educationally effective among those who are already educationally and socially "advantaged."

The most significant difficulty, however, is one that the Coleman Report did not create and cannot solve. What does equality mean in education? Does it mean that the average Negro should be doing as well as the average white, and that the resources devoted to his education should be improved until he does? Or does it point to some sort of parity in resources? Or to something else? Coleman himself said that the focus of his report was not on "what resources go into education, but on what product comes out." He then goes on to say (in an article in *The Public Interest*[2]) that "equality of educational opportunity implies not merely 'equal' schools but equally effective schools, whose influences will overcome the differences in starting point of children from different social groups."

Pedagogically and politically, Coleman's suggestion is pleasant, impossible, and probably undesirable. Pleasant because it has a nice democratic ring, impossible because the haves in the society won't allow it to happen, undesirable because it assumes that all social and cultural differ-

[1] "The Determinants of Scholastic Achievement—An Appraisal of Some Recent Evidence," Winter 1968.

[2] "Toward Open Schools," Fall 1967.

ences should be equalized away, that Negro children (or Chinese or Jews) have nothing to offer *as Negroes* except problems and disadvantage, and that their culture (or perhaps even their genes) gives them nothing special that might be socially, educationally, or personally valuable. A Negro in this context is nothing but a disadvantaged white.

Since we are now beginning to discover the crucial importance of the very early years of childhood, it is likely that we can achieve a greater measure of equality—to narrow the gap between the advantaged and disadvantaged. More effective preschool programs, and a general extension of the social responsibility of the school for children from deprived homes, may make the classroom more effective. But the matter of achieving genuine equality is another question.

As to the politics: the most effective way that a middle-class parent can endow his children is by buying them a superior education, by giving them the head start his advantages can provide, and he is not likely to run slower to let the poor catch up. Given Coleman's standards, the only way to determine whether schools "overcome the differences in starting point of children from different social groups" is when Negro children from Harlem do as well in College Board scores or reading achievement as whites from Scarsdale. Yet when that happens, Scarsdale will have lost its reason to exist. Is the average white afraid of integration or "equality" only because the Negroes would, as he often says, "drag down the standards" or also because, ultimately, they might succeed? What would happen if the prep schools and suburban high schools, let alone the Ivy League universities, were no longer a guarantee of advantage and ultimate success? What if the game were genuinely open? It has often been said that American economic viability depended in part on the existence of a class of individuals who were available for the dirty jobs that the society requires (try the suggestion that we guarantee everyone a living wage, and listen to the prophecies of economic doom), but is it not equally conceivable that, for many, self-esteem and success are themselves defined by the failures of others? We can assert that technology is taking us to some sort of economic nirvana in which menial work is superfluous and we will no longer require Negroes to do it. And yet, doesn't the psychology of success always require a class of failures, and aren't the black, by virtue of their cultural inheritance, always the best candidates? Can we ever maintain a middle class without a lower class, or does it thrive, like Alcoholics Anonymous, on the continued presence of a group of people who, it is assumed, need reform, and from whose failures the successful can draw esteem? Even if we dismiss that as the bleakest kind of cynicism, we are still confronted by the difficulty of a system where cash and power are convertible into educational assets, where educational assets are, in turn, the major qualifications for entry into the life and prerogatives of the middle class, and where the poor have neither. No governmental program is likely to alleviate the inequities.

As to the pedagogy: Coleman's assumption in talking about the different starting points of children "from different social groups" is that all talent is equally distributed through the population, and that inequities are generated only by social, rather than ethnic or cultural characteristics. The current evidence seems to make the assumption doubtful: it points, indeed, to a very different course of action from the one Coleman advocates. For years there was a lot of condescending talk about the attributes and activities of different ethnic groups (all Jews were tailors, the Chinese ran laundries, the Negro had "rhythm"), and we properly reacted with egalitarian indignity when we decided how silly and pernicious that talk had become. Are we now going overboard the other way by suggesting that all talents and interests, of whatever kind, are distributed absolutely equally through the different ethnic sectors of the population? In establishing criteria for academic success—indeed for social success generally—are we emphasizing certain skills and measures at the expense of others that may be equally valuable not only to the individual's personality and self-esteem but to the society generally? In a recent article in the *Harvard Educational Review,*[3] Susan S. Stodolsky and Gerald Lesser report on research that indicates that the relative strengths and weaknesses in different attributes remain constant for various ethnic groups, regardless of whether they are middle- or lower-class. Jews, for example, score higher, relative to the general population, in verbal ability than they do in space conceptualization. For Chinese children, the relative strengths and weaknesses in verbal ability and space conceptualization are reversed. (Similarly, Negroes seem to perform somewhat better in arithmetic skills and space conceptualization than they do in verbal tests; for Puerto Ricans, the pattern is almost the reverse.) Although middle-class children score higher in *all categories,* the relative ethnic differences are not eliminated. To Lesser and Stodolsky, these findings suggest new distinctions, definitions, and a new course of action. To Coleman's call for equalization, they want to add what they consider the equally important objective of diversification, of trading on the strengths of different ethnic groups, and helping them to develop those strengths to the maximum. "Beyond deploying all necessary resources to achieve minimal equality in essential goals, further development of students may well be diverse," they write. "Following our principle of matching instruction and ability we incidentally may enhance the initial strengths which each group possesses. For example, through the incidental enhancement of the space-conceptualization skills of the Chinese children, we may produce proportionally more Chinese than Jewish architects and engineers. Conversely,

[3] "Learning Patterns in the Disadvantaged," Fall 1967.

through incidental enhancement of verbal skills of the Jewish children, we may produce proportionally more Jewish than Chinese authors or lawyers." There is no suggestion here about producing a Jewish or a Chinese curriculum; what they do propose is tailoring the mode and techniques of instruction to the strengths of particular children.

Studies like this are a long way from producing comprehensive solutions, but they demonstrate how complex the problem has become, how little we know about learning, and how ineffective most current remedial programs seem to be. One of the difficulties, indeed, is determining just what the problem really is. The Coleman Report, whatever its weaknesses, has made the definitional problem painfully clear. When we talk about the education of Negroes, or urban schools, or the ghetto, are we talking about ethnic minorities, a social class, or simply the universal difficulties of operating effective schools, no matter who their pupils happen to be? Clearly there is validity in the charge that some teachers are racially and socially biased, and that the phrase "cultural disadvantage" can be used, like assertions about Negro inferiority, as an excuse for failure, a cop-out for bad teachers. The psychologist Kenneth B. Clark has often pointed out that statements about uneducable children tend to become self-fulfilling prophecies, and that teachers who talk this way don't belong in the classroom. At the same time, it's hard to believe that the same attitudes don't operate in classrooms full of lower-class Italians or Appalachian mountaineers, or that the Protestant schoolmarms of the year 1900 were altogether openminded about the Jews and the Catholics.

Before anyone comes back with the declaration that "we made it on our own, why can't they?" let's quickly add that the economy that permitted making "it" on one's own is dead and gone, and that when it comes to many contemporary school systems, *all children* tend to be disadvantaged. What I'm suggesting is that many schools are not educational but sociological devices which destroy learning and curiosity and deny differences as often as they encourage them, and which value managerial order above initiative, good behavior above originality, and mediocrity above engagement. (Yes, of course, there are exceptions.) All too often, they demand styles of behavior antithetical not only to social and ethnic minorities, but also to most other original or "difficult" children, no matter what their background. They are instruments of social selection and as such they screen out misfits for the middle class, regardless of race, color, or national origin. In performing this function, every guidance counselor becomes an immigration officer and every examination a petition for a passport. Lower-class youngsters, wrote Edgar Z. Friedenberg in *The Vanishing Adolescent,* "are handy with their fists and worse; but they are helpless in the meshes of middle-class administrative procedure and are rapidly neutralized and eliminated by it. . . . They quickly learn that the most terrifying creatures are those whose bite passes unnoticed at the time and later swells, festers, and paralyzes; they cannot defend themselves against the covert, lingering hostility of teachers and school administrators." This hostility, says Friedenberg, is generated by a reaction to the personal intensity of young men and women who resist personal repression offered in the name of adjustment. "Any individual through whom subjective intensity may intrude into the processes of bureaucratic equilibrium is extremely threatening to our society." The school, in short, is not an instrument of pluralism, but of conformity. It turns out shoddy goods for the dime store trade; its teachers are not professionals but petty civil servants who teach children to deny their own instincts and honesty, teach them little tricks of evasion, and reject those who are not acceptable for the mold. While the deviants of the upper class may have access to special schools in the suburbs or the hills of New England, the poor have no choice: the law *requires* them to go to one particular school in one community which, as often as not, treats them as inmates. The school in this instance becomes a sort of colonial outpost manned by a collection of sahibs from downtown. Their idea of community relations is telling parents to encourage their kids to stay in school, help them with their homework, and live the life of Dick and Jane. As a result, the neighborhood school is in, but not of or by the neighborhood.

Given these conditions and the failures of the ghetto schools, the current demands for decentralization and community controls are hardly surprising. There is nothing radical about them, except in the view of school personnel who have been trained to suspect community pressure and who regard any overt mixture of politics and education as the ultimate evil. The advocates of decentralization, who feel that ghetto parents should have as much control over the education of their children as the parents of the small suburb, see political action as the only way to make the school effective and responsible: the issue is not a black principal or a black curriculum for their own sake, but making the schools accountable, and developing the sense of participation that is expected to come with it. If parents are involved, they may provide the interest and support that the education of their children requires. The schools will then become *their* schools, the teachers *their* teachers. A principal working for parents is going to try harder than one who is responsible only to bureaucrats downtown.

For many militants, the appeal of decentralization—as an essential component of community power (read Black Power, if preferred)—is extremely powerful. At the same time, the concept of decentralization suffers from some serious ambiguities. There are people like Roy Innis, a leader in CORE, who favor a single Negro school district in Harlem, a system as distinct from that of New York City as the schools of Buffalo.

For most others, including white liberals, the model is a collection of small districts, each hopefully resembling those of suburbs or the small towns, each immediately accessible to the parents and community. The difference between the two is as large as the difference between Thomas Jefferson and John C. Calhoun: one visualizes a thoroughgoing decentralization—educational federalism; the other calls forth the ghost of the doctrine of the current majority. It is based on the presumption that the Negro community is as distinct from the mainstream as the peculiar institution which helped give it birth and on which Calhoun founded his brand of separatism more than a century ago. Both suffer from what may be an excessive belief in the power of formal education and a conviction that racism and bad intentions, rather than educational incompetence, are the major sources of educational inadequacy.

Yet if this were the whole problem—if teachers and schools were guilty of nothing more than middle-class bias or political irresponsibility toward the poor—the situation would not be as difficult as it is. Even if one grants the possibility of effective decentralization as a *political* solution (assuming that parents can run schools without turning them into political battlegrounds or hothouses of nepotism), what of the educational solutions? The pressure for decentralization does not stem from some specific educational program that large systems refuse to adopt and which the militants consider appropriate to the problems of their neighborhoods and children. Indeed, if the Coleman Report has any validity—and there is little reason to doubt that children from different social backgrounds do learn from each other—then decentralization, which will help institutionalize segregation, is a step backward. Thus, the Bundy Report, which outlines a plan of decentralization for New York City, and the Coleman Report, one might think, were composed on different planets.

The great possibility of decentralization (in New York, the proposal is to establish between thirty and sixty semi-autonomous districts) is not some large educational breakthrough, but no more, and no less, than the immediate objective itself: giving the community a great sense of participation and voice in the management of one of its institutions. (In this respect, it is no different from increasing community control, over planning, street-cleaning, or the administration of the local precinct of the police. It is thus a revolt against the "professionals"—the people who took charge, in the name of reform and good government, and apparently failed to deliver the goods. In its unwillingness to trust the experts, the demand for decentralization is a frontier populism come to the city, a rejection of outside planning and expertise. Parents whose children attend decentralized schools may (with luck) learn more about political action and school management than their children learn about reading or mathematics: so far, at any rate, the chances for the first outweigh those of the second. The mystery of power is, for the moment, more fascinating than the problems of instruction.

The fact is that no one, in the ghetto or out, has yet developed a vision of what the ghetto schools ought to do, how they should operate, or what an educated Negro child ought to be if he is to be something different from a dark-skinned middle-class white. The existing ghetto schools fail Negroes not so much because they are different from all other schools—as the integrationist once assumed—but because they are too much like them. Local control may introduce diversity and new ideas, but those changes are far from clear. At this point there are few alternative models to the existing public-school program. The current talk about relevance in Negro education—about more Afro-Americanism in the curriculum, about Negro history, about urban problems—and the peripheral efforts to use the arts (painting, the dance, music) as ways of engaging children's interests have not taken us very far toward genuine educational integration, toward the point, that is, where ghetto children have the skills to compete effectively in the larger world. It has been said again and again that conventional instruction in formalized academic skills is difficult for children whose lives provide few examples of the value of formal education and little reinforcement for work that might pay off in some vague abstract future. Middle-class kids are, in some measure, to the manner born, and they find plenty of reinforcement around them: they often succeed regardless of school. For many ghetto children, instruction, to be successful, has to be immediately attractive or interesting. (There are, to be sure, many ghetto children from families whose ambitions are identical to those of the middle class.) Whether or not "enjoyment," as someone said, "is a prerequisite to competence," it is plain that skills for the larger world may appear only remotely valuable in the immediate life of a child. The humanity of children may be very distant from the problems of negotiating the economy. The problem is how to get from one to the other.

The proposals for solving the problem are endless and, as might be expected, they are often contradictory. There is no consistent Negro demand in education, any more than there is a white one. Some Negro parents are as committed to authoritarian teachers and rote learning as the village schoolmarm; others regard them as racially repressive and pedagogically useless. (Most Negro parents are probably as conservative about education as any others.) I suspect that part of the anger and frustration in all racial school disputes stems from the inability of the parties to be entirely clear about what they want. Should the schools be more middle class, more white than white, turning out suburban doctors and lawyers, or should they be training men and women who can cope with the outside world but whose energies are directed to the black community and whose loyalties remain in the ghetto? (The controversy is similar to a conventional school debate between advocates of vocational training and college preparation, but the race aspect charges it with explosive overtones.) Whatever the position, the issue is clear: almost inevitably it revolves around the problem of moving the child from where he is to the larger world—resolving the inconsistencies between the attitudes and experience of poverty and the formalized skills and motivation that the world demands. There is no disagreement anywhere that there is a common culture that demands certain levels of verbal and social ability. The question slowly emerging from the current debates, however, is whether that ability must become a universal virtue. Should we be concerned only with the preparation of economic functionaries and the development of conventional academic skills, or also with the growth of human beings whose dignity is not necessarily dependent on middle-class standards of success? Is an understanding of algebraic functions any more desirable than the ability to paint or dance? (The mandated requirements for many jobs—nursing, for example—include verbal abilities that are higher than those the jobs actually require; the stipulated credentials are not necessarily related to the characteristics the jobs demand.) Are we establishing norms that tend to undervalue characteristics that all of society could well use, and for which certain children might be especially well prepared, or do we have to make *all* children into replicas of the middle class?

For the next several years we are likely to hear more and more along this line. In its most extreme form, the argument says that not only is the American school an instrument of the white middle class, but that the overriding emphasis—in school and out—on high verbal and cognitive skills is itself a form of racial and social bias. The rational mind, with its emphasis on a high degree of verbal and analytical facility is, in a manner of speaking, our thing. We invented and perfected it, and for the last fifteen years most curricular reform has been directed to the task of putting a larger and more powerful dose of it into the classroom. Thus we have, even more thoroughly than before, arranged education to separate the sheep of privilege from the goats of deprivation. Increasingly, we will now have to confront questions about what has been excluded: Are we missing something more intuitive, personal, and intangible? Is it possible to extend the Lesser-Stodolsky kind of analysis to include—along with assessments of verbal and mathematical characteristics, and the ability to conceptualize space—things like affective and intuitive qualities, creativity, and some general feeling for the poetic, the visual, the musical?

Because these things are difficult to test, and because their cash value has usually been remote, the schools tend to disregard them, or to assign them to a secondary level of importance. Of all the things that make life rich—the arts, the various elements of literary and personal sensitivity, social and political involvement, philosophy, religion—very few have even a minimal place (except as lip service) in the public school program. One may not be able to mandate such activities in a large compulsory school system, but it is possible to offer them as alternatives to the public school, and one can conceive of all sorts of programs for doing so. The issue here is not to turn every ghetto school into an academy of the arts, but to offer diversity—teaching the skills of a trade or of an art with as much of a sense of importance as we teach mathematics or history. The objective, in each instance, is to draw upon the experiences and interests of the kids, to give them a sense of motion and relevance, and to provide choices, not only as to school and school control, but also as to style of learning. We have, with the single public system, and the instruction it offers, created a single standard of success and failure (and the large hippie element seems to indicate that the standard is not acceptable even to some of those who might meet it). Perhaps we have to recognize the principle of pluralism not only in a cultural context but in an educational one as well. A few years ago such suggestions would have been regarded as racist slurs, but it is now the black militant who regards Swahili as desirable for Negroes as Latin.

Carried to its extreme, the argument leads to a romantic trap, a wishful attempt to arm the weakest members of a technological society with the least effective weapons for dealing with it. It may be nice to think that there are dishwashers with the souls of poets (or even with the skills of poets), but that thought provides no foundation on which to base an educational system. There are, in our culture, a variety of important and rewarding functions that require no extensive verbal or mathematical skills (despite the exclusionist tendency of certain trades and professions to impose arbitrary educational standards for membership). Nonetheless, there remain certain levels of verbal ability without which few people can survive, except in the most menial situations. In our ambiguity and guilt about middle-class life, many of us hold a corresponding ambiguity about those who are left outside the mainstream: the happy hillbilly, the engagement and passion of the ghetto, the uninhibited poor. What we disregard is that, given the choice, most of them would elect to live like us; because of educational deficiencies, they do not have the choice. There is, said a Negro sociologist, only one way out of the ghetto, "and that's out." The reason, finally, that so few of them make it has little to do with differences in culture, or the fact that teachers and administrators are ignorant about the lives of the children assigned to them; it is because they still don't know how to teach. Negro schools are bad because all schools are bad. We simply don't know very much about how children learn. This is, in the end, what the Coleman Report proved. It may also be the greatest single contribution of the civil-rights movement.

But to say that greater diversity, the provision of educational options, and a new emphasis on intuitive learning can be carried to extremes is not to deny the validity of the idea, either in the ghetto or anywhere else. For the past decade we masculinized the schools with mathematics, physics, and with a variety of new toughminded curricula. Educational criticism in the next decade may well concern itself more with the soft side of things—with non-cognitive approaches, and with a reaffirmation of Deweyan ideas. There are a number of people who are talking seriously about a "curriculum of concerns," educational programs that begin with the interests and experience of kids, not with predetermined sets of skills to be learned. Most of the ghetto experiments that seem to have potential are pure Dewey: letting children talk their own stories and developing vocabulary and writing skills from them; trips to factories, galleries, and museums; stories and poems about the streets of the city, and even about addicts and junkies; These things, too, can be carried to undisciplined extremes. None is a cure-all, but nothing in education ever is. The very nature of the enterprise is unsettling and troublesome. Education and maturation mean change, and that, in turn, means dealing with new problems, new elements every day. Equality is relatively easy to define in employment, in housing, or in medicine. It is impossible to define in education because the very nature of the enterprise demands distinctions and produces diversity.

Are we then to abandon integration and concentrate exclusively on the problems of the classroom? Plainly the answer is no. No, because it still seems—at least to some of us—morally important; no, because, lacking better tools, it still appears to be an effective technique for education; no, because any alternative to integration is, despite immediate attractions to the contrary, unthinkable. Yet if integration is to have any meaning, it must be a two-way street—integration not only *between* races, going both ways, but also between the school and the community, school and job, culture and culture. If equality of educational opportunity means merely an effort to improve the chances of the disadvantaged to run the race on our terms, things will never be equal and whatever they have to offer will be lost. Are we really courageous enough to provide a broad range of educational options and not to worry about who's at what level in which track? Are we really interested in education or merely in grades, credits, and diplomas? In the structure of the existing school system, segregation, repression, competition, and failure are all essential parts. Every class has a bottom half, and it tends to include, numerically, as many whites as blacks. Until we are ready to stop selecting people out, almost any conception of education is going to involve some sort of segregation. Our democratic professions might be vindicated if the ranks of the successful were as well integrated as the ranks of the failures, but would that solve the problem of education? What would we do with the failures if they were a statistically average shade of tan? The fundamental issue is not the equality of Negro schools, but the lives of all young men and women, no matter what their category of stigma. "If urban educators are failing," says Robert Dentler, the director of the Center for Urban Education, "they are failing where the newly emergent culture of the urban society itself has failed to specify either ends or means for the educator or his clientele. . . . We are in a period when the place of all children in this culture is in transition." What the problem of Negro education has done, or should be doing, is to alert us to a far larger range of social and educational questions, and to the fact that the goal of maximizing human potential is still a long way off.

CHARLES V. HAMILTON | Race and Education: A Search for Legitimacy

An article on public policy, race, and education in the United States in the late 1960's cannot overlook the clear existence of tremendous ferment taking place in the various black communities in this country. The nature of that ferment is such that, if we would devise relevant policy for educating vast numbers of black people today, we cannot focus merely, or even primarily, on achievement in verbal and mathematical skills as criteria for educational improvement. At one time, possibly to the mid-1960's, it was possible to talk about educational policy largely in terms of "integration" (or at least, desegregation) and assume that plans to implement integration would be dealing with the core of the problem of educational deficiency. This is no longer the case.

Today, one hears wholly different demands being raised in the black community. These demands are better represented by the kinds of resolutions coming out of the workshops of the newly formed (June, 1968) National Association of Afro-American Educators than by the conclusions reached by the report on *Equality of Educational Opportunity* (Coleman Report). These demands are reflected more clearly in the demonstrations of black high school students in many cities for more emphasis on Afro-American history and culture and for better science lab facilities than by the findings of the United States Commission on Civil Rights (*Racial Isolation in the Public Schools*). These demands are more clearly illustrated in the position taken by the Harlem chapter of the Congress of

Hamilton, Charles V., "Race and Education: A Search for Legitimacy," *Harvard Educational Review,* 39:4, Fall 1968, 669–75.

Racial Equality (CORE), calling for an independent school system for Harlem, and by many of the Concerned Black Parents groups than in policy recommendations found in the statement issued by the Board of Education of Chicago, Illinois in August, 1967 (Redmond Report).

First, I would like to indicate why it is more important at this time, from a socio-political point of view, to put more credence in the wishes of the black community than in the statements and findings of the experts. Second, I would like to give examples of the kinds of things on the minds of some of those black people taking an active interest in new directions for education in the black community. Third, I want to present a sketch of a proposal for dealing with some of the problems in some of the large, urban areas. I am not sanguine that the proposal will be applicable in all places (I assume it will not be), but neither do I believe it possible or necessary to develop one model to fit all occasions. My proposal attempts to combine some of the fervent wishes of a growing number of black people with the clear need to think in wholly new institutional terms. I am fully aware that public policy in this area has been influenced by such dichotomies as "integration vs. segregation" (*de jure* and *de facto*) and "integrated education vs. quality (compensatory) education." My presentation will not use these terms as primary focal points, but it is clear that the main thrust of my proposal will support the involvement of more parents in the school system and the improvement of educational opportunities within the black community. Some critics will view this as an "enrichment" proposal, or as an effort at "compensatory" education, or even as a black power move to maintain and further divisiveness in the society. I simply acknowledge these criticisms at the outset and intend to let my proposal stand on its own merits.

A Crisis of Educational Legitimacy

It is absolutely crucial to understand that the society cannot continue to write reports accurately describing the failure of the educational institutions *vis-à-vis* black people without ultimately taking into account the impact those truths will have on black Americans. There comes a point when it is no longer possible to recognize institutional failure and then merely propose more stepped-up measures to overcome those failures—especially when the proposals come from the same kinds of people who administered for so long the present unacceptable and dysfunctional policies and systems. Professor Seymour Martin Lipset once wrote:

> Legitimacy involves the capacity of the system to engender and maintain the belief that the existing political institutions are the most appropriate ones for the society. The extent to which contemporary democratic political systems

are legitimate depends in large measure upon the ways in which the key issues which have historically divided the society have been resolved.

While effectiveness is primarily instrumental, legitimacy is evaluative. Groups regard a political system as legitimate or illegitimate according to the way in which its values fit with theirs.[1]

And in another place, he has written:

All claims to a legitimate title to rule in new states must ultimately win acceptance through demonstrating effectiveness. The loyalty of the different groups to the system must be won through developing *in them* the conviction that this system is the best—or at least an excellent—way to accomplish their objectives. And even claims to legitimacy of a supernatural sort, such as "the gift of grace," are subjected on the part of the populace to a highly pragmatic test—that is, what is the payoff?[2]

The United States gradually acquired legitimacy as a result of being *effective*.[3]

The important point here is that loyalty, allegiance, is predicated on performance. What decision-makers *say* is not of primary importance, but it is important what black people *believe*. Do they *believe* that the school systems are operating in their behalf? Do they *believe* that the schools are *legitimate* in terms of educating their children and inculcating in them a proper sense of values? With the end product (i.e., their children graduating from high school as functional illiterates) clearly before their eyes at home and with volumes of reports documenting lack of payoff, it is not difficult to conclude that black people have good reason to question the legitimacy of the educational systems.

They begin to question the entire process, because they are aware that the schools, while not educating their children, are at the same time supporting a particularly unacceptable situation. They know that the schools are one of the major institutions for socializing their children into the dominant value structure of the society. Professor V. O. Key, Jr. concluded in his book, *Politics, Parties and Pressure Groups:*

In modern societies the school system, in particular, functions as a formidable instrument of political power in its role as a transmitter of the goals, values, and attitudes of the polity. In the selection of values and attitudes to be inculcated, it chooses those cherished by the dominant elements in the political order. By and large the impact of widely accepted goals, mores, and social

[1] Seymour Martin Lipset, *Political Man: The Social Bases of Politics* (New York: Doubleday, 1963), p. 64.

[2] Seymour Martin Lipset, *The First New Nation: The United States in Historical and Comparative Perspective* (New York: Basic Books, 1963), pp. 45–46. (Emphasis added.)

[3] Ibid., p. 59. (Emphasis in original.)

values fixes the programs of American schools. When schools diverge from this vaguely defined directive and collide with potent groups in the political system, they feel a pressure to conform.[4]

The relevance of all this is that makers of policy and their advisers must recognize that there is a point beyond which vast numbers of black people *will* become alienated and will no longer view efforts on their behalf, however well-intentioned, as legitimate. When this happens, it behooves decision-makers, if they would search for ways of restoring faith, trust, and confidence, to listen to the demands of the alienated. The "experts" might see integration as socially and educationally sound and desirable, but *their* vision and empirical data might well be, at this juncture, irrelevant. Unless this is understood, I am suggesting that public policy might well find itself in the position of attempting to force its programs on a reluctant black community. And this is hardly a formula for the development of a viable body politic.

A clear example of a paternalistic, objectionable policy is contained in the report of the Chicago Board of Education, *Increasing Desegregation of Faculties, Students, and Vocational Education Programs,* issued August 23, 1967. The Report called for busing black children into all- or predominantly white schools. It contains the very revealing paragraph:

> The assignment of students outside their neighborhood may be objected to by Negro parents who prefer that their children attend the segregated neighborhood school. This viewpoint cannot be ignored. Prior to implementation of such a transfer policy the administration must take steps to reassure apprehensive sending areas parents that transfer will be beneficial not only in terms of integration but of improved education for their children. The generation of a favorable consensus in the designated sending area is important. *If such a consensus is unobtainable, the transfer program would have to proceed without a popular base.* In the light of the dismal alternatives such a program perhaps should proceed even without consensus, but every effort should be made to attain it.[5]

This is a perpetuation of the pattern of telling the black community what is best for it. My point is that this position will only increase alienation, not alleviate it. At the present time, when the educational systems are perceived as illegitimate, it is highly unlikely that such a policy could lead to success. In order for the program to work, support *must* be obtained from the black community. This means that educational achieve-

[4] V. O. Key, Jr., *Politics, Parties and Pressure Groups* (New York: Thomas Y. Crowell Company, 1964), pp. 12–13.

[5] *Increasing Desegregation of Faculties, Students, and Vocational Education Programs* (Board of Education, City of Chicago, August 23, 1967), p. B-20. (Emphasis added.)

ment must be conceived more broadly than as the mere acquisition of verbal and mathematical skills. Very many black parents are (for good reason) quite concerned about what happens to the self-image of their black children in predominantly white schools—schools which reflect dominant white values and mores. Are these schools prepared to deal with their own white racism? Probably not, and for a few summer institutes for white, middle-class teachers cannot prepare them. Are these schools prepared to come to terms with a young black child's search for identity? Will the black child indeed acquire certain skills which show up favorably on standardized tests, but at the same time avoid coming to grips with the fact that he or she should not attempt to be a carbon copy of the culture and ethos of another racial and ethnic group? Virtually all the social scientists, education experts, and public policy-makers who emphasize integration overlook this crucial, intangible, psychological factor. Many concerned black parents and teachers do not overlook it, however. And their viewpoint has nothing to do with black people wanting to perpetuate "separate but unequal" facilities, or with attitudes of "hate whitey." This concern is simply a necessary reaction to the fact that many white (and black) liberal, integration-oriented spokesmen are tuned in to a particular result and overlook other phenomena. They fail to understand that their criteria for "educational achievement" simply might not be relevant anymore.

What I am stating (in as kind a way as possible) is that setting criteria for measuring equal educational opportunity can no longer be the province of the established "experts." The policy-makers must now listen to those for whom they say they are operating; which means of course that they must be willing to share the powers of policy-making. The experts must understand that what is high on the liberal social scientist's agenda does not coincide with the agenda of many black people. The experts are still focusing on the effectiveness of existing educational institutions. Many black people have moved to the evaluation of the legitimacy of these institutions.

American social scientists generally are unable to grasp the meaning of alienation when applied to certain groups in this country. (Most of the recent perceptive literature on alienation and modernization deals with new nations of Africa and Asia.)[6]

[6] See:

Myron Weiner, ed., *Modernization, The Dynamics of Growth* (New York: Basic Books, 1966);

David Apter, *The Politics of Modernization* (Chicago: University of Chicago Press, 1965);

S. N. Eisenstadt, *Modernization: Protest and Change* (Englewood Cliffs, N.J.: Prentice-Hall, Inc., 1966);

Edward Shils, *Political Development in the New States* (New York: Humanities Press, 1964);

Consequently, Grant McConnell, in an important book, *Private Power and American Democracy,* could write:

In general the use of government has depended on a particular group's capacity to isolate the relevant governmental agency from influences other than its own and to establish itself as the agency's constituency—at once giving an air of validity to its own ends and endowing it with the added disciplinary power of public authority over its own members.[7]

And later:

. . . farm migrant workers, Negroes, and the urban poor have not been included in the system of "pluralist" representation so celebrated in recent years.[8]

Then finally:

It can be readily agreed that if explosive mass movements are a genuine threat to America, a politics of narrow constituencies might be desirable to counter the danger. Small associations probably do provide order and stability for any society. In the United States some associations may serve in this manner to a greater degree than others. The American Civil Liberties Union and the League of Woman Voters have given notable service to American democracy. Trade unions and farm organizations have undoubtedly also been similarly useful at various times. Nevertheless, it should be clear that a substantial price is paid for any guarantee against mass movements provided by a pattern of small constituencies. That price is paid in freedom and equality. Although the price would be worth paying if the danger were grave, it can hardly be argued that such an extremity is present.[9]

There are voices in the black community (accompanied, as we well know, by acts of expressive violence) saying precisely that the danger *is* grave and that the extremity *is* present. The educational systems are particularly vulnerable, because of their very conspicuous inability to "pay-off."

Thomas Hodgkin, *Nationalism in Colonial Africa* (New York: New York University Press, 1957);

K. H. Silvert, *Expectant Peoples: Nationalism and Development* (New York: Random House, 1964);

Lucian W. Pye, *Politics, Personality and Nation Building: Burma's Search for Identity* (New Haven: Yale University Press, 1962).

[7] Grant McConnell, *Private Power and American Democracy* (New York: Random House, 1965), pp. 346–347.

[8] Ibid., p. 349.

[9] Ibid., pp. 355–356.

CHRISTOPHER JENCKS | **Private Schools for Black Children**

The public school system of New York City is on the brink of collapse. No compromise between the teachers' union and the school board is likely to resolve the fundamental conflicts between the school staff and the advocates of black community control. Until the basic political framework of public education in New York City is altered, strikes and boycotts—or both—are likely to recur on an annual basis.

Nor is New York unique. It is simply first. All the forces which have brought New York City to its present condition are at work elsewhere, and the New York story will certainly be repeated in dozens of other major cities around the country during the next decade.

The origin of the crisis is simple. The public schools have not been able to teach most black children to read and write or to add and subtract competently. This is not the children's fault. They are the victims of social pathology far beyond their control. Nor is it the schools' fault, for schools as now organized cannot possibly offset the malignant effects of growing up in the ghetto. Nonetheless, the fact that the schools cannot teach black children basic skills has made the rest of the curriculum unworkable and it has left the children with nothing useful and creative to do for six hours a day. Ghetto schools have therefore become little more than custodial institutions for keeping the children off the street. Nobody, black or white, really knows what to do about the situation.

The traditional argument of both black and white liberals was that the problem could be solved by integrating black children into predominantly white schools, but experience has shown that many whites are reluctant to allow this, and that many blacks are not willing to move into white neighborhoods or bus their children across town even if the opportunity is available. Furthermore, studies such as the one done in New York City by David Fox have shown that most black children's academic performance improves only a little or not at all in integrated schools. Most people have therefore abandoned integration as a solution, at least in big cities.

Most educators are not concentrating on "compensatory" and "remedial" programs to bring academic competence in all-black schools up to the level of all-white schools. Unfortunately, none of these programs have proved consistently successful over any significant period. A few gifted principals seem to have created an atmosphere which enables black children to learn as much as whites in other schools, but they have done this by force of personality rather than by devising formulas which others could follow. Programs like More Effective Schools in New York City may eventually prove moderately effective, but evaluations to date have not provided grounds for great optimism.

The widespread failure of both integration and compensation has convinced some black nationalists that the answer is to replace white principals and teachers with black ones. But experience with this remedy is also discouraging. The schools in Washington, D.C., for example, have predominantly black staffs, and yet their black pupils learn no more than in other cities. So, many black militants are now arguing that the essential step is not to hire black staffs but to establish black control over the schools. There is little evidence one way or the other on this score, but the schools in America's few predominantly black towns are not especially distinguished.

The available evidence suggests that only a really extraordinary school can have much influence on a child's academic competence, be he black or white. Within the range of variation found in American public schools —and by traditional criteria this range is quite broad—the difference between a "good" school and "bad" school does not seem to matter very much. James S. Coleman's massive Equality of Educational Opportunity survey, conducted for the U.S. Office of Education, demonstrated this point in 1965. Coleman's work was much criticized on methodological grounds, but most subsequent analyses have confirmed his conclusions. Indeed, recent work at Harvard suggests that Coleman probably overstated the effect of school quality on student achievement. This means that the gap between black and white children's academic achievement is largely if not entirely attributable to factors over which school boards have no control.

There are, of course, both educators and scholars who disagree with this conclusion, and who argue that the schools play a substantial role in perpetuating inequality between the races. Such skeptics must, however, explain two facts documented by the Coleman survey and never seriously disputed since.

First, Coleman's work confirmed previous studies showing that even before they enter school black children perform far less well on standard tests than white children. The typical black 6-year-old in the urban North, for example, scores below five-sixths of all white 6-year-olds on tests of both verbal and nonverbal ability. These tests obviously measure performance on tasks which seem important to educators and psychologists, not tasks which seem important to the children being tested or most of their parents. But for precisely this reason they provide a fairly accurate indication of how well any particular cultural group is likely to do at such "white-middle-class" games as reading and long division. In the case of poor black children, the tests predict disaster.

The prediction, moreover, is all too accurate. Twelve years later, after the schools have done their best and their worst, the typical black 18-year-old in the urban North is still scoring at about the 15th percentile on most standard tests. The schools in short, have not changed his position one way or the other. This obviously means that his *absolute* handicap has grown, for he is 12 years older and both he and his classmates know far more than before, so there is more room for differentiation. Thus a first-grader who scores at the 15th percentile on a verbal test is less than a year behind his classmates; a 12th-grader who scores at the 15th percentile is more than three years behind.

The second fact which must be reckoned with is that while black children go to many different sorts of schools, good and bad, integrated and segregated, rigidly authoritarian and relatively permissive, their mean achievement level is remarkably similar from school to school. By the sixth grade, for example, the typical lower-class Northern black child is achieving a little above the fourth-grade level. There is a great deal of *individual* variation around this average, both because black lower-class families vary considerably in the amount of support they give a school child and because individual children differ in native ability. But there is very little variation from one school to another in such children's *average* level of achievement. The black lower-class average is within one grade level of the over-all black lower-class average in 9 schools out of 10. This uniformly depressing picture cannot be attributed to uniformly depressing conditions in the schools Coleman surveyed. Many of these schools were predominantly white, and some had excellent facilities, highly trained and experienced teachers, relatively small classes and high over-all levels of expenditure. These differences show no consistent relationship to the mean achievement of black elementary school pupils.

The last word has certainly not been written on this subject. Indeed, a group at Harvard is planning another whole book on it. But at the moment I think the evidence strongly indicates that differences in school achievement are largely caused by differences between cultures, between communities, between socio-economic circumstances and between families—not by differences between schools.

None of this provides any adequate excuse for the outrageous and appalling things which are often done in ghetto schools. But it does suggest that even if black schools had the same resources and the same degree of responsibility to parents that the better suburban schools now have, ghetto children would still end up much less academically competent than suburban children.

It follows that the pedagogic failure of the ghetto schools must not be blamed primarily on the stupidity or malice of school boards or school administrators. It must be blamed on the whole complex of social arrangements whose cumulative viciousness creates a Harlem or a Watts. This means that, barring a general improvement in the social and economic positions of black America, black children's school achievement is unlikely to improve much in the foreseeable future, no matter who runs the schools or how they are run.

Some will challenge this depressing conclusion on the ground that black children's achievement scores could be substantially improved if really radical changes were made in the character and organization of black schools. This may well be true, but such changes are unlikely. Nor is it clear that they would be worth the cost. Despite a great deal of popular mythology, there is little real evidence that improving black children's academic skills would help any appreciable number of them to escape poverty and powerlessness.

On the contrary, studies by Otis Dudly Duncan at the University of Michigan suggest that academic competence probably explains only 10 per cent or 15 per cent of the variations in men's earnings. Research by Stephan Michelson at the Brookings Institution likewise indicates that staying in school is not likely to be much help to a Negro who wants to break out of poverty unless he stays through college.

In these circumstances, it seems to me that we should view the present urban school crisis primarily as a political problem, and only secondarily as a pedagogic one. So long as militant blacks believe they are the victims of a conspiracy to keep their children stupid—and therefore subservient—the political problem will remain insoluble. But if we encourage and assist black parents with such suspicions to set up their own schools, we may be able to avert disaster.

These schools would not, I predict, be either more or less successful than existing public schools in teaching the three R's. But that is not the point. The point is to find a political *modus vivendi* which is tolerable to all sides. (After that, the struggle to eliminate the ghetto should probably concentrate on other institutions, especially corporate employers.) How, then, might independent, black-controlled schools help create such a *modus vivendi*?

The essential issue in the politics of American education has always been whether laymen or professionals would control the schools. Conflict between these two groups has taken a hundred forms. Professionals always want more money for the schools, while laymen almost always want to trim the budget. Professionals almost always want personnel hired and promoted on the basis of "fair" and "objective" criteria like degrees, examination results and seniority. Laymen are inclined to favor less impersonal criteria, such as whether the individual has roots, whether they personally know and trust him, whether he gets on well with his colleagues, and so forth. Professionals almost never want anyone fired for any reason whatever, while laymen are inclined to fire all sorts of people, for both good and bad reasons. Professionals want a curriculum which reflects their own ideas about the world, and this often means a curriculum that embodies "liberal" ideas and values they picked up at some big university. Laymen frequently oppose this demand, insisting that the curriculum should reflect conservative local mores.

The development of big-city public schools over the past century has been marked by a steady decline of lay control and an increase in the power of the professional staff. Until relatively recently, this has meant that control was exercised by administrators. Now the teaching staff, represented by increasingly militant unions and professional associations, has begun to insist on its rights. This is, however, an intraprofessional dispute. It has done nothing to arrest the staff's continuing and largely successful resistance to nonprofessional "intervention" by parents, school-board members and other laymen. About the only thing such laymen can still decide in most big cities is the over-all level of expenditures.

The extent to which the professional staff gets its way seems to be related to the size of the administrative unit in which it works. Laymen usually have more power in small school districts, while the staff usually has more power in big districts. Until relatively recently, most liberals saw this as an argument for bigger districts, since they thought that the trouble with American education was its excessive deference to local interests and its lack of professionalism. In the past few years, however, liberals and radicals have suddenly joined conservatives in attacking bigness, bureaucracy and the claims of enterprise. Most people on the left are now calling for more participation, more responsiveness, more decentralization, and less "alienization."

Liberal thinking on this question is in large part a response to black nationalism. More and more Negroes believe there is a cause-effect relationship between the hegemony of what they call "white middle-class" (read professional-bureaucratic) values in their schools and the fact that their children learn so little in those schools. So they think the best way to improve their children's performance would be to break the power of the professional staff. This, they rightly infer, requires Balkanizing big-city system into much smaller units, which will be more responsive to parental and neighborhood pressure. (There are, of course, also strictly administrative arguments for breaking up systems as large as New York City's into units the size of, say, Rochester. But that would not do much for parental control.) So black militants want to strip the central board of education and central administrative staff of authority, elect local boards, have these boards appoint local officials and then let these locally appointed officials operate local schools in precisely the same way that any small-town or suburban school system does.

This scheme has been attacked on two grounds. First, given racial and economic segregation in housing, localism in education means *de facto* segregation in schooling. In New York City, for example, almost everyone agrees the so-called "Bundy Plan" would foreclose any serious effort to reduce racial and economic segregation in the schools. Furthermore, if big-city school systems are broken up, the more affluent neighborhoods will presumably pursue the logic of Balkanization a step further by asking for fiscal as well as administrative autonomy. This demand would be politically difficult to resist. Yet if it were met, the expenditure gap between Harlem and Queens would almost certainly become wider than it now is.

The second common objection to the Balkanization of big-city school systems is that it would produce more parental "interference" (The distinction between "participation" and "interference" is largely a matter of where you think parents' rights end and staff prerogatives begin.) Parental interference would, it is plausibly argued, make it even harder to recruit staff members whose values are significantly at odds with the community's. This would make schools even more homogenized and parochial than they now are. Indeed, a local district which does not give its staff substantial autonomy is likely to have some difficulty recruiting even teachers who have grown up in the neighborhood and share the parents' values, simply because most teachers do not want parents constantly second-guessing them. Once the first flush of idealistic enthusiasm had passed, locally controlled schools in poor areas would probably have a harder time getting staffs than they do now. Like small rural districts confronted with the same problem, small impoverished urban districts would probably have to depend mainly on local people who could not get better jobs elsewhere.

These two arguments against local control of big-city schools naturally carry little weight with black militants. They have little patience with the liberal claim that the way to make black children learn more is to give them more white classmates and more middle-class teachers from Ivy League colleges. When liberals oppose decentralization on the grounds that it would legitimize segregation, the black militants answer: "So what? Integration is a myth. Who needs it?" When professional educators add that decentralization would create working conditions unacceptable to highly trained (and therefore potentially mobile) teachers, the black militants again answer: "So what? Teachers like that don't understand black children. Who wants them?"

Differences of opinion like this probably cannot be resolved by "experimentation"—though more reliable information about the consequences of various school policies would certainly help. For reasons already indicated, the solution must be political.

In seeking such a solution, however, we should bear in mind that a similar crisis arose a century ago when Catholic immigrants confronted a public school system run by and for Protestants. This crisis was successfully resolved by creating two school systems, one public and one private. It seems to me that the same approach might be equally appropriate again today. Since such an idea is likely to shock most liberals, it may be useful to recall certain neglected features of the parochial-school experiment.

The motives of the Catholic immigrants who created the parochial-school system were different in many important respects from the motives of the black nationalists who now want their own schools. Nonetheless, there were also important similarities. Just as today's black nationalist does not want his children infected by alien, white "middle-class" values, so many devout Catholic immigrants did not want their children to imbibe the alien values of white Protestant "first families." Just as today's black nationalist deplores the public schools' failure to develop pride and self-respect in black children, so, too, many Irish immigrants felt they needed their own schools to make their children feel that Catholicism and Irishness were respectable rather than shameful. And just as many black parents now want to get their children out of public schools because they feel these schools do not maintain proper discipline, so, too, many Catholics still say that their prime reason for sending their children to parochial schools is that the nuns maintain order and teach children "to behave."

Why, then, did not devout Catholics press for Balkanization of big-city school systems? Why did they not turn their neighborhood schools into bastions of the faith rather than creating their own separate system?

The answer is that there were very few neighborhoods in which literally all the residents were Catholic. Even where everyone was Catholic, not all Catholics wanted their children educated in self-consciously Catholic schools. Some Catholics, especially those of Irish ancestry, were extremely suspicious of the Anglo-Protestant majority, were strongly attached to the church, and eager to enroll their children in church schools. But others, of whom Italian immigrants were fairly typical, felt as suspicious of the Irish who dominated the church here as of the Anglo-Saxons who dominated the rest of America. Such Catholics were often anticlerical, and they wanted to send their children to schools which would stick to the three R's and skip ideology.

Thus, even in the most Catholic neighborhoods, there was a large minority which thought priests, nuns and theology had no place in the local schools. This minority allied itself with the Protestant majority in other parts of the same state. These state-wide majorities then kept strict limits on local control, so as to prevent devout Catholics from imposing their view of education on local Protestant (or lax Catholic) minorities. In particular, most state constitutions contain some kind of prohibition against the introduction of church personnel and teaching into the local public schools. When they do not, it is only because the Federal First Amendment was thought sufficient to prevent the possibility.

This points to a difficulty with neighborhood control which black militants have yet to face. Blacks are not a majority in many of the areas where they live, at least if these areas are defined as large enough to support a full school system. Nor are black Americans of one mind about Balkanization and its likely consequences. Some black parents still believe in integration. They think the only way to get the social and material advantages they want is to stop being what they have always been, however difficult and painful that may be, and become culturally indistinguishable from the white majority. They therefore want their children to attend integrated schools, to study the same curriculum as white children, and to have teachers from good colleges (most of whom will be white for the foreseeable future). What these families want is thus very similar to what the present professional staffs of big-city school systems want.

Other black parents feel that they can never become indistinguishable from whites, that attempts to acquire white culture only make black children feel miserable and incompetent, and that if such children are to succeed they will have to develop their own style. Such parents want their children to attend schools which try to develop distinctive black virtues and black pride, and which maintain the discipline which is so sorely lacking in the public schools. This cannot, I fear, be reconciled with what the present professional staff wants (or knows how to do).

For convenience, I will label these two sorts of black parents "integrationists" and "nationalists"—though the flavor of the distinction is perhaps better captured in the militants' rhetorical distinction between "Negroes" and "blacks."

Balkanizing big-city school systems would clearly be a victory for the nationalists at the expense of the integrationists. Schools in predominantly black neighborhoods would almost certainly end up with fewer white students and teachers. Local control would also make it easier for white neighborhoods to resist open enrollment, busing and other devices for helping black integrationists send their children to predominantly white schools. The curriculum might or might not be substantially revised once black neighborhood boards held power, but whatever revisions were made would certainly please the nationalists more than the integrationists.

Yet for this very reason state legislatures are unlikely to let black separatists exercise complete control over "their" schools. Just as legislatures earlier protected the rights of Protestant and anticlerical Catholic minorities in devout Catholic communities, so they will almost certainly protect the rights of white and black-integrationist minorities in predominantly black neighborhoods.

If, for example, the local Ocean Hill-Brownsville board wins control over the schools in that part of New York City, the New York State Legislature will almost surely go along with union demands for tight limits on the local board's right to discriminate against whites in hiring teachers and principals. (No such discrimination appears to have taken place in Ocean Hill-Brownsville's hiring of teachers, but the local board does seem to have had a strong and entirely understandable prejudice in favor of black principals.) State certification requirements are also likely to be strictly enforced, so as to restrict black local boards to hiring teachers who have enough respect for white culture and white standards of competence to have got through four or five years of college. New restrictions are also likely to be put on the curriculum, perhaps in the form of a law against teaching "racial hatred," so as to keep LeRoi Jones, etc., out of black schools. Such action would be defended on the same grounds as the rules barring religious teaching in public schools.

Restrictions of this kind are both reasonable and necessary in public institutions which must serve every child in a community, regardless of his race or his parents' outlook on life. They are, however, likely to mean that black nationalists end up feeling that, even though they have a majority on the local board, they do not really control their schools. Once again, whitey will have cheated them of their rightful pride. Local control is, therefore, likely to enrage the professional educators, work against the hopes and ambitions of the integration-minded black and white parents, and yet end up leaving black nationalists as angry as ever. An alternative strategy is badly needed.

The best alternative I can see is to follow the Catholic precedent and allow nationalists to create their own private schools, outside the regular public system, and to encourage this by making such schools eligible for substantial tax support.

The big-city school systems could then remain largely in the hands of their professional staffs. (A major change in the distribution of power between teachers and administrators would still be required, and some decentralization of big cities would also be advisable on bureaucratic grounds, but these are negotiable issues.) The public system would continue to serve white and black integrationists. Separatists who found this system unacceptable would have the option of sending their children to other schools at relatively low cost.

The beginnings of such a parallel system can already be seen in some big cities. Black middle-class parents are already far more likely than their white counterparts to enroll their children in private schools. A number of private "community schools" have also sprung up in the ghettos during the past few years. The Muslims run several schools. These schools have found many black parents are willing to make considerable financial sacrifices in order to send their children to a school they think superior to the public one. What these ventures lack, however, is substantial political and financial support. Without this they are likely to remain isolated and relatively unusual.

Some will ask why an independent black school system should need or deserve white support when the parochial schools get no such support. The most relevant answer is that, without the unity and legitimacy conferred by religion, the black community cannot go it alone. It is, perhaps, an unfortunate historical accident that black America lacks its own church, but it does—and even the Muslims have not been able to remedy the situation. Yet black America still needs its own schools, free to serve exigencies of black nationalism. Given the inevitable hostility of both professional educators and laymen who believe in integration, black nationalists are unlikely to be able to create such schools within the public sector.

Is there any justification for funding black private schools without funding other private schools on the same basis? My answer is "No."

Indeed, it seems to me that the only way a black private-school system could hope to get tax subsidies would be to ally itself with a parochial school system in demanding Federal and state support for all private schools. Many traditional liberals feel this would violate the constitutional separation of church and state. The Supreme Court has never ruled on this question, however; until it does, it seems reasonable to assume that there is no constitutional objection to Federal or state subsidies for private schools—so long as these subsidies are earmarked to achieve specific public purposes, and so long as the schools are accountable for achieving these purposes.

An analogy may clarify this point. Back in the 19th century, the Supreme Court ruled that the Government could legally contract with Catholic hospitals to care for public charity patients, and today only the most strict separatist would argue that the Federal Government cannot contract with a Catholic university or a Catholic hospital to carry out scientific research. Why, then, should it not contract with a Catholic school to teach physics to 16-year-olds or reading to impoverished 6-year-olds?

Private schools should, of course, be required to show that they had actually done what they promised to do, rather than devoting public funds to the construction of chapels or the production of antiwhite propaganda. But accountability of this kind is essential with all tax subsidies, whether to private schools, private corporations or local government.

Even if a coalition between the church and the black community were put together, is it realistic to suppose that white Protestant America would actually support black schools? My guess is that it would, so long as the financial burden remains within reason. Remember, I am *not* proposing that white legislators should help create a private system for blacks which would be more expensive than the one now attended by whites. I am only proposing that black children who attend private schools should be eligible for at least part of the tax subsidy which is now available if they choose to seek an education in the public system. Far from increasing the overall tax bill, then, a scheme of this kind would actually lower it. In particular, it would help slow the rise in local property taxes, by providing black parents with state and Federal incentives to withdraw their children from locally supported schools, thus cutting local costs. Many local white taxpayers would probably greet such a development with considerable enthusiasm. It would also reduce some white parents' anxiety about the public system's being "overrun" by black children. (It would not actually diminish integration-minded blacks' interest in desegregation, but if it reduced over-all black enrollment it might make desegregation seem a little less threatening and more practical.) In addition, the creation of an independent black school system might strike many whites as a relatively easy and painless way to buy political peace and sweep the whole racial problem under the rug. I doubt if it would succeed in doing this, but it might at least help shift the focus of racial conflict away from the schools and into other more critical arenas.

At this point, somebody always says, "Well, what about private schools established by white supremacists to escape integration?" The answer to that question is already clear. The Supreme Court has held subsidies for such schools unconstitutional, and neither legislatures nor Congress should provide them.

Indeed, I would go further and argue that the state should not subsidize any school which is not open to every child who wants to enroll —regardless of race, religion or ability. Not many non-Catholics want to attend parochial schools, but some already do and others will. Their admission should certainly be a precondition for public subsidies. Similarly, black schools should be required to admit white applicants in order to get tax support. No rush of applicants need be anticipated.

One final objection to the establishment of independent black schools should be mentioned. Many whites fear that such a system would preach black nationalism and racial hatred, and that this would make racial reconciliation even more difficult than it now seems.

This is a reasonable fear. The same objections were raised against the Catholic schools for more than a hundred years. Yet despite all sorts of horror stories about anti-Semitism and other forms of prejudice in Catholic schools, a 1964 survey by Andrew Greeley and Peter Rossi of the University of Chicago demonstrated fairly conclusively that Catholics who attended parochial schools were no more intolerant, narrow-minded or socially irresponsible than Catholics who attended public schools. Indeed, the survey suggested that, all other things being equal, parochial schools had a more liberalizing effect on Catholics than did public schools.

And similarly, the Greeley-Rossi survey suggests that the black schools would not have to be especially affluent to do an acceptable job. While the parochial schools spent far less per pupil than the public schools, used less extensively trained teachers, had much larger classes, were housed in older buildings, had smaller libraries and relied on a curriculum even more medieval than did the public schools, their alumni did at least as well in worldly terms as public-school Catholics.

All other things being equal, parochial-school Catholics ended up with slightly more education and slightly better jobs than public-school Catholics. The only really significant difference Greeley and Rossi found between the two groups was that parochial school products were more meticulous and better informed about their religious obligations. This suggests that fears for the future of black children in black-controlled schools may also be somewhat exaggerated.

The development of an independent black school system would not solve the problems of black children. I doubt, for example, that many black private schools could teach their children to read appreciably better than white-controlled public schools now do. But such schools would be an important instrument in the hands of black leaders who want to develop a sense of community solidarity and pride in the ghetto, just as the parochial schools have worked for similarly placed Catholics.

Equally important, perhaps the existence of independent black schools would diffuse the present attack on professional control over the public system. This seems the only politically realistic course in a society where professional control, employee rights and bureaucratic procedures are as entrenched as they are in America. The black community is not strong enough to destroy the public-school bureaucracy and staff. Even if it did, it now has nothing to put in its place. What the black community could do, however, would be to develop an alternative—and demand tax support for it.

Some radicals who expect black insurgency to destroy the whole professional hierarchy in America and create a new style of participatory democracy will regard this kind of solution as a cop-out. Some conservatives whose primary concern is that the lower orders not get out of hand will regard it as an undesirable concession to anarchy. But for those who value a pluralistic society, the fact that such a solution would, for the first time, give large numbers of non-Catholics a choice about where they send their children to school, ought, I think, to outweigh all other objections.

NEIL V. SULLIVAN | ***Myths and Gaps in School Integration***

A rabbit was crossing the highway at night. He stopped suddenly to stare into the headlights of an onrushing car. Frozen with terror, he stood immobile as the car bore down on him. This modern fable applies forcefully to American education. Like the rabbit, our educators and boards of education are paralyzed by indecision as they face the onrushing problem of school integration. They wish it would go away. Some would like to take a backward leap to the "safety" of preintegration days by "upgrading" segregated schools. Some would simply like to play dead and hope the problem would miss them entirely.

The truth is that integration of education must be faced and faced now. Leaders, whether political or academic, who do not face up to integration will be run over as surely as the frightened rabbit.

If any Americans are under the illusion that integration is well under way in the United States, they need only read the first paragraph of the U.S. Office of Education's illuminating "Equality of Educational Opportunity" (the Coleman Report) summary. "White children are most segregated. . . . Almost 80 percent of all white pupils in 1st grade and 12th grade attend schools that are from 90 to 100 percent white."

This report was compiled 11 years after the U.S. Supreme Court's desegregation decision of 1954, and in the three years since the report the percentages have changed alarmingly little.

To solve the integration problem, we must understand it—particularly the emotion-charged myths about it that block a solution.

No one can ignore the fact that a large number of Americans are hostile to integration. Many have very real fears about racially balanced schools, but most of these fears are based on a few deeply rooted half-truths. I have run into all of the myths since becoming superintendent of the Berkeley, California, Unified School District, where we are actively committed to integrating our schools.

A myth is, for our purposes, a widely held belief that contains only a grain of truth.

One of the most persistent myths is that school integration will cause academic achievement to suffer. Those who voice this myth mean that the child in a "privileged" environment (the Caucasian child) will suffer socially and academically if his school becomes racially integrated. But according to the Coleman Report:

> . . . if a white pupil from a home that is strongly and effectively supportive of education is put in a school where most pupils do not come from such homes, his achievement will be little different than if he were in a school composed of others like himself. But if a minority pupil from a home without much educational strength is put with schoolmates with strong educational backgrounds, his achievement is likely to increase.

Even more startling, this massive survey found that the student body was the most important single in-school factor in improving the academic achievements of minority group children. To my surprise, and I'm sure to the surprise of Dr. Coleman and most educators, the mixing factor was more important to raising academic achievement levels of disadvantaged pupils than were good teachers (although these were the second most important), equipment, texts, buildings, or other related factors.

I do not mean to imply that racial and "class" integration will automatically insure academic excellence in a school. Academic excellence has always needed educational leadership, and, in the last analysis, a combination of many factors, especially high-quality teachers. But even the Caucasian child in an unintegrated school suffers from his segregation. As far as can be determined from incomplete surveys, segregation of the white child is a disadvantage to that child.

One of the most difficult myths to combat is that violence in the schools will drastically increase if they are integrated. Despite the lack of conclusive studies on this subject, my own experiences in Berkeley—and we are just across the Bay from San Francisco and its Hunter's Point ghetto, where rioting occurred in 1966—would indicate that race-based violence in our school is amazingly low.

In 1964, we in Berkeley completed the integration of our junior high schools and in the process created an unusual one-year school, called West Campus, for all of Berkeley's ninth graders. Garfield Junior High had been virtually an all-white, privileged school; Willard had been fairly well balanced, and Burbank (which became West Campus) was almost entirely Negro.

Naturally, we were apprehensive about the move. Teachers frankly were afraid academic levels would collapse. (Some of them, too, believe in myths!) Many prophesied wholesale violence. The Berkeley Teachers Association, however, strongly supported both the concept of integration and the courageous board members who voted to implement it.

The first year of complete integration at Garfield was tense, but the way the students worked to make it work was wonderful. At West Campus, also, everyone was determined to make the unusual one-year school work—and they did, beautifully. The second year we had the normal problems expected with first-year high school students, but they were not integration problems, not racial violence.

In the 1967–68 school year, there were racial incidents at one of our junior high schools on the heels of Martin Luther King's assassination, which was a more than symbolic, ultimate act of white racism. It triggered long-standing student resentment against a tracking system which seemed to guarantee segregated classes within the desegregated school. It also reflected some staff insensitivity to the needs of a mixed student body. The immediate racial incidents were met by quick emergency action to keep the peace on campus and in the classroom. Students, parents, and teachers of the various races immediately became deeply involved in improving the whole school scene, and this involvement has continued.

The truth is that disillusionment, hostility, hopelessness, and violence by young people are on the rise everywhere—even in all-white schools and communities where race is not at issue. There is very real confusion about fights between members of different races. Some undoubtedly have racial animosity at their base, but do most of them? Is our habit of attributing racial trouble instantly to any fighting between boys of different races responsible for the persistence of the "violence myth"?

The greatest outbursts of racial violence occur where no steps have been taken toward integration or when those taken are so timid, so obviously phony, that the minority race believes the token integration step was taken to prove total integration would not work. If such a thing were done to whites, they, too, would be fighting mad.

Those who repeat the "violence myth" ignore the fact that it is the Negro who has been on the receiving end of most interracial violence down through American history. The myth-sayers appear unconcerned about violence done to the Negro, except as it disturbs the surface calm of our society. However, no matter which side mounts the racial attack, both white and black are the losers. The cure lies in breaking down the ghetto barriers in education, housing, and employment. Then the violence will cease.

Another myth concerns the "great exodus." This one usually comes up at a board of education meeting, phrased this way: "School integration will be followed by a mass exodus of Caucasians from the community." Again we are faced with an observable element of truth. White families do move away as ghetto conditions advance. Some of the easily alarmed ones flee to all-white suburbs or rural areas at the first sign of an "alien" element in the schools. The flight to the suburbs is well-documented. But is it a "race flight"?

It is in some instances. But I suggest it might also be called a "smog flight" or a "congestion flight." Some families fly from high taxes and deteriorating city services—only to discover that taxes can be higher in the suburbs and services even less satisfactory. Many move out of the dense city simply so their children can see grass growing, sit in the shade of a tree, hear a real, live bird sing.

Recent Berkeley experience was an instinctive one with regard to the "great exodus." We were warned that the city would become a ghost town overnight, that it would soon be all-Negro if we proceeded with integration. The City Council even established a committee to study ways a racially mixed Berkeley could face the years ahead without becoming a ghetto.

Before the committee went to work, we knew that there had been a gradual decline in white enrollment in the schools, a decline that had already tapered off. Some presumed that this reflected the movement of white families away from a system they feared would soon be integrated.

In the fall of 1966, with our efforts to implement racial balance a year along, we took a racial census of students in Berkeley schools. The census showed that, not only had the decline in Caucasian enrollment stopped, it had been reversed. Both the number and the proportion of Caucasian students attending Berkeley schools had increased. The 1967 fall census indicated another slight gain in the number of Caucasians in our student population. For Berkeley, the flight to the suburbs was a myth.

A myth attractive to Negroes and whites alike is that compensatory education, by itself, can solve the problems of racial discrimination and poor education for disadvantaged children, eliminating the need for integration of schools.

What is meant by compensatory education? It means pouring money and teachers into poor ghetto schools. The theory is that by smothering these schools in educational goodies—psychologists, researchers, counselors, top-quality teachers, better school buildings, cafeterias—we can put all-Negro schools on a par with all-white schools of the best quality. This, the story goes, will make it necessary to worry about integration because children of all races will have equal educational opportunities everywhere.

There are individual instances of spectacular success when bright ghetto youngsters are given substantial amounts of special help, but there is no real evidence that the mass of minority children can benefit by this technique.

The Coleman Report and a report of the U.S. Commission on Civil Rights both indicate that one of the most important ingredients in education—hope—is not provided by compensatory techniques. Hope for a better future, hope to become an accepted member of society, hope for an end to discrimination—none of these is satisfied by compensatory education.

Involuntary segregation, no matter how benevolent, is rejection. Segregation is the classic symbol of society's centuries-long tradition of discrimination, and it says unequivocally to black people and other minorities, "You are inferior."

Thus, compensatory education, which does have some very valuable features, can never, in my opinion, be a substitute for integration. Many black children who are kept segregated develop a "What's the use?" attitude. Even if their equipment is improved and they get better teachers and special attention, they have no yardstick by which to measure the improvement in relation to what the "other" or white children are receiving. They cannot be convinced that they are not getting scraps from the table.

Compensatory education can be very useful in helping to make up for the deprivation ghetto children have suffered, but it must be used in conjunction with—not instead of—integration. Then it will show spectacular results.

Many Americans still cling to another myth—that integration is not a problem of the schools. Integration, the argument runs, must start with housing: Minorities now have the right to buy houses and rent apartments anywhere. This does not mean, though, that all segments of the population will be mixed together and that schools will be automatically integrated.

However, when ways of integrating housing are discussed, potent real estate groups and frantic property owners insist that this can only be accomplished when the employment sector has been thoroughly integrated. They say that when the Negro and the other minorities get better jobs, they will have the money to upgrade their ghettos or, presumably, to buy better property.

The discussion with employers and unions on integrating jobs brings out the contention that until Negroes and other minorities have had more education, they cannot hope to get or hold better jobs, etc., etc., and around and around.

The fact is that segregation is a problem in all of these areas and solutions must be found in all of them. We educators are under no illusion that desegregation of education alone will solve the problem completely. Solutions must come also in housing and employment, and ultimately in all phases of society. But it is essential that the educational sector not hang back waiting for integration to begin somewhere else first. Education must not be afraid to assume leadership.

I do not delude myself that the myths will soon be completely destroyed or even that the hostility of many white Americans to integration can be entirely overcome. But we will have to live with the myths and with the hostility, and get on with the job of integration. There is no choice. Events are forcing us to act.

Even an all-white community with all-white schools must face up to the race problem. The children in such a "protected" town bump into the problem on TV, in the press, in comic books. Even if they are not asked to discuss it or confront it in their narrow little world, they bump into it whenever they move out of their cocoon. Will they be equipped to deal with the problem intelligently?

Compelling as the case for school integration is, simply mixing students in classrooms is not enough. Some very real gaps have to be closed to make integration work. Yet since desegregation cannot wait, we must integrate and work to close the gaps at the same time.

To professional educators, the most obvious gap is the academic achievement gap—or chasm. Historically, this gap is easily explained. In many areas of the United States, Negroes were deliberately kept uneducated.

When it could no longer be denied that black people were human beings and even could learn to read, write, and manipulate figures, the U.S. Supreme Court came up with its famous "separate but equal" school facilities ruling. Since then, facilities for Negroes have certainly been separate but never equal.

It was not just that equipment was unequal, but that many teachers in ghetto schools were inexperienced and poorly trained. They were not poor in courage, certainly, but many of them had little more than a high school education, and that from inferior segregated schools. Thus, even those Negro children who did thirst for knowledge and who did do their best to get something out of school were cheated. The gap between their education and that of the whites was enormous, and still is.

Beyond the educational gap there is, in many instances, a cultural gap. The very institution of segregation has forced many minorities—but particularly the Negro—into the role of lowest-class citizens. Unemployment is high, so blacks have to live in cramped, unsafe quarters. Food for their tables is inadequate, and food for their minds is even more deficient.

As a baby and preschool youngster, the ghetto child often did not have any practice at naming things and has difficulty doing so when he finally gets to school. For him, the classroom is a new world where the symbols are all different. In a school outside the ghetto, he runs into children who are quite at home in the world of symbols. Quickly falling behind, he becomes discouraged and is frequently rebellious or apathetic.

The "behavior gap" is related to the cultural gap. If a child's home life places no emphasis on consideration for others, then his behavior is going to be a problem in school. But children are sensitive creatures and, when properly handled, soon learn to follow the socially acceptable behavior of their peers. In a thoroughly integrated school, behavior patterns depend on what the school tolerates—just as they do in all-white schools. The behavior gap depends for its solution primarily on teachers and administrators who know when to be firm and when to be yielding, and are always fair.

As Americans should know by now, merely to put children of all races in one school does not mean integration. You can have complete segregation within the school if Negroes speak only to Negroes in the schoolyard and whites to whites. I have seen it happen. Thus the "friendship gap" must also be closed in the schools.

This is not nearly as difficult as we originally supposed. The solution is to capture the children's interest. West Campus School in Berkeley does it with literally hundreds of clubs and activities. An art club, a science club, a hiking club—you name it and West Campus probably has it. Mutuality of interests quickly transcends race. Friendships develop. The de facto segregation pattern in the schoolyard begins to disintegrate.

A gap that the schools will have great difficulty bridging is the gap between expectations and possibilities. When the black child comes out of the ghetto, he is promised freedom, justice, and equality, and he may get them in school, where he becomes an educated man. In the larger community, he collides with brutal reality. The job he is educated to take may not be open to a Negro. His school years of integration are over, and now his expectation of an integrated life as a fully accepted American citizen is blasted.

This last gap is still a matter of education, but it is not one that educators alone can bridge. It has to be a community effort and a national effort. We can exorcise the myths and close the gaps if we will, but we must get about the job now and with vigor.

CHARLES E. MARTIN | ***The Path to Integration***

Year after year, as new guidelines for desegregation appear, school administrators across the country convene in workshops and planning conferences to design a vehicle in which we can travel over new ground. But to date we are still traveling on foot, still uncertain of our directions. Perhaps the time has come to take a closer look at the ground we have covered and at our destination.

In schools throughout the South we began in a state of segregation, licensed by law and fully realized in fact. Following the Supreme Court decisions of 1954 and 1955, we branched in two directions: A few of us looked for a direct path toward integration; most of us beat a thoroughfare in the direction of desegregation.

In certain select schools we deleted the words "white" and "Negro" from those documents which describe student eligibility for enrollment and cautiously opened their doors. We arranged attendance zones in patterns that would permit some mixing of bodies without greatly changing the racial identity of schools. We contrived the assignment of a handful of teachers across racial lines, called it faculty desegregation, and rested our tongues in our cheeks.

A dual structure of schools in a district is at best a mixture, not a compound. Attendance centers that retain their racial identity as black or white mark a district's divisiveness like a checkerboard. A system singly structured, on the other hand, is dynamically compounded in all its parts. Its attendance centers are comprised of teachers and students in a biracial or multiracial balance which will permit their total and mutual involvement in education and in all those facets of daily living and learning by which education is ultimately shaped.

We know that the thoroughfare to desegregation was the long way around. We have not yet come near a real solution to the basic problems of human rights.

Maybe such an approach was one of those saintly sins we must sometimes live through before we can tolerate the demands of virtue on the other side. For some of us it was just plain stubbornness. Whatever our reason we have reaped 14 years of frustrating experience, sowed dragon seed along the way, and created a host of new obstacles.

From *American Education* (September 1968). Published by the Department of Health, Education, and Welfare, Office of Education. Reprinted by permission.

The course of desegregation has led in some instances to resegregation of our communities. In these areas the mere announcement of intent to desegregate a white school has sometimes prompted such a migration of families to the white suburbs that the composition of the student body has changed from white to predominantly Negro before a new school year has begun.

In the pursuit of desegregation we have cloaked the issues with tokenism—token student integration, token staff desegregation, and personnel assignment to positions of token prestige. The admission of Negro students to white schools *that remain essentially white* or of white students to Negro schools *that remain essentially Negro* has solved nothing. Indeed it has openly invited a kind of segregation that is even more stringent than that of our old separate-but-equal zone lines. Few students are likely to sacrifice the positions they have earned in a segregated school in exchange for the questionable personal value of attending a desegregated school, gaining only a seat on the sidelines from which they are permitted to watch the mainstream of the school's social life pass them by. By admitting small numbers of Negro students to white schools without providing for their active absorption in student affairs, we have helped to create and perpetuate de facto segregation, which defeats every worthwhile goal of our commitment.

The assignment of one or two teachers to a faculty predominantly of another race has served only to spotlight the inequities of the dual system, not to cancel them. The doors within a school building can be closed as tightly as those at its entrance. And wherever we have placed a Negro educator in a position where equality pertains only to the job title but not to its function, we have assuredly added insult to injury. Negroes should be appointed to positions of functional prestige and assigned to some of the limelight positions—athletic coaches and special program directors—where their contributions can extend well into public view.

It is not easy to face the fact that we have dissipated 14 years in pursuit of a false goal. But our concentration on rationalized mechanics, freedom of choice, and letter-of-the-law statistics has not produced appreciable changes in our classrooms or equalized educational opportunities. More often than not it begged the issues.

In a soul-searching look at those issues, I cannot consider it impractical to begin with the basic right of man to direct his drives toward the establishment of systems that will permit maximum self-determination of his own social directions. Nor does it seem cynical to take the position that the *worthwhile* survival of man can be assured only to the extent that his society can be an integrated one, affording maximum equality of opportunity for all its members. We are a gregarious breed; we cannot live in isolation; we are impelled to devise social patterns that are conducive to harmonious interaction.

The schools of this country are a system devised by society, and education is a vital component of total social direction. Therefore the only proper issues for our consideration in this matter are the provision of equal educational opportunity for all students in an integrated school society and the exercise of educational leadership for the eventual integration of the broader society which created our educational system and gives us reason for being. This we can accomplish only in full commitment and full acceptance of the responsibility.

If integration is our proper goal, then our task is one of designing and effecting social change. Educators, by the very nature of their profession, hold a mandate, legally issued and socially decreed, to influence the directions of society. And the processes by which social change may be made begin with the identification of those people in whom change of some kind is needed before new patterns of social living can be designed. Immediately apparent on the educational front are members of school boards, school administrators, supervisors, teachers, the staffs of colleges and universities, pupils, and parents.

Change in people is brought about only as they learn new designs for living, unlearn old patterns, or relearn others which they have forgotten. Surely some of the knowledge we have spent our lives collecting can now be applied to the removal of those forces which presently impede the provision of equal opportunity for all our students.

A close look at our efforts on this matter of human rights points up one major prerequisite to learning, and therefore to change, that is conspicuous by its absence: None of us has ever actually seen or had experience with a totally integrated society. We have no whole role models to emulate. We are literally impelled to create prototypes of integration in every segment of school-related society and to arrange for those whom we hope to influence to have experiences with the best models we can produce.

One such effort to create prototypes occurred in the Chattanooga Public Schools, where we have had some success this year with the development of pilot instructional programs in two elementary units. The programs have received every supportive benefit we could muster in their behalf—additional funds for materials, staff and consultative assistance, para-professional aides, building adaptations, and leeway to stretch the precedents on such things as standard textbook adoptions, curriculum development, and flexible scheduling.

The major purposes for developing these pilot programs were related to our efforts to shift the responsibility for program development to the attendance center level, where we feel it properly belongs; to engage Negro and white teachers in cooperative and creative planning; to give reenforcement to faculties who have shown initiative; and to demonstrate in the school system some different arrangements for learning. The positive relationships formed between Negro and white teachers as they reached for common goals and shared common problems have given us rich food for thought. The instructional programs developed are based on student self-directed study in large learning centers. This pattern, coupled with large group instruction in such subject areas as physical education and music, has released teachers for small group and individual work with students in those skills and content areas where direct instruction is needed.

Because of the pilot nature of their programs, these schools have become goldfish bowls, visited by people in our own system and those from other school districts. This concerned me at first, but the effects have been too positive to overlook. Once the newness of being observed wore off, both students and teachers began to respond to the reenforcement of knowing that what they are doing has meaning and worth to others.

Although the faculties of these first pilot efforts have provided the nucleus for a model of staff integration, the student compositions have not. We too are groping for solutions to the problems of de facto segregation. The smaller of the two pilot schools serves an all white community in a low socio-economic area. The other serves an all Negro community. As prototypes of integration they are incomplete, but they have afforded a design for the creation of such a prototype.

In another part of the city, one of our junior high schools has now reached a racial balance in its student composition. On the basis of what we have seen in the two elementary schools, we have elected to focus for the coming year on the junior high situation, to bring its faculty into an integrated balance, then concentrate the same kind of attention on its instructional program. It will be our purpose to make it a complete prototype of integration.

Obviously the problems of integration cannot be solved on a numerical basis. The tokenism of desegration has permitted the statistical use of a relatively small number of teachers and students to draw attention away from the vast majority who remain uninvolved and untouched. It can be impressive, for example, to report that in a district having 40 school units and 20,000 students, there are 16,000 young people who attend schools having biracial student compositions. But this might be said if no more than one student in each of 35 schools were of a different race from that by which the school is traditionally identified. Even if the average number of students in such minority positions is 50 or more per unit, it remains that the schools are identified as Negro or white, that a handful of students in a few classes may comprise a conspicuous minority, and that hundreds—indeed thousands—of young people of both races are learning to live with the myth of justice in tokenism as surely as our own generation learned to live with the myth of justice in separate-but-equal provisions.

In the same school district the assignment of one or two teachers across racial lines in each of 30 faculties might permit an impressive statistical report to the effect that 15,000 students are taught by biracial faculties. The cold facts may be that no more than 2,000 or 3,000 of the 20,000 students in the district have any regular contract with an adult of a different race, that no more than 60 of the 700 teachers are in regular contact with appreciable numbers of children of a different race, and that not a single child or teacher has any opportunity to see or experience a truly integrated school situation.

No matter what set of statistics we polish for approval, the group with which I am most concerned lies in full view in our classrooms. It is there that we have permitted the most subtle and degrading forms of discrimination to prevail in the name of equal opportunity. It is a point of strong conviction that *equal* means something more than *same*. Large numbers of Negro students, although as capable as their white classmates, find themselves floundering for want of the instructional and personal assistance they need to compensate for inadequate earlier experiences. Whenever the cumulative efforts of racial discrimination have created situations that block students from getting an education which will permit them to attain a position of respect in the total society, then opportunity cannot be considered equal without compensatory provisions. It is no saintly sin we commit when we permit a same-for-all approach to perpetuate hopelessness, when we assume a laissez-faire attitude to deny full participation to Negro students in school clubs, councils, elections, teams, and social events, or when we cry "hands off" of so-called individual freedom that denies any student the right to be a welcomed part of the social order and to achieve due prestige among peers. And neither is it mere chance fumbling when, year after year, we hand out an all white curriculum wrapped around all white materials while we play statistical games in the name of desegregation.

Once and for all let's bury the vehicles we have invented which move solely through the machination of statistics. Even if the numbers never fall into balance, we are nevertheless impelled to write the Negro race into our curriculum for students of both races and to intercede for the deliberate involvement of Negro students in the mainstream social life of our schools. There are good teachers, both Negro and white, who can and will provide the role models and develop the prototypes of integrated curriculums and multicolored materials. There are good principals who can and will intercede to exemplify integration in student affairs. There are students who will willingly involve themselves—and parents who will willingly permit them to be involved—in the creation of integrated student societies. If we must deal only with the statistical few, then let those few draw attention toward the goals of integration, not away from them.

With a few instructional and attitudinal prototypes we will be in a position to arrange new experiences for the uninvolved, whether they are teachers, students, parents, board members, or university friends of the family. We will be in a position to support and reenforce positive social growth patterns. Our instruments of assessment can be put to good use indeed, when we have something deserving of assessment.

For university friends of the family two types of integration are imperative. Public school administrators are frustrated at every turn where teacher training institutions are segregated from the cause of public school education, as so many continue to be by deliberate intent. And the cause of racial integration and compensatory programs aimed at equality of educational opportunity will be manacled and weighted so long as colleges and universities pursue the path of bare tokenism and noninvolvement. Unless there is an about face in teacher training practices, public school administrations will be forced to assume some of the college function and to fight through the red tape of legislation to support the effort.

At whatever costs the public schools and those who train their personnel must create cooperatives for teacher training, research, and educational leadership. There must be common goals established for such ventures and examples of racially integrated college societies. Student teacher programs are a beginning. Public schools can integrate these programs by the requirements they set for the placement of student teachers in schools.

The term "compensatory" has acquired a connotation which I think we must broaden. The provisions of things is not in itself compensatory. Where racial discrimination has been the pattern over a long period of time, things may be no more than the tokens we find it easiest to provide. If we cannot expand the concept of educational compensation beyond this level, we may as well call it patronage and be done with it.

In compensation for economic deprivation, we can hardly expect milk served to undernourished children by the gallon at the age of six years to have the same nutritional value it would have had by the ounce at six months. And in compensation for racial discrimination, not even full respect and the right to participate or to compete in 1968 are likely to compensate for their own lacks through the past 200 years. Situational compensation is a comparatively minor part of our task; psychological compensation must be our primary goal.

In these times the provision of equal educational opportunity carries the burden of centuries of inequality. We are therefore impelled to sacrifice some of the things to which we have accorded high value in our white system in order to bring the goals of this issue into proper balance. In the employment and assignment of personnel, for example, the race of a job candidate must frequently supersede other recommendations which have heretofore been our first considerations. If we are indeed committed to the provision of equal opportunity in an integrated society, then the selection of Negro over white personnel and vice versa, according to the predominant race of a faculty, must be deliberate and immediate.

If we make such school assignments across racial lines in order to create a situation approximating integration, we have begun a situational compensation. If it goes no further we are back to statistics. If we move to the point at which a teacher so assigned becomes a reasonably comfortable and accepted member of the faculty, the situational compensation may be fulfilled.

Again for want of role models, I can only project that psychological compensation may begin when and if the teacher so assigned becomes a positive part of the total life of the school, involved in a shared commitment and secure in the sense of personal and professional competency. The myth of Negro teachers' inferiority has been ingrained in both races. The certainty of racial hostility produces anxiety in both Negro and white teachers. These are integration barriers which will actually require overcompensation before they are removed.

Both Negro and white teachers need greatly increased support to their professional competencies in the move to actual integration. They will hardly be able to function as effective role models for students so long as they themselves are weighted with doubts about their own comparative competencies. I do not believe that psychological compensation can ever take root in an environment rife with unsuccess and defensiveness.

The need to provide positive psychological compensation for students is even more acute. We inflict deep wounds on children whenever we permit them to see themselves day after day as being somehow unworthy to participate on an eye-to-eye level with their peers. True, they will find compensation of one kind or another, and they will build defenses to their own purposes; but the underlying blight of racial divisiveness will remain rooted in our society. I doubt that we can move toward positive psychological compensation except by constructing success for the young people who are now bearing the brunt of our statistical gymnastics.

The commitment to integration carries an obligation to intercede in the conduct of student affairs for the deliberate and total involvement of Negro students in the life of the school. Wherever so-called individual freedom serves to perpetuate a circumstance so debilitating to the whole of society, it ceases to be a right. And such a commitment poses a mandate to curricular revision or reconstruction. These, not the techniques of statistics, are the appropriate topics of concern in our professional consideration of human rights.

If we took a wrong turn when we set out for desegregation, as I feel we did, perhaps we are the wiser for it. Perhaps we can now accord to ourselves and to those whom we hope to influence the fundamental right to make mistakes. If we are committed to the creation of a design so new to us all as an integrated society, we will make other mistakes, but I cannot believe that either the commitment or the effort will be among them.

JOHN HARDIN BEST | *Public and Private Education*

The idea of "public" as distinguished from "private" education in America has undergone considerable shift in past years. Perhaps an idea as complex as "public education" is continually changing along with the society and its values. But certainly at the present time we are in an era in which the idea is undergoing a fundamental shift with certain important new elements emerging as part of the definition.

For the past one hundred years, or at least since the Progressive Era of the late nineteenth century, "public education" as an idea in America has had several generally agreed upon components: first, it has meant systematic public support, i.e., annual budgets coming from tax monies; second, public control by officials either directly or indirectly responsible to the taxpayers; and third, schooling in the service of the public interest which in large terms meant the building of a united America wherein individuals could advance themselves within the democratic framework. Public schooling under this conception was considered to be enormously successful, its triumph seen as the essence in fact of the triumph of American democracy.

The historian of this burgeoning public school was of course Ellwood P. Cubberley who took it as his calling not only to chronicle the rise of public education but also, as has every good historian since Thucydides, to make his history serve his cause. Cubberley promoted this burgeoning by every historical means and, one must conclude, with considerable effect. Generations of American educators shared the pride of Cubber-

From *Educational Leadership* 26 (3): 250–53; December 1968. Reprinted with permission of the Association for Supervision and Curriculum Development and John Hardin Best.

ley's position, such as this one, a summary statement from his monumental textbook, *The History of Education:*

By 1860, we find the American public school system fully established, in principle at least, in all our Northern States. Much yet remained to be done to carry into full effect what had been established in principle, but everywhere democracy had won its fight, and the American public school, supported by general taxation, freed from the pauper school taint, free and equally open to all, under the direction of representatives of the people, free from sectarian control, and complete from the primary school through the high school, and in the Western States through the university as well, was established permanently in American public policy.[1]

Cubberley as a historian has in recent years fallen upon evil days, a victim perhaps inevitably of new generations of historians with new causes. His fate, however, need not concern us here, though of course his decline and fall within the past decade may indicate a geologic fault below the seemingly firm surface of the conception of public education.

The distinction of "public" and "private" education during this hundred years, however, was plain and unambiguous. The private school meant privilege, the institution of the rich and high-born. Or it meant schools controlled by the churches which were at the least narrow, i.e., parochial, or at the worst no more than a sink of superstition. Insofar as private education posed a threat to the public school it was seen as fundamentally not in accord with democratic institutions and practices.

The contrast was clear: nonpublic education did not and should not have public support, was not under public control, and could not serve the democratic public interest. Schoolmen at all levels, from elementary schools to the university, shared this conception and defended the distinction of public and private. Perhaps the century from 1860 to 1960 could rightfully be called, with Cubberley's blessing, the "Era of Public Education."

A New Era

In our society it seems that change itself is the only certainty. By the 1960's the idea of public education which had stood so long, reflected in the great system of American public schools, appeared to shift in basically important ways. The immediate background of the change, however, was a series of attacks on the public school during the decade of the 'fifties. These attacks, though fearsome enough, were not really fundamental in that they never struck at the idea of public education.

[1] Ellwood P. Cubberley. *The History of Education.* Boston: Houghton Mifflin Company, 1920. p. 708.

The various special interest groups, such as the Council for Basic Education, were engaged mainly in efforts to gain influence over the public schools. Their attacks may have damaged certain principles of support and control of public education. Yet the more forceful and effective of the critics were those who set out to bend the principle of service to the public interest in pursuit of "cold war" victories. The public school was to pursue excellence which in turn would pursue Russians which, it was understood, was the national interest.

Such cold-warriors as Rickover and Conant may have bent the principle a bit, but in essential ways they concurred with Cubberley's conception of the public school serving what appeared to be the public interest. The furies of the 'fifties left the public school undeniably shaken, but now it seems clear they were no more than precursors of a reexamination of the basic idea of public education beginning in the 'sixties.

The question being raised today is: Can the conception of public education be reinterpreted to stress the interests of the individual in American society? It is a question in a sense of redefining the idea of the public interest, and with it the ideas of support and control of public education along pluralistic lines, to bring them into accord with current ideas of democracy and individual freedom.

Clearly the old distinction, Cubberley-style, of public *vis-à-vis* private education has become so confused as to be dangerously misleading: historically it has been the private school which stressed the individual interest in contrast to the approach used in the public school. Yet beyond that confusion is a more basic criticism: the public interest as it was spelled out by Cubberley, or the national interest in the terms of the 'fifties, seemed to coincide with the interests of white, middle-class, Protestant America, with very little room for diversity within the consensus.

The public school seemed to find no place for the values of the nonwhite, non-middle-class, non-Protestant child; in fact, the public school had become the truly parochial school. Hence, under this criticism, the idea of the public school and the public interest needed considerable expanding to meet the demands of this new America of the 'sixties.

New Demands

Several situations, urban and suburban, will illustrate this demand for expansion of the idea of public education. In one city with an approximate 50 per cent nonwhite public school population, there is a massive system of Roman Catholic schools which enrolls less than five per cent of nonwhite children. Several of these Catholic elementary schools, however, are almost entirely nonwhite. And in these latter schools a first-grade teacher expects at last 50 children as the normal class size—50 pupils with no aides and no assistants. The problems of racial integration in this city's public schools are made difficult indeed by the racial makeup of the Catholic system of schools. Yet the interests of the child who is learning to read, or more likely failing to learn to read, under seriously overcrowded conditions would seem to cloud the question of the public interest in any effort to make a clear division of public and private schools.

Uptown in the black ghetto with its black public schools similar questions, too, are being raised regarding what the public school is. The ghetto residents demand direct and complete control of their community schools, an end to the management of their schools by a centralized administration and by a city school board which, they maintain, cannot possibly understand what is needed in the black schools. In New York City these demands have been endorsed of course by the so-called Bundy Report, the prestigious Report of the Mayor's Advisory Panel on Decentralization of the New York City Schools.[2]

To dismantle the structure of the city's public schools with all the ramifications to the professionals in regard to hiring practices, "white" certification requirements, contracts with the teacher organization, and the like, as well as the implication of fundamental curriculum revisions, may well mean the opening wedge for the public schools of the city to become "public" in ways quite different from what public schools have been in the past. Local community control in the interests of the health of the black community would seem to be a long way from the "national interest" days of the 'fifties.

Even in white suburbia a new wave of criticism of the public schools is rising. A Bruner-Gardner sort of school system may be beautifully attuned to the suburban majorities, the upwardly-striving, college-oriented, middle class. The excessive burden of school taxes, given the antiquated tax structure in most areas, brings forth a predictable economy-based criticism of the local schools. Yet of more fundamental importance is the rise of critics who denounce the public school mediocrity, who find the pursuit of excellence never quite rigorous enough, and who advocate, with William Buckley, that we "take education away from the bureaucrats and the egalitarians and the politicians and return it to the teachers and to the parents."[3] Or on the other hand, there are those who concur with Edgar Friedenberg or Paul Goodman that the suburban child must be freed from the repressive regimentation of the "uni-

[2] *Reconnection for Learning: A Community School System for New York City.* Report of the Mayor's Advisory Panel on Decentralization of the New York City Schools. New York: the Advisory Panel, 1967.

[3] William F. Buckley, Jr. "The End of the Public Schools." In a syndicated column, "On the Right." *The Home News.* New Brunswick, New Jersey, January 13, 1968.

versal trap," who would reorient the public school toward the style and spirit of a Summerhill. These critics from both the left and the right agree on one point, the traditional idea of the public school, the *via media,* will not do today.

The hue and cry over educational establishments in recent years is directly related, it seems, to this reinterpretation of the idea of public education. The 'sixties have seen the struggle in almost every state's department of education as well as in Washington, in which the old "educationist" establishment has been ousted only to be replaced by the new "reform" establishment.[4] The similarities, in the contest for power, for control over the public schools, between the old and new establishments seem much stronger than any dissimilarities.[5] The effect of these struggles is the demand for an end of this public school bureaucratizing entirely, and the rise of what might be called an educational disestablishmentarianism.[6]

New Formulation of Issues

Given this setting, it seems clear that a new formulation of the issues in American education is needed which abandons the confusions of the traditional, narrow interpretations of public versus private education. Discussion needs directing to the questions of what is the public interest in the pluralistic American society of the 'sixties. In a sense, of course, any educational enterprise is public in that it serves some aspect of the public. How today can the public school (as traditionally defined) become more private (as traditionally defined)? That is, how can the public school serve more adequately the interests of all the varieties of individuals and groups who *are* America, and thereby truly come to serve the public interest?

New discussion of the support and control of education leads to the tangle of problems of feasible ways and means for providing this broadened, reinterpreted public education. Can America move toward a kind of open market of publicly-supported and privately-supported schools as

[4] For a current discussion of establishments see: James E. McClellan. *Toward an Effective Critque of American Education.* Philadelphia: J. B. Lippincott Company, 1968. For the question in historical context see: John Hardin Best and Robert T. Sidwell. *The American Legacy of Learning.* Philadelphia: J. B. Lippincott Company, 1967. p. 454 ff.

[5] Daniel P. Moynihan finds a third educational establishment which he labels the "Research Establishment." In: "Sources of Resistance to the Coleman Report." *Harvard Educational Reveiw* 38(1): 23–36; Winter 1968.

[6] The use of this term, of course, suggests historically the movement in Parliament in the mid-nineteenth century to bring about the "disestablishment" of the Anglican Church in Ireland. Eventually it was Gladstone, the staunchest Anglican of them all, who alone could bring about the necessary legislation to alter the status of the Irish Church.

the extremes, with every conceivable arrangement of support and control in between? For example, should stipends be paid to parents for each child, or to small groups of parents to organize a school as in the Netherlands? Arrangements such as these need to be examined.

A demand for the reinterpretation of public and private education is evident. It is time for American education to clear away the old ideas and the clouds of rhetoric surrounding them.

DONALD A. ERICKSON | ***Public Funds for Private Schools***

The decision of the U.S. Supreme Court permitting New York State to provide textbooks in parochial schools and recent related events in Pennsylvania, Michigan, Rhode Island, Ohio, and Louisiana, suggest strongly that tax funds may soon flow freely to the nation's non-public schools. The major education journals and associations will no doubt declare such a turn of events disastrous, and, in some forms, public money for private education could hurt public education, destroy diversity in non-public education, and magnify current inequities. In other forms, however, the aid could serve the disadvantaged, help reduce racial segregation, and encourage experimentation. In short, the new money might be a way of solving some of the most severe problems created by big-city school systems.

I favor public support to non-public schools because I see little hope that public education as it is now structured in the major cities can bring about the necessary fundamental reforms. There is no systematic, conclusive evidence to support this disillusionment; it is based on my own observations and interpretations. Partly because public school superintendents have resisted National Assessment and other data-gathering efforts in any form that would permit firm comparisons among schools, unequivocal findings on the state of instruction in the core cities of the United States are nonexistent. The available studies are largely impressionistic, importantly influenced by the viewpoints of the researchers. Representative national samples of inner-city schools have never been examined.

My colleague Robert Havighurst insists that big-city schools are rather good, that current criticisms are overdone. But a growing number of careful observers are pessimistic. I have reluctantly concluded that the rigidities of public education in the face of the urban crisis are not a passing phase but advanced arteriosclerosis, a tendency of large, publicly protected institutions to become, as Nathan Glazer puts it, "tired, bureaucratic, and corrupt. . . . At that point, they must be supplemented or supplanted by new institutions, which will hopefully respond more sensitively to the needs of their clients."

While all children are handicapped by these systems and their deification of educational custom, the results are most serious for the poor. The schools were adapted in the first place, albeit imperfectly, to the politically potent middle class. Intent on getting his youngster into a high-status college and vocation, the middle-class parent may encourage a stultifying orthodoxy—an unduc concern for state regulations, accrediting criteria, college entrance requirements, and whatever pedagogical fads are popular at the moment—half of them a waste of energy.

Public education has never been given adequate resources, particularly for helping the disadvantaged, and in the light of public disenchantment it seems unlikely that the institution will receive the massive infusion of funds that effective programs require. To pour new moneys into the existing machinery would produce only negligible improvements. If anything, revolutionary adjustments now seem less likely than before. Federal programs increasingly are channeled through state departments of education, which, with few exceptions, are impossibly hidebound. Most "remedial" programs to date have been spasmodic and piecemeal, spread too thin to upset the status quo or produce much instructional impact. We are saddled with practices that have never worked with oppressed minorities and have no shred of research support behind them; yet they are bolstered by ideology and often enforced by law. Their major function, I fear, is to protect the old breed of educator in the schools and teacher-training institutions.

Like any other professor in my area, I encounter inspiring classrooms and schools. But they are the exception in the inner city. Too uniformly, teachers full of energy and zeal are beaten down by administrative hacks, idealistic principals are stopped in their tracks by crotchety Old Guard faculties, and firebrand superintendents are helpless to redirect the creaking bureaucracies, the faceless incubuses, that weigh down the whole affair. Something drastic ails the system. It needs drastic renovation and the shock treatment of being forced to compete for clients and support. And while it is being rejuvenated, if indeed it can be, we must solve our major problems through whatever instrumentalities are available, public or private.

Non-public schools, too, are often stodgy and establishmentarian. For this reason, I would be reluctant to see public aid doled out indiscriminately. We must carefully arrange the financial carrots to reward the people who are creative. Who cares if they are the duly certified functionaries we have relied on in the past? A broad variety of private educational enterprises should be encouraged to compete for pupils and public funds. Industrial firms should be free to try radical new work-study programs for dropouts, actual and potential. Independent boarding schools may be interested in placing ghetto children with high college potential in their dormitories. Neighborhood organizations may create experimental community schools operated under neighborhood boards. The argument that such people are not qualified to run educational programs should not preclude giving the idea a chance. One of the most exciting schools I know of today is run at Rough Rock, Arizona, by a board of Navahos with a cumulative formal education of three years.

There is no good reason, furthermore, why parents should be required to secure their children's total education from a single source. If one agency offers the best reading program, another the best mathematics program, and another (perhaps not even called a "school") the best exposure to the fine arts, why should the parent not be free to obtain one component here, another there, and a third somewhere else? In the light of the advanced state of technology, the lack of educational flexibility is astonishing. To a lamentable extent it is *illegal* to school children for adulthood in any but the most staid and conventional ways. A parent who has given his child a *superb* preparation for his future can still be fined for failing to do so in the usual manner, as in the incredible case of an Amishman, LeRoy Garber of Partridge, Kansas, who was recently denied a hearing before the U.S. Supreme Court.

But I began by stating that the question of tax support for non-public schools was far from one-sided. I must balance my argument, then, by suggesting a commonly advocated form of assistance that could indeed be unfortunate. Assume that tuition vouchers in identical amounts are made available to all parents of school-age children. For each child in the elementary grades, the parent receives a voucher worth $500 a year, redeemable through any state-approved school, public or non-public. The parent may add funds of his own to this tax-provided sum.

As proponents of the plan insist, it would broaden parental choice. Parents who preferred the public school could stay there. Parents who preferred nonpublic schools, possibly for religious or ethnic reasons, would find it financially more feasible to patronize them. But what if, as a result of this policy, most Lutherans ended up in Lutheran schools, most Catholics in Catholic schools, most Seventh Day Adventists in Seventh Day Adventist schools, and many more Negroes in Black Muslim schools? Would national unity be threatened, as James Bryant Conant once insisted?

The example most cited in this connection is the Netherlands. After years of debate and conflict, that nation extended equal support to public and non-public education in 1920. During the last half of the nineteenth century, between 20 and 30 per cent of primary students were in non-public schools. At least partly as a result of the financial aid, it appears, the figure rose to 44 per cent by 1921, and to 72 per cent by 1958.

To a notable extent social life in the Netherlands is now organized, not so much in terms of socio-economic levels or ethnic groups, but in terms of Roman Catholic, Protestant, and "neutral" segments or "pillars," each with its separate institutions. According to numerous reports, there is a widespread reluctance to patronize schools, libraries, radio stations, newspapers, political parties, sports clubs, travel associations, labor unions, teachers associations, hospitals, or physicians outside one's own "pillar." Discussion of controversial topics is inhibited in the schools and elsewhere. Religious affiliation determines eligibility for political appointments, reclaimed land in various areas, and employment in many organizations. Similar characteristics have been evident in Quebec, where non-public schools are supported in much the same way.

Even if disunity in the Netherlands and Quebec is not as serious as some writers suggest, the tendencies seem unfortunate. It is questionable, however, to attribute them to a method of educational finance. Equal support of secular and religious schools is probably more a result than a cause of the social schisms, for ecumenism and rapprochement are now occurring in spite of the educational arrangements. No serious polarization has been associated with public aid to non-public schools in other Canadian provinces, or in England, France, Denmark, Finland, or Germany, according to several observers. American cities with high non-public school enrollments do not seem unusually fragmented. Religious antagonisms in the United States are more logically explained by historical events, such as the juxtaposition of a Brahmin class of Protestants and an outcast group of Catholics. Though a far higher proportion of Catholic youngsters are in parochial schools in Chicago than in Boston, Catholic-Protestant relationships seem more cordial in Chicago.

Many writers claim, nevertheless, that non-public schools produce a "ghetto mentality"—a disposition to withdraw from the larger society and to associate mainly with one's religious or ethnic group. In their recent national study, *The Education of Catholic Americans,* Andrew M. Greeley and Peter H. Rossi found that church-school attendance had no notable impact on involvement in the "secular" community, choice of neighbors, co-workers, or visitors, or feelings concerning the importance of having friends from the same religious group. Similarly, a study of Lutheran education by Ronald O. Johnstone produced no indications of divisiveness. These results are not startling. Our society is characterized by forces for conformity too powerful for the social good, in the view of many commentators. The major religious communities themselves may have undergone so much assimilation that they represent only embellishments on a common theme.

The evidence does not indicate what results would be produced if denominational schools were more dominant—if 92 per cent rather than 46 per cent of Catholic children were in Catholic schools, for example. But some studies suggest that the emotionally supportive milieu of a school operated by one's religious or ethnic group promotes a stronger, more positive sense of identity and thus renders the individual more capable of participation in the larger society in later years. Despite extensive folklore to the contrary, if more Catholics were educated in Catholic schools, more Lutherans in Lutheran schools, more Jews in Jewish schools, more Amish in Amish schools, and more Negroes in Black Power schools, there might be more national unity rather than less.

The voucher plan, however, has one major shortcoming. It would magnify educational inequalities and accentuate the trend toward separate schools for the rich and the poor. Since the advantage of a superior education is now so obvious, citizens able to add money of their own to the tax-provided vouchers would almost universally seek better instruction by leaving schools attended by the poor. This tendency would probably continue even if schools for the impoverished were supported, through the vouchers, at the maximum level one can imagine to be politically feasible. No doubt the plan would serve in the long run to raise levels of support for all schools, but the *disparities* could be disastrous. Institutions supported through vouchers plus personal funds could always outbid institutions supported through vouchers alone for the supply of competent personnel, to say nothing of differences in facilities and instructional materials. Even if schools for the disadvantaged turned out, through some near-miracle, to be excellent in many respects, the "dumping ground" image could be devastating to the pupil's self-esteem.

If tax credits or deductions were allowed for tuitions in non-public schools, the consequences might be even worse, for the families with the lowest incomes would receive no help at all, while the well-to-do would have more to spend than at present on non-public education. In fact, since non-public education is to such an extent a middle- and upper-class phenomenon, to give it virtually any commonly advocated mode of assistance is to extend benefits primarily to moderate- and high-income families. Current mechanisms of educational finance may respond sluggishly to the impulse for improvement, but at least they help to harness the aspirations and finances of the wealthy to the needs of the poor.

It is precisely on this point that most proponents of aid to non-public schools have been unrealistic. They ignore the disruptions ill-designed assistance would incur. A serious economic bias is exhibited in the private educational sector. In their comprehensive study on this topic, Greeley and Rossi found Catholic school attendance considerably more frequent among wealthier than among poorer Catholics. Similarly, in his recent Chicago study, the Rev. James W. Sanders has documented a direct relationship between the socio-economic condition of Catholics and the attendance of their children in parochial schools. Equally representative research is not available for other non-public schools, but the findings all lead to the same conclusion.

As if racial balance were not difficult enough to achieve, some non-public schools siphon off many white students, leaving public schools with an artificially high proportion of Negroes and Puerto Ricans. The situation in Manhattan is reaching alarming proportions. In Washington, D.C., public education has been deserted by almost everyone with an option. The former president of Washington's school board wonders, consequently, "whether we will have a system composed entirely of poor children."

The inadequacies of public education are a factor in the preference of many parents for non-public schools. There is little point, furthermore, in castigating non-public schoolmen for a selectivity that is fiscally inevitable. But censure is justified when they advocate forms of support that might aggravate the problem. It is not enough to improve the education of all children. We must achieve a vastly greater equality. The hostilities that now threaten us are not alleviated by the fact that the poor in the United States are better off than the poor elsewhere. It is the inequities between rich and poor that may tear the nation apart.

Among the methods that seem promising for granting help to non-public schools, the following is a hypothetical instance: Trinity Lutheran, a middle-class elementary school in Megatown, receives more applications than it can accept. But recently it has lost many clients to the suburbs. Forty of its 300 desks stand vacant, and the enrollment seems destined to drop even further. As a result, per-pupil costs are higher for all patrons, and expensive capabilities go unused while Negro children in a nearby ghetto attend crowded, segregated public schools.

This crisis presents an opportunity, Trinity's board decides, to broaden its pupils' horizons, experiment with new approaches, and demonstrate religious concern. A committee is appointed, including representatives from the Negro community, to design special services for the disadvantaged. Forty "low-achieving" Negro pupils are recruited, and state scholarships are sought to finance their programs at the level of per-pupil expenditure maintained in the public schools.

Under the law authorizing the scholarships, Trinity's program must be approved by an interdisciplinary panel. The state department of education commissions a psychologist, a sociologist, an anthropologist, and an educator who has done experimental work with slow learners to visit the school, not to check for orthodoxy in the manner unfortunately typical of state departments, but to determine whether the plans are promising and whether proper provisions have been made to assess the outcomes. The panel is impressed. It recommends forty state scholarships annually for a three-year period.

In areas where serious fragmentation of effort is threatened, the state approves only a few of the more promising programs. Except when there are compelling reasons to the contrary, no participating school is permitted to "skim off" the more capable Negro students. Each institution must arrange for an evaluation of its work under the scholarships, and the state publicizes the results of the experiments. The new pupils are exempt from all religious activities, except when parents request inclusion. Each child attends at the pleasure of his parents, who may return him to the public school at any time. In annual fiscal reports, the schools must show that state funds have been used for strictly secular purposes and primarily for the benefit of the publicly supported scholars.

Toward the end of the three-year period, Trinity may apply for a five-year extension of its scholarship authorization. Another panel will then study the evaluation report, inspect the instructional activities, and make a recommendation.

By thus extending Trinity's resources to ghetto children, the state is not merely helping non-public schools; it is exploiting private capabilities for the public benefit. In one sense, every roomful of middle-class children near a ghetto represents an opportunity to assist the disadvantaged. There are strong indications in recent research, such as the Coleman report, that ineffective learners benefit by associating with more successful peers, while the latter do not suffer as a result. Isolated from these influences, impoverished youngsters reinforce each other's despair, alienation, and inadequate study habits. There is a shortage of schools to provide this assistance to the poor.

In addition, the scholarship plan puts to use certain unique strengths of nonpublic schools. Lutheran schools have a high proportion of male teachers (usually around 50 per cent of the faculty) with whom boys who have no father in the home may identify. Other non-public schools enjoy special access to oppressed minorities. In some Puerto Rican communities, for instance, distrust of public agencies is so pronounced that the public schools are disabled, yet Catholic institutions are familiar, trusted components in the culture. Many independent boarding schools can offer twenty-four-hour programs on campuses far removed from the ghetto's despair.

When well-to-do patrons move away, impoverished families can fill empty desks in non-public schools, but cannot provide the needed money. After a long period of expansion, enrollments in the nation's non-public schools have declined of late, mostly in response to fiscal pressures. By helping keep Trinity open, the state avoids the expense of providing classroom spaces at about $2,000 each and a major part of an annual operating cost approaching $600 each for 360 pupils. The scholarships dramatically broaden parental choice, for few ghetto families have had any previous option among schools. Socio-economic and racial segregation are reduced at Trinity as a result. Equality of opportunity is advanced.

The public school is kept from becoming a "dumping ground" where all the penniless and hard-to-educate are found. At the same time, it is given some badly needed competition. If other agencies educate the deprived effectively, enormous pressures for improvement will be felt in the public schools. Since nearby public schools are crowded, no defensible economies of scale are sacrificed there, and some are gained in the Lutheran school. The city's instructional resources, public and private, are used more efficiently. Parents are protected against questionable schools by the approval mechanism, yet diversity is not stultified by the "minimum standards" the state department of education might otherwise enforce.

In conclusion, we must abandon simplistic arguments on both sides of the issue of aid to non-public schools and design forms of assistance that will accentuate the advantages and minimize the dangers. I have attempted to demonstrate that the *form* in which financial relief is extended may largely determine the consequences, but it would hardly be possible in these few pages to weigh all options and develop a legislative package that is socially defensible and politically feasible. Different approaches may be dictated in different states, though in all cases, I believe, logic will require a privileged status for underprivileged children. I hold no particular brief for the Trinity Lutheran scholarship plan, except as an example of rationally conceived support for non-public schools.

Other mechanisms are at least equally attractive. State departments of education could be given authority to contract directly with non-public schools for services well designed for the deprived. The state could provide low-interest loans to finance private facilities to serve the poor or could lease plant and equipment for this purpose at nominal rates. Educational parks could be designed to make public services and facilities available to children in non-public schools at parental discretion and to promote meaningful contacts between socio-economic, racial, religious, and achievement-level groups. Non-public schools could be granted much more freedom to share not only public instruction, but public facilities.

Government could provide tuition vouchers sharply graduated to give a purchasing edge to the poor. Vouchers for the impoverished could be large enough to finance a first-class education in either the public or non-public sectors, and families able to purchase such an education on their own could receive only token assistance. Special incentive grants could be offered to all schools, non-public or public, that maintained student bodies that were racially, academically, and perhaps socio-economically integrated.

In general, I think public aid to non-public schools should be designed primarily to conserve and utilize the existing capabilities of non-public schools for serving the disadvantaged; to reduce racial, socio-economic, and academic selectivity in non-public schools, partly as a means of avoiding educational "dumping grounds" for the poor; and to encourage educational competition, broadening parental choice and promoting diversity, experimentation, and broad-ranging research. On the negative side, the assistance must not serve to encourage shoddy schools, indefensible fragmentation of effort, or imposition of traditional state regulations.

There is no shortage of ideas to be explored, nor of evidence concerning the problems that may arise if we either blindly oppose all aid to non-public schools or promiscuously extend whatever assistance seems at the moment to be popular. As educators, lawmakers, and citizens, we have some neglected thinking to do.

OSCAR HANDLIN | ***Federal Funds for Parochial Schools***

As this essay is being written, it seems probable that Congress will sustain the President and will refuse to accede to the demand that any share of federal aid to education go to parochial schools. The issue will not then be settled, however. It is likely to be postponed and to rise again and again in the next few years.

The unequivocal ultimatum by the Catholic bishops that they would oppose any bill that did not provide some assistance to parochial schools caused widespread uneasiness among many Americans. This ultimatum raised troubling questions about the obligations of the individual to the community, about the pressures of organized political power, and about the constitutional relations of church and state in the United States. Above all, however, the whole issue of federal aid compels us to re-examine the place allotted to voluntary activities in a free society. That is the core of the matter.

A good deal of confusion has been generated by the argument that the failure to give public funds to Catholic schools unjustly subjects Catholics to a form of double taxation. These parents, it is claimed, pay levies to the government to support institutions they do not use and also pay tuition to those their children actually attend. Father John Courtney Murray has given eloquent expression to this conception: "The canons of distributive justice ought to control the action of government in allocating funds that it coercively collects from all people. . . . The solution . . . reached in the nineteenth century reveals injustice and the legal statutes that establish the injustice are an abuse of power."

It is worth noting that this was not the point of view of Catholics in nineteenth-century America, when the claimants upon the governmental purse were Protestant; nor is it a position that is widely recognized in countries where Catholics are a majority or hold political control. It seems rather to be the product of the particular pressures of the present situation.

But were Father Murray's argument valid, it might well override all other considerations. Yet nothing in the American experience sustains the accusation of injustice. The community has always assumed the responsibility for performing certain functions of general utility, which it supports with income raised by taxation. In this manner, schools, hospitals, and libraries are maintained because they serve the welfare of the whole community, not because they serve those who pay the costs. There are individuals and groups who prefer to use private libraries or to buy their own books, or who elect to enter private hospitals, or who wish to send their children to private schools or colleges. In so doing, they satisfy their own desires or the dictates of their own consciences—and at their own expense. Yet that does not acquit them of their obligation to the community. Nor can they call, in the name of justice, for a share of the financial resources that the government acquires to perform its own functions in the same spheres.

The freedom of the individual to choose the school or hospital of his own preference is conditioned upon the acceptance of his obligations to the whole community. Without this balance our society would confront equally undesirable alternatives. Either each man would be left to find what services he himself could afford, with the poor dependent upon some form of charity; or the state would assume or delegate complete control of any or all services.

The development of the school system, as of similar institutions, has enabled Americans to escape the necessity of accepting either alternative. Loose pluralistic forms have permitted the spread both of public, governmentally-operated services and, in the same areas, of private, voluntary ones. This balance has been an important element in the maintenance of American liberty.

It does not follow, however, that the public school system of the past hundred and twenty-five years is sacrosanct. This system has not always been a part of our life, but arose in response to historic needs; conceivably, if it outgrew those needs, the people could alter or abolish it. But any change that is made ought to be determined not by the interests of a single group, but on the basis of larger criteria—political expediency, constitutionality, and the effects of the change upon freedom.

In my opinion, federal aid to parochial schools would be most inexpedient politically. Historians of the future will, I suspect, divide the last fifty years into two periods. From 1910 to 1940 there was a steady, tragic rise in intergroup hostility, in religious prejudice, and in overt conflict. It was unthinkable in 1928 that a Catholic should be chosen President; and it remained unthinkable during the next three elections. During the two decades since 1940, the war and the threat of totalitarianism have rapidly eased these tensions; and the election of 1960 revealed that a majority of non-Catholic Americans no longer feared Catholicism as a monolithic force alien to the nation's traditional values. It would be heart-breaking if those gains were in the least to be diminished.

Twice President Kennedy has asked why the question of aiding parochial schools should have been raised this year; it was not raised on previous occasions when Congress considered federal aid to education. The President's query echoes in the minds of many Americans. Were Catholics now to constitute a political bloc which made aid to parochial schools a condition for any federal legislation in the area of education, intergroup relations would certainly suffer.

Considerations of constitutionality are serious, but less decisive. For a century and a half the direction of American constitutional law has been to exclude the government ever more sharply from areas in which faith was involved. That trend could of course be reversed, but such a reversal ought not to be effected without a clear recognition of the consequences.

The framers of the Virginia statute on religious liberty and of the First Amendment to the federal Constitution were groping toward a novel conception of man's relation to God—as an altogether voluntary matter with which the polity ought not to interfere. But since they could not anticipate all the implications of this idea, there was no clean sweep of inherited practices. Well into the nineteenth century vestiges of establishment persisted, sometimes in a modified form, and a few persist even to this day—for example, the chaplains in the armed services and in Congress, the support of Christian missions on Indian reservations, and state bluelaws.

Nevertheless, the main line of development in American constitutional law has moved toward an ever fuller implementation of the conception of religion as properly free of governmental coercion or support. The courts have held that the First Amendment intended to do more than create conditions of equality among the diverse religious groups of the country: it also intended to separate clearly the affairs of the national government from those of the church. With the extension by the Fourteenth Amendment of that wall of separation to the individual states, any doubts about the exclusion of government from the realm of religion were removed. (If the Sunday laws are still sustained, it is under the subterfuge that the state's police powers permit it to enjoin a day of rest upon all its citizens.)

The consequences of total separation were fortunate. Americans were no less devout than other Western peoples, perhaps more so. But their piety was removed from open or concealed compulsion. James Bryce, noting that half the troubles which vexed the Europe of his day arose "from the rival claims of Church and State," concluded: "This whole vast chapter of debate and strife has remained unopened in the United States. . . . All religious bodies are absolutely equal before the law, and unrecognized by the law, except as voluntary associations of private citizens."

But the Constitution is a living document, subject to amendment, reinterpretation, and evasion. Innovations may be introduced by acts of Congress or by the state legislatures in forms which are not testable by the courts, and even if such innovations were to be tested the judges might still push the laws in a new direction. Above all, there remains open the possibility of forthright amendment, should enough citizens desire it. If the American people decide that the ideas of James Madison ought no longer to bind them, there are ample means of escape or accommodation. A candid and public discussion of the alternatives, however, would be preferable to the pretense that no alternatives exist.

The crucial question, therefore, is whether the principle of strict separation—which sprang from a concern with liberating the conscience of man from the rule of force—has outlived its utility.

During the first century and a half of American experience, tightly organized homogeneous communities recognized no distinctions between the sword and the altar. The New England meeting house served both for worship and for government. The Virginia vestry and parish were at once political and religious entities. Everywhere but in Rhode Island and Pennsylvania, the churches were established, supported by taxes, and sustained by legal sanctions. Given such integrated communal organization, there could be no distinction between public and private in the sense we now know it. Colleges and philanthropic institutions, as well as churches, depended upon government aid and accepted government control.

To endow religious bodies with absolute autonomy under these circumstances was a monumental achievement, matched in few other societies. It was made possible by the slow discovery that governmental means were not the only ones available for social action. By the 1780's Americans had learned to work together in voluntary associations which depended not upon coercion but upon the loyalty and willingness of their members to make personal sacrifices in order to attain common goals. That experience was more weighty in establishing religious liberty than formal constitutional guarantees. The churches discovered empirically that the voluntary adhesion of their members was a greater source of strength than the props available from the state. Since the eighteenth century, Americans have preponderantly believed that the instruments of coercion with which government was armed were inappropriate in matters of the spirit; and as a religious people, they were persuaded that religion could best thrive free of such interference.

In the nineteenth century, by a tortuous course (the details of which are not yet clear), a line was drawn between public and private institutions, religious and others. At the opening of the century, churches—like colleges, academies, hospitals, and libraries—though controlled by their own governing boards, still had ties to the state from which they accepted privileges. Gradually the ties loosened and the privileges disappeared. For the price of autonomy was to surrender the claim for aid and the resolve to rely completely upon independent resources. The only surviving privilege is the essentially negative one of tax exemption, which can be bestowed without selection or preference.

Now and again, some private organizations have been tempted by easy access to the public treasury. More generally, they have preferred to allow the government to expend its funds through its own agencies, even when these agencies offered competition to the private ones. Yet the growth of state universities, public schools, and municipal hospitals did not damage private institutions. Indeed, one of the great strengths of the American republic has been the latitude of choice it offered individuals: not everything that had to be done, had to be done through the state. The capacity to choose has been an important element in keeping state power within manageable limits and in allowing diverse groups to seek their own ends in their own ways.

In a period when the growing power of government tends to subdue differences and to subject the individual to total dependence upon the state, it is more important than ever to preserve freedom of action. And nowhere is this principle more important than in education. The issue was fought out over a century ago in New York City when Archbishop Hughes objected to the markedly Protestant character of the society which operated the public schools. The only feasible arrangement was to divorce public education from religious control entirely and to expend all state funds through state institutions, while each sect remained free to conduct its own system at its own expense.

Almost forty years ago that arrangement was implicitly confirmed by the Supreme Court in the case of *Pierce* v. *the Society of Sisters,* which held that the state did not possess a monopoly over the process of education and that particular groups could organize toward their own ends as they wished.

This decision (and similar ones) rested upon two crucial premises. First, the right to conduct schools was not considered to inhere in the particular merit of a private organization such as the Society of Sisters; the Court did not pass upon that question. The right emanated from the parents and the pupils, who were held free to choose whatever form of training they considered appropriate, subject only to certain general regulations of health and safety. What these parents could do was precedent for any other group; the status of all private schools, under whatever auspices, thus became identical.

Furthermore, the unexpressed but assumed premise of the decision was that the private school had no financial ties to the state. The rights of the Society of Sisters were a condition of the organization's willingness to assume the burden of maintaining its own institution.

Any grant of public aid, in any form whatever, diminishes the private voluntary character of the recipient. It is a well-founded principle, and one that has great merit, that the bestowal of a public privilege brings with it public responsibilities, which can only be defined by governmental authority. This has been held true of museums, housing projects, and trade unions; it would certainly be held true of schools or even churches. It is of the essence of the relationship thus created that the grant establishes the subordination of the receiver to the donor.

Senator Joseph Clark of Pennsylvania, for example, has defended aid to the parochial schools on the grounds that the government is responsible for assuring adequate schooling for all children. But if this is so, who is to set the standards of adequacy? There can only be one answer—the government. The states themselves have already gone far, too far, in establishing requisites of instruction; and the resultant damage has only been mitigated by inefficiencies in enforcement. It would be hazardous indeed to establish a basis upon which our government could begin to define, as totalitarian regimes do, what is true, good, and useful.

This danger is remote, but it is nonetheless genuine. If the federal treasury is opened to religious schools, it must be opened to private secular schools as well. Even if the resources of the government were limitless, some standard of selection would have to be employed and, since that could not rest upon the status of the potential recipients, it could only involve a judgment of what constituted adequate schooling.

We are all too ready to close our eyes to the potential danger here because the very voluntarism which government aid threatens has thus far shielded us from it. We can now operate under the convenient fiction that every bachelor's degree and every diploma is equal in value, although in actuality there are vast disparities among the thousands of diverse schools and colleges in the country. We could not sustain that useful tolerance once the question of government aid were injected. Decisions would then be necessary as to whether to spread available funds thin among all applicants, to limit them to the best, or to set minimum standards of adequacy. Any choice would call for political judgments about the goals and methods of education and would put pressure on all institutions to conform. It would make necessary unwelcome comparisons among various types of schools and teachers—unwelcome because they would depend upon the application of uniform criteria which are not universally accepted. Finally, public aid would demand the acceptance of governmentally-defined codes of internal organization and behavior. Just as such aid deprives the trade union and the housing project of the freedom to discriminate among applicants and employees, so it would limit the right of the school to set its own admissions policy and to hire its own teachers.

The alternative is far more safe and fully as feasible—to continue to depend upon the loyalty and devotion of those who have thus far been willing to sustain the private and parochial schools of the country voluntarily. The amount the Catholic bishops have requested to meet their capital needs is not out of line with that recently raised by the Ivy League colleges, and the number of potential contributors is far larger. A historian who has studied the nineteenth-century immigration to the United States is again and again impressed by the ability of humble men of low earning power to dedicate themselves to building institutions in which they really believed. The Irish and Italian and Polish laborers, who gave gladly of the little they had, contributed to an impressive achievement, and in doing so, also expressed their identification with the Church in a totally meaningful way. Is it too much to expect that their affluent grandchildren could do the same and achieve spiritual gains in the process?

Above all, religion in the United States has remained most faithful to its own nature and purpose when it refused to employ the instruments of the government. It has best been able to dedicate itself to the salvation of the individual when it has abjured that power which is the essence of the state. Armies, police, and tax collectors diminish rather than extend the authority of religion, for religion grows only by conversion, by the inner dedication of men to it. Thus religion would be making a poor bargain indeed to pay for some new buildings with the loss of some of its precious old freedom.

WILFRID SHEED | *Don't Junk the Parochial Schools*

The Catholic parochial-school system recently has been under considerable fire—light fire from without and heavy fire from within. (Just as it takes a believer to be a thoroughgoing anticlerical, so it takes a Catholic really to blast the parochial schools.) These schools, it is said, did a good job in the 19th century—and are still doing it: a good, 19th-century job. They are still teaching immigrants how to keep out of mischief and how to be good Americans of the simpler variety; they are frozen, like the Statue of Liberty, in an uncomplicated gesture of welcome.

It is an irony of the situation that, now that the parochial system is at last receiving the kind of abrasive criticism that every institution needs but which for obvious reasons few ecclesiastical institutions get, the critics are calling not for reform but for abolition. They feel that the schools are not only past praying for but not worth praying for. Even a *good* parochial system would not satisfy critics of the New Wave.

Now of course nobody is in favor of bad parochial schools; but good ones might be something else. Surely there is not so much good education going around that we can afford to choke off any source of supply. I should like to suggest, first of all, that anyone who is capable of providing good education should be encouraged, be he Catholic, Protestant, Jewish, or nothing at all. Further, I see no intrinsic reason for parochial schools not to be good. Some of them are good already, and most faults ascribed to the others belong to a certain time and place and can be scraped off like so much rust.

If we abolish the parochial schools, we will have abolished an educational alternative that some of us value. If a parochial school is inferior, we are free not to use it; but if it doesn't even exist, the choice for most of us is down to one. And there is no reason to assume that the choice that is left, the public schools, would improve automatically with the abolition of parochial schools. Public education would certainly become more expensive, more crowded and understaffed; the taxpayers would presumably have to pay some of the money that is exhorted out of Catholics every Sunday, simply to stay in the same place, simply to keep public schools from deteriorating. Where the improvement would come from is harder to say.

But the question of educational choice goes deeper than that. It is not merely a question of comparison shopping but of doing one small thing to counter the natural drift of mass societies toward an oppressive, cultural monotony. If pluralism really is a value—rather than a necessity that we have made into a value—the assimilations of the melting pot must be resisted at some point. Cultural variety belongs in the home, no doubt, but the home nowadays is only a dumping ground for three major television networks, and the neighborhood is only the home repeated to infinity.

The parochial school is one of the few surviving objects of cultural diversity. To my mind, it already mimes the public school much too closely; but it is different enough to preserve a certain openness in an increasingly stuffy society. Modern American life maintains a consensus not only of opinion but of intellectual style probably more overpowering than that of any other civilized country. The consensus is so all-encompassing that many of us are not even aware of its existence. As far as we are concerned, it is simply the only way to think.

I am not suggesting that the public schools are entirely responsible for this state of affairs, nor that the parochial schools have done anything much to improve it. I am saying that a person with a nonpublic-school education has at least a choice in intellectual styles: He knows that a choice exists. With everyone going to what amounts virtually to the same school, this choice would be reduced by that much. This is another reason for supporting schools run by every sort of group. Let the children be melted as much as they like at university and in outside life, but give them first something to melt. At present too many of us are simply empty mirrors of one another.

The question may be asked at this point whether religious groups are the ideal units for carrying out this necessarily divisive mission. Even now, in the flood tide of ecumenicism, there remains a nervous feeling in the backs of many minds that religions are divisive enough, without adding to their opportunities.

It is true that Christianity has a formidable record for factiousness, as has every idea of any importance. But closing the schools, on the grounds that organized Christians can never be persuaded to act like Christians, seems to me an act of despair. If Pope John XXIII's ecumenical spirit fails in the parochial schools, it will be because it has failed in the church at large, and I am not yet resigned to expecting that. If it succeeds in the church at large, it seems unduly pessimistic to insist that the schools will be unaffected by it. An ecumenically minded church would surely express itself in schools different from those of an embattled church.

Like generals who are forever fighting the last war, I think the critics may be looking backward and may have underrated the changes that have already taken place—and are in germ of taking place—in the parochial schools. There are, of course, many stubborn pockets of resistance. Yet the St. Louis schools, for instance, under Cardinal Ritter, are reputed to have made tremendous advances which may serve as models to others. The nuns who have been through the Sister Formation movement are light-years away from the old schoolmarm nun teaching arithmetic on the rosary. This progress does not call for yet another celebration, but to deny it altogether would be equally misleading.

There is a physical limit to this improvement. Bulging classrooms and press-ganged teachers are of no use in any kind of school. It may be fair to say that the system had in the past overextended itself, and that it should confine itself henceforth to what it can do best. There are already moves afoot to eliminate some of the lower grades. Another useful step would be, wherever possible, to increase the number of lay teachers, so as to release priests and nuns from the exigencies of algebra and biology. If the system lacks the flexibility and humility to adapt itself, the abolitionists will have their way after all, for the modern Catholic parent feels less and less obliged to send his child to an inferior Catholic school.

But if the system does evolve as it has shown signs of doing, if it ceases once and for all to see itself as a sort of crowded fallout shelter from popular culture, and if it opens itself without reservation to the spirit of the Ecumenical Council, I think we may find there are still certain advantages in having these schools.

For one thing, the public schools are, as Walter Lippmann and others have pointed out, notoriously uneasy in the teaching of moral motives. No doubt ways can be worked out to teach morals without reference to religion (although even this requires a philosophical consensus, and as soon as you have that, somebody is sure to call it a rival religion, and the judges will have to be called in again). But the public schools seem to walk on eggshells in the whole realm of human behavior. A boy who shuttles between his TV set and his public classroom might come to maturity without ever hearing a definite statement about anything important.

To say that moral training belongs primarily in the home is to take a rather special view of education. (It is ironical in this age of the broken home and the non-home to see so much pressure placed full-weight on that institution.) An education innocent not only of value judgments but even largely of value comments leaves a vacuum that nobody has found a way of filling. Even the mildest moral injunction (such as, "Please don't stab me") depends on some values held in common. But it is not my aim to satirize people who are doing a difficult job as well as they can; I wish only to suggest that if teacher and student can agree on religion as a moral base, it seems reasonable to give them a chance to do so.

There is always the danger, after all, that the concept of God may wither away altogether in this country, not under attack but from sheer disuse. Modern American disbelief has crept like a white fog through our suburban churches. In fact, churchgoing is quite irrelevant to it. Such disbelief is not incompatible with a mild assent to religious truths, or even to a mild religious revival.

This thin atmosphere, drained of all suggestion and mystery, blank as a hospital corridor, is the one thing that people who have been exposed to religion, even in a hostile way, probably fear more than anything else in the world. Better to have your children chanted over by a mad old woman in a witch's gown (religious teaching does not boil down to that, however it may appear to its more hysterical critics) than to have them shaped by people untouched by mystery, by the sacred and by the intense imaginative experience of religion.

While I am not accusing the whole public-school system of this kind of vapid secularism, it must surely take some responsibility for the reflexive and panicky avoidance of controversy, and therefore of inquiry into our religious heritage, that is the first step toward it. It has been said that the parochial schools have been doing a 19th-century job —and in this respect it might also be added that, far from being divisive, they have tended to stress a suffocating Americanism—but perhaps there is something 19th century about the public-school mystique too. In a young nation of raging diversity, there was a lot to be said for getting everyone into the same classroom to be taught the same thing, if only to keep wild sectarians from each other's throats; but now that, as I say, we are all too thoroughly melted, we can surely afford to take a chance on variety, and on religious controversy too. The dangers of life have shifted. Compulsory public schooling for all but the richest smacks of martial law, of some kind of artificial emergency.

For nine out of 10 families today the choice is already as small as it can be—the state school or the truant officer. Those who can afford private schools are above the battle, and yet they pay a price. Their children are usually withdrawn altogether from their own communities and placed in rather limited new ones, where their friends will all be special cases, like themselves. They are likely to be slightly out of context for the rest of their lives.

Since I take education seriously, I would send my children, if they were of school age, to a good private school rather than a mediocre parochial school. Yet I can see that a really good parochial school would have many advantages. The parish is a natural grouping, often highly diversified. The child who attends one for a few years need not be estranged from community life.

Unfortunately, there are comparatively few groups that can afford to run their own schools. This has distorted the issue from a public one to a sectarian one. The parochial schools appear to many as a disturbing advertisement of Catholic power. (Parishioners may make a wry face at this, when they recall how this power has to be squeezed and coaxed out of them every Sunday.) Unchristian boasting about our wonderful school system, as if size and expense were the tests of education, has not helped much. The military pugnacity of the old days dies hard. But a system should not be judged by its worst examples, let alone by caricatures of its worst examples. In many places, parochial schools are demonstrably better than public schools. In such cases, it is not unheard of for non-Catholic parents to use them. (In the same spirit, I would not hesitate to send my own children to a clearly superior Jewish or Quaker school. Education matters.) To abolish good schools because you don't like the system seems, in this season of *aggiornamento,* either vindictive or despairing.

Should these schools receive public aid? To this untrained eye, the constitutional language on this point is loose enough for people to make what they want of it. (Of course, many sincere people find it a clear mandate one way or the other.) I tend to agree with those who feel that good education is a public service, and that any school that provides it up to the required standards should receive some public assistance, as it would in England, Holland and elsewhere. In effect, this would mean that Catholics would get some of their own tax money back, instead of paying extra for the privilege of keeping the public schools less crowded and less expensive to run. Public assistance might also have the further advantage of encouraging other groups to start their own schools. And it would reduce the specter of Catholic power, the upkeep of which most Catholics would be only too happy to dispense with.

However, I do not like to ask for something which others do not want to give. Brutal demands for one's rights (real or imaginary) are, strictly speaking, unchristian; displays of political muscle cancel out any benefits that a Christian education might confer. If public aid causes unholy rancor, it is best forgotten about. The schools are worth saving and certainly worth improving—but not at the expense of hatred.

PHILIP H. PHENIX | ***Religion in American Public Education***

Institutional religion is an important factor in the American social and cultural scene. According to the latest published statistics, there are in

From *Teachers College Record,* 57: 26–31 (1955), Teachers College, Columbia University, N.Y. Reprinted by permission.

the United States 255 religious bodies with a total membership of about 95 million, or nearly 60 per cent of the population. If only adults were considered, the percentage would be substantially higher. Of these, 56 million are Protestant Christian, 32 million are Roman Catholic, 5 million are Jewish and 2 million are Eastern Orthodox. The multiplicity indicated by the number 255 is misleading, since the great majority are members of a relatively small number of major religious bodies. Nevertheless, plurality of religious organizations is a dominant feature of the American scene, of particular importance for the problem of religion in public education.

There are three main issues about which religious persons and groups differ. The first has to do with the nature and authority of the religious organization. At one extreme, among the groups we are considering, are the Roman Catholics, with a centralized, authoritarian, hierarchical church. At the other extreme are the Quakers and Baptists, with traditions of individual freedom and local autonomy. The second issue is the nature and interpretation of the Bible. The right wing is made up of fundamentalists who regard the Scripture as the literal Word of God disclosed through supernatural revelation. The left wing contains the modernists who regard the Bible merely as a record of the history and religious experience of the Hebrews and early Christians. The third issue is the character of worship. On the one hand there are the formal, liturgical, traditional types and on the other hand the informal, free, spontaneous modes.

But what is it that these differing beliefs and practices have in common, that they should all be called "religion"? What *is* religion? There is no standard and universally accepted definition. Yet there is a widely used meaning which is especially useful in analyzing the role of religion in education. Religion may be defined as *comprehensive life-orientation,* or again, as *the pattern of organization of life in relation to values regarded as ultimate* (i.e., involving crucial or life-and-death decisions). Thus, the differing views of the various religious groups are expressions of contrasting convictions about the ultimate meaning of life or about the scheme of crucial values which governs its conduct.

This is what religion aims to be and claims for itself, despite the fact that there are many who are only nominal members of a religious body. Every religion professes and promotes a comprehensive scheme of outlook and motivation, even though its adherents may fail to embody it. Also there may be many who do embody it but do not confess allegiance to the institution promoting it. For this reason the true and complete story of religion is not told by official membership statistics.

If we use this broad, functional definition of *religion,* it follows that everyone has *some* religion, since everyone has some pattern of life-orientation and some ultimate values. Religious institutions are merely social embodiments and historical concretions of certain commonly shared patterns of practical ultimate conviction. The fundamental question about religion, then, is not whether one has it or not, but *what kind* of religion he has. By what ultimate commitments is his life governed? About what supreme loyalties does his existence center? By devotion to what highest ends is his conduct motivated? It is the answers to such questions that reveal the true character of religious faiths. And it is these answers that the essential character of cultures is manifested. Religion is the vital center or innermost principle of culture.

Religion conceived in this fashion is obviously of central importance for education, since the nature of the educative process—goals, methods, materials, motives—will reflect a pattern of ultimate values. Every educational program has an implicit or explicit rationale derived from a pattern of convictions about what is of life-and-death importance. Hence every educational system presupposes some religious faith, and the problems of education require attention to the prior problems of underlying life-orientation.

The special difficulty in connection with American public education is the plurality of religious faiths—not only the 255 bodies officially reporting but the many other varieties of ultimate commitment which find no organized social expression or which are not recognized as "religious" in the conventional sense. For the public school—indeed for any public enterprise, but especially for the school, by whose program the loyalties of a people are transmitted—the basic question is: How can people with differing ultimate values and life-orientations live together and cooperate in a program of public endeavor? Negatively, we need to face the fact that people cannot live together or cooperate in matters governed by opposed values of life-and-death importance. To assume a pre-established harmony in human affairs or the possibility of an easy resolution of differences simply by closer acquaintance or more discussion is to surrender to sentimental illusion.

Living together and operating public enterprises is possible only with *a common faith* in respect to certain human relationships, in which the ultimate values of association are agreed upon, and where differences in values are in the realm of penultimate concerns or relate to matters other than social organization. In particular, the American public school system presupposes a common faith of some kind, at least with respect to the principles of association and cooperation amongst diverse patterns of belief and practice.

Historically, the American people have resolved the general problem of religion in public enterprises by the classic principle of "separation of church and state." This means (1) freedom of religious groups from state domination or interference, (2) individual liberty of conscience in the holding of beliefs and the practice of worship, and (3) freedom of government from any and every form of ecclesiastical control or intervention. This doctrine is embodied in the First Amendment to the Federal Constitution.

But the principle that church and state should be separate does not mean that *religion* and state should be severed. Indeed, according to a fundamental functional definition of religion, as suggested above, such a separation would be impossible, since the very conduct of government presupposes commitment to certain values as ultimate. It is usually said that the common faith of America is the democratic faith. One article of this democratic faith, embodied in the separation principle, is that freedom of belief has priority over any ecclesiastical institution and its claims to authority. American democracy therefore presupposes a particular doctrine of the institutional church as not supremely authoritative and as not coextensive with religion. This is a *theological* doctrine (historically derived from Protestantism) to which all Americans tacitly subscribe, as part of their common democratic faith. In our democracy, preservation of freedom of individual conscience and belief is a matter of life-and-death importance and as such is functionally a religious principle.

The principle of separation of church and state as applied to education has had two consequences. On the one hand, it has confirmed and encouraged the establishment of parochial schools, where sectarian religious instruction may freely and properly be given. On the other hand, it has brought about the progressive secularization of the American public schools.

This secularization has involved three things. First, ecclesiastical control of public schools has been prohibited. The schools have been governed by local boards and state departments of education, operating without regard to church affiliation.

Second, instruction in traditional religion has been largely avoided. Sectarian instruction has been widely recognized as contrary to law, and there has been reluctance in most places to attempt nonsectarian teaching, on the ground either that it too is prohibited by law or that it would lead to conflict and controversy with groups holding a different interpretation and hence considering the supposedly nonsectarian teaching to be actually sectarian. The secularized public school thus tends as far as possible to avoid all reference to specifically religious matters (in the conventional sense), and especially to avoid reference to the articles of belief of the various churches.

Third, the secularization of public education has entailed the substitution of a new scheme of comprehensive orientation and of ultimate values in place of those underlying the traditional religions. It was pointed out above that with a fundamental functional definition of religion the question is not *religion or no religion* but only *what kind of religion.* Thus the secularization of public education does not mean the elimination of a faith basis for the educational enterprise. It simply means the development of a new pattern of practical ultimates by which public education is to be guided. Secular public education is not and cannot be free of first principles or basic assumptions—in short, of religious presuppositions. There is an implicit common faith of secular public education, with distinctive doctrines—of man, of the nature of knowledge, and of the highest goods—which constitute the articles of that faith.

The crucial question for our time concerning religion in American public education is whether this three-fold pattern of secularization is right and proper for the public schools. Should public education be secular in these respects, or should the proper role of religion in education be differently conceived? Should the common faith of public education be the same as for most other public enterprises (e.g., the conduct of government), where the common bond is simply agreement on certain canons of administrative procedure? Or does the special nature of the educational enterprise require a more profound common commitment, and one more directly related to the faiths of traditional religion?

I wish to present my answer to this crucial question by evaluating in order the three components of secularism in public education mentioned above. As to the first, it seems clear that the public schools should remain free of any ecclesiastical control. This is a direct and obvious consequence of the principle of separation of church and state. A publicly supported school under church auspices would involve the state in the propagation of a particular faith. If support were given on a per-pupil or other pro-rata basis amongst the denominations, disputes and rivalries would be inevitable. But more important, such schools would not in any full sense be *public,* since the educational program would inevitably presuppose adherence to or tacit acceptance of a particular church position. On the same grounds, there is no justification for permitting or requiring the use of any prayers, the reading of scriptures (with or without comment), or the corporate exercise of any other religious act in the public school, including, I might add, the pledge of allegiance with the phrase "under God." Such practices are a direct violation of the principle of separation and a denial of religious freedom (particularly for those who profess no religious allegiance).

The second aspect of secularization—the elimination of references to religion in its various forms from the curriculum—seems quite unwarranted. Religion in its many historic forms has been and continues to be an important fact in human culture and as such should be studied in the schools. That the perceptive and fair-minded teaching of the major religious ideas and practices of mankind, in contexts appropriate to their consideration, is not an easy task is readily granted. But it is difficult also to teach mathematics to promote rational understanding rather than routine manipulation of symbols. That religion is controversial and emotion-arousing is no reason for avoiding it. It is all the more important to consider it, for a main objective of education ought to be development of the ability to deal intelligently and constructively with disputed and feeling-charged issues. This applies to economic and political issues as well as to religion. To restrict public education to matters on which everyone agrees would be to shun a primary educational responsibility.

The proposal that religion as a reality of cultural life be given its fair place in the public school curriculum is substantially the intent of the recent recommendations by the Educational Policies Commission (1951) and by the Committee on Religion and Education of the American Council on Education (1953) advocating the "objective" or "factual" study of religion. This ought to be done simply in the interests of intellectual adequacy. That it would not be easy to insure the competence of teachers for this task, or that some churches might object to having their faiths presented along with other faiths by an independent agency, may be granted without in the least detracting from the importance and urgency of the task.

But it is not enough that religion be objectively presented where appropriate to the various school disciplines. As pointed out earlier, religion is not chiefly a matter of rational understanding but of ultimate concern or supreme commitment. Hence to have factual knowledge, however valuable, *about* religion, is not the same as being religious. In fact, a spectator relationship to the varieties of faith may hinder the acknowledgment of one's own ultimate concerns. This prompts the questions: Is it the proper function of the public school to encourage religious commitment? Is it right for the school in some sense to teach religion, as well as to teach *about* religion?

My answer to these questions is that it is not right for the school either to teach any one kind of religion or to encourage students to be religious (in the conventional sense) rather than non-religious (e.g., by urging them to go to church or by judging adversely those who are not affiliated with any religious organization). But I would maintain beyond this that the public school *does* have an obligation and an opportunity to "teach religion" in the fundamental functional sense. To make this clear I must consider the third aspect of secularization referred to above. It was pointed out that the secular public school rests upon certain basic assumptions and presupposes a particular total orientation and scheme of values which constitute its common faith. These provide in the functional sense a religious foundation for public education. The point I want to underline is that this common faith of public education needs to be recognized for what it is, made explicit, criticized, and reconstructed.

Insofar as there are primary commitments underlying the school enterprise, religion is being taught. It is important, then, to ask whether the faith being thus propagated in public education is the highest possible common faith or an inadequate substitute for it. It is not easy to state what the actual faith now underlying the secular public school is. For many it would include belief in the self-sufficiency and autonomy of man, in human society as the arbiter of morality and the master of its own destiny, and in the sole reliability of natural scientific inquiry to provide knowledge. On such assumptions, most historic religion is of minor importance if not positively misleading, and its excision from the school program leads to freedom both from sectarian strife and from concern with outgrown superstitions.

But these fundamental questions about the nature and destiny of man, his place in the larger scheme of things, the foundation of moral conduct, the right methods of inquiry and the criteria for truth—these questions upon which the conduct of the whole educational enterprise depends—are by no means so clearly and finally settled that a common faith for public education can be built upon the answers which many have so confidently set forth. It seems unfortunately to be the case that what has been presented as a means for preserving religious peace and freedom through secularization has to some extent become a method of propagating a particular dogmatic faith, namely, scientific naturalism or, to give it another name, naturalistic humanism.

Then what is to be done? Should doctrinaire humanism give way to orthodox theism as the foundation of public education? By no means. Should the attempt to find a common faith for public schools be abandoned and education be surrendered to sectarian agencies? By no means.

The answer seems to me to lie in the formulation and adoption of a faith more comprehensive and more profound than the warring dogmas of most existing faiths, including scientific naturalism. This faith would rest upon the following premises: (1) that there are ultimate concerns which human beings have about such matters as the origin of existence, the meaning and purpose of human life, and the sources of moral guidance; (2) that these questions arise out of the common and universal human situation or predicament; (3) that to the questions there are many different answers and expressions of these answers, and that no single set of answers to the common questions has been found which will command universal assent; (4) that there is an obligation in the school program to recognize and to acknowledge the ultimate questions and in appropriate ways to help students to confront them; and (5) that the school can and ought to utilize the beliefs and practices of the historic religions (and "anti-religions") to illustrate ways in which men have sought to answer these problems. Indeed, the working out and advancement of such a common faith—one which properly balances the need for unity with commitment to diversity—is the essence of the American common school tradition.

To summarize: The philosophy of the common school is, in my opinion, defective in three respects. (1) It has not been recognized that the secular public school rests upon a faith, a chosen set of highest values and a particular orientation framework. (2) This faith has been in certain respects and in the hands of certain interpreters as narrow, dogmatic, and exclusive as some theological systems. (3) It has been a superficial faith, tending to restrict education to the areas where there are demonstrable and verifiable answers. I believe that a consideration of the religious question points the way to a more adequate philosophy for public education by requiring (1) an explicit recognition and reappraisal of the faith basis of the common school program, (2) concern for the great questions of life, death, and destiny which inhere in the human situation rather than for easy, superficial answers, and (3) forthright and informed reference to the beliefs and practices of the major religious (and non-religious) faiths to illustrate the answers men have found to these questions.

The public school program has been impoverished by being severed from some of the deepest springs of human life. We ought to be wise enough to know that our unity in the human predicament lies deeper than our diversity in ecclesiastical allegiance. We should be mature enough and democratic enough to use religious differences to enrich the life of the common school.

Selected References

Association for Supervision and Curriculum Development (NEA). *Life Skills in School and Society.* Washington, D.C.: The Association, 1969.

———. *Youth Education: Problems, Perspectives, Promises.* Washington, D.C.: The Association, 1968.

BECK, CARLTON E., *et al. Education for Relevance: The Schools and Social Change.* Boston: Houghton Mifflin Company, 1968.

COLEMAN, JAMES. "The Concept of Equality of Educational Opportunity," *Harvard Educational Review* (Winter 1968), pp. 7–21.

DIVOKY, DIANE. "Revolt in the High Schools," *Saturday Review* (February 15, 1969), pp. 83–89, 101–102.

DOUGLAS, WILLIAM O. *The Bible and the Schools.* Boston: Little, Brown & Company, 1966.

DUCKER, SAM. *The Public Schools and Religion.* New York: Harper and Row, 1966.

"Education in the Ghetto," *Saturday Review* (January 11, 1969), pp. 4–61.

FANTINI, MARIO D., and GERALD WEINSTEIN. *The Disadvantaged: Challenge to Education.* New York: Harper and Row, 1968.

FULL, HAROLD. *Controversy in American Education: An Anthology of Crucial Issues.* New York: The Macmillan Company, 1967.

GOLDBLOOM, MAURICE J. "The New York School Crisis," *Commentary* (January 1969), pp. 43–58.

GOLDSTEIN, BERNARD. *Low Income Youth in Urban Areas: A Critical Review of the Literature.* New York: Holt, Rinehart & Winston, 1967.

HICKERSON, NATHANIEL. *Education for Alienation.* Englewood Cliffs, N.J.: Prentice-Hall, 1966.

KENNEDY, ROBERT, *et al.* "Ghetto Education," *The Center Magazine* (November 1968), pp. 46–60.

KEPPEL, FRANCIS. *The Necessary Revolution in American Education.* New York: Harper and Row, 1966.

KOZOL, JONATHAN. *Death at an Early Age.* Boston: Houghton Mifflin Company, 1967.

MILLER, HARRY L. (ed.). *Education for the Disadvantaged.* New York: The Free Press, 1967.

National Society for the Study of Education. *The Changing American School* (65th Yearbook, Part II). Chicago: University of Chicago Press, 1966.

———. *Metropolitanism: Its Challenge to Education* (67th Yearbook, Part I). Chicago: University of Chicago Press, 1968.

PASSOW, A. HARRY, *et al.* (eds.). *Education of the Disadvantaged.* New York: Holt, Rinehart & Winston, 1967.

PICKERING, SIR GEORGE. *The Challenge of Education.* London: Watts and Co., 1967.

ROBERTS, JOAN I. (ed.). *School Children in Urban Slums.* New York: The Free Press, 1967.

SCHREIBER, DANIEL. *Profile of the School Dropout.* New York: Vintage Books, 1968.

SELIGMAN, BEN B. (ed.). *Poverty As a Public Issue.* New York: The Free Press, 1965.

SILBERMAN, CHARLES E. *Crisis in Black and White.* New York: Random House, 1964.

SMILEY, MARJORIE B., and HARRY L. MILLER. *Policy Issues in Urban Education.* New York: The Free Press, 1968.

STOREN, HELEN F. *The Disadvantaged Early Adolescent: More Effective Teaching.* New York: McGraw-Hill Company, 1968.